Clinical Engineering
A Handbook for Clinical and Biomedical Engineers

Clinical Engineering
A Handbook for Clinical and Biomedical Engineers

Second Edition

Edited by

Azzam Taktak
Royal Liverpool University Hospital, Liverpool, United Kingdom

Paul S. Ganney
University College London Hospitals NHS Trust, London, United Kingdom,
University of Liverpool, Liverpool, United Kingdom

David Long
AJM Healthcare, UK & Oxford University Hospitals NHS Foundation Trust, Oxford, UK

Richard G. Axell
University College London Hospitals NHS Foundation Trust, London, United Kingdom;
University College London, London, United Kingdom

ELSEVIER

ACADEMIC PRESS
An imprint of Elsevier

Academic Press is an imprint of Elsevier
125 London Wall, London EC2Y 5AS, United Kingdom
525 B Street, Suite 1650, San Diego, CA 92101, United States
50 Hampshire Street, 5th Floor, Cambridge, MA 02139, United States
The Boulevard, Langford Lane, Kidlington, Oxford OX5 1GB, United Kingdom

Library of Congress Cataloging-in-Publication Data
A catalog record for this book is available from the Library of Congress

British Library Cataloguing-in-Publication Data
A catalogue record for this book is available from the British Library

ISBN: 978-0-08-102694-6

For information on all Academic Press publications visit our website at
https://www.elsevier.com/books-and-journals

Publisher: Mara Conner
Acquisition Editor: Mara Conner
Editorial Project Manager: Andrae Akeh
Production Project Manager: Anitha Sivaraj
Cover Designer: Christian J. Bilbow

Typeset by TNQ Technologies

Working together
to grow libraries in
developing countries
www.elsevier.com • www.bookaid.org

Contents

Section I
Professional practice

1. The role of clinical engineers in supporting patients

John Amoore, Francis Hegarty, Justin McCarthy, Richard Scott and Paul Blackett

2. Health technology asset management

Justin McCarthy, Francis Hegarty, John Amoore, Paul Blackett and Richard Scott

3. Health technology assessment and issues in health economics

Azzam Taktak and Siddhartha Bandyopadhyay

4. Good clinical practice

Anthony Scott Brown

5. Risk management

Anthony Scott Brown

6. Research methodology

Azzam Taktak

7. Leadership

Merlin Walberg

Section II
Information technology & software engineering

8. Information communications technology

Paul S. Ganney

9. Software engineering

Paul S. Ganney, Sandhya Pisharody and Edwin Claridge

10. Web development

Paul S. Ganney, Sandhya Pisharody and Ed McDonagh

Section III
Clinical instrumentation & measurement

Section IV
Rehabilitation engineering & assistive technology

26. Powered wheelchairs

Ladan Najafi and David Long

27. Electronic assistive technology Introduction and assessment

Donna Cowan, Jodie Rogers and Ladan Najafi

Environmental control systems

Donna Cowan

Augmentative and alternative communication (AAC)

*Ladan Najafi, Fiona Panthi and Georgina
Overell*

Access to electronic assistive technology (EAT)

Jodie Rogers and Ladan Najafi

Integrated systems

Ladan Najafi

Using and adapting mainstream technology for assistive technology

Will Wade

Brain computer interfaces

Robert Lievesley

Orthopaedic biomechanics

Tim Holsgrove

Mobile arm supports

Tori Mayhew and
David Long

Robotics

Mike Hillman

Contributors

Tim Adlam, University College London, London, UK & Designability, Bath, UK

John Amoore, Consultant Clinical Engineer (Retired), Edinburgh, Scotland, United Kingdom

Richard G. Axell, University College London Hospitals NHS Foundation Trust, London, United Kingdom; University College London, London, United Kingdom

Dan Bader, Faculty of Health Sciences, University of Southampton, Southampton, United Kingdom

Siddhartha Bandyopadhyay, University of Birmingham, Birmingham, United Kingdom

Paul Blackett, Lancashire Teaching Hospitals NHS Foundation Trust, Lancashire, United Kingdom

Anthony Scott Brown, Health Tech Solutions Ltd, Redruth, United Kingdom

Edwin Claridge, University Hospitals Birmingham NHS Trust, Birmingham, United Kingdom

Donna Cowan, Chailey Clinical Services, East Sussex, UK

Christine Denby, Royal Liverpool University Hospital NHS Foundation Trust, Liverpool, United Kingdom

Paul S. Ganney, University College London Hospitals NHS Trust, London, United Kingdom; University of Liverpool, Liverpool, United Kingdom

Vicky Gardiner, Opcare, Abingdon, UK

Joel P. Giblett, Royal Papworth Hospital NHS Foundation Trust, Cambridge, United Kingdom

Richard Hagan, Royal Liverpool University Hospitals NHS Foundation Trust, Liverpool, United Kingdom

Francis Hegarty, Healthcare Technology Department, Children's Health Ireland, Dublin, Ireland

Mike Hillman, University of Bath, Bath, UK

Tim Holsgrove, University of Exeter, Exeter, UK

Paul Horwood, Oxford University Hospitals NHS Foundation Trust, Oxford, UK

Robert Lievesley, Oxford University Hospitals NHS Foundation Trust, Oxford, UK

David Long, AJM Healthcare, UK & Oxford University Hospitals NHS Foundation Trust, Oxford, United Kingdom

Tori Mayhew, Oxford University Hospitals NHS Foundation Trust, Oxford, UK

Justin McCarthy, Clin Eng Consulting Ltd, Cardiff and School of Engineering, Cardiff University, Wales, United Kingdom

Ed McDonagh, The Royal Marsden Hospital NHS Foundation Trust, London, United Kingdom

Ladan Najafi, Kent and Medway Communication and Assistive Technology Service (KM CAT) – Adults, Kent, United Kingdom; East Kent Adult Communication and Assistive Technology (ACAT) Service, Kent, UK

Georgina Overell, Kent and Medway Communication and Assistive Technology Service (KM CAT) – Adults, Kent, UK

Fiona Panthi, Kent and Medway Communication and Assistive Technology Service (KM CAT) – Adults, Kent, UK

Sandhya Pisharody, Varian Medical Systems, Crawley, United Kingdom

Nicholas P. Rhodes, University of Liverpool, Liverpool, United Kingdom

Jodie Rogers, Kent and Medway Communication and Assistive Technology Service (KM CAT) – Adults, Kent, UK

Richard Scott, Sheffield Teaching Hospitals NHS Foundation Trust, Sheffield, United Kingdom

Adam P. Shortland, Guy's and St. Thomas' NHS Foundation Trust, London, United Kingdom; School of Biomedical Engineering and Imaging Science, King's College London, London, United Kingdom

Martin Smith, Oxford University Hospitals NHS Foundation Trust, UK

Eskinder Solomon, Guy's & St Thomas' NHS Foundation Trust, London, United Kingdom

Thomas Stone, Cambridge University Hospitals NHS Foundation Trust, Cambridge, United Kingdom

Ian Swain, Salisbury NHS Foundation Trust, Salisbury, United Kingdom

Karl P. Sylvester, Royal Papworth & Cambridge University Hospitals NHS Foundation Trust, Cambridge, United Kingdom

Azzam Taktak, Royal Liverpool University Hospital, Liverpool, United Kingdom

Will Wade, ACE Centre North, Manchester, UK

Merlin Walberg, Phoenix Consultancy USA Incorporated, Fort Lauderdale, Florida, United States

Paul A. White, Cambridge University Hospitals NHS Foundation Trust, Cambridge, United Kingdom; Anglia Ruskin University, Chelmsford, United Kingdom

Duncan Wood, Salisbury NHS Foundation Trust, Salisbury, United Kingdom

Habiba Yasmin, University College London Hospitals NHS Foundation Trust, London, United Kingdom; University College London, London, United Kingdom

Foreword

Clinical Engineering is a broad arena and practitioners in this area need to understand a wide range of subjects, some in great detail, and others with just a working knowledge. In my experience although there are many separate books covering the complete subject area, there is no complete book that professes to cover the entire range of subjects, which can be a useful reference for the professional working in this field. Clinical engineers must have a working knowledge of the human body, both in how it functions and its anatomy. They must be able to work with patients, clinical staff and other health professionals. They need to be experts in their engineering areas, but keep up to date in the relevant research and innovations in this field. Finally they must be able to lead and manage, both themselves and their teams. This book seems unique in that the wide range of subjects mentioned is included, some in great detail, others necessary less so, but most chapters are referenced widely, with useful extra reading material presented for further study. There are some innovative parts of the book. For example, a section on leadership is not often included in text books such as this, but this particular chapter is very well presented, in a very personal style, with thought provoking exercises and sections. The excellent chapters making up the section on rehabilitation engineering are unusual to be included in a book such as this, but they make the book seem very complete. The web and computer sections give the book a very up-to-date feel.

Professor Azzam Taktak has edited the book and chosen with care some excellent coeditors and authors to contribute. His concept of the book came out of his vast experience in teaching the subject at his hospital and university, both in the classroom and using electronic learning. He has contributed to the new Modernising Scientific Careers (MSC) NHS programme and this experience has enhanced the book. It is interesting that the MSC course also includes leadership and professional issues as a key component, and it reassuring that this is included in this complete course on clinical engineering.

The contents of the book follow a logical sequence, that take the reader from a brief look at the anatomy and physiology of humans, to statistics, good clinical practice, the role of clinical engineers in hospitals, and information and computer systems. These subjects make up the first two sections of the book, which are about presenting the background 'core' areas and the legal processes involved. The final two sections of the book cover all the main areas of clinical measurement and rehabilitation.

I have had the pleasure of knowing Azzam for many years. It is hard to think of anyone with more knowledge and experience of clinical engineering in its widest form, and he has an extensive network of colleagues he can draw upon to contribute to this work. I have also had the pleasure of knowing most of the excellent authors in the book. Some chapters have been written by single authors, others by multiple ones. The variety in authorship gives a refreshing combination of styles, which keeps the writing alive and accessible.

The book will be a valuable resource for many engineers and clinicians working in this area, and also to refresh the many experts involved in the field of clinical engineering.

Professor Mark Tooley
PhD FIET FIPEM FinstP FRCP
Consultant Clinical Scientist, Royal United Hospital, Bath

Preface

This book is aimed at professionals, students, researchers, or anyone who is interested in clinical engineering. It provides a broad reference to the core elements of the subject for the reader to gain knowledge on how to successfully deploy medical technologies. The book is written and reviewed by professionals who have been working in the field of clinical engineering for decades. Many of the authors are clinical and biomedical engineers working in healthcare and academia and have also acted as trainers and as examiners on the subject.

As well as possessing engineering skills, clinical engineers must be able to work with patients and a range of professional staff. They need to keep up to date with fast-moving scientific and medical research in the field, and to develop their own laboratory, design, analytical, management, and leadership skills. This book is designed to assist the clinical engineer in this process.

The book is organized into four main sections. The first section covers generic aspects of the core skills needed to work in this area. It gives the reader a flavour of how to engage with research and development, data analysis and study design, and management and leadership. It also discusses in detail the important role engineers play in the healthcare environment. The second section covers legislation relevant to information technology based medical devices and standards concerned with security, encryption, and data exchange. There is also material on software development/management and web development, which will be of interest to those working with these technologies across the entire field of clinical science and medical engineering.

The third section deals with clinical measurements and instrumentation. It starts with a quick overview of medical electronics theory before moving on to clinical measurements. It explains in detail the physics and engineering aspects involved in making useful and reliable measurements in the clinical situation. Examples of clinical measurements covered include cardiology, haematology, neurophysiology, and respiratory.

The forth section provides a comprehensive summary of the subject of rehabilitation engineering and assistive technologies. Topics covered include gait analysis, posture management, wheelchair and seating, and assistive technology. It is the first comprehensive and practical guide for engineers working in a clinical environment.

I would like to express my sincere gratitude to my coeditors who spent a considerable amount of time and energy recruiting authors and pulling together the material for their own sections, while working in such a demanding environment. I would also like to thank the authors and the reviewers for the fantastic effort they have put in.

I hope you enjoy reading this book and find it illuminating.

Acknowledgement

Azzam Taktak would like to thank his wife Diane and his children Chris and Sarah for their continued love and support. He would also like to thank the following people who have had a major influence in shaping his career: Peter Rolfe, Paul Record, Iain Chambers, Alicia El-Haj, Justin McCarthy, Malcolm Brown, Tony Fisher, Steve Lake, Antonio Eleuteri, Paulo Lisboa and Bertil Damato.

Paul S. Ganney would like to thank his wife, Rachel, for her continued encouragement and his colleagues for many helpful discussions: especially Paul Ostro, Patrick Maw, Khalil Itani, Justin McCarthy and Bill Webster.

Dave Long would like to thank Jo for her love, encouragement, willingness to tell him when he is wrong, and general sense of fun. He would also like to acknowledge the many people with whom he has had the privilege to work closely over many years, most recently Jo Bates, Bicky Ho, Rick Houghton, Wendy Murphy, Bex Oakes, Kate Parker, Lynda Pearce, Steve Peck, Pat Postill, Nathan Robson and Louise Way.

Richard G. Axell firstly would like to say a big thank you to Azzam, Paul and David for inviting him to be part of the editorial team for this edition. He would also like to thank his partner Elaine, parents, family and friends for their constant support and encouragement. He would like to acknowledge and thank the many colleagues he has had the privilege of working with. He would like to say a special thank you to Anna Barnes, Jalesh Panicker and Tamsin Greenwell who have constantly inspired, supported and continue to mentor him. Finally, he would like to thank Paul White for opening his eyes to the wonderful world of research, as a healthcare scientist in the NHS, and along with both Stephen Hoole and James Hampton-Till for their time, patience and support when completing his PhD.

Section I

Professional practice

Chapter 1

The role of clinical engineers in supporting patients

John Amoore[a], Francis Hegarty[b], Justin McCarthy[c], Richard Scott[d] and Paul Blackett[e]

[a]Consultant Clinical Engineer (Retired), Edinburgh, Scotland, United Kingdom; [b]Healthcare Technology Department, Children's Health Ireland, Dublin, Ireland; [c]Clin Eng Consulting Ltd, Cardiff and School of Engineering, Cardiff University, Wales, United Kingdom; [d]Sheffield Teaching Hospitals NHS Foundation Trust, Sheffield, United Kingdom; [e]Lancashire Teaching Hospitals NHS Foundation Trust, Lancashire, United Kingdom

Chapter outline

Introduction

Technology has been used from the early days of medicine. Records of early Greek medicine describe the use of simple tools, splints, and crude surgical tools (Milne, 1907). The development of healthcare technology can be illustrated by considering the evolution of a simple cutting blade, through carefully designed surgical knives and by way of sophisticated electrosurgical tools, to precise robotic controlled surgical arms, enhancing, but not replacing, the clinical staff who provide the healthcare. As medicine and technology have advanced over the millennia, healthcare technology has become more sophisticated and more complex, but its essential role of extending the ability of people to deliver healthcare remains. Over the past hundred years, healthcare has become increasingly reliant on medical technology with clinicians dependent on it for diagnosis, treatment and rehabilitation, and for improving the overall health of people. The appropriate deployment of technology contributes to the improvement in the quality of healthcare, the containment of cost, and to increased access to services (David and Jahnke, 2004). Thus, an essential activity within hospitals is managing the medical technology and its use, ensuring that the technology supports the strategic aims of the organization (Hegarty et al., 2017). Consequently, healthcare delivery organizations must continuously evolve, investigating and, where justified, adopting new technologies to meet their organizational goals of delivering high quality and equitable healthcare cost-effectively.

An increasing trend is for healthcare to be delivered in the community to address: demographic changes; increasing demands for better access to healthcare; demands for patient-centred care and care close to home and; containing rising costs (Smith et al., 2012). The management, care and support of the healthcare technology in the community will continue to bring new challenges.

Engineers create products and processes to improve the delivery of healthcare. In this chapter the products being considered are medical devices and medical equipment and the processes within which they are used. The terms *medical device*[a] and *medical equipment*[b] are defined by the World Health Organization (WHO, 2011a; p.4). Medical equipment refers to powered medical devices (usually electrically powered) such as MRI scanners, defibrillators, endoscopes, and ECG recorders. Examples of non-powered medical devices are consumables used with medical equipment such as syringes and infusion sets and ECG electrodes; Clinical Engineers have important contributions to make to the management of these passive devices. Medical dramas and science documentaries on TV have brought these devices to the attention of the general public. They are rightly portrayed as complex high-tech machines that are reliable, safe and used expertly by clinicians. As with technology like the aircraft used in the travel industry, the public are optimistic in how they view medical technology and seem content to put themselves and their safety in the hands of professionals who use medical equipment. However, these ubiquitous devices, equipment and systems bring with them risks as well as benefits. All equipment and systems, such as aircraft, bridges and other technology and infrastructure, need active management to ensure that the benefits they bestow far outweigh any risk associated with their use, and that these risks are managed and controlled, with methods in place to minimize them. This is particularly the case for medical devices and equipment to ensure they are safe and optimally used for the benefit of patients. Although the name of the discipline of medical device and equipment asset management has changed over the years, a commonly used term to describe it today is Healthcare Technology Management (AAMI, 2011). Hegarty et al. (2017) have expanded its scope to include a systems engineering and values driven approach, together with active, patient-centred support for clinical applications of technology.

Medical devices incorporate optics, electronics, mechanics, computing, digital signal processing, and sensors of all types. They often make intimate connection with the human body to deliver fluids, or energy in the form of electric current, or ionizing and non-ionizing radiation. They all need to be carefully controlled to ensure they are effective, accurate, and safe.

The complete range of medical devices and systems procured by a hospital constitutes a valuable financial asset with capital and revenue resourcing requirements. Particularly for medical equipment, its selection, procurement, upkeep, and life cycle should be carefully managed to ensure the equipment is cost effective, up to date, and continues to support the corporate objectives of the hospital. Which technology is required to support the healthcare delivered by the hospital? What resources (clinical staff, space, infrastructure, consumables, and finance) are required for its application? When should technology be removed from service and if so should it be replaced? The requirement to actively manage these assets has resulted in the emergence of a specialist strand of engineering dedicated to the pursuit of excellence in the application of technology in the clinical setting. *Clinical Engineering* is the name given to this discipline. Those who practice it are called *Clinical Engineers*. Clinical engineering is a particular specialization of the discipline of biomedical engineering. What differentiates clinical engineering from biomedical engineering is that the activity and those who deliver it are based in hospitals and clinics at the point of care. Clinical engineering as a discipline is concerned with the application of engineering tools and theory to all aspects of the diagnosis, care and cure of disease, and life support in general, all of which are embraced in the delivery of healthcare services (Geddes and Careers, 1977).

Clinical engineers are individuals usually employed in hospitals to advance care through actively supporting the application of technology at the point of care. They assure positive outcomes from clinical practices predicated on the use of medical equipment. On one level this requires measures to be put in place to assure the technical performance, maintenance, and quality control of the medical equipment itself, its usability, and support for its use, both in terms of staff training and in the supply of accessories and consumables. On another level the use of medical equipment requires the provision of expert and independent advice on what technology to deploy and how best to use technology in the clinical setting. This can extend beyond medical equipment to include the range of passive (non-powered) medical devices used in the delivery of care (e.g. syringes, infusion sets, patient support systems etc.) whether they are used in conjunction with medical equipment or stand alone. Sometimes this may extend to the development of a particular or bespoke device, data

---

[a] Medical device: An article, instrument, apparatus or machine that is used in the prevention, diagnosis or treatment of illness or disease, or for detecting, measuring, restoring, correcting or modifying the structure or function of the body for some health purpose. Typically, the purpose of a medical device is not achieved by pharmacological, immunological or metabolic means.

[b] Medical equipment: Medical devices requiring calibration, maintenance, repair, user training, and decommissioning — activities usually managed by clinical engineers. Medical equipment is used for the specific purposes of diagnosis and treatment of disease or rehabilitation following disease or injury; it can be used either alone or in combination with any accessory, consumable, or other piece of medical equipment. Medical equipment excludes implantable, disposable or single-use medical devices.

processing, or other engineering solution to solve a specific problem or to meet and advance a clinical need. Within the complex environment of the modern hospital, clinical engineering activity is concerned primarily with equipment and passive medical devices but recognizes that interactions between people (patients and clinicians), medication, procedures, and equipment occur and must be understood and managed to ensure safe and effective patient care. The clinical engineer is the expert in the engineering and system science underpinning the application of medical equipment, devices and systems. Clinical engineers operate at the point of care and it is this first-hand knowledge of the day-to-day needs within the patient environment and care process that allows the term *clinical* to be used (Aller, 1977).

Clinical engineering services delivered within healthcare delivery organizations are provided by a range of individuals each with specialist expertise, qualifications, and skill. In this chapter the term *clinical engineer* is used to describe all engineers and scientists who provide clinical engineering services regardless of their employment role or level of professional development.

Clinical engineering as applied biomedical engineering

Clinicians working in modern hospitals use medical devices and equipment to diagnose, monitor, treat and rehabilitate patients. These technologies have been developed to improve clinical outcome, reduce trauma, and support day-to-day living. The technology should support clinical staff in optimally delivering effective care.

The developments in medical devices have relied on, and continue to rely on, developments in engineering technologies. Advances in the field of optics have resulted in the development of advanced laparoscopy and endoscopy with high-quality video imaging systems that have revolutionized practices in gastroenterology and surgery, where keyhole surgery has transformed the delivery of care with benefits for patients and healthcare organizations. Developments in keyhole and open surgical procedures have been made possible by sophisticated electrosurgical diathermy devices that allow surgeons to deliver radio frequency electrical currents to the body in precise ways allowing them to cut, dissect, coagulate, and ablate tissue in a highly controlled manner. Advances in modern electronics allow for feedback to be built into these devices so that the device controls and alters the cutting current and waveform in real time in response to changes in the tissue at the treatment site.

Modern anaesthetic workstations are complex electromechanical-optical systems that deliver precise gas mixtures to patients during surgery. The development of small and reliable spectroscopy systems allows these gas mixtures to be measured and displayed in real time. Anaesthetists use different optoelectronic sensors and electrophysiology measurement methods to monitor the patient's physiology during surgery. These devices are configured into systems that allow data from all these sources to be processed and analyzed to provide new information for anaesthetists to help them guide the course of care. Often data from such devices are stored in databases in clinical information systems both for archiving and clinical audit purposes.

Similarly, multiparameter physiological measurement devices are used extensively in intensive care units. Modern intensive care ventilators, like anaesthetic machines, incorporate physiological measurement modules and software that allow the performance of the ventilator to be precisely set up and to act in harmony with the patient's own physiology and breathing patterns. Medical imaging systems use ionizing (CT scanners, X-ray machines, gamma cameras) and non-ionizing (MRI machines, ultrasound scanners, thermal imaging systems) radiation to provide sophisticated images of anatomy and physiological function to support clinical decision making. Data from these systems can be used to make physical models of anatomy using 3D printers, giving clinicians new ways of preparing for surgery, more information and ways of planning interventions in advance.

Technology contributes significantly to the treatment of people with disabilities, whether from birth or through illness, trauma or age. Special seating devices can prevent tissue deterioration, appropriately designed wheelchairs can improve mobility and allow participation in sport. Sophisticated and personalized powered wheelchair controls and speech synthesizing communication aids can allow people with disabilities to make sometimes profound contributions to society (Hawkin, 2013). Artificial limbs can provide function following trauma.

It is no surprise then, that doctors, nurses, and other clinical staff, whose backgrounds and training are in the life sciences, find themselves using complex technology every day in their clinical practice. The technology relies on complex electronic, mechanical, optical, signal processing and information technology systems. Much of this technology is hidden from the clinicians as they rely on it to care for their patients, hidden behind operating consoles whose design requires an understanding of user − device interactions, of ergonomics.

Consequently, clinicians using such technology benefit from collaborating with clinical engineers at the point of care. With knowledge of the engineering, physics and system science underpinning medical devices, equipment and systems, and working collaboratively in the clinical environment, clinical engineers are well placed to help ensure the optimum application of the technology for patient care. Furthermore, clinical engineers have the knowledge and expertise to process, analyze and critically review the data produced by all this technology. They play an important role in ensuring positive outcomes from the use of technology, and in reducing negative outcomes.

Clinical engineers manage the devices and their integration into systems and the clinical environment so that they perform accurately and reliably. Failure or misuse of a device may result in unintended harm to the patient or user. A failure or misuse that results in a data error, if it is not detected, may negatively influence the course of a patient's care. Consequently, in the day-to-day delivery of healthcare, which is predicated on the use of medical devices, equipment and systems, there is a need for clinical engineers to be based at the point of care, to exercise due care, and conscientiously monitor the deployment and use of technology in the clinical setting. In doing so, clinical engineers should imaginatively foresee hazards and act to mitigate them. This can take the form of projects to redesign the processes in which devices are used, advice on how to better utilize equipment or non-active devices within clinical practice, or indeed advice on replacement of devices or equipment with new improved technology.

Clinical engineers can also be directly involved in patient care. Rehabilitation Engineers for example, play a key role in the assessment of the individual needs of people with a disability and in the prescription of all types of assistive technology to meet those needs.

Clinical engineers also use their expertise and particular understanding of the application of devices at the point of care to contribute to international work concerned with the ongoing development of essential standards that new medical device must meet. They also report back to industry and both national and international regulatory bodies on the performance of specific devices. Given the diversity, complexity, and ubiquity of medical equipment in the modern hospital, their safe and effective use requires ongoing training. Clinical engineers contribute significantly to the development and delivery of training courses for all staff who use technology to deliver care. They also contribute to undergraduate and postgraduate education programmes and continuous professional development for doctors, nurses, other clinical staff, and biomedical and clinical engineers.

The practice of clinical engineering draws on all the other sub-disciplines of biomedical engineering. Consequently, you can find clinical engineers who are experts in medical electronics, rehabilitation engineering, clinical measurement, and, increasingly, clinical informatics. In their practice they work directly with clinicians in supporting clinical practice and may work directly with patients as appropriate. What differentiates clinical engineers from other biomedical engineers working in academia, industry, or the regulatory environment is their direct involvement with the delivery of care in hospital and community settings.

Clinical engineering activities — healthcare technology management

The practice of clinical engineering in modern hospitals is difficult to define for two reasons. Firstly, the activity is interdisciplinary. Secondly, the scope of the activity undertaken by a clinical engineering department varies from institution to institution depending on the jurisdiction, regulatory environment, corporate governance, maturity of the organization, and corporate priorities. Within this broad remit, the nature of the work depends on the experience and focus of the individuals, both within clinical engineering and within the healthcare institution. So, it is impossible to describe a single defined approach that would be applicable for all healthcare delivery organizations. The approach taken in this chapter is to develop a generic description, modelled on a large teaching hospital that will be used to explain, illustrate, and justify common approaches taken.

Clinical engineering activities will be discussed under the following two headings shown in Fig. 1.1.

- Healthcare Technology Management - Supporting and advancing care
- Healthcare Technology Management - Medical Device Management

Together these two strands combine to form an overall framework for the professional management of medical devices and equipment, their development and application. The role and activity are referred to as 'Healthcare Technology Management' (HTM). It encompasses not only the medical devices and equipment but also associated medical information technology and systems to which medical equipment is interfaced. Furthermore, it includes the activities associated with supporting the use of the technology so that its value is realized in clinical practice. Therefore, the term *healthcare technology management* describes the role more completely than other terms such as clinical engineering. The management of healthcare technology requires a holistic approach that is first and foremost patient-centred. Black and Amoore (2011) in their paper *Pushing the Boundaries of Device Replacement: Introducing the Keystone Model* proposed that, during all stages of medical devices procurement, the needs of the patient should be kept in mind. The keystone metaphor introduced in that paper can be extended and used to illustrate the value of developing a patient-care-focused model of

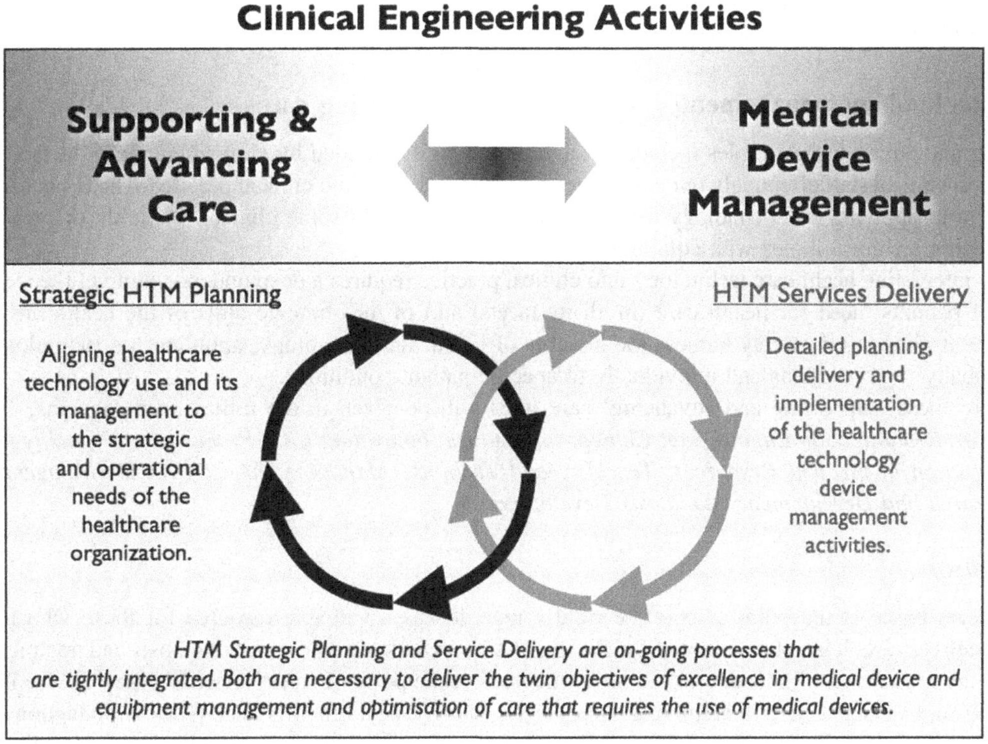

Clinical Engineering Activities

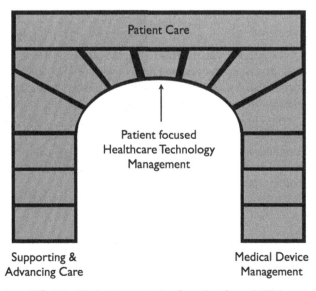

Supporting & Advancing Care ⟷ Medical Device Management

Strategic HTM Planning

Aligning healthcare technology use and its management to the strategic and operational needs of the healthcare organization.

HTM Services Delivery

Detailed planning, delivery and implementation of the healthcare technology device management activities.

HTM Strategic Planning and Service Delivery are on-going processes that are tightly integrated. Both are necessary to deliver the twin objectives of excellence in medical device and equipment management and optimisation of care that requires the use of medical devices.

FIG. 1.1 The two interlocked aspects of Clinical Engineering activities. *Adapted with permission from Fig. 4.12 in Hegarty, F., Amoore, J., Blackett, P., McCarthy, J., Scott, R., 2017. Healthcare Technology Management — A Systematic Approach. CRC Press, Abingdon, UK. ISBN 978-1-4987-0354-3.*

clinical engineering (Fig. 1.2). The supporting and advancing care and the medical device management roles can be considered the pillars of any clinical engineering service. However, it is important to recognize and acknowledge at all times that these roles are complementary and are tightly integrated in practice. The archway shown in Fig. 1.2 represents the integration of these two roles. It is only by fulfilling both roles that clinical engineering can completely support the delivery of patient care. The keystone at the apex of an arch is the final piece placed during construction and locks all the stones into position, allowing the arch as-a-whole to bear weight. We suggest that the keystone of any clinical engineering

Patient Care

Patient focused Healthcare Technology Management

Supporting & Advancing Care

Medical Device Management

FIG. 1.2 The keystone metaphor for patient focused HTM.

service should be that it is focused on delivering processes that improve the patient and carer experience of the application of technology to healthcare.

Healthcare technology management — supporting and advancing care

The supporting and advancing care roles include a range of activities provided by clinical engineers to facilitate hospital management and clinical staff effectively integrating healthcare technology into clinical practice. The focus of these roles is on collaboration in applying the technology or using engineering skills to solve clinical, research, or process problems rather than specific technical issues with equipment.

Effectively integrating healthcare technology into clinical practice requires a deep understanding of the technology that is available, of patients' need for health care (in all its facets) and of the strategic aims of the healthcare organization delivering care. It aims to effectively harness the benefits of healthcare technology, applying the technology to support healthcare, globally to populations and individually to specific patient conditions.

Examples of these 'supporting and advancing' care roles will be given in the following paragraphs. They include: *Clinical Support*; *Rehabilitation Engineering*; *Clinical Informatics*; *Innovating Care Processes and Quality Improvement*; *Optimum Utilization of Medical Resources*; *Teaching and Training; Managing the Clinical Environment; Risk Management; Research and Development; Standards Development*.

Clinical support

Clinical engineers based at the point of care are rightly regarded as a valuable resource for those who use advanced technology to deliver care. It is not uncommon for clinical engineers to contribute to the diagnosis and treatment of patients by facilitating the application of new devices or novel methods at the point of care. Before any new device is trialled in a clinical unit the clinical engineers will assure the equipment's safety. They will also manage the introduction of the device into the clinical working environment ensuring that the necessary training is in place, specialist supplies are available and that the introduction of this new item does not compromise the existing equipment, environment or way of delivering care. Sometimes clinical engineers will work alongside clinicians applying complex or novel technology at the point of care, making measurements and analyzing data. Other clinical engineers based at the point of care assist with the application of technology at the bedside, but do not have a direct clinical role. For example, a specialist vascular surgeon may be assisted in measuring carotid artery blood flow using new medical equipment. Other examples are using multimedia technologies such as 3D imaging and printing, or specialist recording and editing of medical procedures for audit and teaching. With the increase in the reliance on technology comes a requirement for experts in engineering and science to support and advance the application of these technologies by clinicians. Clinical engineers may design and develop new medical devices or adapt existing devices for novel uses. They will work with clinicians, often in multi-disciplinary teams to bring this equipment into use, applying their knowledge of technology and of safety, Regulations and Standards to help advance patient care.

Rehabilitation engineering

Some specialist clinical engineers work directly with patients to meet their specific needs. Rehabilitation engineers are one such group whose practice includes assessing and responding to the needs of people with disabilities. Rehabilitation engineers assess the needs of patients, usually as part of a multi-disciplinary team, then design and build devices and systems to meet a wide range of needs that can assist individuals with mobility, communication, hearing, vision and cognition. In their practice they work closely with individual clients/patients and their carers, fitting or installing these devices or systems to assist with disabilities or aid the recovery of physical and cognitive functions lost because of disease or injury. They are involved in designing artificial body parts and in measuring gait patterns to design and improve the function of artificial limbs and surgical corrections of deformities. In doing all of this they help people with day-to-day activities related to employment and independent living.

Clinical informatics

Interoperability between equipment and information technology has delivered great benefits in many industries. The world is becoming more connected. The 'internet of things' is upon us and it is now common to have personal devices such as phones and watches that can control our own environments such as the home. This connectivity gives rise to real-time data that can be used to examine how systems are used in practice and in turn inform and support improvements in processes. The same opportunities exist in healthcare and so there is a growing demand for medical equipment to be interoperable with medical IT systems, and for experts to avail themselves of the opportunity of new datasets to analyze and improve the delivery of care. This use of information technology in clinical practice is referred to as Clinical Informatics. Clinical Informatics is interdisciplinary, operating at the intersection of clinical care, the health system, and Informatics and Communications Technology (ICT). Supporting this is the integration of medical equipment with the eHealth systems (ECRI Institute, 2008). Increasingly, clinical engineers are taking a lead role in informatics projects. This is not surprising given their well-established role in supporting the application of technology at the point of care and their core training in engineering and system science. Over the years clinical engineers have developed their knowledge and skill in response to the emergence of new technologies and equipment, and the arrival of clinical information systems is no different.

Interoperability of medical equipment with ICT systems is far from the 'plug and play' functionality experienced with domestic equipment. Interoperability may require a physical connection that does not compromise the stringent safety standards to which medical equipment is designed, a communications layer and a semantic layer, where a shared defined context for the data is known at both the transmitting and receiving system. The lack of open standards for medical equipment interoperability means that almost all interoperability projects of any scale and complexity require the use of a middle layer or integration engine that must be locally configured and validated. This need to be carefully planned, implemented, validated and managed. Placing medical equipment on a converged network, shared with other systems can introduce risks. While there are commercial and operational benefits to using converged networks, doing so requires hospitals to set up processes to ensure the associated risks are identified and mitigated in the immediate and long term. These risks include data mapping errors between systems, cyber security and downtime risks to name but a few.

The IEC subcommittee 62A: *Common aspects of electrical equipment used in medical practice* and ISO technical committee 215: *Health informatics*, have jointly produced and published a standard IEC 80001-1 (*Application of risk management for IT-networks incorporating medical devices. Roles, responsibilities and activities*) and a series of technical reports IEC 80001-2-xx. A list of all parts of the 80001 series, published under the general title *Application of risk management for IT-networks incorporating medical devices*, can be found on the IEC website.

Clinical engineers are well placed to act as Medical IT Network Risk Managers as they understand the technology, the regulatory environment and the clinical environment within which these networks are constructed and used.

Innovating care processes and quality improvement

Many hospitals now have continuous quality improvement programmes in place focused on innovating how care is delivered with the aim of improving safety, controlling costs, and making the service more accessible and effective for patients. With both engineering and system science training, and a practical knowledge of the clinical workflow, clinical engineers can take a leadership role in quality improvement initiatives associated with the application of technology. This may include how to optimize the use of new technology; for example, the application support expert working in critical care or introducing new palliative care systems (Case Studies CS1.2 and CS2.1 in Hegarty et al., 2017). It will also include the implementation of health informatics systems and analysis of the data they produce. Where Medical IT Networks are established, the mining of the data sets they generate can give insights into how effective clinical services are. They can also support analysis to help identify process issues.

Quality improvement initiatives can be effectively delivered at the micro level, within individual units or wards. It is at this level, where patient and healthcare provider interact, that quality, safety, reliability, and efficiency are delivered, and the patient's experience of care is created. Clinical engineers actively promote a culture of safety and quality improvement around the use of technology at both the healthcare institution-wide and individual patient-area levels.

Optimum utilization of medical equipment resources

The optimum utilization of medical equipment requires that the type and quantity of medical equipment be correctly specified and procured and that the equipment is appropriately tailored and configured to meet the strategic aims of the healthcare organization and the patients it serves. Clinical Engineers can support the optimum utilization of medical equipment.

'Buy It Right, Use It Right, Keep It Right' (Abraham, 2000) is a catchy phrase well-worth remembered by clinical engineers. Here we are concerned with 'Buy It Right'. It bridges both the 'Supporting and Advancing Care' and 'Medical Device Management' roles (Fig. 1.1), with the strategic planning globally for the whole organization, an advanced HTM activity. This involves multi-disciplinary team work to support the organization's objectives. Based on a clear understanding of how medical devices and equipment support patient care, the activity should be forward focussed, aiming to take the assets available from 'where-they-are' to 'where-they-need-to-be' (Case Study CS5.6, Hegarty et al., 2017). The team work required harnesses the talents and expertise of clinicians and clinical engineers, the later often leading the process (Amoore et al., 2015; Amoore, 2018a).

The first stage of the planning process involves clarifying the current equipment status, 'where-we-are', assessing the inventory in relation to the equipment needed to provide care. Gaps in what is needed will appear. These should be put in context with 'where-we-want-to-be', what equipment is required to support the healthcare objectives, perhaps with strategic planning highlighting the need to prioritize some care activities (for example, increased day surgery). Gathering the evidence requires conversations between clinical engineers, the clinicians and hospital management, including the directorate of finance, to examine whole-life cost of ownership in relation to healthcare benefits (Amoore, 2018b). The multi-disciplinary team assesses what equipment is required to support care, mindful of the care processes and the strategic aims of the organization. It will consider developments in healthcare technology and how they can support care through innovative processes. Patient-focussed, it will consider the needs of patients.

A multidisciplinary forum such as a 'Medical Devices Committee' can facilitate the process, but typically clinical engineers can have a leading role in guiding the process, articulating the global needs of the organization.

The process is illustrated in Fig. 1.3.

Once equipment is procured it will need to be installed correctly. This may involve physical installation and will probably require customization and configuration. Modern medical equipment is complex, often software controlled, offering a range of features, settings, and options. Similar to the typical general-purpose personal computer with its operating systems and general applications packages, the hardware and software features of medical equipment need to be tailored to the clinical requirements. Some of this is achieved before the procurement phase, with the specification of the required options. However, the process also requires that during the commissioning phase the applicable features are

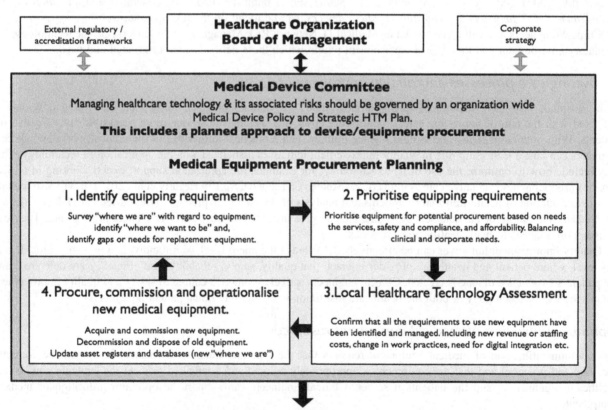

FIG. 1.3 Procurement planning: determining what equipment is required to deliver care. *Copyright Francis Hegarty; used with permission.*

selected and configured. In practice, the configuration is a complex task usually undertaken by a 'super-user' clinician who understands the clinical requirements, working with a clinical engineer who understands the technology.

Equipment configuration planning may be required for equipment unique to specific clinical areas such as neonatal intensive care units but will also be required for medical equipment that is used globally throughout the organization. Standardization of start-up configurations of identical, numerous and widely used devices such as infusion pumps needs to be carefully thought through, a process involving clinical engineers and representative clinicians for the whole organization. Careful equipment configuration and its standardization is a significant contributor to patient safety and effective staff training (Gibson et al., 1998).

Configuration includes mode of operation and selection of parameters and their details. The configuration required varies with the device. For a patient monitor it includes how the various vital signs are displayed and the setting of alarm limits and filters for signals such as the electrocardiogram. For an infusion device it includes infusion rate limits, operating mode, and alarms to help alert the user to problems with the device's operation. Configuration includes tailoring the user-operating environment and connections to networks and hospital information systems. The multidisciplinary expertise of clinical engineers, embracing both clinical and technical knowledge, leads them to be charged with managing the configuration of these devices.

Optimum utilization also requires that the extent to which equipment that is in use is actively considered and managed. Planning the optimum utilization requires an understanding of the criticality of having devices available when required and ensuring their availability at the place and time of need. Equipment libraries have been developed to share commonly used devices such as infusion devices, with processes in place to ensure delivery of the devices to locations where they are needed (Keay et al., 2015). These libraries have traditionally been physical rooms and departments. An alternative is the concept of a virtual library that utilizes equipment-tracking systems (RFID systems) to locate equipment, determine whether it is being used or not and to alert where to find unused equipment within the organization.

Planning equipment numbers to ensure optimum utilization requires an understanding of the function of the equipment and the clinical demand. Planning the deployment of emergency equipment such as life-preserving/restoring defibrillators must consider the requirement for equipment to be available on demand at the point of need within a short period of time.

Teaching and training

Optimal and safe use of medical technology requires more than the device to be properly commissioned, installed, and configured. It requires the user to have an understanding of the technology, its characteristics and limitations, and how it can be used to support healthcare. This knowledge and understanding will include an appreciation of the interplay between the patient, clinical and care staff, the technology, and the environment in which the equipment will be used. Teaching and training is another important activity undertaken by clinical engineers. They contribute to university undergraduate and postgraduate teaching and develop and deliver training programmes within the hospital on issues associated with the application of medical equipment.

Clinical engineers have unique knowledge, skills, and understanding of both the technology (its characteristics and limitations) and of its clinical applications and implementations. This gives the clinical engineer particular skills to support and deliver training. Some clinical engineering departments, recognizing the importance of user training, employ staff to provide this training to medical and nursing staff, working in co-operation with the medical and nursing leadership and training departments. Clinical staff are increasingly required to have demonstrated competence in the use of medical equipment (Leach, 2002).

Managing the clinical environment

Clinical engineers can contribute to the design and control of the clinical environment itself. Where new facilities are being built or existing ones upgraded, clinical engineers can play a pivotal role in developing the design brief and acting as facilitators of a conversation between architects, civil and structural engineers, hospital capital planning teams, and the clinical staff. This includes understanding and discussing the interaction between and requirements for different medical equipment within the clinical environment. For example, the development of a new CT scanning facility must consider the requirement for anaesthetic procedures and hence the supply of anaesthetic gases and the optimum position of the anaesthetic machine and patient monitors. Similarly, the development of a renal dialysis unit must consider the space and utilities required for specialized chairs and dialysis equipment and the requirement for ultra-pure water and dialysis chemicals supply. Development of the equipment-intensive environments of critical care and theatre requires specialized planning for the medical equipment that will support and provide critical clinical services.

Risk management

Problems can occur with medical devices arising from device failures, device usability problems, installation and associated infrastructure problems and failure to operate devices correctly (Amoore and Ingram, 2002; Jacobson and Murray, 2007). The failures may have caused patient harm, or, but for the timely intervention of clinical staff, could have led to patient harm. Where adverse events involving medical devices occur, clinical engineers have an important role in their investigation. For every event it is important to understand the underlying causes. Their investigations can be assisted by a systematic approach that assesses possible contributions from the medical device, the users of the device, the clinical environment and the interactions between device, patient, clinicians and the environment of care (Amoore, 2014). The approach recognizes that adverse events often have more than one cause, as explained by Reason's Swiss Cheese model (Reason, 2000). The approach encourages identifying measures that will minimize the risk of recurrence, 'fixing' the gaps in the Swiss Cheese model. Managing these gaps with appropriate measures, often referred to as risk mitigation, can help prevent recurrence.

Clinical engineers also play a role in implementing the recommendations for improving hospital processes that emerge from such investigations. The need to learn from events and share the findings from investigations has led to national incident-reporting processes. Where an event gives cause for concern regarding the function or design of a medical device the hospital's clinical engineer will need to report this to the local regulatory authority.

Clinical engineers will also play an important part in managing safety notices from national and international bodies often acting in a formal role as Medical Device Safety Officers.

Research and development

Where the hospital has active research programmes clinical engineers contribute scientific support. Research programmes may require computer programming, development of specific unique devices, or application of existing devices. Clinical engineers have the skill and knowledge to deliver solutions through the combination of their engineering knowledge and skill and their knowledge and understanding of the clinical context in which a project will be delivered. Hospital-based clinical engineers, who deal every day with safety and quality assurance issues in the clinical environment, have a lot to offer when it comes to taking a research project out of the lab and into the clinical environment. Consequently, they are also involved in the innovation phase of new device developments and can be key facilitators of getting prototype designs into clinical practice for evaluation. Clinical engineers' involvement with the development of international standards both draws on and contributes to their effectiveness in this regard.

Clinical Engineers are by nature problem solvers. In many instances they solve problems by fabricating technology within their own organizations and deploying it in clinical practice. Such contributions can be small, such as making a bespoke adapter or holder for an item, to the design and build of a bespoke piece of equipment. This activity is always conducted with scientific and technical rigour to ensure safety and effectiveness but may be motivated by clinical need rather than a research activity. This 'Maker' tradition within clinical engineering continues and today can include software and app solutions, novel databases, use of 3D printing, augmented reality and prototyping electronics such as Arduino etc. However, such developments must be done in a manner that is consistent with best practice, compliant with current regulations. Within the European Union, such developments that are both carried out and put into clinical use within the same legal entity, i.e. are not placed on the market, are now subject to a 'light touch' regulation under Article 5.5 of the Medical Devices Regulation 2017 (European Union, 2017). Previously, under the Medical Devices Directive, such activity was unregulated and therefore Clinical Engineering Departments will now have to ensure compliance with the new Regulation (McCarthy, 2018).

Standards and their development

The safety and functional integrity of medical equipment are guided by Standards. Standards set out best practice, the state of the art or minimum performance criteria. They support designers and manufacturers, guiding them as they plan and design, to ensure that the device being developed meets the key criteria. They support procurers of medical equipment by providing reassurance that the equipment considered for procurement meets the criteria.

Standards are formal documents drawn up by national or international Standards bodies such as the American National Standards Institute (ANSI), the British Standards Institute (BSI), the International Organization for Standardization (ISO) and the International Electrotechnical Commission (IEC). These bodies rely on the expertise of professionals to draft and maintain the Standards. The training and experience of Clinical Engineers enable them to contribute to Standards bodies.

Four different types of Standards can be identified: Basic; Group; Product and Process. Basic Standards cover general principles applicable to equipment in general, such as the protection from electrical shock. Group Standards cover the essential requirement of equipment within a particular distinct group, for example medical equipment. An example is IEC 60601-1, stipulating the basic safety and essential performance requirements generally applicable to medical electrical equipment. Product Standards are specific to a particular type of product, for example Anaesthetic Machines or Ventilators. Process Standards describe the processes that support the design and use of medical equipment, for example Standards for asset management (ISO 55000) or quality management (ISO 9001).

Typically, each medical equipment is supported by several standards, its specific Product Standard as well as more general Process Standards such as the human usability Standard (IEC 62366), risk management (ISO 14971) and quality management for regulatory purposes (ISO 13485) as well as Standards for control symbols and for alarm systems (Vincent and Blandford, 2014).

Clinical Engineers can make an important contribution to the development and updating of Standards. In turn, an understanding of Standards and the Standards making process supports Clinical Engineers managing medical equipment.

Healthcare technology management — medical device management

The second pillar of HTM, as shown in Fig. 1.2 above, is Medical Device Management. HTM is concerned with the holistic management of the complete range of medical devices and systems within the hospital. The management of the assets will be explored in greater detail in Chapter 2. Key elements of medical device management are reviewed here to summarize this second pillar of HTM with an emphasis on the management of medical equipment.

The principles of asset management that apply to equipment in other sectors, as codified in the international standard ISO 55000, also apply to medical equipment. Developing a comprehensive asset management and maintenance function is a prerequisite of the healthcare delivery organization achieving its goals. Holistic asset management includes the technical and scientific management but extends to include a comprehensive governance framework for medical equipment and how full life cycle management, financial planning and stewardship is achieved. The American College of Clinical Engineering in 1992 adopted the following definition: 'A clinical engineer is a professional who supports and advances patient care by applying engineering and managerial skills to healthcare technology.' (Bauld, 1991). The inclusion of managerial skills in this definition reflects the fact that within many large hospitals, the clinical engineering department takes direct responsibility for actively managing the medical equipment over its useful life.

Equipment management activity

The equipment management activity includes the technical maintenance and financial management of all the medical equipment within the hospital. The activity covers the full life cycle of the assets from procurement through to eventual write-off and disposal. Given the vast quantity and diversity of devices in the modern hospital, the financial resources required for their management, and the varied support mechanisms that need to be put in place to achieve this, effective equipment management requires clinical engineers to be skilled in management practice.

Clinical engineers who provide institution-wide equipment management usually work closely with the hospital's risk and finance departments to ensure that optimal support can be delivered within a managed cost control environment. The equipment management function provides support for the equipment at each stage in its life cycle. This includes management of healthcare technologies and computer systems that are highly integrated and interoperable. The role extends beyond managing the medical equipment itself, to include associated and networked equipment, in particular where the devices are incorporated into information technology networks. This activity embraces, but is not limited to, a focus on scientific and technical support of medical equipment and clinical information technologies, including financial stewardship.

Inventory of medical equipment

An inventory of the medical equipment within the healthcare organization must be developed and maintained and expenditure associated with their maintenance and upkeep recorded and reported (WHO, 2011b). The inventory is the foundation on which the medical device management activity builds. At its core it includes the details of each item, make, model name and number, serial number, procurement details, software version and status and location. Sharing of information with other organizations to build up pictures of equipment reliability requires the use of uniform nomenclature. International groups have been working on standardized terms for medical devices, with the International Medical Device Regulators Forum recommending the Global Medical Device Nomenclature (GMDN) (see references for internet website).

It is a list of generic names designed to uniquely identify all medical device products. The asset inventory provides the basis for recording the maintenance and breakdown history of each asset, in turn supporting the planning of scheduled maintenance activities.

Maintenance: scheduled, performance verification and unscheduled

The ongoing technical maintenance of healthcare technologies has three key components: *scheduled maintenance; performance verification;* and *unscheduled maintenance.* Scheduled maintenance consists of all proactive activities whose purpose is to reduce the likelihood of failure of equipment in service. Performance verification includes all proactive processes that assure equipment that appears to be working are working optimally. Unscheduled maintenance covers all reactive actions that are initiated as a result of a reported real or suspected fault or failure of equipment or system.

Clinical engineers use risk management methodologies to optimize the available resources to deliver a medical device management programme that is focused on ensuring that the devices and equipment function safely and reliably, playing their part in ensuring that the clinical work can be delivered safely, cost-effectively and optimally. These technology management functions can be delivered by in-house teams of clinical engineers, be contracted to the service engineers of the equipment manufacturers, or be contracted to third-party maintenance groups. In practice it is often a combination of these. One of the key roles of the clinical engineer is to determine the optimum mix of services to best meet the organization's need.

Management of medical equipment takes place within a business model and so clinical engineers work closely with the organization's finance and procurement departments to ensure that not only is the technical equipment management effective but the support arrangements efficiently use the financial resources. Consequently, the clinical engineering role includes the development of strategies for the support of equipment, management and regular review of these strategies, and the management of both fiscal resources and personnel.

Medical equipment planning, including replacement planning programmes

Clinical engineers are often the drivers of the medical equipment management programmes within the hospital and develop processes by which the existing medical equipment inventory is assessed annually to ensure it is efficient and effective. This is a good example of how the two HTM roles, advancing care and device management, are complementary and integrated. To be able to advise effectively, clinical engineers should know both the current state of the existing technology deployed in the hospital (the asset register and the condition of the assets) and be able to provide an overview of new developments, and then be able to articulate how implementing a new technology will affect the hospital's ability to meet its corporate goals.

Clinical Engineers will use their knowledge and understanding of the organization's existing medical equipment to recommend replacement plans. Their knowledge of the corporate goals of the organization and of developments in healthcare technology can assist clinicians seeking to procure additional equipment to advance clinical practice and care.

Summary: patient-focused engineering

In this chapter we have looked at the specific activity of clinical engineering, based within the hospital. Clinical engineers have particular expertise and experience in the application of technology to the delivery of healthcare. They work in support of those delivering care by contributing to the management of healthcare technology, the clinical environment, and by providing direct support to those involved in clinical practice (Fig. 1.4). In doing so, clinical engineers can support a wide range of activities, devices, equipment and systems within the modern healthcare delivery organization.

Clinical engineering works at the point of care, and in many cases clinical engineers have direct patient contact. We have seen that, by its nature, clinical engineering is interdisciplinary. Clinical engineers work collaboratively with doctors, nurses, paramedics and hospital finance, risk and quality departments. To function optimally clinical engineers need to remain connected to the wider biomedical engineering community, the medical device industry, and the Standards and Regulatory community.

The most visible activity of a clinical engineering department engaged in the full gamut of activity described in this chapter is often the maintenance processes: workshops, and test equipment used to deliver the maintenance function. Consequently, clinical engineers are often mistakenly viewed as being primarily maintenance managers of the medical equipment. However, nothing could be further from the truth. The last few decades have witnessed enormous strides in the reliability of equipment, driven by advances in material and manufacturing science and improved standards. This has

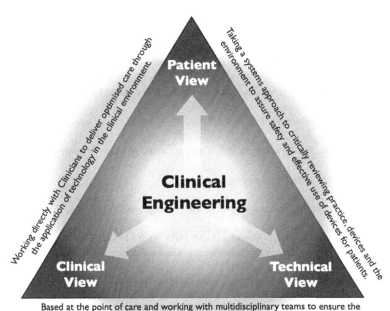

Based at the point of care and working with multidisciplinary teams to ensure the appropriate devices are procured, maintained and used correctly.

FIG. 1.4 Clinical Engineering is centrally placed to facilitate and assist communication. *Adapted with permission from Fig. 8.2 in Hegarty, F., Amoore, J., Blackett, P., McCarthy, J., Scott, R., 2017. Healthcare Technology Management — A Systematic Approach. CRC Press: Abingdon, UK. ISBN 978-1-4987-0354-3.*

shifted the challenge from activities concentrating on repairing and failure-prevention measures, towards optimizing the use and exploiting the potential of new equipment. The objective is to ensure that the medical equipment and systems are optimally deployed and applied to meet the organization's clinical and corporate missions. Clinical engineering is based on sound engineering principles and the application of critical thinking to solve problems. Its application requires imagination and creativity to synthesize solutions followed by a systems approach to implementing the solutions within an evidence-based framework.

Clinical engineering includes the management of diverse equipment and is complex. Achieving the twin roles of supporting and advancing care and device management within a holistic healthcare technology management framework is challenging. Financial controls, constraints, and decision making are complex and often emotional. Managing and balancing competing demands can sometimes blind clinical engineers to the essential focus of the healthcare system: helping the patient. Whether advancing care through the provision of engineering and scientific support, improving the safety and effectiveness of medical technology, or ensuring compliance with regulations and guidelines, clinical engineering should always remain focused on the care of the patient. Clinical engineering should both support and advance patient care. Therefore, patient care is the ultimate reason that clinical engineering exists.

References

Association for the Advancement of Medical Instrumentation (AAMI), 2011. Report of Future Forum to Identify a Unified Name and Vision. Available at: http://s3.amazonaws.com/rdcms-aami/files/production/public/FileDownloads/HTM/Final_Future%20_Forum.pdf.

Abraham, N., June 2000. Can We Gain without the Pain? *Controls Assurance Conference*. Hammersmith Hospital, London, UK.

Aller, J.C., 1977. Technology and people. In: Careers, C.A. (Ed.), The Practice of Clinical Engineering. Academic Press Inc., London, p. 34.

Amoore, J.N., Ingram, P., 2002. Learning from adverse incidents involving medical devices. Br. Med. J. 325 (7358), 272—275.

Amoore, J.N., 2014. A structured approach for investigating the causes of medical device adverse events. J. Med. Eng. 2014. Article ID 314138. http://www.hindawi.com/journals/jme/2014/314138/.

Amoore, J.N., Hinrichs, S., Brooks-Young, P., 2015. Medical equipment specification, evaluation and selection (Chapter 6). In: Clarkson, D. (Ed.), Quality in Clinical Engineering, pp. 58—85. Report 110. Institute of Physics and Engineering in Medicine, ISBN 978 1 903613 58 0. 2015.

Amoore, J.N., April 30, 2018. Strategic Equipment Planning: Teamwork Achieves the Dream. Health GB Conference: Medical Engineering. Informa, Manchester. https://www.healthgbexhibition.com/en/conference/Medical-Engineering-Conference.html.

Amoore, J.N., May 1, 2018. Improving Planned Equipment Management: Integrating the Clinical Engineer into the Supply Chain. Health GB Conference: Procurement. Informa, Manchester. In: https://www.healthgbexhibition.com/en/conference/Health-Procurement-Overview1.html.

Bauld, T.J., 1991. The definition of a clinical engineer. J. Clin. Eng. 403—405.

Black, P., Amoore, J.N., September 2011. Pushing the Boundaries of Device Replacement: Introducing the Keystone Model. European Medical Physics and Engineering Conference. Trinity College, Dublin, Ireland.

David, Y., Jahnke, E.G., 23 (3), May–June 2004. Planning hospital medical technology. IEEE Eng. Med. Biol. Mag.

ECRI Institute, 2008. ECRI Institute, Coping with convergence: a road map for successfully combining medical and information technologies. Health Devices 293–304.

European Union, 2017. Regulation (EU) 2017/745 on Medical Devices. Available at: http://eur-lex.europa.eu/legal-content/EN/TXT/?uri=OJ:L:2017: 117:TOC.

Geddes, L.A., Careers, C.A., 1977. Historical background of interdisciplinary engineering. In: Careers, C.A. (Ed.), The Practice of Clinical Engineering. Academic Press Inc., London, p. 17.

Gibson, C., McCarthy, J.P., Powell, A., Roberts, D., Spark, P., Truran, R.J., 1998. Minimising clinical risk in the use of active intravenous infusion devices. Br. J. Intensive Care 8, 114–119.

GMDN, Global Medical Device Nomenclature, GMDN Agency. Available at: https://www.gmdnagency.org/.

Hawkin, S., 2013. My Brief History. Bantam Press, London, UK.

Hegarty, F., Amoore, J., Blackett, P., McCarthy, J., Scott, R., 2017. Healthcare Technology Management – A Systematic Approach. CRC Press, Abingdon, UK. ISBN 978-1-4987-0354-3.

Jacobson, B., Murray, A., 2007. Medical Devices: Use and Safety. Churchill Livingstone, Elsevier Limited. ISBN-10: 0 443 10259 7.

Keay, S., McCarthy, J.P., Carey-Smith, B., 2015. Medical equipment libraries – implementation, experience and user satisfaction. J. Med. Eng. Technol. 39 (6), 354–362.

Leach, D.C., 2002. Competence is a habit. J. Am. Med. Assoc. 287 (2), 243–244. https://doi.org/10.1001/jama.287.2.243. Available at: https:// jamanetwork.com/journals/jama/article-abstract/194539.

McCarthy, J.P., 2018. MDR – the health institution exemption and MHRA draft guidance. Scope 27 (3), 24–27 (IPEM: York).

Milne, J.S., 1907. Surgical Instruments in Greek and Roman Times. Clarendon Press, Oxford. Available at: https://www.gutenberg.org/files/40424/40424-h/40424-h.htm.

Reason, J., 2000. Human error: models and management. Br. Med. J. 320 (7237), 768–770.

Smith, M., Saunders, R., Stuckhardt, L., McGinnis, J.M. (Eds.), September 2012. Best Care at Lower Cost: The Path to Continuously Learning Healthcare in America. Institute of Medicine. Available at: http://www.nationalacademies.org/hmd/~/media/Files/Report%20Files/2012/Best-Care/Best% 20Care%20at%20Lower%20Cost_Recs.pdf.

Vincent, C., Blandford, A., 2014. Infusion Pump Standards Guide. Technical report IP002. Chi-med. Available at: www.chi-med.ac.uk/research/bibdetail. php?PPnum=IP002.

WHO, 2011a. Development of Medical Device Policies. World Health Organization, WHO Press, Geneva. ISBN 978 92 4 150163 7. Available at: http:// apps.who.int/iris/bitstream/10665/44600/1/9789241501637_eng.pdf.

WHO, 2011b. Introduction to Medical Equipment Inventory Management. World Health Organization, WHO Press, Geneva. Available at: http://apps. who.int/medicinedocs/documents/s21565en/s21565en.pdf.

Chapter 2

Health technology asset management

Justin McCarthy[a], Francis Hegarty[b], John Amoore[c], Paul Blackett[d] and Richard Scott[e]

[a]Clin Eng Consulting Ltd, Cardiff and School of Engineering, Cardiff University, Wales, United Kingdom; [b]Healthcare Technology Department, Children's Health Ireland, Dublin, Ireland; [c]Consultant Clinical Engineer (Retired), Edinburgh, Scotland, United Kingdom; [d]Lancashire Teaching Hospitals NHS Foundation Trust, Lancashire, United Kingdom; [e]Sheffield Teaching Hospitals NHS Foundation Trust, Sheffield, United Kingdom

Chapter outline

Introduction

Clinical engineering has evolved to meet the needs associated with the introduction of medical devices and equipment[1] into the clinical environment. In the early years there was a necessary focus on safety and reliability, technical maintenance and repair. Best practice in clinical engineering was characterized by well-developed technical equipment management processes that operated within a quality system. As the complexity and number of devices increased, there was a need for the equipment management role to expand to include a more strategic dimension. Today the term 'asset management' is used to describe a holistic equipment management approach which includes the important technical processes and also the strategic management of the fleets of medical devices, equipment and interoperable systems. Collectively these are described as healthcare technology.

The strategic plans of a healthcare organization determine its current and future operations. Strategic plans are subject to change, evolving incrementally and responding to the challenge of meeting the needs of the people the healthcare organization serves. The evolution and development of healthcare technologies trigger developments in clinical care which in turn can impact the strategic development of healthcare organizations. The term *healthcare technology management* (HTM) describes the role that embraces, but is not limited to, a focus on scientific and technical support of electromedical devices and clinical information technologies, including their financial stewardship. In Chapter 1 a holistic Healthcare Technology Management approach was described. This included a discussion of the clinical engineering activities that make up such an approach under two heading, Supporting and Advancing Care, and Medical Device Management. In this

---

1. The WHO definitions of medical device and medical equipment are given in Chapter 1.

chapter we focus on the later, the asset management of the medical devices, equipment and associated systems referred to as healthcare technology. The advancing and supporting care activities will not be revisited in this chapter; however, as discussed in Chapter 1, in practice these activities are blended and closely interdependent.

Healthcare Technology Asset Management: a systematic approach

As healthcare organizations develop a holistic healthcare technology management system, one strand of that activity is healthcare technology asset management. This ensures the deployment of the healthcare technology assets in such a way that their value to the organization and its stakeholders is optimized. Such a system will have processes for supporting equipment from the strategic acquisition and deployment of technology down to the day-to-day support requirements (MHRA, 2015). Hegarty et al. (2017) have described in detail a systematic approach to healthcare technology management that is structured so as to add value in its widest sense.

The asset management of healthcare technology is complex and to implement fully requires a number of different processes to run concurrently and in an interconnected way. In the model described in this chapter, the strategic asset management is realized by having a corporate-level Medical Device Policy that brings into being a multidisciplinary group called the Medical Device Committee (MDC). The operational asset management of healthcare technology is developed by specific departments within the organization who are mandated by the MDC to implement the asset management process within their expertise as part of the Medical Device Policy. The Clinical Engineering Department would be one such department which would usually have an organizational-wide responsibility. Laboratory services such as pathology and biochemistry might be tasked with managing the technology particular to their speciality within the context of the MDC guidelines. The roles and responsibilities of any group tasked with managing healthcare technology will be set out within the Medical Device Policy; however each department must develop a specific programme that takes into account the particular healthcare technology in its charge and also the context within which they are used. Each department charged with realizing the strategic asset management policy will therefore develop an HTM Programme for the healthcare technology they look after. This programme in turn will consist of day-to-day detailed operational support plans for groups of specific equipment. These equipment support plans are likely to be numerous and run concurrently.

The overall structure of such a holistic asset management approach for healthcare technology can be considered as two interlocking management processes that form a Healthcare Technology Management System as shown in Fig. 2.1.

The strategic asset management objectives of the organization are thus set out and planned at corporate level in the Medical Devices Policy and implemented and delivered on the ground in the specific equipment support plans. By ensuring that the two layers of the system are interconnected and responsive to each other, the organization can be sure there is a

Healthcare Technology Management System

Aligning healthcare technology and its management to the strategic and operational needs of the organization.

Strategic Planning

Delivery & Implementation

Detailed planning, delivery and implementation of healthcare technology management

FIG. 2.1 The two interlocking cycles of a Healthcare Technology Management System. *Reproduced with permission from Fig. 4.12 in Hegarty, F., Amoore, J., Blackett, P., McCarthy, J., Scott R., 2017. Healthcare Technology Management — A Systematic Approach. CRC Press, Abingdon, UK.*

clear line of sight of responsibility and accountability throughout the organization. Each layer can be run as a quality system with regular reporting built into the system between each layer.

The arrangements outlined match those set out in the international Standard series for Asset Management, ISO 55000 (ISO, 2014) with the equivalences shown in Table 2.1.

Implementing the strategic aspects of the Healthcare Technology Management System

As noted above, a multidisciplinary Medical Device Committee (MDC) is an important mechanism for realizing and implementing the HTM system. The MDC will develop and implement the Medical Device Policy (MD Policy) which sets out the strategic objectives for all aspects of the use and management of medical devices across the organization. Many stakeholders can contribute to such a policy — board members, clinicians, general managers, finance managers, clinical users of healthcare technology — but it is only clinical engineers that have this area of work as a central feature of their role profile. The systems engineering skills of clinical engineers can contribute significantly to the development and review of the hospital-wide strategic asset management approach or plan (Hegarty et al., 2017, Chapter 2).

The MDC would set into action the aspirations set out in the MD Policy by developing the Strategic HTM Plan. Such a Strategic HTM Plan will be reviewed annually and might be altered in response to changes in the organization or the governance within which it operates.

The MDC should analyze the deployment of healthcare technology assets and review their associated risks and benefits, to ensure that their implementation supports the organization's clinical, corporate and financial goals. This would include management and use of medical devices, corporate oversight of risk management, adverse event investigation as well as strategic management of investment in healthcare technology. For example, the MDC should identify the requirements for new acquisitions of healthcare technology either to support service development or as part of a planned replacement programme. The MDC should also coordinate a local healthcare technology assessment activity to ensure that adoption of new technologies will deliver benefits within the specific context of its own organization. Where acquisitions are sanctioned, the MDC should initiate an acquisition project to plan and manage the procurement and commissioning of the new healthcare technology.

Implementing the operational aspects of the Healthcare Technology Management System

The MDC should assign authority and responsibility for the ongoing management of healthcare technology assets to the appropriate departments within the organization. This should be set out in the MDC's Strategic HTM Plan. The MDC acts

TABLE 2.1 Terminology equivalence with ISO 55000.

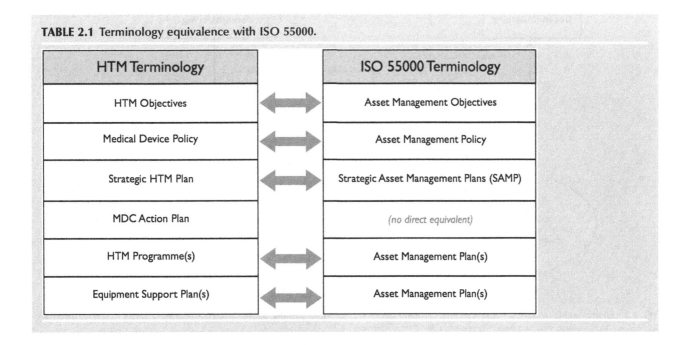

HTM Terminology	ISO 55000 Terminology
HTM Objectives	Asset Management Objectives
Medical Device Policy	Asset Management Policy
Strategic HTM Plan	Strategic Asset Management Plans (SAMP)
MDC Action Plan	*(no direct equivalent)*
HTM Programme(s)	Asset Management Plan(s)
Equipment Support Plan(s)	Asset Management Plan(s)

in a coordinating capacity in this regard ensuring that, through the Strategic HTM Plan, all healthcare technology is assigned to the care of appropriate departments. The Strategic HTM Plan sets into action the operational requirements set out at a high level in the HTM Policy and should be reviewed regularly. A dynamic MDC Action Plan, reviewed and updated at each meeting, is the main working document of the MDC and is used as a means of setting and recording operational goals and responsibilities. The MDC does not develop the specific support solutions; that is done within each department. However, each department will report back to the MDC on the effectiveness of the solutions it develops and delivers. In this way the MDC can assure that appropriate solutions are being applied across the organization and the Board has visibility of this.

The Clinical Engineering Department (CED) is one such department that is typically charged with the task of delivering medical equipment asset management. The CED must develop its healthcare technology management programme (HTM Programme) which sets out the day-to-day workings of how clinical engineers will manage the healthcare technology assets allocated to them, ensuring that equipment is maintained in a satisfactory condition and kept available for use.

The challenge for any CED is how to best deploy resources to optimally manage the diverse and complex range of healthcare technology for which it has responsibility. This has to be achieved within finite resources, which rarely allow for an ideal solution to be put in place. Consequently, some form of benefit and risk evaluation is necessary to identify items that carry a greater management requirement in order to realize benefits and to control the corporate, clinical, and financial risk.

The life cycle of medical devices and equipment is described in Fig. 2.2. The processes for acquisition are shown step by step in the upper right part of the flowchart. As equipment is commissioned, there is a need for a formal plan to be put in place to support the use of the equipment. This is the equipment support plan (ESP) which may be for a single item of equipment particularly if it is a 'one-off' within the organization, or it may be a plan for a generic group of equipment which are dealt with in the same way e.g. all the anaesthetic machines in an operating theatre suite. The ESP will include

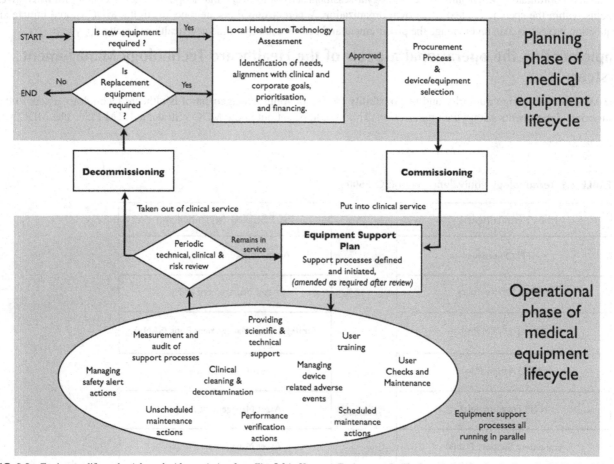

FIG. 2.2   Equipment life cycle. *Adapted with permission from Fig. 5.1 in Hegarty, F., Amoore, J., Blackett, P., McCarthy, J., Scott R., 2017. Healthcare Technology Management — A Systematic Approach. CRC Press, Abingdon, UK.*

some or many of the support processes shown in the bottom section of the flowchart, depending on the level of support considered to be necessary and appropriate. When a new type of device is first put into use, the ESP for the first year will be established. However, over time the support requirements may change and so at regular intervals the ESP may need to be altered. For the purposes of illustration in this chapter we will assume the ESP will be reviewed annually.

So the HTM programme as a whole is an ongoing process that consists of a series of equipment support plans that are reviewed and monitored and amended within a quality management system. This overall structure is illustrated in Fig. 2.3.

At any one time, a clinical engineering department will be implementing an HTM Programme that supports all the devices it has responsibility for. This will include many different devices, each in a different point in its own life cycle and each used within a particular clinical context. The HTM Programme will therefore consist of a number of ESPs each tailored for specific groups of devices and all running concurrently. It is through the development and delivery of the device-specific ESPs that the HTM programmes can focus on the particular requirements of the vast range of devices supported, while also ensuring the HTM Programme as a whole meets corporate, clinical, and financial objectives.

Linking the circles: defining the aims, objectives, and scope of different components of the HTM system

Healthcare organizations will have overarching corporate objectives, goals, and targets for short, medium, and long-term periods which will be used to develop the overall Medical Device Policy, aligning the medical device planning with the strategic aims of the organization. The relevant aims and objectives become more detailed and expanded as they travel down from Board and executive level through the MDC until they arrive at the CED, communicating the organization's

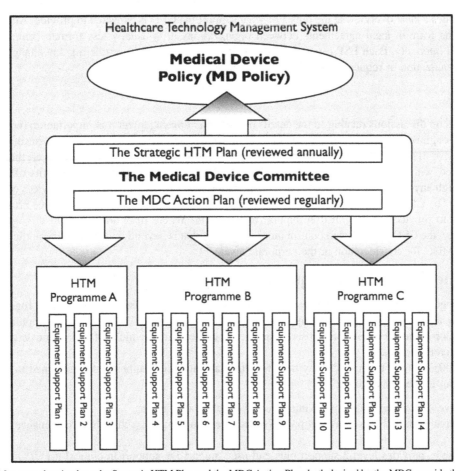

FIG. 2.3 The HTM system showing how the Strategic HTM Plan and the MDC Action Plan, both devised by the MDC, provide the linkage between the Medical Device Policy and the HTM Programmes. Different HTM Programmes may be developed by a number of departments, each programme consisting of a series of Equipment Support Plans. *Reproduced with permission from Fig. 4.14 in Hegarty, F., Amoore, J., Blackett, P., McCarthy, J., Scott R., 2017. Healthcare Technology Management — A Systematic Approach. CRC Press, Abingdon, UK.*

requirements for the local objectives and explaining how they fit into the overall 'big picture'. Review of these corporate goals should inform the development of the local HTM Programmes. By setting out the aims, objectives, and scope of the programmes, the CED can build the corporate overview into its own plan.

Healthcare organizations, whether privately or publicly owned, are usually subject to standards and regulations set by various bodies. Clinical associations and groups, together with professional institutes and numerous government agencies and accreditation bodies, dictate minimum levels of care, safety, and service to be provided by the healthcare organization. The support provided by the CED will be influenced by these standards to which clinical engineers may have contributed, and the CED is strategically placed to provide evidence to support the organization's claim that it is complying with the standards. Equally the CED has an obligation to bring to the attention of any other departments who deliver healthcare technology management programmes, and the various committees and groups within the organization, any shortcomings and failures that need to be addressed to ensure future compliance with standards or regulations.

As with any product design or service delivery, understanding the customer's requirement is an essential ingredient. The delivery of healthcare technology management is an interdisciplinary endeavour. Responsibilities will be shared between the CED and those involved with device procurement and use, with all stakeholders having an active part to play. The most successful clinical engineering services are to be found where the clinical users — the customers — have had a say in the initial service design. In this way, a real sense of shared purpose is achieved. As with any engineering endeavour, it is best practice to build on what has worked successfully, taking objective responses into account, refining, and evolving services for customer benefit. Be adaptable and prepared to change — if that cherished idea has evidently not worked then start again! This plan—do—check—act model will be familiar to those who have worked with formal quality management systems such as ISO 9000 (ISO, 2015) and ISO 13485 (ISO, 2016). But keep in mind always that the end beneficiary of the services provided is the patient.

Defining the aims, objectives and scope for the healthcare technology management programmes at department level in specific ESPs provides a clear overview at the outset of what support the CED is expected to provide. Although this can, in some cases, take the form of legal agreements between organizations, it is usually less formal, being discussed, documented, and agreed internally. Each ESP can and should, be reviewed annually, considering any changes in the strategic direction of the organization or requests from individual clinical services.

Dealing with risk

As we start to focus on discussions relating to the details of equipment management it is important to remember that a key role for the clinical engineering department is to identify, evaluate, and appropriately address risks. In some cases it may be possible to reduce risk to such a low and acceptable level that no further action is required. However, there will always be some risk associated with the delivery of healthcare. The challenge is to ensure that the benefits of any treatment or intervention outweigh any potential harm. So careful consideration needs to be given as to how devices covered by an ESP are used clinically. The CED can contribute to risk reduction not only by implementing maintenance programmes but also by protecting time to provide meaningful user support and training. Where risks are identified through participation in maintenance activity, the CED should act to control those risks or, if that is beyond the scope of the particular ESP, escalate the risk up to the MDC for consideration at the corporate level.

Developing the device-specific equipment support plans (ESP)

Having defined the goal of the HTM programme, the CED must now organize itself to deliver that programme. Given the diversity of devices and clinical environments supported it is not surprising that a 'one size fits all' approach will not work. The CED will develop a number of ESPs for different devices or clinical areas, which define in more detail how the service support will be delivered for each.

Hegarty et al. (2017) suggest that ESPs may be categorized at four levels, appropriately assigned to different types of equipment according to their risk profile:

Level 1: Reactive — provides only unscheduled, reactive technical support
Level 2: Proactive — in addition, provides proactive technical support e.g. scheduled maintenance and performance verification
Level 3: Holistic — provides level 2 support plus end-user support i.e. support in clinical use
Level 4: Audit — provides level 3 support plus annual review as part of a quality cycle.

It can be argued that there is also the possibility of a Level 0 for some devices (typically accessories) where maintenance is not economic and the response should be 'replace on failure'.

The content of a typical ESP with, for some aspects, possible performance indicators (PI), might include some or all of the following:

- An acceptance service for new devices: PI, time from delivery to deployment;
- Device specific scheduled maintenance details: PI, completion time scales and targets;
- Handling of breakdown requests: PI, response times to request, repair time targets, equipment availability targets;
- Provision of medical device management advice: PI, meeting of agreed deadlines;
- Safe disposal of devices;
- Maintenance and access to a medical equipment inventory;
- Delivery of device-specific training: PI, percentage of staff cohort trained;
- Addressing medical device alerts and investigating incidents: PI, percentage of actions taken within deadlines
- Clinical user support.

In developing the ESPs, the CED should carefully consider and balance how to meet the clinical, corporate, and financial requirements of the organization. Ideally the equipment support plan will ensure the efficacy of the equipment and allow the clinical engineers to play a complete role in supporting the clinicians. However, financial constraints rarely allow the ideal to be delivered. It is unlikely that the CED will become expert in the support of all medical devices. The monetary or staffing resources needed to train and maintain competence on a 'one-off' particular model of equipment can become unreasonable and the CED may determine, in consultation with the clinical users, that a Level 2 ESP is required but choose to outsource the support to the manufacturer or an external service supplier. The CED should research how to best support all devices through a mix of in-house and external service support.

Once acceptance checked, recorded and deployed into service, the ongoing technical maintenance of healthcare technologies has three key components. These are scheduled maintenance, performance verification, and unscheduled maintenance. Scheduled maintenance consists of all proactive activities whose purpose is to minimize the likelihood of failure of the device in service. Performance verification includes all proactive processes that assure devices that appear to be working are working optimally. Unscheduled maintenance covers all reactive actions that are initiated as a result of a reported real or suspected fault or failure of a device or system. Clinical engineers use risk management methodologies to optimize the hospital resources to deliver a HTM Programme that is focused on ensuring that the clinical work of the hospital can be delivered optimally. These technology maintenance functions can be delivered by in-house teams of clinical engineers, by a contracted third-party maintenance organization or can be contracted to the service engineers of the equipment manufacturers, or a combination of all three.

One of the key roles of the lead professional clinical engineer is to determine, in consultation with their senior staff, the optimum mix of services to meet the organization's need. Management of the devices takes place within a business model and so clinical engineers work closely with the finance and procurement departments to ensure that not only is the technical equipment management effective but the support arrangements are also an efficient use of financial resources. Consequently, the clinical engineering role includes the development of methodologies for the support of healthcare equipment, regular review and management of these methodologies, and the management of both fiscal resources and personnel.

Clinical engineers understand the devices and the clinical context in which they are used, and in developing the individual support plans they often imaginatively foresee problems that could arise and develop the support strategies to mitigate them.

Assigning the resources

It is axiomatic that funding for the CED is necessary to meet its agreed service specification targets. Staff must be recruited; tools, test equipment, and spare parts be bought; and service contracts placed. The healthcare organization should allocate a staff and revenue budget that allows the CED to deliver the HTM programme. Departments that are fully funded to maintain their establishment's medical devices to manufacturers' specifications and frequency are rare! Pressures brought to bear on the CED of finance, labour, expertise, and materials come up against the requirement to maintain equipment in a safe and operational condition to meet the needs of the clinician and patient. Where the resources allocated are insufficient to deliver a comprehensive solution, the head of CED must first optimize the use of available resources and must then communicate the residual risk to the CEO and the Board. Usually, the cost of labour and parts are associated with work undertaken by in-house clinical engineers and their support staff, while external financial commitments are associated with equipment on service contracts and those items of equipment sent away for repair. The CED needs to implement some form of financial control so that an accurate position regarding finances can be maintained. Working within a larger organization it is likely that other departments such as procurement and finance will have introduced ways to do just this, but smaller or independent departments will need to start from scratch.

A useful and important tool to assist in prioritizing medical devices for time and money to be spent on maintenance is to place devices into risk categories. ECRI Institute[2] has long suggested devices are placed into low, medium, and high-risk categories and usually a record of the category is held on the clinical engineering equipment management database. The categorization can be used to inform decisions regarding maintenance strategy (ECRI Institute, 2007). The choice of risk category however is up to the CED in consultation with clinical users but general definitions are given. For example, high-risk devices would include ventilators and defibrillators — devices whose failure would reasonably be expected to cause immediate patient harm. Medium-risk devices would include ECG recorders and BP monitors which if they fail, could possibly cause delay in treatment. Low-risk devices are those that are unlikely to lead to any serious complications. The risk category itself does not dictate what maintenance a device requires but it can be a useful component of a risk assessment and of deciding which level of ESP may be appropriate. Also it is important to realize that some items of the same type may be put in different risk categories because of different clinical areas or clinical uses to which they are put.

In the context of resources, the difficult issue of "maintaining equipment in accordance with (or in line with) manufacturers' instructions" needs to be considered. Regulatory authorities may stipulate this (MHRA, 2015), but it is unlikely that the allocated resources will allow complete compliance. In 2014 the Centers for Medicare & Medicaid Services (CMS) of the US Department of Health & Human Services (DHHS) amended Appendix A of their State Operations Manual and stated that:

> *A hospital may, under certain conditions, use equipment maintenance activities and frequencies that differ from those recommended by the manufacturer. Hospitals that choose to employ alternate maintenance activities and/or schedules must develop, implement, and maintain a documented AEM program to minimize risks to patients and others in the hospital associated with the use of facility or medical equipment.*

CMS (2014)

If the CED decides to implement an 'alternative equipment maintenance' (AEM) plan, this must only be done on the basis of evidence, experience, and knowledge of local conditions of use, and must be clearly documented. This approach is also supported in a note in IEC 62353 (IEC, 2014) "A RESPONSIBLE ORGANIZATION having appropriate expertise can also take responsibility for modifying MANUFACTURER's proposals based on local conditions of use and risk assessment." The decisions should be reported to the MDC.

It is not acceptable practice for a CED to concentrate slavishly on meeting Level 2 performance verification schedules set by a manufacturer whilst leaving equipment requiring breakdown repair out of service for many weeks at a time.

Implementing an in-house maintenance programme

Once defined in the equipment support plan and the resources assigned, teams are set into action. The scheduling of work is an important task for the team leader. They have to develop and implement a programme that includes routine scheduled maintenance and performance verification processes (Level 2), while also having sufficient resources to respond to breakdowns or unscheduled maintenance events (Level 1). Also remember that ongoing clinical user support and training (Level 3) might be as important to clinical effectiveness and safety as routine performance verification.

Typically, equipment requires some form of inspection perhaps on an annual basis with some devices requiring this more frequently. This performance verification activity is intended to assure that the device is performing to specification and is safe. It is considered good practice for a device to be seen at least once per year, and manufacturers usually provide a checklist to detail what should be checked and how often this should be done. CEDs use manufacturers' guidelines but are also influenced by local experience gained in supporting devices. It should also be noted that some countries have requirements for regular electrical testing of 'portable appliances', the details usually based on an assessment of risk and conditions of use (HSE, 2015).

Additionally, some devices may require scheduled, proactive maintenance, that is, routine replacement of parts such as filters to prevent failures. While these may be replaced at a set frequency, sometimes parts require changing after a number of operating hours, which introduces an additional complexity. Others yet may require parts such as batteries to be replaced at a differing frequency to an inspection. Any system introduced by the CED needs to carefully manage the peculiarities of the medical devices within its care.

---

2. https://www.ecri.org/about/

For particular groups of devices it makes sense for the performance verification and scheduled maintenance activities to be aligned and undertaken at the same time. For example, the team that verifies the performance of all the defibrillators in the hospital will usually manage the planned replacement of the defibrillators' batteries and change the battery in the clinical area during one of its scheduled visits. The planning and monitoring of these proactive maintenance actions is best carried out in conjunction with the medical equipment database. This database will usually automatically generate reminders for scheduled work a set period before it being due. This gives the clinical engineer time to contact the user and arrange a time for the maintenance to be carried out. Likewise, should the device not be available, or not found, a procedure must be in place to advise the user that it has not been maintained.

Corrective maintenance, or repair, is the process of restoring a medical device to a safe, functional, normal condition (see the definition 3.39 in IEC 62353) (IEC, 2014). Corrective maintenance is unpredictable and the department has to put a system into place to handle difficult situations with varying demands on a whole range of devices where specialist knowledge may not be available and conflicting requests made. Clinical engineers with appropriate training and experience are expected to diagnose and rectify these problems, with reference to technical documentation and to the manufacturer if required. The process that gets the device back into use must be done quickly as it is possible that diagnosis or therapy to patients may be delayed due to the device being out of service. All corrective actions will also be documented in the medical equipment database so that it contains a full service history for each device.

Contracting out external maintenance programmes

The contracting of maintenance to an external supplier requires careful consideration. The transfer of work to an outside contractor does not remove liability from the healthcare organization nor responsibility from the CED. Due diligence needs to be exercised that the contractors are suitable. This might entail requesting training records and evidence of knowledge, experience, and skills, examining insurance cover, and considering business continuity issues. These are particularly important when the contractor being considered is not an authorized service agent of the manufacturer, sometimes called a 'third-party contractor'. Even if a contractor is approved by the manufacturer it is still appropriate to request relevant information and review its responses.

With the choice of contractor having been made there is a decision on the level of cover required. Typically this may be a comprehensive Level 2 support which includes all the required proactive actions and any reactive repairs necessary, or a more restrictive Level 2 support, covering only the recommended scheduled actions, or a Level 1 reactive repair service with priority. Many variations exist in-between, parts excluded, onsite or offsite servicing, accidental damage included, parts included to a monetary value, only one repair visit included, and so on. It is usually the CED's decision as to which level of cover is best suited to the organization but consultation with the clinical users is important. If the equipment is new it will probably be reliable so the decision may be taken to only cover the equipment with a basic contract; if it is unreliable it may be financially attractive to have fully comprehensive cover.

One particular approach is to have a contract with the external contractor, yet have the in-house clinical engineering department perform 'first-line fault finding'. These or similar contracts are often called "partnership" contracts. With such a contract, when a fault is reported the CED takes the initiative and looks to see what the fault is and liaises with the contractor. If repairs can be undertaken by the CED then this may done, or at the least, the contractor knows the general condition of the equipment before they attend onsite. This solution allows the CED to retain involvement with the equipment while having technical backup easily at hand.

Whichever method of external contract is made, records need to be kept of the contract and period of cover, along with service reports. The scheduled and unscheduled maintenance delivery by the external service supplier should also be documented within the medical equipment database.

Documenting the delivered programme, the role of the medical equipment management database

An essential component of any HTM Programme is the existence of a register of all medical devices being managed by the CED (WHO, 2011). The department, indeed the organization as a whole, cannot manage what it does not know about, therefore a requirement to establish a medical device inventory is immediately identified. It is important to consider what devices should be included in the database. In many healthcare organizations there are several technical departments that manage specific types of devices. Renal dialysis is a typical example but there are others such as radiotherapy engineering, rehabilitation engineering, and pathology which may have maintenance teams dedicated to their specific equipment. While the CED will probably have the greatest quantity of equipment, a decision will need to be taken whether to include the devices from these other departments or not. The significant advantage of doing so is that the organization has a single point of reference for its medical devices, but a single, common database structure may not be suitable for every department. However there are now a number of commercially available equipment management database systems that will allow the inventory and associated staff and work records to be sectioned such that different teams within the organization can have screen layouts appropriate to their needs and only have day to day access to data relevant to their team. A system manager can, when asked extract data on an organization wide basis.

The management of the HTM programme relies heavily on the upkeep of the medical equipment database. Over the years CEDs have approached this from different directions. Some departments have designed their own database, tailoring it to their own needs, while others have opted to buy a commercially available database. There are advantages and disadvantages in both cases but the major consideration is one of support. In the case where the database has been developed locally, support is usually provided by one person with an interest in information technology. If they leave, retire, or become ill, there is likely to be no robust contingency plan to handle this. On the other hand, a commercially available database will be offered with service support, albeit at a cost. Therefore, it is quite justifiable to have such a crucial part of the department supported professionally.

The medical equipment database is the repository for the medical equipment asset register and the service histories of these assets. The database may also support scheduling of routine work across the different teams. Reports generated from mining the data are useful in the day-to-day management of the delivery of the plans and in measuring the efficiency and effectiveness of the programme as a whole. Data and information from this source will also be part of the significant contribution from the CED to the organization's annual HTM plan.

As the medical device management system (MDMS) equipment database touches on all aspects of the CED it is likely to be the repository and hub of all stored and accumulated data. It is therefore vital that efforts are made to maintain the accuracy of the data. The established database needs regular housekeeping which will highlight areas that have become outdated and records that have not been completed correctly. Although computer systems have many ways of validating inputs it is surprising how small errors can appear, and of course no amount of validation can keep clinical departments from changing their names or moving equipment around! Regular refresher training can remind clinical engineers of the correct ways of using the database and can avert any build-up of poor practice. Finally, robust data backup procedures are essential.

Financial control

All the actions identified as part of the equipment support plan need to be resourced, set into action, and controlled. Controlling costs is an important part of the programme and so some means of measuring resource utilization needs to be established.

The optimum mix of in-house or externally contracted maintenance services needs to be decided and justified. Often the decision to manage devices in-house is made where the CED has the capacity and capability to do so. However, it is important to remember that the HTM programme must also support the hospital's financial goals. Regardless of the mix of service support chosen, there is a need to control the costs associated with it.

Where the service solution is fully outsourced the costs associated with external contractors will be readily available as service contracts will be procured and their cost clearly identified. However, in such situations it is not uncommon for the CED to also provide some degree of front-line support. As a minimum this usually includes managing communications between the clinical staff and the service company so that a complete service history is maintained, but may extend to having a quick first look to rule out user error or user difficulty with operation.

Where service is delivered in-house it can be difficult to assess all the costs associated with its provision. It should include an estimate of staff costs, non-contract external service, spare parts, and cost of staff training as a minimum. However, other overhead costs such as workshop space, tools, test equipment, energy costs, calibration costs, quality management system certification etc. can be less visible in the hospital context. Regardless, the CED should make all reasonable attempts to construct a complete financial analysis of its function and include financial analysis in the decision making when developing the HTM Programme.

Clinical engineering departments may analyze costs in different ways. A top-down approach might be to divide the overall department budget including overheads such as lighting, heating, and IT on a pro-rata basis to each device supported. A bottom-up approach might be to track resource utilization as part of recording each maintenance action within the MDMS database and then aggregate the costs up. The actual method developed should be implemented in conjunction with the hospital's finance department to ensure compliance with the corporate financial policy.

Being able to estimate the total cost of each equipment support plan enables analysis of how cost effective each plan is. An estimate of the cost of the plan can be achieved by looking at the internal and external costs associated with each

Equipment Support Plan Actions	Clinical Engineering Department Internal Costs		Clinical Engineering Department External Costs	
	Staff Costs	Spare parts costs	Service Contract costs	Non Contract costs
End-user Training				
Unscheduled Actions				
Scheduled Actions				
Performance Verification Actions				
Sub-totals				
Cost of Internal support				
Cost of External support				
Total Cost of support				

FIG. 2.4 Template used to estimate the total cost of an equipment support plan.

element. Fig. 2.4 shows a simple template that can be used to get an estimate of the support costs associated with an equipment support plan.

Hegarty et al. (2017) have described in more detail a methodology for assessing the value delivered by an equipment support plan and balancing the resources between different ESPs in Section 6.2.6 of their book.

Evaluating effectiveness

As well as these financial controls, a set of key performance indicators (KPIs) developed for the work undertaken by the CED is a valuable and clear way in which the general performance of the CED can be monitored. The management of the organization and the members of the department will have a keen interest in how well the CED is working and it is usually accepted that KPIs are reported on a monthly basis.

In developing KPIs it is useful to adopt a balanced scorecard approach, where several aspects of the department are taken into account rather than presenting an overwhelming list of technical data. There are no fixed rules as to what should be included but reference to the service specification agreed on would be a good start in developing these. Perhaps KPIs that have been grouped into four categories — service user, internal management, continuous improvement, and financial — would be appropriate. Such a set of KPIs prove a useful tool when looking at trends over a long period of time. Changes in work practice and external influences on the department can be quantified.

Another way of assessing the effectiveness of the service is to ask the user of that service what they think of it. Many ways of obtaining feedback from users of services exist; some are more suitable than others to the healthcare environment. For example, it is unlikely that focus groups would be successful as these would take clinical staff away from patient care and therefore would be costly. Sometimes the simpler solutions are the best and a straightforward customer survey will yield useful results.

Closing the circle

The most effective improvements to service delivery are likely to come from those committed to delivering it. Clinical engineers committed to excellence will strive to improve the service. The annual review provides a structured way of doing this. The effectiveness of the established programme will be assessed by the CED. This should be done objectively, based on evidence and available data. Assessment of how the department is performing against its targets can be achieved through analysis of the KPIs. Qualitative data from customer feedback surveys and a review of the complaints received

No.	Objective	Action	Due Date	Person Responsible	Review	Completed Date
38	Reduce response time for breakdown requests (unscheduled actions) to within 6 working hrs	Introduce named engineer rota to deal with incoming requests	2nd October	John Smith	Weekly until complete	

FIG. 2.5 An example of one line of a simple QIP format.

also inform the review. Finally, critical thinking from all members of the clinical engineering department can help identify ways in which the service can be improved.

As part of the review process the clinical engineering department will write a quality improvement plan. A quality improvement plan (QIP) is an annual, detailed plan that describes the improvement actions identified during the annual review. The usual form of a QIP is a table with actions to address a particular improvement listed alongside other key information as shown in Fig. 2.5 below.

Additional columns could be included to list resources required or challenges to be overcome. The QIP, however, should be understandable by all staff as it is a team plan and everyone needs to play their part in the improvement of quality. A useful acronym to aid creation of QIP actions is SMART (Meyer, 2003).

Actions should be:

- Specific: Not vague or easily misunderstood;
- Measurable, in some form: How do you know the action has been achieved?
- Achievable: Must have the agreement of all parties;
- Realistic: Need to be attainable within availability of resources;
- Timely: Should be deliverable within some agreed time scale.

Where items on the QIP are deliverable within the capability of the department, they will be progressed. Usually these will take the form of changes to specific equipment support plans. Through writing and implementing the QIP the CED closes the quality circle and improves the programme.

As part of the annual review, the CED may identify improvements that are beyond its capability. We have already seen that review of the HTM Programme may identify changes to the Strategic HTM Plan so as to better control a risk. Perhaps, for example, the CED may suggest that the MDC consider managing a group of devices using an equipment library approach rather that devices being owned by an individual department (Keay et al., 2015). Through critical review of the HTM Programme, clinical engineers, informed by working with end users close to the point of care, can often identify actions that improve practice and control risk. We have also seen that the annual review of the HTM Programme can identify equipment for planned replacement. Since many of the risk issues and planned replacement projects are outside the scope of the HTM Programme, to close the quality circle the clinical engineering department should report and escalate them up to the MDC as part of the annual report.

Summary of the Healthcare Technology Management Programme

In summary, we can define the healthcare technology management programme as the concurrent implementation of equipment support plans for different groups of devices. These plans are developed, delivered, and reviewed as part of a quality cycle (Fig. 2.6). The plans may indicate that components of each are delivered by in-house teams or are contracted to third-party or supplier maintenance organizations. Regardless of which, the documentation of the plans and the work undertaken is recorded in a database used to provide statistics for the annual review, and, as required during the year, to provide KPIs that guide the management of the plan's implementation.

The operational support process outlined takes up a significant amount of the working hours within a CED. Much of it is routine and involves equipment maintenance. However, the additional engineering and technical support that a clinical engineering department can provide to a hospital, together with the high-level strategic input described earlier, make up effective HTM and contribute significantly to the safety of patients, to clinical outcomes, and to good governance within the hospital.

It is worth highlighting that all the processes within Fig. 2.6 are developed, delivered, and managed by the CED. Consequently, clinical engineers need to develop their management knowledge and skills. Looking at Fig. 2.6 it is clear why the American College of Clinical Engineering definition of a clinical engineer places equal weight on the application

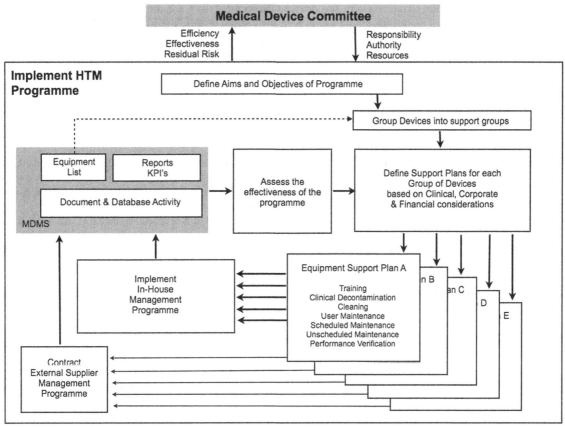

FIG. 2.6 Healthcare Technology Management Programme (HTM Programme) as a quality management cycle.

of management and engineering skills when defining the role of the clinical engineer (ACCE, 1992). It is also worth stressing that since the equipment management practice is operating within a quality cycle, and the review process responds to application issues from the clinicians and to changes in the hospital strategy, the day to day practice of healthcare technology management is also supporting and advancing patient care.

The key role of clinical engineers

Implementing HTM through developing and delivering a Strategic HTM Plan based on the organization's HTM Policy is the process that will maximize the benefit to the patient and to the organization, and reduce and control risk. While the policy and its implementation involves many stakeholders it is only clinical engineers that contribute to all elements of the policy.

Clinical engineers contribute significantly to the development and review of the hospital-wide strategic policy. The CED's links with senior management of the organization and the lead professionals for the different clinical specialties will support the necessary dialogue to ensure effective equipment prioritization decisions, whether these involve the transfer of existing equipment or procurement of additional or replacement equipment. The involvement of the CED and individual clinical engineers is collaborative and interdisciplinary. It is the role of the clinical engineer to apply engineering principles and practice, incorporating their practical experience of supporting healthcare technologies in order to create a framework in which the risks associated with the acquisition and use of medical devices are minimized. Clinical engineers have a commanding expertise in the development and delivery of healthcare technology management programmes. So, it is the clinical engineer who is uniquely placed to develop the overarching management systems. In short, healthcare technology management services, led by clinical engineers working in partnership with clinicians and managers, are essential in delivering robust patient focused healthcare and corporate success.

Clinical engineers will often be the drivers of the HTM Programmes within the healthcare organization and develop processes by which the existing medical equipment infrastructure is assessed annually to ensure it is efficient and effective.

This is a good example of how the advancing care and device management roles are complementary and integrated. To be able to advise effectively, clinical engineers should know both the current state of the existing technology deployed in the hospital and be able to provide an overview of new developments. They are then able to articulate how implementing a new technology will affect the hospital's ability to meet its corporate goals for the benefit of patients.

Glossary

Medical Device Committee (MDC) A multidisciplinary committee established at corporate level within a healthcare organization, charged with responsibility for the development, regular review, and implementation of the organization's HTM Policy and Strategic healthcare technology management plan.

Healthcare Technology Management Policy (HTM Policy) A hospital-wide policy, drafted by the MDC, that identifies the corporate requirements for the deployment and ongoing support of healthcare technology and sets out a course of action by which the corporate objectives are met. The HTM Policy should be approved and issued by the healthcare organization's Board and reviewed at corporate level as part of the regular management of the governance structures within the organization.

Strategic Healthcare Technology Management Plan (Strategic HTM Plan) An annual plan developed by the MDC which outlines how the HTM Policy will be implemented at corporate level in the current year

Healthcare Technology Management Programme (HTM Programme) A planned programme designed by a technical support department to deliver appropriate scientific, engineering, and technical support to ensure healthcare technology remains safe and effective in clinical practice. If there are more than one technical support departments, each will have its own HTM Programme

Equipment Support Plan (ESP) A document that sets out the range and scope of maintenance and support action to be delivered by the clinical engineering department (or other technical support department) for a specific device or group of devices. Also includes details of the information sources on which the plan is based and the means by which the plan's effectiveness can be assessed.

References

American College of Clinical Engineering (ACCE), 1992. Clinical Engineer (defined). Available from: https://accenet.org/about/Pages/ClinicalEngineer.aspx.

CMS, 2014. State Operations Manual. Appendix A — Survey Protocol, Regulations and Interpretive Guidelines for Hospitals (Rev.103, A-0724 Issued: 02-21-14). Available from: https:www.cms.gov/Regulations-and-Guidance/Guidance/Transmittals/Downloads/R103SOMA.pdf.

ECRI Institute, 2007. ECRI-AIMS Overview. Available from: www.ecri.org.uk/wp-bits-and-bobs/uploads/ECRI-AIMS_Overview.pdf.

Hegarty, F., Amoore, J., Blackett, P., McCarthy, J., Scott, R., 2017. Healthcare Technology Management — A Systematic Approach. CRC Press, Abingdon, UK.

HSE (Health and Safety Executive), 2015. The Electricity at Work Regulations 1989 — Guidance. HSE, UK. Available from: http://www.hse.gov.uk/pubns/books/hsr25.htm.

International Electrotechnical Commission (IEC), 2014. IEC 62353:2014 Medical Electrical Equipment — Recurrent Test and Test After Repair of Medical Electrical Equipment, Second Edition. IEC, Geneva. 2014.

International Organization for Standardization (ISO), 2014. ISO 55000:2014 Asset Management — Overview, Principles and Terminology. ISO, Geneva.

International Organization for Standardization (ISO), 2015. ISO 9000:2015 Quality Management Systems — Fundamentals and Vocabulary. ISO, Geneva.

International Organization for Standardization (ISO), 2016. ISO 13485:2016 Medical Devices — Quality Management Systems — Requirements for Regulatory Purposes. ISO, Geneva.

Keay, S., McCarthy, J.P., Carey-Smith, B., 2015. Medical equipment libraries — implementation, experience and user satisfaction. J. Med. Eng. Technol. 39 (6), 354—362.

Medicines and Healthcare Products Regulatory Agency (MHRA), 2015. Managing Medical Devices — Guidance for Healthcare and Social Services Organisations. Available from: www.gov.uk/government/publications/managing-medical-devices.

Meyer, P.J., 2003. What would you do if you knew you couldn't fail? Creating S.M.A.R.T. goals. In: Attitude Is Everything. The Meyer Resource Group Incorporated, ISBN 978-0-89811-304-4.

WHO, 2011. Introduction to Medical Equipment Inventory Management. World Health Organization, WHO Press. Available from: http://apps.who.int/medicinedocs/documents/s21565en/s21565en.pdf.

Suggested Further Reading

Hegarty, F., Amoore, J., Blackett, P., McCarthy, J., Scott, R., 2017. Healthcare Technology Management — A Systematic Approach. CRC Press, Abingdon, UK., ISBN 978-1-4987-0354-3

Willson, K., Ison, K., Tabakov, S., 2014. Medical Equipment Management. CRC Press, Abingdon, UK, ISBN 9781420099584.

WHO, 2011. Introduction to Medical Equipment Inventory Management. WHO Press, Geneva, Switzerland, ISBN 978 92 4 150139 2. Available from: http://apps.who.int/medicinedocs/documents/s21565en/s21565en.pdf.

Chapter 3

Health technology assessment and issues in health economics

Azzam Taktak[a] and Siddhartha Bandyopadhyay[b]

[a]Royal Liverpool University Hospital, Liverpool, United Kingdom; [b]University of Birmingham, Birmingham, United Kingdom

Chapter outline

Introduction

Technology assessment in the healthcare industry is a relatively new name (Banta, 2003). Most hospitals nowadays make decisions about purchasing new technology diffused among many people. Hospital executives benefit the most from this field because they often feel uncomfortable with making decisions regarding the use of technology. The process of making decisions can be broken down into four major elements: assessment, planning, acquisition and management. The most useful definitions of the above elements are outlined in the literature (Berkowitz and Swan, 1993).

Within the concept of Health Technology Assessment (HTA), the term Technology refers to an existing, new or emerging device, pharmaceutical, procedure or protocol. Technology Assessment is the practical process of forming an advisory committee to determine effectiveness, outcome, risk and strategic planning. The term Technology Planning is the systematic method of determining the hospital's technology needs and setting short and long term priorities. Technology Acquisition is the process of determining which manufacturer provides the best equipment and support. And last but not least there is Technology Management which is the process of ensuring that the technology is well used and supported.

It is important that physicians are involved at the early stages of technology assessment by being a part of the advisory committee. This will help ensure that medics are current with training issues especially with the rapid advancement of science and technology. At this stage the person making requests describes the technology or procedure, explains existing arrangements and describes how it will affect outcome. The committee then conducts a more detailed analysis considering financial and other issues. The committee then sets out priorities for this plan according to hospital objectives. Reviewing the value of existing technology is another critical task. Replacement proposals are made for various reasons such as safety considerations, standard of care, age and obsolescence of existing equipment. Acquisitions can also be proposed to consolidate, expand or add a new service. Technology assessment and planning can be conducted for a single department, product line or clinical service. Strategic plans can be developed internally (administrators, planners, directors) or externally with the aid of informed party.

During the planning stage, an extensive audit of existing technology is carried out by looking at reviews, condition, capability, history, statistics and incident reports. An evaluation of other hospitals' technology and a review of technology trends is also carried out. The committee would then develop a long term plan for the deployment of the technology.

At the acquisition and management stages, budget plans are submitted to cover training, spare parts, service, support, upgrades and decommissioning. Large purchases can be phased over several years. Best value costs for supporting the technology in terms of insurance, in-house support or service contracts are looked at to provide 10–30% cost savings (Mallouppas, 1986).

Regional considerations play an important role in HTA. Service providers look for methods to ensure that the technology is distributed rationally. If this is done carefully it can maximize patient experience whilst at the same time enhance the reputation of local hospitals. It is not uncommon nowadays for hospitals to utilize telemedicine and mobile services (e.g. vans, trucks, etc.) to share services between neighbouring hospitals.

Cost analysis

When one carries out a costing exercise for a technology, it is important to bear in mind the cost viewpoint. For example, patient travel costs, loss in earning due to sickness, etc are costs from a patient's viewpoint whereas provision of bed space, linen, food, etc. are costs from a hospital's viewpoint. Costs from a hospital viewpoint could be seen as benefits from a patient or society's viewpoint and vice versa e.g. costs of a lifesaving equipment from a hospital's viewpoint may be a benefit from the patient's viewpoint in terms of longer years lived. It might not always be easy to consider all costs especially costs which are not reflected in market prices such as volunteer time, patients' leisure time, donated clinic space, etc. Cost estimation can be collected from various sources e.g. clinical trial forms, patient's notes, hospital records, patient diaries or questionnaires.

The range of costs considered may determine which programme is considered more expensive. For example, a study in the USA showed that a community-oriented programme for treatment of mentally ill patients costs $1700 per annum more than a hospital-based programme when primary treatment costs where considered. However, when other costs were added to the analysis such as social services, provision of food and shelter and loss of earning to the patient, the final figures showed that the community-oriented programme had a lower net cost of $400 per annum (Weisbrod et al., 1980).

For non-market resources, best fit equivalent costs might be considered. Volunteers' time for example can be made equivalent to unskilled wage rates. Loss of leisure time is sometimes considered to be equivalent to overtime payment.

Market prices do not always reflect true costs and some adjustments may be applied. Physician fees might vary from one procedure to another depending on the level of skill and time required. A health authority might negotiate a deal with a company.

It is also important to consider the time period for the cost analysis. For example, a short-term study has shown that the coronary artery bypass surgery costs more than twice an angioplasty procedure. A 24-month randomized control trial however showed that the two procedures were almost identical in costs since more patients from the angeoplasty group may require additional treatment including bypass surgery (Henderson et al., 1998).

The terms average and marginal costs are often used in cost analysis depending on what is being measured. Average costs are calculated as the total costs divided by the total quantity of output. Marginal costs on the other hand are incremental costs, calculated by dividing small changes in costs by small changes in quantity output. If the costs of a technology vary randomly around a baseline throughout the time period then average costs are used. However, if there is a gradual or sudden shift in the baseline then marginal costs are used. The extra cost of keeping a patient in hospital for another day at the end of their treatment for example might be less than the average daily cost for the whole stay. Marginal costs are therefore used in this scenario.

Overhead costs are shared resources across many departments, e.g. general administration, laundry, cleaning, porters, power, etc. The quantities of service consumed by the patient (days of stay, number of laboratory tests, number of procedures, etc.) are multiplied by the full cost (including overhead, capital, etc.) per unit and sum up the results. Alternatively, a simpler method is to assume all patients cost the same amount in items related to 'hotel services'.

Capital costs are the costs of purchasing large equipment or a piece of land. These have two components:

1. Opportunity cost: by purchasing the capital, you lose the opportunity to invest the money in something else
2. Depreciation: the asset purchased depreciates with time.

A formula that is normally used in calculating capital costs taking into account the two components above is:

$$E = \frac{K - S/(1 + r)^n}{A}$$

(3.1)

where:

> E is the equivalent annual cost.
> K is the purchase price.
> S is the resale value.
> A is the annuity factor.
> r is the interest rate.
> n is the useful lifetime of the capital.

The annuity factor can be calculated as:

$$A = \frac{1 - 1/(1 + r)^n}{r} \qquad (3.2)$$

Cost-minimization analysis (CMA)

The term cost-minimization is used when comparing two or more interventions that have exactly the same outcome. For example, if two drugs that are equally as effective as each other in clearing infection, we would choose the cheaper one. Costs in such a scenario would include cost of drug acquisition, administration, monitoring and management of adverse reactions.

Cost-effectiveness analysis (CEA)

This is a term used for comparing two or more interventions in terms of a single natural common unit. Interventions are compared in terms of cost per additional unit of benefit, e.g. cost per life saved, cost per mmHg BP reduction of blood pressure. A significant limitation is that it does not allow comparison in areas with different outcomes.

For example, a health provider is investigating the cost effectiveness of a vaccination programme. Let us assume that a single vaccination is estimated to cost £70 when considering the cost of the drug, consumables, clinic space, staff time, etc. Next, we assume that the vaccine is 95% effective, that the probability of catching the disease for unprotected subjects is 10% and that it costs £500 to treat the disease. We start by constructing a decision tree as shown below. Notice that the probability of catching the disease without the programme is double that of the unprotected when the programme is in place as there is more chance of cross-contamination (herd immunity https://www.vaccinestoday.eu/stories/what-is-herd-immunity/).

In this example, a protected individual represents a single utility. We multiply the utility by the probability in each arm and sum them up. We do the same for the costs. We see that it costs around £125 to gain a single utility without the programme (100/0.8), whereas with the programme, it costs around £73 per utility gained (72.5/0.995) (Fig. 3.1).

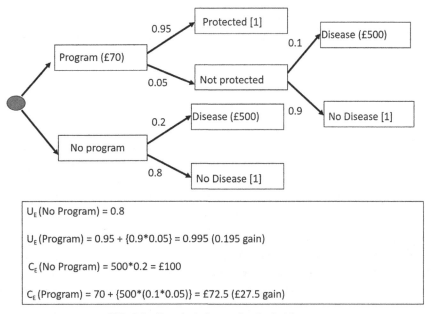

FIG. 3.1 Hypothetical example of a decision tree.

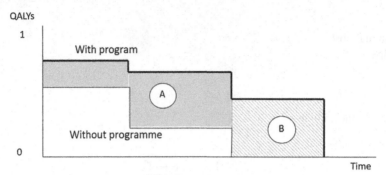

FIG. 3.2 Example on the use of QALYs. Section (A) represents increase in morbidity and section (B) represents increase in mortality.

Cost-benefit analysis (CBA)

This term is used when both costs and outcomes are expressed in monetary units. Financial value can be attached to the benefit by asking patients or the public how much they are *willing to pay*. A treatment is adopted if its cost is less than the value placed on the benefit. It is of course difficult to ask people to place monetary value on health benefits. A simple example illustrates how a person's actual choice can reveal information about benefits.

Suppose the probability of being killed in a car accident is 10 in 100,000. You buy a car and an optional added safety feature that brings this probability to 5 in 100,000 costs £50. If you decide to buy this option, then you value your life to at least £1 million:

£50/(10/100,000 − 5/100,000) = £1,000,000.

Cost-utility analysis (CUA)

This is a special form of cost effectiveness where all the benefits are captured in a single outcome measure. CUA is the preferred method in the healthcare environment.

A very commonly used outcome measure in healthcare is called QALY which stands for Quality-Adjusted Life Years. This is a value between 1 (representing perfect health) and 0 (representing death). A hypothetical example illustrating how a health programme affects patients' life is shown in Fig. 3.2. The figure shows that the programme adds more quality of life during the initial stages (Part A) and more years of living in the latter stages (part B).

QALY's are measured by asking subjects with the condition a series of questions. A very common generic tool that is often used to calculate QALY's is the EQ-5D tool (https://euroqol.org/). It asks the subject to rate their mobility, self-care, usual activities (e.g. housework, study, etc.), pain/discomfort and anxiety. For example, subjects with acute coronary syndrome have rated their condition to be equivalent to a QALY of 0.8 (Karnon et al., 2010). Mild to moderate depression equates to a QALY of 0.7 (Kendrick et al., 2009).

An alternative outcome measure to QALYs is Healthy Years Equivalent (HYE). This is based on a standard gamble scenario where people are asked how many years of living with a certain condition they are willing to trade for perfect health (Towers et al., 2005).

Incremental cost-effectiveness ratio (ICER)

When a new technology is proposed, it is often the case that there is a hypothetical increase in benefit with an associated increase in cost. The ratio of added costs to added benefits is called Incremental Cost-Effectiveness Ratio (ICER). The technology is considered as cost effective if this ratio is below a certain threshold. In the UK, the National Institute of Health Care Excellence (NICE) sets this threshold at around £20,000 − £30,000 per QALY gain (McCabe et al., 2008).

The problem with calculating costs and benefits is that it is often subjective and based on assumptions so it is not an exact science. For example, let us suppose we are trying to introduce a new screening device which would help diagnose subjects with early stages of cancer. We would need to provide an estimate of the costs of making the device, test, clinic, consumables, etc. From the patient's point of view, we need to estimate the costs of travel, parking, accommodation, days off work, etc. To calculate benefit, we might need to make assumptions regarding the increase in QALYs (morbidity and mortality) resulting from detecting the cancer early. There might be other assumption we need to make such as the costs of false positives and false negatives, litigation, anxiety, side effects, etc. Sensitivity analysis is often carried out to test the impact of these assumptions on the true costs.

Feature of health care markets

The concepts discussed above apply in principle not only to HTA but should govern decision making in the healthcare market in general. The marginal principle guides economic decision making in general and while there are difficulties in operationalizing QALYs, it still provides a useful guide in determining cost effectiveness of health care interventions. However, there are certain features in health care markets (see Arrow, 1963) that lead to market decisions not being determined by cost-effectiveness, further the market outcome without regulation is not optimal.

In particular, health care markets have to contend with the following features:

- **Uncertainty** in (individual) demand for health care and uncertainty in product. Over an individual's life cycle, it is often hard to estimate what his/her healthcare needs would be and therefore individual level planning for healthcare costs can be difficult. Further, there is uncertainty in the product being sold with wide individual variability in response to treatment, particularly for serious diseases.
- **Externalities** (other people benefit from your action): An externality can be defined as an unpaid service (or disservice) accruing to a third party (or parties). Being vaccinated against flu does not just benefit the person being vaccinated but also others. There is for example herd immunity mentioned in the discussion of cost effectiveness earlier, where the small number of unvaccinated also face a lower incidence of the disease as most people are vaccinated and do not get infected, thus greatly reducing transmission risk. Hence the privately optimal decision is not in general socially optimal i.e. a person who decides that her cost of getting vaccinated is greater than her benefit is not making a socially optimal decision as she does not regard the benefit to others in terms of lowered probability of catching the disease. The 'standard' correction for this is through taxes (if it is a negative externality e.g. smoking) or subsidies (it has positive externalities as in the vaccination example) which align private and social costs. This 'internalises' the externality as the taxes adds to the costs of the activity and is taken into account when deciding on the activity, if the tax fully reflects the social cost the optimal consumption is now reached (a similar argument holds for subsidizing activities that generate positive externality). A related way to think of externalities is to think of them as 'missing markets' i.e. no one has ownership over e.g. the smoke emitted or can trade in it. If for instance those who benefit from someone else getting vaccinated could pay people who do not, markets would again restore inefficiency (see Coase, 1960; Arrow, 1969) but transaction costs usually make such solutions impractical when the number of parties involved is large. Further, who holds initial ownership of the activity has distributional consequences. Thus, whether we assign the right to smoke to smokers who can then be paid by non-smokers to quit or lower smoking or whether we assign the rights to non-smokers who can be paid to allow people to smoke in their presence would both generate outcomes that are efficient as argued by Coase but the distributional consequences are not the same. Further, in reality, it is hard for individuals to have complete information on the degree of externality generated causing strategic issues in overstating or understating the amount of extra harm or benefit arising from an activity. The strategic issues from informational issues are discussed below.
- **Asymmetric information:** A situation of asymmetric information arises when one party has better information about state of the world (e.g. how effective a medication is on average vs surgical intervention) than the other. For example, doctors know more about treatment and possible effects than patient. This allows for doctors to manipulate how they present treatment options so that they are more beneficial for the doctor than the patient. For example, if surgery is more profitable to the doctor than conservative management of a condition, a doctor may be more inclined to suggest surgery than might be optimal. The class of problems where a (partly) self-interested person knows more about the state of the world than the (less informed) person who is his customer are called principal agent problems where (relatively) uniformed principal has to depend on the expertize of the (informed) agent to do a task for her. The principal's problem is how to the agent to do what is best for the principal. Such problems do not achieve the first best solution i.e. the outcome that would occur had the principal and agent had the same amount of information. In particular, healthcare is what is called a credence good, (see Emons, 1997) where the information asymmetry is not necessarily resolved post-consumption-the complexity of treatment makes it very difficult to verify if one as 'over treated' for example (i.e. prescribed an expensive treatment when a cheaper one would have been just as successful). Thus, in this environment, we seek a second best solution i.e. the best that the principal can achieve given the informational constraint.

Given these features of the healthcare market, where free market forces do not lead to optimality, government intervention is felt to be necessary. Indeed, governments can to an extent solve the problems above. Individual variability of health care demand is why many government directly offer state (taxpayer) funded health care systems (e.g. UK, Canada) or a mix of state funded health care and offering incentives for citizens to buy insurance (e.g. US, France, Germany). Government can certainly also 'solve' the externality problem by taxing or subsidizing appropriately and can also reduce asymmetric information by using exerts to collect data on e.g. treatment options and outcomes so that patients can make informed choices. Yet, this is not without its problems as governments are themselves made up of politicians with possible vested interests and rely on experts who also have their own bias and self-interest. Thus, while governments can mitigate some of the market failure associated with healthcare, it is far from obvious that government intervention leads to optimality. Additionally, government funding of health care also has a redistributive role, and there may be differences of opinion among citizens on the level of desired redistribution. While none of these negate the efficiency arguments made earlier, it is not clear that they are achieved or even how to achieve them.

Healthcare systems around the world

The feature of health care markets as well as the fact that healthcare is considered an essential commodity to an extent has led to government financing or involvement in healthcare across the world. There are however variations on the way healthcare is funded across the globe, with a mix of private and public funding being the norm though the magnitude varies. The UK has a healthcare system which is almost entirely free at the point of service and funded by general taxation. Most developed countries offer near universal coverage through a system of compulsory insurance and subsidies for lower income but often requires upfront payments for services with most of it reimbursed through private/public insurance. Most countries outside the developed world often struggle with providing more than basic care and remain underfunded and poor in quality (see WHO). Among the developed world, the three so called healthcare models are the Single payer model (as e.g. in the UK, Spain), the socialized model (as e.g. in Germany) and the national health insurance model. Some of these differences stem from the historical basis of the system and might differ very little in coverage or costs. The single payer model is where all healthcare is funded by general taxation, is paid for by the government. It is argued that these help keep cost down through the monopoly (government) deciding on what medical providers can or cannot charge.

This taxonomy while helpful does not really shed light on what the efficiency and equity properties of different healthcare systems are. For that we need to understand how the features of healthcare markets interact across different systems. The private system may encourage doctors and other health care providers to push treatments that are more remunerative. State funded salaries systems reduce such distortions while leaving the possibility that doctors paid flat fees (or salaries) may shirk and not innovate. Further, what systems over treat or undertreat does not map neatly into whether they are state of privately funded. Indeed, empirical evidence is at best mixed on this and what system works better is sensitive to the outcomes that we use to measure performance (see Schutte et al., 2018).

Concluding remarks

Health technology assessment is a very important topic when it comes to deciding whether a device, a drug or a procedure should be adopted or not. With every new intervention, there are always costs to consider and these are not always easy to determine accurately. This chapter gives a brief insight into the key issues the reader needs to know such as cost viewpoints and how utility can be measured using QALYs. The second part of the chapter considers specific features of healthcare markets viz. presence of externalities and asymmetric which leads to market failure and causes strategic behaviour among market participants, with the possibility of government intervention doing better. Brief suggestions are offered on how to evaluate different healthcare systems around the world in terms of its implications for efficiency and equity. If the reader wishes to delve into the subject in more details, the books listed below provide an excellent source of material on the subject.

References

Arrow, K., 1963. Uncertainty and the welfare economics of medical care. Am. Econ. Rev. 53 (5), 941−973.

Arrow, K.J., 1969. The organization of economic activity : issues pertinent to the choice of market versus non-market allocation. In: Congress of the United States, the Analysis and Evaluation of Public Expenditures: The PPB System, pp. 47−64.

Banta, D., 2003. The development of health technology assessment. Health Policy 63 (2), 121−132.

Berkowitz, D.A., Swan, M.M., 1993. Technology decision making. A constructive approach to planning and acquisition will require a paradigm shift. Health Prog. (Saint Louis, MO 74 (1), 42−47.

Coase, R., 1960. The problem of social cost. J. Law Econ. 3 (1), 1−44.

Emons, W., 1997. Credence goods and fraudulent experts. RAND J. Econ. 28 (1), 107−119.

Henderson, R.A., Pocock, S.J., Sharp, S.J., Nanchahal, K., Sculpher, M.J., Buxton, M.J., Hampton, J.R., 1998. Long-term results of RITA-1 trial: clinical and cost comparisons of coronary angioplasty and coronary-artery bypass grafting. Lancet 352 (9138), 1419−1425.

Karnon, J., Holmes, M.W., Williams, R., Bakhai, A., Brennan, A., 2010. A cost-utility analysis of clopidogrel in patients with ST elevation acute coronary syndromes in the UK. Int. J. Cardiol. 140 (3), 315−322.

Kendrick, T., Chatwin, J., Dowrick, C., Tylee, A., Morriss, R., Peveler, R., Leese, M., McCrone, P., Harris, T., Moore, M., Byng, R., Brown, G., Barthel, S., Mander, H., Ring, A., Kelly, V., Wallace, V., Gabbay, M., Craig, T., Mann, A., 2009. Randomised controlled trial to determine the clinical effectiveness and cost-effectiveness of selective serotonin reuptake inhibitors plus supportive care, versus supportive care alone, for mild to moderate depression with somatic symptoms in primary care: the THREAD (THREshold for AntiDepressant response) study. Health Technol. Assess. 13 (22), 1−159.

Mallouppas, A., 1986. WHO: Strategy and Proposed Action Concerning Maintenance of Hospital and Medical Equipment. WHO Reports, Geneva.

McCabe, C., Claxton, K., Culyer, A.J., 2008. The NICE cost-effectiveness threshold: what it is and what that means. PharmacoEconomics 26 (9), 733−744.

Schütte, S., Acevedo, P., Flahault, A., 2018. Health systems around the world − a comparison of existing health system rankings. J. Global Health 8 (1), 010407. https://doi.org/10.7189/jogh.08.010407.

Towers, I., Spencer, A., Brazier, J., 2005. Healthy year equivalents versus quality-adjusted life years: the debate continues. Expert Rev. Pharmacoecon. Outcomes Res. 5 (3), 245−254.

Weisbrod, B.A., Test, M.A., Stein, L.I., 1980. Alternative to mental hospital treatment: II. Economic benefit-cost analysis. Arch. Gen. Psychiatr. 37 (4), 400−405.

Further reading

Drummond, M., S, M.J., Torrance, G.W., O'Brien, B.J., Stoddart, G.L., 2005. Methods for the Economic Evaluation of Health Care Programmes. Oxford University Press, Oxford.

Edlin, R., M, C., Hulme, C., Hall, P., Wright, J., 2015. Cost Effectiveness Modelling for Health Technology Assessment: A Practical Course. Springer, Switzerland.

Morris, S., Devlin, N., Parker, N., 2012. Economic Analysis in Healthcare. Wiley.

Chapter 4

Good clinical practice

Anthony Scott Brown

Health Tech Solutions Ltd, Redruth, United Kingdom

Chapter outline

Introduction

The standards of clinical research have developed over many decades during which there have been many trials that today we would frown on or even be horrified by for being unscientific, unethical, or both. There was the Public Health Service syphilis study conducted in Tuskegee, Alabama. This study researched the natural effects of untreated syphilis in black males between 1932 and 1972; it involved 600 participants, of which 399 who had the disease were not treated for its effects. Furthermore there was no informed consent for this study (CDC, 2011). Another early disaster was a trial of the drug thalidomide developed by German scientists during the Second World War. It was prescribed to pregnant mothers as a treatment for morning sickness and resulted in the birth of babies without arms or legs (Foggo, 2009). Thankfully clinical research has moved on considerably and the standards of both clinical and ethical practice have improved immeasurably. That said, unfortunate incidents in clinical trials do still occur.

The risks of clinical trials were brought to a fore by the media in 2006 with the TGB1412 disaster. This drug was developed by the German biopharmaceutical company TeGenero and the trial was run by the contract research organization (CRO) PAREXEL International Limited, at the Northwick Park Hospital in the United Kingdom. Eight healthy volunteers entered into the phase 1 trial of the anti-CD28 monoclonal antibody TGN1412. Two of the volunteers received a placebo and the remaining six who received the new drug became seriously ill within minutes and were admitted to intensive care (Saunders, 2006; Brown, 2011). Although these occurrences are rare, they do raise the awareness of the public, healthcare providers, and the manufacturers to the potential harmful consequences of clinical trials.

Phases of clinical research

Clinical research is undertaken in a series of phases, and with each subsequent phase there is a reduced risk to patient safety. For clinical trials of investigational medicinal products (CTIMPs) there a four phases, whereas for clinical investigations of medical devices there are just two phases. A comparison of the two types is given in Table 4.1.

Clinical Engineering. https://doi.org/10.1016/B978-0-08-102694-6.00004-8

TABLE 4.1 Comparison of the phases of drug and medical device trials.

Clinical trial of investigational medicinal product	Details and purpose	Clinical investigation of medical devices	Details and purpose
Phase I	First time in man (FTIM), healthy volunteers Collection of tolerability data Pilot dose findings and investigation of pharmacokinetic (PK) and pharmacodynamic (PD) profiles	Premarket approval study	To obtain CE marking includes pilot studies
Phase II	Therapeutic pilot study Demonstration of pharmacological activity assessment of short-term tolerability profile		
Phase III	Larger scale study of subjects with target disease Comparison of efficacy with current treatments		
Phase IV	General population Long-term safety data	Evaluation with a CE marked device	Registry and audit-type studies

Standards in clinical research

Probably the first standard to be introduced in clinical research was the Nuremberg Code of 1947. This came about following the legal trials of military war crimes, and one of the most significant requirements set down in the code was that the voluntary consent of the human subject is absolutely essential (Nuremberg Military Tribunals, 1949).

A major step forward was the development of the Declaration of Helsinki (1964) which evolved out of the Nuremberg Code and abuses of human research subjects. There have been seven revisions to this over the years, the current revision was introduced in 2013 and as such it is seen as a living document that responds to the changing environment and scope of research. In the United States the Declaration of Helsinki is not used at all.

The 2013 declaration has made a number of changes in the seventh iteration of the declaration and probably the most important our outlined below.

For the first time researchers are required to justify why minority groups, such as women and children have been excluded from research. It also addresses research conducted in countries with limited resources and, in particular, the availability and access to interventions and are for participants after the trial had ended if proved effective. Another change in the 2013 version is the recommendation for the use of unproven interventions in cases for which proven interventions do not exist.

Informed consent has also been strengthened and now recognises that in some cultures the involvement of community leaders can act as an additional layer of protection for researchers to pass through. There are also on-going discussions about compensation to participants involved in research studies who have suffered harm or sustained injury as a result of their involvement.

Although these are all laudable improvements to the declaration which have served to strengthen the declaration and its core aims probably the most significant change is regarding the dissemination and publication of all research findings irrespective of whether they resulted in positive, negative or inconclusive findings. This is a very bold but enlightening improvement which can only serve to advance research more rapidly. Any research which proves negative or inconclusive can prevent repetition of the same or similar research studies and thereby reducing the burden of suffering on research participants in some instances but also serve to steer prospective researchers in new directions that may result in beneficial findings.

The first Good Clinical Practice (GCP) standard was published in America in 1977 as one of the US Food and Drug Administration (FDA) regulations.

The problems of differing regulations and standards in countries across Europe meant there was considerable repetition of trials and that delayed new pharmaceutical products getting into the marketplace, which consequently put more participants potentially at risk. Results of trials in one country were not accepted in another country because the trial was conducted under a different set of standards.

To provide some standardization, a series of conferences with representation from regulatory authorities was organized: The International Conference on Harmonization of Technical Requirements for Registration of Pharmaceuticals for Human Use (ICH). The cosponsors of the ICH are:

- European Commission (EC), European Union
- Food and Drug Administration (FDA), United States
- Ministry of Health, Labour and Welfare, Japan
- European Federation of Pharmaceutical Industries Associations (EFPIA)
- Pharmaceutical Research and Manufacturers of America (PhRMA)
- Japan Pharmaceutical Manufacturers Association (JPMA)

The aim of ICH is to harmonize the processes within clinical research, focusing on quality. There are a range of guidelines divided into four key areas: quality, safety, efficacy, and multidisciplinary. The ICH E6 Guideline for Good Clinical Practice is widely available.

There are a range of regulations that have been developed over the years which have built on the Declaration of Helsinki and ICH GCP. The two European directives are 2001/20/EC and 2005/28/EC, which each country needs to transpose into law. In the United Kingdom the main regulation is the Medicine for Human Use (Clinical Trials) Regulations 2004 which was implemented into law through Statutory Instrument 2004/1031. The statutory instruments in the United Kingdom can be visualized as a wall with the Declaration of Helsinki being the foundation; it is this "wall" that protects research participants and ensures the research is conducted to the highest standards (Fig. 4.1). Similar arrangements are in place in other European countries.

European Clinical Trails Regulation (No. 536/2014)

The 2001/20/EC directive introduced wide ranging improvements to the conduct of clinical trials in respect of their ethical validity and conduct, safety and the reliability of the data produced from the trials. However this has heavily criticized by the pharmaceutical industry as being over burdensome and as a result in recent years there has been a marked reduction in applications for authorization of clinical trials, The introduction of the European Clinical Trials Regulation (No. 536/2014) introduces a more streamlined approach with more proportionate requirements and hence goes some way towards addressing the criticisms and gaps in the earlier directive. The regulation was adopted in April 2014 by the European

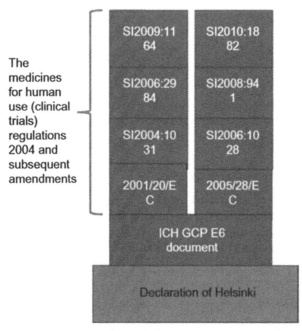

FIG. 4.1 The wall of clinical trials regulations.

Parliament and subsequently came into force in 2017. The other benefit of this new regulation is that it makes Europe as a whole competitive as a place in which to conduct research, by minimizing the regulatory autonomy of Member States. It is unclear at this stage the impact on clinical trials in the United Kingdom once it has left the European Union through "Brexit".

The costs of clinical trials will always be high and pharmaceutical companies need to factor this in when embarking on a new trial considering their longer-term return on investment (ROI). A good example of this led to the recent controversy over Bevacizumab (Avastin®), a drug licensed for Cancer treatment, however when used off-label has also proved to be a cheap and effective drug to treat wet age-related macular degeneration (AMD). The drug companies have been found by the European courts to be guilty of anti-competitive behaviour in their attempts to restrict the use of Avastin. Estimates of potential savings for the NHS over the past decade if Avastin® had been used instead of the licensed drugs Lucentis and Eylea are in the order of £3bn.

According to Tenti et al.:

In order to outline terminology, the regulation defines the term "clinical trial" as a study designed to:

(a) to investigate or confirm the clinical, pharmacological or other pharmacodynamics effects of one or more medicinal products;
(b) to detect any side effects of one or more drugs or
(c) study the absorbtion, distribution, metabolic or excretion of one or more medicinal products, in order to establish the safety and/or efficacy of these medicinal products. (2018, p. 99)

From this we can see that non-interventional studies are not classed as clinical trials and fall outside the regulation.

Good clinical practice

Clinical trials of investigational medicinal products (CTIMPs) are important in developing both the safety and efficacy data around a new drug before it is granted a product license (Brown, 2011, p. 104). Good Clinical Practice (GCP) is a set of internationally recognized ethical and scientific quality guidelines that should be followed to ensure that the rights and well-being of participants are protected and that the data produced from the research are valid and reliable. To put it simply, GCP ensures that the research is conducted to high standards of ethical and scientific integrity. The ICH GCP E 6 document covers the following elements of clinical trials:

- Design
- Conduct
- Performance
- Monitoring
- Auditing
- Recording
- Analysis
- Reporting

Central to the principles of GCP is informed consent and this comprises 21 elements which are briefly outlined in Fig. 4.2. Although these principles are specific to clinical trials involving investigational medicinal products, they underpin all research activity including investigations involving medical devices.

Clinical investigations for medical devices

Although clinical trials for medicinal products (drugs) have been a requirement for many years, it was not until 2010 that the equivalent was required for medical devices. The requirement was introduced in the revision to the Medical Devices Directive 2007/47/EC and this had to be transposed into law in the member states by 21 December 2008; it finally came into force 21 March 2010. The changes can be briefly summarized as follows:

- Clinical data are required for all classes of medical device (i.e., Class I, IIa, IIb, or III) irrespective of whether they are already CE marked or not.
- All serious adverse events (SAEs) must be reported to the competent authority (CA; in the United Kingdom the CA is the MHRA, in the United States it is the FDA).

1. Trial involves research
2. Purpose of the trial
3. Trial treatments; probability for random assignment
4. Trial procedures, including invasive procedures
5. Subject's responsibilities
6. Experimental aspects of the trial
7. Reasonable forseeable risks and inconveniences
8. Alternative (available) procedures and treatment(s)
9. Compensation
10. Anticipated prorated payment
11. Anticipated expenses
12. Subject's participation is voluntary throughout
13. Monitors, auditors, inspectors: access to notes
14. Confidentiality
15. Pledge to inform subject on new information
16. Contacts: information, trial-related injury
17. Forseeable circumstances of termination
18. Duration of subject's participation in trial
19. Approximate number of subjects in the trial
20. Permission to inform the subject's GP/family doctor; the use of tissues, organs, samples, and DNA during and after the trial; data protection 95/46/EC
21. ICH 4.3.3 That the patient's GP (if not involved in the trial) will be informed of their participation in the trial

FIG. 4.2 The elements of informed consent.

Classification of medical devices

The classification of devices was introduced in the Medical Devices Directive (93/42/EEC). The new Directive 2007/47/EC has subsequently amended this earlier directive and also incorporates the active implantable Medical Devices Directive (90/385/EEC).

The classification of a medical device is determined by a set of 18 rules that provide statements relating to situations, functions, parts of the body treated, and properties (EC, 2010). An overview of the classifications, risk, and rules is given in Table 4.2.

The rules are designed to allow the manufacturer to determine the classification of the product. For detailed guidance the reader is directed to the European Commission Medical Devices Guidance Document (MEDDEV 2.4/1 Rev. 9 June 2010; EC, 2010) which sets out the rules and provides a series of simple flowcharts to aid manufacturers in determining the classification of their device. Brief details are also given in the MHRA Bulletin No. 10, The Classification Rules (MHRA, 2011). Examples are:

Class I: Hospital beds/hoists, operating tables, non-invasive electrodes (e.g., ECG or EEG), and plasters
Class IIa: Fixed denture prosthesis, reusable surgical instruments, and tracheal tubes
Class IIb: Radiological equipment, volumetric infusion pumps, and anaesthetic workstations
Class III: Bone cement, biological heart valves, and contraceptive diaphragms

TABLE 4.2 Classification of medical devices.

Classification	Risk	Rules	Application
I	Low	1–4	Noninvasive
IIa	Medium	5–8	Invasive, transient, or short term[a]
IIb	Medium	9–12	Additional rules for active devices
III	High	13–18	Miscellaneous rules

[a]Short-term use >60 min and <30 days.

Accessories are classified in their own right separate from the device.

While this classification holds true for countries in the European Union, the Unites States, whose competent authority is the Food and Drug Administration, has a different system for classification. The FDA has established classifications for approximately 1700 different generic types of devices and grouped them into 16 medical specialties referred to as panels. Each of these generic types of devices is assigned to one of three regulatory classes based on the level of control necessary to assure the safety and effectiveness of the device. The three device classes and the requirements (regulatory controls) that apply to them are:

1. Class I: General Controls
   a. With exemptions
   b. Without exemptions
2. Class II: General Controls and Special Controls
   a. With exemptions
   b. Without exemptions
3. Class III: General Controls and Premarket Approval.

Exemptions relate to devices that will not require premarket notification (510k). The 510k is a premarket submission to demonstrate that the device is both safe and effective before it can be sold commercially. Both Class 1 and Class 2 devices can be exempt, examples include anaesthesiology devices, ophthalmic devices and orthopaedic devices. Further guidance can be found on the US Food & Drug Administration site Medical Device Exemptions (510k) and GMP requirements available from https://www.accessdata.fda.gov/scripts/cdrh/cfdocs/cfpcd/315.cfm [Accessed 25 January, 2019] Without exemptions covers what are termed 'Reserved devices', such as Dental handpieces and accessories but also devices adopting new technology such as electronics being added to prosthetics.

Special controls are subject to certain limitations that re exempt from premarket notification under the FDA Modernization Act 1997. Special controls provide reasonable assurance that the device is safe and effective, examples of evidence include performance standards and postmarket surveillance.

Comparing clinical trials and clinical investigations

It is anticipated that readers of this book are more likely to be involved in clinical investigations of medical devices; however it is useful to have an understanding of the phases of clinical trials as underpinning knowledge. Table 4.1 compares the phases of clinical trials against the stages of a clinical investigation for medical devices.

The key difference is that there are only two phases in a medical device trial. The first phase is a premarket approval study, the purpose of which is to obtain CE marking. Once CE marking has been obtained, the next phase is an evaluation while in clinical use. This second phase tends to be either registry or audit-type studies to monitor long-term safety.

ISO 14155 standard

The international standard for medical device trials is ISO 14155:2011; it is the equivalent and similar in many ways to ICH GCP, the standard for clinical trials of investigational medicinal products (CTIMP). ISO 14155:2011 is published in two parts:

1. Part 1 General Requirements: Defines procedures for the conduct and performance of clinical investigations of medical devices
2. Part 2 Clinical Investigation Plans (CIPs): Provides the requirements for the preparation of a CIP for the clinical investigation of medical devices

The aim of these standards is essentially threefold. Firstly, to ensure that human subjects are protected and understand the foreseeable risks and potential benefits (if any), and having understood this freely give informed consent to participate in the study. Furthermore to ensure that the trial is scientifically well designed and that its conduct will establish the performance of the medical device by providing clinical data that are both valid and reliable; that are reproducible. Finally, it also acts as a reference document for sponsors, monitors, investigators, ethics committees, and regulatory authorities.

For healthcare organizations the responsibilities of the sponsor and clinical investigator will be important as well as the monitor. It may be that some of the duties of the sponsor can be delegated to a clinical trials unit or a contract research organization (CRO) and this should only be undertaken when a contract or a written agreement clearly specifies the duties that have been delegated.

Sponsor responsibilities

The key responsibilities of a sponsor are outlined in the following list; however readers are advised to refer to the ISO 14155 standard for definitive guidance. The standard lists 15 key responsibilities (ISO, 2003, pp. 10–11):

1. Selection of an appropriate clinical investigator (CI) and investigation site
2. Appointment of an appropriate monitor to oversee its conduct
3. Prepare and keep current the clinical investigator's brochure
4. Provide the CI with the Clinical Investigation Plan (CIP) and subsequent amendments
5. Sign the CIP
6. Supply the medical devices as specified in the CIP
7. Ensure the CI is provided with the appropriate training to use the device in accordance with the CIP
8. Ensure all deviations from the CIP are reviewed and reported
9. Appropriate recording and review of all adverse events
10. Inform all principal investigators (PIs) about serious adverse events (SAEs) and all serious adverse device effects during clinical investigations
11. Inform the CI when the clinical investigation is prematurely terminated or suspended and the relevant bodies
12. Inform the CI of the developmental status of the device
13. Review and approve any deviation from the CIP taking appropriate actions as necessary
14. Collect, store, and keep secure all relevant documentation
15. Ensure accurate device accountability and traceability systems

Note that for a device trial the term *clinical investigator* is used, whereas for a drug trial *chief investigator* is the normal nomenclature.

Clinical investigator responsibilities

For those involved in clinical engineering design it is likely that they may at some time become a clinical investigator (CI) for that medical device; the following outlines the responsibilities entrusted to the role.

The clinical investigator must be appropriately qualified, experienced in the field of application, and familiar with the investigation methodology. Paramount is training in informed consent and this could be obtained through attending ICH GCP training. There are 21 elements of informed consent for clinical trials of investigational medicinal products and in general these are also relevant for device trials; these were shown in Fig. 4.2.

The clinical investigator is responsible for the day-to-day conduct of the clinical investigation as well as for the safety and well-being of the human subjects involved in the clinical investigation (ISO, 2011). Full details are given in the International standard ISO 14155:2011.

Clinical investigation plan

The Clinical Investigation Plan (CIP) is the key document in device trials; it is effectively the equivalent of the protocol in a clinical trial. The CIP is defined as follows (ISO, 2003, p. 6):

The CIP shall be a document developed by the sponsor and the clinical investigator(s). The CIP shall be designed in such a way as to optimise the scientific validity and reproducibility of the results of the study in accordance with current clinical knowledge and practice so as to fulfil the objectives of the investigation.

Key elements of the CIP include:

- General information to include a comprehensive list of all the CIs, PIs, coordinating CIs, and investigations centers/sites, name and address of the sponsor, monitoring arrangements, data and quality management, an overall synopsis of the clinical investigation, approval and agreement to the CIP
- Identification and description of the medical device to be investigated
- Preliminary investigations and justification of the study including literature review, preclinical testing, previous clinical experience, and device risk analysis and assessment (this process is described in EN ISO 14971:2007 which is explored in Chapter 6 "Risk Management")
- Objectives of the clinical investigation
- Design of the clinical investigation

- Statistical considerations
- Deviations from the CIP and how they are handled and recorded
- Amendments to the CIP (ISO, 2003, pp. 6—11)
- Adverse events (AEs) and adverse device effects
- Early termination or suspension of the investigation
- Publication policy
- Case report forms (CRF) (the means by which data are captured during the investigation)

Approvals to undertake research

There are generally two regulatory approvals needed prior to undertaking research; namely ethical approval and competent authority (CA) approval. Ethical approval in the United Kingdom is given through the National Research Ethics Service (NRES); other countries have similar bodies, sometimes called ethical review boards (ERBs). The proposed research is reviewed by a research ethics committee (REC) which comprises expert and lay members to give an opinion on whether the rights and well-being of the participants are suitably protected. There are various timelines within which a response from the ethics committee is required and this will vary from one country to another.

The competent authority is concerned with the science of the research and the safety of the patient. In the United Kingdom the competent authority is the Medicines and Healthcare Products Regulatory Agency (MHRA). Tables 4.3 and 4.4 give examples of competent authorities.

TABLE 4.3 Examples of competent authorities for drug trials.

Country	Competent authorities for drug trials
France	Agence française de sécurité sanitaire des produits de santé (AFSSAPS)
Germany	Bundes institut für Arzneimittel und Medizinprodukte (BfArM)
Italy	Agenzia Italiana del Farmaco (AIFA)
Luxemburg	Division de la Pharmacie et des Médicaments
Norway	Statens Legemiddelverk
Sweden	Läkemedelsverket
United Kingdom	Medicines and Healthcare Products Regulatory Agency (MHRA)

TABLE 4.4 Examples of competent authorities for medical device clinical investigations.

Country	Competent authorities for medical device clinical investigations
France	Agence nationale de sécuritéde medicament et des produits de sauté(ANSM)
Germany	BfArM
Italy	Ministry of Health
Luxemburg	Ministère de la Santé
Norway (ETFA)	Helsedirektoratet Norwegian Directorate for Health
Spain	Agencia Española Medicaments y productos Sanitariós
Sweden	Medical Products Agency, Läkemedlesverket
United Kingdom	Medicines and Healthcare Products Regulatory Agency (MHRA)

Glossary

Clinical investigation The systematic testing of medical devices following an ethical and scientifically approved Clinical Investigation Plan.

Clinical investigator The person responsible for the day-to-day conduct of the clinical investigation as well as for the safety and well-being of the human subjects involved in the clinical investigation.

Clinical trial The systematic testing of investigational medicinal products (drugs) following an ethically and scientifically approved protocol to determine the efficacy and safety of a new medicinal product.

Good Clinical Practice (GCP) A set of internationally recognized ethical and scientific quality guidelines which should be followed to ensure that the rights and well-being of participants are protected and that the data produced from the research are valid and reliable.

Medical device Apparatus or instrument used for the diagnosis, prevention, monitoring, and treatment of disease.

References

Brown, A.S., 2011. Clinical trials risk: a new risk assessment tool. Clin. Governance 16 (2), 103−110.

Centers for Disease Control and Prevention (CDC), 2011. U.S. Public Health Service Syphilis Study at Tuskegee: The Tuskegee Timeline. Available from: http://www.cdc.gov/tuskegee/timeline.htm.

European Commission (EC), 2010. Medical Devices: Guidance Document − Classification of Medical Devices. MEDDEV 2.4/1 Rev. 9. Available from: http://ec.europa.eu/health/medical-devices/files/meddev/2_4_1_rev_9_classification_en.pdf.

European Parliament and the Council of the European Union, 2007. Directive 2007/47/EC. Off. J. Eur. Union L247 21−55.

Foggo, D., February 8, 2009. Thalidomide 'was developed by the Nazis': the damaging drug may have been developed as an antidote to nerve gas. Sunday Times.

International Organization for Standardization (ISO), 2011. ISO 14155 Clinical Investigation of Medical Devices for Human Subjects.

Medicines and Healthcare Products Regulatory Agency (MHRA), 2011. Competent Authority (U.K.) Bulletin No. 10 the Classification Rules. Medicines and Healthcare Products Regulatory Agency, London.

Nuremberg Military Tribunals, 1949. Trials of War Criminals before the Nuremberg Military Tribunals under Control Council Law No 10, vol. 2. U.S. Government Printing Office, Washington D.C., pp. 181−182

Saunders, S., 2006. Post-mortem on the TGN1412 Disaster. Institute of Science and Technology. Available from: http://www.i-sis.org.uk/PMOTTD.php.

Tenti, E., Simonetti, G., Bochicchio, M.T., Martinelli, G., September 2018. Main changes in European Clinical Trials Regulation (No 536/2014). Contemp. Clin. Trials Commun. 11, 99−101.

Further reading

Cohen, D., 2018. The 10 −year Fight to Offer a Cheaper Drug. Available from: https://www.bbc.co.uk/news/health-45600433.

Ndebele, P., 2013. The declaration of Helsinki; 50 years later. J. Am. Med. Assoc. 310 (20), 2145−2146.

International Council for harmonization of technical requirements for Pharmaceuticals for Human Use (2016), Step 4 version. Integrated Addendum to ICH E6(R1): Guideline for Good Clinical Practice E6(R2).

Regulation (EU) No 536/2014 of the European Parliament and of the Council of 16 April 2014 on clinical trials in medicinal products for human use and repealing, 2014. Directive 2001/20/EC. Off. J. L158(27.05.2014):1.

World Medical Association (WMA), 1996. Declaration of Helsinki: recommendations guiding medical doctors in biomedical research involving human subjects. Available from: http://www.jcto.co.uk/Documents/Training/Declaration_of_Helsinki_1996_version.pdf.

Useful Websites

National sInstitute for Health Research, www.nihr.ac.uk.

National Research Ethics Service, www.nres.nhs.uk.

Medicines and Healthcare Products Regulatory Agency, www.mhra.gov.uk.

Chapter 5

Risk management

Anthony Scott Brown

Health Tech Solutions Ltd, Redruth, United Kingdom

Chapter outline

Introduction

Preventable mistakes are common in healthcare. The risks associated with healthcare are being highlighted, and hospitals and healthcare organizations are taking steps to manage these through active risk management. An acceptable framework should provide a clear definition of "reasonable risk" and an account of normative justification for this definition. This is largely determined by the risk appetite of the organization—how much risk the organization is prepared to accept. In addition, it should elucidate a set of operational criteria or markers that delineate in an operationally useful way the parameters or boundaries that separate reasonable from excessive risk. Finally, it should articulate practical tests that deliberators can use to determine whether or not these operational criteria have been met in a particular case (London, 2006; Brown, 2011). This chapter is structured loosely in a similar manner to the International Standard ISO 14971:2007 which relates to the application of risk management to medical devices.

Definition

In any discussion about risk management we must first establish what we mean by risk. Risk can be defined as "a situation involving exposure to danger [noun] or exposure (someone or something valued) to danger, harm or loss" (Oxford Dictionaries online). Other definitions include the following.

Rosa et al. (2003) defines risk as "a situation or event where something of human value (including humans themselves) is at stake and where the outcome is uncertain." The Royal Society (1992) uses the definition "the probability that a particular adverse event occurs during a stated time period or results from a particular challenge."

It is accepted that the concept of risk has two components (BSI, 2007, p. V):

1. The probability of occurrence of harm
2. The consequences of that harm, that is, how severe it might be

(*Note*: The European Standard EN ISO 14971:2007 has the status of a British Standard.)

The Office of Government Commerce (OGC) define risk as "an uncertain event or set of events which, should it occur, will have an effect on the achievement of objectives" (OGC, 2007, p. 1).

Consequences and likelihood

Clearly the definition is open to interpretation, but essentially to make it useful in managing risk we must be able to "quantify" it. The basic risk equation is:

$$\text{Risk} = \text{Consequences} \times \text{Likelihood} \tag{5.1}$$

[NB. Consequences is sometimes replaced by Impact and Likelihood by probability]

Third dimension of risk

Most risk assessment systems consider risk in terms of consequences and likelihood (sometimes referred to as probability and impact matrices; APM, 2010), however in some circumstances there is a third dimension: time (Fig. 5.1). The time factor is principally used in project management either for a stage or the overall project (OGC, 2009). Hence there is proximity (i.e., the time before the risk is apparent) and also a duration (i.e., the time period over which the risk is present).

The overrunning of a stage or project can have major implications. According to the OGC (OGC, 2007, p. 26), impacts on an organizational activity are usually considered in terms of the organizational objectives and hence examine the impact on:

- Costs
- Timescale
- Quality/requirements

The OGC guide also introduces the concept of a time dimension which impacts and feeds into the risk assessment. The concept of time-dependent risk is not usually considered in many industries including healthcare, however it may be appropriate for specific risks, for example, a new surgical procedure, a licensed drug being used "off label," or a clinical investigation of a new medical device.

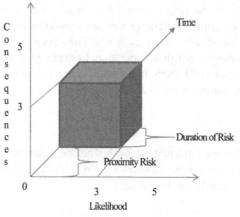

FIG. 5.1 Three-dimensional model of risk.

In reality, medical device risk is time dependent. For example, using a syringe driver or volumetric infusion pump to administer an infusion to a patient. There are a number of risks associated with failure of the device such as the pump stopping and hence not delivering the required prescription, the clinical consequences of this would be dependent upon the drug being administered and the impact on the patient. The syringe driver could also over or under infuse at its set rate and again the outcome of this would be dependent upon the drug being administered. Whilst this accounts for a technical failure there is also the possibility of user error in programming the device; whether malicious or unintentional. These risks have been recognized for some time and most manufacturers have introduced control measures to reduce the likelihood of programming errors with the adoption of Drug Error Reduction Software (DERS) in what is often termed 'smart' pumps. A recent government report estimated medication errors led to an estimated 712 deaths in England every year and could have been a contributing factor to 1708 deaths (Elliott et al., 2018). At a later time the same device may be used again either on the same patient to deliver a further infusion or a different patient. The second infusion might be a different drug and the syringe driver may be operated by a different member of staff with more or less experience and training. In areas such as a Critical Care Units CCU) there may be multiple devices connected to a patient. In this instance the risk consequences and likelihood may be different. This is shown in Fig. 5.2 which shows two risks separated by a period of time. The first risk has a consequence of 3 and a likelihood of 3, whereas the second risk has a consequence of 2 and a likelihood of 4. The time period may be hours or even days in some instances for a particular device or only a few minutes where a device or elements of a device are used almost consecutively. Perhaps a good example would be a patient attending a dental practice or the oral surgery unit in an acute hospital for a planned dental filling. After the administration of local anaesthetic into the gum the dental surgeon need to remove some of the hard outer enamel of the tooth in order to gain access to the decaying dentine. The dental surgeon will first use the high speed air turbine from the Dental operating unit; the turbine is a low torque drill and rotates typically at 400,000 to 500,000 rpm. A number of possibilities exist that might cause the turbine to fail;

- Loss of the air supply (Typically @ 5.5 Bar)
- Failure of the gearbox within the high speed hand piece
- Turbine stalling due to a high torque requirement when cutting.

This part of the procedure represents the first risk; the dental surgeon now swaps to a low speed (high torque) hand piece to remove the dentine. Similar risks relating to this hand piece as the high speed turbine and this is represented by the second risk in Fig. 5.2 where maybe there is a period of only a few minutes between these risks.

In reality, of course, while this may be true for a single medical device, there are for some times of equipment several hundred similar devices in an acute care hospital so the risk is continuous. In areas such as intensive care or the operating theatres there may be multiple devices connected to the patient. In many ways we should consider the number of simultaneous infusions so we can aggregate the risk, but as this is not possible to estimate let alone measure, the risk is treated as though it were continuous.

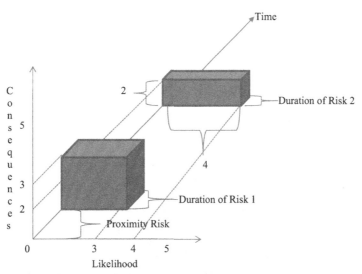

FIG. 5.2 Three-dimensional model of risk showing two distinct events.

Although the overall or average risk over time would be lower, it would not be practical to undertake a formal risk assessment prior to using every medical device. However, it would probably be useful to undertake a further reassessment should there be any significant change of staffing or for a change in the environment.

We can add another dimension of risk is where the level of a particular risk changes. In this instance there could be two risk states; active risk and quiescent or passive risk. The levels of risk would be different in the two states whether the active state poses a higher or lower risk is contextually specific. For example let us consider a road junction where the flow of traffic is controlled by traffic light signals mounted on the lamp posts. Under normal circumstances when the electronic circuitry controlling the traffic light signals is functioning correctly the lights are illuminated in the correct sequence as in Table 5.1. This is the active state for the traffic lights.

Assuming that the road users adhere to the Highway Code (2015) then the risk of a collision is very low. If however the electronic circuitry develops a fault and the traffic light signals are inoperative effectively this becomes the quiescent state. In this instance when there are no traffic light signals illuminated the risk of a collision is much greater as all of the road users try to negotiate the junction at the same time; effectively "uncontrolled". Thankfully modern electronic circuitry is very reliable; Mean time between failures (MTBFs) is likely to be measured in years, and so the quiescent risk rarely occurs.

If we look at another example but this time in the healthcare sector how this scenario works. Consider a patient going the operating theatre for a surgical procedure under general Anaesthetic and we will look at the risks of failure of the anaesthetic workstation.

The patient is taken into the Anaesthetic room where, after patient identification has been confirmed, a cannula is inserted into a vein on the back of the hand. The patient is administered 100% oxygen via a face mask to fully saturate the alveoli in their lungs (pulmones). An injection of typically Thiopental (a barbiturate) is administered to the patient via the cannula and they drift off to sleep. This is followed by administration of a muscle relaxant such as Succinylcholine which provides short term paralysis minimizsing coughing and the gag reflex to aid tracheal intubation. The patient is now connected to the anaesthetic workstation via a breathing circuit and filters where a cocktail of oxygen, air and volatile anaesthetic agent are administered to deepen the level of anaesthesia. Surgical anaesthesia occurs at Stage 3, Plane III (Guedel, 1927) where the anaesthetist would use the integral ventilator to breathe for the patient using Pressure Control (PC) mode of ventilation. The patient is now totally reliant on the ventilator for their breathing and we can consider this period as an "Active" risk. Failure of the ventilator is clearly the hazard in this instance.

A little later on as the surgical procedure draws to an end the anaesthetist reduces the percentage of volatile anaesthetic agent and the patient starts to make some respiratory effort; the ventilator is now switched to Pressure support (PS) mode. In this period of time the patient is breathing spontaneously and the ventilator is "topping up" this effort if required; essentially moving towards a monitoring rather than interventional function and is more of a "Quiescent" risk.

The two risks are shown in Fig. 5.3. Here we can see that whilst the impact to the patient remains the same (3) i.e. not getting sufficient oxygen and becoming hypoxic, the likelihood of the risk occurring is much greater during the active phase because the patient's own breathing is suppressed.

As we can see in this instance that with reference to our risk matrix during the 'active' phase the RRN is (9) which equates to a LOW (Yellow) grading and in the 'quiescent' phase the RRN is (6) and the grading is now VERY LOW (Green).

TABLE 5.1 Typical definitions for consequences.

Negligible (none)	Treatment/diagnosis error resulting in minimal or no detectable effect to patient condition
Minor	Minimum harm/injury to patient with short-term consequences, e.g., additional monitoring or minor treatment
Serious (moderate)	Significant but not permanent harm with medium-term consequences and requiring further treatment
Critical (major)	Significant injury with long-term/permanent consequences
Catastrophic	Resulting in patient death

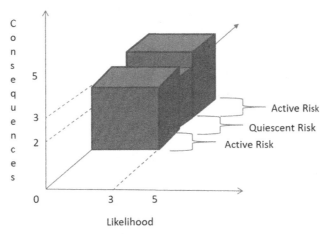

FIG. 5.3 Active and quiescent risk.

The final dimension of risk is when there are two risks present simultaneously. This could be the same risk but due to more than one cause or two entirely different risks. Furthermore, as an added complexity the duration of the risks, if not continuous, could be entirely different as shown in Fig. 5.4.

In reality of course, we are surrounded by many risks in everyday life both at home and when we are at work. Some environments pose a greater risk than others, such as people in the construction industry on a building site compared with working in an office. However, it is only in the work environment that we formally assess risk and develop action plans to manage or mitigate them.

Procurement risk

In recent years we have seen risk used as a tool to inform procurement decision making. Medical devices are expensive and with the ever-increasing adoption and integration with information technology and computerized control equipment is becoming obsolescent sooner. Whilst in the past a medical device might have been seen as an investment that had a working life of 15 or more years we now see this drastically reduced to less than a decade and for some devices only five years. This reduction in useful working life of equipment is placing an increasing burden on capital funding mechanisms.

This cost pressure has been exasperated by an unprecedented slowdown in the growth of NHS funding in England since 2010 leading to productivity improvement Programmes. No doubt the austerity measures have also hit other healthcare providers including the private sector. This has resulted in organizations having to 'sweat' their assets longer as they struggle to fund the technical refresh of the medical device asset base. The slowdown in funding is reported in the Kings Fund paper *The NHS Productivity Challenge* which predicts the proportion of GDP for NHS funding will fall to 6% in 2021 from its peak in 2009 of 8% (Appleby et al., 2014).

The following year the MHRA published its guidance document *Managing Medical Devices* (2015) which, for the first time, advocated a strategic approach to replacement and development equipment procurement planning. For the past few

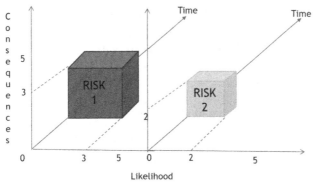

FIG. 5.4 Simultaneous risks.

years this strategic approach has been widely adopted whereby organizations' have developed a rolling replacement programme for medical devices. The concept is to develop a system where we minimize surprises and where the peaks and troughs of capital investment can be 'smoothed' by using a structured approach to the replacement of medical devices. This ensures that medical devices are replaced in a timely manner and the asset base remains fit for purpose. From a clinical engineering perspective our key drivers for replacement are reliability and maintainability which can loosely be aligned to End of Life (EoL) and End of Support (EoS) respectively. Looking at this from a clinical perspective the focus would be on how any breakdown or failure might affect patient safety and/or disrupt service delivery and capacity. For a timely replacement programme we must also build in a period of time for evaluations where necessary and the lead time for delivery of the new devices.

Of course, this approach does not deal with unexpected failures which will occur from time to time, however it has proved extremely useful and met with considerable success in revitalizing aging asset bases of medical devices. In recent years we have seen a drop in real terms in capital funding which is stifling the structured rolling replacement approach. The crisis in funding has led to a more critical focus in immediate patient safety. Prioritization is no longer based on the milestone date of EoS and EoL from the manufacturer or even horizon scanning/technology adoption for improved techniques and greater efficiency. We are prioritizing, and quite appropriately, on replacement of equipment which is deemed likely to lead to patient harm within year. Here we can introduce a new term; 'proximity risk'. For devices not deemed to cause immediate patient harm i.e. the risk is not in closeness, proximity, the risk is reduced and can be considered further away at some time in the future. So, this would include risks which might have an impact on business continuity and service delivery limiting our ability to deliver diagnosis or treatment in a timely manner to the wider population. In such austere times drastic measures are necessary and it becomes increasingly important that underpinning the decision making are robust and transparent governance processes. These governance processes must be informed by realistic and appropriate risk assessments; several techniques in the risk toolbox are described later in this chapter.

Risk appetite

One area of risk not yet mentioned is the concept of risk appetite, or the capacity of the organization; this is usually determined or set by the board. According to the Office of Government Commerce, "Risk appetite plays a vital role in supporting an organization's objectives and orchestrating risk management activities" (OGC, 2007, p. 20). Each organization will take a view on what level of risk they are willing to take or accept; it may well be dependent on how the organization would be able to manage a risk. For example, an organization with substantial financial reserves and capital levels would be better placed to live with financial risk than other organizations with less capacity. Another way of looking at risk capacity is the burden it places on the organization and how it enacts on the way the organization operates. It may, for instance, influence decisions about changing the business direction.

For clinical engineering departments involved in major equipping or re-equipping programs an understanding of corporate risk appetite is essential so that a risk management strategy and escalation rules are appropriately defined (Sowden, 2011, p. 138). Properly defined and communicated risk appetite helps to insulate a program from unwelcome surprises and provides it and its projects with clear tolerances in which to operate.

Risk acceptability

Linked to risk appetite is risk acceptability: the extent to which the organization will accept a given level or risk. Tolerance thresholds may be specified and probably the two simplest to specify are time and cost.

In some countries, a good example being the United Kingdom, healthcare organizations can "pool" risk. The National Health Service Litigation Authority (NHSLA) in the United Kingdom has the Risk Pooling Scheme for Trusts (RPSTs) whereby meeting governance standards in individual organizations will entitle them to reduced insurance premiums.

Medical devices directives

There are a plethora of technical standards relating to medical devices, designed to ensure consistency in the safety of a device throughout its life. These must be seen as the starting point in the risk profile. Underpinning these are the Medical Devices Directives (Fig. 5.5). "The Medical Device Directives are 'New Approach' directives relating to the safety and performance of medical devices which were harmonized in the EU in the 1990's" (BSI, 2018). There are three European Directives concerning medical devices:

British Standards/CE Marking			
Medical Device Regulations (2002) [SI No. 618]		Medical Device Amendment Regulations (2005) [SI No. 2909]	
90/385/EEC	93/42/EEC	98/79/EEC	

FIG. 5.5 Legislation wall of safety.

- Active implantable Medical Device Directive (90/385/EEC)[1]
- Medical Devices Directive (93/42/EEC)
- In vitro diagnostic Medical Devices Directive (98/79/EEC)

The EU Directive 2007/47/EC (which amends the Medical Devices Directive 93/42/EEC) specifies:

- Clinical data will be required on all classes of medical devices (even if already CE marked)
- All serious adverse effects (SAEs) must be reported to the competent authority (CA). The competent authority in the United Kingdom is the MHRA (European Parliament and the Council of the European Union, 2007).

The requirements for Good Clinical Practice in medical device clinical trials are set out in BS EN ISO 14155:2003, Clinical Investigation of Medical Devices for Human Subjects, and was explored in Chapter 3 "Good Clinical Practice."

The Medical Devices Directives were implemented into UK legislation by the Medical Device Regulations 2002 (S.I. No. 618). This statutory instrument consolidates all existing medical device regulations into a single piece of information that came into force on 13 June 2002. Subsequently the Medical Device (Amendment) Regulations 2005 (S.I. 2005 No. 2909) were introduced. In other countries the directive would be implemented through their own legislative processes into regulations. The regulations place obligations on manufacturers to ensure that their devices are safe and fit for their intended purpose. In addition, the majority of medical devices need to be CE marked before being placed on the market.

There are further safeguards in the manufacturing process through British Standards such as the ubiquitous BS EN ISO 60601-1-6:2013 and the amendment A1:2015, Medical Electrical equipment. General Requirements for Basic Safety and Essential Performance, which is further supported by the specific standards for types of devices such as surgical diathermy. This legislation and regulations are easily conceptualized as a brick wall to protect the safety of patients and staff.

The safety of medical devices is overseen by the competent authority (CA) in each country whose remit is the regulation of medicines and medical devices and equipment used in healthcare and the investigation of harmful incidents. Their guidance on managing medical devices recommends that healthcare organizations should strive to ensure that the service departments that maintain their equipment should be registered to BS EN ISO 9001 or similar. BS EN ISO 9001:2015 is a general quality management standard that is not specifically targeted at medical devices but is more concerned with having processes and checks in place to ensure a consistent quality and is underpinned by the ethos of continuous improvement. Increasingly, in-house electrobiomedical engineering (EBME) departments are becoming registered to this standard. There is tacit knowledge surrounding the rationale for routine maintenance, and in particular maintenance schedules are hotly debated.

Healthcare organizations, their staff, and patients take on faith that medical devices are intrinsically safe based on the safeguards put in place through the legislation. In the United Kingdom the safety of medical devices is overseen by the MHRA, an executive agency of the UK Department of Health, whose mission is "… to protect and promote public health and patient safety." (MHRA, 2015, p.5).

BS ISO 31000:2018

This is an international standard that outlines the principles and generic guidelines on the principles and practice of risk management within an organization. A useful accompanying standard is BS ISO 31100, the code of practice that provides guidance on the implementation of BS ISO 31000. The standard 31000 sets out a framework to embed risk management in any organization. The framework comprises seven elements:

1. Understanding the organization and its context
2. Risk management policy
3. Embedding risk management into processes within the organization
4. Identifying lines of accountability

---

1. These standards were incorporated into U.K. law in a new standard 2007/47/EC on 21 March 2010.

5. Recognition of the need and identification of resources
6. Internal reporting mechanisms, such as risk registers, and communication channels
7. External communication and reporting (if required)

   Overall the risk management framework must not be seen as a one-off task, but must be continually revisited to ensure that it remains fit for purpose. The basic review cycle is shown in Fig. 5.6.

Risk management policy

Like all policies the risk management policy must be subject to periodic review. To ensure risk management is core to the business it must link in to other policies and the objectives of the organization. For organizations involved in medical devices, whether that be manufacturing or in use, one of the key objectives must be patient safety. The organization's risk appetite must be clearly articulated in the policy and this may be informed by legal and financial aspects.

   The policy must also clearly define the roles and responsibilities for managing risks; often in large organizations there is a risk manager who oversees the risk management framework and processes. It is usual for each risk to have a named risk owner. The risk owner is responsible for the identification of the hazard, the evaluation and grading of the risk, and subsequent control measures. There needs to be in place a regular review process whereby each risk is reviewed to ensure that the control measures are effective and that the residual risk is correctly graded.

   The policy must set out the process, methods, and tools used to manage the risks within the organization. Typically, this will comprise a risk matrix to grade the consequences and likelihood and then the recording of risks, traditionally by means of a risk register. There can be different levels of risk register, for example, in a hospital the ward or department would hold a risk register, and risks that cannot be managed at this level would sit on a higher-level risk register at the directorate or division. Finally, there would be an organization risk register held by the board.

AS/NZS 4360:2004

The AS/NZS 4360 risk management standard (now in its third revision in 2004 from the original 1995 standard) is the basis of many risk management standards across the world and underpins the new International Standard ISO 31000. The latest revision places more emphasis on embedding risk management within the organizational culture rather than merely "quantifying risk." Furthermore, it considers risk as an opportunity in addition to risk as a threat. This represents a sea

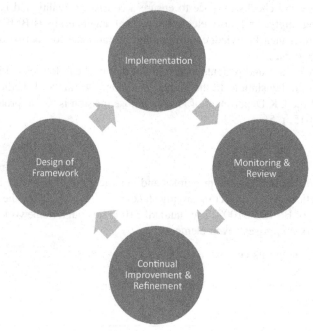

FIG. 5.6   Risk management review process.

change in risk management which was once linked closely with the blame culture and has now matured into a fair and just culture.

Essentially the process comprises four steps:

1. Risk identification
2. Risk analysis
3. Evaluation of risk
4. Risk control

Like any management process, communication and monitoring is essential at every stage.

ISO 14971:2007

This international standard on the application of risk management to medical devices is aimed at the manufacturing industry and outlines in some detail a process to identify the hazards associated with all medical devices. It describes a method of risk assessments, identification of control measures, and review. This standard should be read in conjunction with BS EN ISO 60601-1-6:2013 + A1:2015, Medical Electrical Equipment − Part 1: General Requirements for Basic Safety and Essential Performance, and any specific ISO 60601 standards for the device in question. It is strongly recommended that the implementation of a risk management system for medical devices becomes part of an overall quality management system (QMS); the associated international standard is ISO 9001:2015, Quality Management Systems − Requirements.

The ISO 14971 standard states (BSI, 2007, p. 5):

The manufacturer shall establish, document and maintain throughout the life-cycle an ongoing process for identifying hazards associated with a medical device, estimating and evaluating the associated risks, controlling these risks, and monitoring the effectiveness of the controls.

The process is divided into four parts:

1. Risk analysis: The identification of the hazards and estimating the potential risk that they pose
2. Risk evaluation: Determining if the risk is acceptable or if further reduction is necessary
3. Risk control: Identification and analysis of possible control measure options and their implementation
4. Product and post-production information: A system to collect and review information about the medical device during the production stage in manufacturing but also subsequently in use during installation, maintenance, or operation

Failures "in the field" may well be reported back to manufacturers through the competent authority (CA) and will result in an incident investigation. Readers are directed to the International Standard ISO 13485:2016, Medical Devices − Quality Management Systems − Requirements for Regulatory Purposes, for additional guidance.

To demonstrate that a device has been designed to be safe, manufacturers are required to undertake risk assessments and compile a risk management file. BS EN ISO 14971:2007, Medical Devices, Application of Risk Management to Medical Devices, provides a framework to systematically assess the risks. Any EBME department undertaking the design and manufacture of devices for use either in their hospital or to be placed "on the market" should therefore undertake a systematic estimate and evaluate the associated risks and ensure that this is documented appropriately.

The resultant risk management file can be used to inform the basis of subsequent reliability centered maintenance. Readers are directed to Moubray (1992), which gives a detailed insight into reliability centered maintenance.

The risk management process as outlined in BS EN ISO 14971 includes a subset of risk assessment. There are six phases to the risk management process: risk analysis, risk evaluation, risk control, residual risk evaluation, risk management report, and production/post-production information.

Risk analysis

Theoretical perspectives on risk will not be elaborated on here as they have already been discussed in a recent Institute of Physics and Engineering in Medicine (IPEM) report entitled Risk Management and its Application to Medical Device Management (Brown and Robbins, 2007). Risk analysis requires the identification of key safety characteristics of the device, and identification of the hazards. For each of the hazards an estimation of the risk should be made. Essentially this is about considering the consequences (severity) and likelihood (probability) of a hazard becoming a risk. This is a systems approach to failure as conceptualized by Reason's (2000) "Swiss cheese" model. "The systems approach concentrates on

TABLE 5.2 Typical definitions for likelihood.

Improbable (rare)	Rarely occurs, >1–5 years
Remote (unlikely)	Not expected to happen more than yearly
Occasional (possible)	May reoccur occasionally, >6 monthly
Probable (likely)	Likely to reoccur > monthly
Frequent (almost certain)	Frequently reoccurs > weekly

the conditions under which individuals work and tries to build defenses to avert errors or mitigate their effects" (Reason, 2000, p. 768).

To ensure consistency, each of these terms should be defined or quantified in the risk management file. Typical definitions are given in Tables 5.1 and 5.2.

When considering medical device design, a risk may be the failure of a safety critical component, in which case the likelihood may be estimated in mean time to failure (MTTF), for risks where is not possible to estimate the likelihood, for example, of software failure, or malicious tampering the worst-case scenario should be used. ISO 14971 gives some useful examples of sources of information or data for estimating risks (BSI, 2007, p. 10):

- Published standards
- Scientific technical data
- Field data from similar devices already in use, including published reported incidents
- Usability tests employing typical users
- Clinical evidence
- Results of appropriate investigations
- Expert opinion
- External quality assessment schemes

Risk evaluation

Having estimated the risk for each hazardous situation, the risk must be evaluated.

For most practical purposes this will be "measured" using a risk matrix. Most healthcare organizations use a 5 × 5 risk matrix based on the Australian Standards AS/4360:2004 where the two axes correspond to scales for consequences, sometimes call severity and likelihood. A typical example is shown in Table 5.3.

Risk control

Following on from risk evaluation we must now put in place processes to control the risks. The introduction of control measures (barriers) can reduce the consequences (severity) or reduce the likelihood (probability), either way this will diminish the risk. There is a hierarchy for controlling risks. The first and most preferable is elimination by using a different

TABLE 5.3 Example of 5 × 5 risk matrix.

Consequences	Likelihood				
	Improbable	Remote	Occasional	Probable	Frequent
Negligible	1	2	3	4	5
Minor	2	4	6	8	10
Serious	3	6	9	12	15
Critical	4	8	12	16	20
Catastrophic	5	10	15	20	25

FIG. 5.7 Hierarchy of risk control. *Source: CIEH, 2005.*

approach to achieve the same goal. Where elimination is not feasible then control measures must be put in place. The hierarchy of control is (CIEH, 2005, Fig. 5.7):

1. Elimination or avoidance
2. Substitution
3. Controlling risks at source
4. Separation and isolation
5. Safe working procedures
6. Training, instruction, and supervision
7. Personal protection
8. Other considerations: welfare facilities, first aid, emergency procedures (Table 5.4)

Lack of control can compromise risk, however careful attention to manufacturing process can minimize the risk. Techniques such as hazard and operability (HAZOP) studies, which originated in the British chemical industry, could prove useful.

Risk management report

Having put in place systems to either minimize or eliminate risk, there now remains only overall residual risk. It is therefore necessary to re-evaluate the risks to determine whether the overall residual risk posed by the medical device is acceptable. Inevitably there will be some risks that cannot realistically be eliminated. There are two possible outcomes from the evaluation of the overall residual risk:

1. Risk unacceptable: This will require the collation of further evidence/literature to determine if the clinical benefits outweigh the overall risk. If judged acceptable the evidence to justify this decision should be included in the risk management file; if this is not the case the risk remains unacceptable.
2. Risk acceptable: The manufacturer should decide what evidence is pertinent to include in the accompanying document in the risk management file.

TABLE 5.4 Risk rating numbers.

Risk rating	Risk rating number
Very low	1–7
Low	8–12
Medium	13–15
High	16–25

According to ISO 14971 "Compliance is checked by inspection of the risk management file and the accompanying documents" (BSI, 2007, p. 13).

Production and post-production information

The risk management report is an important document in the risk management file and acts as a check or quality control which provides an assurance that the risk management plan has been implemented correctly, the overall residual risk is acceptable, and that mechanisms are in place for the compilation of production and post-production information. This information can be drawn on for the issuing of Field Safety Corrective Actions (FSCAs) through the MHRA, and, where necessary, Medical Device Alerts (MDAs).

One way of ensuring that processes are consistently followed is through the introduction of a quality system that is externally certified, such as BS EN ISO 9001:2015.

Risk tools

Monte Carlo modeling

Monte Carlo analysis is a widely used qualitative risk analysis technique. It is a powerful technique but does require considerable preparatory work and judgment to ensure it models the risk appropriately. Although traditionally used in project management, it could be successfully used in clinical engineering for a major re-equipping project or a new operating theater suite.

Monte Carlo simulation is a complex stochastic technique used to solve a wide range of mathematical problems. Monte Carlo methods randomly select values from a given distribution to create multiple scenarios of a problem. Each time a value is randomly selected, it forms one possible scenario and solution to the problem (Cummins et al., 2009).

A key feature of this technique is that it offers an approach that comprises the assessment of any number of individual risk events with the analysis that concerns overall project risk. Essentially there are three elements (APM, 2010, p. 153):

- Risk estimates
- Monte Carlo modeling
- Simulation and analysis of results

Risk estimation

The first step is risk estimation and is based on the assumption that it is possible to estimate the outcome of a risk event on a continuous probability distribution. Cost and time are common parameters in clinical engineering, though patient safety may be a more useful parameter. The *Project Risk Analysis and Management Guide* (APM, 2010, pp. 148–150) suggests five factors to be considered when estimating risk:

1. Understand the implications of the probability distribution shape (e.g., Beta PERT, triangular, and general triangular).
2. Consider all relevant sources of uncertainty.
3. Follow a process designed to avoid bias and unrealistic low-income variance.
4. Avoid assumptions that the most likely value is the one that is planned.
5. Adopt a lessons-learned approach to compare estimate against actual incomes.

Hazard and operability study

A hazard and operability (HAZOP) study is a systematic process for examining a system to identify potential hazards and potential operability problems. Hence HAZOP can be used to inform risk assessments.

HAZOP studies require more detail than other techniques, such as failure mode and effects analysis (FMEAs) and fault tree analysis (FTAs), regarding the systems under consideration, but produce more comprehensive information on hazards and errors in the system design (IEC 61882:2016). The international standard IEC 61882 was prepared by the International Electrotechnical Commission (IEC) Technical Committee 56. Readers are directed to this standard for further guidance and specific examples of the study process.

The HAZOP process is designed to be used by multidisciplinary teams, therefore in the healthcare sector this could be the clinical engineer in conjunction with a clinical colleague. The composition of the clinical team (e.g., surgeons, physicians, nurses, physiotherapists, and radiographers) will very much depend on the type of system being examined. Alternatively, if this is part of a design or development process for a new medical device the team would comprise the designer of the electronic circuitry, the mechanical engineer who specified the enclosure and interface ports, for example, a clinical engineer, and a maintenance technician.

The HAZOP study procedure has four key steps and is shown as a flowchart in Fig. 5.8.

The following four subsections look at each of the steps in more detail.

Definition

Before a study is started both the scope and objectives must be clearly defined. This is paramount for a successful study and will ensure that "the system boundaries and its interfaces with other systems and the environment are clearly defined …" (BSI, 2016, p. 17). The objectives of a study can be best described as stepping stones toward the overall aim, and these must be specific and measurable.

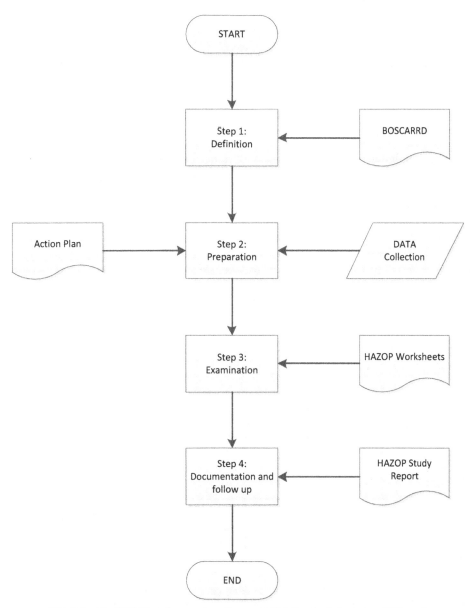

FIG. 5.8 The HAZOP study procedure. *Source: British Standards Institution, 2001, p. 9.*

An example of a team in the healthcare sector was described earlier; each member of the team must be assigned a role. The key roles include the study leader, a recorder, designer, user, specialist, and a representative from the maintenance staff.

Preparation

The study leader has a pivotal role and must be trained in HAZOP techniques. This person assumes the responsibility for all of the preparatory work including obtaining and formatting the information, and organizing the meetings. In many ways, for a HAZOP study, the leader will act as the project manager and use similar techniques to the PRINCE 2® project management methodology.

Key to the preparatory work is the identification of a team of specialists from various disciplineds and the development of a study plan which will include:

- Objectives and scope of the study
- Technical details
- An outline design divided into nodes (parts and elements)with defined design intent, and for each node a list of components, materials, and activities and their characteristics
- A list of proposed guide words to be used and the interpretation of the guide word-element/characteristic combinations
- A list of appropriate references (this may include data sheets, relevant design standards, etc.)
- Administrative arrangements, schedule of meetings including their dates, times, and locations
- Form of recording required (usually recorded using a word-processing package on a PC)
- Templates that may be used in the study

Design description

In clinical engineering the design description may include functional block diagrams, electronic circuit diagrams, printed circuit board layouts, component data sheets, and mechanical engineering diagrams. For programmable systems this would include programming information, logic and timing diagrams, and state transition diagrams. The combination of these technical diagrams will provide a rich source of reference material to inform the examination process.

Guide words and deviations

It is the study leader's responsibility to compile the initial list of guide words, and care must be taken to ensure that they are neither too specific that they may limit ideas or too broad, so they are not well defined. The compilation of the list of guide words is therefore of paramount importance. Some examples of guide words suitable for clinical engineering are given in Table 5.5.

The guide word/element associations as shown in Table 5.5 can be thought of as a risk matrix. To produce comprehensive hazard identification, all possibilities must be considered. There may be gaps in the matrix where combinations are not credible or realistic. There are many variations on risk matrices, for example: probability—impact grid, risk map, and

TABLE 5.5 Guide word examples.

Deviation type	Guide word	Example
Negative	No	No physiological, control, or data signal passed
Substitution	Reverse	Of no consequence
	Other than	The physiological, control, or data signals are not correct
Time	Early	Signal not synchronized to clock, arrives early
	Late	Signal not synchronized to clock, arrival delayed
Order or sequence	Before	Signals or events occurred in the wrong sequence, before intended
	After	Signals or events occurred in the wrong sequence, after intended

summary risk profile. Further guidance can be found in the OGC book entitled *Management of Risk: Guidance for Practitioners* (OGC, 2007).

Once a deviation is identified and its risk impact in terms of consequences and probability is determined, the next step is to determine what actions, if any, can be taken to mitigate or reduce the risk. Following the implementation of these actions there may still be a residual risk present which must be graded, and then a decision is made whether this risk is considered acceptable for the organization.

The examination process should be well documented and the study leader will have determined the requirements for documentation at the planning stage. There are several iterations of the examination process for each guide word applied to every element or component of the system.

Examination

The examination meetings are where the deviations to elements of the system are considered, and they must be structured according to the study plan to achieve the best outcomes. A particular element/node (characteristic) should be selected and analyzed following its (correct) sequence and then the next element should be considered. It is often helpful to sequence the examination logically following either a process from the start to its destination or tracking a signal from the input to the output.

Central to the examination is the use of guide words, which structure a specific search for deviations from the intent of the design. This demonstrates the importance placed on developing an adequate guide word list with suitable definitions.

Each element is examined, physical systems and processes may be broken down into more manageable steps or, individual signals [in clinical engineering this may also be psychological waveforms]. The size of an element may depend on the complexity of the system. For a simple system this may be an individual component (e.g., a sensor, transducer, or valve actuator); for a larger system this may be a functional block such as the ECG front end in an electrocardiograph.

It is useful to express the element in terms of its input signals, functionality, and the output to either the destination (such as an LCD display) or linked to the next processing stage of the system that will be the next element for investigation.

Documentation

Like many systematic logical processes, HAZOP is extremely powerful if used with diligence and thoroughly documented. The extent of the documentation and recording may be determined by the complexity of the study, legislation, and regulatory or contractual obligations. Essentially recording falls unto one of two types: full recording or recording by exception. Full recording is obvious, whereas exception reporting is only documenting the problems highlighted, whether they are hazards or operability. For robustness, full recording is the gold standard.

The use of templates or worksheets assist in providing clarity and consistency and one worksheet should be used for each element or node. The design of the worksheet and level of detail recorded will be dependent on individual needs. Proprietary word-processing packages or spreadsheets provide simple and convenient solutions to recording. The header should include the project title, design intent, element or part under examination, and names of the team members. The footer will include the file name, date, and page number.

A table can then be constructed using the following column titles: reference number, element or part, guide word, deviation, cause, consequences, control measures or barriers, severity, risk rating, action plan, priority, the actionee, and finally the status.

For completeness it is useful to record all of the reference documents referred to during the examination, such as circuit diagrams, exploded views, and regulatory documents and design standards. The culmination of all the examinations will lead to the study report. The report should comprise:

- An executive summary
- Conclusions from the study
- Agreed scope and objectives of the project
- Identified hazards and operability problems
- Recommendations for changes in particular aspects of the design, and actions required to mitigate uncertainties and problems

Appendices to the report will include:

- Completed worksheets

TABLE 5.6 Probability impact grid.

Probability	1.0	Certain 81%–100%	0.2	0.4	0.6	0.8	1.0
	0.8	Almost certain 61%–80%	0.16	0.32	0.48	0.64	0.8
	0.6	May happen 41%–60%	0.12	0.24	0.36	0.48	0.6
	0.4	Unlikely 21%–40%	0.08	0.16	0.24	0.32	0.4
	0.2	Very unlikely 0%–20%	0.04	0.08	0.12	0.16	0.2
			No harm				Death
			0.2	0.4	0.6	0.8	1.0
			IMPACT				

Values given are for illustrative purposes only, representing patient safety.

- Listings of diagrams and drawings
- Reference list of standards and regulations together with relevant information from previous studies

Probability impact grid

The probability impact grid is one of the techniques used to assess the likelihood of a threat or opportunity materializing and their potential impact. It is a qualitative technique used to rank previously identified risks. The probability (sometimes called consequences or impact scale) is a measure derived from percentages. The scale can be divided into any number of parts; typically, a five-point scale is used together with a five-point impact scale, thus producing a 5 × 5 risk matrix.

The Australian Standard AS/NZS 4360:2004 and the International Standard ISO 14971:2007 both use a 5 × 5 risk matrix. The scales for each access do not need to be the same and can equally be linear or logarithmic. Table 5.6 shows an impact scale where the bands are all less than 1. Typically, this may describe cost or time; in clinical engineering we would be interested in patient safety and reliability (failure rates).

Table 5.6 shows qualitative words to describe the impact scale specific to patient safety.

Risk map

Another form of risk estimation is the risk map (Table 5.7). In this case the term *likelihood* is used instead of probability. The classifications of risk at maximum would be high, medium, and low, which produces a 3 × 3 risk matrix. However, more often this is extended to a 5 × 5 matrix. Examples of this application are a tool for assessing the situational and contextual risk factors when using medical devices (Brown, 2004, 2007) and also assessing the risks associated with undertaking clinical trials to highlight the patient risk, PR risk, and financial risk for the organization (Brown, 2011).

Clearly this taxonomy of grading risk has little meaning unless each of the terms is given an explicit meaning. Failure to provide a definition will expose the term to be interpreted differently by people dependent partly on their experience and knowledge in the particular area where the assessment is taking place.

TABLE 5.7 Example of a risk map.

Likelihood	Very high					
	High					
	Medium					
	Low					
	Very low					
		Very low	Low	Medium	High	Very high
	Impact					

TABLE 5.8 Example of RAGB grading.

Color	Status
Red	No progress, remains high risk
Amber	Moderate progress bus still poses a significant risk
Green	Good progress made with evidence of deliverables
Blue	Action completed and deliverables achieved

RAGB status

Both the probability impact grid and risk map can be further enhanced by the use of RAGB (red, amber, green, blue) status which can translate them into risk registers/profiles (see Table 5.8). The RAGB status can be simplified to RAG rating (red, amber, and green) as is commonly used across many aspects of the healthcare sector from pressure score assessments to preventative maintenance requirements.

Glossary

Competent authority An agency or body that holds the power to regulate and conduct inspections. This is also sometimes referred to as the regulatory authority.

Mean time to failure (MTTF) The mean or average time to failure of a component or piece of equipment.

Medicines and Healthcare products Regulatory Agency (MHRA) The regulatory body and competent authority in the United Kingdom that oversees the safety of medical devices and equipment.

Quality management system (QMS) A system of documents that describes the planned and systematic work practices to ensure a consistent quality. It usually includes standard operating procedures (SOPs) and work instructions (WIs).

Risk A situation involving exposure to danger, or exposure (someone or something valued) to danger, harm, or loss.

Risk appetite This describes the level or amount of risk that an organization or individual considers to be acceptable and to which they are prepared to be exposed.

Statutory instrument The formal method by which a directive is enacted into British law.

References

Appleby, J., Galea, A., Murray, R., 2014. The NHS Productivity Challenge. The King's Fund, London.

Association for Project Management (APM), Project Risk Analysis and Management Guide. Association for Association for Project Management (APM), 2010. Project Risk Analysis and Management Guide, second ed. Princes Risborough, Buckinghamshire, Association for Project Management (APM), Princes Risborough, Buckinghamshire.

British Standards Institution (BSI), 2001. Hazard and Operability Studies (HAZOP Studies) − Application Guide BS IEC 61882. British Standards Institution (BSI), London.

British Standards Institution (BSI), 2016. Hazard and Operability Studies (HAZOP studies) − Application Guide BS IEC 61882. British Standards Institution (BSI), London.

British Standards Institution (BSI), 2007. Medical Devices − Application of Risk Management to Medical Devices BS EN ISO 14971. British Standards Institution (BSI), London.

British Standards Institution, 2018. European Medical Device Directives. Available from: https://www.bsigroup.com/en-IL/medical-devices/our-services/european-medical-device-directive1.

Brown, A.S., 2004. Finding the hidden risks with medical devices: a risk profiling tool. J. Qual. Prim. Care. 12, 135−138.

Brown, A.S., 2007. Identifying risks using a new assessment tool: the missing piece of the jigsaw in medical device risk assessment. Clin. Risk. 13 (2), 56−59.

Brown, A.S., 2011. Clinical trials: a new risk assessment tool. Clin. Governance 16 (2), 103−110.

Brown, S., Robbins, P., 2007. Risk Management and Its Application to Medical Device Management − Report. Institute of Physics and Engineering in Medicine, New York.

Chartered Institute of Environmental Health (CIEH), 2005. Risk Assessment: Principles and Practice − Level 2 Course.

Cummins, E., Butler, F., Gormley, R., Brunton, N., 2009. A Monte Carlo risk assessment model for acrylamide formation in French fries. Risk Anal. 29 (10), 1410−1426.

Elliott, R.A., Camacho, E., Campbell, F., Jankovic, D., St James, M.M., Kaltenthaler, E., Wong, R., Sculpher, M.J., Faria, R., 2018. Prevalence and Economic Burden of Medication Errors in the NHS in England. Policy Research Unit in Economic Evaluation of Health & Care Interventions (EEPRU).

European Parliament European Parliament and the Council of the European Union, 2007. Directive 2007/47/EC. Off. J. Eur. Union L247.

Guedel, A.E., 1927. Stages of anesthesia and re-classification of the signs of anesthesia. Curr. Res. Anesth. Analg. 6 (4), 157–162.

London, A.J., 2006. Reasonable risks in clinical research: a critique and proposal for the integrative approach. Stat. Med. 25 (17), 2869–2885.

Medicines and Healthcare Products Regulatory Agency (MHRA), 2015. Managing Medical Devices. MHRA, London.

Moubray, 1992. Reliability Centered Maintenance, second ed. Industrial Press Inc, New York.

Office of Government Commerce (OGC), 2007. Management of Risk Guidance for Practitioners. The Stationery Office, Norwich.

Office of Government Commerce (OGC), 2009. Managing Successful Projects with Prince 2. The Stationery Office, Norwich.

Reason, J., 2000. Human error: models and management. BMJ 320, 768–770.

Rosa, E.A., Pedgeon, N.F., Kasperson, R.E., Slovic, P., 2003. The logical structure of the social amplification of risk framework (SARF): metatheoretical foundations and policy implications the social amplification of risk. In: Pedgeon, N.F., Kasperson, R.E., Slovic, P. (Eds.), The Social Amplification of Risk. Cambridge University Press, Cambridge.

Royal Society, 1992. Risk: Analysis, Perception and Management. Report of a Royal Society Study Group. The Royal Society, London.

Sowden, R., 2011. Best Management Practice: Managing Successful Programmes. The Stationery Office, Norwich.

Further reading

Brown, S., Robbins, P. (Eds.), 2007. Risk Management and its Application to Medical Device Management Report. Institute of Physics and Engineering in Medicine, New York.

ISO 13485, 2016. Medical Devices — Quality Management Systems — Requirements for Regulatory Purposes.

Chapter 6

Research methodology

Azzam Taktak

Royal Liverpool University Hospital, Liverpool, United Kingdom

Chapter outline

Introduction

Before embarking on a study, it is very important to carefully consider all the issues and potential pitfalls that can make the study fail or, worse still, give the wrong result. At the focus of study design should be the final objective (or objectives); what is the question we would like to answer. The question should not be "how do I analyse my data" but rather "Is there a link between X and Y and if so, is it linear, positive, negative, etc.". The answer to the question and the type of data will determine what analysis to perform and how to interpret the results.

Broadly speaking, there are two types of studies, observational and experimental (Altman, 1991). In observational studies, data are collected on one or more groups of subjects purely from an observer's point of view. That is, we do not interfere with the clinical management of these subjects. An example would be to compare the survival rate of infants with low birthweights compared with those with average birthweight. Another example is to look at the prevalence of heart disease in groups of subjects from the general population with different socio-economic status. Data for these studies can either come from clinical records or from surveys. Experimental studies on the other hand require the researcher to deliberately influence the clinical management of the subjects in order to investigate the outcome. Typical examples of these types of studies include drug trials.

There are two types of observational studies, case-control studies and cohort studies. In case-control studies, a number of subjects with the disease in question (cases) are identified and compared with a group of subjects without the disease but who are otherwise comparable (controls). The past history of these groups is examined to determine their exposure to a particular risk. In cohort studies, two groups are identified, one exposed and one not exposed to a particular risk. The groups are followed up over time and the occurrence of the disease in question in each group is identified.

In both designs it is possible to have more than one case group. For example, if we are studying the association between smoking and lung cancer, we might have two case groups, present smokers and those who have smoked in the past but stopped smoking prior to being recruited for the study. We might go on further to divide the present smokers group into heavy smokers and light smokers (measured in a unit called pack-years).

The advantage of cohort studies is that they do not rely on the accuracy of medical records which can sometimes contain errors or be incomplete. The disadvantage is that if the disease in question is rare, they will need a large number of subjects to be recruited and may take years which can be costly. Another problem with cohort studies is that subjects sometimes drop out of the study. They might for example stop smoking half way through the study, or refuse to take part or

Clinical Engineering. https://doi.org/10.1016/B978-0-08-102694-6.00006-1

move to a new house or die of an unrelated cause. These problems are known as loss to follow-up. Another problem that can occur in both types of studies is that certain aspects can change over time. Clinical practice might change over time, certain risk factors might affect older subjects more than younger ones and so on. Moreover, there are issues related to feasibility and ethics to consider with cohort studies. Consider for example a study looking at association between car accidents and drivers being under the influence of alcohol. Here, a case-control study is the only feasible option. As blood samples are always taken from drivers who have been involved in a crash and analysed for alcohol, reliable data should be possible to obtain.

A serious problem that some clinical studies can experience is the effect of confounders. A confounder is a variable that has not been taken into account and that can completely skew your results. A well-known example from the literature is a study by Charig (Charig et al., 1986) on the effectiveness of keyhole surgery on the treatment of kidney stones. In this study, 350 subjects treated with keyhole surgery (cases) were compared with another 350 subjects treated with the more traditional open surgery (controls). They concluded that keyhole surgery had higher success rate than open surgery. Suppose however we separated the subjects according to the size of the stone. It is highly likely that those with smaller stones (<2 cm diameter) were more likely to undergo keyhole surgery than open surgery. They also had better chance of removal of the stone due to its small size. The size of the stone is a confounder. Results of the two groups separately can show an association in the opposite direction with open surgery proving to be more successful in both groups.

Bias

Bias can occur when studies are not carefully designed. Let us suppose we are conducting a drug trial and we split our subjects into two groups; those who receive the drug and those who do not. We might consciously or subconsciously be biased in our judgment so that we only include in the treatment group subjects who we think will benefit the most from the drug, e.g. patients with early stages of cancer only. We might introduce further bias when we analyse the data by giving more weighting to positive results or trying to find reasons to exclude negative results by labelling them as outliers for example. The study subjects themselves can also consciously or subconsciously bias the results. Those receiving the treatment might start behaving differently knowing they are being monitored. Other bias errors might occur due to measurement error. Supposing for example we ask subjects to record their own blood pressure. They may only do so if they felt well, take the measurement at different times of day, make inaccurate measurements or lie about their results.

Randomisation is a process designed to eliminate or at least reduce errors due to bias. For example, in a drug trial, if we decided to give the first 100 subjects the new drug and the next 100 subjects the existing drug or placebo, we might introduce bias if some clinical settings which influence outcome could have changed with time. In such study, we would allocate the subjects to the cases or controls groups at random. To do this, we need a random sequence of numbers which we can obtain from software packages or statistical tables. Let us consider the following random sequence:

91470387540015331276.

If we decide that any number in the range 0−4 will be allocated to the cases group (N) and 5−9 allocated to the controls (C) group, we will have the following sequence:

CNNCNNCCCNNNNCNNNNCC.

So, the first subject is allocated to the controls group, the second to cases and so on. The problem with this type of allocation is that we are not guaranteed a 50:50 split especially if the total number of participants is small. In the above example, 8 subjects were controls and 12 were cases. In such cases, we can either repeat the process until we get an even split or increase the number of subjects significantly.

Now, suppose we are comparing the performance of 4 blood pressure devices in 4 normal subjects to see if the devices produce similar results. Since the subjects are normal healthy volunteers of a limited age group, say 20−30 years old, we are not expecting any significant variation between subjects. The only bias to consider here is the order in which these measurements is taken. It is hypothetically possible that there is an upward trend in the measurements due to subject fatigue. We would therefore randomise the process using something known as a block design as shown in Table 6.1.

The numbers inside the boxes are the order of the measurements. This is known as a balanced design as subjects were all observed an equal number of times. In some cases, it is not possible to observe all subjects an equal number of times. For example, let us consider a study that is looking at the physiological cost index of disabled people using different types of wheelchairs. Let us say we have 6 wheelchairs and 12 subjects. It is only feasible to test each subject on 2 wheelchairs a day due to time constraints and level of effort involved. We could bring subjects back but that will introduce error as subjects might be feeling more or less tired on different visits. It will also inconvenience the subjects and increase the costs of the study. To get around this problem, we would randomise subjects using an incomplete block design as shown in Table 6.2.

TABLE 6.1 An example of a balanced randomized block design.

Subject	Device			
	B	A	C	D
4	1	2	4	3
1	4	3	1	2
3	3	4	2	1
2	2	1	3	4

TABLE 6.2 An example of an incomplete randomized block design.

Subject	Wheelchair					
	3	5	1	2	6	4
3	✔	✔				
8			✔	✔		
5					✔	✔
1	✔		✔			
7		✔		✔		
11			✔		✔	
10				✔		✔
2	✔			✔		
9		✔			✔	
12			✔			✔
6	✔				✔	
4		✔				✔

We should also where possible make the observer unaware of the conditions of the experiment to reduce the possibility of bias. This process is known as blinding. If the observer and the subject were both unaware of the conditions, this is known as double blinding. However, this is not always feasible. For example, if a trial is being conducted to investigate the efficacy of surgery against other form of treatment, blinding would not be an option. Sham surgery is sometimes carried out in these situations to blind the subject but not the observer. In such cases, it might be possible for someone else other than the surgeon to conduct the analysis without knowing whether the subject had surgery or not.

Setting a hypothesis

Let us consider a simple case of a drug trial where we are trying to assess the efficacy of a new drug on maintaining blood pressure in a group of adults. Suppose the mean blood pressure in the treatment group is μ_T and that in the control group is μ_C. If these measurements are different, we would like to know if the difference is significant or could it have occurred by chance.

To answer this question, we need to define our null hypothesis. The null effect here is that the drug has no effect, i.e.:

$$\mu_T = \mu_C \tag{6.1}$$

Now if the null hypothesis is indeed correct and if we repeat this experiment many times (theoretically, an infinite number of times), each time calculating the difference between μ_T and μ_C, we will get a distribution that looks like the one shown in Fig. 6.1.

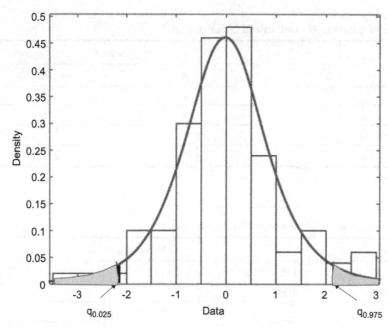

FIG. 6.1 A histogram distribution of differences in means for repeated experiments. The continuous curve is a best fit probability density function.

This is a distribution of the difference in means called a t-distribution (explained later). A best-fit probability density function has a peak around zero and tails off to $+\infty$. This means that all values are possible; the more extreme the value, the less likely we are to observe such difference. Experimenters often do not have the luxury of repeating the experiment many times; they only do a one-off experiment. We then need to carry out statistical tests to determine how likely it is to obtain such data (or more extreme) if the null hypothesis is correct. For example, in Fig. 6.1 we see that the 2.5th and 97.5th quantiles for this distribution are -2.262 and 2.262 respectively. That means that in repeated experiments, 5% of the experiments will show differences that are greater than 2.262 or less than -2.262. If therefore our one-off experiment results in differences in those regions, we can say that the probability of obtaining such result is <5%, or $P < 0.05$. If we deem this probability to be too small, this gives us some evidence in favour of the alternative hypothesis expressed as:

$$\mu_T \neq \mu_C \tag{6.2}$$

This is called a 2-sided alternative since μ_T can be greater than or less than μ_C. Sometimes the alternative can only go one way, e.g. $\mu_T < \mu_C$. This is known as a 1-sided alternative. These however are rarely used as it is not always possible to know in advance which way the association can go.

Significance and power

In the above example it was decided that a probability of 5% or less of obtaining extreme data was small enough to reject the null hypothesis. This is called the level of significance and it must be decided upon prior to observing the data. It is the probability of falsely rejecting the null hypothesis, otherwise known as a Type I error. Choosing the threshold is dependent on the application. In the context of a drug trial, this translates to 5% chance of using an ineffective drug. This is a very undesirable outcome as new drugs are often expensive and the long-term effects are unknown. There has been much debate in the literature recently warning against this threshold (Baker, 2016, Chavalarias et al., 2016). Ideally you would like this to be zero or very close to zero. This however comes at a cost. The smaller this figure is, the more likely we are to not be able to reject the null hypothesis when it is false. This is called a Type II error. The probability of avoiding Type II error is called the power of the study. Setting the power should also be done prior to observing the data. Ideally this should be 1 or very close to 1. So, there is a trade-off between the level of significance and the power, and it depends on the sample size and the amount of overlap between the two groups.

Hypothesis testing

Let us look at how to formally test a hypothesis using a statistical test. A study was conducted to investigate the association between birth weight and death in infants with severe idiopathic respiratory distress syndrome (SIRDS) (Van Vliet and

Gupta, 1973). A group of 50 infants with SIRDS were recruited, 27 died and 23 survived. The average weight of the survivor group was 2.21 kg compared to an average of 1.86 kg in the deceased group. We wish to know whether the difference in weight is significant or is it due to chance only.

The appropriate test to do here is a 2-sample t-test for difference in means. The test requires that 3 assumptions are met:

- The data are normally distributed
- The samples are independent
- The 2 groups have equal variances (a rule of thumb can be applied here that the two variances do not differ by a factor of more than 3).

Although the t-test assumes normal distribution of the populations, if normality is not satisfied the test will have a lower power. Therefore for non-normal data we will need larger sample sizes to achieve the nominal power.

Once we are satisfied that the above assumptions are met, we can proceed to analyse the data. There are many statistical packages that can carry out statistical analysis. Examples of which include SPSS, SAS, Minitab, GenStat, R, MATLAB (Statistics Toolbox), etc. Even Microsoft Excel, which is primarily a spreadsheet tool, can carry out a number of sophisticated statistical analysis but only after installing the Data Analysis add-on. There are also nowadays many online packages that carry out the analysis, but the reader must take care that they trust them first before using them. In this section, we will demonstrate some statistical analysis using the following website which was developed by the author:

https://mpceweb.liverpool.ac.uk/medstats/MedStats_Demos.htm.

Go to the website above and click on Student's 2-sample t-test. Click the View button next to About This Program line. This will open a window that describes the test. Here, you will also be able to download the SIRDS data. Upload the data as described and click Evaluate. The program displays a t statistic of -2.2538 and a P-value of 0.029 (2-tailed). There is therefore moderate evidence from the data that the difference in weight is statistically significant but we probably need to collect more data to be sure.

If there are more than 2 groups to compare, a family of statistical tests called ANOVA (ANalysis Of VAriance) are used. ANOVA is a very wide and complex topic and we will only cover the basics of it here. For more information on the subject, the reader is referred to the list of recommended books at the end of this chapter.

We will now visit some of the basic aspects of ANOVA using a hypothetical example. Let us suppose we collected data from a number of subjects using 10 different instruments. A 1-way ANOVA test tells us whether the instruments produce similar results or not. The null hypothesis is that the distributions of results between instruments are the same. If the P-value is small ($P < 0.01$, say) this provides evidence against the null hypothesis, i.e. there is a difference somewhere in the measurements. ANOVA does not tell you where the difference is. If we want to informally find out where the difference is, we must carry out more analysis like box-whisker plots to visually analyse these differences. A box-whisker plot of this hypothetical dataset is shown on Fig. 6.2. We can also carry out pairwise t-tests but this increases the chances of false discoveries due to chance (Type I error). To avoid these false discoveries, the significance level must be corrected for the number of tests. If we assume a 0.05 threshold of significance and we carry out n-pairwise tests then the new significance level is 0.05/n.

The P-value for the above dataset is 0.013 indicating moderate evidence against the null hypothesis. On close examination of Fig. 6.2, we notice that instrument number 10 produced slightly lower results on average than some other instruments. This is the most likely contributing factor to the small P-value. In fact, all measurements were sampled from the same normal distribution but with random noise. Notice that the number of samples does not have to be equal for each instrument for this analysis. However, the 3 assumptions needed for the t-test above are also required for ANOVA.

An alternative to the t-test is the z-test. This test is usually used for other types of data that can be approximated by a normal distribution when certain conditions are met. Examples of such data include proportion data which can be modelled using binomial distribution and count data which can be modelled using Poisson distribution. To view an example of where this test might be used, visit the above website and click on "Significance Test for Difference in Proportions".

Testing for normality

The t-test is used when the data can be reasonably modelled by a normal distribution, like for example taking mean blood pressure readings from 100 normal subjects. A histogram is a very quick method to check the distribution of the data although there are some pitfalls when using histograms. Another tool to assess the normality of the data visually is the normal probability plot that most statistical software packages offer. This tool plots the ordered values of the variable against normal scores from the standard normal distribution. More formally, there are statistical tests to assess the normality of the data such as the Lilliefors test or the chi-squared test. If the data appears to be skewed, we can apply some

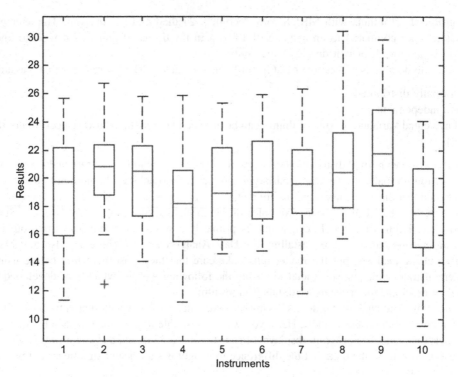

FIG. 6.2 Box-whisker plot of results of 10 instruments on independent samples.

transforms such as taking the natural logarithm or the square root to make the data look "more normally" distributed, but note that this may destroy important features of the data, for example outliers, that could be relevant to the analysis. In general, data transformations should be applied with caution.

Confidence intervals

The confidence interval is a term used to denote the variability of estimators. Instead of quoting a single value (point estimator), we acknowledge the fact that there is some amount of uncertainty in our estimation and we call this the confidence interval. If we are trying to estimate a parameter θ and we obtain a 95% confidence interval (θ_L, θ_U), the interpretation of this interval is this: if we repeat the experiment a large number of times (theoretically infinite) then the true value of θ would be included in this interval in 95% of the experiments. Of course, most often, we only carry out an experiment once, so the implication is that there is a 5% probability that our interval misses out θ completely.

For example, supposing we had 2 groups with 100 subjects in each group. Go back to the Significance Test for Difference in Proportions website. Enter 100 in the number of samples in groups 1 and 2. Now enter 45 successes for group 1 and 40 for group 2. The program returns the following values:

$$P1 = 0.45 \ (95\% \ \text{C.I.} \ 0.35 - 0.55)$$

$$P2 = 0.4 \ (95\% \ \text{C.I.} \ 0.3 - 0.5)$$

As can be seen, there is a significant overlap between the two confidence intervals so we cannot rule out the possibility that the two proportions are similar. The program also returns the z statistic and the *P*-value which in this case are 0.716 and 0.474 respectively. This is a high *P*-value indicating that there is little evidence against the null hypothesis that the two proportions are the same.

Now let us suppose that we based our estimation of proportions from a sample of 1000 in each group. We now enter 1000 in the number of samples in each group and 450 and 400 in the number of successes. We get a different picture:

$$P1 = 0.45 \ (95\% \ \text{C.I.} \ 0.42 - 0.48)$$

$$P2 = 0.4 \ (95\% \ \text{C.I.} \ 0.37 - 0.43) \tag{0.43}$$

The z statistic is much higher now with a value of 2.265 and the *P*-value is much smaller at 0.024 indicating moderate evidence against the null hypothesis of equal proportions. We can keep going like this and we notice that the evidence gets stronger with more data.

Nonparametric tests

These tests do not make any assumption about the distribution of the data as they perform the analysis on the ranks of the data rather than the values themselves. Examples of such data may include comparing responses to a questionnaire from two groups whereby responses are graded as: 1- Excellent, 2- Good, 3- Average, 4- Poor, 5- Diabolical. There is a clear ordering in the sequence of the above numbers but the distances between them are not defined. The test to do in this case is called a Mann-Whitney test.

Although nonparametric tests are more convenient in that they do not make any explicit assumption on the distribution of the data, they are less powerful than parametric tests since they ignore the values. For example, if we apply a Mann-Whitney test to the SIRDS dataset above, we would obtain a *P* value of 0.076 (2-tailed) which provides only weak evidence against the null hypothesis that the two distributions are the same. If we then apply a threshold of 0.05 for the *P*-value as is common practice in medical literature, we would reject the null hypothesis under the 2-sample *t*-test and not reject it under the Mann-Whitney test.

Knowing something about the data is very important in making a judgement regarding the distribution of the data. Data representing weight, height, blood pressure in a normal population should be adequately modelled by a normal distribution. Responses to questionnaires on the other hand are very unlikely to be normally distributed. Age is likely to have some right skew.

Correlation and regression

These two terms are often used synonymously, and the difference can be quite subtle. Correlation is a term that refers to the fact that knowing something about one variable tells you something about the other. Regression is a mathematical equation that allows you to predict the value of one variable (known as the response variable) from another (known as the explanatory variable). We can see why the two terms are often quoted together since if the two variables are not well correlated, it is meaningless to try to generate a regression model for these variables. The simplest form of a regression model is the linear regression model. If the explanatory variable is represented by x and the response variable by y, the linear regression model describing the relationship between the two can be modelled by the equation of a straight line:

$$y = mx + c \tag{6.3}$$

Note that if we came across the following relationship:

$$y = mx^2 + c \tag{6.4}$$

This is still considered as a linear model since x^2 can be easily replaced by another variable, say t. This is also true for any of the following:

$$y = me^x + c \tag{6.5}$$

$$y = m\log(x) + c \tag{6.6}$$

$$y = 1/x \tag{6.7}$$

If we have a set of x and y of continuous measurements on a number of samples and we wish to see how they are correlated, the first step is to do a scatter plot of the data. We could do this task quite easily on any software such as Microsoft Excel. Below is a plot of a hypothetical set of values. We then perform linear regression analysis on the data and again we can do this with Excel or any other package. The plot below shows the best fit line to the data (Fig. 6.3). We can use the equation of the best fit line to predict values of y for given x. The r^2 value that the software calculated is known as the coefficient of determination. It tells us how much of the variation in the data can be explained by the best fit line with the rest of the variation being noise. The square root of this value, i.e. r, is called Pearson's correlation coefficient. It takes an absolute value of 1 if the correlation was perfect and 0 for no correlation. Most statistical packages will give you a *P*-value or a confidence interval with the r-value and it is good scientific practice to quote these as well as the r-value itself. Note that regression analysis as implemented in most software packages assumes that y is normally distributed, so that the regression model can be interpreted as the expectation of y conditional on x.

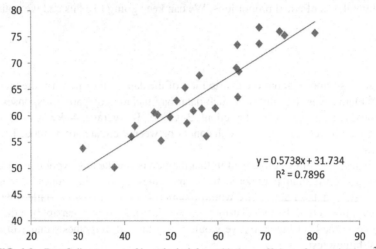

FIG. 6.3 Best fit line to a set of hypothetical data with the coefficient of determination r^2.

It is often said that correlation does not imply causation. Just because x and y correlate strongly does not mean one causes the other. It might be that the correlation we find is due to a third factor that we have not considered that is also correlated with these two variables and is the true causation. To determine causality, we need to ask ourselves, does the association make scientific sense? Is it consistent with current knowledge and can it be repeated under different settings? (Greenhalgh, 2010).

A summary of statistical tests with some clinical examples is shown in Table 6.3.

TABLE 6.3 Summary of statistical tests with clinical examples.

Purpose	Example	Parametric	Nonparametric
Compare paired samples	Taking heart rate measurement before and after exercise on a number of healthy volunteers	1-sample t-test	Wilcoxon signed rank test
Compare two unrelated samples	Measuring birth weight of infants with SIRDS and comparing the survived against deceased groups	2-sample t-test	Mann-Whitney test
Compare more than two sets of observations on the same sample	Taking measurements on a number of subjects using different instruments to assess the differences between devices (but not difference between samples)	One-way ANOVA	Kruskal-Wallis
Compare more than two sets of observations on a single sample under different conditions	Different operators making measurements on a number of samples using different methods of preparing the samples	Two-way ANOVA	Friedman
Investigate correlation between two continuous variables	Correlation between systolic and diastolic blood pressure in a group of patients with hypertension	Pearson correlation	Spearman correlation
Investigate correlation between two categorical variables	Correlation between smoking and lung cancer	None	χ^2
Investigate correlation between two ordinal variables	Agreement between disease severity and QALY score	None	Kappa

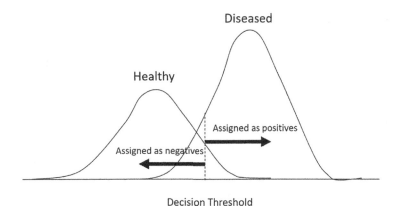

FIG. 6.4   Setting a decision threshold to decide whether an individual is affected or no affected.

Receiver-operator characteristic (ROC) analysis

ROC analysis is used to assess the performance of diagnostic tests. The typical setup considers two groups of subjects under different conditions (e.g. "normal" and "disease"), and a diagnostic test which should discriminate between the two classes which essentially acts as a classifier. Perfect separation is not possible in general, resulting in a classification error.

In Fig. 6.4, the graph shows the number of patients with and without a disease arranged according to the value of a diagnostic test. We notice that the two groups are not perfectly separable with the test and that there is an area of overlap in the distributions. This area of overlap indicates where the test cannot distinguish normal from disease without error. If we are using this test clinically we must choose a threshold above which we consider the subject to be affected and below which we consider the subject to be unaffected.

Fig. 6.4 shows that depending on when we set a threshold, there will be a certain number of True Positives (TPs), True Negatives (TNs), False Positives (FPs) and False Negatives (FNs). Using this type of analysis, the following terms are defined:

$$Sensitivity = TP/(TP + FN) \tag{6.8}$$

$$Specificity = TN/(TN + FP) \tag{6.9}$$

$$Accuracy = (TP + TN)/(TP + FP + TN + FN) \tag{6.10}$$

So for different thresholds, we can get different pairs of sensitivity and specificity figures. A ROC curve is a plot of sensitivity vs 1-specificity. The area under the ROC curve (AUROC) is a measure of discrimination power of the test. An AUROC of 0.5 corresponds to a useless discriminator which is no better than decisions obtained by chance (such as tossing a coin). An AUROC of 1 on the other hand represents the perfect discriminator. In reality, most tests have an AUROC figure between 0.5 and 1 with an AUROC of 0.8 and above being generally considered as a good discriminator.

The choice of the threshold therefore represents a trade-off between sensitivity and specificity and is application-dependent. If we are using a test for screening purposes where we would like to identify as many subjects at high risk as possible, we would maximise sensitivity at the cost of low specificity. If on the other hand if we are using a test for diagnostic purposes where the outcome is likely to be an intervention, then we would go for a high specificity at the cost of low sensitivity.

Literature searching and referencing

Searching medical literature has never been easier with the availability of online tools such as PubMed, Scopus, Web of Knowledge, etc. PubMed is the tool most widely used by Clinicians, Healthcare Scientists and other Healthcare Professionals. It is a free resource that is developed and maintained by the National Centre for Biotechnology Information (NCBI), at the US National Library of Medicine (NLM), located at the National Institutes of Health (NIH). PubMed comprises millions of citations for biomedical literature from Index Medicus and MEDLINE. There is an online tutorial and a link to a YouTube demo on how to use PubMed.

To demonstrate how PubMed works, let us assume we want to do a search for publications on sudden infant death syndrome (SIDS). We type the first word "sudden" and we immediately get a drop-down box with some suggestions. We select Sudden Infant Death Syndrome from the list and press Select. We get a list of nearly 10,000 publications dating back to 1945. We also get a histogram showing how many articles were published each year since 1945. Now let us refine our search a little bit by looking at publications in the last decade i.e. starting from 2000. Click the Custom Range on the left-hand side and specify the date range from the first of January 2000 to the present date. We now get around 3500 publications. Let us refine the search even further by search for Clinical Trials and Randomised Controlled Trials only. We click on these two links on the left-hand side and we now get a much smaller number near 100.

Now let us suppose we are doing research looking for any association between SIDS and breast feeding. We click meta-analysis on the left and we find that there is an article by K.L. McVea et al. published in the Journal of Human Lactation in February 2000 on this subject (McVea et al., 2000). An examination of the abstract tells us that study is a summary of 23 cohort and case-control studies and the combined evidence shows that infants who were bottle fed were twice as likely to die from SIDS than those who were breast fed. It is very important however not to jump to conclusions here. Remember; correlation does not imply causation. In fact the paper could not rule out the presence of confounders.

If you are doing the search from a computer that is connected to an educational institution's network, the chances are you will be able to read the full article taking advantage of your institution's library subscription with the Publisher, sometimes through a third party. The paper tells us that the analysis was conducted by searching MEDLINE database between 1966 and 1997. The search included a number of MeSH (Medical Subject Heading) terms such as sudden infant death, cot death, crib death, breastfeeding and infant nutrition.

In Biomedical Engineering, we are probably primarily interested in review articles that assess a particular technology. For example, Lisboa and Taktak published an article on the use of Artificial Neural Networks in cancer (Lisboa and Taktak, 2006). In the period between 1994 and 2003, there were 396 studies published with only 27 being either Clinical Trials or Randomised Controlled Trials. The majority of these latter studies showed an increased benefit to healthcare in the use of this technology. The uptake of this technology in the manufacturing of medical devices remains low sadly with only a handful of devices utilising the technology to date.

There are other powerful online literature search engines besides PubMed. One such engine is called Scopus which is again free to access via most academic networks. From a Clinical Engineering point of view, Scopus has the advantage over PubMed in that it also searches for scientific and technical journals and books that are not included in MEDLINE.

Another useful tool is Google Scholar. Although it is slightly less structured than PubMed and Scopus, it has the advantage that it can be accessed from anywhere and it trawls the whole Internet to find matches to your query. Sifting through the results however can be time consuming and you cannot limit your search to Clinical Trials or Meta-Analysis only for example. Another major drawback with Google Scholar is that it finds publications that have not gone through a peer-review process as well as those that have so use it with caution.

If you are embarking on a literature search from new, it is a good idea to build yourself a database if you haven't got one already. There are a number of bibliography software packages available such as Reference Manager, EndNote, etc. These packages link to word processing software such as Microsoft Word which helps a great deal in taking care of citations and generating a reference list when writing a scientific paper.

Let us look at an example of how to import references from PubMed into EndNote and linking it to a document in Word. First re-visit the PubMed site with the search for meta-analysis studies in SIDS since 2000. Tick 3 studies that related to SIDS and breastfeeding. Click Send To, Select File and select MEDLINE as the format and save the file to the hard disk. Next, open EndNote, create a new library and choose "Import" from the file menu. In the Import dialogue box choose the MEDLINE filter as the import function and select the file you have just downloaded. You should see all 3 references you have just selected appear in your library.

Next open Microsoft Word. There should be an EndNote menu item in the menu bar. You can insert references in your document in many different ways. If EndNote is still open, you can highlight the reference you want to insert and click Insert Selected Citation from the menu. Alternatively, type the name of one of the authors (e.g. McVea) and click Insert Citation. If there is more than one reference for this author you will be presented with a list that you can choose from. Once you have finished typing your document, you will want to format your references in the style of the journal you are submitting to. In the Style drop down box you will notice numerous styles such as Harvard, Vancouver or other styles that are more specific to certain journals such as the BMJ.

References

Altman, D.G., 1991. Practical Statistics for Medical Research. Chapman & Hall/CRC, London.

Baker, M., 2016. Statisticians issue warning over misuse of P values. Nature 53 (7593), 151.

Charig, C.R., Webb, D.R., Payne, S.R., Wickham, J.E., 1986. Comparison of treatment of renal calculi by open surgery, percutaneous nephrolithotomy, and extracorporeal shockwave lithotripsy. Br. Med. J. 292, 879—882.

Chavalarias, D., Wallach, J.D., Li, A.H., Ioannidis, J.P.A., 2016. Evolution of reporting P values in the biomedical literature, 1990—2015. J. Am. Med. Assoc. 315 (11), 1141—1148.

Greenhalgh, T., 2010. How to Read a Paper: The Basics of Evidence-Based Medicine. Wiley-Blackwell.

Lisboa, P.J., Taktak, A.F.G., 2006. The use of artificial neural networks in decision support in cancer: a systematic review. Neural Netw. 19, 408—415.

Mcvea, K.L., Turner, P.D., Peppler, D.K., 2000. The role of breastfeeding in sudden infant death syndrome. J. Hum. Lactation 16, 13—20.

Van Vliet, P.K., Gupta, J.M., 1973. THAM v. sodium bicarbonate in idiopathic respiratory distress syndrome. Arch. Dis. Child. 48, 249—255.

Further reading

Armitage, P., 2000. Statistical Methods in Medical Research. Blackwell Scientific, Oxford.

Cohen, L.H., Holliday, M.E., 1996. Practical Statistics for Students: An Introductory Text. Sage Publications Ltd.

Harrell Jr., F.E., 2006. Regression Modeling Strategies: With Applications to Linear Models, Logistic Regression, and Survival Analysis. Springer.

Peat, J., Barton, B., Elliott, E., 2008. Statistics Workbook for Evidence-Based Healthcare. Wiley-Blackwell.

Van Belle, G., Heagerty, P.J., Fisher, L.D., Lumley, T.S., 2004. Biostatistics: A Methodology for the Health Sciences. Wiley, New Jersey.

Chapter 7

Leadership

Merlin Walberg

Phoenix Consultancy USA Incorporated, Fort Lauderdale, Florida, United States

Chapter outline

Introduction

One afternoon, I was sitting in the lobby of a very luxurious hotel in North Carolina, waiting for a client meeting to begin. A member of staff walked through the lobby, noticed a small piece of paper on the carpet, bent down, picked it up, and carried on his way.

This tiny behaviour made a big impression on me. It demonstrated true, DNA-centered leadership! We are certain that nowhere in his job description did it say, "responsible to always look for bits of paper on the lobby floor."

In essence, this was a true (if small) demonstration of leadership: seeing a need, deciding that you are responsible, determining the outcome wanted, taking initiative, changing something, modeling the behaviour you wish to see in others. *Walking the talk.*

Clinical Engineering. https://doi.org/10.1016/B978-0-08-102694-6.00007-3

This chapter is to introduce you to *leadership* as it applies to you, a *scientist*. Our goal, outcome wanted, #EndInMind is for you to make the connection that it is not only your skills as a scientist that determine your effectiveness and ability to make a difference, it is those skills, that mindset and inner rigor, combined with DNA-centered leadership that will enable you to achieve your dreams. We are talking about self-leadership (as demonstrated in the little vignette above) and leadership of others—bringing people together around a common goal and achieving it.

By way of further introduction, we invite you to read everything here with two different pairs of spectacles: professional spectacles and personal spectacles. What we describe in this chapter applies to being successful in work and in life overall. Amazing and true; see if you agree. By trying out what is proposed here you will be able to tell if it is true and works, just as with your scientific training. Learn, try out, practice, reflect on what worked and what did not, revise your practice, try some more, and get better and better at making things work.

There is a fundamental difference between learning leadership and everything else you learned to be a scientist. As a scientist you start with a big picture and look at possibilities, then narrow down those possibilities with the goal of finding the one right answer. It is very exact and specific. As a leader, you look at a very specific situation and back up from that issue to broaden your picture, find out who else is or needs to be involved, explore possible ways forward, and then make a plan and enact it. There are always different approaches possible and never one right answer, which is what makes it tricky.

So what is leadership? Hundreds of books are written each year in an attempt to answer that question.

Exercise

Start by thinking for a moment about a great leader that you have known in your life. A person who, according to you, demonstrated leadership as part of his or her way of being, had the skills, qualities, abilities, and attributes that caused other people to follow voluntarily. This last point is important, as we really want to be talking about positive forms of leadership, not the kind that provides heavy penalties for *not* following (though that can be very effective in the short term).

What did he or she do? How did they behave? What were (are) they like? How did (do) they make you feel? Scribble down a list.

The list probably includes the following:

- Has vision
- Communicates clearly and often
- Listens
- Is strategic
- Is approachable
- Values others
- Has a certain confidence, gravitas
- Is knowledgeable
- Sees the big picture
- Good at delegating, negotiating, influencing, and making decisions
- Can deal with conflict and differences
- Engenders trust and respect
- Is consistent and fair
- Vales and empowers others
- Is flexible
- Makes me feel valued

The list indicates who a leader is as well as what a leader does. We depict these two aspects as *inner* and *outer* (Fig. 7.1).

As a scientist, you will be very familiar with the symbol shown in Fig. 7.1. In terms of leadership however, the symbol demonstrates the ever-present relationship between what is going on *inside you*, all invisible and hugely powerful in your experience of the world:

- Your thoughts
- Your health
- Beliefs about yourself and others
- Emotions
- Interpretation of the behaviour of others and previous experiences

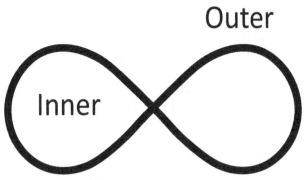

FIG. 7.1 Inner and outer loops.

- Attitudes
- Values

  and that which is visible *in the world*:

- Behaviours
- Skills
- Interactions with others
- Words you and others speak
- Your abilities
- How you spend your time
- How others view you

Why does this matter? Think about it this way: A tennis player learns a set of skills and strategies and rules, gets good tools, and goes out to play the game. What affects how that game is played? Does the particular opponent matter? Does the player's view of court surface matter? Does the history of matches played between the two on the court matter? Does the crisis at home just before the game matter?

What matters the most is our tennis player's view of these things, his or her ability to focus on what is important, to manage things that are not important, and be totally present to what is needed in this situation right now.

The ability to be self-aware, learning to notice the impact of what is happening inside of ourselves and others and learning to manage all of that enables the leader to have desired outcomes more frequently; and with more positive impact.

It is very easy to see the experienced high-level tennis player working with this knowledge. Much time is spent training for the *inner game* as well as on the outer game (Gallwey, 1986).

Exercise

Think of a situation that happened recently which did not go as you would have liked. Can you find anything that was happening in your inner world that contributed to that?

Think of a situation that happened recently that did go as you wished. Can you notice anything in your inner world that contributed to that? What are the conditions that enabled that? How can you create more of those conditions in the future?

Leadership and management

Before we go any further, let us be clear about these two interrelated concepts. *Leadership*, by definition, indicates that one is going somewhere, hopefully forward! If you are leading yourself, you are both leader and follower. If you are leading a team, as we have already said, you want followers to join you on the journey. When you are in leadership mode you are thinking about an end goal and how whatever you are about to say or to do is moving you closer or further away from that goal. *Management* is about handling what currently exists and improving it, making it more efficient, smoothing out the wrinkles, and so on.

Everyone needs to do both, lead and manage. Sometimes at the same time. So how can you tell what you need to do when?

If you are delegating a new task to someone with the intention of helping that person to develop new skills, you are leading. If you are delegating just to find a more efficient way to divide the work load, you are managing. Get the difference?

If you are a scientist with no line management responsibilities, these both still apply to you. For example:

- Ensuring your work is done in time to pass it on to the next link in the chain: management
- Recommending a new link in the chain to create a better service: leadership
- Keeping up to date with scientific journals: self-management
- Training for new skills: self-leadership
- Prioritizing work delegated to you: management
- Offering to join a project team: leadership

In his classic article "Managing the Dream: Leadership in the 21st Century" Warren Bennis clarifies the distinction between leadership and management. The following list is from that article (Bennis, 1989):

- The manager administers; the leader innovates
- The manager is a copy; the leader is an original
- The manager maintains; the leader develops
- The manager focuses on systems and structure; the leader focuses on people
- The manager relies on control; the leader inspires trust
- The manager has a short-range view; the leader has a long-range perspective
- The manager asks how and when; the leader asks what and why
- The manager has his eye on the bottom line; the leader has his eye on the horizon
- The manager accepts the status quo; the leader challenges it
- The manager is the classic good soldier; the leader is his own person
- The manager does things right; the leader does the right thing

Exercise

Think about your workload. How much time do you spend managing things? How much time do you spend leading? Is there more scope to develop either? Both?

What is one aspect of your work that is calling out for more leadership on your part? Will you make a commitment to respond to that challenge? Even if no one asks you to do so, or even notices?

A tremendous amount of self-awareness, clarity about values, and personal goals gives one the strength and insight to tackle such things.

Emotional intelligence

This brings us to the subject of emotional intelligence. This is often described as the key to outstanding performance, particularly at senior levels.

Here is a working definition: Emotional intelligence is the ability to understand one's own emotions and those of others and their impact on behaviour, and then to use them intelligently.

Exercise

Think for a moment about the role emotions play in everyday work situations. What do they affect? Be specific. What sort of impact do they have? How much do they affect performance? Morale? Productivity?

The previous exercise demonstrates how emotions play a huge part in almost everything. Positive emotions can be contagious. Negative emotions too. And yet, emotions are rarely discussed or valued as part of the way we conduct business. We do, however, speak indirectly with others about the emotions that impact the way of working offline.

That being said, it becomes easier to understand just why having high emotional intelligence is considered *the* differentiator between good and great performance. Daniel Goleman's research of outstanding leaders showed that intellect was a driver of outstanding performance, but emotional intelligence (EQ) proved twice as important for jobs at all levels (Goleman, 1996). And the more senior one gets, the more important it is. Technical knowledge is not a differentiator at senior levels; influencing, team effectiveness, motivation, inspiring others are. All of these require more senior EQ.

How can that be true? It is because the technical skill to perform your job is expected as the baseline. What makes the difference is how you put those skills to work with other people. The good news is that emotional intelligence can be learned; that is, you can increase your EQ, unlike your IQ which stays the same throughout life.

Daniel Goleman is the man who popularized emotional intelligence. He describes the key components in great detail. In the following we touch on just a few of the first characteristics of these components.

Self-awareness

- Know which emotions you are feeling and why
- Realize the links between your feelings and what you think, do, and say
- Recognize how your feelings affect your performance
- Have a guiding awareness of your values and goals

Once you are aware of these things, the next step is to manage or regulate them. This does not mean denying your feelings, rather managing the way they are used instead of having them unconsciously determine your behaviour. For example, speaking about being angry rather than shouting because you are angry. See the difference?

Self-regulation or self-management

- Manage impulsive feelings and distressing emotions well
- Stay composed, positive, and unflappable even in trying moments
- Think clearly and stay focused under pressure

Self-motivation

Self-motivation is about taking responsibility for your behaviour, goals, and about persevering despite obstacles, which is a very important part of self-management.

Social awareness

Social awareness is fundamentally about intending to understand the moods and needs of others. Let's focus again on the first aspect, empathy. Emotionally intelligent people share the following traits:

- Attentive to emotional cues of others and listen well
- Show sensitivity and understand others' perspectives
- Help out based on understanding other people's needs and feelings

You can see that if you include other people's frame of reference, lots of things change. You will then be looking for opportunities to meet the needs of others, ways to ensure diverse backgrounds and viewpoints can flourish, and have a coaching attitude, where one intentionally develops the skills and abilities of others.

Social skills and relationship management

This is about managing relationships through applying the other skills and connecting more with people to improve how people respond to you. Emotionally intelligent people share the following:

- Skilled at persuasion
- Deal with difficult issues straightforwardly
- Foster open communication and stay receptive to bad news as well as good
- Fine-tune what they say to appeal to the listener

Exercise

Do a bit of research. Study yourself and your emotional reactions to things. Begin to develop your awareness of what affects you, why, how your behaviour changes when your emotions are getting the best of you. This awareness raising is the first step in developing your emotional intelligence further than it already is. As a leader, the more you can develop this, the more you can choose responses and behaviours that will encourage others to follow your lead.

TABLE 7.1 The consequences of not listening.

Speaker	Non-listener	Organization
Feels: • Undervalued • Demotivated • Irritated • Frustrated • Anger	Loses respect Looks foolish Gets avoided Misses opportunities Wastes time Is considered rude	Loses commitment Increases poor performance Wastes resources Deals with increased mistakes Has higher costs Has reduced quality

Emotional intelligence begins with listening. Listening to yourself and then listening to others. In fact, when I go to a new client organization and ask people that work there to describe the leaders, they usually say "he/she listens."

Daniel Goleman, 1996.

Why is listening important? Listening is the key skill that enables us to understand each other. Unlike speaking, in most educational systems we are never taught to listen. It is often assumed that if we are fortunate enough to have two ears that work well, we listen well. This is not necessarily so. You have probably heard it said that the single most important human need is the need to be loved. One can go further and say that the most important need we have is the need to be understood. A key component of being understood is having others who are willing to give their attention to you and to listen. This is a hugely valuable gift that you have to offer in every interaction. It costs you nothing, except a bit of your time.

Listening to understand what motivates and has meaning for others offers the single most powerful tool to influence others. Choosing to influence others is leadership. Listening is an essential ingredient in a wide range of work activities: understanding and solving problems, dealing with enquiries, responding to customer needs, attending meetings, staff supervision and development, team work, conflict resolution, effective negotiation, delegation, building cooperative alliances, and leading and implementing change. The list could go on. Table 7.1 outlines the consequences of not listening from the point of view of the speaker, the person who is not listening, and an organization as a whole.

The consequences of poor listening are severe and dramatic. Not listening includes half-listening: reading, writing, or thinking about other things while someone is speaking to us. In an organization where the predominant culture is one of not listening or only half-listening, staff contribution decreases hugely over time, morale suffers, and absenteeism increases.

Listening does not necessarily mean agreeing. We are really only talking about listening and giving attention to someone.

Note: Active listening is only possible for short periods of time. In fact, we spend much of our time cutting out noises and distractions. However, it is critical to know when to listen, and to have the skill and motivation to do it.

Listening on three levels

To really understand what someone is saying, we need to learn to listen to the whole person: not just the words that are being said, but also what lies between and behind the words. This is described as listening on three levels: to the content, the feelings, and the intentions.

1. *Content*: This is what we usually listen for: the facts, information, the details, the story line. However, as we think at about 500 words per minute, and speak at about 125 words per minute, there is a lot of time for our mind to wander to similar experiences we have had, preparation for a counter argument, or the day's shopping list! Developing the capacity to listen accurately to content is helped by trying to be as objective as possible. This means holding back our own feelings about what we are hearing, resisting thinking about our own experiences, and trying to capture the speaker's words.

2. *Feelings*: By listening to the feelings we can discover the relationship between the speaker and the "story." We listen between the lines of a perfectly rational story to hear feelings of resentment, frustration, excitement, hope, and so on. It is important to hear these feelings, because they can linger far longer than the events to which they are related, and will have a tremendous impact on future behaviour. Developing the capacity to listen accurately to feelings is helped by holding back our own feelings, likes and dislikes, and trying to develop empathy. Empathy allows us to pick up the feelings of the speaker, rather than our own. This is done by listening to the words people choose, the tone of voice used, and looking at facial expression and changes in body language.

3. *Intentions*: Listening to the "will" of the speaker will enable us to find their motivation, commitment, and direction. This information is vital in negotiations and agreements, to know what the prospects for implementation and support are. Developing the capacity to listen accurately for the intentions of the speaker requires that we hold back our own wishes, suggestions, and advice, and that we are interested in the outcome for the speaker. Despite the fact that intentions are often buried and unconscious it is possible to hear them by listening to the emphasis given, the amount of detail, the first and the last thing said, and the energy used to describe different aspects. It can be very helpful to the speaker if you are able to hear their intentions and reflect them back.

One more important thing about listening: You will note that in all cases, to listen to someone else's story to hear the content, feelings, or intentions requires that your inner space is clear of your own story. If you really want to listen to someone else, do not start talking about the time the same thing happened to you, how you would feel if it were happening to you, or giving them advice that is based on what you would do if you were them.

Remember: The goal is to understand them better, not to get them to understand you.

Exercise

Try it out. In a one-on-one situation, see if you can hear and repeat the story without embellishment. You can stop the speaker by saying "Hang on a minute, I just want to check that I got what you have just been saying."

To capture feelings, listen to the words they choose, any change in the tone of their voice, and any changes in body language that might be indicating feelings. Ask about those, rather than assume you know what they mean. "Can I just check? You said you are fine with this idea only the way you said 'fine' so emphatically makes me want to ask if there is anything more you might tell me to help me understand more of how you feel about this."

Listening for someone's will is actually pretty easy. Does it sound like they are really committed to taking action? Or just like it's a good idea? Or does it sound like they are saying "yes" just to get you to finish? You might say "Thank you for agreeing to do this. When can I expect the first step?" or "I hear that you think this is a good idea, I am just not hearing that you are really committed to acting on it. Is that so? What can I due to help get you more committed? Is there something still concerning you?" or "I hear you speaking a bit about the two possible options and you describe option one in great detail and option two only briefly. It sounds to me like option one is the one you prefer. Is that so?"

If you are going to a meeting with a colleague, why not speak with that colleague before the meeting and ask him or her to notice what is actually said, how important it is, what actually applies to you and your team, and what will really happen as a result. Or something similar. You get the idea.

Making listening visible

For the speaker to feel valued, motivated, worthwhile, and encouraged they need to know that they are being listened to. Therefore it is important to avoid doing things like doodling and shuffling through papers. Instead:

- Give the speaker your full attention, even if it is only for long enough to say that you are unable to listen at the moment and to arrange another time to talk.
- Keep eye contact with the speaker while being sure to avoid staring.
- Sit or stand reasonably still; fidgeting indicates impatience, doing other activities indicates disinterest.
- Periodically summarize and reflect back what you have heard. This helps both you and the speaker to keep track of what's being said. Do not change subjects!
- Allow silence to help you communicate patience and to enable the speaker to draw more out of themselves.

Remember: The thing that will most indicate you are listening is giving your full, relaxed attention and concentration to the speaker.

Creating the right environment

- Find a quiet space: wherever possible ensure an atmosphere of privacy.
- Eliminate distractions: divert phone calls, put up a "do not disturb" notice, put your work aside.
- Eliminate barriers: come out from behind the desk, be at the same height level, use understandable language.

TABLE 7.2 Challenges of listening on three levels.

		Listening on three levels				
		This level is	This level expresses	What are we listening for	Where is it coming from?	Challenge for the listener
Content	P A S T	Objective Level Most common, surface	Ideas Information	What is said	Head	To be open minded
Feelings	P R E S E N T	Subjective Level Between the lines	Values Attitudes	How it is said	Heart	To be Empathetic
Intentions	F U T U R E	Operational Level What is behind, or underneath	Motivation Commitment	What is intended	Hands & feet	To retain interest in the speaker

©Merlin Walberg Phoenix Consultancy USA, Inc. 1988.

Create the right "inner" environment by clearing your mind, so as to make a space for what the speaker has to say.

Remember: What you think you are hearing on the three different levels must never be assumed to be correct. Test it out with the speaker by reflecting back what you have heard and asking if it is right.

Table 7.2 summarizes the challenges of listening on three levels.

Seven habits of effective leaders

In addition to active, empathetic listening, what else are the key behaviours of excellent leaders? Stephen Covey's excellent book *The Seven Habits of Highly Effective People* describes these behaviours perfectly (Covey, 1989).

Briefly, Covey researched what successful people had in common and discovered that there were seven habits consistently present. Habits are behaviours that people use regularly, so much so, that they do not require conscious thought (eventually!). Habits are things that can be learned and changed so *anyone* who wishes to adopt these habits can do so. We translate into meaning that excellent leadership can be learned, which is good news. That's not to say that everyone can be a chief executive or a leader of a social movement or a prime minister; all of these things require more than good habits. However, good habits are required for all of them. As described earlier, there is a baseline of skill and knowledge that is expected for senior positions, it is emotional intelligence, and having excellent self-discipline and interpersonal habits, that make the difference between good and great (Collins, 2001).

Here are the habits:

Habit 1: Be proactive

This means to fundamentally accept that you are responsible for your own behaviour. "What? Of course I am," you might say. Really? Do you ever think or say: "It wasn't my fault because," "I didn't have …," "He makes me angry," "I have to …," "What can *I* do?" "If only … then I would …," "I don't have time," "I can't."

You can see how easy it might be to say one of those, right? What lies behind each of those statements is someone saying "I am not responsible for my feelings, behaviours, or thoughts."

How different would it feel to say: "This is not what I would have wanted. Given this situation, I will," "The big decision is out of my control and so what I think is important for us to focus on is …," "My time is very limited, I will look at my priorities," "I prefer …," "I choose …," "I feel angry when …"

Proactivity means choosing your response to whatever comes your way, rather than reacting unconsciously. Make sense? So, on what basis do you make decisions about those choices?

Another key way to determine how proactive you are is to think about how you spend you time and energy. If you are focused on things you can influence, make decisions about, and achieve, you are spending your time in your *circle of influence*. Here is where positive energy rises and you feel a sense of making things happen and contributing. Are you thinking and focusing on things you cannot influence? If so, you are in the arena that Covey calls the *circle of concern*. This is where your energy gets drained, because you are not able to impact these things, and indeed you are less effective in your circle of concern as you waste energy that could be better used elsewhere.

Things in the circle of concern might be very important, such as decisions about policy, funding, the skills of others on whom you rely, for example. Yet, if they are outside your ability to influence, the proactive response is to accept them for what they are and deal with *that* reality rather than the one you wish were true—even if you are right! Think about it.

Exercise

Reflect on the conversations you have with others over and over again. Are they about things in your circle of concern? Is that why you keep having the same conversation, because there is nothing you can do about it? Do you know people who do that? How does it feel?

Habit 2: Begin with the end in mind

This is the habit of personal leadership. It means thinking about what you want the outcome to be and having that as your guiding light for all decisions. Covey talks about having a personal mission statement comprised of your values and things that are important to you.

Exercise

You are attending your retirement party. What would you like to hear people say about you? About what you stand for? What you would not stand for? The impact you had on them? The workplace? Your profession? The answers to those questions will lead you toward your core values, which, no matter how challenging or restricted you find the situation you are in, will give you peace of mind, knowing that you have done the best you can from your own point of view.

Begin with the end in mind is useful for small things as well. Someone comes to your office, or the lab, and starts speaking to you. You are wondering what on earth they are talking about. You can say: "I only have a few minutes at the moment. What is it you would like from this conversation?" "What do you need from me?" or "How can I help?"

As important, when you are about to speak with someone, think first of your ends in mind for that conversation. Have you ever walked out of a meeting with your supervisor knowing that it did not go well, that you did not get what you wanted? Not sure quite what happened? This is often because you were not clear before you went in about what you wanted.

There are always two ends in mind:

- Content of issue outcome
- Relationship or interpersonal outcome

Thinking about having two ends in mind will certainly have an impact on how you say what you say, bearing in mind that you want to have the relationship continue or get better.

Habit 3: Put first things first

Now that you have decided that you are responsible for your own behaviour and have more clarity about what you are responsible to achieve, this habit, the habit of self-management, will help you to get there. There is a quote of Goethe's that is the essence of this habit: "The things which matter most must never be at the mercy of the things which matter least."

This habit is asking you to actively think about how you choose to spend your time and to prioritize important things. Table 7.3 illustrates this beautifully.

TABLE 7.3 Prioritizing your activities.

Important →	Quadrant I. Activities Important and urgent	Quadrant II. Activities Important not urgent
	• Crises • Pressing problems • Deadline driven projects	• Crisis prevention • Values clarification • Preparation & planning • Relationship building • Renewal & evaluation
	Quadrant III. Activities **Urgent not important**	**Quadrant IV. Activities** **Not urgent and not important**
	• Interruptions, some phone calls • Mail, some reports • Some meetings • Some pressing matters • Many popular activities	• Trivia, busy work • Some mail • Some phone calls • Time wasters • Many pleasant activities
	Urgent ←	

Exercise

For one week keep track of how you spend your time. You can use a model of these four quadrants to log your activities. How much of your time falls into the different quadrants? Be honest with yourself. What changes would you like to make? How might you make one or two to give you some more quadrant II time?

The first three habits are what Stephen Covey calls the "private victory." That means no one need know you are doing them. Doing them is your own personal victory. Others will certainly notice the results of those habits, and they do not need to participate for you to succeed with them.

The next three habits are referred to as the "public victory." These habits do indeed involve others in a more obvious way. You will see that they provide a very powerful role model about the way to engage with individuals and teams. In fact, all of us would like to be treated in the way these habits prescribe. We just don't always remember to do it for others!

Habit 4: Think win-win

This is a very interesting habit. The habit is called *think* win-win, not win-win. Pedantic? Maybe, but maybe that one word is central. The habit means that in all interactions with others it is your job to *always* be thinking about yourself and the other and how the situation in which you are both involved can have mutual benefit. In fact, if I were naming the habit, I would call it "think mutual benefit." Mutual benefit implies the ever-present intention to look for positive outcomes, no matter how difficult and different the points of view. This is the way to build long-term relationships. Win-lose or lose-win are always a setup for someone to try to get even; not a good prescription for long-term sustainability and certain implementation of agreements. Think about it: You feel screwed into the ground by someone who thinks they have just negotiated a great deal. How likely are you to work really hard to make sure the arrangement works perfectly?

Mutual benefit even applies if you are saying "no" to someone or telling someone they no longer have a job in your department. How is that possible? The way you give the information can either enable someone to walk out of the door with their head held high or crawling. Very different.

Habit 5: Seek first to understand, then to be understood

This is the habit of empathetic listening. We have already discussed listening in great detail. The key to the effective use of this habit is that you do it *before* giving your point of view. The idea is that if you listen first and speak second, you will have information that can help you pitch what you want to say in a way that makes it as meaningful and accessible as possible. After all, that is what you want isn't it? To be listened to? So this habit, as with the others, asks you to model it first. It is guaranteed to save you time by helping you to only have to say it once to be understood. It will help you to not have to go back and ask again, as you will have been listening the first time. Also, as you have been listening on three levels you really have the full story. It is hugely motivating for someone to feel heard and you may gain the added benefit of having someone listen to you as well. Nonetheless, whether they do or not, it is your job to continue to do so. Eventually they will too.

Habit 6: Synergize

This is the habit of creative cooperation or teamwork. Covey calls it the highest form of human interaction. Have you ever experienced real synergy? When you and another person or group of people are all focused on something creative, interesting, and engaging and are working away at it? No point scoring, no worrying about who speaks more or less, only interest in the topic itself and everyone contributing what they have to offer. Suddenly two or 3 h have passed.

What are the conditions necessary for this to possibly happen? To lead the possibility of synergy, your job is to enable diversity of opinion and create a culture where it is okay to express opinions, even if they turn out not to be the ones chosen for implementation; where it is safe to try to have a go. Of course, we are not suggesting that this is suitable for everything. Scientific tests, for example, should not be done creatively. They must be exact and follow strict protocols. However, there are many real synergies in science. Indeed it is often synergy that creates breakthroughs in science. It is the leader's job to determine whether precision or divergent thinking is needed and to be flexible enough to foster both.

Habit 7: Sharpen the saw

Last of all, and perhaps the most important of all, is this final habit of self-care. It is the habit of taking care of yourself so you are in the best shape to carry out all of the other habits. This requires courage to take breaks, nourish oneself with good food, and create a life with spiritual, social, and intellectual nourishment, for you to be your best. Great leaders know that burnout or operating at 50% capacity is just not going to yield top-notch results all the time. It takes some strength to resist "working so hard" that others may perceive you as really committed. Here you are asked, again, to be the role model for the way of life that actually yields the highest returns.

Examples

"So what is all this Leadership stuff? Surely it is just common sense dressed up with a few long words and some catchphrases. The real problem is that they don't listen to the real experts ..."

Sound familiar? It is something I still hear from many scientific colleagues, and I would admit to having shared many of the underlying beliefs myself. Having undergone some leadership training, and even more powerfully, having had to lead scientists across a wide range of specialisms without formal hierarchical authority, my views are now radically different. Here are a few examples:

Emotional intelligence

"Working in safety critical areas like radiotherapy physics means getting the right balance between essential checking and safety procedures, and providing prompt personalised radiation dose treatment for patients. When someone has this balance wrong, engaging in purely objective discussions about safety checks and QA frequency may only embed their views, leading to conflict. You need to understand their (and your) emotional commitment to these views, and the values which underpin them. Only then can you reach a consensus which is right for the patient."

The 7 step process of change

"Given that scientists are committed to rational evidence based decisions, once new evidence is available and tested, of course we will all happily change to a new procedure or process ... except we don't. Scientists are human too, and we need to go through the same adaptions to change as any other group. When merging (and reorganising) medical physics and clinical engineering colleagues working in the same organisation in related but historically separate groups, the process took longer than needed and was more distressing than it should have been because we didn't acknowledge the need for people to undergo change processes. A more structured approach, which would have acknowledged the concerns, hopes and fears of the individuals, would also have been more efficient."

Asking questions rather than giving answers — empowering others

"Scientists are good at questions, after all we are professional sceptics, and we are trained to spot the flaws in arguments and to expose them forensically. That approach is fine for purely scientific discourse, but is terrible training for dealing with people that we want to motivate. People give of their best (and give much more) when engaged and empowered. Wanting a junior colleague to take responsibility for a new area of work in the safe use of medical equipment, motivation came from discussing the scope of the clinical problem with them, and asking for their ideas on how scientists could contribute, how best to engage with nursing and medical colleagues, etc. The outcome was an improved clinical service as well as a motivated individual aware of her capabilities to take on bigger tasks in future."

Taking responsibility to lead, even when it is not your job

"The more we learn, the more there is to learn, and we love our personal area of scientific expertise, so we go deeper rather than broader. Fine, and sometimes necessary, but also limiting. Being the expert in a specialised field doesn't preclude us from being good in other fields as well. When the opportunity came to move out of my specialist area of science, to a role which encompassed all the applications of science in medicine, my first reaction was to question whether anyone could be an expert in all these areas. Once you realise that no-one can be, then the issues become clearer: who is best placed to lead the experts who do work in these diverse scientific disciplines? And if not us, then who?"

Using leadership tools in a scientific environment

"The value of leadership tools has been to develop personal awareness and listening skills, and I have also had the opportunity to put the skills I have learned into practice when implementing a 7 day service within a multi disciplinary team. Previously our team only provided a five day service, so moving to working over seven days was quite different.

When faced with a challenge or difficult situation I have learned to listen to my inner self, developing my self confidence and being able to project that confidence to my outer self which is the face that others see. A valuable skill to develop in becoming a good leader; enabling you to deal with your fears and face challenges.

When introducing anything new to an established service it is crucial to recognise that the staff in that service will have some resistance to that change.

Possession of leadership tools puts you in a strong position to resolve this resistance to change and find solutions that empower others.

I found it important to use emotional intelligence and the skill of listening on 3 levels, as so little of our communication is verbal, it was through the actions and non verbal communication of the team that I was able to identify particular issues, including concerns about how a seven day rota would operate and the impact on individual team members.

By being aware of the 7 Stage Process of Change I was able to anticipate and understand the process the staff were going through. The change process was discussed as a team and everyone in the team was able to voice their ideas and any concerns.

Initially there was staff resistance, some staff stated problems with childcare, and this was followed closely by an awareness and recognition of the need to change, to offer a better service, increased results and outcomes for patients. Staff quickly realised that there might be benefits for them as well, the 'what's in it for me?' Staff decided that they would like to have a day off on the week in lieu of weekend working.

By thinking win-win the strategies that resulted in mutual benefits and solutions were employed. I was able to outline the benefits to the patients and service. As a leader I value and respect others, I like to put myself in their place, and it was important to allow the staff to realise the benefits themselves without pressurising them.

The next stage in the process was to have a mental try out of the process—what will the benefits be if we do this? Staff, patients, unit, we could have better results and outcomes.

- Improve the quality of care
- Offer greater patient choice
- Reduce cancelled treatment cycles
- Reduce risk
- Reduce complaints
- Service expansion and development
- Increase success rates

- Increase business
- Increase service profile
- Generate additional income

This was quickly followed by a real world try out as a pilot study, with a planned review after 6 months. The cost of offering weekend services was not as much as anticipated and offset by additional income generation.

The staff gave their commitment to the arrangement and after the trial period we had evidence based improved outcomes, and staff took pride in offering the best options possible to the patients, enjoying the increased success.

After the six month pilot the weekend working was integrated and became part of normal service, with staff finding additional things to do on a Saturday morning, including extra patient clinics."

The successful implementation was due to the use of the leadership tools, using the appropriate tool at the right time.

Emotional intelligence/listening on three levels

Example

"I had recently taken over line management responsibility for a member of staff who had been working in the department for a couple of years, although only just been rotated into my laboratory. Within a few months of this rotation, the annual appraisal of this person was due. I had been very pleased with the progress they had made and was impressed by the quality of their work and obvious commitment to the job. I expected the appraisal to be straight forward.

Initially the appraisal went well. The discussion of recent achievements was straightforward and the feedback I was giving was very positive. Appropriate responses were being received to the questions I was posing yet I began to feel that something was out of synch. Whilst the content of the conversation was stating everything was fine, the feelings that I was picking up on were telling me the exact opposite. At the time I couldn't quite put my finger on what it was but in retrospect I think it was the lack of visible emotion displayed, as if the person was simply going through the motions. The appraisal ended with an opportunity for the member of staff to raise any additional concerns they may have. I was told that everything was fine and there was nothing else they wished to raise. The expression on their face was not in keeping with their words so I pushed the point several times but their answer did not change. I ended the appraisal with an offer for them to come and have a chat with me at any time.

I wrote up the appraisal paperwork that afternoon and was still convinced that something was very wrong. Having only known this person for a relatively short period of time, and in a professional capacity, I had no idea what it could be and whether it was even work related. I was also unsure what the best way to approach them with my concerns would be. In the end I chose to go with my gut instinct and the following day I asked to speak to them again. At this point the person became extremely upset and confided in me.

Acting on what I heard and using my emotional intelligence to offer a gentle and repeated opportunity for the member of staff enabled this person to trust me enough to speak so that we could work together on the issue at hand."

Power

One more thing for us to look at that is essential to understand as a leader is the use of power in organizations and how people get things done. It is not as simple as it might seem.

The understanding of power and how it works among people is central to achieving impactful leadership. Often one thinks about power in terms of hierarchy in organizations, and that those who are the most senior have the most power. In fact, we usually think of power as a weapon to use to get your own way.

We admire it in men and are very wary of it in women. There is much to be done in our understanding of power to enable power to have the same value for both genders. Here is something that might help. Let us define power as "the ability to make things happen."

How does that definition make sense in terms of leadership within the scientific professions and in the professional world in general? Can one have too much ability to make things happen? Can it be that making things stable and consistent is powerful? That enabling exceptional teamwork is powerful? That joining together with colleagues to solve complex problems is powerful? If so, would it be hierarchical power that was most effective? Let's have a look.

Positional power—formal authority

This type of power is invested in a title or position. Whoever occupies that position has that authority. True, it takes some doing to get into that position in the first place, but the amount of power is the same for anyone in that position. Some examples are CEOs, police officers, parents, athletic coaches, head teachers, heads of departments, clinical directors, and so on.

The use of this type of power is *very* effective for quick short-term results. Those responding to this power do so because the person in the powerful position has the ability (either perceived or real) to make things difficult or unpleasant for the follower.

"Put away your toys or you will not be allowed to …"

"Follow my instructions or I will have to find someone else who will."

"This is the way we do it on this team."

"The decision has been made to change this protocol. You are required to change the way you do it. Today."

Positional power is highly respected to get someone to change their behaviour really short term, perhaps in emergency situations, to avoid an accident, move a group of people quickly, or make a quick decision as in changing direction on a sailboat. It is highly valued in the military.

However, if positional power is overused in ordinary situations, the followers feel invisible, devalued, and unable to contribute. One consequence of this is that people often do what they are asked, but do as little as is possible to be safe.

Research shows that there is 30% discretionary effort that employees have at their disposal to offer their workplaces. Not one single percent of that will go to a leader who simply uses his or her position to get people to behave in the way they want. So what else can one due to influence people?

Expertise

We have heard it said that knowledge is power, and this is true! Think about meetings you have attended where the chairperson is a very senior person who has an idea or plan for making a change. You, the subject expert, in front of a room full of senior people might be in a position to say: "That is an interesting idea and unfortunately, it will not work. The reason is …" In such situations expertise is considerably more powerful than position. Of course, it makes sense.

The fewer people that have the knowledge, the more powerful expertise is. This is also a source of power for people who are not very high up in the hierarchy. Think of the person who schedules holidays or takes care of the payroll. An important side note here: Sometimes, when someone's experience of their power is tied to their area of expertise (like being the only one who knows the method for running the payroll), you might try to offer help so that they do not feel "too burdened to take a holiday." This offer would be to have them train someone else to do what they do. It is your job as a leader to ensure that the person in charge of payroll has a way to contribute, feel valued, and experience themselves as powerful if you plan to take away their unique expertise.

Exercise

Take 2 min to think about and jot down all of the areas in which you have expertise and knowledge. Think broadly. These could include computer skills, knowledge about processes, about people, about what is happening in your field, and more.

Resource control

We know that holding the key to resources is powerful. The finance team, the CFO, the auditors; all powerful people. What other resources that you control are a further source of power for you? Your time; the time of those on your team; information; perhaps some machinery or equipment? As with expertise, resources can be highly valued, especially if they are rare. There is a great opportunity here to build relationships and expand your influence: You can trade resources!

You can offer to help another colleague with a short-term deadline and build up "credit" with that colleague for future needs you may have. This can be adapted and bring great benefit to multiple parties over long periods of time. Look for opportunities to offer to help, no matter how busy you are. It makes you visible, gets you to be viewed as a positive contributor, shows what you are capable of, and builds up knowledge of your expertise and resources so that your power is magnified.

Exercise

Think about and jot down as many resources that are within your gift as you can. Think about those around you who you have easy access to as well as yourself.

Interpersonal skills

Have you ever known a brilliant professor who was such a boring speaker that his or her brilliant ideas and knowledge just didn't get heard? Or someone who was extremely capable, got lots of things done and done well, and could have done so much more if they were able to delegate, share, and communicate better with others?

What about someone who seems to be able to build relationships with anyone, get people on board easily with new ideas, who is a great listener who makes others really feel heard? A person who others are happy to work with and who somehow finds ways to cooperate even when there are differences?

This type of power trumps everything we have discussed so far. The people who possess it know that interpersonal skills are by far the biggest source of personal power that anyone can have. They have the skills and awareness needed to make others feel valued and important: the ability to listen, communicate clearly and gently, understand the impact of emotions, and work with others positively. These include the skills of self-awareness and self-management and knowing that asking questions is a much better way to engage people in a conversation than making statements about what you want.

Exercise

How good are your interpersonal skills? Which ones need some attention? Which ones serve you really well and can be built upon and expanded?

Exercise

The power net

To get a visual representation of your political situation you can draw yourself and your relationships and the power that flows between you in both directions.

1. Draw a circle in the center of a page to represent yourself.
2. Draw circles to represent specific people with whom you interact. Draw these circles closer to you for people with whom you spend a lot of time and further away for those who have an important effect on your work though they may not spend much time interacting with you (patients, suppliers, commissioners, for example).
3. Draw lines to connect yourself with all of the people. On the lines write what type of power each person in your net has in relation to you. Do they have the right to decide what you do? What information do you need? What is the basis of their power? What sort of power do you have in relation to them?

You can also think of the power net in terms of dependence: who depends on you for what? And who do you depend on for what?

Information

Information is one of the most important political resources, and politically useful information cannot be gained through formal channels only. Tuning in to informal information networks is a vital part of understanding organizational politics and hence of being able to manage power.

Change and opportunity

Managing power not only involves being able to analyze the political framework in which you find yourself, but also recognizing when this changes and taking the opportunity that this may present. The ability to act assertively (rather than passively or aggressively) may be important if you are to make the most of such opportunities.

Conclusion

To be a leader requires a paradigm shift: to feel deep inside that you are responsible. It is about getting it in your DNA; "I matter, what I see matters, what I do matters, and how I do it matters most of all." Every day you interact with people, processes, and problems that will benefit greatly from your commitment to thinking about what you can due to make things and relationships with people better. To think from the other person's perspective: why would he or she do, think, or say that? Then to pitch what you want to say in language that they understand, always being aware that there are two ends in mind in every situation: the content of what you want to achieve and the relationship/interpersonal outcome that you want. Keeping the relationship intact makes it possible to work on the content further. Forgetting the relationship and only working on the content may mean that the content gets sabotaged, because the other party feels hard done by.

At all levels of your scientific career you can be a leader, if you choose to do so. The decision is yours. Enjoy the journey.

References

Bennis, W.G., 1989. Managing the dream: leadership in the 21st century. J. Organ. Chang. Manag. 2 (1), 6–10.

Collins, J., 2001. Good to Great. Random House.

Covey, S.R., 1989. The Seven Habits of Highly Effective People. Simon & Schuster.

Gallwey, W.T., 1986. The Inner Game of Tennis. Pan Books.

Goleman, D., 1996. Emotional Intelligence: Why it Can Matter More Than IQ. Bloomsbury.

Section II

Information technology & software engineering

Chapter 8

Information communications technology

Paul S. Ganney[a,b]

[a]University College London Hospitals NHS Trust, London, United Kingdom; [b]University of Liverpool, Liverpool, United Kingdom

Chapter outline

The regulation of clinical computing

The use of a computer as a clinical device — MHRA, FDA

Introduction

Putting a computer into clinical use, as opposed to administrative use, brings with it additional requirements in the form of regulations. The requirements of the IEC 601 family of standards on Medical Electrical Equipment, of which IEC 60601 is the most pertinent, and of the **Medical Devices Regulation** (MDR) need to be addressed and are discussed later — see

"Regulatory standards". One thing worth noting here, though, is that any electrical device which is within 1.5m of a patient is deemed to be in the "Patient Environment"[1] and thus becomes subject to the safety requirements of IEC 60601, even if its primary purpose is not clinical. Equipment on trolleys may therefore be considered as likely to come into this environment and should be assessed in the same way as equipment permanently there.

It is allowable to bring non-medical equipment into the Patient Environment provided that:

- it meets the safety standards relevant to its own type e.g. IEC 60950 (safety of information technology equipment) AND
- it meets the single fault touch current requirements for medical equipment, i.e. 500 μA.

The **Food and Drink Administration**, USA (FDA) and **Medicines and Healthcare products Regulatory Agency**, UK (MHRA) are national regulators setting standards of compliance which must be achieved before a product can be placed on the market in that country.

The MHRA

The MHRA is an executive agency of the Department of Health and is *"the UK's regulator of medicines, medical devices and blood components for transfusion, responsible for ensuring their safety, quality and effectiveness."*[i] The agency is responsible for:

- *"ensuring that medicines, medical devices and blood components for transfusion meet applicable standards of safety, quality and efficacy*
- *ensuring that the supply chain for medicines, medical devices and blood components is safe and secure*
- *promoting international standardisation and harmonization to assure the effectiveness and safety of biological medicines*
- *helping to educate the public and healthcare professionals about the risks and benefits of medicines, medical devices and blood components, leading to safer and more effective use*
- *supporting innovation and research and development that's beneficial to public health*
- *influencing UK, EU and international regulatory frameworks so that they're risk-proportionate and effective at protecting public health"*[ii]

Of particular interest to this chapter are the medical device role and the reporting of incidents.

The FDA

FDA regulations are generally regarded as being "tougher" than MHRA ones, although whether this refers to the stringency of the regulations or the regulation process is unclear. The main difference is that MHRA is concerned with safety, whilst the FDA is also concerned about clinical effectiveness. In the UK that is a separate role, dealt with by **The National Institute for Health and Clinical Excellence** (NICE). The FDA is responsible for:

- *"protecting the public health by ensuring the safety, efficacy, and security of human and veterinary drugs, biological products, and medical devices; and by ensuring the safety of our nation's food supply, cosmetics, and products that emit radiation.*
- *regulating the manufacturing, marketing, and distribution of tobacco products to protect the public health and to reduce tobacco use by minors.*
- *advancing the public health by helping to speed innovations that make medical products more effective, safer, and more affordable and by helping the public get the accurate, science-based information they need to use medical products and foods to maintain and improve their health."*[iii]

The FDA also plays a significant role in the USA's counterterrorism capability, by *"ensuring the security of the food supply and by fostering development of medical products to respond to deliberate and naturally emerging public health threats."*[iv]

In the realm of medical devices, **Premarket Approval** (PMA) is the most stringent type of device marketing application required by the FDA and is based on a determination by the FDA that the PMA contains sufficient valid scientific evidence providing reasonable assurance that the device is safe and effective for its intended use or uses. PMA is therefore

---

1. Although some educators quote 3 m, being the distance a person might reach when holding onto the patient.

required before a Class III product[2] can be placed on the market. One interesting form of regulation the FDA offers is humanitarian device exemption. This is a form of PMA but is for Humanitarian Use Devices (HUDs). These are devices that are intended to benefit patients by treating or diagnosing a disease or condition that affects fewer than 8000[3] individuals in the United States per year. Thus the "effectiveness" section of a full PMA submission is not required.

Recalls

So far we have considered only the regulatory nature of the two agencies. Additionally, they both issue alerts and recalls. It is therefore important that a healthcare provider has someone tasked with receiving these and disseminating the information appropriately, although only from their own agency (i.e. the NHS need not receive FDA alerts — these are more likely to be monitored by the MHRA, which will then (if appropriate) issue their own alert).

From a Medical Physics/Clinical Engineering perspective, therefore, there are three main areas where interaction with MHRA/FDA is required:

- Ensuring that devices deployed have the correct accreditation/approval.
- Determining when in-house developments require accreditation/approval (and seeking it when it is required).
- Receiving and disseminating alerts and recalls.

This has covered the overall organizational arrangements in the US and the UK, the latter as typical of Europe. The next section covers the detail of IEC 60601, the MDR and CE marking.

Regulatory standards including IEC601, the Medical Devices Regulation and CE marking as applied to software

IEC 601

IEC 60601-1 Medical electrical equipment — Part 1: General requirements for basic safety and essential performance, was first published in 1977. It is now in its third edition and became effective in Europe in June 2012. It is the main standard for electromedical equipment safety and is first in a family of standards, with 11 collateral standards[4] (numbered 60601-1-N) which define the requirements for certain aspects of safety and performance, e.g. Electromagnetic Compatibility (IEC 60601-1-2) and over 60 particular standards (numbered 60601-2-N) defining the standards for particular products, e.g. nerve and muscle stimulators (IEC 60601-2-10). Two important changes from the previous versions are the removal of the phrase "under medical supervision" from the definition of medical electrical equipment and the inclusion of the phrase "or compensation or alleviation of disease, injury or disability" (previously only diagnosis or monitoring) meaning that many devices previously excluded are now included in the standard's coverage. Possibly the largest change, though, is the requirement for manufacturers to have a formal risk management system that conforms to ISO 14971:2007 Medical devices — Application of risk management to medical devices, in place.[v]

A risk management system includes within it two key concepts:

- Acceptable levels of risk
- Residual risk

Once acceptable levels of risk have been established, all residual risks (as documented in the hazard log — a part of the risk management file) can be measured against them. That way, risks can be demonstrably determined to be acceptable prior to manufacture and certainly prior to deployment.

Furthermore, there are two compulsory **Data Coordination Board** (DCB) standards that are mandatory under the Health and Social care Act 2012. DCB0129 ("Clinical Risk Management: its Application in the Manufacture of Health IT Systems") describes the risk management processes required to minimize risks to patient safety with respect to the manufacture of health software products either as new systems or as changes to existing systems. DCB0160 ("Clinical Risk Management: Its Application in the Deployment and Use of Health IT Systems") is similar, describing the deployment of such products. Thus many healthcare sites need to comply with DCB0129 and all with DCB0160. A fully populated hazard

---

2. One that supports or sustains human life, is of substantial importance in preventing impairment of human health, or which presents a potential, unreasonable risk of illness or injury. Note that FDA classification does not correspond to MDR classification.
3. Previously 4000 — this was increased in 2016.
4. Of which 1, 5 and 7 are now discontinued.

log may be used to demonstrate compliance, and compliance with DCB0160 will encompass compliance with IEC 80001-1, which we will look at later in this chapter.

IEC 60601-1 covers all aspects of the medical device, including classifying the parts that connect (directly or indirectly) to patients. Of interest to this section of this book, though, is its applicability to computer-based medical devices. It is almost certain that a standard PC power supply will not meet the regulation so this must either be replaced or an isolation transformer must be placed in line. As it is unlikely that any computer-based medical device will exist in isolation, the connections to other items of equipment must also be examined. One commonly overlooked connection is to a network — this can be isolated either via transformer or optically. However, some on-board network adaptors are unable to supply the power required to drive such an isolator which may not pose a problem to a desktop machine (as a separate adaptor can be added), but would to a laptop, netbook or tablet device (especially if it is operating on battery power). Wi-fi may provide the best electrical isolation, but brings with it other problems leading to a risk balancing exercise.

IEC 60601-1 applies to medical devices and for a definition as to what constitutes such a device, we must turn to the Medical Device Regulation.

The EU Regulation on Medical Devices 2017/745 (MDR)

At the time of writing (summer, 2019) there is some uncertainty about the continued application of the MDR within the UK, assuming Britain leaves the EU. It seems unlikely that use of the regulations will be abolished but this is not known for certain. Regardless, the regulations will continue to provide a robust framework of reference for anyone seeking to design a medical device.

The MDR replaced the previous **Medical Device Directive** (MDD) and the **Active Implantable Medical Devices Directive** (AIMDD) in 2017. These defined essential requirements, introduced harmonized standards helping to demonstrate conformity to the essential requirements, defined conformity assessment procedures, and organized market surveillance functions by **Competent Authorities** (CAs) and **Notified Bodies** (NBs).[5] In this they satisfied the three conditions of the "blue guide" on the implementation of EU products[vi]:

1. Essential requirements for the products involved must be defined;
2. Methods must be established to describe how product compliance with the requirements is addressed;
3. Mechanisms to supervise and control the actions of all Economic Operators and others involved in the manufacturing and distribution of the products must be created.

However, changes in technology and medical science demanded additional legislation and the interpretation of the Directives was not consistent across all national governments. Directive 2007/47/EC modified the MDD and AIMDD in an attempt to address these concerns, but this amendment did not achieve all goals. The scandal involving defective breast implants manufactured by **Poly Implant Prosthesis** (PIPs) in France demonstrated additional weaknesses in the system and a further level of revision was required.

The major difference between a regulation and a directive is that a Directive is placed into member state law through each different legislative system (thus giving scope for different interpretations in different member states), whereas a Regulation becomes law as written in all member states. There is no room for differences of interpretation or application unless explicitly stated in the Regulation that aspects are left up to member states.

The member states of the **European Union** (EU) had three years in which to implement the regulation, with a deadline of May 2020. We will now consider some significant elements of the MDR, presenting quotations in italics.

The MDR "*lays down rules concerning the placing on the market, making available on the market or putting into service of medical devices for human use and accessories for such devices in the Union. This Regulation also applies to clinical investigations concerning such medical devices and accessories conducted in the Union.*"[vii]

The MDD focussed on the path to CE marking, whereas the MDR promotes a life-cycle approach (in this it is similar to the FDA and many other international standards). Previous guidance documents (MEDDEVs) have been incorporated into the regulation,[6] making the previously optional guidance mandatory.

In common with all EU regulations, Articles provide definitions and Annexes describe an application. Article 1 of the MDR brings products without an intended medical purpose that are listed in Annex XVI into the scope of the MDR.

---

5. A Notified Body is an organization that has been nominated by a member government and has been notified by the European Commission. They serve as independent test labs and perform the steps required by directives. Manufacturers are not required to use notified bodies in their own country but may use any within the EU.
6. Possibly not all, but certainly Guidance on Authorized Representation, Clinical Evaluation, Vigilance, and Post-Market Clinical Follow-Up.

Medical devices, accessories and the products in Annex XVI are referred to as "devices". In the definition of accessories, no exception is made for products without a medical purpose that will be considered medical devices and therefore their accessories will also fall within the scope of the MDR. Annex XVI may have new groups of products added during the lifetime of the MDR.

Article 2 lists 71 definitions, compared to the MDD's 14. Amongst these, **In-Vitro Diagnostics** (IVDs) are covered and accessories are now defined to "assist" as well as to "enable" a medical device's usage. Likewise, "label" is defined, as is "risk".

"Standalone software" is no longer mentioned. "Software may have a medical purpose," in which case it falls within the scope of the MDR. Annex VIII, Classification Rules now refers to "software that drives a device or influences the use of a device" versus software that is "independent of any other device."[viii]

There is now only one definition of a medical device, whereas previously there were three. This definition reads:

"(1) 'medical device' means any instrument, apparatus, appliance, software, implant, reagent, material or other article intended by the manufacturer to be used, alone or in combination, for human beings for one or more of the following specific medical purposes:

— *diagnosis, prevention, monitoring, prediction, prognosis, treatment or alleviation of disease,*
— *diagnosis, monitoring, treatment, alleviation of, or compensation for, an injury or disability,*
— *investigation, replacement or modification of the anatomy or of a physiological or pathological process or state,*
— *providing information by means of in vitro examination of specimens derived from the human body, including organ, blood and tissue donations,*

and which does not achieve its principal intended action by pharmacological, immunological or metabolic means, in or on the human body, but which may be assisted in its function by such means.
The following products shall also be deemed to be medical devices:

— *devices for the control or support of conception;*
— *products specifically intended for the cleaning, disinfection or sterilization of devices as referred to in Article 1(4) and of those referred to in the first paragraph of this point.*

Additional clauses deal with accessories, custom-made devices etc.

(2) 'accessory for a medical device' means an article which, whilst not being itself a medical device, is intended by its manufacturer to be used together with one or several particular medical device(s) to specifically enable the medical device(s) to be used in accordance with its/their intended purpose(s) or to specifically and directly assist the medical functionality of the medical device(s) in terms of its/their intended purpose(s);

(3) 'custom-made device' means any device specifically made in accordance with a written prescription of any person authorized by national law by virtue of that person's professional qualifications which gives, under that person's responsibility, specific design characteristics, and is intended for the sole use of a particular patient exclusively to meet their individual conditions and needs.

However, mass-produced devices which need to be adapted to meet the specific requirements of any professional user and devices which are mass-produced by means of industrial manufacturing processes in accordance with the written prescriptions of any authorized person shall not be considered to be custom-made devices;

(4) 'active device' means any device, the operation of which depends on a source of energy other than that generated by the human body for that purpose, or by gravity, and which acts by changing the density of or converting that energy. Devices intended to transmit energy, substances or other elements between an active device and the patient, without any significant change, shall not be deemed to be active devices.

Software shall also be deemed to be an active device[7];"[ix]

Software was previously considered to be passive — the change may thus increase the risk rating of existing software. Further definitions of interest from a software perspective are:

---

7. Previously passive — this may thus increase the risk rating of existing software.

(12) " *'intended purpose' means the use for which a device is intended according to the data supplied by the manufacturer on the label, in the instructions for use or in promotional or sales materials or statements and as specified by the manufacturer in the clinical evaluation;*

...

(25) *'compatibility' is the ability of a device, including software, when used together with one or more other devices in accordance with its intended purpose, to:*
   (a) *perform without losing or compromising the ability to perform as intended, and/or*
   (b) *integrate and/or operate without the need for modification or adaption of any part of the combined devices, and/ or*
   (c) *be used together without conflict/interference or adverse reaction.*
(26) *'interoperability' is the ability of two or more devices, including software, from the same manufacturer or from different manufacturers, to:*
   (a) *exchange information and use the information that has been exchanged for the correct execution of a specified function without changing the content of the data, and/or*
   (b) *communicate with each other, and/or*
   (c) *work together as intended.*
(29) *'putting into service' means the stage at which a device, other than an investigational device, has been made available to the final user as being ready for use on the Union market for the first time for its intended purpose;*
(30) *'manufacturer' means a natural or legal person who manufactures or fully refurbishes a device or has a device designed, manufactured or fully refurbished, and markets that device under its name or trademark;*
(31) *'fully refurbishing', for the purposes of the definition of manufacturer, means the complete rebuilding of a device already placed on the market or put into service, or the making of a new device from used devices, to bring it into conformity with this Regulation, combined with the assignment of a new lifetime to the refurbished device;"*[x]

Additionally, clause 19 from the preamble is also worth mentioning[8]*: "It is necessary to clarify that software in its own right, when specifically intended by the manufacturer to be used for one or more of the medical purposes set out in the definition of a medical device, qualifies as a medical device, while software for general purposes, even when used in a healthcare setting, or software intended for life-style and well-being purposes is not a medical device. The qualification of software, either as a device or an accessory, is independent of the software's location or the type of interconnection between the software and a device."*[xi]

There has been much concern over paragraph 4 of chapter II's statement that *"Devices that are manufactured and used within health institutions shall be considered as having been put into service."*[xii] as it would require one-off products such as rehabilitation engineering devices and most software for use in Medical Physics and Clinical Engineering departments to be CE marked. Paragraph 5 and Article 10 (referred to as the **health institution exemption** (HIE) by MHRA) tempers this and provides requirements that, if met, mean that CE marking is not required. However, if they are not met, then the full regulation applies. These are:

"With the exception of the relevant general safety and performance requirements set out in Annex I, the requirements of this Regulation shall not apply to devices, manufactured and used only within health institutions established in the Union, provided that all of the following conditions are met:

(a) the devices are not transferred to another legal entity,
(b) manufacture and use of the devices occur under appropriate quality management systems,
(c) the health institution justifies in its documentation that the target patient group's specific needs cannot be met, or cannot be met at the appropriate level of performance by an equivalent device available on the market,
(d) the health institution provides information upon request on the use of such devices to its competent authority, which shall include a justification of their manufacturing, modification and use;
(e) the health institution draws up a declaration which it shall make publicly available, including:
   (i) the name and address of the manufacturing health institution;
   (ii) the details necessary to identify the devices;
   (iii) a declaration that the devices meet the general safety and performance requirements set out in Annex I to this Regulation and, where applicable, information on which requirements are not fully met with a reasoned justification therefore,

---

8. As it means that "Lifestyle" software (activity trackers etc.) are not classified as medical devices.

(f) the health institution draws up documentation that makes it possible to have an understanding of the manufacturing facility, the manufacturing process, the design and performance data of the devices, including the intended purpose, and that is sufficiently detailed to enable the competent authority to ascertain that the general safety and performance requirements set out in Annex I to this Regulation are met;

(g) the health institution takes all necessary measures to ensure that all devices are manufactured in accordance with the documentation referred to in point (f), and

(h) the health institution reviews experience gained from clinical use of the devices and takes all necessary corrective actions. Member States may require that such health institutions submit to the competent authority any further relevant information about such devices which have been manufactured and used on their territory.

Member States shall retain the right to restrict the manufacture and the use of any specific type of such devices and shall be permitted access to inspect the activities of the health institutions.

This paragraph shall not apply to devices that are manufactured on an industrial scale."[xiii]

Article 10 also specifies requirements for custom-made devices, such that full technical documentation is not required but documentation in accordance with Section 2 of Annex XIII is. Custom-made and investigational devices are also exempt from the requirement to draw up an EU declaration of conformity. Investigational (but not custom-made) devices are exempt from the requirement to maintain a **Quality Management System** (QMS). Article 5.5 (above) sets out the conditions for what the MHRA refer to as the HIE. As previously mentioned, if this light-touch regulation is not met, then the Regulation applies in full.

This review of the MDR raises several questions for Clinical Engineers, often because some definitions need interpretation. In particular should the NHS be regarded as one legal entity or several and what is an appropriate QMS? From a software perspective, it is as yet unclear whether a new version of software is a new device and also how software relates to the definitions of parts and components. These issues are already subject to UK discussion, coordinated by the MHRA, who are developing guidance.

What is clear, is that the ability to run software that is a medical device on a computer that is not originally designed as a medical device thus re-designates the hardware as a medical device and must be evaluated and controlled accordingly. It is also worth noting that it is recognized that software may consist of multiple modules, some of which are medical devices and some are not.

Finally, we consider the issue of scripts. These are small pieces of programming code, or modules, that may run within a medical device, performing some function upon it, such as extraction of data or implementing a new diagnostic metric. Crucially, new scripts can be developed by end users. It may be argued that such scripts are covered by the device's CE mark as the device is intended to host scripts and therefore is operating as intended. However, this does not make the manufacturer liable for any errors in programming, as the author is still responsible for the safe application of the device (and therefore script). An alternative view is that scripts form software modules and therefore are independent of the device. The MDD defined software as being able to be broken down into modules where each one correlates with an application of the software, some having a medical purpose and some not,[xiv] so this may assist — especially with scripts performing non-medical device functions such as averaging and aggregating.

CE marking

CE marking[9] on a product:

- is a manufacturer's declaration that the product complies with the essential requirements of the relevant European health, safety and environmental protection legislation.
- indicates to governmental officials that the product may be legally placed on the market in their country.
- ensures the free movement of the product within the European Free Trade Association (EFTA) & European Union (EU) single market (total 28 countries), and
- permits the withdrawal of the non-conforming products by customs and enforcement/vigilance authorities.

CE marking did not originally encompass Medical Devices, but they were brought into the scope of the general directive by a series of subsequent directives from 2000 onwards. It is worth noting that a device must comply with all relevant directives (i.e. all the ones that apply to it).

---

9. "CE" is an abbreviation of the French phrase "Conformité Européene" ("European Conformity"). Whilst the original term was "EC Mark", it was officially replaced by "CE Marking" in the Directive 93/68/EEC in 1993 which is now used in all EU official documents.

Products with minimal risk can be self-certified, where the manufacturer prepares a "Declaration of Conformity" and affixes the CE mark to their own product. Products with greater risk are usually (depending on the directive) independently certified, which must be done by a NB.

Custom made devices, devices undergoing clinical investigation and in-vitro medical devices for clinical investigation do not currently require CE marks but must be marked 'exclusively for clinical investigation'.

The MHRA provides advice and guidance on matters concerning the relationship between the MDR and the CE requirements and their website[xv] contains helpful documents, including flowcharts and decision trees to assist in determining whether a device is a medical device and, if so, the class to which it belongs.

Integrating medical devices into an IT network: IEC 80001

Adding medical devices to a standard IT network greatly increases the risk of a clinical event. Examples of failures through poor implementation of such a network are: Radiotherapy treatment sessions being suspended when the treatment equipment lost connection with its server via the network during a virus attack; 'broadcast storm' events causing widespread disruption and unplanned reversion to less efficient downtime backup procedures; arson attacks destroying 70% of the network capacity for a substantial period; a loose network cable being plugged into an empty port, thus creating a loop causing a router to talk to itself, bringing network traffic to a crawl in the affected area.

IEC 80001-1 (2010) "Application of risk management for IT-networks incorporating medical devices – Part 1: Roles, responsibilities and activities", provides some standards for integrating medical devices into IT networks. The standard is in two parts (part 1 is the standard itself and part 2 consists of technical reports to support implementation of the standard) and has 4 goals:

- patient safety
- effectiveness (as in the enhancement of the delivery of care through safe and effective connectivity)
- data and system security, and
- interoperability

The IEC 80001 family of standards attempts to balance these goals using a risk management framework.

The main definition for consideration here is that of the *"Medical IT Network"*, which is defined as *"an IT-NETWORK[10] that incorporates at least one MEDICAL DEVICE."*[xvi] An IT-NETWORK is defined as *"a system or systems composed of communicating nodes and transmission links to provide physically linked or wireless transmission between two or more specified communication nodes"* and is adapted from IEC 61907:2009, definition 3.1.1. The MEDICAL DEVICE definition is from the MDD and will therefore be replaced by the one from the MDR. A hospital that connects even one medical device into its standard network (or, indeed, loads medical device software onto a non-medical device so connected) has thereby created a medical IT-Network. The bounds of this network are that of the responsible organization but do bring different responsibilities into play, as detailed in the standard. In particular the role of the medical IT-network risk manager is specified.

IEC 80001-2-1_2012 describes a 10-step process[11] for implementing this standard:

- STEP 1: Identify HAZARDS.
- STEP 2: Identify causes and resulting HAZARDOUS SITUATIONS.
- STEP 3: Determine UNINTENDED CONSEQUENCES and estimate potential severities.
- STEP 4: Estimate the probability of the UNINTENDED CONSEQUENCE. By estimating probability and severity of UNINTENDED CONSEQUENCE, you have estimated RISK.
- Iterate STEPS 1 through 4, using both top-down and bottom-up approaches. There can be multiple HAZARDOUS SITUATIONS per HAZARD, multiple causes per HAZARDOUS SITUATION, multiple HAZARDOUS SITUATIONS per cause.
- STEP 5: Evaluate RISK against pre-determined RISK acceptability criteria.
- STEP 6: Identify and document proposed RISK CONTROL measures and re-evaluate RISK (i.e. return to STEP 3).
- STEP 7: Implement RISK CONTROL measures.

---

10. Words in CAPITALS are terms with specific definitions in the standard. This is a common notation in such documents.
11. Or more than 10, depending on the "iterate" step.

- STEP 8: Verify RISK CONTROL measures.
- STEP 9: Evaluate any new RISKS arising from RISK CONTROL.
- STEP 10: Evaluate and report overall RESIDUAL RISK.

IEC 80001-2-3_2012 addresses wireless networks (including possible sources of interference such as microwave ovens and radar), along with asking "does the use case of the device require wireless connectivity?" i.e. would a wired connection actually be better.

IEC 80001-2-4_2012 addresses the use of third party suppliers and their responsibilities — the RESPONSIBLE ORGANISATION has to ask them the same questions it is asking itself as to risk management, disaster recovery and contingency.

IEC 80001 is currently undergoing revision. While the main points are still considered to be sound, the lack of drivers for implementation and the complexity of some of the standard are being considered in the revision.[xvii]

Other standards

There are two major sets of standards that we are concerned with: regulatory, especially around Medical Devices, and developmental, around software. The most important UK legislation designed to protect the patient is the MDR, which is described earlier.

Three international standards offer valuable contributions to those working to provide and support Medical Devices:

- IEC 62304-2015: Medical Device Software Lifecycle — Software Lifecycle processes. This offers a risk based approach and makes reference to the use of **Software of Unknown Provenance** (SOUP).
- IEC/ISO 90003-2004 Guidelines for the application of ISO 9000-2000 to computer software, which offers similar concepts to those embraced in the TickIT scheme.[xviii]
- ISO 13485-2003 Medical Devices — Quality Management Systems - Requirements for Regulatory Purposes. This deals with the production and management of Medical Devices in a manner that parallels ISO 9000.

Process standards relevant to the in-house production of medical software include:

- ISO/IEC 62366: 2015. Medical Devices — Part 1: Application of Usability Engineering to Medical Devices
- ISO 14971: 2012. Application of risk management to medical devices
- IEC 60601:2006+A12:2014. Safety requirements for programmable electronic medical systems.
- IEC 61508: 2000. Functional Safety of Electrical/Electronic/Programmable Electronic Safety-related Systems.
- ISO 15189: 2012. Medical laboratories - Requirements for quality and competence.

NHS Digital produced a helpful document summarizing the key data protection, data governance and medical device regulatory requirements involved in the development of decision supporting and decision-making software applications, or devices incorporating such technology, in the NHS and Adult Social Care. Whilst not intended as a comprehensive guide to all relevant legislation, it signposts detailed guidance and acknowledges ongoing work aimed at providing clarity and covering several issues not currently well catered for in the existing legislative framework.[xix]

The Data Protection Act, the GDPR, the Freedom of Information Act and the Caldicott Committees

There are two main pieces of general legislation covering the use of information/data and the right to disclosure. Personal data is covered by the **European Union General Data Protection Regulation** (EU GDPR — more often just called GDPR) and official information by the **Freedom of Information** (FOI) Act. Both of these are described below. A third item, the Environmental Information Regulations (with a separate version for Scotland), covers more public bodies but is only likely to impact upon the NHS in terms of buildings and waste disposal. The particular sensitivities surrounding medical data were considered by the Caldicott committee in 1997, with a second consideration in 2013. The legislation will first be discussed, followed by consideration of required practice within the medical environment.

The General Data Protection Regulation

The GDPR came into effect on 25th May 2018. It is enshrined in UK law as the **Data Protection Act** of 2018 (DPA, 2018) which replaced the DPA:1998 of 2000. It applies to processing carried out by organizations operating within the EU as well as organisations outside the EU that offer goods or services to individuals in the EU. The GDPR does not apply to certain activities including processing covered by the Law Enforcement Directive,[12] processing for national security purposes and processing carried out by individuals purely for personal/household activities. It is stronger than preceding legislation and the fines for a breach are higher: for the most serious instances of non-compliance, an organization can expect a fine of up to 4% of annual global turnover or €20 million, whichever is greater.

The GDPR applies to controllers and processors. A controller determines the purposes and means of processing personal data (how and why), whereas a processor is responsible for processing personal data on behalf of a controller. The GDPR places specific legal obligations on processors. For example, the requirement to maintain records of personal data and processing activities. Controllers are not relieved of their obligations where a processor is involved — the GDPR places further obligations on them to ensure their contracts with processors comply with the GDPR. The GDPR has seven main principles, which are recorded in Article 5 and reproduced here in italics:

"1. Personal data shall be:

  (a) *processed lawfully, fairly and in a transparent manner in relation to the data subject ('lawfulness, fairness and transparency');*

  (b) *collected for specified, explicit and legitimate purposes and not further processed in a manner that is incompatible with those purposes; further processing for archiving purposes in the public interest, scientific or historical research purposes or statistical purposes shall, in accordance with Article 89(1), not be considered to be incompatible with the initial purposes ('purpose limitation');*

  (c) *adequate, relevant and limited to what is necessary in relation to the purposes for which they are processed ('data minimisation');*

  (d) *accurate and, where necessary, kept up to date; every reasonable step must be taken to ensure that personal data that are inaccurate, having regard to the purposes for which they are processed, are erased or rectified without delay ('accuracy');*

  (e) *kept in a form which permits identification of data subjects for no longer than is necessary for the purposes for which the personal data are processed; personal data may be stored for longer periods insofar as the personal data will be processed solely for archiving purposes in the public interest, scientific or historical research purposes or statistical purposes in accordance with Article 89(1) subject to implementation of the appropriate technical and organisational measures required by this Regulation in order to safeguard the rights and freedoms of the data subject ('storage limitation');*

  (f) *processed in a manner that ensures appropriate security of the personal data, including protection against unauthorised or unlawful processing and against accidental loss, destruction or damage, using appropriate technical or organisational measures ('integrity and confidentiality').*

2. *The controller shall be responsible for, and be able to demonstrate compliance with, paragraph 1 ('accountability')."*[xx]

"Personal data" is defined as: *"'personal data' means any information relating to an identified or identifiable natural person ('data subject'); an identifiable natural person is one who can be identified, directly or indirectly, in particular by reference to an identifier such as a name, an identification number, location data, an online identifier or to one or more factors specific to the physical, physiological, genetic, mental, economic, cultural or social identity of that natural person."*[xxi]

Personal data is therefore information that relates to an individual. That individual must be identified or identifiable either directly or indirectly from one or more identifiers or from factors specific to the individual. The **Information Commissioner's Office** (ICO)'s website lists five factors that need to be considered to determine whether personal data is being processed. These are:

- identifiability and related factors
- whether someone is directly identifiable
- whether someone is indirectly identifiable
- the meaning of 'relates to'
- when different organizations are using the same data for different purposes

---

12. An EU directive that *"lays down the rules relating to the protection of natural persons with regard to the processing of personal data by competent authorities for the purposes of the prevention, investigation, detection or prosecution of criminal offences or the execution of criminal penalties, including the safeguarding against and the prevention of threats to public security."* — http://eur-lex.europa.eu/legal-content/EN/TXT/PDF/?uri=CELEX:32016L0680&from=EN.

The key to personal data is identifiability — whether the information allows an individual to be specifically identified. Whilst a name is probably the most common means of identifying someone, whether any potential identifier, including a name, identifies an individual depends on the context. The GDPR gives a non-exhaustive list of common identifiers, such as name, identification number and online identifiers such as IP addresses and cookie identifiers. Any identifier, or combination of identifiers, can be sufficient to identify a single individual. An individual is also identifiable if you can distinguish that individual from other members of a group.

Indirect identification is possibly the hardest part of "personal data" to ensure compliance with. An individual that cannot be directly identified from the information being processed (for example where all identifiers have been removed) may still be identifiable by other means, either from information already held, or information that is needed to be obtained from another source.

However, the GDPR only applies to living individuals — information relating to a deceased person does not constitute personal data.

There are eight rights for individuals under the GDPR:

- The right to be informed. (Individuals must be provided with the purposes for processing personal data, the retention periods for that personal data, and who it will be shared with. This set (together with some other information) is called 'privacy information').
- The right of access. (Individuals have the right to access their personal data, commonly referred to as "subject access". See later).
- The right to rectification. (Individuals have the right to have inaccurate personal data rectified or completed if it is incomplete. This request can be verbally or in writing, there is one calendar month to respond to a request, but in certain circumstances a request for rectification may be refused).
- The right to erasure. (Also known as "the right to be forgotten", individuals can demand under certain circumstances that all copies of their personal data be erased by the data controller).
- The right to restrict processing. (Individuals have the right (in certain circumstances) to request the restriction or suppression of their personal data. When this applies the personal data may be stored but not used).
- The right to data portability. (Individuals have the right to forward personal data from one data controller to another. The data must be provided in a structured, commonly used machine-readable format such as CSV, XML or JSON).
- The right to object. (Individuals have the right to object to the processing of their personal data in certain circumstances. Specifically, they have an absolute right to stop their data being used for direct marketing. In other cases where the right to object applies processing may be allowed to continue if a compelling reason for doing so can be shown).
- Rights in relation to automated decision making and profiling. (Automated individual decision-making (making a decision solely by automated means without any human involvement) and profiling (automated processing of personal data to evaluate certain things about an individual) require additional information to be provided and require explicit consent).

Of particular interest to a clinical setting are these issues, which we will now examine:

- Anonymisation
- Medical Opinion
- Consent
- The "right to be forgotten"

Anonymisation

Anonymized data no longer relates to a specific person or can be attributed to them, so the GDPR no longer applies. However, the GDPR does apply to the process of anonymisation as the data is being processed. Pseudonymisation (where, for example, all identifying information is removed and replaced with a reference number that is stored separately) is effectively only a security measure and (as recital 26 makes clear) the data remains as personal data and the GDPR still applies to it.

Medical opinion

A record of an opinion (not just a medical one) is not necessarily inaccurate personal data if it is later proved to be wrong. Opinions are, by their very nature, subjective and not intended to record matters of fact. *"An area of particular sensitivity is medical opinion, where doctors routinely record their opinions about possible diagnoses. It is often impossible to conclude with certainty, perhaps until time has passed or tests have been done, whether a patient is suffering from a particular condition. An initial diagnosis (which is an informed opinion) may prove to be incorrect after more extensive examination or further tests. However, if the patient's records reflect the doctor's diagnosis at the time, the records are not inaccurate, because they accurately reflect that doctor's opinion at a particular time. Moreover, the record of the doctor's initial diagnosis may help those treating the patient later, and in data protection terms is required in order to comply with the 'adequacy' element of the data minimisation principle."*[xxii]

Consent

In order to process data, a "Lawful Basis" must be established. There are six such, of which consent (where the individual has given clear consent for the processing of their personal data for a specific purpose) is likely to be the most used in healthcare. *"Consent under the GDPR must be a freely given, specific, informed and unambiguous indication of the individual's wishes."*[xxiii] There needs to be a clear affirmative action (a positive opt-in − consent cannot be inferred from silence, pre-ticked boxes or inactivity) and must be verifiable. Consent must also be separate from other terms and conditions, and it must be an easy process for consent to be withdrawn.

The "right to be forgotten"

The "right to be forgotten" has raised concern amongst medical professionals. However, Article 17 of the GDPR states that *in certain circumstances* an individual can submit a request to the data controller to have personal information erased or to prevent further processing of that data. This applies when:

- The personal data is no longer necessary or relevant in relation to the purpose for which it was original collected
- The individual specifically withdraws consent to processing (and if there is no other justification or legitimate interest for continued processing)
- Personal data has been unlawfully processed, in breach of the GDPR
- The data must be erased in order for a controller to comply with legal obligations (for example, the deletion of certain data after a set period of time)

In conjunction with this, those collecting health data will normally choose to rely on consent. *"However, an organisation does not have to rely on consent (as its ground for processing sensitive personal data) and can collect and use health data if the processing is necessary for the purposes of preventive or occupational medicine, medical diagnosis, provision of health or social care or treatment, management of health or social care systems and services, under a contract with a health professional or another person subject to professional secrecy under law (the 'medical care' ground). Additionally, consent is not required if the processing is necessary in the public interest for public health reasons (the 'public health' ground), or if the organisation can argue that the processing is necessary for scientific research."*[xxiv]

Thus, it may be argued, the "right to be forgotten" does NOT apply to medical data.

Subject access request

The GDPR, like the DPA before it, gives individuals the right to access their personal data. This is known as a "subject access request". Individuals can make a subject access request verbally or in writing, and the organization has one month in which to respond to a request. This can be extended by a further two months if the request is complex or if several requests have been received from the individual. The individual must be informed within one month of receiving their request and given an explanation as to why the extension is necessary. A fee to deal with this request cannot be charged in most circumstances.

Individuals have the right to obtain confirmation that their personal data is being processed, a copy of their personal data and other supplementary information. This includes:

- the purposes of processing
- the categories of personal data concerned
- the recipients or categories of recipient the personal data is disclosed to
- the retention period for storing the personal data or, where this is not possible, the criteria for determining how long it will be stored
- the existence of their right to request rectification, erasure or restriction or to object to such processing
- the right to lodge a complaint with the ICO or another supervisory authority
- information about the source of the data, where it was not obtained directly from the individual
- the existence of automated decision-making (including profiling)

- the safeguards provided if personal data is transferred to a third country or international organization.

Much of this information may already be provided in the organization's privacy notice.

The Freedom of Information Act 2000

The FOI is a UK law (although there are many similar laws elsewhere, especially in Europe) that describes the rights of groups and individuals to request information and the obligations of the organization to respond to such requests. All public authorities in England, Northern Ireland and Wales and those which are UK-wide have a legal obligation to provide information through an approved publication scheme and in response to requests. Scotland has a similar Act, the Freedom of Information (Scotland) Act 2002 which is regulated by the Scottish Information Commissioner's Office.

Under the FOI Act,[13] a member of the public has the right to ask for any information they think a public authority may hold. The right only covers recorded information which includes information held on computers, in emails and in printed or handwritten documents as well as images, video and audio recordings.

A request is made directly to the relevant authority, in writing. The request may be in the form of a question and must contain the requester's real name and a contact address for the reply.

The request must be responded to within 20 working days. This response can take one of the following forms:

- *provide the information requested;*
- *respond that the authority doesn't have the information;*
- *respond that another authority holds the information.* The authority may (but does not have to) transfer the request;
- *respond that the information is available and can be provided for a* fee (but there are rules surrounding this);
- *refuse to provide the information,* and explain why; or,
- *respond that more time is required to consider the public interest in disclosing or withholding the information,* and state when a response should be expected. This should not be later than 40 working days after the date of the request. The time limit can only be extended in certain circumstances, and an explanation as to why the information may be exempt must be provided.

The request may be refused for the following reasons:

- *It will cost too much to provide.* The limit is currently set at £600 for any government department, Houses of Parliament, Northern Ireland Assembly, National Assembly for Wales, Welsh Assembly Government and armed forces and £450 for any other public bodies. This is interpreted as being 24 and 18 hours' effort, respectively. (i.e. about two and a half days' work for the NHS).
- *The request is vexatious or repeated.*
- *The information is exempt from disclosure under one of the exemptions in the Act.* There are 23 exemptions in the Act, broadly divided into three categories:
  - Those that apply to a whole category (or class) of information, for example, information about investigations and proceedings conducted by public authorities, court records and trade secrets.
  - Those that are subject to a 'prejudice' test, where disclosure would, or would be likely to, prejudice for example the interests of the United Kingdom abroad, the prevention or detection of crime or the activity or interest described in the exemption.
  - Requests that should be dealt with under the DPA either as a subject access request, or releasing the information would contravene the DPA (e.g. where the FOI request is about a third party).
- It is worth noting that a request may not be refused because part of a document that would have to be provided is exempt. In this case, a redacted version of the document with the exempt information removed must be provided.

There are some very good examples on the ICO web site[xxv] of how to interpret these exclusions.

This leads to the question of anonymized data, where all person-identifiable information has been removed. For example, a request to provide an anonymized MRI image. This would seem to satisfy the requirements of a FOI request, but is not one of the purposes for which the data was collected, so is exempt via the DPA (unless, of course, it was included in the consent form).

---

13. Essentially an addenda to the Public Records Act, which itself had to be modified to take account of the FOI.

The Caldicott Committee

The Caldicott Committee was established in 1997, to review the flow of patient-identifiable information around and out of the NHS. Its work resulted in an instruction to all NHS Chief Executives to appoint Caldicott Guardians by the end of March 1999.

The Caldicott Guardian is a senior member of staff whose role is to:

- *establish the highest practical standards for handling patient information;*
- *produce a year on year improvement plan for ensuring patient confidentiality;*
- *monitor yearly improvement against the improvement plan;*
- *agree and review protocols governing the protection and use of patient identifiable information;*
- *agree and review protocols governing the disclosure of patient information;*
- *develop the Trust security and confidentiality policy.*

The implication of this is that approval of the Caldicott Guardian must be gained for all new flows of patient data. The decision of the Caldicott Guardian is final and may not be challenged.

The second Caldicott Committee

The Caldicott2 Review Panel in 2013 revised the Caldicott Principles and recommended that they should be adopted and promulgated throughout the health and social care system. The Government accepted this recommendation in their response to the Caldicott2 Review ("To share or not to share"). Dame Fiona Caldicott became the **National Data Guardian for Health and Care** (NDG) in 2015.

The revised principles (Revised September 2013) are[xxvi]:

Principle 1. Justify the purpose(s) for using confidential information

Every proposed use or transfer of personal confidential data within or from an organization should be clearly defined, scrutinized and documented, with continuing uses regularly reviewed, by an appropriate guardian.

Principle 2. Don't use personal confidential data unless it is absolutely necessary

Personal confidential data items should not be included unless it is essential for the specified purpose(s) of that flow. The need for patients to be identified should be considered at each stage of satisfying the purpose(s).

Principle 3. Use the minimum necessary personal confidential data

Where use of personal confidential data is considered to be essential, the inclusion of each individual item of data should be considered and justified so that the minimum amount of personal confidential data is transferred or accessible as is necessary for a given function to be carried out.

Principle 4. Access to personal confidential data should be on a strict need-to-know basis

Only those individuals who need access to personal confidential data should have access to it, and they should only have access to the data items that they need to see. This may mean introducing access controls or splitting data flows where one data flow is used for several purposes.

Principle 5. Everyone with access to personal confidential data should be aware of their responsibilities

Action should be taken to ensure that those handling personal confidential data — both clinical and non-clinical staff — are made fully aware of their responsibilities and obligations to respect patient confidentiality.

Principle 6. Comply with the law

Every use of personal confidential data must be lawful. Someone in each organization handling personal confidential data should be responsible for ensuring that the organization complies with legal requirements.

Principle 7. The duty to share information can be as important as the duty to protect patient confidentiality

Health and social care professionals should have the confidence to share information in the best interests of their patients within the framework set out by these principles. They should be supported by the policies of their employers, regulators and professional bodies.

The original terms of reference for the first review did not explicitly cover data for research and it was assumed to be covered by the ethics committee instead. Caldicott2 more clearly acknowledges the importance of data being available for research.

On the international scene information is protected through the ISO 27000 family of standards. In particular, ISO 27799: 2008 'Health Informatics − Information Security Management in Health using IEC/ISO 20002' covers the principles described, together with the provision of accredited Information Security Management Systems.

In summarizing the principles surrounding the proper protection of data the NHS Information Strategy adopted the acronym CIA (Confidentiality, Integrity and Access). Whilst data must be kept confidential and its integrity is paramount; it must also be readily accessible to those who need it. This section has dealt with the legislative aspects; the next section covers the engineering aspects used to help achieve the objectives. Overriding Clinical Governance issues will be discussed after both aspects have been described, in a separate section.

Data security requirements

Information Communications Technology (ICT) security − firewalls, virus protection, encryption, server access and data security

Introduction

There are great advantages in connecting together ICT equipment to enable data sharing, together with the enhanced safety from a reduction in transcription errors and the increased availability and speed of access to information. However, this connectedness brings with it additional system security issues: a failure in one part may be swiftly replicated across the IT estate. There are many ways to tackle these issues and this section details some of these. It should be noted that best practice will utilize a range of security methods.

Firewalls

The first method is one of segregation, using a firewall. A firewall is, in the simplest sense, a pair of network cards (or a router - see later for a description) and a set of rules. A network packet arrives at one card (or port), is tested against the rules and, if it passes, is passed to the other card (or port) for transmission. In this way, a part of a network can be protected from activity on the rest of the network by restricting the messages that can pass through it to a predefined and pre-approved set. The rules controlling this may be as simple as only allowing a predefined set of IP addresses through. Refinements include port numbers, the direction the message is travelling in, whether the incoming message is a response to an outgoing one (e.g. a web page), specific services (e.g. videoconferencing − which may be further restricted to certain external IP addresses only) and specific exceptions to general rules. This is all achieved via packet filtering, where the header of the packet is examined in order to extract the information required for the rules.

The above description is of a hardware firewall. Software firewalls run on the device after the network traffic has been received. They can therefore be more sophisticated in their rules in that they can have access to additional information such as the program that made the request. Software firewalls can also include privacy controls and content filtering. As the software firewall runs on the device, if the device becomes compromised then the firewall may also be compromised. The Windows 7 firewall only blocks incoming traffic, so for example it will not prevent a compromised device from sending malicious network packets. It is possible to adjust the settings of the Windows firewall (usually to allow a program to operate through it), but a user will rarely need to do this as it will be done by programs during installation.

Tackling malware

Probably the most common security issue faced by NHS IT systems is that of viruses. Whilst the term "virus" is often used, it covers many different types of malicious software (or "malware") such as Trojans, worms, spyware and rootkits. There are two important features of such malware: it does something malicious and it can replicate itself, thereby passing from one device to another. The Trojan (named after the famous Trojan horse) is probably the simplest of these. This is a piece of software that purports to perform some useful function (such as a system scan), which it may do. However, it also contains within it another program that performs the malicious action (such as seeking out passwords and emailing them to the Trojan's author). By purporting to perform a useful system-level function, a user will permit the program to operate in administrator mode without anticipating the risk. The Trojan may also copy itself to all other programs on the device, so that deleting the original program does not remove the Trojan from the system.

A worm (so called because it "burrows" into the system) is a program that seeks to exploit vulnerabilities in a device (or network), usually by probing certain access points or by appearing to be a "trusted" service. Having installed itself on the device ("infected" it), it is then able to activate its malicious element (the "payload").

Viruses may be resident or non-resident. Both types will have attached themselves to a legitimate executable program in order to be executed by the device. They will initiate (possibly complete) and then pass control to the host program. A non-resident virus will search for other files to infect and do so by copying its code into the new host (thereby replicating itself). A resident virus will not perform this action immediately but will instead install itself into memory and attach itself to an operating system function, running each time this function is called. A virus scanner that fails to recognize such a virus may itself become the initiator, thereby causing each scanned file to become infected (via replication) as soon as the scan completes.

Virus technology is not new. John von Neumann described them in 1949,[xxvii] but it is the modern high level of connection in networks (and especially the Internet) that has seen the most widespread proliferation.

An anti-virus program will work in many ways, such as trapping unpermitted behaviour, but the most common is the file scan. In this method, a file[14] is examined byte by byte. The virus scanner has a set of binary patterns known as "virus definitions" that it is looking for. These are unique to the virus in question and are therefore not simply a few bytes long. In this way, Trojans and spyware can also be trapped. Once found, the scanner will perform some kind of corrective action, the most common of which are quarantine (moving the infected file somewhere else for further examination) or deletion. "Cleansing" the file is the removal of the virus but as viruses become more sophisticated this is not always successful.

In order for an anti-virus program to be successful, it must scan the files on the system. There are two main ways to do this: scheduled scanning and on-access scanning (frequently the two are combined).

On-access scanning scans files as and when they are accessed. In the case of an executable, this is just prior to its execution. Scheduled scanning scans the full system at a predefined time. On-access scanning is clearly the most secure, yet is not always applicable due to the processing overhead and time delay it introduces. This may not have any critical effect on entering figures into a spreadsheet, but is likely to in real-time control and acquisition software. For this reason most medical devices employ scheduled scanning, but it is therefore imperative that the scan is scheduled for a time when the device is operational.[15]

Virus signatures generally do not change. However, new viruses continually appear — either as a new variant on an old idea or in response to a new security flaw being discovered. Therefore virus signature files need to be kept up-to-date. In an enterprise,[16] this will generally be done by a local update server. This communicates with the main online repository (e.g. Sophos) and then distributes the updates on a regular basis (usually daily) around the enterprise. Using such a system means that the updates only have to be downloaded once, thus reducing Internet traffic and potential delays.

Some specific examples from healthcare

Conficker, 2009 The Conficker group of computer worms targeted several Microsoft Windows operating systems, using flaws in Windows OS software and dictionary attacks on administrator passwords to propagate while forming a botnet.[17] It proved unusually difficult to counter because of its combined use of many advanced malware techniques.

It was initially unclear as to the payload, as Conficker simply resided and replicated. However, it then started sending packets of data to numerous internet addresses, the content of which was not clear. The risk to patient care, however, was.

---

14. Usually an executable program — but remember that many spreadsheets and word processing documents contain executable code in the form of macros.
15. Scheduling the scan for 3 am and switching the device off when the staff go home is poor planning.
16. Such as a hospital, not a starship.
17. A number of Internet-connected devices, each of which is running one or more bots (software applications that run automated tasks over the Internet). They can be used to perform distributed denial-of-service attack (DDoS attack), steal data, send spam, and also allows the attacker to access the device and its connection.

Infected Trusts, such as West Middlesex University Hospital, implemented business continuity plans (such as manual systems) while it shut down its entire network in order to isolate the virus and clean the system. The trust managed to get a number of computers working in priority areas such as A&E, ITU, theatres and outpatient departments within a few days.

Conficker was widespread but the response was swift and the remedy relatively simple to apply: the fix was to take an infected server off of the network, run a tool to disinfect the files, apply the patch and then restart. Whilst this affected service, the downtime was minimized by this robust approach.

WannaCry, 2017 According to the National Audit Office, WannaCry started on 12 May, 2017 and is thought to have affected 81 Trusts and almost 600 GP surgeries. WannaCry is a ransomware cryptoworm, based on the original WannaCrypt. It works by exploiting a security flaw in order to enter the system (in this case, Windows' **Server Message Block** (SMB) protocol, although the original suspected route was non-secure email services such as gmail and yahoo), checks for a "kill switch"[18] and (if not present) encrypts all the data on the device. It then uses the SMB vulnerability to infect other devices on the same network. The payload then displays a message informing the user that files have been encrypted, demanding a payment of around US$300 in bitcoin within three days, or US$600 within seven days.

The general advice in dealing with the incident was not to pay, for two reasons:

1. There is no guarantee that once paid, the data would be restored.
2. Paying encourages others to try the same approach.

Different NHS Trusts dealt with the incident in differing ways. Those which had not yet been infected (such as University College London Hospitals), rapidly closed down the currently understood attack vectors (such as email). Those that had been infected (such as The Royal Berkshire Hospital) implemented their business continuity and disaster recovery plans. After switching to paper reporting, they wiped all memory, rebuilt servers (and ensured that all patches — including ones fixing the SMB vulnerability — were applied) and restored from backup. Of these affected Trusts, Papworth was possibly the luckiest — the attack took place on a Friday and the hospital does not operate over a weekend, so had two clear days to reinstall and rebuild.

The most disappointing part of the whole story is that the vulnerability had been reported before the attack and patches were available to defend against it. Most NHS Trusts hadn't applied them. The **Department of Health and Social Care** (DHSC) reported that WannaCry cost the NHS an estimated £92 million.

Specific concerns for medical devices

Medical devices often have a consumer operating system at their heart (Windows XP embedded is particularly prevalent) and thus the same vulnerabilities. As more are networked (see "IEC 80001" above) they are more at risk than before.

Medical devices have a heightened risk of malware infection due to the nature of their operation: a software patch may alter the operation of the device and therefore each one requires testing prior to deployment. In most cases, this deployment will only take place after the manufacturer (or authorized representative) has given permission for the patch or update to be applied. Such permission has historically not been swift. This changed with the Conficker outbreak (see above) when medical device manufacturers more commonly started to provide permission for device owners (such as NHS Trusts) to apply security patches immediately. Other updates (such as those providing enhanced or corrected functionality) were still "paused". As a risk-balancing exercise this proved to be the best approach.

Encryption

Assuming that devices are secure and the connection is also, the next issue to address is that of interception. Data may be deliberately intercepted (via packet logging) or simply mislaid. In either case, the next level of security is encryption. Successful encryption means that only the authorized receiver can read the message.

Encryption is, of course, a very old science. It has gone from simple substitution ciphers (where each letter of the alphabet is exchanged for another — decryption is a simple matter of reversing the substitution), through the complexity of the Enigma machine, to today's prime-number based techniques. The most common encryption in use today is RSA developed by **Rivest, Shamir and Adelman** in 1978 and relies upon the difficulty of factoring into prime numbers. It works as follows:

---

18. A "kill switch" exists so that the malware can determine whether it is being run in a security environment, the idea being that if this is the case, then the malware does not execute and so does not reveal its workings or purpose. In the case of WannaCry, the switch was checking whether a specific internet domain existed — the attack was thus halted when the domain was discovered and registered.

- Let p and q be large prime numbers and let $N = pq$. Let e be a positive integer which has no factor in common with $(p - 1)(q - 1)$. Let d be a positive integer such that $ed - 1$ is divisible by $(p - 1)(q - 1)$.
- Let $f(x) = x^e \bmod N$, where a *mod N* means "divide N into a and take the remainder."
- Let $g(x) = x^d \bmod N$.
- Use $f(x)$ for encryption, $g(x)$ for decryption.

[Clay Mathematics Institute[xxviii]]

Therefore, in order to transmit a secure message only the numbers e and N are required. To decrypt the message, d is also required. This can be found by factoring N into p and q then solving the equation to find d.[xxix] However, this factorization would take millions of years using current knowledge and technology.[19]

A simpler method is **Pretty Good Privacy** (PGP) developed by Phil Zimmerman in 1991[xxx] and subsequently multiply revised. In this there is a single public key (published) which is used for encryption and a single private key which is used for decryption. In PGP a random key is first generated and is encrypted using the recipient's public key. The message is then encrypted using the generated (or "session") key. Both the encrypted key and the encrypted message are sent to the recipient. The recipient then decrypts the session key using their private key, with which they decrypt the message.[20]

So far we have only considered data transmissions. Encryption can also be used on data "at rest", i.e. on a storage device. RSA encryption is therefore useable in this context, although PGP isn't. There are two forms of encryption: hardware and software. Both use similar algorithms but the use of hardware encryption means that the resultant storage device is portable as it requires no software to be loaded in order to be used. A device may be fully encrypted (i.e. the entire storage, sometimes including the master boot record) or filesystem-level encrypted, which just encrypts the storage being used, often leaving the file names and structure in plain text, so it is worth being careful when naming files and folders. Devices may use multiple keys for different partitions, thereby not being fully compromised if one key is discovered.

Three final concepts must be considered before we move on from encryption: steganography, checksums and digital signatures. Steganography is a process of hiding files within other files, often at bit level — image files are therefore very suitable for this, as reducing 24-bit colour depth to (say) 16-bit is rarely noticeable to the human eye (which is the basic rationale behind lossy compression) and so the other 8 bits can be used for the hidden information.

Checksums were originally developed due to the unreliability of electronic transmission. In the simplest form, the binary bits of each part of the message (which could be as small as a byte) were summed. If the result was odd, a bit with the value 1 would be added to the end of the message. If even, then the bit would be 0. Thus, by summing the entire message's bits, the result should always be even.

As an example, consider 9. As a 7-bit number this is 0001001. It has 2 1s, so the check digit is 0, giving 00010010. It is therefore vital to know whether you are using even or odd checksums (often called parity).

Extensions to this basic sum were developed in order to detect the corruption of multiple bits (as a simple checksum can really only reliably detect one error) and also to correct simple errors.[21] Developed to ensure the integrity of the message due to electronic failure, these techniques can also be used to detect tampering (also see "RAID", later).

A full-file checksum is commonly used to ensure the reliable transmission of the file (e.g. from memory stick to PC) and is calculated using a hashing function. *"The most common checksums are MD5 and SHA-1, but both have been found to have vulnerabilities. This means that malicious tampering can lead to two different files having the same computed hash. Due to these security concerns, the newer SHA-2 is considered the best cryptographic hash function since no attack has been demonstrated on it as of yet."*[xxxi] A checksum is calculated by the transmitting (or source) system prior to transmission and also by the receiving (or destination) system after receipt and then compared. If they are the same, then the file is presumed to have been transferred without corruption.

Digital signatures verify where the information received is from. They use a similar asymmetric cryptography technique to PGP, in that a message is signed (encrypted) using a public key and verified (decrypted) using a private key. A more complex version also uses the message, thereby demonstrating (in a similar fashion to checksums) that the message has not been altered. A valid digital signature provides three things: a reason to believe that the message was created by a known sender, that the sender cannot deny having sent the message, and that the message was not altered in transit.

Digital signatures are commonly used for software distribution, financial transactions, contract management software, and in other cases where it is important to detect forgery or tampering. They are also often used to implement electronic signatures. "Electronic signature" is a broader term that refers to any electronic data that carries the intent of a signature,

---

19. It is not worth beginning to speculate on how a mathematician discovering a fast factorization method may affect global security.
20. See also "Public and Private Key Encryption" in Chapter 10.
21. Hamming codes, for example.

FIG. 8.1 Access control under Windows 10.

but not all electronic signatures use digital signatures. In many countries, including the United States, Algeria, Turkey, India, Brazil, Indonesia, Mexico, Saudi Arabia, Uruguay, Switzerland and the European Union, electronic signatures have legal significance.

In the UK, the **Electronic Prescription Service** (EPS) implements an electronic signature via a smartcard, thus guaranteeing that the electronic prescription has been appropriately authorized.

Access control

We now consider access controls on a server. There are two methods to consider here: direct (shared filesystem) and remote (or terminal). Both require a system of authentication. Some of these methods will be under the control of corporate IT and some under the control of Clinical Engineering.

For filesystem access (such as to a shared folder[22]) the server administrator will grant permission for the folder (and subfolders) to be accessed by specific users. This may be individually, or by groups. The latter is simpler to maintain, but takes longer to set up. A mixture of methods is possible. Permissions on a folder include permission to read, to write, to delete and to create/delete subfolders — all of which may be granted or denied individually. It is also possible to grant/deny these permissions on individual files. Where this is not done, files inherit the permissions of the folder they are contained in. An example of the control interface that an administrator might use is shown in Fig. 8.1.

Direct access will usually be achieved by mounting the server's shared folder as a remote folder on the accessing device (that is, make the remote folder appear as though it is part of the local filesystem). If there are insufficient privileges, then mounting will fail.

Remote access may be required by system suppliers, to assist with Medical Device management, or to give departmental staff access to systems from outside the work environment. Such access must be carefully controlled and the use of **Virtual Private Networks** (VPNs) to assure encrypted security is recommended. Used for these purposes the corporate IT department will manage the server facility. In general, remote access is achieved through a separate program, such as Telnet, **Secure Socket Layer** (SSL) or **Remote Desktop Protocol** (RDP). For all of these, the server must be configured to

---

22. Or directory, on UNIX and Linux servers.

accept such connections and will need to be verified via a username/password combination. Additionally, any firewalls along the route must be configured to allow such access. Telnet is the most trusting of the three and SSL the most secure, but once they are set up the experience of using them is very similar.[23]

Other access problems arise in segregating clinical Medical devices, such as radiotherapy machines and their networks. The use of VLANs on the corporate network is a valuable tool here and can be more convenient than using separate networks and bridges. In handling research data both VLANs and VPNs can make significant contributions to the provision of effective data access, where the use of VPNs to separate responsibilities (for which the crafting of router rules is key) and the running of a research network where strong firewall rules enables some communication with the main IT network while keeping risk to the minimum.

Further access control is considered in Chapter 11 where we examine distributed applications via the Web.

The human factor

Finally, we consider the security of the data itself. **Data Loss Prevention** (DLP) is of particular interest to NHS organizations as the movement and transfer of patient-identifiable data is tightly controlled (see "Caldicott", above). DLP may take many forms: system-wide policies[24] can be applied in which no data can be written to removable devices (or restricted to encrypted ones); emails may be examined to determine if they contain patient-identifiable information (usually via keyword searches); all emails to non-NHS addresses may be encrypted on departure; firewall rules may permit data to be sent from certain devices only at specified times. Sadly, the most common cause of data loss in the NHS is human error. Technology merely reduces this.

One useful such technology is the NHSmail service, which is a secure service. It is authorized for sending sensitive information, such as clinical data, between NHSmail and:

- NHSmail addresses (i.e. from an '.nhs.net' or '.hscic.gov.uk' account to an '.nhs.net' or '.hscic.gov.uk' account)
- Government secure email domains (between *.nhs.net and *.gsi.gov.uk, *.gse.gov.uk and *.gsx.gov.uk)
- Police National Network/Criminal Justice Services secure email domains (between *.nhs.net and *.pnn.police.uk, *.cjsm.net)
- Ministry of Defence secure email domains (*.mod.uk and *.mod.gov.uk).
- Local Government/Social Services secure email domains (*.nhs.net and *.gcsx.gov.uk)

  Sensitive data may be exchanged outside of the above secure domains, using the NHSmail encryption tool.

Server/database replication, backup, archiving, RAID, bandwidth and infrastructure

A reliable data centre, be it for a web presence, a clinical database or document repository requires resilience to be built into the design. As with security, there are many ways of achieving this and the best designs will incorporate a mixture of these. In this section we consider four such.

Replication

Replication, either of a server or a database (or both) is what the name implies: a copy exists of the server/data enabling it to be switched to in the event of a failure in the primary system. There are two main ways of achieving this, and the required uptime of the system determines which is the most appropriate. This will be determined by the business continuity process — how long the service can continue without the server/database. The simplest replication to achieve is a copy, taken at a specified time, to a secondary system. The two systems are therefore only ever briefly synchronized and in the event of a system failure bringing the secondary system on line means that the data will be at worst out-of-date by the time interval between copying. Replication of this form is usually overnight (thereby utilizing less busy periods for systems) meaning that the copy is at worst nearly 24 hours out-of-date. If changes to the system have been logged, then these may be run against the secondary system before bringing it on-line, but this will lengthen the time taken to do so.

The most common use of this form of replication is in data repositories (see "Links to Hospital Information Systems" for a description), thereby removing some of the workload from the primary system and improving its reliability (and response time). It also means that the secondary system is doing useful work while also on standby.

---

23. Although beware versions — you may have to set one tunnel up differently to another, depending on what is at the other end.
24. Security rules run at network level.

The second method of replication is synchronized: that is, both copies are exactly the same at all times. There are two primary ways of achieving this. The simplest is via a data splitter: all changes sent to the primary system are also sent to the secondary (we will cover this in HL7 for details on messaging). This is clearly the best method when the system receives changes via an interface (which may be from an input screen or from a medical device) as the primary system only has to process the incoming message and the work of replication is external to it (e.g. in an interface engine). The second is where every change to the primary system is transmitted to the secondary for it to implement, using a similar messaging protocol. This introduces a processing overhead on the primary system, especially if it has to also receive acknowledgement that the change has been applied to the secondary system. As this method introduces a messaging system, the system could instead be designed to use the first method described. If the organization already utilizes an interface engine, then this approach is strongly recommended.

The most basic (and therefore most common) method of replication, though, is the backup. This is simply a copy of the system (or a part of it) taken at a specified time, usually onto removable media (for high volumes, this is usually tape so our descriptions will use this, although other media may be substituted). As such backups are generally out-of-hours and unattended, systems that exceed the capacity of the media are backed up in portions, a different portion each night.

Whilst a backup enables a quick restore of lost or corrupted data (and simplifies system rebuilds in the case of major failure — see "WannaCry" above for an example), data errors are usually not so swiftly noticed and may therefore also exist on the backup. The **Grandfather-Father-Son** (GFS) backup rotation system was developed to reduce the effect of such errors. In this, three tapes are deployed: on day one, tape 1 is used. On day 2, tape 2 is used and on day 3 tape 3 is used. On day 4 tape 1 is re-used and so on, meaning that there are always three generations (hence the name) of backup. Most backup regimes are variants on the GFS scheme and may include a different tape for each day of the week, 52 tapes (e.g. every Wednesday) also rotated or 12 tapes (e.g. every first Wednesday). In this way data errors tracing back as far as a year may be corrected.

Archiving

Despite the massive increases in storage capacity in recent years, medical imaging has also advanced and thus produces even larger data sets. It has been estimated that 80% of PACS (**Picture Archiving And Communications System**) images are never viewed again. However, as a reliable method for identifying those 80% has not yet been achieved, all images must be kept, but keeping them online (on expensive storage) is not a sensible option. Thus old images are generally archived onto removable media (again, tape is usual) or onto a slower, less expensive system and the original data deleted to free up space.[25] There are several algorithms for identifying data suitable for archiving, but the most common is based on age: not the age of the data, but the time since it was last accessed. In order to implement such a system it is therefore imperative that each access updates the record, either in the database (for single items) or by the operating system (in the case of files).

Resilience using RAID

Probably the most common type of resilience, especially on a server, is **Redundant Array of Independent Discs** (RAIDs).[26] There are several forms of RAID and we consider two (levels 1 and 5) here. RAID level 1 is a simple disc image, as per replication above — only in real-time. The replication is handled by the RAID controller (a disc controller with additional functionality) which writes any information to both discs simultaneously. If one disc fails, then the other can be used to keep the system operational. The failed disc may then be replaced (often without halting the system — known as "hot swapping") and the RAID controller builds the new disc into a copy of the current primary over a period of time, depending on the amount of data held and the processing load.

Other forms of RAID do not replicate the data directly, but spread it across several discs instead, adding in some error correction as well. The form of spreading (known as "striping") and the type of error correction are different for each level of RAID.

RAID 5 uses block-level striping and parity data, spread across all discs in the array. In all disc storage, the disc is divided up into a set of blocks, a block being the smallest unit of addressable storage. A file will therefore occupy at least one block, even if the file itself is only one byte in size. A read or write operation on a disc will thus read or write a set of

---

25. There may be several "layers" of such storage, each slower to access than the previous, eventually reaching a removable media layer.
26. "I" was originally rendered "Inexpensive", but as the technology became adopted the acronym shifted.

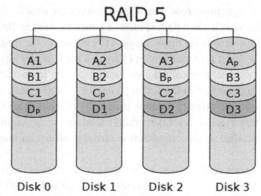

FIG. 8.2 Diagram of a RAID 5 setup.[xxxii] Each letter represents the group of blocks in the respective parity block (a stripe).

blocks. In RAID 5 these blocks are spread across several discs, with parity data stored on another one (see Fig. 8.2). Thus RAID 5 always requires a minimum of three discs to implement.

Parity, which we met in "encryption", is a computer science technique for reducing data corruption. It was originally designed for data transmission and consisted of adding an extra bit to the data.[27] This extra bit forced the sum of the bits to be odd (odd parity) or even (even parity). It was added at transmission and checked at reception (although this would only detect one error).[28] More complex forms used more bits which enabled the data not just to be better checked, but also to be corrected. Such codes are known as Hamming codes.[29] The parity used within RAID 5 not only checks that the data is correct, but enables it to be re-built, should a disc fail and have to be replaced.[30] A RAID controller is also able to recreate the missing data in real time, resulting in minimal degradation of service.

In the figure, the distribution of the blocks and the parity can clearly be seen. Distributing the parity blocks distributes the load across all the discs, as this is where bottlenecks may appear (to read blocks B3 to C1, for example, also requires two parity blocks to be read — in this case each disc only has one read operation to perform). RAID 5 has found favour as it is viewed as the best cost-effective option providing both good performance and good redundancy. As write operations can be slow, RAID 5 is a good choice for a database that is heavily read-oriented, such as image review or clinical look-up.

As has been mentioned, a RAID controller can keep a system operational even when a disc has failed, so much so that users may not notice. It is therefore imperative to monitor such clusters as one failure may be easily fixed but two may be catastrophic.

Traditionally computer systems and servers have stored operating systems and data on their own dedicated disc drives. With the data requirements expanding it has now become more common to have separate large data stores using NAS or SAN technology. These differ in their network connectivity but both rely on RAID for resilience. NAS uses TCP/IP connections and SANs use Fibre Channel connections.

Bandwidth

Finally, for this section, we consider bandwidth. Bandwidth in a computer network sense is its transmission capacity, which (as it is a function of the speed of transmission) is usually expressed in **bits per second** (bps). The most common wired bandwidths are 1 Gbps (often called "Gigabit Ethernet"), 10 Mbps (standard Ethernet) and 100 Mbps (fast Ethernet). Wireless is generally slower — 802.11 g supports up to 54 Mbps, for example. Note that these are maximums and a wired network stands a better chance of providing the full bandwidth due to less interference. 802.11 g normally only provides 20 Mbps and the fastest current one — 802.11ac, operating in the 5 GHz band — has a theoretical bandwidth of 1300 Mbps but only provides 200 Mbps. 802.11ax[31] is due for release sometime in 2019 and claims a 4-times increase over 802.11ac. As bandwidth is actually the capacity, binding together several cables can increase the total bandwidth whilst not increasing the speed — although this would not normally be done in a departmental network, the point at which a hospital

---

27. An alternative was to use one of the 8 bits in each byte for parity. Hence ASCII only uses 7 bits and simple integers often only have a range of 0–127.
28. For a 7-digit binary number, 3 bits are required to check for all possible errors.
29. After Richard Hamming, who invented them in 1950.
30. Therefore a failed disc can be temporarily ignored as the data on it can be computed in real time by the RAID controller.
31. Also known as "Wi-Fi 6".

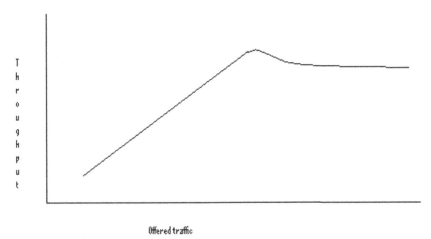

FIG. 8.3 A generalized throughput verses offered traffic curve showing a deterioration in performance when optimal levels are breached.

Throughput

Offered traffic

meets the national N3 network may be implemented this way (provided both sides of the connection can handle it — which is usually by routing pre-defined packets to specified lines, e.g. by IP address range).

It is never a good idea to reach 100% bandwidth utilization and the average in order to avoid this may be as low as 30%, although 50% would be more common (see Fig. 8.3). The amount of "spare" capacity is often termed "headroom". At 75% the throughput verses offered traffic curve starts to depart from a linear proportional increase of throughput for increase of offered traffic. At 80% the channel could be approaching overload. Much is dependent upon the traffic type — data traffic can cope with higher utilization levels than voice as delay and jitter have more effect on the user experience for voice traffic than data traffic. Optimization techniques such as **Quality-of-service** (QOS — a Cisco product) can be used to prioritize voice traffic (or any other traffic that is time-critical).

The above utilization levels are generally for non collision based channels. In the case of Ethernet which uses **Carrier Sense Multiple Access** (CSMAs)[32] with collision detection as the access mechanism, utilization should be much lower. An overdriven CSMA channel can result in a throughput reduction rather than an increase with increasing offered traffic. Retrys as a result of a collision lead to more retrys and more collisions and so on. Collision detection with a limitation on the number of retrys and a back off between the retrys is intended to keep the channel stable but throughput will tail off. Kleinrock[xxxiii] provides good further reading.

The use of different network transport protocols can also improve throughput. For example, Skype uses TCP for video (which guarantees delivery) and UDP for audio (which doesn't). On first inspection this appears to be the wrong way round, but TCP waits until a missed packet is delivered, whereas UDP just carries on. Thus the video freezes whereas the audio doesn't — a small glitch in the audio feed (50fps) is not going to be noticed.

All resilience methods require a level of redundancy: be it a copy, checksums or headroom. Thus a resilient system will always be over-engineered — in the case of bandwidth, over-engineering can remove the need for optimization systems such as QOS, thus making the design (and therefore the support) simpler.

Infrastructure

The core of modern hospital infrastructure is the supervised, air-conditioned server room, with redundant power supply provision. The users link to this facility by Ethernet and offsite electronic replication is likely. The bulk of the front line data storage will use SAN or NAS and racks of servers will often be running Virtual Systems. Clinical Scientist/Engineer user specialists will have remote administrator access to their systems. Critical Clinical Systems, such as Radiotherapy facilities will be likely to have some form of segregations, such as VLANs or firewalls. Virtual systems are particularly useful for enabling the local testing of commercial software upgrades, as it is relatively simple to destroy the server and re-create it. See Chapter 10 for a further discussion.

---

32. A protocol in which a node verifies the absence of other traffic before transmitting on a shared transmission medium.

Networking

Whilst a computer on its own is a powerful device, the possibilities and the power increase greatly when such devices are linked together to form a network. There are more aspects to networking that this chapter can contain, so we will only consider four here: the network packet, the three main components of a network, common topologies and the IP address.

The network packet

All networking is described in terms of packets. A network packet is a formatted unit of data carried by a packet-switched network. Computer communications links that do not support packets, such as traditional point-to-point telecommunications links, simply transmit data as a bit stream.

A packet consists of control information and user data, which is also known as the payload. Control information provides data for delivering the payload, for example: source and destination network addresses, error detection codes, and sequencing information. Typically, control information is found in packet headers and trailers.

Different communication protocols use different conventions for distinguishing between the elements and for formatting the data. For example, in Point-to-Point Protocol, the packet is formatted in 8-bit bytes, and special characters are used to delimit the different elements. Other protocols like Ethernet establish the start of the header and data elements by their location relative to the start of the packet. Some protocols format the information at bit level instead of at byte level.

A good analogy is to consider a packet to be like a letter: the header is like the envelope, and the data area is whatever the person puts inside the envelope.

The three main components of a network

The three main components are a hub, a switch and a router, which we will now examine.

A hub is a simple connection box. Like a transport hub, it's where everything comes together. Unlike a transport hub, though, whatever comes in on one connection goes out on all other connections. It's up to the receiver to decide whether or not the message is for them. Hubs therefore work well for small networks, but get messy and slow down for larger ones. It is therefore often common to find them in small networks (e.g. at home) or in sub-networks (e.g. in an office). Additionally, a 10/100 Mbps hub must share its bandwidth across each and every one of its ports. So when only one device is broadcasting, it will have access to the maximum available bandwidth. If, however, multiple devices are broadcasting, then that bandwidth will need to be divided among all of those systems, which will degrade performance.

A switch is a device that filters and forwards packets between **Local Area Network** (LAN) segments. Switches support any packet protocol. LANs that use switches to join segments are called switched LANs or, in the case of Ethernet networks, switched Ethernet LANs (as you might expect). A switch keeps a record of the **Media Access Control** (MAC) addresses of all the devices connected to it. With this information, a switch can identify which system is sitting on which port, thus only sending incoming data out on the correct port. And, unlike a hub, a 10/100 Mbps switch will allocate a full 10/100 Mbps to each of its ports. So regardless of the number of devices transmitting, users will always have access to the maximum amount of bandwidth. For these reasons a switch is considered to be a much better choice than a hub in many situations. Both hubs and switches may be referred to as "bridges".

A router forwards data packets along networks. A router is connected to at least two networks[33] and is located at a gateway, the place where two or more networks connect. Routers use headers and forwarding tables to determine the best path for forwarding the packets, and they use protocols such as **Internet Control Message Protocol** (ICMP) to communicate with each other and configure the best route between any two hosts. A router's job, as its name implies, is to route packets to other networks until that packet ultimately reaches its destination. One of the key features of a packet is that it not only contains data, but the destination address of where it's going.

So, in summary, a hub glues together an Ethernet network segment, a switch can connect multiple Ethernet segments more efficiently and a router can do those functions plus route TCP/IP packets between multiple LANs and/or WANs; and much more. It may seem that routers are therefore significantly better than bridges for connecting parts of a network together. However, bridges pass all network traffic whereas routers only handle directed traffic. Network wide broadcasts are inherently local in scope which means that they are passed along by hubs and switches, but not by routers. The Windows "Network Neighborhood"[34] file and printer browsing depends upon network broadcasts to allow locally

---

33. Commonly two LANs or **Wide Area Networks** (WANs) or a LAN and its **Internet Service Provider** (ISP)'s network. For example, a home network and the Internet.
34. Updated to "My Network Places" from Windows 7 onwards.

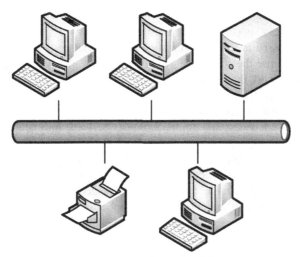

FIG. 8.4 Bus topology.[xxxiv]

connected machines to find each other on the LAN — these broadcasts therefore stop at the router, so placing a shared printer on the wrong side of a router is not only poor design, it also leads to significant user frustration.

Common network topologies

The topology of the network can be thought of as its shape. Not its physical shape, but its logical one: much like the London Underground map shows how stations connect, not where they are. The five basic topologies are bus, ring, star, tree and mesh, which we will now examine

Bus networks (Fig. 8.4) use a common backbone to connect all devices. A single cable, the backbone, functions as a shared communication medium that devices attach or tap into with an interface connector. A device wanting to communicate with another device on the network sends a broadcast message onto the wire that all other devices see, but only the intended recipient actually accepts and processes it.

Ethernet bus topologies are relatively easy to install and don't require much cabling compared to the alternatives. However, bus networks work best with a limited number of devices. If more than a few dozen computers are added to a network bus, performance problems will be the likely result. In addition, if the backbone cable fails, the entire network effectively becomes unusable

In a ring network (Fig. 8.5), every device has exactly two neighbours for communication purposes. All messages travel through a ring in the same direction (either "clockwise" or "anticlockwise"). A failure in any cable or device breaks the loop and can take down the entire network.

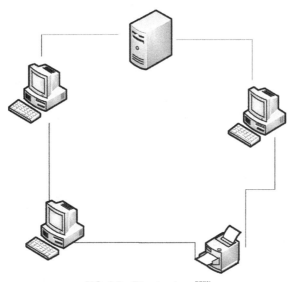

FIG. 8.5 Ring topology.[xxxv]

A common method for implementing a ring network is the "Token Ring". In this, a "token" is passed around the network. The device holding the "token" is permitted to transmit — nothing else is. If a device has nothing to transmit, it passes the token on. The token is passed in the same direction as the messages.

Most small (e.g. home) networks use the star topology (Fig. 8.6). A star network features a central connection point called a "hub node" that may be a network hub, switch or (more likely) a router. Devices typically connect to the hub with **Unshielded Twisted Pair** (UTP) Ethernet.

Compared to the bus topology, a star network generally requires more cable, but a failure in any star network cable will only take down one computer's network access and not the entire LAN (If the hub fails, however, the entire network also fails).

Tree topologies (Fig. 8.7) integrate multiple star topologies together onto a bus. In its simplest form, only hub devices connect directly to the tree bus, and each hub functions as the root of a tree of devices. This bus/star hybrid approach supports future expandability of the network much better than a bus (which is limited in the number of devices due to the broadcast traffic it generates) or a star (which is limited by the number of hub connection points) alone.

Mesh topologies involve the concept of routes. Unlike each of the previous topologies, messages sent on a mesh network can take any of several possible paths from source to destination. (Recall that even in a ring, although two cable paths exist, messages can only travel in one direction.) Some WANs, most notably the Internet, employ mesh routing, specifically for the resilience that it brings.

A mesh network in which every device connects to every other is called a full mesh. As shown in Fig. 8.8, partial mesh networks also exist in which some devices connect only indirectly to others.

The IP address

People prefer to communicate using names. Therefore we call our devices "Linac B PC", "Endoscopy control" and so on. Computers however prefer numbers. When they're communicating, they require unique numbers. Therefore they use **Internet Protocol** (IP) addresses. An IP version 4 address is formed of 4 groups of digits, separated by dots. Each group of digits can range in value from 0 to 255—256 unique numbers (2^8). The combination of these 4 groups should uniquely identify the device on the network.

In order to call our devices by names, a network service called a **Domain Name Service** (DNS) is usually available to translate "LinacA" into 123.45.67.89 so that the command "ping LinacA" (a command that sends an "are you there" message) can be issued and a reply can come from 123.45.67.89 without the user having to know the IP address of LinacA.

Standard IP addresses allow for 4,294,967,296 (256^4) unique addresses but there are many ways to extend this, of which **Network Address Translation** (NAT) and IP masquerading are probably the most common. It seems like a large number, but with a world population running at 7 billion, that's only 0.5 IP addresses each.

IP masquerading is a technique that hides an IP address space (e.g. your home network) behind a single (public) IP address. The outgoing address thus appears as though it has originated from the router, which must also do the reverse mapping when replies are received. The prevalence of IP masquerading is largely due to the limitations of the range of IPv4 addresses and the term NAT has become virtually synonymous with it.

IPv6, launched in 2011, provides for (2^{96}) unique addresses. Uptake has been slow but most operating systems and most major UK ISPs now support it. It is beyond the scope of this chapter to discuss in more detail but is worth noting that ISPs provide links between users on the two systems.

Information Governance

Information Governance (IG) is the function of corporate governance that ensures the confidentiality, integrity and availability of an organization's information assets. There is a range of complex legal and professional obligations that limit, prohibit or set conditions in respect of the management, use and disclosure of information and, similarly, a range of statutes that permit or require information to be used or disclosed. There is a full set of legislation, standards, codes of conduct and guidelines in "NHS Information Governance — Guidance on Legal and Professional Obligations" (available on the Department of Health and Social Care web site[xxxix]).

IG is achieved through a mix of policy and protocol. It is not unusual for IG policies to form part of an employee's contract. The major tension in IG for Healthcare (and arguably any organization) is between openness and confidentiality. Too confidential (restrictive) and the delivery of healthcare suffers; too open and patient confidentiality suffers (so might the financial integrity of the organization which in turn would impact upon healthcare delivery: thus an imbalance results in reduced healthcare, whichever way the imbalance lies). There is also the tension of the adoption of leading edge

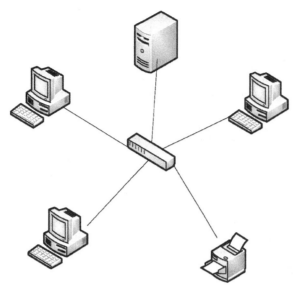

FIG. 8.6 Star topology.[xxxvi]

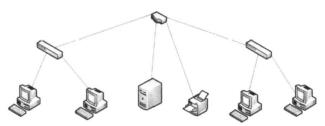

FIG. 8.7 Tree topology.[xxxvii]

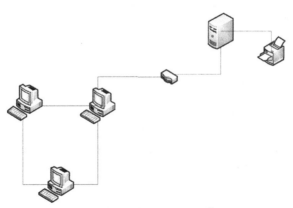

FIG. 8.8 Mesh topology.[xxxviii]

technology without introducing unacceptable levels of risk — the protocols must be open enough to permit this advance, whilst being restrictive enough to prevent breaches.

IG protocols need to recognize the need to share information between health organizations and other agencies in a controlled manner consistent with the interests of the patient (and in some circumstances, the public interest). Underpinning this is the need for electronic and paper information to be accurate, relevant, and available when required and processed appropriately.

It is impossible to create policies which achieve complete restriction and complete openness. Therefore a large element of IG is in risk reduction: a pragmatic approach to ensuring the organization can function and develop, without leaving it open to damage.

IG polices will cover all "Information Assets" which include all information and data held by the organization, whether held electronically or in manual, paper based systems and all information processing/computer systems and networks owned or operated by the organization including all systems operated on behalf of it by third parties and those entrusted to it by third parties.

All organizations will have an IG manager/officer/director who will have top-level (e.g. Executive Board) influence and authority. It is their responsibility to interpret legislation, devise the organization's implementation of this and to advise and rule on risk.

Two systems are required to implement IG: Firstly, in order to monitor compliance, an organization should have a reporting mechanism for incidents and this will most likely be as a part of an existing incident reporting system. Secondly, an Information Asset's inability to comply fully with policies and procedures does not necessarily mean it cannot be deployed. However, it must be fully risk assessed and entered onto a risk register in order to do so.

Information Governance may include computer forensic readiness, which is the ability of an organization to maximize its potential to use digital evidence whilst minimizing the costs of an investigation. This is normally utilized after an incident (criminal or otherwise) and may involve log files, emails, back-ups etc. Which therefore need to be retrievable in a suitable interpretable format.

Part of the restriction IG implements comes under the heading "data security" and the NHS has adopted the BS ISO 27000 series of Information Security Standards[xl,xli,xlii] which address this. Data security addresses:

- the physical security for data centres and communication/hub rooms
- technical measures/standards to achieve appropriate access control (e.g. password complexity and expiry)
- standards for the development of software
- standards for the procurement of software
- disaster recovery/business continuity standards
- technical standards and process to prevent malicious code attack (e.g. intrusion detection systems and anti-virus)
- standards for technical documentation etc.

Whilst IG can at first appear to be a restrictive mechanism and the role of the IG Manager one of bottleneck or killjoy, if implemented properly with all aspects of the organization's activities considered, it can assist in releasing information, especially for research purposes. As such it should be regarded more as an enabler (by doing things properly and efficiently) than a disabler.

Data exchange protocols

Data exchange standards — digital imaging and communications in medicine (DICOM) and healthcare level 7 (HL7)

Introduction

We have now considered legislation and data protection. To make clinical computing work we also need to deal with protocols and standards surrounding data communication and exchange. In order for computer systems to be able to process data produced by other systems, a data standard must be agreed. Even in proprietary systems from the same manufacturer, the format of the data has to be consistent so that different modules can access that data and understand its meaning. We will consider structured data later in the section on Databases in Chapter 9, but a few concepts require consideration here.

The simplest form of this is *positional meaning*. In this standard, the data will always consist of the same items in the same order (and each item may be of a fixed length). For example, the data below may be converted for transmission to an external system via the process shown in Figs. 8.9—8.11.

The items in the first row are field names (but may also be thought of as column headings). The field sizes should be defined as per Fig. 8.10.

The data record string can then be defined, noting that unused characters are rendered with ^ and not as spaces, as these appear in the data itself as per Fig. 8.11.

Machine	Manufacturer	Model	IP address
Cardio 1	GE	Vivid T8	138.25.114.7
Urology 5	GE	Logiq F8	138.64.25.9
Vascular 3	Philips	Epiq 7	138.34.34.5
Breast 1	Siemens	Acuson S2000	138.17.19.21

FIG. 8.9 A set of ultrasound machine data, arranged in a table.

Machine	10
Manufacturer	7
Model	12
IP address	12

FIG. 8.10 The maximum length of the data in each field.

Cardio 1^^GE^^^^^^Vivid T8^^^^138.25.114.7Urology 5^GE^^^^^Logiq
F8^^^^138.64.25.9^Vascular 3PhilipsEpiq 7^^^^^^138.34.34.5^Breast
1^^SiemensAcuson S2000138.17.19.21

FIG. 8.11 The data converted into one long data stream.

Simplicity is the main advantage of this system for data sharing, so it is easy to implement. Limitations are also obvious: for example, consider adding just one field to the table, or increasing the length of a field. In order to overcome these, we might introduce a header to the data stream that describes the data that is to follow. Such a header might, for this example, be as shown in Fig. 8.12.

This header first states the number of items per record (and thus also the number of items in the header), then the name and length of each field in turn, all separated by a special character. Extensions to this to describe the type of data (numeric, currency, textual, boolean etc.) are also possible.[35]

Two particular standards for data exchange in the healthcare field concern image sharing and clinical data exchange. We will now consider these two in more detail.

Digital imaging and communications in medicine

The addition of a header solves the data length problem and the "new field" problem in our introductory example and can be seen to be very flexible. However, there are still proprietary elements to this data: specifically the construction of the header and the control character selected. It was to overcome such problems (and more besides) that the **American College of Radiologists** (ACRs) and the **National Electrical Manufacturers Association** (NEMA) proposed a standard. ACR/ NEMA 300 was published in 1985 and (after several revisions and additions) was re-named DICOM (**Digital Imaging and Communications in Medicine**) in 1993. DICOM specifies not only the file format but also a network communication protocol (based on TCP/IP) and a set of services. DICOM, as the name implies, is used extensively in digital imaging. Its initial success lead to extensions for some textual information exchange, such as worklists and then other specialized information, such as a Radiotherapy treatment plan data (DICOM-RT). Standardisation also addresses one additional problem: longevity. Data format standards ensure the data can still be read in many years' time, a key consideration for medical data.

The DICOM file format is based on data sets and embeds data such as the patient identifier into this, ensuring that the image cannot be separated from the patient to whom it belongs. A DICOM data object consists of multiple data elements, each of which is tagged[36] in order to describe the data it contains, such as Name, Date of Examination, etc. A tagged version of the example in Fig. 8.9 is shown in Figs. 8.13 and 8.14. It can be seen from this example that a tagged format is not suitable for data sets which are comprised of multiple rows, as the tags appear in each row and therefore are repeated throughout the data stream.

A DICOM data object contains only the one image element, although this may in turn be comprised of several frames. A DICOM data element consists of the tag, an optional value representation (the values for which are defined as part of the standard), the length of the data and the data itself. When a DICOM data object is exported as a DICOM file, several of the

---

35. The dBase 3 file format is a very good example.
36. Two very common tagged file formats in current use which may assist in the understanding of DICOM are TIFF and MP3.

```
4^Machine^10^Manufacturer^7^Model^12^IP address^12
```

FIG. 8.12   A header for the data stream in Fig. 8.11.

FIG. 8.13   The first two records of the data stream from Fig. 8.9, complete with header from Fig. 8.12.

```
4^Machine^10^Manufacturer^7^Model^12^IP address^12 Cardio
1^^GE^^^^^Vivid T8^^^^138.25.114.7Urology 5^GE^^^^^Logiq
F8^^^^138.64.25.9^
```

FIG. 8.14   The same data stream, in a tagged format. Note the "EOF" indicating the end of the stream. Also that the order of the fields is now unimportant as they are prefixed by their tag in all cases.

```
Machine^10^Cardio 1^^ Manufacturer^7^GE^^^^^ Model^12^Vivid T8^^^^ IP
address^12^138.25.114.7^Machine^10^Urology 5^ Manufacturer^7^GE^^^^^
Model^12^Logiq F8^^^^ IP address^12^138.64.25.9^EOF
```

key elements are formed into the header (although they do also exist within the object — they are purely copies), along with details of the generating application. This simplifies the import of objects as the entire object need not be read prior to storage.

DICOM information objects are definitions of the information to be exchanged. They are effectively templates into which a new image is placed. Each image type, and therefore information object, has specific characteristics — an MRI image requires different descriptors to an ultrasound image, for example. These information objects are identified by unique identifiers, which are registered by NEMA. An **Information Object Definition** (IOD) is an object-oriented abstract data model used to specify information about Real-World Objects. An IOD provides a common view of the information to be exchanged.

An IOD does not represent a specific instance of a Real-World Object, but rather a class of Real-World Objects which share the same properties. An IOD used to generally represent a single class of Real-World Objects is called a Normalized Information Object. An IOD which includes information about related Real-World Objects is called a Composite Information Object.

As mentioned above, DICOM also defines services. These are again defined in the standard, but include such as:

- Query/Retrieve
- Storage Commit
- Worklist management
- Print
- Verification

As there have been multiple versions of the DICOM standard and no application is required to implement the full standard (for example, a service may not be applicable to it) the "DICOM conformance statement" is an essential part of any system, describing the parts of DICOM that it implements (and to which version). Just as "runs on electricity" does not fully explain how to connect up a device, neither does "DICOM compliant".

DICOM is very useful for the exchange of a large quantity of data, such as a worklist or an image. It is not so useful, though, for exchanging incremental changes within a database. This case is very common in Healthcare where many clinical systems take a "feed" from the **Patient Administration System** (PAS) and return results to it. Here the PAS exchanges small changes such as date of appointment, time of arrival at reception etc., as well as large ones such as a new patient being registered (although, in a database of over a million patients this may also be considered "small").

HL7

Such incremental changes are achieved through a messaging interface and the most common standard adopted for these is HL7. HL7 is administered by Health Level Seven International,[xliii] a not-for-profit **American National Standards Institute** (ANSI)-accredited organization. Although HL7 develops conceptual standards, document standards and application standards, it is only the messaging standard that we will consider here.

Version 2 of HL7 was established in 1987 and went through various revisions (up to 2.7). Version 2 is backwards-compatible, in that a message that adheres to 2.3 is readable in a 2.6-compliant system.

Version 3 (the latest version) appeared in 2005 and, unlike v2, is based on a formal methodology (the **HL7 Development Framework**, or HDF) and object-oriented principles. The HDF *"documents the processes, tools, actors, rules, and artifacts relevant to development of all HL7 standard specifications, not just messaging.*[xliv]*"* As such it is largely **Universal Modelling Language** (UML) compliant, although there are currently exceptions.

The cornerstone of the HL7 v3 development process is the **Reference Information Model** (RIM). It is an object model created as part of the Version 3 methodology, consisting of a large pictorial representation of the clinical data. It explicitly represents the connections that exist between the information carried in the fields of HL7 messages.

An HL7 v3 message is based on an XML encoding syntax. As such it is far more versatile than v2, but with an attendant overhead. Due to the installed userbase of v2 and the difference in message structure, v3 is not yet in widespread use. A very good comparison of the two formats can be found on the Ringholm web site,[xlv] of which a small part is reproduced in Figs. 8.15 and 8.16.

A further layer of data exchange is **Cross-enterprise Document Sharing** (XDS) which allows structured data documents of any type to be shared across platforms. Key elements in this are the document source (e.g. a PAS), the document repository (a shared store) and the document registry (essentially an index on the documents). Because the data is structured, the registry is able to index not only the title or metadata from within a header, but the data contained within the document itself. This makes searching the registry more powerful. XDS is of particular interest in a healthcare setting where the source material may be produced from a large range of systems and devices (e.g. for a PACS or a PAS).

Links to hospital administration systems

Traditionally the major hospital information system in use was the PAS, handling all patient registrations, demographics, clinic appointments and admissions (planned and emergency). It will normally be regarded as the "gold standard" for data, holding the "most correct" version, especially the demographics and GP contact information. As systems evolve, they are now frequently replaced by **Electronic Patient Record** (EPR) systems, adding fuller medical records, including correspondence.

An EPR will have a heavy processing load. For this reason, it is common practice to have a second data repository which is a copy of the data, created via an overnight scheduled task. Reports may thereby be run against this data without incurring a performance hit on the main system. The data is at worst 24 hours out of date, but for most administrative reporting (as opposed to clinical reporting) this is acceptable. A notable exception is bed state reporting, which is therefore normally a feature of the main system.

The functionality of the EPR is greatly enhanced via interfaces to clinical systems. This will usually be via HL7 messages (see earlier) and may be outbound (where the data flow is from the EPR to the clinical system), inbound (the other direction) or two-way. Demographics are usually outbound, test results are usually inbound and bed state information may be two-way.

The most recent move in the UK has been towards an **Electronic Health Record System** (EHRS) which contains all the information in an EPR but with additional data such as that from medical devices and specialized systems: it is a longitudinal record bringing together patient data such as demographics and medical history, treatment information, diagnostic information, operational information[37] and clinical care information. In doing so it provides a fuller picture of the patient pathway and provides opportunity for data mining such as operational and clinical analytics.

Interfaces and interface engines

An interface is a point where two systems, subjects, organizations, etc. meet and interact. In computing, an interface is a shared boundary across which two or more separate components of a computer system exchange information. The exchange can be between software, computer hardware, peripheral devices, humans or combinations of these. We can therefore see that there are several types of interface which we might be interested in:

- User interface, where the user interacts with the software.
- Hardware interface, where electronic components interact.
- Software interface, where software components, including operating systems, interact.
- Systems interface, where software systems interact in order to pass information (synchronization and interrogation).

---

37. In this case, appointments as opposed to surgery.

FIG. 8.15 A section of a HL7 v2.4 message, detailing the patient a test is for.

```
PID|||555-44-4444||EVERYWOMAN^EVE^E^^^^L|JONES|19620320|F|||153 FERNWOOD DR.^
^STATESVILLE^OH^35292||(206)3345232|(206)752-121||||AC555444444||67-
A4335^OH^20030520<cr>
```

FIG. 8.16 A similar section to the message in Figure 20, using HL7 v3.

```
<recordTarget>
  <patientClinical>
  <id root="2.16.840.1.113883.19.1122.5" extension="444-22-2222"
    assigningAuthorityName="GHH Lab Patient IDs"/>
  <statusCode code="active"/>
   <patientPerson>
    <name use="L">
      <given>Eve</given>
      <given>E</given>
      <family>Everywoman</family>
    </name>
    <asOtherIDs>
      <id extension="AC555444444" assigningAuthorityName="SSN"
        root="2.16.840.1.113883.4.1"/>
    </asOtherIDs>
   </patientPerson>
  </patientClinical>
</recordTarget>
```

As an EPR (and more so, an EHRS) will interface to many other systems, the use of an interface engine is usual. This may be thought of as a sophisticated router, in that not only will it pass on the relevant messages to the appropriate systems, it can also process these messages, so that codes used by the EPR/EHRS may be converted into ones used by the downstream system. Examples of such processing that an interface engine would perform in order to ensure that the downstream system receives information in a form it can interpret are: postcode layout, date format and where a coding system, such as ethnic origin, may have more granularity on one system than on the other.

An interface engine will normally include a large cache, so that downstream systems that go offline (e.g. for upgrade work) are able to collect the relevant messages when they come back on line. Therefore acknowledgement messages form an important part of the interface engine protocol.

Co-ordination between CE and IT

As technology advances and more and more specialized devices become mainstream, there needs to be agreement between the device specialists (in the context of this book, Clinical Engineers) who are used to dealing with one-off and unusual scenarios and the technology generalists of an IT (or ICT) department who are responsible for the smooth running of ICT equipment and services across the entire enterprise.

Whilst there are some clear areas that fall under the jurisdiction of each group (Clinical Engineering should not be supporting the office functions, whereas ICT should not be updating medical devices) there will always be the devices that fall close to the boundary or, indeed, move across it (sometimes several times). Once agreement has been reached that ICT will not update medical devices and that CE will not modify a standard desktop PC or server without first prior discussion attention needs to be turned towards these "boundary devices". It is here that standards such as IEC 80001 come into play – a risk-based discussion with a focus on patient safety can normally establish the correct placement of responsibility. Collective policies on issues such as software, updates, supplier access and procurement strategy all fall comfortably within the scope of IEC 80001. The requirement is for all the corporate players to be co-operating.

Abbreviations

ACR — American College of Radiologists
AIMDD — Active Implantable Medical Devices Directive
ANSI — American National Standards Institute
bps — bits per second

CA	Competent Authorities
CIA	Confidentiality, Integrity and Access
CSMA	Carrier Sense Multiple Access
DDoS	Distributed Denial-of-Service
DCB	Data Coordination Board
DHSC	Department of Health and Social Care
DICOM	Digital Imaging and Communications in Medicine
DLP	Data Loss Prevention
DNS	Domain Name Service
DPA	Data Protection Act
EFTA	European Free Trade Association
EHRS	Electronic Health Record System
EPR	Electronic Patient Record
EPS	Electronic Prescription Service
EU	European Union
EU GDPR	see GDPR
FDA	The Food and Drink Administration
FOI	Freedom of Information Act
GDPR	(European Union) General Data Protection Regulation
GFS	Grandfather-Father-Son
HDF	HL7 Development Framework
HIE	health institution exemption
HUD	Humanitarian Use Devices
ICMP	Internet Control Message Protocol
ICO	Information Commissioner's Office
IG	Information Governance
IOD	Information Object Definition
IP	Internet Protocol
ISP	Internet Service Provider
IVD	In-Vitro Diagnostics
LAN	Local Area Network
MAC	Media Access Control
MDD	Medical Devices Directive
MDR	Medical Devices Regulation (The EU Regulation on Medical Devices, 2017/745)
MHRA	Medicines and Healthcare products Regulatory Agency
NAT	Network Address Translation
NB	Notified Bodies
NDG	National Data Guardian for Health and Care
NEMA	National Electrical Manufacturers Association
NICE	The National Institute for Health and Clinical Excellence
PACS	Picture Archiving And Communications System
PAS	Patient Administration System
PGP	Pretty Good Privacy
PIP	Poly Implant Prosthesis
PMA	Premarket Approval
QMS	Quality Management System
QOS	Quality-of-service
RAID	Redundant Array of Independent/Inexpensive Discs
RDP	Remote Desktop Protocol
RIM	Reference Information Model
RSA	Rivest, Shamir and Adelman
SMB	Server Message Block
SOUP	Software of Unknown Provenance
UML	Universal Modelling Language
UTP	Unshielded Twisted Pair
VPN	Virtual Private Network
WAN	Wide Area Network
XDS	Cross-enterprise Document Sharing

Endnotes

i   https://www.gov.uk/government/organisations/medicines-and-healthcare-products-regulatory-agency/about.
ii   See endnote i.
iii   https://www.fda.gov/AboutFDA/WhatWeDo/default.htm.
iv   See endnote iii.
v   Sidebottom, C., Rudolph, H., Schmidt, M., Eisner, L., 2006. IEC 60601-1 — the third edition. J. Med. Device Regul. 8—17. Available from: http://www.eisnersafety.com/downloads/IEC60601-1_JMDRMay2006.pdf.
vi   The 'Blue Guide' on the Implementation of EU Product Rules 2016. Available from: http://ec.europa.eu/transparency/regdoc/rep/3/2016/EN/C-2016-1958-F1-EN-MAIN-PART-1.PDF.
vii   Off. J. Eur. Union L117. 60, May 5, 2017. Available from: http://eur-lex.europa.eu/legal-content/EN/TXT/?uri=OJ:L:2017:117:TOC.
viii   Loh, E., Boumans, R., May 2017. Understanding Europe's New Medical Devices Regulation. Emergo. Available from: https://www.emergogroup.com/resources/articles/whitepaper-understanding-europes-medical-devices-regulation.
ix   See endnote vii.
x   See endnote vii.
xi   See endnote vii.
xii   See endnote vii.
xiii   See endnote vii.
xiv   MEDDEV 2.1/6.
xv   https://www.gov.uk/government/organisations/medicines-and-healthcare-products-regulatory-agency.
xvi   https://www.iso.org/standard/44863.html.
xvii   MacMahona, S.T., Cooper, T., McCaffery, F., 2018. Revising IEC 80001-1: Risk management of health information technology systems. Compute. Stand. Interfac. 60, 67—72.
xviii   http://www.tickitplus.org/.
xix   https://digital.nhs.uk/services/solution-assurance/the-clinical-safety-team/clinical-safety-documentation.
xx   https://eur-lex.europa.eu/legal-content/EN/TXT/PDF/?uri=CELEX:32016R0679&from=EN.
xxi   https://ico.org.uk/for-organisations/guide-to-the-general-data-protection-regulation-gdpr/what-is-personal-data/what-is-personal-data/.
xxii   https://ico.org.uk/for-organisations/guide-to-the-general-data-protection-regulation-gdpr/principles/accuracy/.
xxiii   https://ico.org.uk/for-organisations/data-protection-reform/overview-of-the-gdpr/key-areas-to-consider/.
xxiv   https://www.hldataprotection.com/2016/01/articles/health-privacy-hipaa/the-final-gdpr-text-and-what-it-will-mean-for-health-data/.
xxv   https://ico.org.uk/for-organisations/guide-to-freedom-of-information/refusing-a-request/.
xxvi   https://www.gov.uk/government/uploads/system/uploads/attachment_data/file/192572/2900774_InfoGovernance_accv2.pdf.
xxvii   von Neumann, J., 1949. Theory and Organization of Complicated Automata. Institute for Advanced Study in Princeton, New Jersey.
xxviii   Clay Mathematics Institute, The RSA algorithm. Available from: http://www.claymath.org/posters/primes/rsa.php.
xxix   Milanov, E. The RSA Algorithm. Available from:https://sites.math.washington.edu/~morrow/336_09/papers/Yevgeny.pdf.
xxx   https://cs.stanford.edu/people/eroberts/courses/soco/projects/2004-05/cryptography/pgp.html.
xxxi   https://www.online-tech-tips.com/cool-websites/what-is-checksum/.
xxxii   Cburnett, 2006. Used under GNU License via Wikimedia Commons.
xxxiii   Kleinrock, L., 2011. Queuing Systems, vols. 1—3. John Wiley & Sons.
xxxiv   Ganney, P., Maw, P., White, M., 2018. In: Ganney, R. (Ed.) Modernising Scientific Careers the ICT Competencies. UCLH Medical Physics.
xxxv   See endnote xxxiv.
xxxvi   See endnote xxxiv.
xxxviii See endnote xxxiv.
xxxix   https://www.gov.uk/government/publications/nhs-information-governance-legal-and-professional-obligations.
xl   BS ISO/IEC 27002:2013 Information Technology — Security Techniques — Code of Practice for Information Security Controls.
xli   BS ISO/IEC 27001:2013 Information Technology — Security Techniques — Information Security Management Systems — Requirements.
xlii   BS ISO/IEC 27005:2011 Information Technology — Security Techniques — Information Security Risk Management.
xliii   www.hl7.org,.or.www.hl7.org.uk for the UK version.
xliv   HL7 Development Framework Project, Project Charter, HL7 2002.
xlv   http://www.ringholm.de/docs/04300_en.htm.

Chapter 9

Software engineering

Paul S. Ganney[a,b], Sandhya Pisharody[c] and Edwin Claridge[d]

[a]University College London Hospitals NHS Trust, London, United Kingdom; [b]University of Liverpool, Liverpool, United Kingdom; [c]Varian Medical Systems, Crawley, United Kingdom; [d]University Hospitals Birmingham NHS Trust, Birmingham, United Kingdom

Chapter outline

Software development and management

Operation systems

Having covered significant governance and general hardware issues we can now turn our attention to software. This is executed under the control of a software **operating system** (OS) and for completeness we should first give a brief review of the ones that we commonly encounter. An OS is a very complex piece of software that interfaces directly with the hardware upon which it is running: all user software runs under the OS and will call routines within the OS in order to achieve hardware effects, such as displaying information (on screen, printer or other display device), receiving input (from keyboard, mouse, graphics tablet, touch screen etc.) and reading from or writing to storage (hard discs, RAM drives, tape systems or network-based storage[1]). The first three introduced here are all multi-user, multi-tasking OSs which is why they

---

1. These are, of course, simply the same types of storage only differently attached. It has often been said that "the cloud" is simply someone else's computer.

are to be found on servers as well as end-user machines, with the fourth appearing more commonly in healthcare over the last decade but mainly as an end-user system.

Microsoft windows

There are two families of this OS: end-user (currently Windows 10) and server (normally dated and currently Windows Server 2019 (Long-Term Servicing Channel)). A developing trend is to offer cloud services; these can cover **Infra-structure as a Service** (IaaS) or **Software as a Service** (SaaS). There is also a move towards subscription services rather than OS and applications purchase.

Windows offers a graphical user interface, employing the WIMP (**Windows, Icons, Mouse**,[2] **Pointer**) paradigm pioneered by Xerox and brought into popularity by Apple and Atari. It is an event-driven OS, in that events are generated (e.g. by a mouse click, a keyboard press, a timer or a USB device insertion) and these are offered by the OS to the programs and processes that are currently running (including itself) for processing. For this reason a program may not necessarily cancel just because a user has clicked on a button labelled "Cancel" — the event will merely sit in a queue, awaiting processing.[3]

Windows has gained great popularity, partly because of its relative openness for developers (compared to, say, Apple) but mostly due to its common user interface: similarly displayed buttons and icons perform similar functions across programs (e.g. the floppy disc icon for saving — even though the program is unlikely to be saving to a floppy disc) and almost-universal keyboard shortcuts (e.g. Ctrl-C for "copy"). This makes the learning of new programs easier and more intuitive. It is also a demonstration of one of the many benefits of adhering to a standard.

Windows is most likely to be found running desktop end-user machines, departmental servers and (in its embedded form) medical devices.

Unix

Unix is also a family of OSs (such as Unix 98, Posix and SunOS) and may run on end-user machines as well as on servers. However, it is on the latter that it is now most prevalent, due to its robust stability. Whilst there are graphical user interfaces, it is most commonly accessed through a command-line interface, a "shell" (such as Bourne or C) that accepts certain commands (usually programs in their own right rather than embedded into the OS) and logic flow. Originally developed for dumb-terminal access (where all the user has is a keyboard and VDU, the processing taking place on the server) it can therefore be accessed easily via a terminal emulator on any end-user machine (e.g. a Windows PC or an Android phone).

A key concept in Unix is that of the pipe. In this, the output of one program can be "piped" as the input to the next in a chain, thereby producing complex processing from a set of relatively simple commands. For example,

ls -al | grep 'd'

This command takes the output of the "ls -al" command (which lists all the files in the current directory) and pipes it into the "grep 'd'" command which only displays those lines beginning with the letter d. These piped commands therefore list only the sub-directories of the current directory. This facility is used throughout the OS, so that text is piped to printers and files to storage.

This example also introduces another key concept of Unix — that of regular expressions,[4] a simple example of which might be "organi[sz]e" in a text search, which would match both spellings of the word (i.e. "organise" and "organize").

Unix is generally seen as an "expensive" OS, which is one of the reasons it is less likely to be found on end-user machines.

Unix is most likely to be found running departmental and critical enterprise servers.

Linux

Linux was developed as an open-source variant of Unix by Linus Torvalds. It gained rapidly in popularity in that, due to its open-source nature, developers are able to access the source code to the OS and produce new versions of the programs within it, thereby expanding functionality and correcting errors. The caveat is that this new version must also be freely

---

2. Some variants interpret "M" as "menus" and "P" as "pull-down menus.
3. Therefore well-written code will frequently "peek" the event queue for such an occurrence.
4. Regular expressions pre-date Unix, but the syntax defined in Unix is now the most widely used.

available, with source code, to anyone who wishes to use it. There are therefore various different versions (referred to as "flavours") of Linux, such as Ubuntu and openSUSE.

As with Unix, Linux is mostly command-line, yet graphical user interfaces not only exist but have increased in power and usability over the last decade and (as the cost pressure does not exist) are now more likely to be found on end-user machines. The low processing overhead (compared to Windows, for example) has led to the introduction of cheap yet powerful systems, such as the Raspberry Pi, which has seen Linux systems appearing in many areas of healthcare.

Linux is most likely to be found running desktop end-user research machines, departmental servers and especially web servers.

iOS/macOS

iOS and macOS are OSs created and developed by Apple Inc. exclusively for its hardware. iOs is the mobile version (powering devices such as iPhone, iPad[5] and iPod) with macOS found on devices such as iMac and MacBook. They are very similar in terms of user experience, meaning that moving from one Apple device to another is very intuitive, once the first has been mastered (see the comment on Microsoft and standards, above).

Whereas macOS uses fairly traditional input devices (such as keyboard and mouse), the iOS user interface is based upon direct manipulation, using multi-touch gestures. Gestures such as swipe, tap, pinch, and reverse pinch all have specific definitions within the context of the iOS OS and its multi-touch interface.

The tight development relationship between the hardware and software (compared to Linux which is designed to run on a vast range of hardware) means that both benefit from optimisations.

iOS is most likely to be found in mobile healthcare settings (such as clinical record taking) whereas macOS is more found in graphics-heavy settings, such as image processing. They are more likely to be end-user machines than servers.

Language selection

There are many factors which influence the selection of a programming language with which to tackle a specific problem. Below are listed 9 criteria for consideration (although see Table 9.1 for a different take on this). The key consideration (repeated often in this list) is of maintainability of the produced code. It is tempting to think that code is written once and that the stable system never requires re-working. Whilst true of some projects, it is not true of the majority.

1. Ease of learning. Does the project timescale provide sufficient time for the programmer to attain the required level of competence?
2. Ease of understanding. Whilst a language will be learned once, the code produced will be read many times (especially during de-bugging). If the code statements are very complex then code maintenance becomes problematic. This can be mitigated to an extent by documentation, especially in-code comments.[6]
3. Enforcement of correct code. Development is frequently time-pressured and there is always a temptation to write "quick and dirty" code and "tidy it up later". It is possible to write good, well-structured code in every programming language. One that forces good practice (e.g. variable typing) produces code that is easier to maintain.
4. Productivity of the language. All development systems contain tools to increase the programmer's productivity. These include the IDE (**Integrated Development Environment**), the debugger and libraries (for example, to provide DICOM support).
5. The availability of peer support, both inside and outside of the organisation/department (e.g. Internet forums). Whilst programming can be a very solitary activity, someone who knows how to implement a poorly-documented feature is worth a hundred textbooks.
6. Applicability to the problem domain (e.g. writing a device driver in a scripting language is a poor choice).
7. Performance of the compiled code. Whilst computing power is always increasing, some projects still require more: hardware acceleration (for example in a graphics card) or the use of a low-level language may provide better speed.
8. Platforms. If the solution is only ever required for one platform, then the language should be chosen accordingly. Likewise, if multiple platforms are required, then a cross-platform language such as Java is required.
9. Portability. If the base platform changes, how portable is the code? How portable does it have to be?

---

5. In 2019 iOS for iPad became iPadOS and at this point the OSs diverged.,
6. See the discussion on comments in the section "Software coding and coding management" in this chapter.

TABLE 9.1 Ratings of SASEA (selecting appropriate software engineering assets) language characteristics. The specific problem provides the weights, from which the rest of the table is completed.

Language	SQL	C++	Fortran	Java	Assembly
Language characteristic					
Clarity of source code	5	6	5	8	1
Maintainability	5	7	2	9	0
Object-oriented programming support	0	10	0	10	0
Portability	1	7	3	9	1
Reliability	3	5	1	8	0
Reusability	1	8	3	8	1
Safety	0	3	0	4	0
Standardization	1	5	5	8	0

Extracted from Lawlis, P.K., 1997. Guidelines for Choosing a Computer Language: Support for the Visionary Organization. Available from: http://archive.adaic.com/docs/reports/lawlis/content.htm – a full table with explanations is available at the referred website.

There are formalised methods for selecting a language, by listing the attributes of each and weighting them in importance.[7] Each weight is multiplied by the score for that attribute for each language and summed. The final score then indicates the language that should be used. A sample of such scoring is in Table 9.1.

Finally, we consider mixed-language projects. These are often found in large software projects, where layers (or components) of the project are written in different languages in order to take advantage of the features (thereby implementing point 4 above). Another reason is when components for the project already exist and are being re-used (either from in-house development or purchased modules/components).

In this case, the primary language chosen for the project will be the interface between these components, ensuring that the system operates safely and efficiently. Once this language has been selected, it may be appropriate to develop new code in it also.

Mixing languages is never as straightforward as using just one language and it may prove simpler to redevelop the paradigms of one component into another language (thereby enforcing point 9 above).

One major exception to this is, of course, web development: it is not at all unusual (and indeed satisfies many of the criteria listed above) for each component of the web site to be written in a language optimised for the function that it is performing. Perl may be utilised for the front-end gathering of data, C++ for the back-end processing of that data (with SQL for any database functions required) and JavaScript (with a library such as Chart.js) for the data display. Such an approach may also be able to re-use code from other projects and maximise the use of in-house expertise in the different environments.

Software coding and coding management

There isn't enough room in this section to completely describe the art of Computer Programming – indeed, Donald Knuth devoted several large volumes to it (Knuth, 2011).[8] What we will consider here are instead those elements of software coding that are to be found in most high-level (and in some cases low-level) languages. Illustrations will be provided in several languages. Additional examples can be found in a later section, "procedural, object-oriented and functional programming" and in the section on "web programming" in the next chapter.

The first thing that any program requires is somewhere to store variables, whose values may change during execution. The base types are usually numbers (integers, text, booleans) but from these bases more complex types can be built (see the section on "Object-Oriented programming" in this chapter for examples). Some languages require this storage to be declared prior to use (e.g. C), whereas others (e.g. shell script) allow declaration at use. The naming of variables may be

---

7. Weights are from 1 to 10, attributes from 0 (no support) to 10 (full support).

8. His planned 7-volume opus on the topic saw the first 3 published in 1968–1973 with volume 4A appearing in 2011 and 4B is expected to appear in sections from 2019 onwards.

prescribed by the language (e.g. in some forms of BASIC a variable ending in "$" is of type text; in FORTRAN variables whose names start with a letter between I and N are integers; in M (formerly MUMPS) variables prefixed with "^" indicate disc (permanent) storage). The most common form of variable naming is what is known as "Hungarian notation"[9] where the variable name (starting with a capital letter) is prefixed with lower case letter(s) that denote its type, e.g. nTotal is numeric, sName is string (text) and bCapsLockOn is boolean.

Assigning values to variables is generally accomplished using the "=" operator, although Algol 68 used ":=" in order to distinguish assignment from comparison (see later). More complex variable types may use a "set" operator so that multiple values can be assigned at once to a single variable.[10]

All languages contain key words which are part of it and form instructions. These are called "reserved words" and cannot be used as variable names (although they can be used as part of a name, e.g. "If" is a reserved word so cannot be used as a variable name, whereas "IfPrinting" is an acceptable name — although "bIfPrinting" would be better).

The "intelligence" within software, though, is provided through the flow-of-control mechanisms. Through these mechanisms decisions are made and different algorithms invoked according to the current state of the variables. Simple flow control is achieved through the *if-then-else* mechanism. An example in **Visual Basic** (VB) would be:

```
If nMonth=9 or nMonth=4 or nMonth=6 or nMonth=11 Then
    nDays=30
ElseIf nMonth<>2 Then
    nDays=31
Else
    nDays=28[11]
End If
```

Note the use of "EndIf" to terminate the clause. The reserved word "Then" is optional, but does improve the readability of the code.

The other control mechanism we will consider is *switch*. This takes an input value and executes a clause corresponding to it. The above example might thus be rendered in C as:

```
switch (nMonth)
{
    case 9:
    case 4:
    case 6:
    case 11:
        nDays=30;
        break;
    case 2:
        nDays=28;
        break;
    default:
        nDays=31;
        break;
}
```

Note the use of "break" to indicate that processing should continue after the *switch* clause. It is therefore superfluous in the final "default" clause. Although it doesn't aid readability (or greatly reduce it) it is good practice as other "case" clauses can be added after it and it may thus prevent erroneous processing.

The other mechanism we shall consider here is repetition. The simplest of these is the *for-next* loop, such as this one in JavaScript, which generates the first 10 powers of 2:

---

9. Named after Charles Simonyi, a Hungarian employee at Microsoft who developed it. Hungarian names are, unusually for Europe, rendered surname first — i.e. family (type) name, followed by individual (specific) name.
10. See the date examples in the "object oriented programming" section in this chapter.
11. The special processing for leap years is left as an exercise, in this and all subsequent examples.

```
n=1;
for (i=0; i<10; i++)
{
    n=n*2;
    document.write ("2^" + i + " = " + n + ", ");
}
```

The *for* statement has three clauses: the starting condition (i=0), the continuing condition (i<10) and the iterative condition (i++ - i.e. i is increased by 1 on each circuit around the loop). Some languages (e.g. MATLAB) prefer to specify an end value instead of an end condition.

An alternative repetition is *while*. Whereas *for* executes the given code a set number of times (although there are alternatives in languages such as C), *while* executes the code until a condition is no longer true. Thus, to output powers of 2 that are less than 1 million, a C program might be[12]:

```
n=1;
i=0;
while (n<1000000)
{
    n*=2;
    i++;
    cout << "2^" << i << " = " << n << ", ";
}
```

The final item a language requires is a mechanism for input and output. In VB this is achieved through statements such as:

```
FileOpen (1, "PATIENTLIST", OpenMode.Input)
Input (1, sPatName)
Debug.WriteLine(sPatName)
```

Some languages use the same statements to input from the user as to input from a file, and to output to a file as to output to screen or printer. Whilst this aids the speed of learning the language, it does not assist code readability.[13]

Whilst all the above aid the development of computer programs, one common feature (sadly probably the poorest-used) greatly aids the maintenance of code: the comment. This is a piece of text which is ignored by the compiler/interpreter and plays no part whatsoever in the execution of the program. It does, however, carry information. There have been many attempts to codify the use of comments, from the simple "one comment every 10 lines of code" (resulting in useless comments such as "this is a comment" and failing to document more complex coding), to a more complex rigidly-defined comment block at the head of every subroutine describing variables used, the execution path and all revisions to the code since it was originally authored. An example for one of the routines above might be, in C:

```
/* *****************************************
Routine to calculate number of days in a month
Written: Paul Ganney, 10/5/85
Edit: Paul Ganney, 11/2/88 correction for leap years
Edit: Paul Ganney, 5/1/00 correction for 2000 not being a leap year

Inputs:
nMonth: month number (Jan=1, Dec=12)
nYear: year number as 4 digits

Outputs:
nDays: number of days in month

Execution: simple switch statement
*/[14]
```

---

12. Actually this code also outputs the first power of 2 over a million. It is left to the reader to correct this.
13. See "overloading" in the section on "object-oriented programming" in this chapter.
14. Note the use of /* and */ to denote the start and end of a comment block.

The most prevalent use of comments is probably as an aide-memoire to the programmer: if a line of code required great thought to create it, then it will probably require great thought in order to understand it when it requires modification — therefore any hints that the creator can leave are always welcome. This though, is insufficient when multiple programmers are working on a system at the same time and a solid commenting methodology should form part of the design. There are two useful rules of thumb: "you cannot have too many comments" and "there are not enough comments yet".

One approach to writing code is to first write pseudocode, which describes the logic/action to be performed but in a human-readable form. Converting this into comments means that the logic is preserved when the pseudocode is converted into actual code. Optimisations may therefore be written/introduced yet the logic is still clear.

As with any document, version control is vital in software development. There are two elements to this:

- Ensuring developers are all working on the latest version of the code.
- Ensuring users are all executing the latest version of the code.

There are multiple ways (and multiple products) to achieve this, so we will examine only one example of each.

A common code repository enables multi-programmer projects to be successfully developed. This repository allows all developers access to all the code (although some allow version locking). When a developer wishes to work on a piece of code, this is "checked out" and no other developer may then access the code for alteration until it is "checked in" again. Dependency analysis is then utilised to alert all developers to other code modules which depend upon the altered code and may therefore require revision or re-validation. Possibly the most commonly used repository is Git,[15] developed by Linus Torvalds while he was developing Linux. Unlike other **Version Control Systems** (VCSs), which log changes, Git stores snapshots of committed code. This means that rollback to a previous version is much simpler. GitHub is a commonly used online Git repository, for organisations who do not want to set up their own service.

In a database project (or any software that accesses a database, regardless of whether that is core functionality — and it is worth remembering that a password list is a simple database) it is possible to ensure that all users are using the latest version of the software by hard-coding the version into the source code and checking it against the version in the database. If the database has a later version number, then the program can alert the user, advising them to upgrade or even cease to progress (depending on the nature of the upgrade).

Open source software

There has been a lot of interest in the use of open source software and here we examine the issues surrounding the use of such software in a healthcare setting.

Open source software is software where the source code has been made available for inspection and modification. Such software is usually released under a licence allowing such modification, even for commercial gain, provided that the modified software is also provided complete with source code. Three of the most widely-used such pieces of software are the Linux OS, the Python programming language and the apache web server (on which most of the Internet's web services run).

Whilst a lot of open source software is free, it is not a requirement (otherwise "commercial gain" would not be possible). Open source software programs (whole systems or just modules) may come with a fee. Because an open source license usually requires the release of the source code when the software is sold,[16] some programmers/companies prefer to charge users for software services and support (rather than for the software itself).

Four common reasons for using open source software rather than proprietary software are:

- Control — it is possible to examine the code to ensure it functions exactly as required, removing unwanted features and modifying desired behaviour to be an even closer match to requirements.
- Training — as open source code is publicly accessible, programmers can study it in order to improve their own code.
- Security — open source software is often considered to be more secure and stable than proprietary software. As anyone can view and modify open source software, errors and omissions can be fixed, updated, and upgraded more quickly than proprietary software, due to the number of people using and inspecting the code.[17]
- Stability — as the source code for open source software is distributed with the product, users relying on that software for critical tasks can be more confident that their tools won't disappear or fall into disrepair. Additionally, open source software usually adheres to open standards.

---

15. Possibly because it is free and open source, as well as doing the job.
16. It is rare for this not to be the case.
17. Obviously this is truer of software such as Apache than more niche software, e.g. Fred's image inverter.

Two further concepts require clarification before we can examine the use of such software.

Firstly, **off-the-shelf** (OTS) software,[18] which is defined in an FDA guidance document as "*a generally available software component, used by a medical device manufacturer for which the manufacturer cannot claim complete software life cycle control*" (Off-the-Shelf Software Use in Medical Devices, 1999). There is a subset, **Commercial Off-The-Shelf Software** (COTS), which commands a fee.

Secondly, **Software Of Unknown Provenance** (SOUP), introduced in IEC 62304: 2006 and described as "*a software item that is already developed and generally available and that has not been developed for the purpose of being incorporated into the medical device (also known as "off-the-shelf software") or a software item previously developed for which adequate records of the development processes are not available*". This therefore effectively defines all OTS software as SOUP. The FDA/IEC definitions of OTS software and SOUP are roughly equivalent (thus reinforcing this view), although COTS is not necessarily SOUP (as you may know its provenance — see the comment on MATLAB below) and vice versa (as you may not have paid for it).

One key question over the use of open source software (and especially over whether or not the developer is responsible for quality assurance of the final system) is this: has the software been modified by the end user? If it is not, then the FDA guidance makes it clear that the medical device manufacturer assumes full responsibility for software assembled using third party components. Such software should thus be treated as SOUP and then IEC 62304: 2006 outlines a range of measures to ensure that such software is suitable for use in a safety related environment (Got SOUP? - Part 2: OS, drivers, runtimes, 2013). A system developed using a product such as MATLAB (see later for a fuller description of this product) is likely to be a series of pre-existing library routines, joined together via a user-written script, and thus falls into this category. Such products are often described as "Clear SOUP", where the supplier has made available the development methodology, as well as independent reports from standards auditing bodies — for example, MathWorks (MATLAB's owner) appreciates that this information might be required by developers using their software in a safety-related environment and so does exactly this (FDA Software Validation, 2017).

Software lifecycle

The lifecycle of a software system runs from the identification of a requirement until it is phased out, perhaps to be replaced by another. It defines the stages of software development and the order in which these stages are executed. The basic building blocks of all software lifecycle models include[19]:

1. Requirements Specification
2. Software design
3. Software Development and Coding
4. Software Testing
5. Software Maintenance

Each phase produces deliverables required by the next stage in the life cycle. Requirements are translated into design. Code is produced driven by the design. Testing verifies the deliverable of the coding stage against requirements. Tested software is installed and maintained for its lifespan. Maintenance requests may involve addition or revision to requirements and the cycle repeats (Fig. 9.1).

To see how software progresses through its lifecycle, let us consider an example wherein a need has been identified to develop software for recording training and competencies of staff within a department. In the following sub-sections, we'll look at what's involved at each stage of this software's lifecycle.

Requirements specification

This phase of the lifecycle identifies the problem to be solved and maps out in detail what the user requires. The problem may be to automate a user task, to improve efficiency or productivity within a user group, to correct shortcomings of existing software, to control a device, and many more. Requirements on software are usually a complex combination of requirements from a variety of users associated with a problem.

For our example, this would be staff as users who would enter their details, supervisors who might use the system to verify competencies and managers who would use it to ensure staff are competent for the tasks assigned.

---

18. Sometimes rendered OTSS to avoid ambiguity.
19. There are others, but these five are common to all and so we will focus on them here.

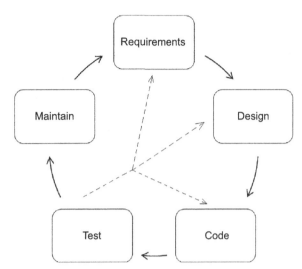

FIG. 9.1 The software lifecycle. If testing reveals errors, then the process may return to any one of the three preceding stages. Release would normally come between "Test" and "Maintain".

Various techniques are available for requirements gathering and analysis:

1. Observation of existing workflows, pathways and processes and any related documentation
2. Interviews with potential users − individually or in groups
3. Prototyping the concept, not necessarily as software but as mock screenshots or storyboards
4. Use cases from different perspectives − user, programmer, maintainer

Requirements should be analysed for consistency and feasibility. It is essential for software requirements to be verifiable using available resources during the software acceptance stage. A change management process for requirements will also be helpful depending on the expected lifespan of the software.

The final step is to record these requirements including functional ones (e.g. what training data needs to be recorded), non-functional ones (e.g. how to ensure data confidentiality), design (what tools are required to build the software), etc. in a **Software Requirements Specification** (SRS). A prototype may also be built during this stage to help the user visualize the proposed software solution.

Software design

Software design typically involves 2 levels of design − namely architectural and detailed design.

- The Architectural design specifies the basic components of the software system such as user interface, database, reporting module, etc. often using tools such as **Data Flow Diagrams** (DFD) and **Entity-Relation Diagrams** (ERD).
- Detailed design elaborates on each of these components in terms of tables and fields in the database, layout and data to be displayed on the graphical user interface, and often pseudo-code for any data analysis modules (Bennett et al., 2010).

Common design strategies adopted include:

1. Procedural − Software is broken down into components based on functionality following a top-down approach and the process continues with each component until enough detail has been achieved (Fig. 9.2).

For our example above, this could mean different components dealing with staff login, data management, user-specific functionalities, etc. Data management could then be further split into data entry, data storage, data retrieval and so on.

2. Object-oriented − Software is described in terms of objects and their interactions with each other. This enables a component-based approach to be followed, enabling modular deployment and improving reuse. In developing object-oriented software, the design can be greatly assisted through the use of **Unified Modelling Language** (UML) tools such as Use Case and Activity diagrams and Class diagrams (Figure 9.3) (Bennett et al., 2010; Miles and Hamilton, 2006).

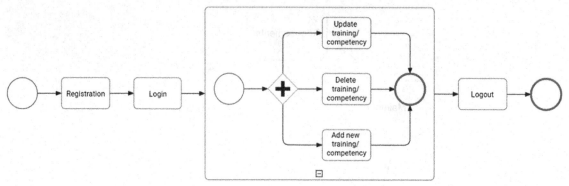

FIG. 9.2 Sample high-level procedural design diagram.

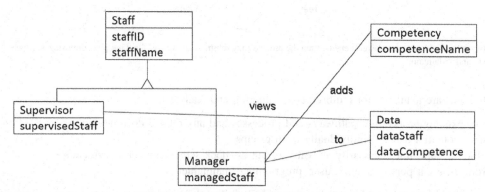

FIG. 9.3 Sample object-oriented design diagram.

For our training records system, the objects could be staff member (which could then be used as a base class for specialised objects for supervisor and manager[20]), data record, competency, database handler, etc. Interactions are defined between objects. For example, 'staff member' adds 'data record' which includes one or more 'competencies'.

3. Data-oriented — In this case, the input and output data structures are defined, and functions and procedures are simply used as a tool to enable data transformation (Fig. 9.4).

For our example, you could have data structures defined for a competency record and defined functions for its insertion, updating, verification and deletion and build the software around this basic framework.

A **Requirements Traceability Matrix** (RTM) is used to map design components to requirements and can be used to ensure that all the key requirements have been captured.

Risk analysis and management options are commonly carried out at this stage. Identifying potential problems or causes of failure here can influence the development stage of the software.

Software development and coding

This phase of the software development lifecycle converts the design into a complete software package. It brings together the hardware, software and communications elements for the system. It is often driven by the detailed design phase and must take into consideration practical issues in terms of resource availability, feasibility and technological constraints.[21] Choice of development platform is often constrained by availability of skills, software and hardware. A compromise must be found between resources available and ability to meet software requirements. A good programmer rarely blames the platform for problems with the software.

---

20. See "Object-oriented programming" in this chapter.
21. There almost always is something that was not picked up during design.

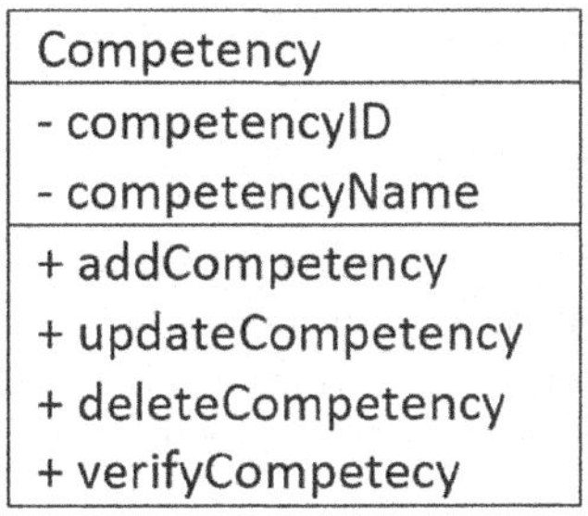

```
┌─────────────────────────┐
│ Competency              │
├─────────────────────────┤
│ - competencyID          │
│ - competencyName        │
├─────────────────────────┤
│ + addCompetency         │
│ + updateCompetency      │
│ + deleteCompetency      │
│ + verifyCompetecy       │
└─────────────────────────┘
```

FIG. 9.4 Sample data-driven design diagram.

Installing the required environments, development of databases, writing programs, refining them, etc. are some of the main activities at this stage. More time spent on detailed design can often cut development time, however technical stumbling blocks can sometimes cause delays. Software costing should take this into account at the project initiation stage.

For the training and competency software example, a database will need to be created to hold the staff details and records. User interfaces will need to be built for inputting data, signing off competencies and other user interactions. Database handling routines for insertion, updating and validation of data records, logic for supervisor and management roles, etc. are some of the functional modules required. The back-end chosen should consider the number of records expected to be held, simultaneous multi-user accessibility and of course, software availability.[22] As far as possible it is a good idea for departments to select a family of tools and to use them for several projects so that local expertise can be efficiently developed.

Software coding should adhere to established standards and be well documented. The basic principles of programming are simplicity, clarity and generality (Kernighan and Pike, 1999). The code should be kept simple, modular and easy to understand for both machines and humans. There are several books [e.g. Bennett et al., 2010; Knuth, 2011] which describe best practices in programming both in terms of developing algorithms as well as coding itself. Code written should be generalised and reusable as far as possible and adaptable to changing requirements and scenarios. Automation and reduced manual intervention will minimise human errors.

Unit testing is often included in this phase of the software lifecycle as it is an integral part of software development. It is an iterative process during and at the end of development. This includes testing error handling, exception handling, memory usage and leaks, connections management, etc, for each of the modules independently.

Software testing[23]

Software testing is an ongoing process along the development to maintenance path. There are 3 main levels of testing

1. Unit testing — where individual modules are tested against set criteria.
2. Integration testing — where the relationships between modules are tested.
3. System testing — which tests the workings of the overall software system.

Test criteria should include functionality, usability, performance and adherence to standards. Test cases are usually generated during the design stage for each level of testing. These may be added to or modified along the pathway but should, in the least, cover the basic criteria. Testing objectives also influence the set of test cases. For example, the test cases for acceptance testing might differ from those for a beta test or even a usability test.

Software maintenance

Software maintenance is defined in the IEEE Standard for Software Maintenance (IEEE 14764-2006 - ISO/IEC) as the modification of a software product after delivery to correct faults, to improve performance or other attributes, or to adapt the product to a modified environment. It lasts for the lifespan of the software and requires careful logging and tracking of change requests as per the guidelines for change management set out at the end of the requirements phase.

A maintenance request often goes through a lifecycle similar to software development. The request is analysed, its impact on the system is determined, any required modifications are designed, coded, tested and finally implemented.

---

22. Sadly, this is often the major deciding factor within Medical Physics/Clinical Engineering.
23. See "Software Validation and Verification" later in this chapter for a fuller discussion.

Training and day-to-day support are also core components of the software maintenance phase. It is therefore essential for the maintainer to be able to understand the existing code. Good documentation and clear and simple coding at the development stage will be most helpful at this point especially if the developer is not available or if there's been a long gap since development.

There are many tools that provide help with the discipline of software development, such as, in Unix/Linux, SCCS (**Source Code Control System**), SVN (**Apache Subversion**) and MAKE, which codifies instructions for compiling and linking. In addition, OSS wiki and Q-Pulse document management systems can help departments log their activities, including the queries that are raised during the complete software life cycle.

Software lifecycle models

The software lifecycle models help manage the software development process from conception through to implementation within time and cost constraints. We consider four popular ones here.

Waterfall model

The Waterfall model is one of the most common and classic of life cycle models, also referred to as a linear-sequential life cycle model. It is based on the factory assembly-line process. It follows a structured sequential path from Requirements to Maintenance, setting out milestones at each stage which must be accomplished before the next stage can begin (Fig. 9.5).

The rigidity of the Waterfall model aids project management with well-defined milestones and deliverables. It does however restrict flexibility and does not provide much scope for user feedback until software development has been completed. It is only suitable for insular projects where user requirements can be clearly defined at the outset and are unlikely to change over the software lifespan.

Incremental model/prototyping model

The incremental model is an intuitive approach to the waterfall model. There are multiple iterations of smaller cycles involving requirements, design, development, and testing, each producing a prototype of the software. Subsequent iterations improve or build on the previous prototype. In situations where there is no manual process or existing system to help determine the requirements, the prototype can let the user plan its use and help determine the requirements for the system. It is also an effective method to demonstrate the feasibility of a certain approach for novel systems where it is not clear whether constraints can be met, or whether algorithms can be developed to implement the requirements. Testing and managing is easier with smaller cycles and errors can be detected early. It provides a better system to users as users tend to change their mind in specifying requirements and this method of developing systems supports this.

A drawback however is the "scope creep" that can often result from frequent user feedback and the associated risk of getting stuck in a never-ending development loop. Also, since the requirements for the entire system are not gathered at the start of the project, the system architecture might be affected at later iterations. Another issue is the risk of a build-and-patch approach through development, leading to poor code design (Fig. 9.6).

Spiral model

The Spiral Model was designed to include the best features from the Waterfall and Prototyping Models. It is similar to the incremental model, but each iteration (called a spiral in this model) produces a robust working version of the software which is released for user evaluation. The development of each version of the system is carefully designed using the steps

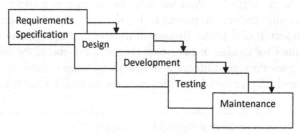

FIG. 9.5 The waterfall model.

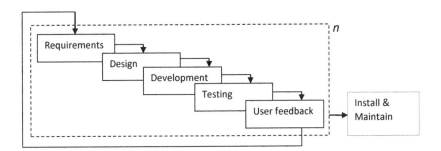

FIG. 9.6 The incremental waterfall model.

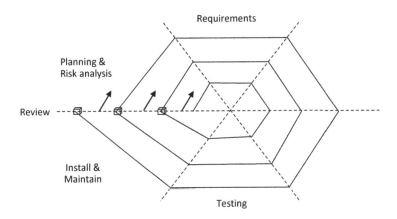

FIG. 9.7 The spiral model.

involved in the Waterfall Model. The first version is called the 'baseline spiral' and each subsequent spiral builds on the baseline spiral, each producing a new version with increased functionality. The theory is that the set of requirements is hierarchical in nature, with additional functionality building on the first efforts. The spiral model specifies risk analysis and management explicitly which helps to keep the software development process under control. This is a good model for systems where the entire problem is well defined from the start, such as modelling and simulating software, but not so much for database projects where most functions are essentially independent (Fig. 9.7).

Agile methodology

With the advent of web-based software and mobile applications, the older software lifecycle models were felt to be too restrictive and time-consuming. The focus shifted to quick releases and lesser focus on the traditional requirements → design → development process. This methodology stresses collaboration over documentation and constant evolution over detailed design.

Agile software development is a set of frameworks and practices based on the Agile Manifesto[24] that provide guidance on how to adapt and respond quickly to requirement changes in a constantly evolving environment.

Popular Agile frameworks include Scrum and Kanban. An agile software development process always starts by defining the users and the vision for the problem to be solved. The problem is then further sub-divided into user stories which are prioritised and delivered in chunks at regular intervals called *Sprints*. Each sprint delivers a releasable product increment.

The main difference with the agile methodology is a change in mindset. Unlike the waterfall model where a solution to the entire problem is considered at the outset, Agile aims to look at specific use cases or user stories at a time and develop and test those with users. This provides the ability to change tracks quickly when requirements change. More and more clinical software is now starting to adopt an agile development approach (Fig. 9.8).

The models discussed above are some of the basic models and individual software projects may sometimes combine techniques from different models to suit their specific needs. Medical Physics/Clinical Engineering projects often follow an

24. https://agilemanifesto.org/.

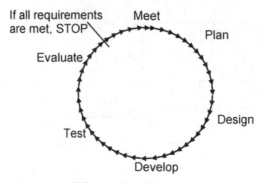

FIG. 9.8 The agile model.

iterative or agile approach since the requirements are not always clearly defined and may undergo frequent revisions. It is essential in such cases to maintain a robust software change control process (see "Software Quality Assurance" later in this chapter).

Procedural, object-oriented and functional programming

In the early days of computing, when memory was small and processing power slow (compared to today), many programs were short and simple. They followed a linear path from start to finish. As computers grew in complexity and memory (both internal and external) increased, along with processing power[25] more complex programs were possible. Whilst modern computing power means that less efficiently designed programs will still run in an acceptable time (and for a one-off result that may be acceptable), procedural programming will better utilise what are still limited resources.

Procedural programming

Procedural programming breaks a problem down into several subproblems and identifies similarities between these. For example, a program that displays a set of test results, together with the reference range and a note as to whether the result is inside or outside of this, will format the same type of output several times. By moving this formatting code to a separate routine (often called a subroutine) and parameterising it, the code becomes easier to write and more efficient to store (see Fig. 9.9). It also has two added advantages: firstly, that a change to the way in which these results are to be displayed (for example, wanting results outside of the reference range to be displayed in red) only needs to be made in one place. The second advantage is that if a subsequent program is written that requires the same formatting, it is easy to extract the relevant code and re-use it elsewhere.

The above description also provides two examples of code reuse: internally and externally. Code that is to be reused externally often requires a more stringent design (as it is impossible to predict exactly all the uses the code may be put to) and provides the basis for a code library. A code library may be pre-compiled so that other programs may use the routines, but not alter the source code, thereby ensuring continued integrity.

Procedures are used by calling them. The values in the brackets following the procedure name (in its definition) are the parameters. They are given the values, in order, that are in the brackets when the procedure is called. These may be explicit values (3.14, "Pi", etc.), the values stored in variables (e.g. nPi) or pointers to variables (e.g. *nPi). The latter of these three forms means that the procedure can not only use the value passed to it, but — as it is only a pointer — it can alter the value also. In this way a procedure can return more than a single result. In the example in Fig. 9.9B, the procedure does not return anything (hence it is declared as having type void) but if it did not contain the display code, it might have been of type CString and returned the value of sText which it had assembled, for the calling program (which itself may have been a procedure) to display.

The variable sText in Fig. 9.9B is worthy of further investigation. As it is declared inside a procedure, it only exists there. As soon as the procedure completes, sText is destroyed and the memory it occupies is freed up for use by other procedures. sText is therefore known as a local variable. A global variable is one which exists throughout the entire program and is declared differently. In aiming for code reuse, it is unwise to rely on global variables, as they may not exist

---

25. Moore's Law states that the number of transistors on a microprocessor (and thereby the processing power) will double every two years. This was stated prophetically (and was originally every year, but he revised it to 2 years in 1975) rather than empirically, but it does seem to have held.

(A)

```
sText.Format("Potassium: %.2f. Reference range: 0-60. This value is
%s",nPotassium,(nPotassium>0 && nPotassium<60?"Normal":"Suspect");
pDC->TextOut(100,100,sText);

sText.Format("Sodium: %.2f. Reference range: 0-60. This value is %s",nSodum,(nSodium>0 &&
nSodium<60?"Normal":"Suspect");
pDC->TextOut(100,200,sText);

sText.Format("Urea: %.2f. Reference range: 0-60. This value is %s",nUrea,(nUrea>0 &&
nUrea<60?"Normal":"Suspect");
pDC->TextOut(100,300,sText);
```

(B)

```
DisplayResult("Potassium",nPotassium,0,60,pDC,100,100);
DisplayResult("Sodium",nSodium,0,60,pDC,100,100);
DisplayResult("Urea",nUrea,0,60,pDC,100,100);

void DisplayResult(CString sName, float nValue, float nLower, float nUpper, DC *pDC, int x, int y)
{
        CString sText;
        sText.Format("%s: %.2f. Reference range: %.2f-%.2f. This value is
        %s",sName,nValue,nLower,nUpper,(nValue>nLower &&
        nValue<nUpper?"Normal":"Suspect");
        pDC->TextOut(x,y,sText);
}
```

(C)

```
Potassium: 30. Reference range: 0-60. This value is Normal
Sodium: 30. Reference range: 0-60. This value is Normal
Urea: 30. Reference range: 0-60. This value is Normal
```

FIG. 9.9 (A) Non-procedural code in C++ with **Microsoft Foundation Classes** (MFC). sText is a CString (a text string) and pDC a device context on which the results will be displayed. nPotassium etc. are numbers calculated elsewhere. (B) The code from Fig. 9.9A written in a procedural style. (C) The output from both pieces of code.

in the next use of the code. It is therefore always better to pass all variables required by the procedure into it. The parameters of the procedure are also local to it. Therefore, a procedure may freely alter the value that these variables are initially given, for the variable that the procedure was called with will remain untouched. (Unless it is passed as a pointer, as discussed above). As sText is local to the procedure, it does not matter if a variable outside of the procedure also has the name sText: the procedure can only use what it knows about. If there exists a global variable called sText then the procedure will still use the local variable. There are ways to get a procedure to use a global rather than a local variable, but it is generally better to use different names — this avoids confusion and makes the code more readable and therefore more maintainable, another key consideration when writing code for reuse and especially for inclusion in a library. Where a variable exists is known as its *scope* — a procedure will therefore always use the ones that are in scope. Ones outside of a routine's scope are inaccessible.

The program keeps track of the local variables and which ones are currently in scope by use of a stack (see the section on Artificial Intelligence in this chapter for a description of this).

Examples of procedural programming languages are ALGOL, BASIC, C, COBOL, JavaScript, FORTRAN, Java, MATLAB, M (also called MUMPS), Pascal, Perl, Python and R.

Object-oriented programming

Object-Oriented programming (OOP) builds upon procedural programming and introduces the concept of an object. The paradigm is to analyse the problem by identifying real life entities, with data and operations that they contain and perform. The construction and interaction between the objects forms the basis of the programming. OOP is a major programming paradigm and has been used in the construction of Radiotherapy treatment planning systems and the modelling of biological systems.

There are two main concepts to cover in order to explain OOP: *encapsulation* and *polymorphism*. As an introduction to these, we will first consider a *structure*, expanding it to describe a *class*. Encapsulation and Polymorphism will then follow.

A structure is a collection of data items into one. It can therefore be manipulated as a single item, passed around the program as a single item and stored and retrieved as a single item. The data items that comprise the structure do not need to be of the same type (indeed, it would be unusual if they were). As an example, let us consider a structure that holds information about an event. For the sake of simplicity, we will restrict an event to having a name, a location and a date on which it will occur. Two structures to represent this might be:

struct date {int nDay; int nMonth; int nYear};
struct event {CString sName; CString sLocation; date dDate};

The individual members of the structure are addressed using dot notation. For example, if we have a variable of type event called evWedding, then the location is evWedding.sLocation and the year is evWedding.dDate.nYear.

It can be seen that, using multiple structures, the tables of a relational database can be simply represented in code, which makes the manipulation of the data simpler (see later in this chapter for a discussion of relational databases).

Operations upon structures such as this can then be written, for example to determine the day of week that the date represents or to move an event forwards or backwards in time (e.g. for implementing a To Do list, a recurrent action might be moved to a week later upon completion rather than deleted). However, these are external to the structure and must also be moved to another program should the structure be re-used (which, in the case of simple structures like the ones above is very likely). This is the issue that *encapsulation* addresses. A *class* is a combination of one or more data items that describe that class (i.e. a structure) together with one or more methods that act on or for it. An instance of a class (i.e. a variable defined as having this type) is called an *object* and leads to object-oriented programming. The methods are addressed in the same way as the data items, using dot notation, e.g. evWedding.dDate.GetDayOfWeek () or evWedding.SetLocation ("Westminster Abbey"). These are called *methods* in order to avoid confusion with operators.

Operators are similar to mathematical operators and can also be defined for classes. Thus, it is possible to create a method dDate.AddDays (7) and also an operator + which adds the number of days to the date and delivers a new date, so that you can write dDate2=dDate1 + 7. It can be seen that dDate.AddDays (1) and dDate ++ will yield the same result in this case. The operators are defined by the programmer for the class so need not bear any similarity to a mathematical one. Hence evWedding ++ could reverse the letters in the name of the location, although this is not helpful for maintainability and would be better accomplished through a method ReverseLocation ().

Object orientation encourages code reuse in that classes developed for one application can easily be used in another. As they encapsulate the methods as well as the data, all the functionality is in one place making it easily transportable.

Polymorphism, the other prime concept in object orientation, means "many forms". There are three forms of polymorphism: method polymorphism, operator polymorphism and class polymorphism. Method and operator polymorphism are similar in nature and implement overloading. An overloaded operator (or method) is one where there are more than one definitions with the same name — the difference being either the type of the result, or the type of the operand, or type (or number) of the parameters. Fig. 9.10 gives some examples.

Class polymorphism relies upon another concept in object orientation: *inheritance*. Consider an event planner application: there may be several different types of event, a wedding, a birthday, a party. All require slightly different data members and may require different operators of methods. However, they also have a lot in common. Inheritance allows a class to be derived from another, *base class*. A derived class automatically inherits all the member data and methods of the

```
dDate2 = dDate1 + 7;
dDate3 = dDate1 + dDate2;
dDate1.SetDay(5);
dDate1.SetDay("Wednesday");
sText = dDate1.GetDay();
nDay = dDate1.GetDay();
```

FIG. 9.10 Some overloaded methods and operators. The one used depends upon the operands, parameters or assignment. The first pair are distinguished by the data type being added (integer or date), the second pair are distinguished by the data type of the parameter (integer or text) and the third pair are distinguished by the type of the returned value (text or integer).

base. These can be overridden (in much the same way as a local variable replaces a global) if different functionality is required or added to. Class polymorphism allows a descendant class to be used where the base class is defined, e.g. if the sub-class dateofbirth is created which inherits from the class date (with the addition of a place name and registering office, for example) then the operator = which is defined for type date will also accept an operand of type dateofbirth, using only the date data member.

Examples of Object-Oriented programming languages are C++, Java, LabVIEW, PHP and Python.

Functional programming

Functional Programming is a paradigm that evaluates mathematical functions, avoiding state and mutable[26] data. It contrasts with the imperative style (as used elsewhere in this chapter) in that it emphasises the application of functions rather than changes in state (in other words, it evaluates expressions, whereas imperative programming evaluates statements). Its roots are in lambda calculus which was developed in the 1930s to investigate function definitions, function application and recursion (see later). As functional programming cannot alter the state of the program, it cannot be affected by it either. Thus, a function will always return the same output for a given input, which may not be true of imperative programming. It is therefore much easier to validate a functional program than an imperative one.

The most likely languages a scientist or engineer will meet which implement functional programming are Mathematica, Lisp and (implemented to a lesser extent) SQL. C# and Perl, although strictly imperative languages, have constructs which allow the functional style to be implemented. Many functional concepts can be implemented in other languages.

The most important concepts are first-class and higher-order functions; pure functions; recursion; and lazy evaluation. We now describe these.

Functional programming requires that all functions are first-class: that is, they can be treated as any other values and can thus be used as arguments to other functions or return values from them. Such a function that takes another as an argument is a *higher-order function*. A good example of such a function is *map*, which takes a function and a list as its arguments. When executed, *map* applies the function to all the elements of the list. For example, to subtract a given number from every element in a a list lNum:

```
subtractFromList lNum nNum = map (\x -> x - nNum) lNum
```

Some functional programming languages allow actions to be yielded as well as return values. These actions are termed *side effects*, indicating that the return value is the most important part. Languages that prohibit side effects are known as *pure*. Thus, a *pure function* is one with no side effects.

Recursion is where a procedure calls itself. The classic example of this is in the evaluation of the mathematical function factorial (denoted !), where n! is defined as 1 when n=1 and n x n-1 when n is greater than 1. It is only defined for positive integers. A simple implementation would be:

```
factorial (int n);
{
    if (n<1) return 0; // error value
    if(n==1) return 1;
    return n*factorial (n-1);
}
```

Note the use of zero as an error value (see the section on software validation and verification in this chapter for another error condition in such a function). Many procedures return pre-defined values to indicate that an error has occurred (usually in the input values, but sometimes in terms of failing to retrieve data from an external source, such as a networked device). The only occasions on which this error condition need not be tested is when the error conditions have been pre-evaluated — for example when the input could never be less than 1 due to previous calculations.

Lazy evaluation is the deferment of the computation of values until they are needed. For example, in Python 2:

```
r = range(10)
print r
    output: [0, 1, 2, 3, 4, 5, 6, 7, 8, 9]
```

---

26. Mutable data is data that may change — immutable data is data that does not.

```
print r [3]
   output: 3
```

All members of the list are calculated at declaration, whereas in Python 3:

```
r = range(10)
print(r)
   output: range(0, 10)
print(r[3])
   output: 3
```

The value of r [3] is not computed until it is referenced. This can have a great saving in execution time when not all of a range might be referenced.

The documentation for Haskell, a functional programming language, purports that "Functional programming is known to provide better support for structured programming than imperative programming. To make a program structured it is necessary to develop abstractions and split it into components which interface each other with those abstractions. Functional languages aid this by making it easy to create clean and simple abstractions. It is easy, for instance, to abstract out a recurring piece of code by creating a higher-order function, which will make the resulting code more declarative and comprehensible.

Functional programs are often shorter and easier to understand than their imperative counterparts. Since various studies have shown that the average programmer's productivity in terms of lines of code is more or less the same for any programming language, this translates also to higher productivity."

The Haskell Programming Language

Real-time system programming

Real-time programming relates to programming where no delays are acceptable in the data processing. For example, a cardiac monitoring system must alarm the instant an event is detected, not 5 min later when other processing (such as a routine database copy) has completed. The correctness of the system therefore depends not just on the logical result, but also on the timeframe in which it was delivered.[27] A failure to respond is as critical an error as an incorrect result. Probably the most common use of real-time programming in a Medical Physics/Clinical Engineering sense is that of signal processing and most real-time systems are part of an embedded system (see the next section).

Nothing is instantaneous and therefore real-time programming works according to a "real-time constraint", i.e. the acceptable limit between an event and the system response. It is also worth noting that a system may have real-time and non-real-time elements, probably as independent threads. In this scenario a real-time thread will receive and process the incoming data/event within the required time frame, thereby being ready to process the next one. The other thread will take the result of this action and process it further, for example by displaying only certain events or by implementing a localised trendline.

There are three forms of real-time, as defined by Burns and Wellings (2009):

- Hard real-time, where it is imperative that the system delivers a response within the required deadline, e.g. a flight control system.
- Soft real-time, where the deadlines are important but the system still functions correctly if occasional deadlines are missed, e.g. data acquisition.
- Firm real-time, where a missed deadline is tolerable but there is no benefit from the late delivery of service.

Systems may be time-triggered (e.g. every 25 ms or at 18:00) or event-triggered (where an external or internal event triggers activity).

Important characteristics of a real-time system are guaranteed response times, concurrency (rather than parallel processing), an emphasis on numerical computing (and algorithms), hardware interaction and extreme reliability and safety.

The difference between concurrent, parallel and sequential processing can be illustrated in Ada in Fig. 9.11.

---

27. There is a large debate over the clocks used to timestamp such data, especially with regard to daylight saving.

(A)

```
procedure guitar-solo is
begin
        left-hand-fingers-on-fretboard;
        right-hand-pluck-strings;
        face-screwed-up;
end
```

(B)

```
procedure guitar-solo is
        task right-hand;
        task body right-hand is
        begin
                right-hand-pluck-strings;
        end right-hand;
        task left-hand;
        task body left-hand is
        begin
                left-hand-fingers-on-fretboard;
        end left-hand;
        begin
        face-screwed-up;
end
```

FIG. 9.11 (A) Sequential programming, which does not achieve the desired effect as each procedure (defined elsewhere) completes before the next commences. (B) Concurrent and parallel programming. The "begin" just before "face-screwed-up" activates the two previously defined tasks concurrently, after which face-screwed-up will run in parallel. Thus the desired effect is achieved.

Examples of real-time programming languages are Ada, C, Java (although these two require extensions), RTL/2, Modula-2 and Mesa. There is insufficient space to reproduce sample code here, but good examples can be found on Andy Welling's web pages.

Embedded system programming

An embedded system is one which is contained ("embedded") into the electronics of the device itself. There are several reasons for wishing to do this:

- Safety — an embedded system is very difficult to tamper with.
- Speed of execution — an embedded system is often pre-loaded into **Read-Only Memory** (ROM) and so starts "instantly".
- Optimisation — code written for and developed around electronics to serve a specific purpose will always be more optimal (and hence faster to execute) than code written for a generalist machine (e.g. a standard PC).

This final point is a major characteristic of embedded systems — they are designed for specific purposes rather than general. Thus a more complex device may actually be composed of several modules[28] each with its own embedded code.

The simplest form of embedded code is machine code (the lowest language of all) but this is by no means the simplest to create and maintain.[29] For many years embedded systems and languages were reflections of the electronics and especially of the microprocessors at the heart of them. Such electronic systems are often termed "microcontrollers" and the program that controls them "firmware". This firmware is traditionally loaded into a ROM but is more likely to be an **Electrically Programmable Read-Only Memory** (EPROM) now. The widespread use of the Internet means that such firmware can be easily updated — whereas older systems remained as they were once deployed, or required engineering expertise to update them.

---

28. For example: an input module, a computation module, a data logging module and an output module.
29. Although it is the fastest. The author learned to write C6502 code by implementing a version of the game "Breakout". He then learned how to implement delay loops as it was too fast to play.

Whilst traditional embedded systems used very specialised programming languages and OSs (the more specialised being both), three more general ones have widespread use, which we will consider further: Android (from Google), Windows Embedded (from Microsoft) and Java (from Sun). They can be found in devices as diverse as mobile phones and coffee machines.

Java is built on a tiered model. The key to this is the intermediate stage, or **Java Virtual Machine** (JVM). There are JVMs available for all the most common hardware and software platforms. A Java program does not need to interact directly with the local OS or with the hardware – the JVM does that. The Java program thus instructs the JVM, which instructs the OS or hardware. A Java program can therefore run on multiple platforms, just by using different JVMs.

Windows Embedded (originally Windows CE[30]) originally appeared in PDAs and was developed to have a small footprint, thereby fitting into a low-RAM device. It has the advantage that developers used to working with Visual Studio and Silverlight can quickly produce embedded systems. It has been supplanted by embedded versions of later Microsoft OSs, with Windows XP Embedded particularly prevalent in medical devices. Windows 8.1 is currently the latest version and Microsoft is recommending an upgrade path to Windows 10, so a future for this software (despite the huge user base) is unlikely.

Android is a relative newcomer to the field. Originally developed for mobile phones, it has also appeared in tablet computers (thus blurring the division between specialised and general). It is close to being open source, enabling developers to work closer to the heart of the OS. The distribution model for Apps so produced is simple (certainly compared to Apple's) meaning that developers can release them swiftly. However, the openness of Android is also seen as its greatest weakness, in that it is viewed as being less secure for critical operations and data.

None of these more general systems are as efficient as a microcontroller-specific system, but with increased storage and faster processing that is rarely an issue any more. There is also a shorter development lifecycle as the tools to develop for these OSs are more likely to be familiar, and the multi-platform support means that new skills do not need to be learned for each new project.

Software validation and verification

The primary purpose of validation and verification (when applied to medical software) is safety. Functionality is a secondary purpose, although without functionality the code is pointless. The way to reconcile this is to enquire as to the failure of the code: a system that is 75% functional but 100% safe is still useable (albeit annoying) – if the figures are reversed, it is not.

In validating and verifying a system as safe, one starts from the premise that all software contains "bugs". These "bugs" may be classified as faults, errors or failures. A fault is a mistake in the design or code, which may lead to an error (but equally may not), such as declaring an array to be the wrong size. An error is unspecified behaviour in execution, which may lead to a failure, such as messages starting with non-numeric codes being discarded as they evaluate to zero. A failure is the crossing of a safety threshold due to an uncontained error.

There are two main approaches to testing, often referred to as "black box" and "white box". Applying this to software testing, the "box" is the program, or module, that is to be tested.

In black box testing, the contents of the box are unknown.[31] Therefore, tests comprise of a known set of inputs and the predetermined output that this should provide. This is very useful when the software has been commissioned using an **Output-Based Specification** (OBS) or for end-user testing. It also removes any effect that may be caused by the application of the debugger environment itself.[32]

In white-box testing (also known as clear box, glass box or transparent box testing, which may be a better descriptor of the process) the contents of the box are known and are exposed. In software terms, this may mean that the source code is available or even that the code is being tested in the development environment via single-stepping. It is therefore usually applied to structures or elements of a software system, rather than to its whole. It is also not unusual for a black box failure to be investigated using white box testing.

In generic terms, therefore, black box testing is functional testing whereas white box testing is structural or unit testing. A large system comprising multiple components will therefore often have each component white box tested and the overall system black box tested in order to test the integration and interfacing of the components.

---

30. Compact Edition.
31. But not in a Schrodinger sense.
32. It is extremely annoying to find that code runs perfectly under the debugger but not outside of it.

Testing should normally be undertaken by someone different from the software author. A draft BCS standard (Standard for Software Component Testing) lists the following increasing degrees of independence:

a) the test cases are designed by the person(s) who writes the component under test;
b) the test cases are designed by another person(s);
c) the test cases are designed by a person(s) from a different section;
d) the test cases are designed by a person(s) from a different organisation;
e) the test cases are not chosen by a person.[33]

There are multiple test case design techniques with corresponding test measurement techniques. ISO 29119 lists the following:

- Equivalence Partitioning
- Boundary Value Analysis
- State Transition Testing
- Cause-Effect Graphing
- Syntax Testing
- Statement Testing
- Branch/Decision Testing
- Data Flow Testing
- Branch Condition Testing
- Branch Condition Combination Testing
- Modified Condition Decision Testing
- LCSAJ (**Linear Code Sequence And Jump**) Testing
- Random Testing

It is instructive to examine one of these, together with its corresponding measurement technique. The one we will select is Boundary Value Analysis. This takes the specification of the component's behaviour and collates a set of input and output values (both valid and invalid). These input and output values are then partitioned into a number of ordered sets with identifiable boundaries. This is done by grouping together the input and output values which are expected to be treated by the component in the same way: they are thus considered equivalent due to the equivalence of the component's behaviour. The boundaries of each partition are normally the values of the boundaries between partitions, but where partitions are disjoint the minimum and maximum values within the partition are used. The boundaries of both valid and invalid partitions are used.

The rationale behind this method of testing is the premise that the inputs and outputs of a component can be partitioned into classes that will be treated similarly by the component and, secondly, that developers are prone to making errors at the boundaries of these classes.

For example, a program to calculate factorials[34] would have the partitions (assuming integer input only):

- Partition a: $-\infty$ to 0 (not defined)
- Partition b: 1 to n (where n! is the largest integer the component can handle, so for a standard C integer with a maximum value of 2147483647, n would be 12)
- Partition c: n+1 to $+\infty$ (unable to be handled)

The boundary values are therefore 0, 1, n and n+1. The test cases that are used are three per boundary: the boundary values and ones an incremental distance to either side. Duplicates are then removed, giving a test set in our example of {-1, 0, 1, 2, n-1, n, n+1, n+2}. Each value produces a test case comprising the input value, the boundary tested and the expected outcome. Additional test cases may be designed to ensure invalid output values cannot be induced. Note that invalid as well as valid input values are used for testing.

It can clearly be seen that this technique is only applicable for black-box testing.

The corresponding measurement technique (Boundary Value Coverage) defines the coverage items as the boundaries of the partitions. Some partitions may not have an identified boundary, as in our example where Partition a has no lower bound and Partition c no upper bound. Coverage is calculated as follows:

---

33. i.e. an automated testing system is deployed.
34. See the section on Functional Programming (in this chapter) for a definition.

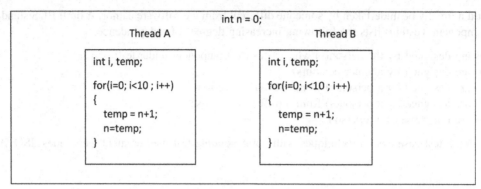

FIG. 9.12   A simple two-threaded program.

$$\text{Boundary Value Coverage} = \frac{\text{number of distinct boundary values executed}}{\text{total number of boundary values}} \times 100\%$$

In our example, the coverage is 100% as all identified boundaries are exercised by at least one test case (although $+\infty$ and $-\infty$ were listed as the limits of partitions c and a, they are not boundaries as they indicate that the partitions are unbounded). Lower levels of coverage would be achieved if all the boundaries we had identified were not all exercised, or could not be (for example, if 2147483647 was required to be tested, where 2147483648 is too large to be stored). If all the boundaries are not identified, then any coverage measure based on this incomplete set of boundaries would be misleading. The cited paper contains fuller worked examples.

Let us now consider a further level of complexity.

In theory, a software system is deterministic. That is, all of its possible states can be determined and therefore tested, and the resultant system verified. However, although the states and the transitions between them may be finite, the use of multithreaded code and of multicore processors means that the number of test cases becomes unfeasibly large to process. This resultant complexity means that it is more practical to treat the system as being nondeterministic in nature and test/validate accordingly.

Testing therefore becomes a statistical activity in which it is recognised that the same code, with the same input conditions, may not yield the same result every time. In order to demonstrate this, consider the code in Fig. 9.12.

On simple inspection, this code would be expected to produce a final value of x of between 10 and 20. However, it can produce values as low as 2 in 90 steps. (As an aside on complexity, this simple piece of code has in excess of 77,000 states) (Hobbs, 2012).

Hobbs defines "dependability" as "*A system's [...] ability to respond correctly to events in a timely manner, for as long as required. That is, it is a combination of the system's availability (how often the system responds to requests in a timely manner) and its reliability (how often these responses are correct)*" (Hobbs, 2012). He goes on to argue that, as dependability is inseparable from safety and dependability results in increased development cost, systems only need to be "sufficiently dependable" where the minimum level is specified and evidenced.

In conclusion, validation and verification may be fully possible. However, it may only be statistically demonstrable.

Software quality assurance

The terms "**Software Quality Assurance**" (SQA) and "**Software Quality Control**" (SQC) are often mistakenly used interchangeably. The definition offered by sqa.net is:

Software Quality Assurance [is] the function of software quality that assures that the standards, processes and procedures are appropriate for the project and are correctly implemented.

Software Quality Control [is] the function of software quality that checks that the project follows its standards processes, and procedures, and that the project produces the required internal and external (deliverable) products.

SQA Definition

The two components can thus be seen as one (SQA) setting the standards that are to be followed with the other (SQC) ensuring that they have been. The process for SQC is one that should be specified as part of SQA so that the method for measurement and thus the criteria for compliance are known up-front. For example, the SQA may specify that ISO 14915 be used to define the multi-media user interfaces. SQC will therefore test to ensure that all multi-media user interfaces comply. It is thus clear that SQC will be undertaking a level of testing and it is not unusual for the full test suite to be part of the SQC process − testing not just the standards employed, but the functionality and safety of the software also.

It is common to break the software down into attributes that can be measured[35] and in this there is a similarity with software testing (see "Software Validation and Verification" in this chapter). There are several definitions of software quality attributes: McCall (1977), Boehm (1978), Robert Grady's FURPS+[36] and Microsoft's Common Quality Attributes. Some such attributes are:

- Accuracy − the ability of the system to produce accurate results (and to what level of accuracy this is required).
- Availability − the proportion of time that the system is functional and working.
- Compatibility − the ability of the system to work with, for example, different input devices.
- Functionality − what the system is actually supposed to do.
- Manageability − the ease with which system administrators can manage the system, through tuning, debugging and monitoring.
- Performance − the responsiveness of a system to execute a required action with a set time frame.
- Security − the ability of a system to resist malicious interference (see "ICT security" in Chapter 8).
- Supportability − the ability of the system to provide information to assist in rectifying a performance failure.
- Usability − how well the system meets the users' requirements by being intuitive and accessible. (Standards may seem limiting and anti-creative, but Microsoft's success is built on them, especially the common Windows user interface[37]

Three further areas fall into the remit of SQA, all of which assume that the system (and especially the software at the heart of it) will not remain constant over time (it is often said that software is never finished, only implemented and passed to users): Configuration Management, Change Control and Documentation, which we will now examine.

Software Configuration Management (SCM) is the tracking and controlling of changes in the software. It therefore requires a robust **Change Control** (CC) method. The TickIT guide (TickITplus − A Path to Excellence in IT) has two quality control elements covering this: "Maintain and Enhance" and "Support"[38] listing as the control mechanisms:

- Change control approval points: authority to proceed with change
- Full release approval
- Regression tests
- System, integration and acceptance test
- Reviews and audits
- Configuration and change management
- Quality plans and projects plans

It can therefore be seen that changes to a live system should not be undertaken lightly. They require possibly more consideration than the initial system to ensure that a fix doesn't cause more problems. A risk assessment, covering both the risk of making the change as well as the risk of not doing so, must be undertaken. Requiring authorisation ensures that SQA is undertaken.

Like the software, the documentation must be kept up to date. It must form an accurate reflection of the software in use and should thus undertake the same version control as the software (see "Software coding and coding management" in this chapter) at the same time. It is therefore clear that the system documentation (in several parts: user guide, programmers' guide, system administrators' guide, etc.) must have a clear structure to it. Without such structure, the documentation becomes difficult to maintain. In order to enable programmers to work across multiple projects employing several languages, it is vital that the documentation has a consistent format to it so that information can be swiftly found and easily updated. In other words, the documentation also requires a standard, which should be part of the SQA process that it also enables.

There are three main types of documentation that we are concerned with:

---

35. If it can't be measured, then there's not a lot of point in specifying it.
36. Functionality, Usability, Reliability, Performance, Supportability, constraints (such as design, implementation, interface and physical).
37. Left-click to select, right-click for a context menu, commonality of icons so "save" always looks the same, etc.
38. The difference between the two is primarily that support may not change the software, whereas maintain & enhance will.

- User documentation, describing to the user how the system works and how to interact with it in order to achieve the desired results.
- Technical documentation, describing to technical staff how to maintain the code, how to install it and what to do when something goes wrong. This technical file (which includes the technical design) is often required when seeking certification such as a CE mark. A Technical file has three possible audience scenarios and should be written with these in mind:
  − Routine maintenance
  − Emergency maintenance
  − Enhancement implementation
- Safety documentation, describing the safe operation of the software, the limits of usage (in order to remain safe) and any fail-safe modes and error messages that may appear.

Databases

Data can take many forms and this section is concerned mainly with data that can provide information through structured assembly and subsequent formal analysis. This is the concept of **Relational Database Management Systems** (RDBMSs). These systems continue to be valuable and have evolved to be the foundation for paperless management systems.

The simplest data structure is perhaps the paper list: a single column of items. It is an easy step to expand a 'list' into a 'table', or flat file structure, with multiple columns.[39] The structure can be further enhanced by adding unique column headings to the first row and unique row identifiers to the first column, so that it is possible to uniquely identify each cell. This is the structure of the basic computer spreadsheet, without any formulae or computed cells and it will provide the starting point for our discussion of structured databases. The row and column identifiers are called primary keys and their importance will become clearer as more structure and abstraction are added to our data. We are concerned here with data storage and interrogation and so the use of spreadsheets in numerical processing will not be covered. It should be noted, however, that such use in clinical engineering activities requires considerable software engineering discipline.

In preparing tabular data for entry into a computer it is useful to add a unique separator between each item in the rows. The most common separator is the comma (hence "**comma separated values**," or CSV, a common file format used for data exchange), however this can produce problems of its own when recording data containing commas, for example addresses. There are two common solutions to this: encapsulating the data within double inverted commas and using an "escape character." The first of these brings problems where double inverted commas are present (e.g., addresses again). The second, although more robust, requires slightly more processing. An escape character is a character that changes the interpretation of the character that follows it. A common escape character is "\". Hence, a comma that separates data would stand alone: , whereas a comma that should be taken to be part of the data would be preceded: \,. This notation does not suffer from the problems mentioned above, in that a backslash simply becomes \\.

Whilst a flat file data structure can equally be represented as lines of data items, with one line per row, in a computer spreadsheet such structures soon become unwieldy. We will therefore introduce some formal relational database terminology (Table 9.2) and develop a specific introductory example.

For our example, The ICT department of the University of ClinEng wish to record the contents of their racks of equipment. They decide to create a database in order to catalogue this. Being computer scientists, they want to create a relational database. A simple preparation might use a single-table spreadsheet, (Table 9.3). It is clear that this design is inefficient, considering how many spaces there are in a rack, and then how many times all those fields will need to be filled. An inefficient design is difficult to maintain.

The spreadsheet data in Table 9.3 can be regarded as a first step towards a relational database, where each cell is a field and each row is a record. Ignoring the labels 1 in Table 9.3 the items in row 1 can be viewed as field names, column headings or attributes and the numbers in column A as unique identifiers. Note that field names do not contain spaces or punctuation, the underscore character often being used to denote a word break. While some systems allow punctuation, delimiters are then required. The structure provided by the relational approach aims to avoid data redundancy, so

---

39. Technically, a flat file has no internal hierarchy, containing records that have no structured interrelationship. A typical flat file is a text file, containing no (or having had removed) word processing or other structure characters or markup (such as paragraph mark, tabs etc.). The term has been commonly been expanded to include structures such as those described here.
40. The "7" is an internal identification number, distinguishing this fan from others in other racks. Similarly for the "2" and "8" for the RAID array and Keyboard.

TABLE 9.2 Relational database terminology.

Relational database: A data structure through which data are stored in tables that are related to one another. The way the tables are related is described through a relationship (see later definitions).

Data: Values stored in a database.

Entity: A person, place, thing, or event about which we want to record information; an object we're interested in.

Field: The smallest structure in a relational database, used to store the individual pieces of data about the entity; stores a single fact about an entity that we're interested in; represents an attribute.

Record: A single "row" in a table; represents the collection of information for a single occurrence of the entity that the table represents.

Table: The chief structure in a relational database, composed of fields and records, whose order is unimportant. A single table collects together all of the information we are tracking for a single entity; represents an object or an entity.

Entity-relationship diagram (ERD): Identifies the data/information required, displaying both the relevant entity and the relationships between them. Sometimes called the database schema.

Key: A field in the database (or an attribute in an ERD) that is used to uniquely identify records and establish relationships between tables or entities; used for the retrieval of data in the table.

Primary key: Uniquely identifies each record in a table, the key is part of the table for which it operates. (Note that this is normally a single field but may be a combination of fields—a composite key).

Foreign key: A key from another table that is used to define a relationship to another record in another table. It has the same name and properties as the primary key from which it is copied.

Rules for Foreign Keys
- 1-1: Primary key from the main table is inserted into the second table.
- 1-many: Primary key from the "1" table gets inserted into the "many" table.
- Many-many: Primary key from each side gets placed into a third intermediate linking table that (usually) includes nothing but both keys.

Non-key: A "regular" field; describes a characteristic of the table's subject.

Relationship: Establishes a connection or correspondence or link between a pair of tables in a database, or between a pair of entities in an ERD.

One-to-one relationship: A single record in table A is related to only one record in table B, and vice versa. (Note that this and the following two relationships are intentionally similar to the rules for foreign keys).

One-to-many relationship: A single record in table A can be related to one or more records in table B, but a single record in table B can be related to only one record in table A.

Many-to-many relationship: A single record in table A can be related to one or more records in table B, and vice versa. There are problems with many-to-many relationships in that one of the tables will contain a large amount of redundant data, both tables will contain some duplicate data, and it will be difficult to add/update/delete records because of the duplication of fields between tables.

Normalisation : Formal design methodology to enable robust systems.

Schema: Diagrams showing the database tables and key linkages.

minimising the possibility of insertion, update or deletion anomalies. This is achieved through the process of normalisation. Table 9.3 satisfies the first normal form (1NF) requirement because each cell contains only one item of data. Example problem fields might contain multiple telephone numbers or complete addresses.

We will now work through a process to modify the design, making entry and modifications much less error prone and later processing more efficient. We must remove subsets of data that apply to multiple rows of a table and place them in separate rows in new tables. We will do this for Manufacturers, Models and Units, as shown in Table 9.4. In each new table the rows are identified by a primary key and when that key appears in its predecessor table it is called a foreign key. This makes the system more secure by avoiding the repeat of the same data in many fields.

Table 9.5 shows the result of using foreign keys to link to the three new tables in table Racks − some details in Table 9.3 no longer appear, only the ID values. Considering the relationship between the remaining columns we note first that it is not clear whether this data set is really intended just for server racks or not. For server racks only we do not need a Rack_type column but for greater flexibility we would. If we choose to remove that column, we achieve second normal form (2NF). The remaining columns have more subtle dependencies. The Rack_position column is probably best absorbed with Rack_model (or Rack_type), as are Cost, Copies and Total_value (the latter being a calculated cost). The example

TABLE 9.3 A set of data arranged in a spreadsheet.

	A	B	C	D	E	F	G	H	I
1	Rack_ID	Rack_type	Rack_manufacturer	Rack_model	Unit_description	Rack_position	Copies	Cost	Total_value
2	1	Server	Prism	P1	Fan 7[39]	1	2	1000	2000
3	2	Server	Prism	P1	2Tb RAID 2	2	2	1000	2000
4	3	Server	Prism	P1	Keyboard 8	3	2	1000	2000

TABLE 9.4 Tables for manufacturers, models and units.

Manufacturers

Manufacturer_ID	Manufacturer_Name
1	Prism

Models

Model_ID	Model_Name
1	P1

Units

Unit_ID	Unit_Description
1	Fan 7
2	2Tb RAID 2
3	Keyboard 8

TABLE 9.5 Table racks, after applying all these changes to our original data (in Table 9.3).

Rack_ID	Rack_type	Rack_manufacturer	Model_ID	Unit_ID	Rack_position	Copies	Cost	Total_value
1	Server	1	1	1	1	2	1000	2000
2	Server	1	1	2	2	2	1000	2000
3	Server	1	1	3	3	2	1000	2000

TABLE 9.6 Table for racks reduced to 3NF form having put some data aside.

Rack_ID	Manufacturer_ID	Model_ID	Unit_ID
1	1	1	1
2	1	1	2
3	1	1	3

suggests server racks and any media library racks will require additional entities. In short planning database structures is complex and to progress with our analysis section we will put aside the problematic columns to move to the third normal form (3NF), seen in Table 9.6. Here there are no questionable dependencies.

We can see that this final structure has the following relationships (naming the tables Racks, Manufacturers, Models, and Units respectively):

- Manufacturers to Racks is one-to-many.
- Models to Racks is one-to-many
- Units to Racks is one-to-one.

In this simple example there is little efficiency gained from this abstraction, but by the addition of just one extra field (e.g. adding Serial_Number to table 'Units) it can be seen how this structure is more adaptable than the one we started with.

The table 'Racks' has a primary key (Rack_ID) and foreign keys (Manufacturer_ID, etc.) which are the primary keys in their own tables. An analogy from programming would be the use of pointers: not the data itself, but a link to where the data may be found (an analogy with the World Wide Web is similar).

The three normal forms may be summed up as follows:

- Duplicate columns within the same table are eliminated. (1NF)
- Each group of related data is in its own table with a primary key to identify each row. (1NF)
- Each cell contains just one item of data (1NF)
- Subsets applying to multiple rows of a table are in their own table. (2NF)
- Relationships are maintained by creating foreign keys. (2NF)
- Any columns not dependent upon the primary key are removed from the table. (3NF)

Normalisation increases search efficiency and reduces the likelihood of data entry, update and deletion errors. 4NF and 5NF constraints also exist but are beyond the scope of this text.

One issue does arise through the use of normalising a database, however. The relationships are achieved through the use of indexes. These are rapidly-changing files which therefore have a risk of corruption. If a corrupt index is used to retrieve records matching a certain key, the records returned may not all match that key. It is therefore imperative (depending on the criticality of the data retrieved) that these data are checked prior to use. This can be as simple as ensuring that each returned record does contain the key searched for. This will ensure that no erroneous results are used but does not ensure that all results have been returned. To achieve this, a redundant data item, such as a child record counter, must be used. In most cases, this is not an issue but it does need to be considered when the criticality of the results is high (e.g. a pharmacy system).

Our rack equipment example is quite simple. In a practical clinical example, we might have several major entities, such as Patients, Therapy Equipment, Appointments, etc. These will require separate table hierarchies, still linked through primary and foreign keys. It is very helpful to create entity relationship diagrams, representing the tables and the links between them, often called the database schema. When purchasing a management tool based around a relational database it is essential to have access to the schema, otherwise constructing queries (see later) can be a trial-and-error affair, leading to the introduction of unnecessary risk.

The theoretical material, explaining the relational database principles, is based on the work of Codd (1970). To put it into practice his work was followed by the introduction of the **Structured Query Language** (SQL). The many current commercial and open source RDBMS provide a comprehensive set of tools to create, populate and interrogate data, based on SQL. There are various dialects, in spite of the existence of ISO/IEC 9075, but the underlying principles are the same and there is much tutorial material available on line. Most systems are designed for Client − Server environments and form the core of many clinical systems such as PACS and EPR. In contrast, SQLite is intended for stand-alone machines and provides a useful route for exploration. It is also embedded in many common devices and software tools.

The four most common SQL commands are SELECT, INSERT, UPDATE, and DELETE. Commands do not need to be in uppercase but are written this way here for clarity. The basic structure of a SELECT command is:

SELECT (fields) FROM (table) WHERE (condition)

Using the tables described in Table 9.4 (Units)

SELECT Unit_Description FROM Units WHERE Unit_ID=2

will return one result: "2Tb RAID 2".

The WHERE clause is a logical statement, using Boolean logic, and can therefore include Boolean operators which will evaluate to either TRUE or FALSE. The statement thus finds all rows for which the WHERE clause is TRUE and then returns the fields listed in the SELECT clause.

To gain benefit from the relational structure, we need to return data from more than one table. Two main ways of doing this are, firstly:

SELECT (fields) FROM (tables) WHERE (condition, including the relationship)

As an example using the Racks, Manufacturers, Units and Models tables:

SELECT m.Manufacturer_Name, u.Unit_Description
    FROM Manufacturers as m, Units as u, Racks as r
    WHERE m.Manufacturer_ID = r.Manufacturer_ID
    AND u.Unit_ID = r.Unit_ID
    AND u.Model_ID=1

Note the use of the notation "Manufacturers as m" in the FROM clause, providing an alias for the table name. The alias is used in the SELECT clause, which otherwise would have included Manufacturers. Manufacturer_Name. Alias usage is temporary and can be used to rename tables or columns. Its importance can be seen from the table structures: several field names appear in multiple tables (as can be seen from the WHERE clause); SQL requires that no ambiguity exists in the statement and the use of aliases helps in this.

A second form, to achieve the same result, is:

SELECT (fields) FROM (table) JOIN (table) ON (relationship) WHERE (condition)

Applied for our example:

SELECT m.Manufacturer_Name, u.Unit_Description FROM RacksAS r
    JOIN Manufacturers AS m ON m.Manufacturer_ID = r.Manufacturer_ID
    JOIN Units AS u ON u.Unit_ID = r.Unit_ID
    WHERE u.Model_ID=1

Both forms return:

Manufacturer_Name[41]	Unit_Description
Prism	Fan 7
Prism	2Tb RAID 2
Prism	Keyboard 8

An INSERT statement adds a record to a single table. To add the item "UPS 3" to the example above would require the following statements:

INSERT INTO Racks (Rack_ID, Manufacturer_ID, Model_ID, Unit_ID) VALUES (4, 1, 1, 4)
INSERT INTO Units (Unit_ID, Unit_Description) VALUES (4, "UPS 3")[42]

The field list is not always necessary: if the list is omitted it is assumed that the values are in the same order as the fields. If the primary key is an auto-number field (i.e. one that the system increments and assigns) then this cannot be specified, meaning that the field list is required. However, if the primary key is an auto-number field, adding data may require several steps, as the value assigned will have to be retrieved so it can be provided to the other INSERT statements.

An UPDATE statement has the form:

UPDATE (table) SET (field 1 = value 1, field 2 = value 2,...) WHERE (condition)

Had we retained Rack_position in the Racks table we would have been able to alter it using UPDATE, for example to move the UPS down a position:

UPDATE Racks SET Rack_position = Rack_position +1 WHERE Model_ID = 1 AND Rack_position >3

or

UPDATE Racks SET Rack_position = 5 WHERE Rack_ID = 4

The first form enables update of multiple records, whereas the second will update only one, as it uses the primary key to uniquely identify a single record.

---

41. Note that the manufacturer here listed makes the rack, not the item.
42. Note the use of double quotes. Some systems use single quotes in order to delimit strings (or can be set to do so), although this can cause problems with surnames such as O'Connor.

Finally, the DELETE statement has the form:

DELETE FROM (table) WHERE (condition)

If the condition is omitted, then all records from the specified table will be deleted. An example might be:

DELETE FROM Units WHERE Unit_ID = 4

This statement alone would create a referential integrity error, in that Racks now includes a reference to a record in Units that no longer exists. To correct this, either a new Item with Unit_ID of 4 must be created, or the following must be done:

DELETE FROM Racks WHERE Unit_ID = 4

RDBMS were introduced with a small range of data types, such as integer, real and text, with text relating to short character strings. This was sufficient for the commercial and management systems of the day. The range of data types has gradually increased. More recently we encounter the concept of paperless management systems. RDBMS systems have evolved to help satisfy this desire and most now have some ability to reference **Binary Large Objects** (BLOBs), allowing documents to be included, or for document stores to be referenced. Applications common in hospital informatics and clinical computing, based around RDBMS software, include oncology management systems, the electronic patient record, cardiology patient monitoring systems and equipment management systems. The latter are considered in the Applications section of this chapter. A common feature of such systems is the use of web-based user interaction pages. The link between the RDBMS and their web interfaces is discussed in Chapter 10.

In addition to pure RDBMS other systems have been developed under the generic heading NoSQL. Interpreted as **Not Only SQL** these include systems with a relational foundation. Interpreted as **No SQL** there are systems designed to access data that has no predefined structure. The main approaches are to use key-value pairs, documents, or graphs (thought of as maps) as data objects, coupled with sophisticated search tools. NoSQL takes one into the world of Big Data and is beyond the scope of this book.

Typical applications

Image processing software

Image Processing is the application of a set of techniques and algorithms to a digital image to analyse, enhance or optimise image characteristics such as sharpness and contrast. Most image-processing techniques involve treating the image as either a signal or a matrix and applying standard signal-processing or matrix manipulation techniques respectively to it.

Terminology

A '*pixel*' or 'picture element' is the smallest sample of a two-dimensional image that can be programmatically controlled. The number of pixels in an image controls the resolution of the image. The pixel value typically represents its 'intensity' in terms of shades of grey (value 0−255) in a greyscale image or RGB (red, green, blue, each 0−255) values in a colour image.

A '*voxel*' or 'volumetric pixel' is the three-dimensional counterpart of the 2D pixel. It represents a single sample on a three dimensional image grid. Similar to pixels, the number of voxels in a 3D representation of an image controls its resolution. The spacing between voxels depends on the type of data and its intended use. In a 3D rendering of medical images such as CT scans and MRI scans, the size of a voxel is defined by the pixel size in each image slice and the slice thickness. The value stored in a voxel may represent multiple values. In CT scans, it is often the Hounsfield unit which can then be used to identify the type of tissue represented. In MRI volumes, this may be the weighting factor (T1, T2, T2*, etc.).

Image Arithmetic is usually performed at pixel-level and includes arithmetic as well as logical operations applied to corresponding points on two or more images of equal size.

Geometric transformations can be applied to digital images for translation, rotation, scaling and shearing as required. Matrix transformation algorithms are typically employed in this case.

For binary and greyscale images, various *morphological operations* such as image opening and closing, skeletonisation, dilation, erosion, etc. may also be employed for pattern matching or feature extraction.

An *Image Histogram* represents the distribution of image intensity values for an input digital image. Histogram manipulation is often used to modify image contrast or for image segmentation when the range of values for the desired feature is clearly definable.

Some common Image Processing applications are introduced below.

Feature extraction is an area of image processing where specific characteristics within an input image are isolated using a set of algorithms. Some commonly used methods for this include contour tracing, thresholding and template matching. Image segmentation is a common application of feature extraction which is often used with medical imaging to identify anatomical structures.

Pattern and Template Matching is useful in applications ranging from feature extraction to image substitution. It is also used with face and character recognition and is one of the most commonly used image processing applications.

There are several image processing software packages available from freely distributed ones like ImageJ to expensive suites such as Matlab and Avizo that range in functionality and targeted applications. We'll only discuss a few of the commonly used ones within Medical Physics/Clinical Engineering here.

The image format most commonly used in medical applications is DICOM, providing a standardized structure for medical image management and exchange between different medical applications (see "DICOM" in Chapter 8 for a description of this standard).

Image processing software packages

ImageJ[43] is an open source, Java-based image processing program developed at the National Institute of Health. It provides various in-built image acquisition, analysis and processing plugins as well as the ability to build your own using ImageJ's built-in editor and a Java compiler. User-written plugins make it possible to solve many bespoke image processing and analysis problems.

ImageJ can display, edit, analyse, process, save, and print 8-bit colour and greyscale, 16-bit integer and 32-bit floating point images. It can read many standard image formats as well as raw formats. It is multithreaded, so time-consuming operations can be performed in parallel on multi-CPU hardware. It has built-in routines for most common image manipulation operations in the medical field including processing of DICOM images and image stacks such as those from CT & MRI.

Mimics[44] (**Materialise Interactive Medical Image Control System**) is an image processing software for 3D design and modelling, developed by Materialise NV. It is used to create 3D surface models from stacks of 2D image data. These 3D models can then be used for a variety of engineering applications.

Mimics calculates surface 3D models from stacked image data such as CT, micro-CT, CBCT (**Cone Beam Computed Tomography**), MRI, Confocal Microscopy and Ultrasound, through image segmentation. The **Region Of Interest** (ROI) selected in the segmentation process is converted to a 3D surface model using an adapted marching cubes algorithm that takes the partial volume effect into account, leading to very accurate 3D models. The 3D files are represented in the STL[45] format.

The most common input format is DICOM, but other image formats such as TIFF, JPEG, BMP and Raw are also supported. Output file formats differ, depending on the subsequent application, but common 3D output formats include STL, VRML, PLY and DXF.

Mimics provides a platform to bridge stacked image data to a variety of different medical engineering applications such as **Finite Element Analysis** (FEA − see the next section), **Computer Aided Design** (CAD), Rapid Prototyping, etc.

MATLAB[46]

MATLAB is a programming environment for algorithm development, data analysis, visualisation, and numerical computation.

It has a wide range of applications, including signal and image processing, communications, control design, test and measurement, financial modelling and analysis, and computational biology. The MATLAB Image Processing Toolbox™ provides a comprehensive set of reference-standard algorithms and graphical tools for image processing, analysis,

---

43. https://imagej.nih.gov/ij/.
44. https://www.materialise.com/en/medical/software/mimics.
45. An abbreviation of "stereolithography", this is a file format native to the stereolithography CAD software created by 3D Systems.
46. https://www.mathworks.com/products/matlab.html.

visualisation, and algorithm development. It also has built-in support for DICOM images and provides various functions to manipulate DICOM datasets. This makes it a widely used tool in various Medical Physics/Clinical Engineering research groups and related academia.

Interactive data language

IDL (**Interactive Data Language**)[47] is a cross-platform vectorised programming language used for interactive processing of large amounts of data including image processing. IDL also includes support for medical imaging via the IDL DICOM Toolkit add-on module.

The image processing software packages mentioned here are but a few of the commonly used ones within a Medical Physics/Clinical Engineering environment partly due to their extensive libraries for medical image processing and partly for historical reasons.[48] There are many more free-for-use as well as commercial software packages available providing varying degrees of functionality for different applications and if there is a choice available, it would be advisable to explore the options available for a particular task.

Finite element analysis

The finite element method is an engineering technique used for analysing complex structural problems. FEA is an effective and widely used computer-based simulation technique for modelling mechanical loading of various engineering structures, providing predictions of displacement and induced stress distribution due to the applied load (Pao, 1986).

The basic idea of the finite element method is to break up a continuous model into a geometrically similar model made up of disjoint linked components of simple geometry called *finite elements*. The behaviour of an individual element is described with a relatively simple set of equations. These elements are made up of a collection of *nodes* which define both the element's shape as well as its degrees of freedom.

The geometry of the element is defined by the placement of the geometric nodal points. Most elements used in practice have fairly simple geometries. In one dimension, elements are usually straight lines or curved segments. In two dimensions they are of triangular or quadrilateral shape. In three dimensions the most common shapes are tetrahedra, pentahedra and hexahedra.

Elements are joined together at nodes along *edges*. When adjacent elements share nodes, the response field is shared across boundaries. Material and structural properties such as Young's Modulus are assigned to each element that describes how it would respond to applied loading conditions. Nodes are assigned at a certain density throughout the material depending on the anticipated stress levels of a particular area. Regions which will receive large amounts of stress (for example, areas of fracture-risk) usually have a higher node density than those which experience little or no stress. The response of each element is then defined in terms of the nodal degrees of freedom. The equations describing the responses of the individual elements are joined into an extremely large set of simultaneous equations that describe the response of the whole structure. Analysis of the model provides nodal displacements and induced stress distribution due to the applied load (Fig. 9.13).

FEA has become a solution to the task of predicting failure due to unknown stresses by showing problem areas in a material and allowing designers to see all of the theoretical stresses within. This method of product design and testing is far superior to the manufacturing costs which would accrue if each sample was actually built and tested.

In practice, a finite element analysis usually consists of three principal steps (Roylance, 2001):

1. Preprocessing: The discretised model of the structure is divided up into nodes and elements. Constraints and loads are then applied as required. Several commercial finite element analysis packages such as ANSYS, FEMtools and Quick-Field have graphical user interfaces for this stage. Some of these packages also offer an option to import CAD models and overlay a mesh on these to generate the FE model.
2. Analysis: The dataset prepared by the pre-processor is used as input to the finite element code itself, which constructs and solves a system of linear or nonlinear algebraic equations that compute displacements corresponding to externally applied forces at the nodal points.
3. Postprocessing: Most FEA packages present FE analysis results graphically with colour coding or contours depicting hotspots and the range of deformation.

---

47. https://www.harrisgeospatial.com/Software-Technology/IDL.
48. Although these two factors can be seen to feed each other.

FIG. 9.13 (A) A FEM model of cancellous bone with uniform load applied across the top. (B) The same model showing the deformation due to this loading, after 16 iterations.

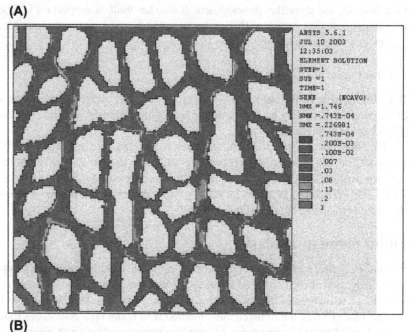

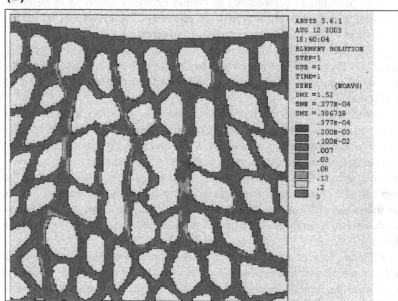

Artificial intelligence and expert systems

The creation of **Artificial Intelligence** (AI) has been a human goal for a very long time. One of the most famous examples, the Grand Turk (a chess-playing automaton) was a hoax, the perpetration of which was aided by the desire for such a device to exist.

In computer science terms, AI is popularly perceived to be something that can pass the "Turing Test" (Turing, 1950) in which an interrogator puts questions to a "thinking machine" and a human and is unable to tell the difference between the two. Currently AI is defined more as "*the study and design of intelligent agents*" (Poole et al., 1998)

AI is predominantly concerned with the solution of problems and can be best illustrated using a maze problem.

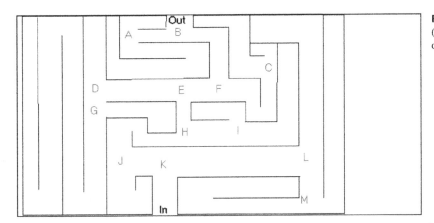

FIG. 9.14 A simple maze. The "decision points" (i.e. the points at which a decision must be made in order to progress) are labelled as capital letters.

In Fig. 9.14, the quickest route through the maze can be seen to be In-K-J-H-E-F-B-Out. Artificial Intelligence is concerned with how the decision is made at each point, using a set of rules, or heuristics.[49] A simple heuristic might be "turn left" (in order to avoid confusion, "left" is taken to be "not right" where "right" is clear but left may not be — there are no cases in this example where neither left nor right is clear). This yields the path In-K-J-Fail. "Turn right" yields In-K-L-M-Fail, whereas "alternate left and right" gives either In-K-J-H-E-F-B-A-Fail (the best result so far) or In-K-L-Fail (an equal worst result). Additional complexity is therefore required and may be introduced as follows:

4. If the decision point has not been encountered before, turn left.
5. If a dead end is reached, return to the most recently encountered decision point and turn right.
6. If both routes from a decision point reach dead ends, return to the most recently encountered decision point before this and turn right.

This yields the result In-K-J-Fail-J-H-E-D-G-Fail-G-Fail-D-Fail-E-F-B-A-Fail-A-Fail-B-Out, which is successful but long-winded. It does, however, demonstrate the use of heuristics to solve a problem. It also introduces a new requirement not previously present: that of recording the decision points encountered and the order in which they were encountered. A more complex maze would also require the decision made at that point to be recorded.

Assuming that we have some knowledge of the final target (for example, its co-ordinate position) we may postulate a further enhancement where the direction of turn (left or right) is determined by taking a small step in each direction and determining the absolute distance to the target from each and taking the direction yielding the minimum value. An absolute rule (e.g. "turn left") is still required in the event of a tie. Such a heuristic adds the requirement to record the decision taken at each point encountered and would yield the path In-L-Fail-L-M-Fail-M-Fail-K-J-H-E-F-B-Out which (aside from a poor start) is very efficient.

The best way to record this process is by using a *stack*. This is also known as a *heap*[50] and consists (as the name implies) of a **last-in-first-out** (LIFO) list[51] (just like a pile of paper on your desk). The stack might progress as follows (Table 9.7) for the heuristic outlined above in points 1—3 (using "r" and "l" to represent "right" and "left" — note that this implementation records the action(s) left to be taken should you return, not the one(s) taken, which is thus more scalable):

It can be seen that such rigid heuristics may occasionally give rapid success, but may equally give poor results. Whilst this example will always produce a result (as the number of options is finite) other problems may not do so or may lead into a cyclic path from which there is no escape.[52] One vital component of intelligence is missing from this heuristic-based system: the ability to learn. Artificial Intelligence therefore seeks to develop algorithms that are self-modifying, based upon the results that have been achieved. In order to illustrate this, we will investigate the **Artificial Neural Network** (ANN).

An ANN is an information-processing paradigm whose intention is to take a large number of inputs (for example, parameters from an ECG trace) and produce an output representing a decision (for example, whether or not this trace is

49. Wikipedia defines a heuristic as "a way of directing your attention fruitfully".
50. Although specific implementations in programming languages such as C++ and Java give these different meanings (primarily to do with scope) they are essentially the same structure.
51. A similar structure, the queue, is a **first-in-first-out** structure, often referred to as FIFO.
52. Minotaurs are an end to the problem but not necessarily a solution. The reader may select their own analogy as to what a Minotaur may represent.

TABLE 9.7 A stack implemented to record the maze tracing.

Step	Action	Stack
1	Turn left @ K	Kr
2	Turn left @ J	KrJr
3	Dead end — retrace. Take top element from stack and follow this (turn right @ J)	Kr
4	Turn left @ H	KrHr
5	Turn left @ E	KrHrEr
6	Turn left @ D	KrHrErDr
7	Turn left @ G	KrHrErDrGr
8	Dead end — retrace. Turn right @ G	KrHrErDr
9	Dead end — retrace. Turn right @ D	KrHrEr
10	Dead end — retrace. Turn right @ E	KrHr
11	Turn left @ F	KrHrFr
12	Turn left @ B	KrHrFrBr
13	Turn left @ A	KrHrFrBrAr
14	Dead end — retrace. Turn right @ A	KrHrFrBr
15	Dead end — retrace. Turn right @ B	KrHrFr
16	Success	

normal). It does this through a collection of highly interconnected processing elements (called neurones) which are trained to produce reliable output. In Fig. 9.15, the two outputs might be labelled "normal" and "requires investigation" (continuing the ECG example).

In the example in Fig. 9.15, information flows forwards only (in the case of this diagram, from left to right). At each point processing occurs and this is fed forwards into the next layer. It is not difficult to extrapolate this model into one with multiple hidden layers and/or feeds backwards as well as forwards. The hidden layer is so called because this auto-tunes itself. In order to achieve this, data with known results are divided into two sets: a training set and a test set. The training set is used to tune the processing in the hidden layers (this may be as simple as assigning weights to the input values in order to determine the value to feed forwards). Once tuned, this processing is fixed and the test set is used to determine how successful the tuning has been. If the results are not as good as required (and the required level of success may depend on the problem being posed and the consequences of an incorrect output) then redesign is required: either in the processing neurones or the structure of the network. The process is then repeated. At no point must the test set be used to train the network or vice versa (otherwise it has become a data-fitting exercise rather than a machine learning one) and the importance of adequately dividing the data into training and test sets can clearly be seen.

One of the successful areas of AI has been the expert system. An expert system seeks to replicate the decision-making processes of a human expert and as such combines the principles described above: it is heuristic (some inputs produce a definitive output), can account for noisy data (some inputs produce a probabilistic output) and is adaptive (it can be trained). It comprises two parts: an inference engine and a knowledge base. The knowledge base is a set of rules in an IF...THEN structure, for example:

- IF the chest wall is moving THEN respiration is taking place.
- IF the stain of the organism is gramneg and the morphology of the organism is rod and the aerobicity of the organism is aerobic THEN there is strongly suggestive evidence (0.8) that the class of the organism is enterobacteriaceae (Medical Expert Systems)

The inference engine (as the name implies) infers new rules based upon the ones already present in the knowledge base. It may do this by chaining together the outputs from several different rules (possibly in a network structure akin to the ANN) or by requesting clarification from the operator. A key output of the expert system as opposed to the ANN is that the logic used in reaching the result is displayed along with the result. In an ANN, the logic remains hidden.

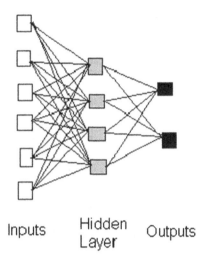

Inputs   Hidden   Outputs
              Layer

FIG. 9.15   A simple feedforward network, where processing flows "forwards" from inputs to outputs.

Equipment management database systems

An equipment management database system is, as the name implies, a database of equipment around which a system has been constructed to manage that equipment. As such, it shares a lot of features with asset management database systems but contains additional features to aid in the management of equipment, which for the focus of this book means medical equipment.

An asset management database will contain such information as the equipment name, manufacturer, purchase cost and date, replacement cost (and planned replacement date if known), location and a service history (if appropriate). Reports may then be run against this data to produce information on capital spend and assistance in forecasting future spend. It may also be used to highlight unreliable equipment, commonalities of purchasing (in order to assist in contract negotiations and bulk buying) and equipment loss due to theft or vandalism.

An equipment management database system will include all of these features but will also include information so that the equipment may be managed appropriately. Probably the most common example of this additional functionality is the PPM (**Planned Preventative Maintenance**).[53] In order to implement PPMs, all equipment managed must be assigned a service plan. In its simplest form, this is a set time frame: for example, a set of scales that requires calibration once a year. A more complex plan might include different tests or calibrations to be performed at different times. This type of service plan will generally still include a fixed time interval but will also include a service rotation. On the first rotation, it might be visually inspected to ensure that all seals are still in place. On the second rotation a calibration might be added and on the third a **Portable Appliance Test** (PAT) renewal might be undertaken in addition to the inspection and calibration. The system will keep track of all work that is due (producing worklists for a particular time period), the service rotation that is due, parts and labour used in the maintenance and so on.

Inspecting, calibrating and testing all of a hospital's medical equipment is not a minor task: most such services spread the load across the entire year, which the management system is also able to assist in planning by reporting on peaks and troughs in the planned workload, adjusting for planned staff absences and potential peaks and troughs in emergency repairs (from historical data).

Further functions that such a system can assist with are the management of contracts (where equipment is maintained by a third party), the recording of repairs undertaken (thus determining when equipment has reached the end of its economic life) and the recording of medical device training.

In this latter example, all staff of the hospital are recorded along with the equipment they have been trained to use. Thus, training can be kept current and a mechanism for preventing the unsafe use of equipment implemented.

In order to achieve all this functionality, an equipment management database system will need to be interfaced to other systems, such as a capital asset management system, a human resources system and a contracts management system. See "Links to hospital administration systems" in Chapter 8 for information on interfacing.

---

53. Sometimes simply referred to as "servicing".

Device tracking systems

Electronic tracking devices are a growing element of hospital practice and their role is considered here in terms of potential, rather than system design. The benefits of tracking devices are numerous, from the reduction in time spent looking for equipment (estimated as being 2.5% of nurse time by UCLH in 2011[54]), to theft prevention. Other potential benefits are improved servicing due to having a reliable equipment asset register and the ability to run a more efficient equipment library.

Broadly, there are three types of technology to consider, as described below. Each requires the asset to have a tag attached, which communicates with the central system. The tags may vary in size, depending on the amount of data required and the distance from the transponder that it is required to communicate with. This means that such a system may be deployed for multiple purposes. For example, it may describe bed occupancy, the stocking of a pharmacy cabinet or track the whereabouts of babies and/or vulnerable patients, as well as staff in lone working situations.

The first technology is via a wireless network, usually the organisation's WiFi network. Tags transmit a WiFi signal, which is picked up by WiFi access points — if the signal is picked up by 4 or more access points, the location of the device can be triangulated in three dimensions. This system may be supplemented by additional ultrasound "beacons" to more accurately locate devices within a particular room. There is a claimed accuracy of location to 2m (although there exists some scepticism about this and it is probably only possible with the addition of ultrasound beacons), but it does make use of an existing WiFi infrastructure so no additional hardware is required (thereby also minimising disruption during installation). It does, though, require many more WiFi access points than is needed just for wireless computing in order to get proper triangulation. Using an existing infrastructure places an additional load on the network and tags are relatively expensive.

The second technology is **Radio Frequency Identification** (RFID), where a network of RFID receivers is positioned across the organisation, connected to the **Local Area Network** (LAN). Tags (which can be either active or passive) communicate with these receivers, which can then track their location. Passive tags respond to a signal from gateways (from where they also draw their power to do so), whereas active ones will transmit data to a nearby receiver and have on-board power. Active tags can also transmit additional information, such as battery status for portable equipment. This is a proven technology, being used in many industries, including retail, where passive tags are attached to stock, and their location/presence is tracked. Tags are very cheap, but the granularity of the mapping is not very precise. An additional network (of RFID transponders) is required, which determines the granularity.

The third technology is RFID with **Infra-Red** (IR) which uses RFID technology, supplemented by infra-red transmitters/detectors. IR can be used to track devices to a very granular level (bed space, or even a drawer), and information is then communicated centrally via an RFID network. This provides an accurate location of items at a very granular level and is fully scalable for patients, assets and staff. However, an additional network of RFID transponders needs to be installed and the solution is quite complex in that there are several technologies involved. The risk of failure is therefore higher.

Abbreviations

AI Artificial Intelligence
ANN Artificial Neural Network
BLOB Binary Large Object
CAD Computer Aided Design
CBCT Cone Beam Computed Tomography
CC Change Control
COTS Commercial Off-The-Shelf Software
CSV Comma Separated Values
DFD Data Flow Diagram
EPROM Electrically Programmable Read-Only Memory
ERD Entity-Relationship Diagram
FEA Finite Element Analysis
FIFO First-In-First-Out
IaaS Infrastructure as a Service
IDE Integrated Development Environment
IDL Interactive Data Language

---

54. Internal document, not externally published.

IR Infra-Red
JVM Java Virtual Machine
LAN Local Area Network
LCSAJ Linear Code Sequence And Jump
LIFO Last-In-First-Out
MFC Microsoft Foundation Classes
MIMICS Materialise Interactive Medical Image Control System
NoSQL Not Only SQL or No SQL
OBS Output-Based Specification
OOP Object-Oriented Programming
OS Operating System
OTS Off-The-Shelf (software)
OTSS Off-The-Shelf Software
PAT Portable Appliance Test
PPM Planned Preventative Maintenance
RDBMS Relational Database Management Systems
RFID Radio Frequency Identification
ROI Region Of Interest
ROM Read-Only Memory
RTM Requirements Traceability Matrix
SaaS Software as a Service
SASEA Selecting Appropriate Software Engineering Assets
SCCS Source Code Control System
SCM Software Configuration Management
SOUP Software Of Unknown Provenance
SQA Software Quality Assurance
SQC Software Quality Control
SQL Structured Query Language
SRS Software Requirements Specification
SVN Apache Subversion
UML Unified Modelling Language
VB Visual Basic
VCS Version Control System
WIMP Windows, Icons, Mouse, Pointer
Windows CE Windows Compact Edition

References

Bennett, S., McRobb, S., Farmer, R., 2010. Object-Oriented Systems Analysis and Design Using UML. McGraw-Hill.

Burns, A., Wellings, A., 2009. Real-Time Systems and Programming Languages. Addison-Wesley.

Codd, E.F., 1970. A relational model of data for large shared data banks. Association for Computing Machinery (ACM) 13 (6), 377–387.

FDA Software Validation, 2017. Available from: https://uk.mathworks.com/solutions/medical-devices/fda-software-validation.html.

Got SOUP? – Part 2: OS, Drivers, Runtimes, May 24, 2013. Available from: https://blog.cm-dm.com/post/2013/05/24/Got-SOUP-Part-2-OS%2C-Drivers%2C-Runtimes.

Hobbs, C., 2012. Build and Validate Safety in Medical Device Software. Medical Electronics Design. Available from: http://www.softwarecpr.com.php72-38.lan3-1.websitetestlink.com/wp-content/uploads/Free/Articles/Article-BuildandValidateSafetyinMedicalDeviceSoftware-010412.pdf.

IEEE 14764-2006 – ISO/IEC/IEEE International Standard for Software Engineering – Software Life Cycle Processes – Maintenance. Available from: https://standards.ieee.org/standard/14764-2006.html.

ISO/IEC 9075-1 2016, 2016. "Information Technology – Database Languages – SQL" Part 1: Framework. SQL/Framework, Geneva.

ISO/IEC/IEEE 29119-3:2013 Software and Systems Engineering – Software Testing. Available from: iso.org.

Kernighan, B.W., Pike, R., 1999. The Practice of Programming. Addison-Wesley.

Knuth, D.E., 2011. The Art of Computer Programming, vols. 1–4A. Addison-Wesley.

Lawlis, P.K., 1997. Guidelines for Choosing a Computer Language: Support for the Visionary Organization. Available from: http://archive.adaic.com/docs/reports/lawlis/content.htm.

Medical Expert Systems. University of Brighton. Available from: http://www.it.bton.ac.uk/staff/lp22/CS237/CS237MedicalXSys.html.

Miles, R., Hamilton, K., 2006. Learning UML 2.0 – A Pragmatic Introduction to UML O'Reilly.

Off-the-Shelf Software Use in Medical Devices, September 9, 1999. Available from. https://www.fda.gov/downloads/MedicalDevices/.../ucm073779.pdf.

Pao, Y.C., 1986. A First Course in Finite Element Analysis. Allyn and Bacon Inc.

Poole, D., Mackworth, A., Goebel, R., 1998. Computational Intelligence: A Logical Approach. Oxford University Press, New York.

Roylance, D., 2001. Finite Element Analysis. MIT. Available from: http://web.mit.edu/course/3/3.11/www/modules/fea.pdf.

SQA definition. Available from: http://www.sqa.net/index.htm.

Standard for Software Component Testing. Available from: http://www.testingstandards.co.uk/Component%20Testing.pdf.

TickITplus — A Path to Excellence in IT. Available from: http://www.tickitplus.org/.

The Haskell Programming Language. Available from: http://www.haskell.org/haskellwiki/Haskell.

Turing, A., 1950. Computing machinery and intelligence. Mind LIX (236), 433—460. Available from: https://academic.oup.com/mind/article/LIX/236/433/986238.

Wellings, A. 2004 Book Web Page for Concurrent and Real-Time Programming in Java. A collection of sample programs and an introduction to Java for those familiar with C++/C and OOP. Available from: http://www.cs.york.ac.uk/rts/books/CRTJbook.html.

Chapter 10

Web development

Paul S. Ganney[a,b], Sandhya Pisharody[c] and Ed McDonagh[d]

[a]University College London Hospitals NHS Trust, London, United Kingdom; [b]University of Liverpool, Liverpool, United Kingdom; [c]Varian Medical Systems, Crawley, United Kingdom; [d]The Royal Marsden Hospital NHS Foundation Trust, London, United Kingdom

Chapter outline

Hosting strategies

Software

Content or applications accessible via a web browser can be served from almost any computer device — from an Internet-of-Things lightbulb to a server-farm distributed across continents. The computers providing these web services can be running almost any operating system from the last 20 years and there is also a large choice of web server software.

The majority of active websites are hosted on UNIX-like operating systems (mainly various flavours of Linux), with most of the rest being hosted on Microsoft Windows.[i] About half of active websites use the Apache HTTP server or NGINX (pronounced engine-x) software, both of which are primarily used on Linux but can be installed on Windows and some other operating systems. Microsoft's IIS is used for about 6% of active sites, with a similar proportion using Google's web server software. The rest is made up of software with a small market share, or server software that is configured not to reveal itself to the client, and therefore could be one of the applications already discussed.[ii]

Static websites can be hand-coded or built using website generator software using code or graphical website building software. Dynamic websites might use server-side-scripting with **Hypertext Preprocessor** (PHP), Python or Ruby scripts, or using the **Common Gateway Interface** (CGI) to execute compiled binaries, Perl or Java, and they might have client-side-scripting in JavaScript. More details on these technologies can be found further on in this chapter in the 'Programming' section. A LAMP stack is a term used to refer to a set of open-source software used for web applications and hosting, commonly consisting of Linux, the Apache HTTP web server, the MySQL database and the PHP scripting language. Each of these elements can be swapped out of course, for example using NGINX instead of Apache; MariaDB or PostgreSQL instead of MySQL; and Perl, Python or Ruby instead of PHP. A similar stack can also be hosted on Windows using Apache or IIS.

---

i Usage of operating systems for websites. Available from: https://w3techs.com/technologies/overview/operating_system/all.
ii January 2019 Web Server Survey. Available from: https://news.netcraft.com/archives/category/web-server-survey/.

Containers and virtualization

It is common to provide multiple web services from a single host, and there are many ways to do this. The first is to provide a hypervisor[1] type virtualization, such as Xen, KVM, Hyper-V, VirtualBox or VMWare. The first two of these run on Linux operating systems, Hyper-V runs on Windows operating systems and the final two run on both. They can all host multiple virtual machines (guests) running Linux or Windows. With this sort of virtualization, each guest operating system runs as though it were installed directly on real hardware. The resources of the host system must be divided up between the guest, with limited scope for overcommitting system memory and processors — this therefore limits the number of virtual machines that can be run on a host. However, depending on the capabilities of the guest operating system, resources such as memory, CPUs and storage can be dynamically changed as required, and depending on the hypervisor software, virtual machines can also be moved from host to host and copied and backed up.

It is possible to host many more guests on a single machine by using a container technology such as LXC or LXD.[iii] This allows Linux containers to be created that share the same kernel, memory and processors as the host operating system and the other containers. This limits the host and guest operating system to Linux. Within a container, the operating system has full access to memory, CPUs, network and storage, managed by the host kernel and limited only by what is available, current usage and any limits imposed by the configuration. With shared resources, security can be a concern, but this has been addressed with LXD using 'unprivileged' containers by default with various provisions to prevent a container accessing storage or memory being used by another. Containers can be created, copied and destroyed in milliseconds, and they can be moved to different hosts and have resources dynamically changed as was possible with virtual machines.

A third method of running many services from one host is to use application containerization, for example using Docker.[iv] This time each container runs just one service — that might be a database or a web server, with just enough operating system in the container for it to run. The containers share a network and storage stack, and are connected to each other using configuration on the host computer to provide a service such as a website application. With application containers, each container can be updated when a newer version of that component is released, with data being held in a separate location. Application container services can be hosted on Windows or Linux, with Linux Docker containers. In addition, Windows Server 2016 and Windows 10 release 1607 and later allow Windows based Docker containers.

With each form of containers or virtualization, it is possible to have software that will 'orchestrate' creation, moving or destroying of machines or containers as demand for a service changes or resources become available or degrade.

On-premises hosting

The easiest way to get started with creating a web server and providing a web service of some kind is to install the software on a computer already running on the network, for example a desktop PC (assuming the necessary administration rights have been granted). All the software can be installed for free and there are many guides available on the internet detailing the steps required. This can be useful for prototyping new ideas and quickly provide services to the local network, but isn't a solution for a production service — uptime/availability will be limited by when the PC is on and not too busy and the service cannot scale. However, if virtual machines or containers are available then migration to dedicated servers when available becomes possible.

Another option is to make use of a computer that has reached the end of its useful life as a desktop computer or a clinical server for example. With a fresh installation of a Linux operating system, they can relatively easily be used for hosting web services, or with virtualization or containers many services. This is inexpensive in that no new hardware or software needs to be purchased, though a knowledge of server operating system configuration and maintenance is required (or needs to be acquired). Again, many guides are available. One should take into consideration when re-using older computers that they may be less efficient than a newer computer and therefore might cost more in power or cooling.

If a new server can be purchased, then suitable hardware will range from a cheap, single board computer such as a Raspberry Pi providing a single service through to a suite of multi-processor servers providing high-availability and redundancy. If local services are to be provided in a production environment for the department, then it is usually worth procuring two or three servers for the purpose to enable redundancy and resilience, potentially with a separate server providing the storage.

---

1. A hypervisor creates and runs virtual machines. It may be software, firmware or hardware.
iii Infrastructure for Container Projects. Available from: https://linuxcontainers.org.
iv Docker. Available from: https://www.docker.com.

It is essential when setting up new computers, virtual machines or containers to liaise with the IT services/department. They may have policies that constrain what is possible locally, and they will almost certainly need to configure network switches to enable the use of more than one IP address per port if many virtual machines or containers are to be provided from a single PC or server.[2]

The IT department is also likely to have a virtual machine facility of some kind, and it might be possible to make use of it to create servers and run web services for the department from their infrastructure. This might have the advantage of having storage, networking and backups taken care of by the IT department, but may incur costs and limitations as to what can be done with the servers and services.

Modern web browsers are increasingly requiring or promoting encrypted (https) connections between the web browser and the server, even for local servers. Getting appropriate security certificates for web servers that are not on the internet is not easy, but it is possible to generate 'self-signed' certificates on a web server. However, these are not trusted by the web browsers. It is likely that an institution will have a corporate security certificate installed on all the computers on the domain, which can be used to sign the key via a **Certificate Signing Request** (CSR) which will mean that it is trusted by the web browser.

Off-premises hosting

If a web service that is available on the internet is to be provided, either the IT department will need to install a server in their internet-facing facility, or more likely a commercial hosting company would be utilized. The easiest end of the spectrum is shared hosting. This will provide a web-based control panel to manage email and website content, with **file transfer protocol** (ftp) access to upload content and — depending on the host — a variety of web applications that can be used; from building simple websites to installing and configuring content management systems. Shared hosting is usually low cost (from a few pounds per month), easy to use with limited knowledge, and has no server maintenance requirements beyond maintaining any software deployed. The disadvantages are that there is usually no 'shell' access, i.e. it is not possible to run commands on the server or install software outside of that provided by the host and there is little or no control over which version of PHP, Perl or MySQL is installed nor how they are configured. Each server is usually used to serve hundreds or thousands of websites in others' control, which can leave the site vulnerable to resources being used up by processes on other accounts, and the IP address all the sites share being blacklisted if another account on the server has been compromised or misused. A variation on this approach is managed hosting, where usually a particular application (such as the content management system WordPress) is installed and maintained by the host company, so customization and content are all that is required rather than maintaining the software.

Dedicated servers are at the other end of the spectrum, with control of whole servers configured to the requirements of the user, who then has responsibility for all the operating system and server software installation and maintenance. This service is expensive, but until recently was the only way to guarantee the performance obtainable by not sharing resources in any way. The advantage of dedicated servers is that you can install whatever software is needed, with no sharing of processor, memory, storage or networking; the server is physically isolated from other servers, improving security. The disadvantages are the cost and the limitations on making changes to the hardware resources.

Virtual Private Servers (VPSs) and Cloud servers share many characteristics. Both offer a share of physical resources by means of virtual machines with all the inherent advantages. They are available with a wide range of configurations and an associated wide range of costs, with different applications being able to take advantage of servers tailored to their needs, for example lots of memory compared to the CPU numbers or vice-versa. Each will normally have access to its own IP address(es) and local as well as additional provisioned storage of different speeds and cost models. Both VPS and Cloud servers will require the user to install and manage the operating system and all the software, though operating system images will normally be provided to get started. The difference will mainly be in the flexibility, the payment models and the ability to control the servers programmatically. VPS servers will usually be paid on a monthly basis. If a server is turned off, it remains as a dedicated resource, and the cost doesn't change. Cloud provisioned servers are usually paid for by the minute or by the hour. Unless the resource is reserved, when a server is turned off it is destroyed (logically), and costs cease to be incurred. If a small server has been provided, but there is a requirement for some more demanding processing for the next 15 min, the CPU and memory profile can be changed, the extra processing done and then the changes are reversed, with costs for the extra resources only being for those 15 min. Cloud servers can also be created, modified and destroyed using an **Application Programming Interface** (API). An application may sometimes have higher demand, and when it does the server resources can be scaled up or new servers created to meet that demand automatically,

---

2. You may find your port is automatically blocked if you don't tell them first!

then when the demand drops off, they can be scaled back down and any extra servers that were provisioned destroyed. This then allows for massive resources to be utilized when needed, but not paying for them the rest of the time. Software that can orchestrate server and services provision can work with both on-premises and off-premises hardware, with the ability to move virtual machines and services between an on-premises cloud and an off-premises cloud automatically if required.

Obtaining security certificates is even more important when running services from the internet, but it is also easier to do. Many providers of certificates to enable the running of a trusted https site are available at a variety of costs, but for all but the shared hosting it is easy to obtain a free certificate that is trusted by all modern browsers and operating systems from the "Let's Encrypt"[v] certificate authority. Some shared hosting providers also allow or provide Let's Encrypt certificates.

For all servers that are not owned and located within the institution, extra attention must be given to the information governance of the data held on that server. For example, it must be known where the server is physically located — even for VPS or cloud provisioned servers — as there is a distinction in the legal requirements depending on which country it is located in (see Chapter 8 for a discussion of such issues).

Summary

The choice of hosting strategy will depend on many factors — the task to be achieved, the audience, the sensitivity of the data, the budget, the available skills, how mission critical it is or might become. The points discussed here can be used to guide and inform the decision-making process.

Programming
Web programming

The world-wide web is an information sharing concept that resides on the Internet. The roots of it are in work done by Sir Tim Berners-Lee in 1989 when he worked at CERN in Geneva. The basic concepts are:

- The separation of content storage from content display.
- The use of mark-up languages to describe but not enforce the layout (**Hypertext**[3] **Markup Language,** or HTML being the main one in use).
- The use of links to jump from one page to another (**Hypertext Transfer Protocol**, or HTTP).
- The use of a **Uniform Resource Locator** (URL) to describe the location of information.

Web pages reside on Web servers and are delivered to Web browsers, where they are displayed. A basic page consists of the content and a series of tags describing how that content should be displayed. Originally these were not prescriptive and left the browser to determine how they should be displayed, but later additions to HTML have allowed such prescription, especially through the use of **cascading style sheets** (CSS).

HTML is a stateless protocol, in that it is a communications protocol in which no information is retained by either sender or receiver. The sender transmits a packet to the receiver and does not expect an acknowledgment of receipt. Statelessness means that no client context is stored on the server between requests, so each request from any client must contain all the information necessary to service the request. This means that once the server has sent a page to a browser requesting it, nothing is retained. Revisiting a web page is therefore treated as though this were the first visit, every time. This can lead to user frustration as information such as access to protected pages and user preferences need to be re-entered. Cookies[4] were invented by Netscape to solve this problem and give "memory" to web servers and browsers. There are other ways to solve it (and for protected access a server-side solution is preferable), but cookies are easy to maintain and very versatile, with any session state information held in the client. One of the side-effects of the GDPR (see Chapter 8 for further detail) is the requirement for web sites to expressly seek permission to store cookies on the client machine.

A very simple web page might consist of the code and display shown in Fig. 10.1.

---

v Let's Encrypt. Available from: https://letsencrypt.org.
3. Hypertext is structured text that uses logical links (called hyperlinks) between text-based information resources.
4. A cookie is simply a small text file stored on the requesting machine.

(A) **(B)**

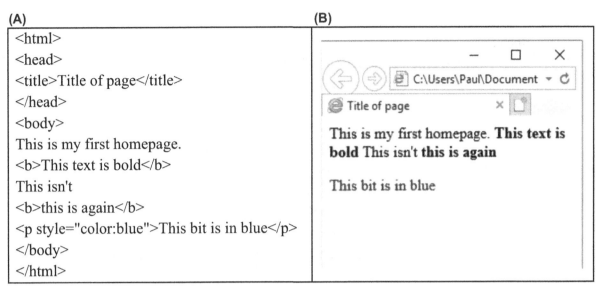

```
<html>
<head>
<title>Title of page</title>
</head>
<body>
This is my first homepage.
<b>This text is bold</b>
This isn't
<b>this is again</b>
<p style="color:blue">This bit is in blue</p>
</body>
</html>
```

FIG. 10.1 (A) The HTML code. (B) The display.

Note the following:

- Each tag begins with < and ends with >.
- For each tag <tag> there is an opposite </tag> denoting the beginning and end of that tag's influence. (There are some exceptions to this, but adding an end tag is never an error, merely unnecessary in some cases).
- Although the source has line breaks, the display does not — it needs to be told where the breaks should appear.
- There are two main parts to the page: the <head> and the <body>. Most of the display content resides in the <body>. The <head> is optional, the <body> is not.
- All tags are lower case (although this is convention and earlier versions of HTML specified upper case).
- Tags are nested and do not interweave — i.e. you cannot do <a><b></a></b>[5]
- The <p> tag has a style attribute, which overrides the default browser style.

Some key formatting tags are:

<b>	bold text
 	Line break — this is an empty tag so does not require a </br>[6]
<i>	italic text
<h1>	Heading style 1 — there are 6 predefined heading styles
<p>	Paragraph break — originally a larger break than ,[7] but now denotes a section of text complete with attributes — therefore the spacing is defined by the style.

Further complexity is added by the ability to program the page. This can be achieved in multiple ways and using various languages. For brevity, only JavaScript is considered here. Such programming adds interactivity to the page, for example a simple calculator, as shown in Fig. 10.2.

Note that, in this code, the bulk of the JavaScript is contained in the <head> section of the page. This separates the code from the display and means that the page renders quicker. The second piece of JavaScript is in the line

<input type="button" value="Calculate" onclick="self.docalc();">

---

5. One useful way to remember this is to consider them as sets of brackets, where you cannot close an outer set before an inner set.

6. In XHTML the <br> tag must be properly closed, like this: <br/>.

7. Although most browsers will interpret <p> without a corresponding </p> it is contrary to the standard and the use of attributes means that the browser does not know where to stop applying them.

(A)

```html
<html>
    <head>
        <script type="text/javascript">
            function docalc()
            {
                var form=self.document.calc
                form.week.value=form.packs.value*form.cost.value*7;
                year=form.packs.value*form.cost.value*365;
                year=year/100;
                year=Math.round(year);
                form.year.value=year;
                form.cds.value=Math.round(year/15); // assumes cost of CD
                is £15
            }
        </script>
    </head>

    <body>
        <h1>Chips calculator</h1>
        <form name="calc">
            How many packets of chips do you buy per day? <input type=text
            name="packs">
            <p>
            And how much does a packet cost (pence)? <input type=text
            name="cost"></p>
            <p>
            <input type="button" value="Calculate" onclick="self.docalc();">
            </p>
            <p>
            This costs you <input type=text name="week" disabled> pence per
            week
            and <input type=text name="year" disabled> pounds per year</p>
            <p>
            Instead of this you could have bought <input type=text name="cds"
            disabled> CDs per year</p>
        </form>
    </body>
</html>
```

FIG. 10.2   (A) The HTML code. (B) The display.

(B)

Chips calculator

How many packets of chips do you buy per day? [_____]

And how much does a packet cost (pence)? [_____]

[Calculate]

This costs you [_____] pence per week and [_____] pounds per year

Instead of this you could have bought [_____] CDs per year

FIG. 10.2 cont'd

Which calls the function in the <head> section when the button is clicked. JavaScript in the <head> section is usually for calling later, whereas that in the <body> section is for immediate execution. Note also the indentation — white space is ignored by the browser, so this is purely for the benefit of the programmer.

It is also worth noting the use of the variable "form" (assigned the value self.document.calc) which is then used as a prefix to all the input fields within the form. Without this, the prefix "self.document.calc" would have to be used on all input fields to identify them. Whilst "form" is a reserved word in HTML (and then only inside a tag), it is not in JavaScript so is a valid variable name.

Such functionality as the above form provides a web page with a degree of interaction, but programming web pages can go far beyond this. Because a web page as served to a browser is simply a stream of text, it is possible to program the entire system in languages such as C++, Python and PHP. The page that is served depends completely on the choices made on previous pages or visits. PHP is a server-side scripting language (unlike JavaScript which is client-side) and is therefore pre-processed, the text passing through the PHP pre-processor before being sent to the browser.

PHP files consist of standard HTML (and therefore can also contain JavaScript for executing on the browser) with specific PHP commands embedded. For example this code:

```
<html>
<body>
<?php echo "Hello World";?>
<p>" ... again"</p>
</body>
</html>
```

Is sent to the browser as:

```
<html>
<body>
Hello World
<p>" ... again"</p>
</body>
</html>
```

In this example there is a clear similarity with command-line script files but both are capable of much more — as with all programming tasks, selecting the most appropriate language for the task at hand is an important part of the project.

Fig. 10.3 shows some examples in different languages which produce the same output. Note that, apart from Fig. 10.3A, these are code snippets and require some additional code to produce the output in Fig. 10.3D and that the comments in Fig. 10.3A also apply to the code in Fig. 10.3B and C. See the section "Forms and data" for a further example. It is possible to embed one system in another. The C++ version in Fig. 10.3B could, of course, just mimic the JavaScript in Fig. 10.3A (prefixed by "cout <<" on each line). This might be appropriate for JavaScript in the <head> section, for example, for execution once the web page has been rendered in the client's browser and in response to a user action.

(A)

```
<html>
    <head>
    </head>
    <body>
        <script type="text/javascript">
            //If the time on your browser is less than 10,
            //you will get a "Good morning" greeting.
            var date=new Date()
            var time=date.getHours()

            if (time<10)
            {
                document.write("<b>Good morning</b>")
            }
            else
            {
                document.write("Good day!")
            }
            document.write("<p>")

            //You will receive a different greeting based
            //on what day it is. Note that Sunday=0,
            //Monday=1, Tuesday=2, etc.

            theDay=date.getDay()
            switch (theDay)
            {
                case 3:
                    document.write("Woeful Wednesday")
                    break
                case 5:
                    document.write("Finally Friday")
                    break
                case 6:
                    document.write("Super Saturday")
                    break
                case 0:
                    document.write("Sleepy Sunday")
                    break
                default:
                    document.write("Roll on the weekend!")
            }
            document.write("</p><p>")
            document.write(time)
            document.write("</p><p>")
            document.write(theDay)
            document.write("</p>")
        </script>
    </body>
</html>
```

FIG. 10.3 (A) JavaScript, (B) C++, (C) PHP, and (D) The browser rendering.

(B)
```
time_t now=time(NULL);
struct tm *localtm=localtime(&now);
int hours=localtm->tm_hour,day=localtm->tm_wday;
cout << "<html>\n<head>\n</head>\n<body>";
if(hours<10) cout << "<b>Good morning</b>";
else cout << "Good day!";
cout << "<p>";
switch(day)
{
        case 3:
                cout << "Woeful Wednesday";
                break;
        case 5:
                cout << "Finally Friday";
                break;
        case 6:
                cout << "Super Saturday";
                break;
        case 0:
                cout << "Sleepy Sunday";
                break;
        default:
                cout << "Roll on the weekend!";
}
cout << "</p><p>" << hours << "</p><p>" << day << "</p>";
cout << "</script>\n</body>\n</html>";
```

FIG. 10.3 cont'd

One key issue in web development is the location of the executing software. The term "executing software" is used in order to distinguish it from where the software actually resides and where the data resides. Indeed, it is possible to deploy systems where the data, the software and its execution are all in separate places.

The key difference is in whether the code executes on the client device or on the server. If it executes on the client, then a loss of connection is no problem, there is a lack of contention for processing power and the code can use data from the host device without it being transmitted. Additionally code may be re-used.

If the code executes on the server, then the resulting download may be smaller, confidential information residing on the server may be used and not transmitted and the server is probably a much more powerful processing device than the client. Additionally, especially for scripting, the workings of the algorithm are hidden from the end-user.

As an example, let us consider again the methods of generating the page in Fig. 10.3: JavaScript is client-side processing, where the web page is downloaded and the final display is generated on the client, whereas PHP and C++ are examples of a server-side technique, where the dynamic content is determined at the server and only the correct information for display is generated.

A mixture of techniques could, of course, be deployed, so that a system may take advantage of both client- and server-side processing and minimize the disadvantages. One such might be a patient monitoring system for home use: the patient's medical history is used to generate a series of criteria, without disclosing the history. These are sent to the patient's browser and the patient enters some fresh figures. These are tested using the downloaded criteria and a result given

(C)

```
<html>
        <head>
        </head>
        <body>
            <?php
                    $now=getdate();
                    if ($now[hours]<10) echo  "<b>Good morning</b>";
                    else echo "Good day!";
                    echo "<p>";
                    switch ($now[wday])
                    {
                            case 3:
                                    echo "Woeful Wednesday";
                                    break;
                            case 5:
                                    echo "Finally Friday";
                                    break;
                            case 6:
                                    echo "Super Saturday";
                                    break;
                            case 0:
                                    echo "Sleepy Sunday";
                                    break;
                            default:
                                    echo "Roll on the weekend!";
                    }
                    echo "</p><p>";
                    echo $now[hours];
                    echo "</p><p>";
                    echo $now[wday];
                    echo "</p>"
            ?>
        </body>
</html>
```

FIG. 10.3 cont'd

(D)

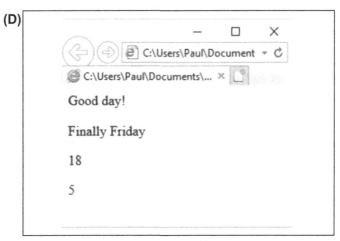

FIG. 10.3 cont'd

(e.g. "normal" or "contact clinic") without transmitting the actual results. At no point has sensitive data been transmitted, yet the patient is given tailored advice.

Forms and data

Whilst displaying information was the primary use of web technology, increasingly it is being used to collect data also. The example in Fig. 10.2 uses a form and it is worth investigating its structure.

As with other HTML, the form is enclosed between tags, in this case <form> and </form>. Within the form lie the input fields (named "packs", "cost") and the output fields (in this case they are the disabled input fields named "week", "year" and "cds"). Note that the form itself is given a name (an attribute within the <form> tag) meaning that multiple forms can exist within a web page, they can be nested and the processing of one form may address data from another.

The most important part of a form, though, is its action. In the form in Fig. 10.2, this action is initiated by the input button (labelled "Calculate"), which calls the embedded JavaScript. In contrast, the form in Fig. 10.4 uses probably the

(A)

```
<form action="/cgi-bin/register.exe">
        Who are you? <input name="name" maxlength=40> (Max 40)
        <p>And the password you wish to use? <input name="paswd" maxlength=10>
        (Max 10)</p>
        <p><input type="submit" name="button1" value="Register"></p>
</form>
```

(B)

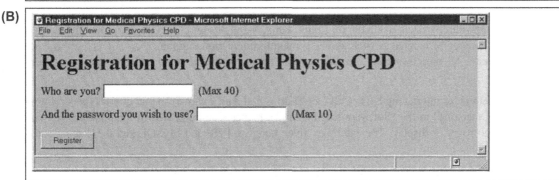

FIG. 10.4 (A) The HTML code for the input form. (B) The code in Fig. 10.4A as rendered by the browser.

most commonly used action, that of calling an external routine described in the <form> tag itself and initiated by clicking a "submit" type of input element. This external routine is a CGI which by default usually resides in the cgi-bin folder of the web server.[8]

We illustrate this by considering an example, that of registering a user into a CPD (**Continuing Professional Development**) database system. The back-end database for this example (PostgreSQL) comes complete with C and C++ libraries (although it should be noted that libpq++ is a merely a wrapper for libpq and therefore both need to be included at the linking stage), which can be used to simply produce CGI scripts.

The registration for the CPD database takes place in two parts: an HTML form to gather the data, as shown in Fig. 10.4, and the action (which also produces a web page) shown in Fig. 10.5. Note that the gathered data from Fig. 10.4 is posted to the CGI application register.exe, the code for which is shown in Fig. 10.5.

This code is for example purposes only, as it contains 3 specific pieces of poor practice:

- The maximum length of a password is 10 characters.
- The password is transmitted and stored in plain text.
- The password is displayed in plain text, both on initial entry and on confirmation.

Dynamic content

A dynamic web page (as opposed to a static one) is a page which changes as a result of user interaction with it. The simplest form of such interaction is access — in this case, the page is generated for display in real-time, but to all other intents is a static page. See Fig. 10.3 for such an example. At the other end of the scale are the continuously updating pages: they may use RSS feeds or continually refresh. In between these are the buttons and forms that we have seen in "Forms and data" above.

The techniques for implementing the dynamic content may be either client-side or server-side, as we saw in "Web programming". We shall therefore consider just one technique here: the page refresh.

A page refresh does as the name implies: it refreshes the page. In the case of the sample code in Fig. 10.3, this would have the effect of keeping the page current as time progresses, moving through the phases of the day and days of the week. JavaScript to accomplish such an effect (and therefore is client-side) is shown in Fig. 10.6. This page refreshes every 10 s, using the 'onload' attribute to call the function Refresh(). The parameter value '10000' equals 10 s.

In itself, this is interesting but not especially useful. An AJAX refresh method, such as shown in Fig. 10.7, allows control of individual elements in a page, for example a bed state query refreshing every minute or an outstanding job counter refreshing every hour.

A refresh attribute does take control away from the user, though. Therefore it must be part of the functionality of the page to display changing content otherwise it will contravene the W3C's accessibility guidelines. It may be better in such cases to have a "refresh" button on the page which would call a function such as the "Refresh()" one of Fig. 10.6.

Interfacing with databases

The first question that must be answered when interfacing with databases is "which database engine?" In most settings, this will have been determined prior to the project's commencement due to the hosting structure and pre-existing applications. Three very common databases, all of which are suitable for web development, are:

- MySQL — the community edition is free to install. Originally only available for Linux, this is now available for many platforms.
- PostgreSQL — An open-source system available on Linux, Unix, Windows and MacOS platforms, this has some very useful programming libraries in languages such as C++ making interaction simpler.
- Microsoft SQL Server — a Windows-only installation, this scales well and is suitable for large, mission-critical databases.

The most common method for interfacing is via CGI (see "Forms and data", above) so that queries (generally written in SQL — see "Structured Databases" in the "Software Engineering" chapter) can be posted to the database engine and the results returned to the web page for display. The examples given here use PHP and MySQL and the database structure is shown in Fig. 10.8.

---

8. For example, on a Raspberry Pi running Apache, the folder is /usr/lib/cgi-bin.

(A)
```
#include <libpq++.h>
#include <strstream.h>
#include "parse.h"
#include "parse.cpp"

void main()
{
        char *query_str=getenv("QUERY_STRING"),buf[4];
        Parse list(query_str);
        int id;
        PgDatabase data("cpd");
        ostrstream os;

        cout << "Content-type: text/html"<<endl<<endl<<endl;
        cout << "<html>"<<endl<<"<head>"<<endl
              <<"</head>"<<endl<<"<body>"<<endl;

        if(data.ConnectionBad()) cout << "<h1>Error:Bad connection</h1>" << endl;
        else if(data.ExecTuplesOk("select * from config") && data.Tuples()==1)
        {
                id=atoi(data.GetValue(0,"next_id"));
                os << "insert into person values ('" << list.get_item_n("name") << "', "
                      << id << ", '" << list.get_item_n("paswd") << "')" << ends;
                if(data.ExecCommandOk(os.str()) &&
                      data.ExecCommandOk("update config set next_id=next_id+1"))
                {
                        cout << "<h2>CPD Registration</h2>"<<endl;
                        cout << "name    : "<<list.get_item_n("name")<<"<p>";
                        cout << "password: "<<list.get_item_n("paswd")<<"</p><p>";
                        cout << "Has been registered on the Medical Physics CPD system
                              </p><hr>";
                }
                else cout << "<h1>Error: Registration failure</h1>" << endl;
                os.rdbuf()->freeze(0);
        }
        else cout << "<h1>Error:Next ID not collected</h1>";
        cout << "</body>"<<endl<<"</html>"<<endl;
}
```

FIG. 10.5 (A) The C++ code (register.cpp) for processing the data and returning a confirmatory web page. (B) The confirmatory page from the code in Fig. 10.5A as rendered by the browser.

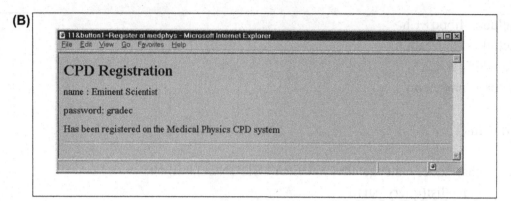

(B)

CPD Registration

name : Eminent Scientist

password: gradec

Has been registered on the Medical Physics CPD system

FIG. 10.5 cont'd

The PHP script connects via

$db=mysqli_connect('localhost',$username,$password,$database) or die('Error connecting to MySQL server.');

where $username and $password have been defined earlier in the script. This is not a security risk as the script is processed on the server side, not the client side. $database is the name of the database, similarly pre-defined in the script. SQL commands are then used to interact with the database, via commands of the form

mysqli_query($db,$query);

(A)
```
<html>
    <head>
        <script type="text/JavaScript">
            <!--
            function Refresh(timeout) {
                setTimeout("location.reload(true);",timeout);
            }
            // -->
        </script>
    </head>
    <body onload="JavaScript:Refresh(10000);">
        <script type="text/javascript">
            var date=new Date()
            var time=date.getSeconds()
            document.write("<b>time passing... <b>")
            document.write(time)
        </script>
    </body>
</html>
```

FIG. 10.6 (A) JavaScript code to refresh the page every 10 s. (B) The resultant page.

(B)

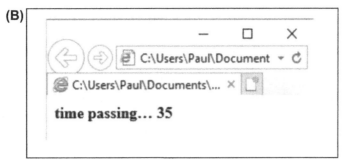

FIG. 10.6 cont'd

$query is a text variable containing the SQL command. This is preferable to the command being written directly as the mysqli_query() parameter as processing can take place in formulating the command. Data can thus be added to the database via $query values such as

$query = "INSERT INTO doctor {name} VALUES {'Whittaker'}";

Note the use of single quotes to delimit text strings.

Let us assume that we wish to display the list of Patients in our database, in alphabetic order of surname. This would be accomplished via

$query = "SELECT * FROM patient ORDER BY Surname";

$result = mysqli_query($db, $query) or die('Error querying database.');

$num = mysqli_num_rows($result);

The second command places the results into an array ($result) and the third command returns the number of rows in that array. The full script to produce this information is thus:

```php
<?php
  $username="dbuser";
  $password="password";
  $database="appts";
  $db = mysqli_connect('localhost',$username,$password,$database)
  or die('Error connecting to MySQL server.');
?>
<html>
  <head>
  </head>
  <body>
    <h1>PHP connect to MySQL</h1>
```

```javascript
var table = $('#sample').DataTable( {ajax: "data.json"} );

setInterval( function () {

        table.ajax.reload( null, false );

}, 60000 );
```

FIG. 10.7 JavaScript to reload table data every minute.

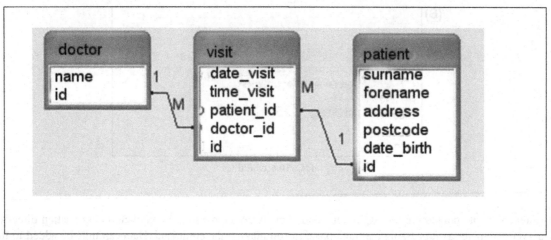

FIG. 10.8 The database structure for the example code in this section. Relationships are denoted by lines joining the tables on the appropriate fields, with "1" and "M" referring to "one" and "many" respectively.

```
<h2> list of all patients</h2>
<?php
    $query = "SELECT * FROM patient ORDER BY Surname";
    mysqli_query($db, $query) or die('Error querying database.');
    $result = mysqli_query($db, $query);
    $num = mysqli_num_rows($result);
    $row = mysqli_fetch_array($result);
    while ($row = mysqli_fetch_array($result)) {
            echo $row['Forename'] . ' ' . $row['Surname'] . '<br />';
    }
    echo "$num listed";
    mysqli_close($db);
?>
</body>
</html>
```

Note that, as we have a count of the number of rows, the list could be done via a for … next loop or a while loop using a counter, such as:

```
$i=0;
while ($i < $num) {
    echo $row['Forename'] . ' ' . $row['Surname'] . '<br />';
    $i++;
}
```

From our example above, this gives the output in Fig. 10.9.

Security

Limiting access

Although most web pages and content are designed to be viewable by all, some pages require, by design, a restriction in access. Examples of this may be research work as yet unpublished and telephone lists, as well as the commercial applications such as banking and paid-for content (such as journals). In clinical computing terms a common access restriction is for data repositories: collection via an internet interface is desirable due to its ease of use, yet it must be secure enough to prevent unauthorised access to that data.

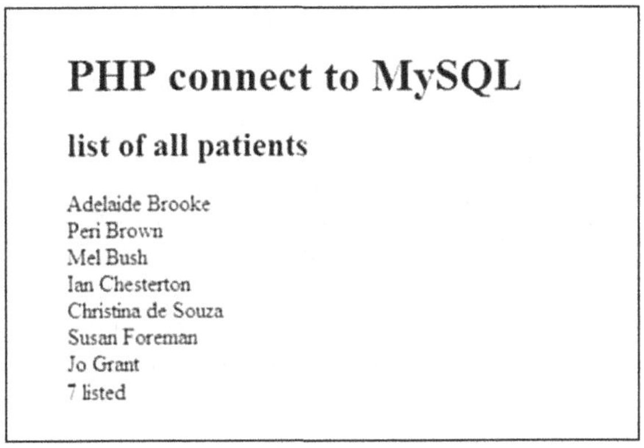

PHP connect to MySQL

list of all patients

Adelaide Brooke
Peri Brown
Mel Bush
Ian Chesterton
Christina de Souza
Susan Foreman
Jo Grant
7 listed

FIG. 10.9   The output from the example PHP code, as rendered by the browser.

There are various ways of restricting access, all of which require some form of authentication. For Unix systems running an Apache web server, the .htaccess file is one method. This is a plain-text file that resides in the same directory as the page that it protects.[9] The following five lines in this file:

```
<Limit GET POST>
order deny,allow
deny from all
allow from .clineng.ac.uk
</Limit>
```

will only allow access to the pages to users from the university of Clinical Engineering. Any other users attempting to access these pages will receive a "403 Forbidden" error.

The .htaccess file can control redirections (e.g. redirecting "clineng.ac.uk" to www.clineng.ac.uk), custom error pages (rather than the default ones in the web server), mime types (so those unknown to the server can still be correctly server to the end user) and **server-side includes** (SSIs) which have many features, a common one being presenting contact information on every page across the entire site, without having to update each page when something changes.

Here, though, we are only interested in the access limitations provided by this mechanism. These lines:

```
AuthUserFile /security/web/passfile
AuthGroupFile /dev/null
AuthName ByPassword
AuthType Basic
<Limit GET POST>
require valid-user
</Limit>
```

mean that access is via a username and password combination, validated against the file/security/web/passfile. The disadvantage of this system is that the password file probably has to be maintained on the Unix system, although this may also be viewed as an advantage, depending on the web site's functionality.

Other methods of restricting access depend a lot on the language the system has been written in. PHP provides functionality to require a password, as in this example:

```
<?php
    if ( $PHP_AUTH_USER != "user" || $PHP_AUTH_PW != "please" ) {
        header("HTTP/1.1 401 Unauthorized");
        echo "Failed to log in.";
        exit();
    }
    else {
```

---

9. It also protects subdirectories from this point down.

```
        echo "You are logged in successfully as: ".$PHP_AUTH_USER;
        echo "Welcome";
    }
?>
```

This has a hard-coded password, which is not ideal, but does illustrate the technology. It is clearly possible to replace this with a database look-up (see "Interfacing with databases"). It is also more secure than a similar JavaScript-based system as it is server-side. The JavaScript version, being client-side can be bypassed by simply viewing the HTML sent to the browser via "View Source".

Finally, on an ASP.NET —based server,[10] the relevant controls would be placed in the web.config file. For example, the following section would allow only the users Clinical and Engineering to access the site:

```
<authorization>
    <allow users="Clinical, Engineering"/>
    <deny users="?"/>
</authorization>
```

Public and private key encryption[11]

In an increasingly online world, it is imperative that software systems remain operational in the event of error or malicious access attempts. In a clinical setting, there are several instances where digital security is applicable. For example, when drug lists or drug information is stored in a central database and accessed electronically, it needs to be ensured that the data is not tampered with either accidently or intentionally. Similarly, electronic access to patient records requires strong user authentication measures and any patient data that passes through an open network needs to be encrypted. In this section we aim to introduce the basic concepts of encryption and some of the key encryption techniques.

Introduction

Cryptography is an algorithmic process of converting a plain text (or clear text) message to a cipher text (or cipher) message based on an algorithm that both the sender and receiver know, so that the cipher text message cannot be read by anyone but the intended receiver. The act of converting a plain text message into its cipher text form is called *enciphering*. The opposite action, converting cipher text form into a plain text message, is called *deciphering*. The terminology enciphering and deciphering are more commonly referred to as *encryption* and *decryption*, respectively.

To start off with, it is useful to define some common terminology associated with encryption[vi]

- *Cryptosystem* or cipher system is a method of disguising messages so that only certain people can see through the disguise.
- *Cryptography* is the art of creating and using cryptosystems.
- *Cryptanalysis* is the art of breaking cryptosystems — seeing through the disguise even when you're not supposed to be able to.
- *Cryptology* is the study of both cryptography and cryptanalysis.
- *Plaintext* is the original message input to the encryption system.
- *Ciphertext* is the disguised message output from the encryption system.
- The letters in the plaintext and ciphertext are often referred to as *symbols*.
- *Encryption* is any procedure to convert plaintext into ciphertext.
- *Decryption* is any procedure to convert ciphertext into plaintext.
- *Cryptology Primitives* are basic building blocks used in the encryption process. Examples of these include block ciphers, stream ciphers and hash algorithms.

---

10. ASP.NET is an open source web framework developed by Microsoft for building web apps and services. It is based on the .NET developer platform and contains tools and libraries specifically for building web apps.

11. See also "Encryption" in Chapter 8.

vi Anderson, R., 2001. Security Engineering: A Guide to Building Dependable Distributed Systems, first ed. Wiley. Available from: www.cl.cam.ac.uk/~rja14/Papers/SE-05.pdf

Block and stream ciphers

One of the first known examples of encryption is the Caesar cipher[12] which involves replacing every letter by the letter 3 places ahead of it in the alphabet, for e.g. Caesar becomes Fdhvdu. This is known as a *substitution cipher* — substituting a letter for another throughout the text. It is also one of the easiest to decrypt given that certain letters occur much more frequently in English words than others.

Another encryption option is the *stream cipher* where a string of characters known as the *keystream* is repeatedly combined with the plaintext to form the cipher. For example, one of the earliest known stream ciphers, the Vignere stream cipher, considers each letter of the alphabet to correspond to a number such as A=0, B=1, ..., Z=25, and simply adds the position numbers of the plaintext symbols and substitutes the corresponding letter in the ciphertext. So if we used 'Julius' as the key, in this case, the first letter 'C' becomes 'M' (C=3 + J=10 → 13=M). Continuing this through, 'Caesar' would be encrypted as 'Mvqbvk'. To crack this type of cipher requires a long enough extract of ciphertext on which frequency analysis of phrases may be used to guess the key.

Unlike stream ciphers that encrypt a symbol at a time, *block ciphers* encrypt blocks of plaintext at a time using unvarying transformations on blocks of data. One of the simplest examples of block ciphers is the Playfair cipher where the plaintext is divided up into blocks of 2 letters and a random arrangement of alphabets in a 5x5 block is used to encrypt each of these blocks individually. Given a large enough extract of ciphertext, it might be possible to reconstruct the coding matrix. One way around this is to have large block sizes and iterative encryption. Some of the common encryption technologies used today such as the **Advanced Encryption Standard** (AES) used worldwide, use a form of block cipher incorporating large (64—128-bit) blocks and pseudorandom encryption keys.

Public-key cryptography

Both stream ciphers and block ciphers are types of *symmetric* key cryptography, i.e. the same key is used both for encryption and decryption (see Fig. 10.10).

Asymmetric key cryptography on the other hand uses 2 separate keys — one of these keys will encrypt the plaintext and the other will decrypt it. This prevents the need for and the associated risks with transmitting keys either with or without the message (see Fig. 10.11).

This technique of sending, receiving and sending again is known as the three-pass protocol for secure transmission of messages without key exchange. It may be explained as follows: consider a situation where a box of valuables needs to be securely sent from one location to another. Sending the key to unlock the box either with it or separately would both be risky. So the sender puts a padlock on the box to which only he has the key. At the other end, the receiver adds his own padlock and sends it back. The sender can now remove his padlock using his key leaving the box locked with just the receiver's lock on it. Back at the other end, the receiver unlocks the box to retrieve the contents. In this case, the need to send any keys is completely eliminated and both the encryption and decryption keys are private.

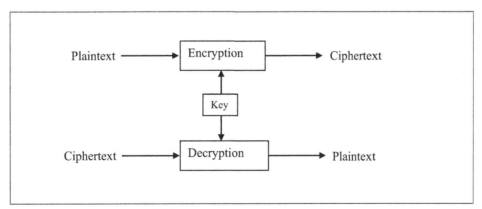

FIG. 10.10 Symmetric key cryptography.

---

12. Accredited to Julius Caesar, hence the name.

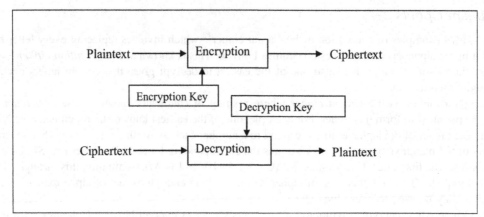

FIG. 10.11 Asymmetric key cryptography.

In public key cryptography, one of the keys is made public, typically the encryption key. So, when a message is transmitted, it is encrypted using this public key to the recipient. The matching decryption key is kept private and known only to the recipient who can then use it to decrypt the ciphertext.

The primary advantage of an asymmetric cryptosystem is the increased security since private keys never need to be transmitted, unlike the symmetric key system where the secret key must be communicated between the sender and receiver as the same key is required for both encryption and decryption. Interception of this secret key can compromise the security and authenticity of future data transmissions.

Digital signatures are an application of public-key cryptography often used in e-commerce applications. These are provided via a *certification authority*. The certification authority manages a repository of public keys that it signs with its own private key to confirm authenticity. A sender can then digitally 'sign' a message using his own private key and the recipient can confirm authenticity of the sender by validating the signature against the public key authenticated by the certification authority.

A drawback of using public-key cryptography for encryption is speed. The multi-step validation and verification process as well as the hashing algorithms typically used with public-key cryptography tend to be slower than symmetric key algorithms for large amounts of data. *Digital envelopes* are a way of combining the best of both by using the more secure public-key encryption to exchange secret keys and then using the faster secret-key encryption on the message itself.

The choice of encryption methodology depends on the application. In circumstances where it is possible to securely exchange secret keys, for example by meeting in person, there is then no need to use public-key encryption. This is also the case for users protecting their own documents with a password. Public key cryptography is advantageous in a multi-user scenario across open networks.

This section has touched only a small area in the vast field of cryptography. But it has hopefully introduced some of the basic concepts and key terminology.

Abbreviations

AES Advanced Encryption Standard
API Application Programming Interface
CGI Common Gateway Interface
CPD Continuing Professional Development
CSR Certificate Signing Request
CSS Cascading Style Sheets
FTP File Transfer Protocol
HTML Hypertext Markup Language
HTTP Hypertext Transfer Protocol
PHP Hypertext Preprocessor
SSI Server-Side Includes
URL Uniform Resource Locator
VPS Virtual Private Servers

Section III

Clinical instrumentation & measurement

Chapter 11

An introduction to clinical measurement

Richard G. Axell[a,b]

[a]University College London Hospitals NHS Foundation Trust, London, United Kingdom; [b]University College London, London, United Kingdom

Chapter outline

Introduction

Measurement underpins science and good measurement forms the basis of good science. A measurement tells us a property of the quantity to be measured and by assigning that property a number and expressing it in the correct SI unit within a healthcare environment allows us to interpret the patient's condition to provide a diagnosis or appropriate intervention. Clinical measurements are obtained using invasive and noninvasive methods, with blood pressure being an ideal example of both. The gold standard technique for the accurate measurement of blood pressure is to use an invasive catheter and advancing the catheter tip to the exact point in the aorta to be measured. However, the most common technique used to measure blood pressure within a clinical environment is to perform the measurement noninvasively. Noninvasive blood pressure measurement is performed by placing a cuff around the patient's arm and listening for Korotkoff sounds due to the turbulence of the blood underneath the cuff. Although the most accurate method of measuring blood pressure is to perform an invasive measurement, this is at an increased risk to the patient when compared to noninvasive measurement techniques. It is the responsibility of the clinician to decide on the condition of the patient and whether the patient will benefit most from the most accurate, potentially harmful invasive measurement of blood pressure, or if the slightly less accurate noninvasive measurement is sufficient. This chapter provides an introduction into the theory and concepts of accuracy and precision of measurement and measurement errors, as well as identifying the importance of calibration, sensitivity, and specificity of measurements that are common across many different clinical measurement modalities.

Accuracy and precision

Firstly, to understand the concept and scientific requirement of the equipment calibration needed to perform a clinical measurement, we must consider the accuracy and precision of the measurement. Resolution is the smallest incremental value that can be measured. The digital measurement display on an ultrasound scanner with a larger number of digits (0.001 mm) has a higher measurement resolution than one with fewer digits (0.01 mm). Similarly, an analogue measurement display on a sphygmomanometer with a tick mark every 1 mmHg has a higher measurement resolution than one with a tick mark every 5 mmHg. However, a higher resolution does not imply higher measurement accuracy; it provides a high measurement precision. Measurement precision is the repeatability of obtaining the output values from repeated measurements under identical input conditions over a period of time. Fig. 11.1A shows low precision where the

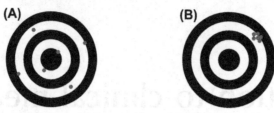

FIG. 11.1 (A) Low precision and (B) high precision.

FIG. 11.2 (A) Low accuracy and (B) high accuracy.

measurement values are scattered all over the target. Fig. 11.1B shows high precision where the measurement values are tightly clustered on the target. Measurement accuracy is given by the difference between the true value and the measured value divided by the true value. Fig. 11.2A shows that although the measurement values are tightly clustered with high precision, they have low accuracy to the true value. Fig. 11.2B shows high accuracy and high precision. When using electronic devices to measure physiological systems, the foremost consideration is selecting the measurement device with the highest possible precision, repeatability, and accuracy.

Although good repeatability would suggest a valid result, a second operator should repeat the experiment using different test equipment to confirm the observed outcomes are the same. There are many different factors that can cause an inaccuracy or error in the result. These inaccuracies or errors can typically be characterized in two groups (1) errors intrinsic with the measured system, or measurement device errors, or (2) errors intrinsic to the measuring system, or measurement errors. Measurement device errors can include mechanical, electronic, software, scale, environmental, and human errors. A measurement error could be classified as systematic or random. To improve the measurement accuracy a strict measurement protocol should be utilized to ensure all measurements are collected in the same manner and that the measurement equipment is calibrated against a national standard. However, even after following this measurement protocol there will always be some measurement uncertainty.

Measurement device errors

A mechanical, electronic or software fault within the measurement device can cause the relationship between the input signal to output reading to be altered by a fundamental characteristic built into the measurement device. For example, a digital filter may have been set with an inadequate sampling frequency, so a component of the input data is being lost and will not correctly displayed on the output signal.

To perform a clinical measurement, the measurement device must have a visual output display to allow the observer to perform the measurement. As previously alluded to, this could be in the form of an analogue scale or a digital display. Going back to the analogue measurement display on a sphygmomanometer with a tick mark every 5 mmHg, the total error with the reading can be no better than the intrinsic error from the manufacturer marking the scale on the display combined with the human interaction when reading the scale. A reading error is one that arises from the pointer-scale-reader interaction, which makes the reading differ from the actual indication on the display. This is twofold: A pointer positioned between two points marked on a scale means the observer has to make some form of assumption on the true value of the indicated point; secondly, if the observer was to take a reading from any point other than normal to the plane of the scale there would be a parallax error associated with the measurement. Parallax errors can also occur from the incorrect use of measurement equipment; for example, if a thermal camera was set up so that the object to be measured was not parallel to the field of view, the measurand would not be entirely covered by the focal region of the thermal camera and errors with the accuracy of the temperature measurement would be induced.

A digital display can only measure to the precision of its most significant digit. So a scale with a precision of 1 g cannot measure to the precision of a set of 0.001 g scales. There may also be some fluctuation with the value displayed on the scale, and so, again, the observer has to make some form of assumption on the true value indicated on the display.

An environmental error arises from factors external to the instrument due to the environment that the measurement device is operated in. Some of the most common types of environmental error are temperature, humidity, pressure, and sound. A temperature change in an environment in which an electrocardiogram (ECG) machine is being operated may cause electronic components in the internal amplifier to have an undesired slow change in the voltage output, called drift. A thermally induced voltage across the amplifier may also cause an undesired random voltage to be measured across the electronic component, called noise.

Measurement errors

A systematic measurement error relates to the magnitude of the output signal across the entire measurement output range of the device. If a measurement device output was 3% higher than the true value, or if the scale was offset by 2 units higher than the true value, the error is termed *systematic*. This error could arise if the zero point of the measurement device scale shifts or if the calibration of the measurement device scale is incorrect. Since a systematic error is constant across the entire output range of the measurement device, it would normally be easy to detect and correct for.

A random measurement error stems from a fluctuation in the conditions within a system being measured which has nothing to do with the true signal being measured. The complexity of any biological system will mean the measurement conditions are continually varying with time, and these variations will appear to the measurement device as differences in the input signal and be displayed as such on the output signal as noise. This will only significantly impact the accuracy of the reading if the magnitude of the noise level is a considerable proportion of the output signal itself. The signal-to-noise ratio (SNR), the ratio of signal magnitude to noise magnitude, is used to define the quality of the output of the measurement device. For example, to be able to detect and measure an electroencephalography (EEG), a high SNR is required to distinguish the relatively small measurement signal from background noise.

Calibration

The basic concept of measurement calibration is that the test equipment should be periodically compared against a standard of higher accuracy. The organisation performing the calibration against the standard of higher accuracy will then provide a calibration certificate. If errors are identified the measurement device may be adjusted so that the measurement is more accurate or correction factors will be specified in the calibration certificate. These correction factors will allow the user to continue using the measurement device and the user can correct for the systematic error ensuring that the measurements recorded are within an acceptable tolerance of measurement accuracy. The calibration certificate will be provided with an accompanying statement of uncertainty. This is where uncertainty analysis is performed on the calibration to specify the uncertainty of the measurement. Within the healthcare environment, a label is attached to the measurement device that indicates the calibration certificate number and the date that it is due for recalibration. A measurement device that is uncalibrated may also be used, however, it should be clearly indicated as such, with a label such as "for indication only".

If the measurement device is linear in its operation, the output can be set to zero for zero input. A one-point calibration can then be used to define the calibration curve that plots output versus input. If the linearity of the measurement device is unknown, a two-point calibration must be performed with these two points plus the zero point used to plot the calibration curve to guarantee linearity. However, if the resulting calibration curve from the two-point calibration is nonlinear, a multipoint calibration must be plotted to obtain the calibration curve. Due to the possibility of environmental effects influencing the performance of the measurement device, calibration curves should be calculated for the range of different temperatures expected during normal use conditions to determine temperature drift effects on the zero point and the gain.

Traceability

For calibration to be considered traceable there must be an unbroken chain of measurements back to a national or international standard. This will ensure that the measurement taken is an accurate representation of the true value by way of its traceability back to a known standard. The National Metrology Institute (NMI) exists to maintain primary standards of measurement to provide traceability for the calibration of measurement devices. Within the United Kingdom, the National Physics Laboratory (NPL) is the accredited national measurement institute and, as such, measurements performed using a calibrated device should be traceable back to their reference standard (accurate to 0.002%). However, the chain of calibrations is only traceable if the correct calibration calculations and uncertainties are correctly applied at every step of the chain back to the reference standard; and with every step along the chain away from the reference standard the measurement uncertainty increases. For instance, NPL's reference standard may be calibrated to an accuracy of 0.002%. A calibration laboratory's "laboratory standard" device may then be calibrated against the reference standard to an accuracy of 0.01%; a calibration laboratory "field use" device may then be calibrated against the "laboratory standard" device to an accuracy of 1.0%; a calibration laboratory would then use the "field use" device to calibrate the clinical measurement device used within a clinical environment to an accuracy of 5.0%.

Uncertainty

With any clinical measurement, there always exist some doubt about the true value of the measurement. A correct understanding of uncertainty is fundamental to good quality measurements for: (1) calibrating a measurement device; (2) correctly interpreting a calibration certificate for the measurement device; and (3) using a measurement device to perform a measurement. Any potential source of error whose value is unknown is a potential source of uncertainty. As such, the overall uncertainty in the measurement will be calculated from the combination of all the individual sources of uncertainty within the measurement device. By performing this analysis of the clinical measurement it will allow the operator to work at reducing the source of greatest uncertainty in the measurement. However, it is important to understand that a mistake when performing the measurement is not a source of measurement uncertainty.

To carry out an uncertainty analysis for a clinical measurement, all the potential sources of error must be defined, and then perform the measurements following a strict measurement protocol. If an operator is inadequately trained, or the operator performs each measurement differently, or an inappropriate measurement device is used to carry out the test, there will be no scientific validity to the result. After using a strict measurement protocol to record the measurement, there are two different methods to express the uncertainty, Type A or Type B. Statistical or Type A uncertainty is used to express the uncertainty in a measurement by calculating the standard deviation of many repeated measurements using the equation,

$$u = \frac{s.d}{\sqrt{n}}$$

where u is the standard uncertainty, $s.d$ is the standard deviation, and n is the number of measurements performed.

Type B uncertainty is used to express uncertainty from supplementary information provided for the measurement device. This could include calibration certificates, specifications, and previously published information on the measurement device. By expressing the individual uncertainties in consistent units, the individual uncertainties calculated for both Type A and Type B can be combined using the "root sum of all squares" equation:

$$Combined\ Uncertainty = \sqrt{a^2 + b^2 + c^2 + ... + n^2}$$

Finally, the combined uncertainty should be expressed as a confidence interval to indicate the confidence level that the true measurement is within the stated range. The expended uncertainty is calculated by multiplying the combined uncertainty by a k factor using the equation,

$$Expanded\ Uncertainty\ U = Coverage\ Factor\ k \times Combined\ Standard\ Uncertainty$$

The k factor is specified depending on the required confidence level, as shown in Table 11.1.

TABLE 11.1 k factor.

Required confidence level (%)	k factor
99.7	3
99.0	2.58
95.0	2
68.0	1

TABLE 11.2 Sensitivity and specificity testing.

	Clinical measurement/test result (T)	
True status of pathology (S)	Positive (+)	Negative (−)
Pathology (+)	a	b
No pathology (−)	c	d

Sensitivity and specificity of measurement technique

We have already determined that clinical measurement is subject to error, be it random, systematic, or human. The random variation with the measurement will mean that if an automated blood pressure monitor to record a patient's blood pressure more than once, the values obtained for systolic and diastolic blood pressure will differ slightly. These differences could be due to variations in the measurement method, the observer, an equipment fault, or physiological differences in the patient. The variations may also increase further by introducing a second observer to perform the measurement and interpret the results.

The operator uses sensitivity and specificity to determine the probability that a clinical measurement test correctly identified the pathology. When a clinical measurement is performed there are two possible test results: (1) the test result is positive, indicating the presence of pathology, or (2) the test result is negative indicating the absence of pathology. There are also two possible clinical outcomes: (1) the patient has the pathology, or (2) the patient is pathology free. Table 11.2 shows the test results in columns and the true status of the patient under test in rows. Sensitivity is defined as the probability that the clinical measurement correctly identifies the patient has the pathology when in fact they do have the pathology. Sensitivity is a measure of how likely the clinical measurement is to detect the presence of pathology in a patient who has the pathology. Sensitivity is given by,

$$P(T^+|S^+) = \frac{a}{a+b}$$

Specificity is defined as the probability that the clinical measurement correctly identifies the patient does not have the pathology when in fact they are pathology free. Specificity is given by,

$$P(T^-|S^-) = \frac{d}{c+d}$$

The ideal clinical measurement test should have a high sensitivity and high specificity, but in a real life clinical environment there may have to be some tradeoff between sensitivity and specificity. Usually a clinical measurement test can be chosen with relatively high sensitivity and specificity, however, there are still false positives and false negatives. A false positive is when the clinical measurement test reports a positive result for a patient that is, in fact, pathology free. A false positive rate is given by,

$$P(S^-|T^+) = \frac{c}{a+c}$$

In an ideal world the number of patients who test positive to pathology that are in fact pathology free would be zero ($c = 0$). In reality, due to the errors associated with clinical measurement techniques, this would be impossible to achieve as soon as the test population increases in number. For small study numbers, random chance could dictate no false positives are observed within the result. Conversely, a false negative is when the clinical measurement test reports a negative result for a patient that has pathology. A false negative rate is given by,

$$P(S^+|T^-) = \frac{b}{b+d}$$

The clinical implications of a false positive or a false negative depend on the type of test being performed. A false positive would indicate that a patient is informed that they have pathology when in fact they do not, causing them unnecessary worry and concern and they could also be given inappropriate intervention or treatment. On the contrary, a false negative indicates that a patient is informed that they do not have pathology when in fact they do. This could lead to withholding intervention or treatment, with an absolute worse-case scenario ending in death.

TABLE 11.3 Hypothesis testing.

True status of pathology (S)	Clinical measurement/Test result (T)	
	Positive (+)	Negative (−)
H_a true (+)	a	b (Type II)
H_0 "true" (−)	c (Type I)	d

Type I and type II errors

Significance tests are used to test a hypothesis, and sensitivity and specificity relate to the correct decisions, whereas a false positive and false negative relate to Type I and Type II errors respectively. When a hypothesis is tested there are two possible outcomes: (a) the test result is positive, a statistically significant rejection of the null hypothesis, or (b) the test result is negative and is not statistically significant, so we decide not to reject the null hypothesis. Table 11.3 shows that if the true status of the pathology is positive (the pathology is present; hence what we are testing for is true) then the alternative hypothesis is true, whereas if what we are testing for is not true (there is no pathology) then the null hypothesis is true. Test result a represents a correct decision to reject the null hypothesis, as the alternative is really true. A high value of a results in a high probability of rejecting a null hypothesis, corresponding to a highly sensitive test. Test result b represents an incorrect decision not to reject the null hypothesis when in fact it is not true. This represents Type II error and corresponds to a false negative. However, a low value of b would represent a low probability of Type II error. Test result c represents an incorrect decision to reject the null hypothesis when in fact it is true. This represents Type I error and corresponds to a false positive. However, a low value of c would represent a low probability of Type I error. Test result d represents a correct decision not to reject a "true" null hypothesis when it should not be rejected. A high value of d results in a high probability of not rejecting a "true" null hypothesis, corresponding to a test with high specificity.

Abbreviations

ECG Electrocardiogram
EEG Electroencephalography
NMI National Metrology Institute
NPL National Physics Laboratory
SNR Signal-to-Noise Ratio

Further reading

International Organization for Standardization (ISO), 2010. ISO 21748:2010 Guidance for the Use of Repeatability, Reproducibility and Trueness Estimates in Measurement Uncertainty Estimation.
Webster, J.G., 2008. Bioinstrumentation. John Wiley & Sons.
Webster, J.G., 2009. Medical Instrumentation Application and Design. John Wiley & Sons.

Chapter 12

Medical electronics and instrumentation

Thomas Stone[a], and Richard G. Axell[b, c]

[a]Cambridge University Hospitals NHS Foundation Trust, Cambridge, United Kingdom; [b]University College London Hospitals NHS Foundation Trust, London, United Kingdom; [c]University College London, London, United Kingdom

Chapter outline

Introduction

This chapter provides a basic summary of medical electronics, basic circuit design, and the importance of differential amplifiers and instrumentation commonly used in clinical measurement systems.

Electronic components

There is a huge, and some would say bewildering, range of electronic components available to the designer. It is vital to have a well-constructed specification for your design to inform your decisions. To know what to specify it is important to have a grasp of the variety of factors that define a component, from the operational factors (electronic function) to the physical factors (size, mounting, etc.). We start with the passive devices, those that store energy and resist current flow, before moving on to the active devices, those that can "actively" change the electrical signal by amplification.

Resistor

A resistor is a passive device with two terminals (Fig. 12.1). It has an ideal voltage−current relationship of

$$v(t) = Ri(t) \tag{12.1}$$

where R is the resistance in ohms and $v(t)$ and $i(t)$ are voltage and current, respectively.

Resistors in series are equivalent by the definition

$$R_{eq} = R_0 + R_1 + R_2 + \cdots + R_n \tag{12.2}$$

Clinical Engineering. https://doi.org/10.1016/B978-0-08-102694-6.00012-7

FIG. 12.1 A resistor symbol and a variety of devices.

Resistors in a parallel network are equivalent to

$$\frac{1}{R_{eq}} = \frac{1}{R_0} + \frac{1}{R_1} + \frac{1}{R_2} + \cdots + \frac{1}{R_n} \qquad (12.3)$$

Resistors are specified by several parameters, however, many will have specific parameters if they are designed for specific tasks:

- Resistance in ohms
- Tolerance in percent: This means that the actual value of resistance is within this percentage of the value quoted as the resistance
- Power in watts: The power rating of the resistor is the power ($P = i^2 R$) above which the resistor will fail; it is a bad idea to operate anywhere near this value
- Working voltage: The appropriate voltage range that should be applied to the resistor
- Temperature coefficient of resistance (TCR) in ppm/°C: The change in the actual resistance with a change in temperature; a value of 10 ppm/°C would imply a change of 10 Ω in every 1 MΩ for every 1 °C
- Voltage coefficient in ppm/V: The change in the resistance with the change in voltage (within the working voltage range); described as a change in parts per million

Resistors are constructed in many ways. Each method has certain benefits and weaknesses and will impact on design consideration.

Metal and carbon film resistor

Carbon film resistors are created by laying a thin carbon film over a nonconductive substrate. The carbon is then etched away (Fig. 12.2) and the pitch of the etch will dictate the resistance of the device.

Metal film resistors are created by depositing a thin film of a metal or metal oxide over a ceramic core. The resistance is again controlled by cutting a helical path into the deposited metal.

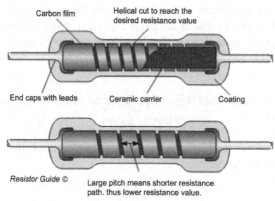

FIG. 12.2 Metal and carbon film resistor.

Thin film and thick film

Thin film resistors are created using a technique called sputtering which permits a very thin and controlled layer of a material, tantalum nitride or Nichrome, to be deposited onto a substrate. The environment in which the film is laid and without the necessity for high power laser trimming ensures a very stable and accurate resistor.

Thick film resistors are constructed from a resistive paste which is printed onto an insulating substrate and then fired. The paste includes glass particles that when fired help fix the resistive material in place; however, it also causes random imperfections within the printed material that can change the conductive properties of the resistor. Thick film resistors are also laser trimmed, as the conductive paste does not have an accurate ohmic property, to achieve the correct resistance value (Fig. 12.3). Laser trimming can have the undesired effect of causing microfractures in the fired paste which cause imperfections in the conductance properties of the resistor.

Away from the ideal

There are several reasons why a resistor may not act in the way described earlier in this section. There are times when a resistor may stop acting as an ideal resistor. For example, if we were to move away from a direct current (DC) application and into higher-frequency applications (AC) the helical cut in a carbon film resistor would increasingly act as an inductor, which is essentially what it is. In addition, a resistor has inherent capacitance, most significantly between the terminals of the device. The model of a resistor that includes all these less than ideal characteristics is shown in Fig. 12.4.

Network and circuit analysis

Kirchhoff's voltage laws state that the sum of voltages, both positive and negative, around a closed circuit must equal zero. Equally, Kirchhoff's current laws state that the sum of all currents, both positive and negative, flowing into a node must equal zero. From these principles we can analyze circuits in terms of loop currents (Fig. 12.5):

$$\begin{cases} i_1R_1 + R_2(i_1 - i_2) + R_3(i_1 - i_3) = 10 \\ R_2(i_1 - i_2) + i_2R_6 + R_4(i_2 - i_3) = 0 \\ R_3(i_1 - i_3) + R_4(i_3 - i_2) + i_3R_5 = 0 \end{cases} \tag{12.4}$$

Using Gaussian elimination, the result for each current can be isolated.

Thévenin equivalent circuits use the principle that any combination of voltage sources and resistors can be reduced to a single voltage source and single series resistance (Fig. 12.6).

Equivalently, the Norton equivalent circuit is a combination of a current source and a parallel resistance (Fig. 12.7).

We calculate the Thévenin equivalent circuit by calculating the open circuit voltage of the circuit and dividing it by the short circuit current.

$$V_{TH} = V(\text{open circuit}) \tag{12.5}$$

$$R_{TH} = \frac{V_{TH}}{I(\text{short circuit})} \tag{12.6}$$

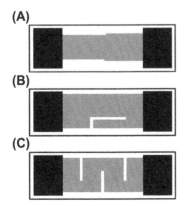

(A)

(B)

(C)

FIG. 12.3 Trim methods: (A) edge, (B) L-cut, (C) S-cut.

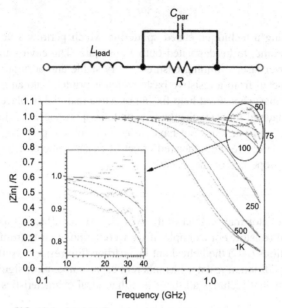

FIG. 12.4 Model of a real resistor and frequency response.

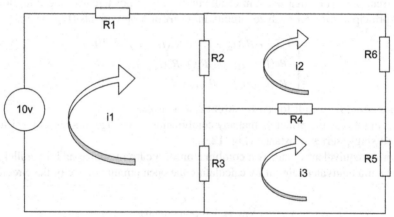

FIG. 12.5 Loop currents, network analysis.

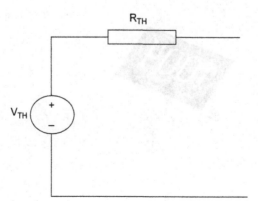

FIG. 12.6 Thévenin equivalent.

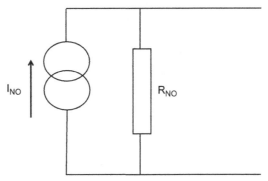

FIG. 12.7 Norton equivalent.

Capacitor

A capacitor is a two-terminal device described schematically in Fig. 12.8.

Capacitance can be defined by

$$C = \frac{\varepsilon_0 \varepsilon_r A}{d} \tag{12.7}$$

where ε_0 is the permittivity of a vacuum, ε_r is the relative dielectric constant of the material between the plates, A is the area of the plates, and d is the distance between the plates.

The charge on a capacitor is described as

$$q(t) = Cv(t) \tag{12.8}$$

where C is the capacitance in coulombs. We can define current as

$$i = \frac{dq(t)}{dt} \Rightarrow i = C\frac{dv(t)}{dt} \tag{12.9}$$

which is the ideal voltage−current relationship of a capacitor.

As mentioned, Thévenin's law states that the sum of voltages around a closed circuit must equal zero. If we want to know the charge on a capacitor at some time t for the circuit in Fig. 12.9 we can write

$$\left(V_s - \frac{Q}{C}\right) - IR = 0 \tag{12.10}$$

$$\therefore \left(V_s - \frac{Q}{C}\right) - \frac{dQ}{dt}R = 0 \tag{12.11}$$

This is a linear first-order differential equation and can be solved by the separation of parts; it is of the form $\frac{dy}{dx} + P(x)y = Q(x)$ with $Q(x) = 0$.

$$\Rightarrow \frac{dQ}{dt}R = \left(V_s - \frac{Q}{C}\right) \tag{12.12}$$

$$\frac{dQ}{dt} = \frac{1}{R}\left(V_s - \frac{Q}{C}\right) \tag{12.13}$$

FIG. 12.8 Capacitor symbol.

$$\frac{dQ}{dt}C = \frac{1}{R}(V_sC - Q) \tag{12.14}$$

Separate by parts and take the definite integral for both sides:

$$\frac{dQ}{(V_sC - Q)} \equiv -\frac{1}{RC}dt \tag{12.15}$$

$$\int_{Q=0}^{Q=Q(t)} \frac{dQ}{(V_sC - Q)} \equiv -\frac{1}{RC}\int_{t=0}^{t} dt \tag{12.16}$$

Recalling $\ln(m/n) = \ln(m) - \ln(n)$

$$\ln\frac{Q(t) - CV_s}{-CV_s} = -\frac{t}{RC} \tag{12.17}$$

$$\therefore Q(t) = CV_s\left(1 - e^{-t/RC}\right) \tag{12.18}$$

which gives the charge on the capacitor after time t. Remembering that $q(t) = Cv(t)$ we can also derive the voltage across it.

The energy stored on a capacitor is defined by

$$E = \frac{1}{2}CV^2 \tag{12.19}$$

Capacitors in a parallel network (Fig. 12.10) are equivalent by the definition

$$C_{eq} = C_0 + C_1 + C_2 + \cdots C_n \tag{12.20}$$

Capacitors in series (Fig. 12.10) are equivalent to

$$\frac{1}{C_{eq}} = \frac{1}{C_0} + \frac{1}{C_1} + \frac{1}{C_2} + \cdots + \frac{1}{C_n} \tag{12.21}$$

Capacitors are specified by a variety of parameters:

- Capacitance in farads (F), defined mathematically previously
- Operating voltage in volts (v), the highest voltage that can safely be applied across the terminals of the device
- Equivalent series resistance (ESR) in ohms (Ω)

Capacitors are also defined by their construction, which tailors them to their application. What was not mentioned in the list of parameters is the material of the dielectric, which defines the energy storage characteristics of the device.

Ceramic

Ceramic capacitors are constructed of layers of ceramic separated by layers of metal. Ceramic capacitors have the lowest equivalent series resistance.

Electrolytic aluminum

Electrolytic aluminum capacitors can be manufactured with large capacitances. The plates of the capacitor can be coated with a very fine layer of aluminum oxide, which has a very high dielectric constant (~ 10). Therefore, if we look at Eq. (12.21) we can see that we are able to construct a large dielectric without taking up too much space and increasing the distance between the plates too much; this equates to larger potential capacitances.

Electrolytic capacitors suffer from higher dissipation factors than other capacitors. The dissipation factor is the combination of all the energy losses within a capacitor under nonideal operation. The dissipation factor is defined as

$$D = \frac{R_s}{X_c} \tag{12.22}$$

where R_s is the series equivalent resistance and X_c is the series equivalent reactance, which is equivalent to

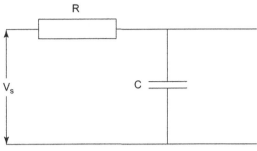

FIG. 12.9 RC circuit.

$$X_c \equiv \frac{1}{j2\pi fC} \tag{12.23}$$

It is for this reason that ripple current is a limiting factor for both aluminum and tantalum capacitors (see next). An alternating current resulting from the ohmic and dielectric losses causes temperature rises in the capacitor that could significantly reduce the capacitor's operational life. Therefore, electrolytic capacitors are often given a rated ripple current that should not be exceeded.

Tantalum

Capacitors have a similar construction to electrolytic aluminum in terms of a deposited fine layer of an oxide of tantalum, which has a high dielectric constant (approximately 27). Therefore, tantalum capacitors tend to have the same benefits of large capacitances as with electrolytic aluminum capacitors. In addition, however, they tend to have lower ESR which increases the stability of the capacitor. As a tradeoff for a high capacitance in a small space but with good stability, tantalum capacitors tend to have a higher cost.

Film

Film capacitors are the jack-of-all-trades in the capacitor world. They provide a low-cost stable capacitor with good leakage characteristics. They are formed by using layers of plastic film between layers of conductor. Modern capacitors have more complex layering techniques which produce equivalent series capacitance. By this process the equivalent series resistance can be significantly reduced in this type of capacitor. Film capacitors are flexible nonpolarized capacitors that are widely used.

Inductor

Inductors, like capacitors, store energy. An inductor is a two-terminal device with the symbol shown in Fig. 12.11.

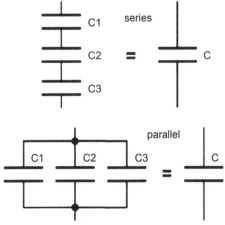

FIG. 12.10 Capacitor in series and in parallel.

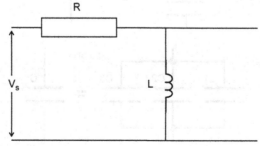

FIG. 12.11 Inductor symbol.

The inductance of a coil can be calculated as

$$L = \frac{\mu_0 N^2 A}{l} \tag{12.24}$$

where μ_0 is the permeability of the core, N is the number of turns of wire, A is the cross-sectional area of the coil, and l is the length of the coil.

The voltage−current relationship (Fig. 12.12) of an inductor is given by

$$\psi(t) = Li(t) \tag{12.25}$$

$$v(t) = \frac{d\psi(t)}{dt} \tag{12.26}$$

$$\Rightarrow v(t) = L\frac{di(t)}{dt} \tag{12.27}$$

In a similar fashion to the capacitor we can derive the current flowing in the inductor for any time t. Recalling Thévenin's rule

$$L\frac{di(t)}{dt} + Ri + V_s \tag{12.28}$$

Separation of parts gives:

$$\frac{di(t)}{V_s - i} \equiv \frac{R}{L}dt \tag{12.29}$$

Integrate both sides and take the natural logarithm:

$$\frac{i - V_s}{V_s} = e^{-tR/L} \tag{12.30}$$

$$\therefore i = V_s\left(1 - e^{-tR/L}\right) \tag{12.31}$$

The energy stored in an inductor is given by

$$E = \frac{1}{2}LI^2 \tag{12.32}$$

Inductors placed in a parallel network are equivalent by the definition (Fig. 12.13)

$$\frac{1}{L_{eq}} = \frac{1}{L_0} + \frac{1}{L_1} + \frac{1}{L_2} + \cdots + \frac{1}{L_n} \tag{12.33}$$

Inductors placed in series are equivalent by the definition

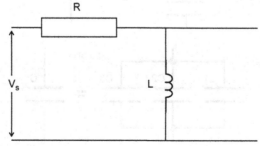

FIG. 12.12 Inductor symbols and common electronic packages.

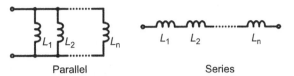

FIG. 12.13 Inductors in parallel and in series.

$$L_{eq} = L_0 + L_1 + L_2 + \cdots + L_n \tag{12.34}$$

Diode

A diode is a nonlinear passive device indicated by the symbol in Fig. 12.14.

Diodes only permit current flow in one direction, and that direction is indicated by the arrow in the symbol. Diodes have a voltage—current relationship as described in Fig. 12.15.

The diode will conduct when the anode is approximately 0.6 V above the cathode.

Transistor

The transistor is an active device, that is, it can perform tasks such as amplification. The bipolar junction transistor, or BJT, is shown as the symbol in Fig. 12.16.

Bipolar transistor

The bipolar transistor has two formations: NPN type and PNP. Transistors permit charge to flow from the collector to the emitter depending on the current flow within the base:

$$I_c = \beta I_B \tag{12.35}$$

where β is the current gain of the transistor.

The flow of current is governed by an increase in free electrons as the forward-biased base and emitter junction reduces the depletion layer between these two regions. Having gathered sufficient energy within the electric field, the excess electrons cross the narrow base layer and are swept across the reversed biased base and collector junction generating a net current flow.

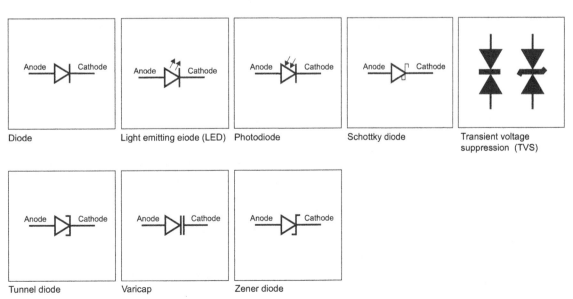

FIG. 12.14 Diodes and their symbols.

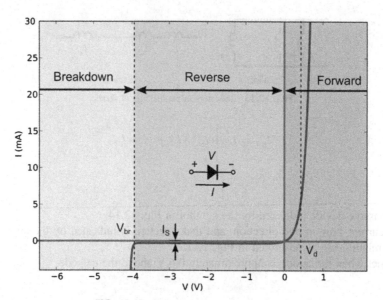

FIG. 12.15 Voltage relationship of a diode.

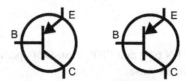

FIG. 12.16 Symbols for bipolar transistors.

A bipolar transistor has maximum values for the current that the base I_B and the collector I_c can sink. In addition, a maximum voltage between the collector and the emitter V_{ce} will be defined.

Field effect transistor

Whereas the bipolar transistor can be considered a current-controlled device (the current in the base), the field effect transistor is a voltage-controlled device. The field effect transistor, or FET, has the symbol shown in Fig. 12.17 shows the family of transistors.

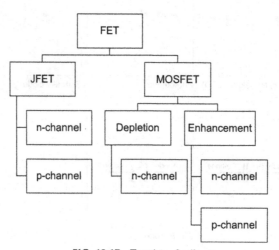

FIG. 12.17 Transistor family.

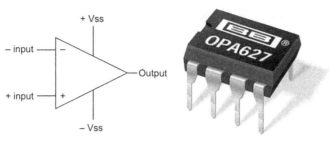

FIG. 12.18 An op-amp.

The terms *base*, *collector*, and *emitter* are now replaced by *gate*, *source*, and *drain*, respectively. The voltage applied to the gate now controls the current through the drain. The electric field generated from the drain can be thought of as "pinching" the flow of charge carriers through the source.

Operational amplifier

The operational amplifier is a three-terminal device (excluding power and balance terminals). It has an inverting input and a noninverting input defined by − and +, respectively. The op-amp is a high gain, high input impedance, low output impendence device which can be used, among a vast number of other possibilities, for amplifying a signal or buffering it from another part of a circuit (Fig. 12.18).

In simple terms the output of an op-amp will try and do whatever it can, if fed back to the input, to make the voltage difference between the two inputs zero. Ideally the inputs draw no current.

AC signals' complex Ohm's law

When an alternating signal is applied to a capacitor or an inductor we have to consider the impact of the varying voltage and current. We take the capacitor as our first example.

We know that the current relationship for a capacitor is

$$i(t) = C\frac{dv(t)}{dt} \tag{12.36}$$

Let the voltage be a sine wave

$$v(t) = V\sin(\omega t) \tag{12.37}$$

$$\therefore i(t) = \omega V\cos(\omega t + \varphi) \tag{12.38}$$

These can be rewritten in the complex polar form

$$i(t) = Re\{I_0 e^{-j\omega t}\} \tag{12.39}$$

$$v(t) = Re\{Ve^{-j\omega t}\} \quad \text{where } V = V_0 e^{-j\varphi} \tag{12.40}$$

$$i(t) = C\frac{dv(t)}{dt} = C\frac{d}{dt}e^{-j\omega t} = Cj\omega e^{-j\omega t} \tag{12.41}$$

$$i = Cj\omega e^{-j\omega t} \equiv Cj\omega v \tag{12.42}$$

$$\frac{1}{Cj\omega}v \equiv \frac{V}{R} \therefore \frac{1}{Cj\omega} \equiv R \text{ is the impedance } Z_{cap} \tag{12.43}$$

Equivalently for an inductor

$$v = Lj\omega e^{-j\omega t} \equiv Lj\omega i \tag{12.44}$$

$$Lj\omega i \equiv IR \therefore Lj\omega \equiv R \text{ is the impedance } Z_{ind} \tag{12.45}$$

The impedance for a resistor of resistance R remains R and there is no phase lag in the resistor.

Basic circuit design in instrumentation

Voltage divider

The ubiquitous voltage divider (Fig. 12.19) has a voltage output that is a fraction of the voltage in

$$I = \frac{V_{in}}{R_1 + R_2} \tag{12.46}$$

The output voltage is the voltage across R_2, therefore

$$V_{out} = IR_2 = \left(R_2 \cdot \frac{V_{in}}{R_1 + R_2} \right) = \frac{R_2}{R_1 + R_2} V_{in} \tag{12.47}$$

We can produce a Thévenin equivalent of this circuit, as shown in Fig. 12.20. We know that the Thévenin equivalent voltage is given by

$$V_{TH} = open\ circuit\ voltage = V_{in}\frac{R_2}{R_1 + R_2} \tag{12.48}$$

In addition we know that the Thévenin equivalent resistance R_{TH} is given by

$$R_{TH} = \frac{V_{TH}}{short\ circuit\ current}$$

$$= V_{IN}\frac{R_2}{R_1 + R_2} \cdot \frac{R_1}{V_{IN}} \tag{12.49}$$

$$= \frac{R_1 R_2}{R_1 + R_2}$$

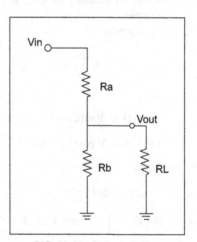

FIG. 12.19 Voltage divider.

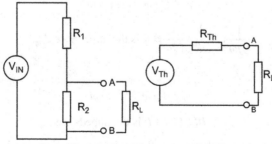

FIG. 12.20 Thévenin equivalent voltage divider.

If we add a load across the output of this equivalent circuit we find

$$V_{out} = V_{TH}\frac{R_L}{R_{TH} + R_L}$$ (12.50)

The load resistance causes the output of the voltage divider to drop. This is an important consideration in the design of measurement equipment. We must ensure that the load resistance is very large compared to the source resistance $R_L \gg R_{source}$. Equivalently, the source resistance should be as low as possible; there are only a few exceptions, for example, if the signal is a current, in which case we want a small input impedance.

Simple signal amplifier built using an op-amp

Because the noninverting input is grounded and because the output acts to equalize the difference between the inputs, the inverting input is also at ground (known as a virtual ground), as shown in Fig. 12.21. As already mentioned, the inputs draw no current, so the current flowing through R_1 and R_2 is the same. Therefore

$$I = \frac{V_{out}}{R_2} = -\frac{V_{in}}{R_1} \Rightarrow \frac{V_{out}}{V_{in}} = -\frac{R_2}{R_1} \equiv \text{voltage gain}$$ (12.51)

The noninverting amplifier is shown in Fig. 12.22.

The inverting input has a voltage

$$V_{inv} = V_{out}\frac{R_1}{R_1 + R_2}$$ (12.52)

$$V_{in} = V_{inv} \rightarrow V_{in} - V_{out}\frac{R_1}{R_1 + R_2}$$ (12.53)

$$\frac{V_{in}}{V_{out}} = \frac{R_1}{R_1 + R_2} \Rightarrow \frac{V_{out}}{V_{in}} = \frac{R_1 + R_2}{R_1} = 1 + \frac{R_2}{R_1}$$ (12.54)

which is the gain of the noninverting amplifier.

Importantly the input impedance of this circuit is, in theory, infinite and in practice very high ($10^{12}\Omega$).

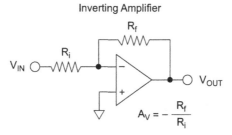

FIG. 12.21 An inverting amplifier.

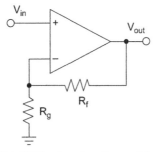

FIG. 12.22 A noninverting amplifier.

Difference amplifier

There are many applications where the important information within a signal is contained in the presence of significant and relatively high amplitude noise. We might think of the electrical signal from a muscle amplifying speech in a noisy environment. The information can be extracted if we improve the signal-to-noise ratio. This can be done by recording a signal from two spatially different points and removing the signal that is *common* to both. The amplifiers seen thus far have only a single input so we need something different (Figs. 12.23 and 12.24).

The operational amplifier seen earlier is essentially a difference amplifier; the difference between the two inputs is reflected by a change in the output. However, because of the huge common mode gains of an operational amplifier very small differences in voltage between the input terminals produce huge swings in the output, so it does not make a practical device for instrumentation. A solution is shown in Fig. 12.25.

In this circuit

$$V_{out} = (V_1 - V_2)\frac{R_2}{R_1} \tag{12.55}$$

Unfortunately this is not an ideal solution as V_2 "sees" an input impedance of $R_1 + R_2$ but V_1 only sees an input impedance of R_1. This imbalance of impedance means that if we were to apply a voltage to one terminal and ground the other than reverse the configuration, different currents would flow through V_2 and V_1 whereas ideally they would be the same. This affects the common rejection ratio as similar signals would not appear so and would not be rejected.

The common mode rejection ratio (CMRR) is defined as

$$CMRR = A_{diff}\left(\frac{V_{cm}}{V_{out}}\right) \tag{12.56}$$

That is, it is a ratio of the common signal present at both terminals (V_{cm}) and the output (V_{out}) multiplied by the differential gain (A_{diff}). The logarithmic expression of the CMRR, the common mode rejection (CMR), can be defined; you may also see this expressed as a logarithmic term $CMR = 20_{log10}CMRR$.

The CMR in dB can be defined in terms of the amplifier gain and the *n* resistor tolerances, *Kr*, or total fractional mismatch.

$$CMR = 20\,log_{10}\left(\frac{1 + \frac{R_2}{R_1}}{nKr}\right) \tag{12.57}$$

It can be seen that if typical values of resistors were used where the tolerances were in the order of 0.1%, the CMR would be very poor.

It should also be noted that the input impedances of the inputs mentioned earlier are really rather low. If we remember what happened to the voltage divider network when $R_L \not> R_{source}$ we can see that we need to maintain a high input impedance so as not to force a reduction in the divider output, which is the signal we are trying to measure. It should be noted that if the signal is acting as a current source, the inverse is true and we want a small input impedance.

The disparity between input currents can be overcome by introducing unity gain (gain = 1) buffer amplifiers to the inputs of the circuit (Fig. 12.26). This essentially produces a very high impedance input to the differential amplifier

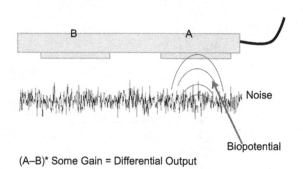

(A–B)* Some Gain = Differential Output

FIG. 12.23 Differential amplifier operation. The noise is common to both electrodes; the biopotential is present predominately at one. *Source: Thomas Stone, Measuring the Motor System, Biomedical Lecture Series Birmingham University 2009.*

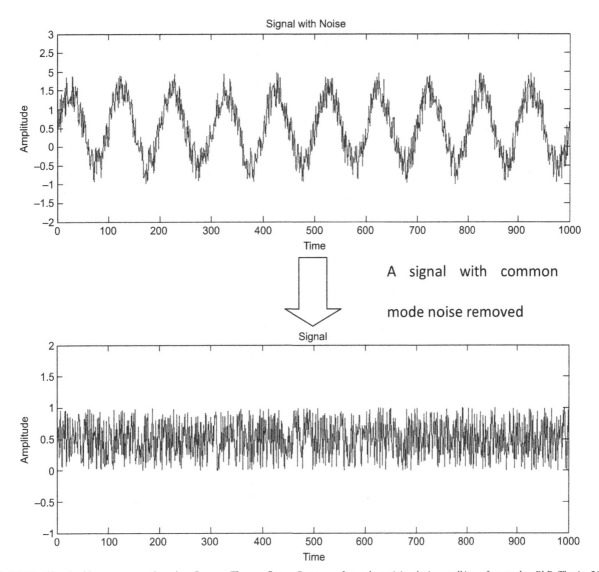

A signal with common mode noise removed

FIG. 12.24 Signal with common mode noise. *Source: Thomas Stone, Patterns of muscle activity during walking after stroke, PhD Thesis, 2006, Bournemouth University.*

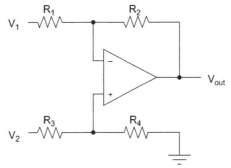

FIG. 12.25 Differential amplifier.

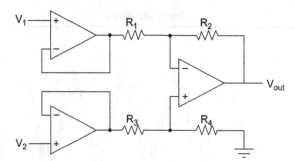

FIG. 12.26 Differential amplifier with buffered inputs.

network; because op-amps typically have very high input impedances, they ideally draw no current through their inputs. The buffer simply provides feedback of the output to the noninverting input which *follows* the inverting input; as such, it merely buffers the input.

The gain of this differential amplifier is set similarly to the inverting amplifier, except the voltage at the noninverting input is not ground. The gain is therefore the ratio of R_1 to R_2; however, to change the gain we must remember that the circuit must remain balanced, and small changes in the resistor pairs will produce different gains on the inputs. How do we solve these problems? The instrumentation amplifier is one solution.

Instrumentation amplifier

The instrumentation amplifier is a precision differential amplifier that is prepackaged in a monolithic device. The circuit shown in Fig. 12.27 can be adapted as described in the following.

The gain of this circuit is defined by R_{gain}. Because the inputs of the two buffer op-amps draw no current, the voltage drop across R_{gain}, which is proportional to the differential voltage V_1 and V_2, produces a current that runs entirely through the resistors R. This produces a voltage that forms the input to the differential amp we saw previously.

$$V_{out} = (V_1 - V_2)\left(1 + \frac{2R}{R_{gain}}\right)\frac{R_1}{R_2} \tag{12.58}$$

It is important to remember that the function of an amplifier is frequency dependent (Fig. 12.28).

Filter

A basic filter can be constructed from a capacitor or an inductor (Fig. 12.29). As we saw earlier, the frequency response of a capacitor is equivalent to saying that it is increasingly resistant to lower-frequency signals. In fact, a capacitor will block DC signals and can be useful for preventing DC offsets from disrupting measurement devices. The same can be said, but inversely, for inductors.

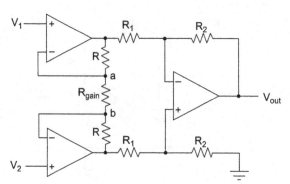

FIG. 12.27 Instrumentation amplifier.

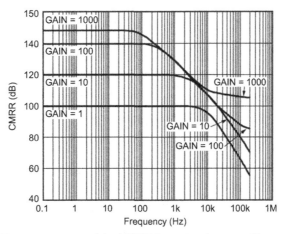

FIG. 12.28 Frequency response of the AD8221 instrumentation amp with respect to CMRR.

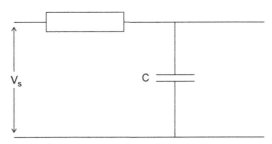

FIG. 12.29 Low pass filter resistor capacitor network.

Signals we have considered thus far have been considered in the *time domain*, that is, they vary with time; we can just as easily consider a signal within the *frequency domain*. If this is the case, the signal now varies with respect to frequency (Fig. 12.30).

We use the frequency domain to understand the response of a signal to a filter; specifically we can use the concept of a *transfer function*. A transfer function can define the response of a linear system given knowledge of its input; nonlinear systems are more complex and require different treatment. Importantly, the input can be arbitrary. The transfer function is defined as the Laplace transform of the system's output over the Laplace transform of the system's input:

$$H(s) = \frac{Y(s)}{X(s)} \tag{12.59}$$

So, for example, if the input were a sine wave, the output would be the Laplace transform of the sine wave input multiplied by the transfer function of the system.

$$Y_s = H_s \mathscr{L}\{A \sin \omega t\} \tag{12.60}$$

$$Y_s = H_s \left(\frac{A\omega}{s^2 + \omega^2} \right) \tag{12.61}$$

For the simple capacitor resistor first order network shown in Fig. 12.29, the relationship of the input to the output as a frequency response can be defined by using Kirchhoff's voltage analysis and taking the Laplace transform of the result.

$$V_{out} = \frac{1}{RCs + 1} V_{in} \tag{12.62}$$

which means that

$$H(s) = \frac{1}{RCs + 1} \tag{12.63}$$

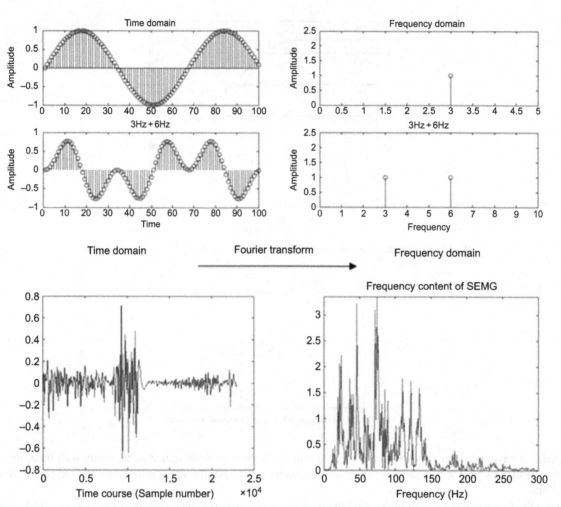

FIG. 12.30 Time and frequency domain. *Source: Thomas Stone, Patterns of muscle activity during walking after stroke, PhD Thesis, 2006, Bournemouth University.*

The transfer function allows us to understand how the system will change with respect to the magnitude and the phase of the output signal. The magnitude of the output is the modulus of the transfer function and the phase is the inverse argument of the transfer function.

We can express the transfer function H(s) in its polar form:

$$H(s) = |H_s|e^{-j\varphi(s)} \qquad (12.64)$$

Therefore, the magnitude can be defined as

$$|H(s)| = \sqrt{\Re\{H_s\}^2 + \Im\{H_s\}^2} \qquad (12.65)$$

and the phase can be defined as

$$\varphi(s) = \tan^{-1}\left(\frac{\Im\{H_s\}}{\Re\{H_s\}}\right) \qquad (12.66)$$

where $\Re\{H_s\}$ and $\Im\{H_s\}$ represent the real and imaginary parts, respectively, of the transfer function H(s).

It is possible to replace s with $j\omega$. Thus, complex representation of the transfer function (Eq. 12.63) can be defined as

$$H_{(j\omega)} = \frac{1}{1 + R^2C^2\omega^2} - j\frac{RC\omega}{1 + R^2C^2\omega^2} \qquad (12.67)$$

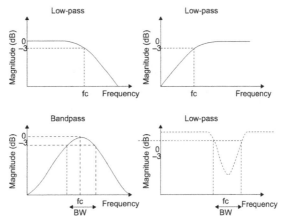

FIG. 12.31 Different forms of filters.

Therefore, the magnitude is

$$\left|H_{(j\omega)}\right| = \sqrt{\frac{1}{(1 + R^2 C^2 \omega^2)^2} - j\frac{R^2 C^2 \omega^2}{(1 + R^2 C^2 \omega^2)^2}} \tag{12.68}$$

and the phase is

$$\varphi_{(j\omega)} = \arg\left(H_{(j\omega)}\right) = -\tan^{-1}(RC\omega) \tag{12.69}$$

These results can be plotted to provide a phase and magnitude response with respect to frequency. Often a special format of plot called a Bode plot is used to visualize the nature of a transfer function.

Filters can be grouped into four main types: low pass, high pass, band pass, and band stop (Fig. 12.31). Filters attenuate a signal and this attenuation is measured in dB. The range of frequencies over which a signal is allowed to pass without attenuation is called the pass band. The frequencies over which the signal is stopped is called the stop band. There are many different types of filters, which provide different characteristics in their pass bands. For example, the Butterworth filter provides a very flat pass band where the signal is not modulated very much over these frequencies. In contrast, the Chebyshev filter has a very oscillatory pass band which means that the signal will be distorted within this band. The advantage of the Chebyshev filter is that it has a much sharper *knee*. That is, signals of the frequency within the stop band are attenuated much more aggressively, as shown in Fig. 12.32. The frequency beyond which the signal should be sufficiently attenuated is called the *cut-off frequency*. The level at which a signal is considered to be attenuated sufficiently is often 3 dB, though this will be application specific.

Filtering has a vital role in conditioning signals during measurement and great care is required when specifying the characteristics of a filter to ensure useful information is not removed from the signal. Fig. 12.33 shows how a rectified surface electromyogram can be turned into a more visually intuitive envelope representation but also how many of the more subtle characteristics of this signal are removed in the process.

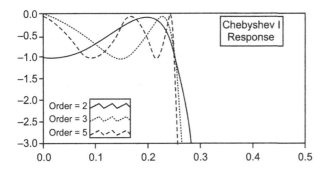
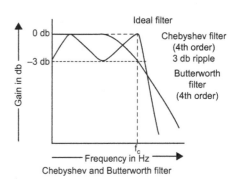

FIG. 12.32 Butterworth filter compared to a Chebyshev filter.

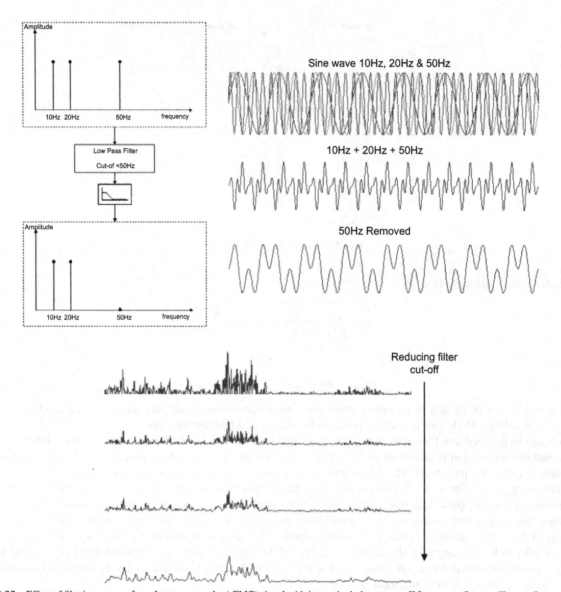

FIG. 12.33 Effect of filtering on a surface electromyography (sEMG) signal with increasingly lower cut-off frequency. *Source: Thomas Stone, Patterns of muscle activity during walking after stroke, PhD Thesis, 2006, Bournemouth University.*

Further reading

Brown, W.F., Bolton, C.F., Aminoff, M.J., 2002. Neuromuscular Function and Disease: Basic, Clinical, and Electrodiagnostic Aspects. W.B. Saunders.

Chiappa, K.H., 1997. Evoked Potentials in Clinical Medicine. Lippincott-Raven Press.

Glisson, T.H., 2010. Introduction to Circuit Analysis and Design. Springer Limited, London.

Horowitz, P., Hill, W., 1998. The Art of Electronics. Cambridge University Press, Cambridge.

Metzer, D., 1981. Electronic Components, Instruments and Troubleshooting. Prentice Hall, New Jersey.

Mississippi, A.A.L.A.P.N.U., Mississippi, V.C.T.N.R.U., 2000. Atlas of Electromyography. Oxford University Press, USA.

Oh, S.J., 2003. Clinical Electromyography: Nerve Conduction Studies. Lippincott, Williams & Wilkins.

Ziemer, R., Tranter, W., Fannin, R., 1998. Signals and Systems, fourth ed. Prentice Hall, New Jersey, Prentice Hall, New Jersey.

Chapter 13

Electrical safety of medical equipment and systems

Azzam Taktak[a] and Justin McCarthy[b]

[a]*Royal Liverpool University Hospital, Liverpool, United Kingdom;* [b]*Clin Eng Consulting Ltd, Cardiff and School of Engineering, Cardiff University, Wales, United Kingdom*

Chapter outline

Introduction

Electrical safety testing of Medical Electrical (ME) Equipment has always been an integral function of Clinical Biomedical Engineers working in hospitals. It is a very important part of the job to ensure that the organisation complies with the law, meets national guidance (e.g. Medicines and Healthcare products Regulatory Agency (MHRA) in the UK), meets good engineering practice, complies with manufacturer's requirements and addresses clinical staff and patients' expectations.

Whereas healthcare organisations follow national guidelines to do these tests, local practice can vary between institutions. A survey was conducted in 2005 regarding electrical safety testing practice in the UK and Ireland (Taktak and Brown, 2005) with 26 responders (Fig. 13.1). Half the respondents said that they test equipment once a year whilst the rest varied depending on equipment type, class, and risk etc. Whilst everyone tested their equipment regularly, only 58% always tested loan items, 61% tested domiciliary medical equipment and 70% tested ME systems (e.g. endoscope or anaesthetic trolleys). All respondents said they label equipment to show that it has passed the test. However, only 38% always recorded the actual test values. All respondents said that they calibrate their test equipment regularly.

The IEC 60601 standard

The IEC 60601 series is an International set of standards for electrical safety of ME equipment. It sets out the requirements for the design and manufacture of ME equipment including type test requirements, construction, rules for the user interface and labelling.

The reason for having a standard for ME equipment which is different from other electrical equipment such as household equipment is that in most cases ME equipment are attached to a patient who is more vulnerable to an electric shock than a healthy person due to:

- Age; they might be a neonate for example
- Sedation

FIG. 13.1 Responding institutions to a national survey on electrical safety testing of ME equipment from Taktak and Brown, (2005).

— Disability
— Deliberate lowering of skin impedance
— Having multiple equipment attached thereby increasing the probability of an electric shock

By setting a common set of internationally recognised standards, manufacturers of medical equipment are able to sell their products anywhere in the world without having different requirements imposed on them in different countries. They also provide the means for the manufacturer to demonstrate compliance with the law.

The IEC 60601 series of standards is structured in four groups. Part 1 of the standard (IEC 60601-1) is the general standard for all types of medical electrical equipment. Complementing that there is a number of additional Part 1 standards known as collateral standards, numbered IEC 60601-1-xx. These either address particular issues relating to a large sub-group of ME equipment, for example equipment designed for use in the home healthcare environment (IEC 60601-1-11) or radiation protection in diagnostic X-ray equipment (IEC 60601-1-3). Alternatively, collateral standards address a specific characteristic that is not fully addressed in the general standard but apply to the vast majority of medical electrical equipment. Examples are electromagnetic compatibility (IEC 60601-1-2) and alarms (IEC 60601-1-8).

Part 2 standards in the series, known as particular standards, add, modify or delete requirements from the general and collateral standards. They take priority over the general and collateral standards. For example, the particular standard for Surgical Diathermy (IEC 60601-2-2) will allow 'Functional Currents' through the patient greatly in excess of allowable leakage currents (explained later). If a particular standard in the series is produced jointly with ISO or published by ISO then it is given an 80601-2-xx number, for example ISO 80601-2-13 *Medical electrical equipment. Particular requirements for basic safety and essential performance of an anaesthetic workstation.*

There are no longer any current Part 3 standards in the series. These were used for performance requirement for some types of equipment. However, from the third edition of the general standard, 'essential performance' as well as 'basic safety' is built into all Part 1 and Part 2 standards.

From 2015, the IEC technical committee responsible for the production of the 60601 series (TC62 *Electrical equipment in medical practice*) has started to produce Part 4 documents. These are all titled … *Guidance and interpretation* … and as such do not contain normative requirements. For example IEC/TR 60601-4-4 *Medical electrical equipment. Guidance and interpretation. Guidance for writers of particular standards when creating alarm system-related requirements.* Fig. 13.2 is a diagrammatic illustration of this structure.

The tests in IEC 60601 standards are Type Tests. These are a set of stringent tests on a representative sample of the equipment with the objective of determining if the equipment, as designed and manufactured, can meet the requirements of this standard. The IEC 60601 standards do not set out any requirements for hospitals nor say anything about testing after

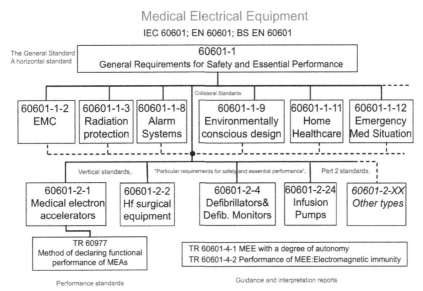

Medical Electrical Equipment
IEC 60601; EN 60601; BS EN 60601

FIG. 13.2 The structure of the IEC 60601 suite of standards.

sale. However, they can enable hospital staff to more effectively evaluate medical equipment and fault-find electrical problems. The general standard is also the basis for other field-testing standards derived from 60601 (e.g. IEC 62353 which assumes that the equipment has been designed to meet the IEC 60601 standard).

Physiological effects of electricity on the human body

There are three main physiological effects of electricity on the human body:

1. Electrolysis - (mainly near d.c.)
2. Neuromuscular effects - (Mainly 10−100 Hz though reduced effects will extend further)
3. Heating (ohmic and dielectric - (mainly 100 kHz-30 Mhz))

The mechanism of very low frequency flow of electric charge (i.e. electric current) through tissue is the movement of ions rather than electrons as in metallic conductors. Electrolysis effects are due to ionic current causing a migration of sodium and chlorine atoms between two electrodes. This creates a build-up of sodium atoms at the negative plate and chlorine atoms at the positive plate, causing chemical reactions and destruction of cells. Very small currents of the order of 50 μA and greater can cause ulceration to the skin beneath the electrodes if contact with tissue is prolonged. This effect diminishes as current frequency rises above a few Hz due to ionic current being replaced by capacitive current, and above 10 Hz there will be no electrolysis effects. Device design must take this into account so that d.c. currents are kept well below harmful levels. The IEC 60601-1 standard allows maximum of 10 μA d.c. leakage in normal conditions and 50 μA in single fault conditions. However, in the healthcare environment electrolysis is used deliberately for therapies such as the removal of unwanted hair.

Neuromuscular effects happen mainly due to the fact that the nerves which communicate between the sensors (touch, pain, sight, smell etc.), the actuators (muscles, glands), and the processing centres (brain, reflex loops etc.) operate through a series of voltage pulses of about 100 mV. Externally applied a.c. voltages causing electrical fields or current flow in the vicinity of nerves can interfere with their action causing sensation or actions. The heart is especially sensitive during certain parts of the cardiac cycle.

The effects of a 10−100 Hz current passing through human tissue will vary with both magnitude and duration. Up to around 0.5 mA, whatever the duration, perception of the current is possible (often described as a 'buzz') but usually there will be no 'startle' reaction. Above 0.5 mA, for a duration of 1 s, the following effects are expected. Between around 0.5 and 15 mA, perception and involuntary muscular contractions are likely but usually there will be no harmful electrical physiological effects. At the higher end of this range, it may not be possible to let go of a conductor grasped in the hand. Above 15 mA and up to 50 mA for this duration, the subject is likely to experience strong involuntary muscular contractions. If the current pathway is across the chest, there may be difficulty in breathing and reversible disturbances of heart function. Immobilization may occur. Effects will increase with current magnitude within this range. Usually no

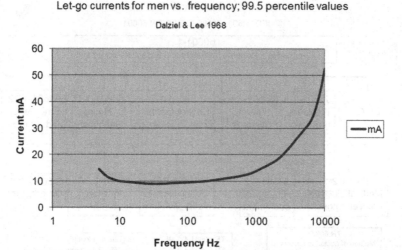

FIG. 13.3 Perception and frequency. *Adapted from Dalziel, C.F., Lee, W.R., 1968. Re-evaluation of lethal electric currents. IEEE Trans. Indus. Gen. Appl. IGA-4 (5), 467.*

organic damage is to be expected. Above 50 mA for this and longer duration, physiological effects may occur such as breathing arrest, cardiac arrest, and burns or other cellular damage. The probability of ventricular fibrillation increases with current magnitude and time. Above 200 mA for a duration of 1 s, the probability of ventricular fibrillation is above 50%. By contrast, for a duration of 30 ms (the maximum allowed disconnection time for a residual current breaker) currents up to 100 mA will produce only perception and involuntary muscular contractions and up to 500 mA will produce only strong involuntary muscular contractions. These figures are taken from IEC/TS 60479-1:2005 +A1:2016 published by BSI as PD IEC/TS 60479-1:2005 +A1:2016 (BSI 2016). It is worth remembering that there is considerable individual variation of susceptibility to electric shock, and variation in the exact circumstances and current pathways in every incident.

At d.c. once the onset has occurred, the body's perception is only about one quarter of that at mains frequency. As frequency increases much beyond 500 Hz or so, the effects decrease in inverse proportion in kHz. Beyond 10 kHz the electric shock effects are negligible (Dalziel and Lee, 1968) (Fig. 13.3) but heating effects may occur.

There are two types of heating effects:

1. Ohmic — low frequencies
2. Dielectric — high frequencies

Ohmic heating occurs at frequencies up to around 100 kHz due to I^2R, causing burns to the skin. At higher frequencies skin impedance reduces and capacitive current is more dominant. This will produce heating in the lossy dielectric in the body. The heating effects of high current at high frequency have been utilised in surgical diathermy for many years. Because of the frequencies involved, (typically 200 kHz-30 MHz) there are no neuromuscular effects, only heating of the target tissues. Heat is concentrated at the tip of the active probe due to the very high current density, whereas at the large area return plate it is low. Heating would only occur at the plate if it is too small for the currents being used e.g. in ablation procedures, or if it becomes partially detached from the patient.

In everyday life, the term 'electric shock' is used to refer to electric current passing through the skin and producing the physiological effects described above. In the medical situation there is a need to distinguish between this type of shock which is named *macroshock*, and shock caused by current applied directly to the heart which can only occur during medical procedures. This is referred to as *microshock*. These terms appeared in the 1960s around the time when heart transplant surgery was getting underway (Spalding et al., 2009). There was particular alarm when it was discovered that currents as small as 50 μA if applied directly to the heart could interfere with heart action, especially as the levels of current concerned were too small to feel and higher levels of currents leaked from equipment that was functioning normally (Lee, 1970).

For a comprehensive explanation of the considerations that led to the values for macro and micro shock adopted in the IEC 60601-1 standard, see Annex A of that standard under the entry for subclause 8.7.3.

Electrocution hazards

In order to mitigate against the risk of electrocution from ME equipment, we must first understand where the hazards are and what is the likelihood of them happening. Electrocution hazards are divided into four main areas:

1. Earth seeking mains supply
2. Faults in mains plugs and leads
3. Mechanical damage to equipment
4. Leakage currents

In a TN mains supply system, each of the nominal (in the EU) 230 V three phase secondary supplies are connected to earth at the sub-station transformer. The protective earth conductor is then either run as a separate conductor throughout the installation from this neutral star point (TN-S), or is combined with the neutral conductor up to the entry point to a building and then must be run separately within the building (TN-C-S). Either arrangement means that the live conductor has a reference voltage to earth at the consumer end. Therefore, if an operator or a patient is exposed to a live voltage, some current will flow through their body to earth.

Faults in the mains plugs and leads are quite common due to their flexible nature and extensive use. They can often suffer from rough treatment such as being pulled, bashed, trampled on, etc. The equipment might still be working normally even if a fault has occurred. For example, if the earth lead comes off at the mains plug, the equipment will carry on working normally, except one means of protection has been lost. The use of moulded plugs has become the norm in recent years as they offer much better grip on the lead insulation and thus better protection against any wires coming loose. Fuses are also used to protect the equipment against further damage or fire. Fuses are chosen so that the rating allows normal current but only a short period of excess current before the fuse opens. How short a period depends on fuse type and the current.

Leakage currents are non-functional currents, usually capacitive a.c. from the mains part of the equipment due to stray capacitance within the equipment and mains lead. If the protective earth is disconnected the leakage current will attempt to flow from the enclosure of the equipment, or through the patient connections to earth. ME equipment is designed so that leakage currents are minimized below the level of perception even under a single fault. However, any ingress of fluids or dust can increase capacitive coupling or provide a resistive pathway between conductors causing leakage currents to increase.

Methods and degrees of protection

There are two methods of protection against electrocution according to the electrical safety class of the equipment. Class I equipment relies on basic insulation plus earthing of all accessible conductive parts other than those which are double insulated. This provides two means of operator protection (two MOOP). The protective earth terminal is marked, usually internally, with the symbol shown in Fig. 13.4A. This terminal and symbol may not always be visible from outside the equipment.

Class II equipment on the other hand does not rely on protective earth but must have double insulation between mains and any accessible conductive parts to provide the required two MOOP. Note that double insulation can consist of basic plus supplementary insulation or these can be combined into a single layer of reinforced insulation. This class of equipment must be labelled with the symbol shown in Fig. 13.4B.

(A)   **(B)**

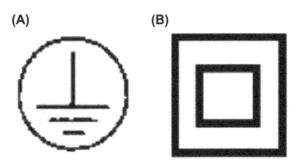

FIG. 13.4   (A) Protective earth symbol on a Class I device and (B) Class II device symbol.

Internally-powered equipment is equipment with an internal battery or power supply. For internally powered equipment that has an alternative mains connection, e.g. for charging, the equipment must meet the safety requirements of Class I or II as appropriate while so connected.

The Applied Part of ME equipment is the part of the equipment that in normal use necessarily comes into physical contact with the patient for the equipment to perform its function. For example an ECG electrode is an applied part as is the patient table of an X-ray machine. An item of ME Equipment may have more than one Applied Part. The IEC 60601-1 standard requires that the patient be provided with two means of patient protection (MOPP) of which one can be provided by two MOOP.

There are three different types of applied parts depending on the degree of protection provided by the combination of the equipment and the applied part:

Type B: Provides protection by way of a *limited range* of allowable leakage currents.

Type BF: Provides protection by way of an *isolated* (floating) Applied Part, and having a very limited range of allowable leakage current.

Type CF: Provides a level of protection by way of an *isolated* (floating) Applied Part and *extremely* limited leakage currents that makes the Applied Part suitable for connection within the heart.

The symbols for these different types are shown in Fig. 13.5.

Type B Applied Parts may be connected directly to earth, or have a higher impedance conductive or capacitive connection. Connection to an earthed and conductive Type B Applied Part may considerably increase risk of electrocution because of the low impedance route to earth for currents from other faulty devices. Since 2005, the IEC 60601-1 standard specifies that 'An APPLIED PART that includes a PATIENT CONNECTION that is intended to deliver electrical energy or an electrophysiological signal to or from the PATIENT shall be a TYPE BF APPLIED PART or TYPE CF APPLIED PART'. Examples of Type B Applied Parts include an examination couch, chin rest, etc.

F- Type Applied Parts reduce to an acceptably low level any currents leaving or entering the equipment via the patient and provide protection should mains potential get onto the patient. This is usually achieved by optically coupling the signal between the pre-amplifier in the patient connected circuit and the electronics in the earth referred intermediate circuits, and providing a power source to the patient circuit using a very high insulation transformer to transfer the small amount of power required.

Electrical safety testing

The IEC 60601-1 standard describes what are called as type tests. These are tests that are performed on a sample of the ME equipment to determine its safety. These tests can be destructive or put the equipment under stress. Some of these tests also require specialist equipment. For these reasons, it is not recommended or appropriate that these exact tests are carried out in the field but test configurations derived from IEC 60601-1 can be used.

Field testing is usually carried out on commissioning, after repair or modification and on a periodic basis. The IEC 62353 standard describes what tests can be carried out in the field and it assumes that the ME equipment has been designed to meet the IEC 60601-1 standard. In addition, government agencies and professional bodies have issued guidance documents on field testing of ME equipment.

For the purposes of this book, we will concentrate on field testing only.

Visual inspection

Visual inspection is a crucial and perhaps the most important part of the electrical safety checks, especially for Class II equipment where the majority of the hazards are due to physical damage. Visual inspection should start with the mains

FIG. 13.5 Applied Part symbols (A) Type B, (B) Type BF and (C) Type CF.

plugs. These should be inspected for any signs of physical damage and for appropriate fuse ratings. For rewirable plugs, it is advisable to open up the plug to check for any signs of damage such as fluid ingress and that fixings such as screws and grips are all tight. The mains lead should be inspected throughout its length for any signs of damage such as cuts, abrasions, wrinkles, etc. and that adequate strain relief is present at both ends. Next, the appliance coupler and the device enclosure should be inspected for any signs of damage or unauthorised modification.

Earth resistance

For Class I equipment, the resistance of the earth wire should be regularly checked to ensure that a) it is still connected and b) its resistance is sufficiently low, thereby providing low resistance path for fault currents, resulting in rapid opening of fuses, and in the normal situation, an easy path for leakage currents to escape. This test is done by applying a large current between the earth pin at the plug-end and the protective earth terminal and measuring the resistance. The measured resistance should be no higher than $0.2 \, \Omega$ when new and no higher than $0.3 \, \Omega$ in service (IEC 62353). The IEC 60601-1 standard calls for test currents of 25 A to flow for 5−10 s for type tests. This is not appropriate for field-testing and most field testing devices apply a test current that is much less than that (200 mA−1 A). Some more modern field testers apply a high current of (8−10 A) for a very short period (<1 s) and ramp it down quickly to around 1 A. This is due to the fact that some old equipment exhibits high resistance when measured at low currents due to oxidization with age of metallic joints such as the pins of the mains plug. It has been noticed that this effect is reduced when a large current is passed for a short period of time so that the resistance becomes low and stays low. It has been argued that this test methodology masks the fact that metallic joints have oxidised but in practice, a fault to earth will result in an instantaneous current very much greater that 25 A and the oxidation will be penetrated, and the slightly higher resistance will make no difference to leakage current since this comes from effectively a constant current source.

Insulation test

This test measures the electrical resistance between the mains part (live and neutral joined together) and earth. This test is carried out in lieu of the dielectric strength test (flash test) which the standard calls for in type testing. It is usually done by applying a d.c. voltage (350−500 V) between the mains part and earth and measuring the current and thus the resistance. The pass levels for this test varies in different sources but most institutions set a level of $>50 \, M\Omega$ to pass the test. If low resistances are measured, it is advisable to check the reason for this as it could be due to mains filters, chokes or mineral insulated heaters. Insulation resistances less than $1 \, M\Omega$ or significantly less than previous results are not acceptable.

Leakage currents

The following leakage current measurements are carried out routinely in field tests:

1. Earth leakage: current that flows down the earth wire in normal operation and under a single fault condition
2. Touch current: current that flows from any accessible metal part of the enclosure to earth via the operator or the patient should they come into contact with the enclosure. This again is done in normal and single fault conditions.
3. Patient leakage current: current that flows from the Applied Part via the patient to earth in normal and single fault conditions.
4. Patient auxiliary current: current that flows between different Applied Parts and through the patient in normal and single fault conditions.

The recommended measuring device is shown in Fig. 13.6. R_2 at $1 \, k\Omega$ represents a minimum body impedance modified by the low pass filter with a cut-off frequency at 1 kHz with a 6 dB/octave roll off. This is in order to simulate the human body's response to electricity for neuro-muscular effects.

For earth leakage currents, the pass limits are 5 mA and 10 mA in normal and single fault conditions respectively. Single faults in this case are the interruption of one of the mains conductors at a time.

For touch currents, the pass levels are 0.5 mA and 1 mA in normal and single fault conditions respectively. Single faults in this case are the interruption of the protective earth conductor or one of the mains supply conductors.

It is important to understand that the IEC 60601-1 standard states that for permanently installed ME equipment, the interruption of the protective earth conductor is not applied as a single fault condition because it is 'considered unlikely to become disconnected' ((IEC 60601-1, 8.1b) fourth dash). Thus in practice, for a Class I plugged-in item of ME equipment that has accessible earthed conductive parts, the effective maximum allowed earth leakage current under normal conditions

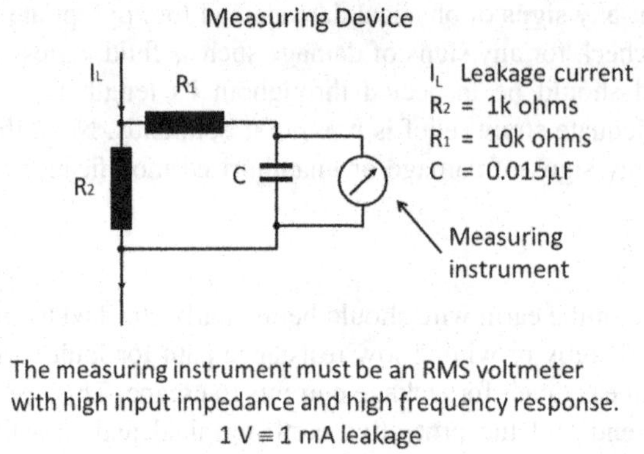

Measuring Device

I_L Leakage current
R_2 = 1k ohms
R_1 = 10k ohms
C = 0.015μF

Measuring instrument

The measuring instrument must be an RMS voltmeter
with high input impedance and high frequency response.
1 V ≡ 1 mA leakage

FIG. 13.6 Leakage current measuring device.

is 0.5 mA (not 5 mA) since this current will become single fault touch current when the protective earth is broken. In contrast, a plugged-in item of Class I ME equipment that has no accessible earthed conductive parts but has an internal protective earth connection, for example some monitors, may have earth leakage current up to 5 mA provided the touch current to any non-earthed accessible conductive parts remains less than 0.5 mA with the protective earth connection open circuit.

For patient leakage and patient auxiliary currents, the pass levels are 0.1 mA and 0.5 mA for Types B and BF applied parts and 0.01 mA and 0.05 mA for Types CF applied parts in normal and single fault conditions respectively. The above limits are root-mean-squared (r.m.s.) a.c. values. For d.c, the limits are much lower due to electrolysis effects.

Safety testers

In recent years, there has been a considerable shift towards fully automated electrical safety test equipment. These offer some advantages; they automatically configure the tests and identify results that are outside the allowable limits, they can also save time and can be used by less qualified staff. The main disadvantages of using such tester is that the operator may not have a full understanding of the tests and may perform some tests incorrectly (touch current can be a repeat of earth leakage current). There is also a potential error of the equipment under test not being in the correct state (on/off) for the test.

A further disadvantage is that some automated testers only give an indication of pass or fail and do not give a result of the measured value. It is very important when carrying out routine electrical safety tests or tests after repair to compare the test results with reference values, usually the 'as new' values (IEC 62353, 6.1). An item of ME equipment that had earth leakage current of say 125 μA when new and now has 450 μA passes the test (<500 μA), but clearly something has changed and needs further investigation.

Abbreviations

BSI British Standards Institution
ECG Electrocardiogram
IEC International Electrotechnical Commission
ISO International Organization for Standardization
ME Medical Electrical
MHRA Medicines and Healthcare products Regulatory Agency
MOOP Means of Operator Protection
RMS Root-Mean-Squared

References

BS PD IEC/TS 60479-1:2005 +A1, 2016. Effects of Current on Human Beings and Livestock − Part 1: General Aspects (BSI 2016).

Dalziel, C.F., Lee, W.R., 1968. Re-evaluation of lethal electric currents. IEEE Trans. Ind. Appl. IGA-4 (5), 467.

IEC 60601-1, 2012. Medical Electrical Equipment − Part 1: General Requirements for Basic Safety and Essential Performance, Edition 3.1.

IEC 62353, 2014. Medical Electrical Equipment − Recurrent Test and Test after Repair of Medical Electrical Equipment, second ed.

Lee, W.R., 1970. The hazard of electrocution during patient monitoring. Postgrad. Med. J. 46, 355–359. https://pmj.bmj.com/content/postgradmedj/46/536/355.full.pdf.

Spalding, L.E.S., Carpes Jr., W.P., Batisttela, N.J., 2009. A Method to detect the microshok risk during surgical procedure. IEEE Trans. Instrum. Meas. 58 (7), 2335–2342.

Taktak, A.F.G., Brown, M.C., 2005. Electrical safety testing of medical equipment: results of a National Survey. Scope 14 (3), 6–8.

Further reading

IEC 62353, 2014. Medical Electrical Equipment – Recurrent Test and Test after Repair of Medical Electrical Equipment, second ed.

Aucott, G., Brown, M.C., Grant, L., Lee, P., Hegarty, F., McCarthy, J.P., Jones, R., Smithson, P., Taktak, A.F.G., Walsh, C., Wentworth, S., 2009b. In: Wentworth, S. (Ed.), IPEM Report 97: Guide to Electrical Safety Testing of Medical Equipment: The Why and the How. IPEM Publication.

Chapter 14

Basic anatomy and physiology

Nicholas P. Rhodes

University of Liverpool, Liverpool, United Kingdom

Chapter outline

Introduction

The following pages summarize some basic yet important principles of anatomy and physiology. This chapter is intended to be just the starting point for your understanding of the subject area, rather than representing the complete biology of human beings.

Cell physiology

The human body can be thought of in terms of physiological systems, for example:

- Nervous system
- Endocrine system
- Myoskeletal system
- Cardiovascular system
- Lymphatic system
- Respiratory system
- Digestive system
- Urinary system
- Reproductive system
- Haematopoietic system (blood)
- Immune system (reticuloendothelial system)
- Special senses (vision, hearing, etc.)

Clinical Engineering. https://doi.org/10.1016/B978-0-08-102694-6.00014-0

Each of these systems has unique and special properties that allow them to function in what seems an almost self-contained fashion, having positive and negative feedback loops, external sensing and multiple action steps. However, each is constructed from many millions of specialized cells. An interesting feature is that almost all cells have very similar biology, with internal chemistry that can sometimes be difficult to differentiate. The study of a "typical" cell allows us to understand the processes occurring in many other cell types, and therefore, tissues and physiological systems (Fig. 14.1A).

The cell can be thought of as an individual factory, having its own computer code and power station. Most cells contain the following:

- Cell Membrane
- Nucleus
- Endoplasmic reticulum
- Golgi complex
- Mitochondria
- Lysosomes
- Microfilaments and microtubules
- Vesicles

Remember that this is a two-dimensional representation of a three-dimensional structure. In reality, there is a much closer association between the endoplasmic reticulum and nucleus, as can be seen in Fig. 14.1B.

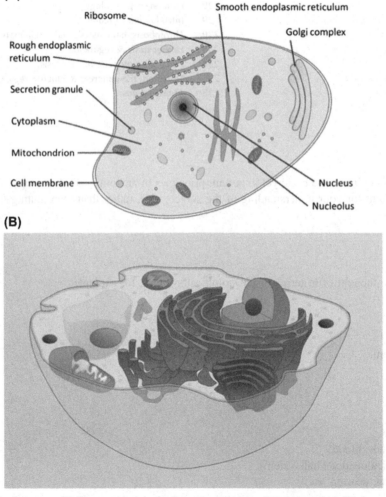

FIG. 14.1 (A) Generalized cell structure (B) 3D representation of cell structure. *(A) https://pixabay.com/en/cell-information-animal-biology-48542. (B) From Wikipedia.org, Creative Commons Attribution-Share-a-like 3.0 License (CC BY-SA 3.0). https://en.wikipedia.org/wiki/File:Eukaryoticcell.png.*

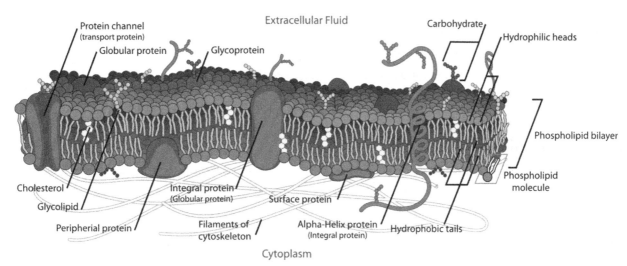

FIG. 14.2   Structure of cell membrane. *From https://pixabay.com/en/biology-cell-diagram-science-41522.*

Cell membrane (Fig. 14.2)

- Separates cell internals from external environment
- Support for sensing receptors
- Allows active uptake and output of chemicals

Nucleus

- Houses a copy of the master blueprints of the host (DNA)
- Handles copying of DNA to allow protein synthesis
- Performs cell replication

Endoplasmic reticulum (ER)

Fluid filled membrane system that synthesizes:
- Lipid (smooth ER)
- Proteins (rough ER)

Golgi complex

- Organizes trafficking of proteins and lipids to the external environment

Mitochondria (plural of mitochondrion)

- Energy centre for cells
- Derived from bacteria (evolutionarily)

For cells to undertake their primary function, they require energy. This is principally achieved by conversion of glucose in food to Adenosine tri-phosphate (ATP), which cells use as an energy source, and CO_2.

The primary function of a cell generally requires it to do one or more of the following:

- Sense the environment, using surface receptors
- Synthesize proteins
  - building blocks, e.g. Collagen
  - *action* molecules, i.e. Enzymes
- Create and use energy
- Output an action,

- Create a force, e.g. Muscle
- Build new tissue
- Dispose of unwanted cells or molecules

Glycoproteins sense the environment that is external to the cell, with receptors using a "lock and key" connection to ligands, with "activation" of such a receptor leading to a cascade of intracellular reactions, resulting in upregulation of specific genes, transcription of proteins that the genes encode, and a particular action, as listed above.

Principles of cell replication

Organisms are organized in terms of their biology, from their simplest component parts to more complex systems, as follows:

- DNA
- Proteins and peptides
- Cells
- Tissues
- Organs
- Whole organism (e.g. animal)

DNA is responsible for maintaining the organism in its correct state and allowing the replication of new cells, as it comprises the full code for life (Figs. 14.3 and 14.4). DNA has the following features:

- It contains *all* information required to build the whole organism
- There is an identical copy in *every* cell
- In humans, there is approximately 2 m of DNA in each nucleus
- DNA is composed of only 4 types of nucleotide base
- It is normally unravelled, but wrapped up into chromosomes during cell division
- DNA codes for proteins only
- Each cell has DNA with approximately 3 billion base pairs
- Less than 1% of DNA is coding information (genes)
- Humans have approximately 20,000 genes (the precise number is still controversial)
- Almost all genes in all people are identical

Proteins are generally either catalytic (known as enzymes — they enable reactions to occur) — or structural (e.g. collagen) in nature.

The question most people ask is "How can people be different from each other if their genes are the same!". The answer to this conundrum lies with the timing of expression of a particular gene. DNA is a genetic library which encodes sophisticated regulatory and timing mechanisms. This fourth dimension is where differences generally occur. The 99% of DNA content is where the scientific knowledge of genetics is currently lacking. As cells mature, enzymes chemically

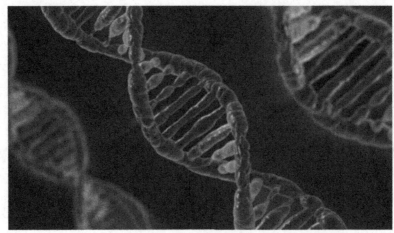

FIG. 14.3 DNA — the code for life. *From https://pixabay.com/en/dna-biology-medicine-gene-163466.*

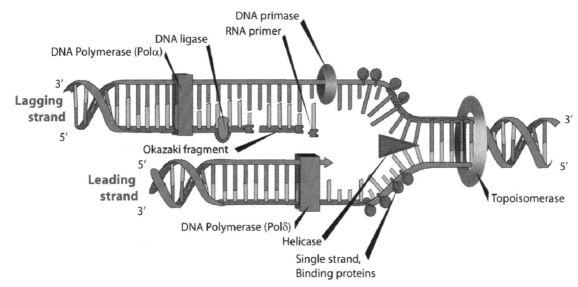

FIG. 14.4 DNA replication by formation of complimentary strands after helix dissociation. *From https://pixabay.com/en/diagram-dna-biology-labeled-41531.*

modify the DNA (e.g. methylation, acetylation, telomere shortening), known as epigenetic modifications, modifying gene expression, which may be inherited.

DNA has only 4 different base types, connected together in a chain and attached to a complimentary (i.e. mirror image) chain. There are only 2 different base pair (bp) combinations:

- Adenine — Thymine
- Guanine — Cytosine

Proteins are composed of covalently bonded amino acids (in the order of 100 in a typical protein). There are only 20 different amino acid types. Each amino acid is coded by a 3 bp sequence (Table 14.1).

TABLE 14.1 Genetic code — how combinations of bases are coded in DNA.

1st base	2nd base				3rd base
	T	C	A	G	
	(Phe/F) Phenylalanine	(Ser/S) Serine	(Tyr/Y) Tyrosine	(Cys/C) Cysteine	T
					C
	(Leu/L) Leucine		**Stop**	**Stop**	A
			Stop	(Trp/W) Tryptophan	G
C		(Pro/P) Proline	(His/H) Histidine	(Arg/R) Arginine	T
					C
			(Gln/Q) Glutamine		A
					G
A	(Ile/I) Isoleucine	(Thr/T) Threonine	(Asn/N) Asparagine	(Ser/S) Serine	T
					C
			(Lys/K) Lysine	(Arg/R) Arginine	A
	(Met/M) Methionine				G
G	(Val/V) Valine	(Ala/A) Alanine	(Asp/D) Aspartic acid	(Gly/G) Glycine	T
					C
			(Glu/E) Glutamic acid		A
					G

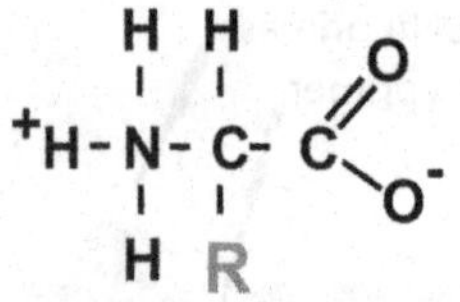

FIG. 14.5   General amino acid structure.

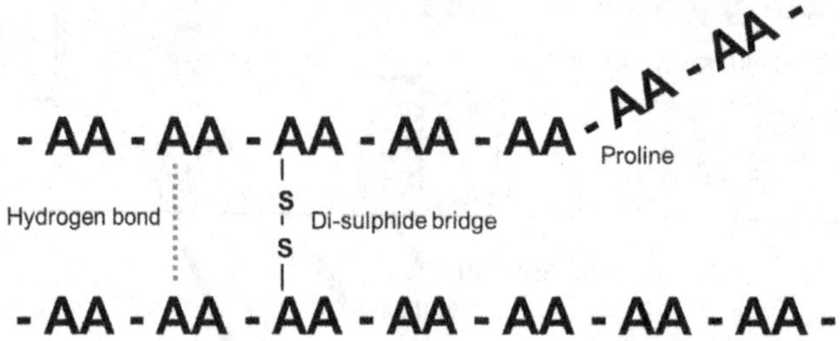

FIG. 14.6   Amino acids joined in a typical dipeptide structure.

The structure of an amino acid allows variation in charge, hydrophilicity, or acidity through variation in the "R" group (Figs. 14.5 and 14.6).

Gene transcription occurs inside cells continuously, resulting in proteins being formed (expressed) all the time. Some proteins (and therefore genes) are expressed *constitutively* (i.e. continuous without a change in expression). For other genes, higher expression of one usually leads to increased or decreased expression of another (like a cascade or sequence).

An example is weak bone. Osteoblasts (bone-forming cells) detect excessive stretching (weak bone is *bendy*), and this turns on the *bone-forming master gene* (cbfa/Runx2). The presence of this protein leads to the activation of other genes over time (collagen I, alkaline phosphatase, osteonectin, osteopontin, osteocalcin, etc.). This strengthens the bone and reduces the activity of the bone formation mechanism.

For a protein to be transcribed, double-stranded DNA in the nucleus is unravelled then a single-stranded messenger RNA (mRNA) is created as a copy of the required gene. This travels out of the nucleus where ribosomes attach, which then attracts the correct transfer RNA (tRNA) molecule for each 3-base mRNA code in the sequence. Each tRNA molecule has a different amino acid attached to it. In this way, a peptide is built by the ribosome as it travels along the mRNA, decoding the base sequence.

Each time a gene is accessed, histones unravel the correct section of DNA. Specific pieces of DNA can be modified (acetylation, methylation). These can make transcription harder or easier over time, because the DNA is wound around histones. Ultimately, this could lead to a cell being killed off (apoptosis) if transcription becomes too difficult.

Bone and skeletal physiology

The skeletal system (Fig. 14.7) can be described simply as comprising four different components:

- Bones: Rigid support
- Cartilage: Flexible support
- Tendons: Bone-Muscle attachment
- Ligaments: Bone-Bone attachment

Bones represent the structural support of the body, a connective tissue that has the potential to repair and regenerate. It is composed of a rigid matrix of calcium salts deposited around protein fibres. The minerals provide rigidity and the proteins provide elasticity and strength.

There are four main bone types:

- Long bones (e.g. femur)
- Short bones (e.g. finger bones)
- Flat bones (e.g. skull)
- Irregular bones (e.g. spine)

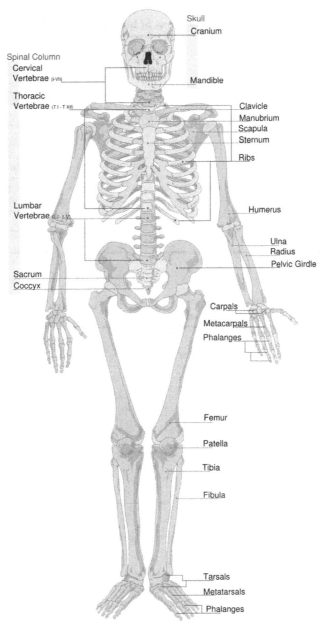

FIG. 14.7   Major bones in a human skeleton. *From https://pixabay.com/en/skeletal-labeled-worksheet-skeleton-40500.*

Long bones are hollow to save weight and are the engine of blood cell manufacture. They are a reservoir for the body's mineral content and are constantly remodelled. Long bones have a dense and rigid exterior of cortical compact bone, surrounding a flexible, protein-rich interior of cancellous (also known as trabecular or spongy) bone (Table 14.2).

Bone consists of extracellular matrix and 3 principal bone cell types:

- Osteoblasts (bone making)
- Osteocytes
- Osteoclasts (bone resorbing)

There are three main types of joint:

- Cartilaginous Joints
- Fibrous Joints
- Synovial Joints

TABLE 14.2 Description of the properties of different forms of bone in long bones.

	Cortical	Cancellous
Physical description	Dense protective shell	Rigid lattice designed for strength; interstices are filled with marrow
Location	Around all bones, beneath the periosteum; Primarily in the shafts of long bones	In vertebrae, flat bones (e.g. pelvis) and the ends of long bones
Proportion of Skeletal Mass	80%	20%
Strength	Withstand greater *stress*	Withstand greater *strain*
Direction of Strength	Bending and torsion, e.g. in the middle of long bones	Compression; Young's modulus is much greater in the longitudinal direction
Stiffness	Higher	Lower
Fracture Point	Strain > 2%	Strain > 75%

TABLE 14.3 Differences in the various types of cartilage.

Cartilage type	Structure	Location	Function
Hyaline	Collagen and abundant proteoglycans	Articular surfaces of bones; growing long bones	Support - rigid yet flexible
Fibrocartilage	More collagen (thick bundles) than proteoglycans	Pubic symphysis, articular disks	Support, resists tension and compression
Elastic	Elastic fibres & collagen	Ear, epiglottis, auditory tubes	Flexible support

and three type of cartilage, as described in Table 14.3:

- Hyaline cartilage
- Elastic cartilage
- Fibrocartilage

Bones can break in many different ways: complete, incomplete, comminuted, transverse, impacted, spiral or oblique fractures. Bone repairs itself by forming a haematoma around the break, the periosteum supplying stem cells into the cavity, followed by callus formation, a substance rich in collagen fibres and cartilage. This callus then becomes ossified, and ultimately remodelled into the same structure that existed before the facture occurred.

Under normal circumstances the structural integrity of bone is continually maintained by remodelling. Osteoclasts and osteoblasts assemble into Basic Multicellular Units (BMUs). Bone is completely remodelled in approximately 3 years. Under normal conditions, the quantity of old bone removed is equal to new bone formed. When too much bone density is removed, osteoporosis occurs. The major factors involved in remodelling are hormones (estrogen or testosterone) and cytokines (growth factors, interleukins [1, 6 and 11], tumour necrosis factor-α and transforming growth factor-β). This is the principal reason that osteoporosis is prevalent in older people.

Nerve physiology

The collections of nerve cells and supporting structures that are distributed throughout the body represent the nervous system (Fig. 14.8). The central nervous system is encased in bone and comprises the brain and spinal cord. The peripheral nervous system is not encased in bone and has peripheral nerves and ganglia.

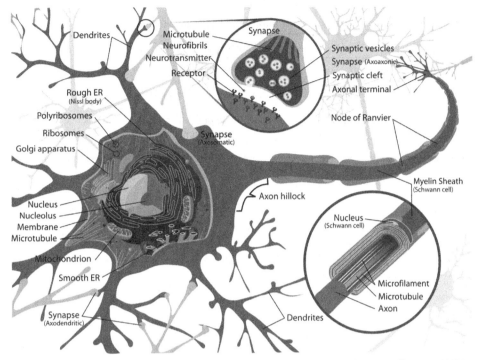

FIG. 14.8   Structure of a nerve cell. *From https://pixabay.com/en/red-science-diagram-cell-neuron-41524.*

Autonomic nervous system

● The afferent and efferent nerves that innervate the bodily organs to coordinate the internal environment (homeostasis).

Somatic nervous system

● The afferent and efferent nerves that innervate the musculoskeletal and integumentary systems for the purposes of motor function and sensation.

Enteric nervous system

● The network of nerves that innervate the gut and coordinate gut function.

Vascular nervous system

● The network of nerves that innervate the blood vessels and coordinate vascular smooth muscle function.

The autonomic nervous system is divided into sympathetic and parasympathetic nerves. The sympathetic system is responsible for hyperarousal at a time of danger, whereas activation of the parasympathetic system results in promotion of rest (Table 14.4).

The resting membrane voltage of a neuron is −70mV. A nerve impulse is an electrochemical event that occurs in nerve cells following stimulation. It is an all-or-nothing process which is fast acting and quick to recover, an event that is described by a voltage curve known as an action potential. The nerve impulse can conduct itself along the entire length of a nerve cell without diminishment (a "domino effect").

Muscle physiology

There are three main muscle types: cardiac, skeletal and smooth. Cardiac muscle is the muscle type of the heart whereas skeletal muscle, also known as striated muscle, is located in all parts of the body where actuation or movement occurs, including, for example, the muscles that create facial expressions. Smooth muscle is utilized in soft organs where

TABLE 14.4 Comparison between sympathetic and parasympathetic systems.

Sympathetic	Parasympathetic
• Fight or flight • Thoracolumbar • Short preganglionic nerves connecting to the sympathetic chain • Long postganglionic nerves connecting to organs • Postganglionic nerves use norepinephrine (mostly)	• Rest and digest • Craniosacral • Long preganglionic nerves connecting to organ associated ganglia • Short postganglionic nerves connecting to organs • Postganglionic nerves use acetylcholine on muscarinic receptors (mostly)

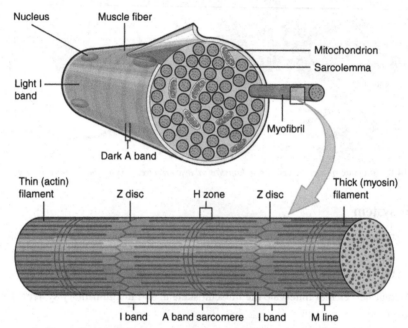

FIG. 14.9 Structure of a muscle fibre and a myofibril, the major component of a fibre. *From Version 8.25 of OpenStax Anatomy and Physiology Wikipedia.org: https://cnx.org/contents/FPtK1zmh@8.25:fEI3C8Ot@10/Preface. https://commons.wikimedia.org/wiki/File:1002_Organization_of_Muscle_Fiber.jpg.*

constriction or motility can occur, such as in the walls of arteries, sphincters, the stomach, intestines and the urinary bladder. Skeletal muscle fibres are innervated directly by axons deriving from the spinal cord. Each muscle fibre, regarded as an individual cell of a skeletal muscle, is composed of many myofibrils (Fig. 14.9).

In turn, muscle fibres are bunched together in what are known as muscle fascicles, and fascicles are bundled together into a gross skeletal muscle.

Muscle movement occurs when a signal is received from the nervous system. Every skeletal muscle fibre receives innervation from a motor neuron at a specialized structure called a neuromuscular junction (Fig. 14.10):

After a signal is received at a skeletal muscle fibre, through rapid control of calcium ion pumps, T-tubules and the associated sarcoplasmic reticulum which envelope individual microfibrils (Fig. 14.11), are flooded with calcium ions. This availability of calcium ions causes the simultaneous contraction of the individual functional units of the microfibrils, known as sarcomeres, causing muscle contraction. Sarcomeres are joined end-to-end, so that small contractions in each add up to a substantial overall muscle contraction.

The functional unit of contraction, the sarcomere, comprises two key elements, the thin and thick filaments, which slide over each other, providing contraction in the muscle fibres (Fig. 14.12). The thin filaments are composed of a protein called actin, around which are wound tropomyosin molecules, that hide the binding sites for the myosin heads of the thick

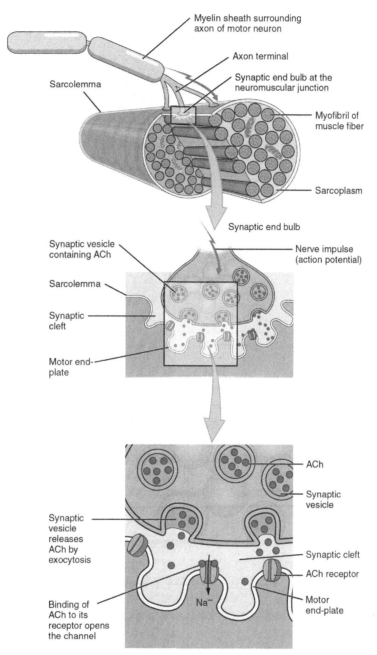

FIG. 14.10 Neuromuscular junction structure and function. *From Version 8.25 of OpenStax Anatomy and PhysiologyWikipedia.org: https://cnx.org/ contents/FPtK1zmh@8.25:fEI3C8Ot@10/Preface. https://commons.wikimedia.org/wiki/File:1009_Motor_End_Plate_and_Innervation.jpg.*

filaments in the absence of calcium ions. After a contraction signal, the tropomyosin slides out of the way, allowing the thin and thick filaments to bind. The release of a phosphate group from adenosine tri-phosphate (ATP) provides the energy to ratchet back the myosin heads through a conformational change in the geometry of the protein structure. It is this change in geometry of the myosin heads that provides the motive force for sarcomere contraction.

Cardiac muscles have similar molecular contraction machinery to skeletal muscle, although the signalling mechanism is different, conduction occurring within specialized high-speed tissues called Purkinje fibres towards the apex of the heart, contraction occurring as a wave throughout the organ. Cardiac muscle has a very large number of mitochondria, up to 40% of the total cell volume, to ensure that the heart never tires. Cardiac muscle cells are connected end-to-end via intercalated discs.

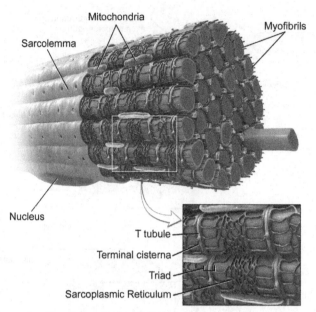

FIG. 14.11 System of T-tubules and sarcoplasmic reticulum that surrounds each microfibril in order to provide calcium ions as the signal to contract skeletal muscles. *From Blausen.com Staff, 2014. Medical gallery of Blausen Medical 2014. WikiJournal of Medicine 1 (2). https://doi.org/10.15347/wjm/ 2014.010. ISSN:2002-4436. https://commons.wikimedia.org/wiki/File:Blausen_0801_SkeletalMuscle.png.*

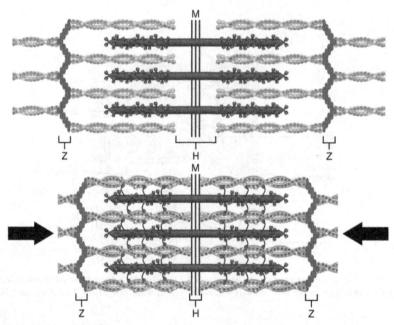

FIG. 14.12 Arrangement of thin (actin) and thick filaments (myosin) that comprise microfibrils and form the functional unit of skeletal muscles, the sarcomere. The arrangement of a sarcomere in a myofibril can be seen in Fig. 14.9. *From Version 8.25 of OpenStax Anatomy and Physiology Wikipedia. org: https://cnx.org/contents/FPtK1zmh@8.25:fEI3C8Ot@10/Preface. https://commons.wikimedia.org/wiki/File:1006_Sliding_Filament_Model_of_ Muscle_Contraction.jpg.*

Smooth muscle does not have sarcomeres, hence the lack of striations in histological slides of smooth muscle-containing tissue. They have actin and myosin molecules that contract against dense bodies. The control of calcium is different from that of skeletal muscles. Smooth muscle uses calmodulin to control calcium, and a stimulation event can result in a contraction that lasts for an extended duration, several hours in some cases.

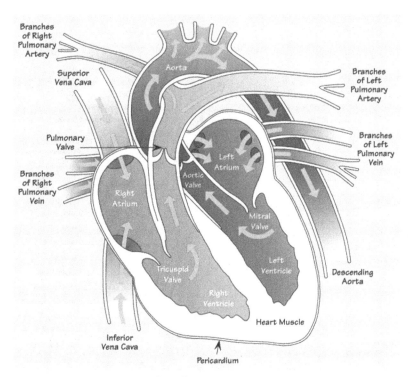

FIG. 14.13 Structure of the heart. *From https://pixabay.com/en/vertical-heart-inner-structure-heart-3076624.*

Cardiac physiology

The circulation has the following principal functions: oxygenation, waste disposal, hormonal/signalling and nutrition. The heart is the major organ within the circulation (Fig. 14.13). Cardiac muscle cells are cylindrical in shape and shorter than skeletal muscle cells. Cell fibres are branched. No nerves are involved in the spread of contraction through the muscle.

Atrial contraction (systole): blood is forced through into the ventricles due to the presence of valves. Ventricles contract as the atria relax (diastole): blood is forced from the ventricles to the tissues (aorta) or lungs (pulmonary artery). Relaxation allows blood to flow into the different chambers.

There are some important principals associated with blood flow:

- Preload: increased volume of blood returned to the heart from the veins. An increase in blood volume stretches the cardiac muscles, increasing stroke volume.
- Afterload: increased blood pressure in the circulation downstream of the aorta. An increase in blood pressure reduces the volume of blood pumped.
- Starling's Law: The strength of the heart's systolic contraction is directly proportional to its diastolic expansion.

The heart beats at a rate such that CO_2 is effectively replaced in the tissues by O_2. As CO_2 builds up the heart beats faster. An action potential builds up in the sino-atrial node. This is transmitted via the cardiac muscle around the atria. The action potential reaches the atrio-ventricular node 40 ms later.

Vascular physiology

A system of blood vessels which carries blood around the body, principally to oxygenate tissues (Fig. 14.14).

Arteries deliver blood that has been oxygenated by the lungs to the tissues and veins which carry carbon dioxide-rich blood back again to the lungs. Waste materials and toxins are removed from tissues, which are mostly processed in the liver. The circulation also acts as an efficient systemic signalling system, where small concentrations of hormones can bring about profound physiological changes.

Arteries are similar in structure to veins, except that the muscle layer (tunica media) is much thicker in arteries, to withstand the extra blood pressure that they are exposed to, since they are much closer to the heart and are required to resist

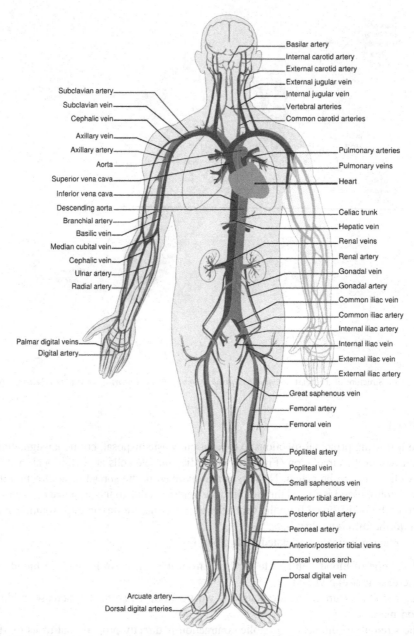

FIG. 14.14 Major arteries and veins. *From https://pixabay.com/en/circulatory-system-labels-biology-41523.*

higher blood pressures (see Table 14.5 and Fig. 14.15). In addition, veins in the legs have valves to prevent back flow during cardiac diastole.

Blood is pumped through the arteries to the venous system. Blood perfuses through tissues by way of muscular control of capillaries. Access to the tissues occurs in response to an increase in:

- CO_2
- Lactic acid
- AMP (adenosine mono phosphate)
- K^+ ions
- H^+ ions

Although the vascular system is a leak-free system, hydrostatic pressure within the circulation causes a significant volume of water to travel through the tissues, returning on the venous side due to osmotic pressure (Fig. 14.16).

TABLE 14.5 Diameters of different blood vessel types.

Blood vessel	Diameter
Capillary	7–9 μm
Arteriole or venule	10–40 μm
Artery or vein	0.04–10 mm

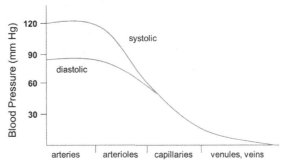

FIG. 14.15 Typical blood pressures in different parts of the circulation.

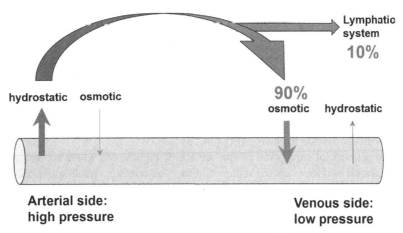

FIG. 14.16 Fluid flow in the circulation.

The main regulators of blood pressure are the sympathetic nervous system, which causes vasoconstriction and the kidneys, which modulate fluid removal and therefore blood viscosity.

Juxtaposition of the leg muscles and venous circulation allows a boost in venous blood pressure during walking and running. This allows blood to return to the heart more easily and increases preload, resulting in a larger heart stroke volume.

The main morbidities of the circulatory system are:

- Heart valve disease, where valves are torn (allowing blood flow reversal), not closing properly (causing regurgitant jets) or are stiff (requiring greater effort to pump blood under normal circumstances)
- Atherosclerosis, where the vessel wall becomes less elastic, allowing connective tissue to build up and plaque and calcium to be laid down, leading to platelet activation, thrombosis and embolism
- Aneurysm, where the inner, muscular lining becomes breached, causing swelling of the artery prior to its catastrophic rupture
- Stroke/seizure, loss of blood flow to all or part of the brain caused by haemorrhage, thrombosis or embolism
- Hypertension, possibly caused by poor diet. It can be the cause of heart failure, damage to the kidneys and an increase in atherosclerosis.

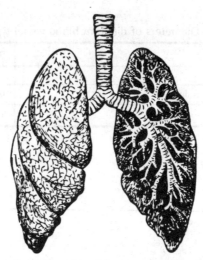

FIG. 14.17   Gross view of the human lungs. *From https://pixabay.com/en/lungs-organ-human-diagram-medicine-37824.*

Pulmonary physiology

The primary role of the lungs is:

- Exchange of oxygen & carbon dioxide
- Neuro-hormonal function
- Cellular processing
- Filtration of gases

Anatomically, the lungs are intimately associated with the heart, with both generally transplanted together if a recipient's heart function is poor (Fig. 14.17).

The larger tubes leading into the lungs are known as bronchi, and the smaller tubes bronchioles, the inside of which are coated with many tiny cilia. These are responsible for mechanical filtration. The bronchioles branch off to millions of alveoli, the site of oxygen-carbon dioxide exchange (Fig. 14.18).

There is a highly dense network of capillaries on the surface of the alveoli, where oxygen is exchanged for carbon dioxide. The inside of the alveoli surface is coated with a thin mucous coating, enabling dissolution of the lung gases to occur.

The connective tissue of the chest wall determines the minimum and maximum volume of the chest cavity, but does not ultimately control minimum or maximum lung volume. The connective tissue of the lung is primarily elastic and tends to collapse. There is some stiffness from these connective tissues. Pathologies that increase stiffness lead to difficulty in breathing.

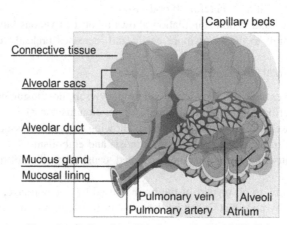

FIG. 14.18   Structure of lung alveoli. *From https://pixabay.com/en/health-labelled-science-organic-41510.*

There are two main laws of physics associated with lung function:

- **Boyle's Law** ($P \cdot V = K$): In a container filled with gas, if you decrease the volume, the pressure will correspondingly increase and vice versa.
- **Dalton's Law**: In a mixture of gases, each gas behaves as if it were on its own: it exerts a *partial pressure* that is independent of that exerted by other gases in the mixture.

Immunological function in lungs is important because the lungs have close contact with ambient air. Lung lymphoid tissue synthesises immunoglobulins (predominantly IgA). Mucous secretions are the first line of defence and filter-out gaseous microbubbles.

Lungs have prodigious biochemical processing capabilities, mainly peptides (e.g. angiotensin, bradykinin, vasopressin), amines (serotonin, histamine, dopamine, norepinephrine) and prostaglandins.

Introduction to blood

Blood is composed of cells, proteins, carbohydrates, lipids, ions and water. Table 14.6 shows the specific functions of each blood component. It has non-formed and formed elements (cells), whose characteristics are described in Table 14.7.

The major roles of red blood cells (erythrocytes) within the circulation are:

- Transport of O_2 to tissues
- Transport of CO_2 from tissues

Platelets (thrombocytes) are involved in:

- Clotting — haemostatic plug, surface for reactions to occur
- Store of bioactive compounds (chemotactic factors, growth factors, enzymes, etc.)

TABLE 14.6 Functions of the different constituents of blood.

Constituent	Specific function
Cells	Oxygenation Clotting Host defence
Proteins	Mainly regulation
Carbohydrates	Energy
Lipids	Building blocks
Ions	Isotonic balance Cell regulation
Water	Volume

TABLE 14.7 Concentrations of the different cell types in blood.

	Normal cell concentration × 10⁶/mL	Diameter (µm)
Red blood cells (erythrocytes)	5000	10
Platelets (thrombocytes)	150–400	2
White cells (leukocytes)	4–10	
Neutrophils	60%	14
Lymphocytes	30%	8
Monocytes	6%	17
Eosinophils	3%	15
Basophils	0.5%	15

White blood cells (leukocytes):

- Lymphocytes: Produce antibodies and maintain the memory of infectious agents
- Neutrophil: Phagocytose bacteria (first line defence)
- Monocyte: Phagocytose bacteria (second line), major component of inflammatory response (become macrophages)
- Basophil/Eosinophil: Phagocytosis

In addition to cells, there are many protein systems within blood:

- Clotting system: Thrombosis and haemostasis
- Fibrinolytic system: Destruction of clots
- Complement system: Immune defence
- Immunoglobulins: 5 subclasses, highly specific
- Protein inhibitors: Negative feedback
- Transport proteins: Waste disposal, etc.

Thrombosis, haemostasis and inflammation

Blood comprises a cellular component (platelets, red blood cells, white blood cells) and a non-cellular component:

- Coagulation cascade (clotting)
  - intrinsic pathway: important in contact with medical devices
  - extrinsic pathway: prevents haemorrhage
- fibrinolytic system
- system of inhibitors

These systems interact allowing the body to maintain a leak-free circuit that does not clot internally (Fig. 14.19).

When a blood vessel is injured, a number of stages of action occur aimed at preventing haemorrhage, as shown in Tables 14.8.

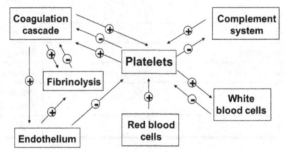

FIG. 14.19   Interaction of cells and protein systems within blood.

TABLE 14.8 Blood vessel injury and response.

Action	Response
Injury to vessel	Spasm of vessel
Platelets stick to exposed collagen	Causes release of platelet granules
ADP stimulates other platelets	Platelet aggregate plugs hole
Tissue factor released into blood	Extrinsic cascade activated
Blood around injury clots	Red blood cells get caught up in fibrin
Endothelium releases tPA	Clot dissolves

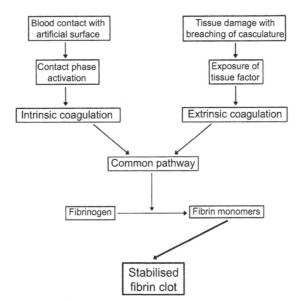

FIG. 14.20   Outline representation of the clotting cascade.

The blood coagulation system is controlled and perpetuated by a system of serine proteases (Fig. 14.20). There are a number of common themes to all the reactions:

- Surfaces are required for many of the complexes to form:
  - activation of fXII, fXI, fX, fII (prothrombin)
- Surfaces are provided by platelets
- All active factors are serine proteases (except fXIII), cleaving the subsequent factor
- All active factors can be inhibited by plasma inhibitors

Homeostasis & regulation

The general principles of homeostasis are that actions are performed to ensure maintenance of the status quo, for example, body heat regulation (Fig. 14.21).

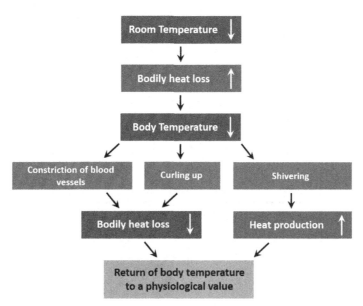

FIG. 14.21   Homeostasis of temperature regulation.

The principal physiological systems that are regulated are:

- Muscular
- Skeletal
- Skin
- Respiratory
- Digestive
- Circulatory
- Immune
- Excretory
- Nervous
- Endocrine
- Reproductive

Systemic calcium levels are maintained by use of the skeleton as a reservoir (Fig. 14.22).

In the circulation, blood pressure, O_2/CO_2 balance, pH, salt balance (Na^+, K^+, etc.) are regulated. This is achieved using specialized receptors and sensors:

- Baroreceptors: Blood pressure
- Chemoreceptors: O_2/CO_2 balance & pH
- Osmoreceptors: Salt concentration

Baroreceptors measure blood pressure and are found in the walls of large arteries of the neck, particularly in the carotid sinus, base of internal carotid artery and the aortic arch. They are sensitive to changes in pressure. They fire off a greater rate of signals when the pressure builds, signalling to the two centres in the brain (medulla oblongata):

- Cardioregulatory centre: increases/decreases parasympathetic stimulation of the sino-atrial node in the heart
- Vasomotor centre: increases/decreases vasodilation

Short-term control of heart rate is by parasympathetic stimulation and vasodilation by sympathetic stimulation. These regulate blood pressure within seconds, and the effects last seconds to minutes. This comes into effect when pressure drops dramatically, e.g. after standing up.

Various long-term regulation mechanisms that control blood pressure over a span of hours are:

- Kidneys: release renin from juxtaglomerular apparatus
- Adrenal glands: release of aldosterone from adrenal cortex (Fig. 14.23)
- Capillaries: fluid movement into/out of tissues
- Blood vessels: mechanical stretching leading to vasodilation
- Baroreceptors: Stimulation of posterior pituitary gland leading to the release of ADH (anti diuretic hormone) causing the kidneys to resorb more water (Fig. 14.24)
- Heart atrial cells: mechanical stretching of these cells leading them to release atrial natriuretic hormone, causing the kidneys to increase the volume of urine

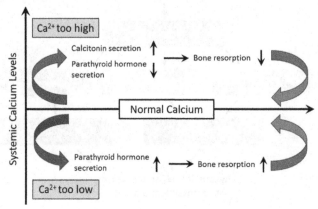

FIG. 14.22   Control of systemic calcium levels.

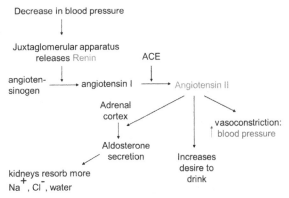

FIG. 14.23 Mechanisms of regulation in the kidneys.

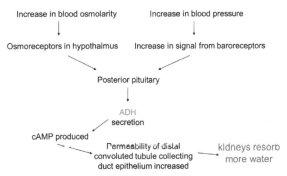

FIG. 14.24 ADH (vasopressin) mechanism of regulation of kidneys.

Control of blood volume by regulation of kidneys ensures the correct isotonic balance. No urine production occurs at 50 mm Hg blood pressure whereas 8 times normal volume is produced at 200 mm Hg blood pressure. The effects last minutes to hours and corrects the gross mis-matching of volume.

There are two chemo-centres in the brain (medulla oblongata) that detect changes in chemistry (pH, O_2, CO_2) and also within the vascular system (carotid/aortic bodies). The sensors in the brain are analogous to baroreceptors and stimulate the same neural pathways.

The chemoreceptors in the medulla oblongata only function during a *"Central Nervous System Ischaemic Response"*, which occurs when blood pressure < 50 mm Hg and extreme concentrations of H^+ & CO_2 build up.

The circulation regulates the core temperature of the body. When the hypothalamus detects changes in core temperature, constriction or dilation of blood vessels in the skin occurs. A decrease in skin temperature below a critical value causes dilation of skin blood vessels to prevent frostbite.

Gross mechanical trauma leads to rapid vasoconstriction. Extreme vascular shock (loss of blood pressure) due to mechanical trauma or anaphylaxis leads to movement of blood from the least important organs.

Renal physiology & homeostasis

The renal system (kidneys) controls the blood content of a number important solutes and electrolytes (Fig. 14.25). It controls blood osmolarity (concentration), acid-base balance, and volume (hyper/hypo-volemia), mostly by osmosis.

Regulation is principally achieved through hormones, the most important being:

- Renin − Angiotensin − Aldosterone Axis
  − Absorption of NaCl and H_2O
- ADH (Antidiuretic Hormone)
  − Absorption of free H_2O

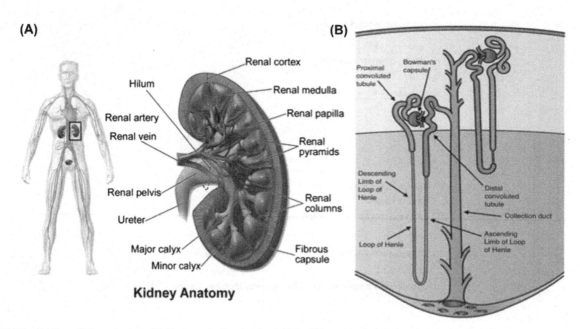

FIG. 14.25 (A) Gross kidney anatomy; (B) Nephron, the functional unit of the kidney. *(A) From Wikipedia.org, Creative Commons Attribution-Share-a-like 3.0 License (CC BY-SA 3.0). https://en.wikipedia.org/wiki/Kidney#/media/File:Blausen_0592_KidneyAnatomy_01.png. (B) From Wikipedia.org, Creative Commons Attribution-Share-a-like 3.0 License (CC BY-SA 3.0). https://en.wikipedia.org/wiki/Kidney#/media/File:Kidney_Nephron.png.*

Blood volume is the parameter undergoing greatest regulation, generally avoiding volume that is too low rather than too great. Kidneys try to conserve volume and solutes. Too great a volume is due to too much water. Smaller volume correction is achieved through osmolarity. High sodium concentration is controlled by reducing further adsorption.

In the kidneys, the molecules that are reabsorbed in the proximal tubule are:

- Glucose
- Amino acids
- Vitamins
- Chloride
- Potassium (K^+)
- Bicarbonate (HCO_3^-)

Following this, molecules are absorbed in the Loop of Henle, using a process known as the counter-current multiplication system:

- Only water escapes on the descending limb (by osmosis)
- Only salt escapes on the ascending limb (by active pump)

Molecules adsorbed after the loop, in the distal tubule are (by osmosis):

- Ammonia
- Urea
- H^+

Water balance is maintained by permeability of the collecting duct:

- If the blood is too dilute, the collecting ducts become impermeable — water goes out to bladder (up to 8× normal urine rate)
- If blood is too viscous, collecting ducts become permeable, water is reabsorbed (down to zero urine production)
- Tubule absorbance is controlled by ADH (anti diuretic hormone)

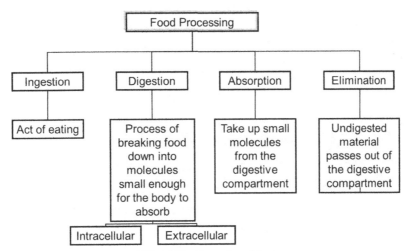

FIG. 14.26 Processing of food.

Nutrition, the pancreas & glucose regulation

Food that is ingested goes through several processes as shown in Fig. 14.26.

Food is composed of protein, carbohydrates and lipids, all of which have different nutritional values (Fig. 14.27). At a basic level, proteins are digested into amino acids, carbohydrates undergo glycolysis and fats are degraded into fatty acids and the glycerol backbone (Fig. 14.28) All of these components are processed ultimately by the Krebs cycle and electron transport chain.

Regulation of appetite mostly occurs through hormonal feedback (Fig. 14.29).

Leptin is produced by adipose (fat) tissue and suppresses appetite as its concentration increases. As body fat decreases, leptin levels fall, increasing appetite. The hormone PYY is secreted by the small intestine after meals, acting as an appetite suppressant that counters the appetite stimulant ghrelin. Ghrelin is secreted by the stomach wall and is a signal that triggers feelings of hunger as mealtimes approach. In dieters who lose weight, ghrelin levels increase, one reason it is difficult to stay on a diet. A rise in blood sugar levels after a meal stimulates the pancreas to secrete insulin. In addition to its other functions, insulin suppresses appetite by acting on the brain. Energy is stored in the body as glycogen (Fig. 14.30).

Glucose levels in the blood are dictated by insulin secretion from the β-cells of the islets of Langerhans in the pancreas. When the ability to produce insulin stops, the patient becomes diabetic. Glucagon acts in the reverse direction to insulin.

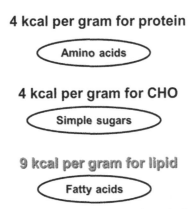

FIG. 14.27 Net energy values of different food groups.

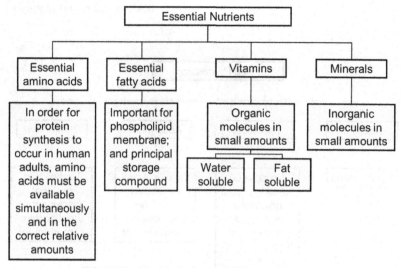

FIG. 14.28 Physiological uses of different food groups.

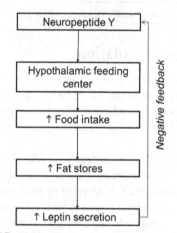

FIG. 14.29 Hormonal regulation of appetite.

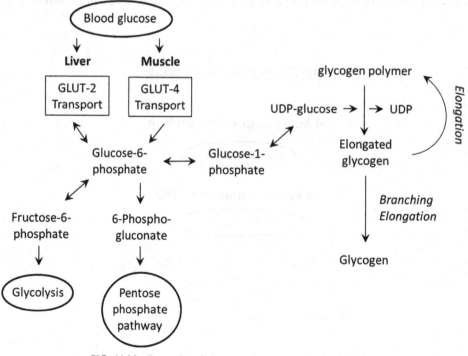

FIG. 14.30 Processing of glucose and energy storage in the body.

Abbreviations

ADH Anti-Diuretic Hormone
AMP Adenosine Mono-Phosphate
ATP Adenosine Tri-Phosphate
DNA Deoxyribonucleic Acid
ER Endoplasmic Reticulum
RNA Ribonucleic Acid
tRNA Transfer Ribonucleic Acid

Chapter 15

Respiratory measurement

Karl P. Sylvester[a] and Paul A. White[b,c]

[a]Royal Papworth & Cambridge University Hospitals NHS Foundation Trust, Cambridge, United Kingdom; [b]Cambridge University Hospitals NHS Foundation Trust, Cambridge, United Kingdom; [c]Anglia Ruskin University, Chelmsford, United Kingdom

Chapter outline

Introduction

The lung function laboratory carries out a number of tests to assess pulmonary function. The purpose of which includes but is not limited to, assisting in diagnosing pulmonary disease, monitoring the response to intervention, for example pharmaceutical or surgical, or risk stratification for undergoing interventions such as chemotherapy or surgery. The tests performed include those that assess lung volume, such as spirometry or plethysmography or those that assess the ability of the respiratory system to exchange respirable gases. More advanced tests can be utilized when basic tests are inconclusive. More complex tests include bronchial challenge tests where a bronchoconstricting agent is inhaled and the response in airway caliber monitored or cardio-pulmonary exercise testing where the system is stressed by symptom limited exercise and the cardiovascular and ventilatory systems assessed. The three procedures undertaken most frequently are spirometry, whole body plethysmography, and single breath gas transfer. These three tests are discussed in this chapter.

Anatomy and physiology

The lungs are situated within the thoracic cavity and are made up of the right and left lung. The right lung has three lobes while the left has two. The predominant role of the lungs are to ensure oxygen enters into the cardiovascular system via alveolar-capillary membrane gas exchange for transportation to cells and exercising muscles where it is utilized for energy production. Bi-products of energy production, such as carbon dioxide, are then excreted into the atmosphere via the lungs.

Air enters the lungs via bulk flow due to a negative pressure being generated within the thoracic cage. This negative pressure is generated via the contraction of the diaphragm pulling the lungs downward and the intercostal muscles pulling the ribcage up and outward. According to Boyle's Law under conditions of constant temperature there is an inverse relationship between pressure and volume (Boyle, 1660). This means that if pressure decreases gas volume increases. So by creating a negative pressure within the chest there is an increase in gas volume. Inspiration, where gas enters the lungs, is an active process during rest and exercise. At rest the main muscle groups involved are the diaphragm and the intercostal muscles. During exercise there is further recruitment of accessory muscles to breathing.

Expiration is predominantly a passive process during rest, where the diaphragm relaxes and the lungs return to a state known as the functional residual capacity or end-expiratory lung volume. This is the state whereby the opposing elastic recoil forces of the lungs and chest wall are in equilibrium. During exercise expiration becomes a more active process, with abdominal and intercostal muscles playing a greater role (Aliverti, 2016).

The lungs are attached to the chest wall via the pleurae. The visceral pleurae cover each lung and the parietal pleurae attach to the chest wall. Between each pleurae is the pleural cavity which contains a thin film of serous fluid. When air enters this space the lung can partially or fully collapse due to a pneumothorax.

The drive for ventilation under resting conditions and small changes in activity is controlled by the respiratory centres within the brainstem (Cotes et al., 2006). The structures involved include the medulla oblongata and pons. The medulla consists of two groups of neurons known as the dorsal and ventral respiratory groups and one within the pons, the pontine respiratory group. The latter includes two areas known as the pneumotaxic centre and the apneustic centre. There are many neural inputs into the respiratory centres that react to basic concentrations of oxygen, carbon dioxide and pH, but there are other inputs such as a response to hormonal changes and the ability to consciously control ventilation via the cerebral cortex.

The pathway down which oxygen is transported to the cells/muscles and carbon dioxide is then transported to the atmosphere starts at the nose and mouth. During quiet resting breathing most individuals will breathe through the nose. The lungs function best in warm and moist conditions and the nose, with its rich plexus of capillaries, acts to warm and humidify air from the atmosphere. Air then enters the larynx, which is the last structure where there is common passage of both food and air, the lungs being protected from aspiration via the glottis. The larynx also contains the vocal cords, which in conjunction with arytenoid cartilage, are used to produce sound for speech.

Air now enters the trachea, which is a cartilage rich structure containing cilia and rich in seromucous glands, acting as another line of defense aiming to prevent pathogens and particles from entering the lungs. The trachea then splits into the two primary bronchi and this continued bifurcation continues all the way down to the alveolar ducts where the majority of gas exchange takes place. Weibel's model of the airways (Weibel, 1963) classifies each bifurcation of the airways as one generation. There are approximately 23 generations of the airways with air travelling via bulk flow through the conducting airways down to approximately generation 16−17. From here air travels to the alveoli via diffusion and from this point onwards gas exchange begins to take place with the major gas exchange occurring within the alveolar ducts and individual alveoli. With increasing airway generation there is a reduction in cartilage tissue. Airway tone is then maintained via an increase in smooth muscle, which under normal conditions contracts and relaxes appropriately to external factors. In conditions such as asthma and increased bronchial reactivity, there is an exaggerated smooth muscle response with increased smooth muscle contraction causing a reduction in airway patency.

Once air reaches the gas exchange zones, oxygen must diffuse across the airway epithelium into the pulmonary capillaries and combine with haemoglobin in the erythrocytes to be transported around the body. Combination of oxygen with the haemoglobin molecule takes approximately 0.25 s. Under resting conditions pulmonary capillary transit time is approximately 0.75 s and so there is plenty of time for uptake of oxygen onto the haemoglobin molecule before blood leaves the lungs (Johnson et al., 1960).

Volume conversions

Measurement of lung volumes is important clinically as many pathological states change specific lung volumes or their relationships to each other (Cotes et al., 2006). The lung can be divided into four irreducible volumes, which can then be combined to form various different capacities, as shown in Table 15.1 and illustrated as part of a spirometric measurement

TABLE 15.1 Definitions and abbreviations of lung volumes and capacities measured during lung function testing.

Volume/capacity	Abbreviation	Description
Tidal volume	TV	Volume inspired and expired in quiet breathing
Expiratory/inspiratory reserve volume	ERV/IRV	Volume that can be ins-/expired above/below that contained in the lungs at the end of a normal tidal ins-/expiration
Residual volume	RV	Volume contained in the lungs at all times due to the elasticity of the alveoli
Inspiratory capacity	IC	IRV + TV, not often used
Functional residual capacity	FRC	ERV + RV, volume left in the lungs at the end of a tidal expiration, when the lungs are in equilibrium
Vital capacity	VC	IC + ERV, maximum volume that can be inhaled (IVC) or exhaled (EVC) in one breath
Total lung capacity	TLC	VC + RV, the total volume of the lungs

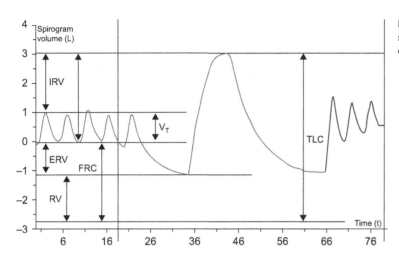

FIG. 15.1 A screenshot of typical output for unforced spirometry. RV, and thus FRC and TLC, are estimates based on reference values.

in Fig. 15.1. The differing environments and conditions under which lung volumes are measured needs to be taken into account to ensure the measurements made are accurate. Ambient air and that in the lungs are at different temperatures and aqueous vapor partial pressures. Thus, when measuring volumes in lung function it is necessary to know the current conditions of the gas and which conditions the volume is usually reported at.

Air in the lung will be at body temperature and saturated with water vapor. This is referred to as BTPS (body temperature and pressure saturated). Ambient temperature and pressure is known as ATP, which includes the partial pressure due to the ambient humidity. This can be corrected for to give the dry ATP (ATPD). Volumes are sometimes quoted at "standard" temperature and pressure (STP), usually 0°C and 760 mmHg. The lung volumes referred to in Table 15.1 are almost universally quoted at BTPS. An equation, based on the ideal gas law, is used to convert between ATP and BTPS:

$$V_{\text{BTPS}} = \frac{310(P_{\text{amb}} - P_{\text{H}_2\text{O,S}}(t)H)}{T_{\text{amb}}(P_{\text{amb}} - P_{\text{H}_2\text{O,S}}(37))} V_{\text{ATP}},$$

where P_{amb} is ambient pressure, T_{amb} is ambient temperature (in K), H is relative humidity, and $P_{\text{H}_2\text{O,S}}(t)$ is the saturated partial pressure of water at temperature t (measured in °C).

Lung conditions

In the lung there are two main forces acting on the airways and alveoli. The first is the elastic recoil of the lung tissue, which alone would lead to the collapse of the lung. However, this is opposed by the outward recoil of the chest wall, which holds the lungs open. At the end of relaxed expiration (at functional residual capacity — FRC), these two forces are in equilibrium. During inspiration, the inspiratory muscles (primarily the diaphragm, along with the external intercostals) increase this outward force, leading to the expansion of the lung tissue and the inflow of air, at a rate controlled by the airway resistance, into the alveoli. In so-called "quiet" expiration, these inspiratory muscles relax and the lung returns to its equilibrium volume, driven by the elastic recoil of the lung parenchyma. In forced expiration, however, the expiratory muscles (the internal intercostals and abdominal muscles) are used to increase the force inward on the lungs to expel air more rapidly, and enabling expiration down to the residual volume (RV). In lung disease, these forces are altered, and lung function testing is used to measure these changes.

In most lung function laboratories four main conditions are most commonly encountered. These are asthma, emphysema, chronic bronchitis, and pulmonary fibrosis. Emphysema and chronic bronchitis are often seen together in the same patient and have similar symptoms, so are often grouped together as chronic obstructive pulmonary disease (COPD). Asthma, emphysema, and chronic bronchitis are examples of obstructive lung conditions, whereas fibrosis is an example of a restrictive lung condition. Table 15.2 shows the effect of these diseases on the frequently measured physiological variables.

The hallmark of an obstructive disease is an increase in the airway resistance, R_{aw}, due to a narrowing of the airways in the lung. This is reflected in the low values of FEV₁/FVC. The FEV1/FVC ratio is the ratio of the forced expiratory volume expired in the first second to the forced vital capacity of the lungs. The normal value for this ratio is in the region of 0.8, though this is age dependent with the lower limit of normal declining with age. A low ratio suggests airflow obstruction.

TABLE 15.2 Typical impact of different conditions on physiological measurements of the lung (N indicates Normal, ↑ an increase, and ↓ a decrease).

	RV	FRC	TLC	FEV$_1$/FVC	$T_{l,CO,sb}$	R_{aw}
Asthma	↑ or N	↑ or N	↑ or N	↓	N or ↑	↑
Emphysema	↑	↑	↑↑	↓	↓	↑
Chronic bronchitis	↑	↑	↑	↓	N or ↓	↑
Fibrosis	↓	↓	↓	N or ↑	↓	N or ↓

An elevated value suggests a restrictive lung abnormality. In asthma, this is due to contraction of the smooth muscle lining the bronchioles. In chronic bronchitis, the narrowing occurs because of inflammation and excess mucous buildup. Emphysema causes airway narrowing because of the destruction of the alveolar walls. This reduces the elastic recoil of the lung and the bronchioles collapse slightly. Forced expiratory maneuvers exacerbate this effect and lead to dynamic compression, in which the inward pressure due to the expiratory muscles collapses the small airways because the reduced elastic recoil is not sufficient to keep them open.

Restrictive diseases are characterized by a decrease in lung volumes, usually due to an increase in alveolar elastic recoil because of an excess of fibrous tissue in the lung. This extra elastic recoil can lead to an increase in FEV$_1$/FVC, and by stenting the airways open, a decrease in R_{aw}.

Reference values

To compare whether the lung function values measured for a particular individual are normal or not, it is necessary to know what constitutes normal. For this purpose, reference values are used, which consist (for adults) of equations based on height and age, with separate equations for men and women. These are based on measurements taken on large healthy populations, usually excluding smokers. The primary tables in use have been published by the European Community for Coal and Steel (ECCS; Quanjer et al., 1983). However, ethnic origin also has an impact on the values, with non-Caucasian subjects having smaller lungs, on average, for a given height (Cotes et al., 2006). To attempt to improve prediction of lung function a new set of predicted ranges have been published for spirometry from the Global Lung Initiative (Quanjer et al., 2012). These have assisted with the interpretation of spirometric indices during the pubertal growth spurt for which older reference ranges created some confusion. They are also multi-ethnic allowing more accurate prediction in the non-Caucasian population. New GLI reference ranges have recently been published for single breath gas transfer also (Stanojevic et al., 2017) with those for lung volumes currently in progress as of 2018. The upper and lower limits in these normal ranges are based on the mean $\pm 1.64 \times$ standard deviation. This means that one in 20 subjects is likely to fall outside this range and must be borne in mind when assessing test results.

Spirometry

Spirometry comes from the Greek language and means the measurement of breath. Specifically in spirometry, lung volumes and flows are measured. In most modern equipment, spirometers actually measure flows which can then be integrated to obtain the lung volumes. There are two main types of airflow measurement device (pneumotachometer) used in spirometry: Fleisch- and Lilly-type pneumotachometers (Cotes et al., 2006). Both consist of resistive elements placed into the flow. Assuming laminar flow, the pressure drop across the resistive element is proportional to the flow rate.

In a Fleisch pneumotachometer, the resistive element consists of a bundle of fine capillary tubes. Their small radius reduces the Reynolds number so that the flow is laminar up to higher flow rates. The pressure is measured near the middle of the capillary bundle.

In a Lilly pneumotachometer, the resistive element consists of one or more mesh screens, with the pressure measured on either side of the screen(s). In this case, the range of flows that remain laminar is increased by tapering the tube outwards. For a given flow rate

$$Q = \pi r^2 v$$

an increase in r will lead to a drop in gas speed v. Substituting back into the Reynolds number we find that, all other things being equal,

$$\mathrm{Re} \propto \frac{1}{r}$$

so that an increase in the tube radius leads to a drop in the Reynolds number and the flow is more laminar. Generally the Fleisch-type are linear up to higher flow rates and more accurate (Cotes et al., 2006), but the Lilly-type are cheaper and easier to clean, making them more practical for hospital use. Pneumotachometers are heated typically to 32°C to avoid water vapor from the saturated breath condensing on the screen and disturbing the airflow.

A typical spirometric output is shown in Fig. 15.1, with the lung volume plotted as a function of time. As well as measuring the lung volumes and flow parameters, spirometers can provide a graphical output of flow rate plotted against lung volume, known as a flow-volume curve. Particularly useful are forced flow-volume curves. A screenshot from the spirometry software is shown in Fig. 15.2, illustrating the relationship between spirograms and the flow-volume curve. Forced flow-volume curves can provide useful feedback when assessing lung function as different conditions often have very distinct curve shapes.

Spirometry and other pulmonary function tests have to be carried out in a standardized fashion, as otherwise there could be large variations between centers, operators, and patients. European guidelines (Miller et al., 2005) exist to facilitate standardization. Lung function tests are unusual as they can be quite technically demanding for the patient, who needs enough coordination to carry out the tests successfully. The operator therefore acts almost as a coach, enabling the patient to perform the maneuver so that useful measurements are taken.

Spirometers are calibrated using a large syringe to inject a known volume of air into the instrument, and values of temperature, pressure, and humidity are entered into the system for volume correction purposes. Infection hazards are minimized by using separate mouthpieces for each patient, with a filter that is stated to remove 99.999% of bacteria and viruses. The pneumotachographs are taken apart and sterilized weekly.

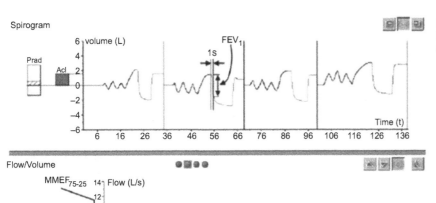

FIG. 15.2 Flow-volume curves for normal lung function along with accompanying spirograms.

Case study 15.1

When performing spirometry the shape of the flow-volume loop provides a good indication of the presence of pathophysiology. In these examples, (A) represents a normal flow-volume loop, with a rapid rise to peak flow before a gradual decline in flow as lung volume reduces down to residual volume. The inspiration when normal results in a semi-circle shape. The difference in expiratory and inspiratory shape of the flow-volume loop is caused by the increased positive pressure on the airways limiting flow, whereas on inspiration the negative pressure on the airways causes them to open and allow air to flow reasonably freely into the lungs. In example (B) the destruction of connective tissue causes an exaggerated collapse of the airways resulting in a reduced peak expiratory flow and a rapid reduction in flow throughout the whole expiration. The inspiratory flow is affected less due to negative pressure opening up the airways.

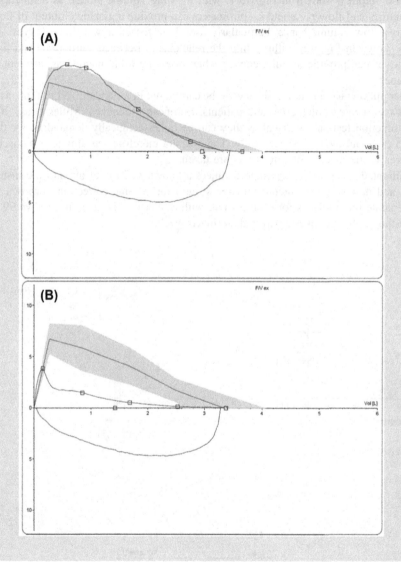

Whole body plethysmography

Whole body plethysmography is the measurement of changes in gas volume of the thorax due to differing amounts of air in the lungs. Due to the nature of the measurement it will also measure gas volumes that may be present in other areas of the thorax, e.g. oesophagus or buccal cavity, but these are likely to be minimal and techniques can be used to minimize the impact. It enables the estimation of both the airway resistance and functional residual capacity (FRC) (and thus total lung capacity — TLC). Measurements are carried out with the subject in a closed chamber of approximately 800 L containing a pneumotachometer and shutter mechanism. Pressure changes at the mouth and in the box when the tube is shut off, are related to changes in the volume of the thorax. A screenshot of the airway resistance and FRC measurement is shown in Fig. 15.3.

During a whole body plethysmography measurement, the subject sits down in the box, which is then sealed and left for 1 min for the temperature inside the box to stabilize. Any excess pressure from the rise in temperature due to the presence of the subject leaves via a high-resistance tube so that there is no pressure buildup. The resistance of the tube is such that the time constant is much greater than the breathing period. Then the higher frequency pressure changes due to the change in the subject's thoracic volume are not excessively diminished by the presence of the leak.

Measurement of the thoracic gas volume (TGV) is carried out by having the subject breathe normally through the pneumotachometer. At the end of a tidal expiration, a shutter comes down and the subject tries to pant against the closed shutter. In this process they rarefy and compress the gas in their lungs. This pressure change is measured at the mouth, while the change in pressure of the box is related to the change in volume of the lungs.

The volume of gas is measured using Boyle's law where PV is a constant. Then (Cotes et al., 2006):

$$PV = (P + \Delta P)(V - \Delta V)$$

$$= PV + V\Delta P - P\Delta V - \Delta P\Delta V$$

By cancelling, rearranging, and assuming that $\Delta P\Delta V$ is small, we obtain

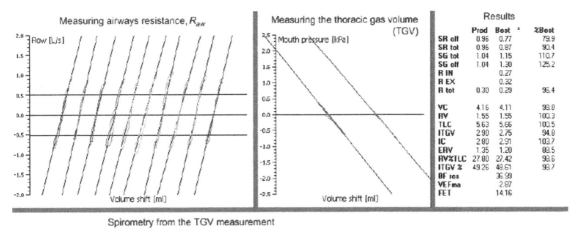

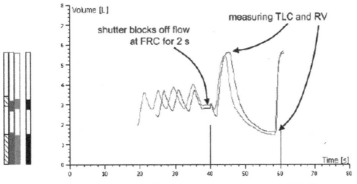

FIG. 15.3 A screenshot of measurements of healthy volunteers using a full body plethysmograph. The linear fits are offset for clarity. Top left are the linear fits for the determination of airway resistance, top middle shows the linear fits for the TGV measurement, and top right are the numerical values. The TGV is sometimes called the ITGV, the intrathoracic gas volume. The horizontal axes are labeled "volume shift" and are equivalent to $P_{box}C_{box}$. The bottom panel shows the spirometric output from the pneumotachograph.

$$V_L = P_{\text{atm}}\frac{\Delta V_L}{\Delta P_{\text{mouth}}}$$

$$= P_{\text{atm}}\frac{\Delta P_{\text{box}}}{\Delta P_{\text{mouth}}}C_{\text{box}}\left(\frac{V_{\text{box}} - M_{\text{body}}/1.07}{V_{\text{box}}}\right),$$

where $C_{\text{box}} = V_{\text{box}}/P_{\text{box}}$ is the compliance of the box, measured at calibration, and the term in parentheses corrects the volume of gas in the box compared to that at calibration, by subtracting the subject's estimated volume. Their mass, M_{body}, is known and 1.07 kg m^{-3} is the average density of the human body.

The changes in box and mouth pressure are monitored as the subject makes small panting attempts against the shutter. The gradient of the straight line plot of ΔP_{box} against ΔP_{mouth} is inserted into the above equation to obtain the volume of the lungs at the time of measurement, the TGV. This corresponds to the subject's FRC. Once the shutter is open again, the subject takes a breath in to TLC, out to residual volume (RV) and back up to TLC. This enables measurement of all the lung volumes. Cancelling the term $\Delta P\Delta V$ depends on the volume and pressure differences being small. The subject attempting to pant against the shutter ensures this. The panting rate should not be too high (>1 Hz) and the magnitude less than 2 kPa, however, as otherwise the airway resistance means that the assumption that $P_{\text{mouth}} = PA$, the alveolar pressure, does not hold. Even at lower breathing frequencies, this can be a problem for very obstructed patients and can lead to an overestimate of lung volume.

In a clinical study, the first measurement taken is that of the airway resistance. The subject breathes shallowly and quickly through the pneumotachometer, which is open to the air in the box, with a frequency of 30–60 breaths per minute. Data are collected until 10 consistent breaths are obtained.

If there was no airway resistance, there would be no change in pressure of the box during panting as air would flow instantly into the lungs as a result of the change in volume of the thorax. However, a pressure gradient is required to shift the air into the lungs, so that when the thorax expands to inspire, there is a pressure rise in the box. Using the relation between P_{mouth} and P_{box} measured during the TGV maneuvers and remembering that we assumed $P_{\text{mouth}} = PA$, the airway resistance is given by

$$R_{aw} = \frac{\Delta P_A}{Q}$$

$$= \frac{\Delta P_{\text{mouth}}}{\Delta P_{\text{box}}}\frac{\Delta P_{\text{box}}}{Q}$$

By measuring the flow rate through the pneumotachometer, Q, and the change in box pressure, and taking the inverse of the gradient of the straight line obtained, we can calculate the airway resistance. The equation assumes that the air entering and leaving the lungs is all at BTPS. This is not strictly true, but is made closer to being so by panting with low flow rates, so most of the air remains in the pneumotachometer (Fig. 15.4). In practice, corrections are made for this error electronically. R_{aw} also changes with lung volume (as the caliber of the airways changes) and with flow rate, so panting also helps to keep the curves linear.

A linear fit associates the Q–P_{box} curves to measure R_{aw}, referred to in Fig. 15.3 as R_{tot}, in the top left pane and P_{mouth}–P_{box} curves. The resistances are therefore measured by simply plotting a straight line through the two volume

FIG. 15.4 Showing the effect of early airway closure on the measurement of airway resistance.

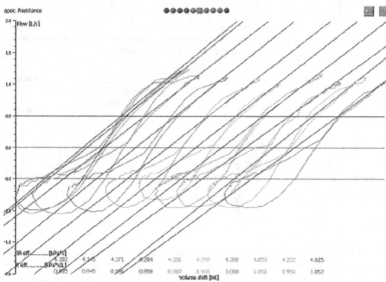

extremes, and that gives R_{tot}. Multiplying R_{tot} by the volume at which the measurement is made gives SR_{tot}, the specific airway resistance. Calculating SR_{tot} removes almost all the dependence of resistance on lung volume. The inverse is SG_{tot}, the specific airway conductance. Another measure is to take the average gradient over the whole loop, which gives the effective specific airway resistance and conductance:

$$SR_{eff} = \frac{1}{SG_{eff}}$$

This value relates to the actual work of breathing the subject experiences. SR_{eff} and SR_{tot} usually only differ significantly if there is substantial noise present in the measurement, which artificially increases SR_{eff}. Because of this susceptibility to error, SR_{tot} is usually the most reliable measure clinically.

The box used for whole body plethysmography is transparent, making the test less intimidating for subjects. There is a handle on the inside of the box so the subject can open the door at any time should they feel the need. However, whole body plethysmography cannot be carried out with very claustrophobic subjects. In these instances lung volumes need to be measured using a gas dilution technique. A vent in the bottom of the box is opened while the subject is in the box, except when tests are taking place. This helps to stabilize the temperature and ensures the oxygen concentration remains normal. As mentioned earlier, a calibrated leak in the side of the box ensures no pressure buildup during tests. If the door handle should break, there are tabs on the door panel so that the frame can be removed for the subject to exit the box.

Calibration of the plethysmograph has two stages: Firstly, the leak decay time is checked by pumping a known volume of gas into the box. The decay in pressure is fitted to an exponential and ensures that any reduction in the pressure readings due to the leak can be accounted for. Secondly, a calibrating syringe pumps a small volume of gas sinusoidally in and out of the box while the pressure is monitored. This enables the compliance of the box to be measured. Each test is carried out three times and the median value for the time constant and compliance are used.

Case study 15.2

This example demonstrates the utility of body plethysmography to identify the presence of gas trapping, which is gas trapped behind closed airways usually as a result of obstructive lung disease (COPD). Early airway closure can occur due to exaggerated contraction of smooth muscle lining the airways or through destruction of connective tissue increasing the compliance of the airways and causing them to collapse

sooner. Elevation in Residual Volume (RV) as denoted by the increased standardized residuals (SR) above the upper limit of normal of +1.64 SRs denotes the presence of trapped gas.

Source Wikipedia.org. https://www.commons.wikimedia.org/wiki/File: Copd_2010Side.JPG. License: Creative Commons CC0 Universal (CC0 1.0) Public Domain Dedication. Link to license: creativecommons.org/ publicdomain/zero/1.0.

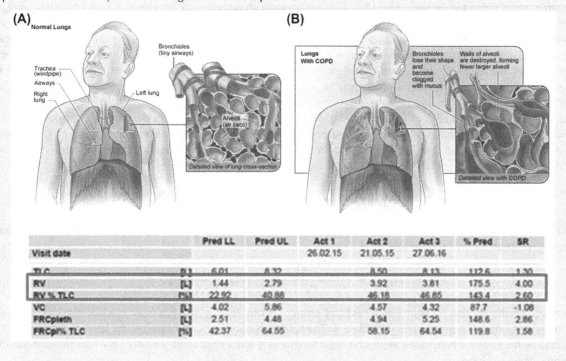

		Pred LL	Pred UL	Act 1	Act 2	Act 3	% Pred	SR
Visit date				26.02.15	21.05.15	27.06.16		
TLC	[L]	6.01	8.32		8.50	8.13	112.6	1.30
RV	[L]	1.44	2.79		3.92	3.81	175.5	4.00
RV % TLC	[%]	22.92	40.88		46.19	46.85	143.4	2.60
VC	[L]	4.02	5.86		4.57	4.32	87.7	-1.08
FRCpleth	[L]	2.51	4.48		4.94	5.25	148.6	2.86
FRCpl% TLC	[%]	42.37	64.55		58.15	64.54	119.8	1.58

Gas transfer

Gas transfer measures how well gases can diffuse into the bloodstream and bind with the hemoglobin in the erythrocytes. It is quantified using the transfer factor T_l, sometimes also known as the diffusing factor. The transfer factor can be expressed as (Cotes et al., 2006)

$$\frac{1}{T_l} = \frac{1}{D_m} + \frac{1}{\Theta V_c},$$

in which D_m is the diffusing capacity of the alveolar membrane, Θ is the rate of combination of a gas with haemoglobin and V_c is the pulmonary capillary blood volume. Diffusion across a membrane is governed by $D \propto A/t$, where A is its area and t its thickness. Therefore diseases that increase the thickness of interstitial lung tissue, such as fibrosis, or diseases that decrease the alveolar area, such as emphysema, will decrease D_m. The hemoglobin concentration in the blood will affect ΘV_c and so test results are usually corrected with a recently measured value of hemoglobin for that individual. For a given gas, G, the model used for T_l is usually

$$T_l = \frac{\text{uptake of gas per minute}}{P_{A,G} - P_{c,G}}$$

where $P_{A,G}$ is the partial pressure of gas in the alveoli and $P_{c,G}$ is the partial pressure of gas in the capillary blood. This treats the lungs as if they are a balloon with perfect gas mixing and contact with the diffusion membrane. In a real lung, there is regional variation in ventilation (the bottom of the lungs tends to fill before the top) and there is always some ventilatory unevenness within regions, even in healthy subjects.

A method to measure gas transfer is the single-breath method. This has the advantage that, because it is measured at total lung capacity, regional variations in ventilation are minimized. However, the uneven ventilation of the lung is not taken into account and this tends to lead to low values of the alveolar volume, V_A. This can give an estimate of gas trapping in the lung, however, which can be a useful diagnostic tool.

The test gas used is carbon monoxide (CO), for two main reasons. Firstly, CO is removed from blood plasma by binding with hemoglobin very quickly. Thus, its partial pressure in blood plasma rises very slowly and does not saturate during the time the capillary blood is in diffusive contact with the alveoli. Therefore, CO is said to be diffusion limited. This makes it ideal for measurements of T_l, as gas will continue to be removed from the alveoli as long as it is in contact with the membrane. The other major advantage to using CO for T_l measurements is that in most subjects, $P_{c,Co} = 0$ before the test begins. However, this is untrue for very heavy smokers or those who have recently smoked.

A spirogram of the test is shown in Fig. 15.5. The test begins with normal tidal breathing. A larger breath is taken in and exhaled down to RV. Close to the bottom, the operator triggers the system so that the room air is shut off. When the subject begins to breathe in, a demand valve opens and the test gas mixture is inhaled up to TLC. The subject holds their breath for 10 s and then exhales so that the test gas can be collected. The first ~ 750 mL of the expired gas are discarded to account for instrumental and anatomic dead space, and then between 0.5 and 1 L of gas are collected and analyzed. The breath holding time is defined from one-third of the way into the inspiration to half of the way through the collection volume, labeled in Fig. 15.5.

The test gas consists of 0.28% CO, 9.5% Helium (He), and 18% Oxygen (O_2), with the remainder made up of Nitrogen (N_2), which is supplied premixed. 18% O_2 is used because this leads to a roughly constant fraction of O_2 in the lungs however much gas is inspired. The uptake of CO in the lungs is proportional to its fractional concentration (assuming zero CO partial pressure in the capillaries), so that

$$\frac{dF_{A,CO}}{dt} = -\frac{F_{A,CO}(P_B - P_{H_2O,S}(37°C))T_{l,CO,sb}}{kV_A}$$

where κ is a constant converting V_A from a volume into a quantity of gas, equal to 1/22.4 mol/L at STP. Integrating and rearranging we find

$$T_{l,CO,sb} = \frac{kV_A}{(P_B - P_{H_2O,S}(37°C))t} \ln\left(\frac{F_{A,CO}(0)}{F_{A,CO}(t)}\right).$$

where $F_{A,CO(t)}$ is the fraction measured in the expired sample. However, $F_{A,CO}(0)$ has to be calculated because the gas left in the lungs at the start of the maneuver will dilute it. The helium fraction is used to measure the level of dilution, and this is assumed to be the same for both gases. Helium is ideal for this as it is not lipid soluble so does not pass through the alveolar membrane. Then we have

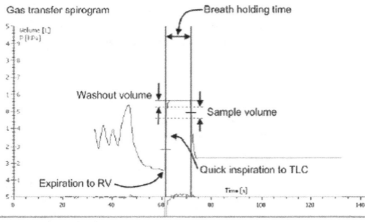

Gas transfer spirogram

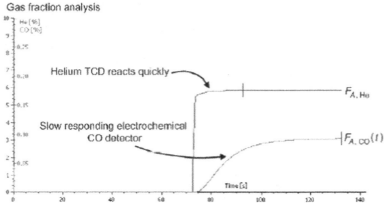

Gas fraction analysis

FIG. 15.5 A screenshot for a gas transfer measurement, showing the spirogram for the test in the upper pane and the gas analysis in the lower pane.

$$F_{A,CO} = F_{I,CO}\frac{F_{A,He}}{F_{I,He}}$$

where F_I is the inspired fraction of gas. Helium dilution is also used to estimate V_A, the alveolar volume. This is the volume of the lungs that actually participates in gas transfer, so excludes the anatomic dead space. It is given at the ambient temperature and pressure saturated (ATPS) by

$$V_{A,\text{eff}} = (V_{I,\text{ATPS}} - V_{ID} - V_{DS})\frac{F_{I,He}}{F_{A,He}}$$

where, V_{ID} is the instrument dead space, including that of the mouthpiece used, and V_{DS} is the anatomic dead space, usually estimated using the empirical observation that dead space volume in ml equals the sum of the subject's age in years and body weight in pounds. This then requires conversion into BTPS (body temperature and pressure saturated). It is labeled as the effective V_A because, as mentioned earlier, it underestimates the true alveolar volume due to uneven ventilation. If the ratio $V_A/V_{A,\text{eff}}$, where V_A = inspired volume plus the RV measured by full body plethysmography, is less than about 0.8, this indicates significant gas trapping.

Note that in single-breath gas transfer measurements, the value measured directly is $K_{CO,sb}$, the gas transfer per unit volume. This is then multiplied by $V_{A,\text{eff}}$ to obtain $T_{l,CO,sb}$. $K_{CO,sb}$ that gives a measure of how well diffusion occurs in ventilated parts of the lung and thus an indication of tissue thickening or loss, whereas $T_{l,CO,sb}$ gives a measure of the overall ability of the lungs to supply oxygen and remove carbon dioxide into and out of the bloodstream.

Gas analysis is shown in the lower half of Fig. 15.5. The CO content of the expired sample is measured using an electrochemical cell, and the He content is measured using a thermal conductivity method (Cooper et al., 2003). In the electrochemical cell, carbon monoxide is oxidized to carbon dioxide and water at the cathode is reduced. A current will flow due to this reaction and this is what is measured. The response time is around 30 s to reach 90% of full signal due to the time needed for the CO gas to diffuse into the electrolyte in the cell. The time response is improved by having a stabilized flow of gas across the circuit elements, so that it takes as little as 3 s to reach 95% of full signal. Thermal conductivity detectors for helium are very linear and stable. The transfer factor is affected by the quantity of hemoglobin in the blood, so it is often standardized by this value to remove any variation that is simply due to anemia.

The equation for this corrected, $T_{l,CO,sb}$ is

$$T_{l,CO,c} = T_{l,CO} + 1.4(Hb_{stand} - Hb_{meas})$$

where Hb_{stand} is 14.6 g dL^{-1} for adult men and 13.4 g sL^{-1} for adult women.

As with spirometry, performance of the test is important to avoid errors. Errors can often be identified by inspecting the spirogram and including stepwise inspiration or expiration, inspiration not from RV, and an inspiration that is too slow. These either invalidate the assumptions made about the breath-holding time, or mean that the volume calculation by helium dilution is inaccurate. Subjects should not have eaten recently, as this will decrease $T_{l,CO,sb}$, and should not have engaged in heavy activity, as this increases $T_{l,CO,sb}$. The test will also be inaccurate if subjects have recently smoked as there is likely to be an appreciable partial pressure of CO in the blood already. A 4-min interval is left in-between tests to enable the CO to diffuse out of the blood as a result of the previous test, and two tests agreeing to within 10% are a minimum for an acceptable determination of $T_{l,CO,sb}$. Historically, it was not possible to carry out the single-breath measurement of $T_{l,CO}$ in patients with a VC less than 1.5 L, however, with the introduction of rapid gas analyzers gas exchange can theoretically be measured at any lung volume. The gas analyzers are calibrated twice daily. They undergo a two-point calibration, checking the zero and that the pre-prepared gas mixture reading agrees with the stated value. The primary risk involved in gas transfer measurements is related to the compressed gas bottles. By using appropriate regulators, high-pressure tubing, and connectors minimizes this risk. The bottles are held in an enclosure so that they cannot fall and either cause injury or be damaged.

Case study 15.3

In lung conditions such as Emphysema there is destruction of the alveolar walls. This destruction reduces the surface area available for gas exchange. In this example we can see that both total lung gas transfer (TLCO SB) and gas transfer per unit lung volume (KCO SB) are declined below the lower limit of normal as denoted by a standardized residual (SR) value less than −1.64.

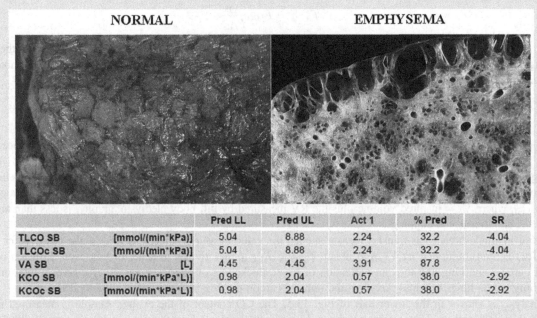

		Pred LL	Pred UL	Act 1	% Pred	SR
TLCO SB	[mmol/(min*kPa)]	5.04	8.88	2.24	32.2	-4.04
TLCOc SB	[mmol/(min*kPa)]	5.04	8.88	2.24	32.2	-4.04
VA SB	[L]	4.45	4.45	3.91	87.8	
KCO SB	[mmol/(min*kPa*L)]	0.98	2.04	0.57	38.0	-2.92
KCOc SB	[mmol/(min*kPa*L)]	0.98	2.04	0.57	38.0	-2.92

Abbreviations

ATP Ambient Temperature and Pressure
ATPD Ambient Temperature and Pressure Dry
ATPS Ambient Temperature and Pressure Saturated
BTPS Body Temperature and Pressure Saturated
CO Carbon Monoxide
COPD Chronic Obstructive Pulmonary Disease
ECCS European Community for Coal and Steel
FEV$_1$ Forced Expiratory Volume in 1 s
FRC Functional Residual Capacity
FVC Forced Vital Capacity
Hb Hemoglobin
He Helium
N$_2$ Nitrogen
O$_2$ Oxygen
RV Residual Volume
SR Standardized Residuals
TGV Thoracic Gas Volume
TLC Total Lung Capacity
VA Alveolar Volume

References

Aliverti, A., 2016. The respiratory muscles during exercise. Breathe 12, 165–168.

Boyle, R., 1660. New Experiments Physico-Mechanicall, Touching the Spring of the Air, and its Effects s.n., Oxford.

Cooper, B.G., Evans, A.E., Kendrick, A.H., Newal, C. (Eds.), 2003. Practical Handbook of Respiratory Function Testing, Part 1, second ed. Association for Respiratory Technology and Physiology.

Cotes, J.E., Chinn, D.J., Miller, M.R., 2006. Lung Function: Physiology, Measurement and Application in Medicine, sixth ed. Wiley, Chichester.

Johnson, R.L., Spicer, W.L., Bishop, J.M., Forster, R.E., 1960. Pulmonary capillary blood volume, flow and diffusing capacity during exercise. J. Appl. Physiol. 15 (5), 893–902.

Miller, M.R., Hankinson, J., Brusasco, V., Burgos, F., Casaburi, R., Coates, A., 2005. Standardisation of spirometry. Eur. Respir. J. 26, 319–338.

Quanjer, P.H., Temmeling, G.J., Cotes, J.E., Pedersen, O.F., Peslin, R., 1983. Standardised lung function testing. European Community for Coal and Steel. Bull Eur Physiol Res 19 (5), 1–95.

Quanjer, P.H., Stanojevic, S., Cole, T.J., Baur, X., Hall, G.L., Culver, B.H., Enright, P.L., Hankinson, J.L., Ip, M.S., Zheng, J., Stocks, J., 2012. Multi-ethnic reference values for spirometry for the 3-95-yr age range: the global lung function 2012 equations. Eur. Respir. J. 40 (6), 1324–1343.

Stanojevic, S., Graham, B.L., Cooper, B.G., Thompson, B.R., Carter, K.W., Francis, R.W., Hall, G.L., 2017. Official ERS technical standards: global lung function initiative reference values for the carbon monoxide transfer factor for Caucasians. Eur. Respir. J. 50 (3).

Weibel, E.R., 1963. Morphometry of the Human Lung. Springer, Berlin.

Chapter 16

Cardiovascular measurement

Richard G. Axell[a,b], Paul A. White[c,d] and Joel P. Giblett[e]

[a]University College London Hospitals NHS Foundation Trust, London, United Kingdom; [b]University College London, London, United Kingdom; [c]Cambridge University Hospitals NHS Foundation Trust, Cambridge, United Kingdom; [d]Anglia Ruskin University, Chelmsford, United Kingdom; [e]Royal Papworth Hospital NHS Foundation Trust, Cambridge, United Kingdom

Chapter outline

Introduction

The heart is an organ that functions as a pump, and is responsible for circulating blood around the body; delivering essential oxygen and nutrition to the tissues; and carrying away waste products. This chapter describes routine physiological measurement techniques used to assess the hemodynamic, electrophysiological and biomechanical function of the heart. Physiological measurement of pressures and flows allow the diagnosis of disease and enable its severity to be assessed. This chapter describes principles that are fundamental to the measurement of blood flow within the human body. The measurement of blood pressure is described using both invasive and noninvasive measurement devices. Invasive hemodynamic monitoring techniques are explored in detail. These techniques include the Swann—Gantz catheter, which allows the determination of cardiac output using the thermodilution method. Echocardiography ultrasound is routinely used to noninvasively assess cardiac structure and function. Doppler ultrasound physics are briefly introduced and how changes in blood velocity can be measured and used to determine cardiac performance. Electrocardiography (ECG) is routinely used to noninvasively record electrophysiological signals generated during the cardiac cycle. Three- and 12-lead ECGs are extensively used within a healthcare environment to provide information on the electrical characteristics of the heart.

Anatomy and physiology

The human heart is about the size of a clenched fist and is located in the mediastinum, within the thoracic cavity between the sternum and the vertebrae. The heart is a pump connected to a system of blood vessels, which can transport oxygen and nutrients to the tissue, and carrying away waste products. This is known as the circulatory system, and is composed of the heart, the pulmonary circulation, and the systemic circulation. Flow in this circulation is unidirectional, and is fixed. The basic structure of the heart is illustrated in Fig. 16.1. The heart is composed of four chambers: blood returns to the heart from the inferior and superior vena cava, entering first the (i) right atrium. Blood then passes by a combination of passive and active filling into the (ii) right ventricle through the tricuspid valve. The right ventricle is connected to the pulmonary artery and sends deoxygenated blood to the lungs (pulmonary circulation). Oxygen and carbon dioxide exchange occurs in the capillaries of the pulmonary circulation. Once the blood has passed through the pulmonary capillaries it returns to the

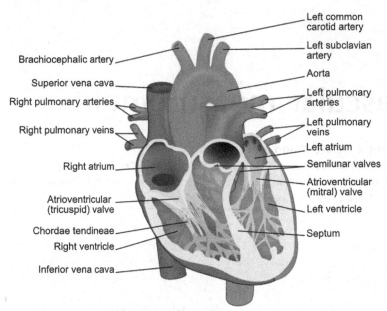

FIG. 16.1 Basic structure of the heart.

left side of the heart via the pulmonary veins. The oxygenated blood enters through the (iii) left atrium, and passes in the (iv) left ventricle through the mitral valve, which is connected to the rest of the body via the ascending aorta (systemic circulation). Arteries form a tree like structure of increasingly small size until they reach the arteriole. Beyond these vessels, blood enters microscopic vessels known as capillaries, where nutrients and oxygen are removed by both passive diffusion and active transport. Waste products including carbon dioxide enter the bloods and are transported back to the heart through the lower pressure venous system.

A cardiac cycle is a series of events that occur during a single heartbeat. It consists of two distinct phases known as systole and diastole. In systole, the ventricles contract and blood leaves into the systemic or pulmonary circulations. In diastole, the ventricles relax and blood fills the chamber from the atria. The atria also experience systole and diastole although these are timed differently and atrial systole aids ventricular filling. The heart contains four one-way heart valves that aide the unidirectional blood flow. The valves are positioned so that they open and close passively due to the pressure differences between the heart's chambers and arteries. The tricuspid (consists of three cusps or leaflets) and mitral (bicuspid, consists of two cusps or leaflets) atrioventricular (AV) valves are positioned between the atrium and ventricle on the right and left sides of the heart, respectively. When ventricular pressure falls below atrial pressure during diastole the valves are forced open to allow the blood to pass into the ventricle (ventricular filling). As the pressure within the ventricle rises during systole, and exceeds atrial pressure, the AV valves close to prevent the back flow of blood into the atria during ventricular emptying. As the ventricle continues to contract during systole, the ventricular pressure eventually exceeds the pressure in the ascending aorta or pulmonary artery, the semilunar (aortic and pulmonary) valves open and allow blood flow into these arteries. As the ventricles relax the ventricular pressure falls below arterial pressure and the semilunar valves close to prevent the blood flowing from the arteries back into the heart.

The timing of events in the cardiac cycle is controlled by a complex electrical system. In the normal situation, initiation of the cardiac cycle occurs at the sinoatrial (SA) node, which acts as an internal pacemaker. The SA node is located in the wall of the right atrium and consists of specialized muscle tissue which combines the characteristics of muscle and nerves; when it contracts it generates electrical impulses similar to those produced by the nervous system. Virtually all myocardial tissue is self-excitable and can contract without any signal from the nervous system. The nodal is the most active and therefore usually begins the contraction that continues in surrounding tissue. Nonetheless, this tissue is sensitive to both neurological and endocrine input, which acts to accelerate or slow the rate of SA node firing. When the SA node contracts it generates a wave of depolarization which travels through the walls of the atria; the impulse spreads rapidly causing both to contract simultaneously. The ventricles are separated from the atria by nonconductive tissue except for a second patch of nodal tissue positioned at the bottom of the atrial septum (the wall separating the two atria) called the atrioventricular (AV) node. As the wave of excitation reaches the AV node it is delayed by approximately 0.1 s to allow the atria to fully contract before the ventricles. After the delay, the excitation wave is conducted through specialized fibres known as the bundle of

His to the apex of the ventricles, then spreading upward through the ventricular walls along the Purkinje fibres. The ventricles contract simultaneously. The depolarization wave is followed by repolarization, creating a refractory period, during which further depolarization is not possible.

Heart rate monitoring

Heart rate is the simplest form of cardiovascular measurement and is the number of times the heart beats per minute (BPM). A normal adult resting heart rate ranges between 60 and 100 BMP. However, endurance athletes can have resting heart rates well below 60 BPM due to high levels of cardiovascular conditioning. Resting heart rates above 100 BPM can indicate an underlying pathology and should be investigated by a clinician. Heart rate is affected by stress, exercise, smoking, caffeine and what the person was doing immediately beforehand. So care must be taken to ensure that resting heart rate is measured after a period of rest. Heart rate is measured manually by checking the pulse rate. This can be performed by supination of the hand so that the palm faces upwards. An index and middle finger are placed along the radial artery (below the thumb side of the wrist) to detect the pulse. Once the pulse is identified it can be counted for 30 s and multiply that number by 2 to identify the heart rate in BPM. Pulse rate can also be used to identify irregular heart rhythms that may be an indication for an underlying heart condition. Heart rate can automatically be measured non-invasively using ECG and invasively during cardiac catheterization, both discussed later in the chapter.

Blood pressure measurement

Movement of fluid through the body is essential to life, providing the body with energy for cellular processes and eliminating toxic waste products. In the simplest model, flow in a tube such as a small blood vessel or bronchiole can be expressed in analogy to electrical flow:

$$Q = P/R$$

where Q is the volume flow rate, P is the pressure change across the tube, and R is the resistance, given by Poiseuille's law:

$$R = \frac{8\eta l}{\pi r^4}$$

where η is the viscosity of the fluid, l is the tube length, and r is its diameter. Note the very strong dependence on r. This demonstrates the close relationship between pressure and flow: in cardiovascular physiological measurement, often a pressure difference will be used as a surrogate for flow, which is often substantially more challenging to measure. The above model is very simple, but works reasonably well in laminar flow, which occurs when the Reynolds number is less than about 2000 or so:

$$\mathrm{Re} = \frac{2\rho v r}{\eta}$$

where ρ is the fluid density and v is its velocity. Above 4000 the flow is fully turbulent; between these numbers the flow is partially turbulent and partially laminar, known as transitional flow.

In the cardiovascular system, reduced flow of blood into the tissues can be due to either an increase in resistance, for example because elevated pulmonary venous pressure in left ventricular failure, or a decrease in pressure gradient, for example in anaphylactic shock, where there is substantial vasodilation, particularly in peripheral arterioles. Inadequate perfusion of tissues due to low flow can ultimately lead to ischemia and death. However, absolute pressure also has physiological significance, particularly in the cardiovascular system, in which a high blood pressure is a strong risk factor for coronary heart disease, stroke, and hypertensive nephropathy. Physiological measurements of pressures and flows allow diagnosis, assessment and monitoring of cardiovascular disease.

Methods of blood pressure measurement

Blood pressure is one of the most common physiological measurements carried out in clinical practice. It is straightforward and provides essential information about the health of the cardiovascular system. For most of the twentieth century, routine blood pressure measurements were made by the auscultatory method. This method is accurate but the reliability of blood pressure readings rely on a careful and precise measurement technique. The method involves occluding the brachial artery by encircling the upper arm with an inflatable bladder attached to a mercury sphygmomanometer (the blood pressure cuff).

The cuff is inflated to above the systolic pressure and then gradually deflated by approximately 2–3 mmHg per second. A stethoscope is held over the antecubital fossa to note the cuff pressures at which the first and fifth Korotkoff sounds are heard. These points are taken to represent the systolic and diastolic blood pressures. Patients should preferably sit for approximately 5 min prior to BP measurement and have an empty bladder to ensure an accurate assessment.

For patients in critical and intensive care situations, continuous monitoring is required so that rapid clinical decisions can be made as a result of change in status. Intra-arterial blood pressure is a commonly used as a monitoring tool in these environments. It is measured using a continuously flushed, fluid-filled catheter which is connected to a pressure transducer, often a strain gauge. The physics of fluid-filled catheters for pressure measurement is discussed in more depth in the next subsection. These measurement systems provide a continuous readout of arterial blood pressure, from which systolic, diastolic, and mean arterial pressures can be determined.

In the 1970s, the first automatic blood pressure monitor was put on the market, the DINAMAP ("Device for Indirect Noninvasive Automatic Mean Arterial Pressure"). This worked on the oscillometric principle, measuring the amplitude of oscillations in the cuff pressure to determine mean arterial pressure. The cuff is pumped up to a certain pressure and the device waits for a predefined time to check for oscillations in cuff pressure. If none are noted, it steps down to the next pressure. Once it detects oscillations in pressure due to the contractions of the heart, it always waits until it has two close readings for the oscillation amplitude before moving on to the next pressure. This is shown diagrammatically in Fig. 16.2. The requirement for two similar oscillations to be detected is used in artefact rejection. Examples of intrinsic and extrinsic artefacts are shown in Fig. 16.2.

In oscillometric measurements, only mean arterial pressure is well defined as the pressure at which maximum cuff oscillations occur. Systolic and diastolic pressures are then calculated using proprietary algorithms from the oscillation amplitude at different cuff pressures. Unfortunately, there are two differing standards for oscillometric blood pressure monitors (also commonly known as non-invasive blood pressure (NIBP) monitors). The Association for the Advancement of Medical Instrumentation (AAMI) in the United States compares NIBP to an intra-arterial reference (FDA, 1997), with the requirement that the mean difference be ≪5 mmHg and the standard deviation of the differences ≪8 mmHg. In contrast, the British Hypertension Society advocates the referencing of NIBP to auscultatory measurements. To obtain an A-rating in this system, 60% of readings must be within 5 mmHg, 85% within 10 mmHg, and 90% within 15 mmHg of the reading taken by the auscultatory method (O'Brien et al., 2001).

In principle, these two standards should be complementary, but this assumes that the values of blood pressure measured intra-arterially and by the auscultatory method agree. There is a wide range of scatter in results of studies comparing auscultatory to intra-arterial blood pressure, but in general, the auscultatory method measures a systolic pressure that is too low and a diastolic that is too high, when compared with the intra-arterial method (Nielsen et al., 1983; Darovic, 1995). Thus, companies have tended to develop more than one algorithm, one referenced to intra-arterial and the other to auscultatory methods. Safety issues specific to oscillometric automated blood pressure monitors are addressed in BS EN

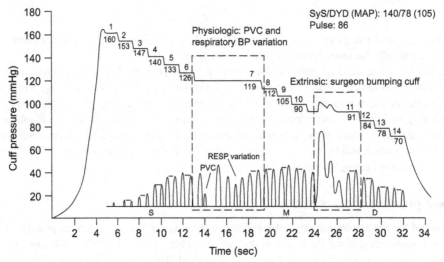

FIG. 16.2 An oscillometric noninvasive blood pressure measurement with artefacts rejected by the automated algorithm. A premature ventricular contraction (PVC) results in a lower than normal blood volume and so is ignored by the algorithm, along with the following larger than normal compensatory beat. Similarly, the large pressure variation due to the surgeon bumping the cuff is ignored.

IEC 80601-2-30 (BSI, 2019). As well as complying with general electrical safety standards, there are particular requirements due to the hazard of the pressurized cuff around the patient's arm. Specifically, excessive pressure could damage the tissues in the patient's arm and cause significant pain, whilst prolonged cuff pressure could cause venous blood pooling, and even limb ischemia. The standard sets out limits for the maximum pressure and the maximum inflated time in both normal and single fault conditions for such devices.

Invasive hemodynamic monitoring

The physiological state of the heart, heart chambers, and heart valves can be assessed by the direct measurement of cardiac pressures. In the cardiac catheterization laboratory (cath lab), catheters are inserted into the heart chambers, usually via the venous or arterial vessels, to measure cardiac function to determine if intervention is required, and post intervention to evaluate the outcome of the procedure. A basic monitoring catheter will incorporate a strain gauge or set of strain gauges to measure the change in pressure by applying the Wheatstone bridge principles. A more advanced conductance catheter typically used in a clinical research setting also allows estimation of blood volume within the heart chamber, derived by measuring the changing conductance within the chamber. Cardiac catheters can also be used to inject radiopaque dye into the chambers or arteries in the heart to undertake measure of cardiac function, and assessment of coronary artery disease. This is known as angiography. Coronary angiography can be followed with a number of interventions including angioplasty (ballooning) and stent deployment in order to treat coronary artery disease — collectively known as percutaneous coronary intervention (PCI). A catheter is typically a flexible tube which can be inserted via a sheath into the narrow opening of an artery or vein and then fed along the vessel into the heart chamber of interest. Arterial catheters are normally introduced from the radial, brachial or femoral arteries, whilst venous (right-sided catheterization) catheters are usually introduced in the internal jugular or femoral vein. Modern best practice would suggest that using ultrasound to guide placement reduces the risk of vascular complications for patients.

Cardiac pressure can be measured using a catheter-type system or catheter tip sensor. A catheter-type sensor measures blood pressure using a fluid-filled catheter with an open tip. The catheter is of known length and diameter so an external pressure sensor can be attached to the end of the catheter outside the patient's body to measure the blood pressure within the heart chamber. This type of catheter is sensitive to damping and resonance which can be avoided by using the more accurate catheter tip sensor. A catheter tip sensor unit is placed at the tip of the catheter and in direct contact with the blood to be measured.

Cardiac output is the effective volume of blood expelled by the ventricles per unit time (usually given in liters per minute) and is used as an overall measure of the performance of the heart. Cardiac output will vary depending on the oxygen and nutrient needs of the body, rising in exercise or disease states. Maintaining cardiac output is essential for the delivery of metabolic oxygen to the body and elimination of unwanted waste products from the tissues. Cardiac output (CO) is given by the following equation:

$$(CO) = HR \times SV$$

where the heart rate (HR) is in beats per minute and the stroke volume (SV) (L) is the volume of blood pumped from a ventricle in a single heartbeat. SV can be difficult to measure directly without specialized blood conductance equipment. Patients come in different shapes and sizes. The cardiac output needed to maintain a 50 kg female may be significantly lower than that needed to maintain an 110 kg male. The cardiac output (CO) (L/min) can be indexed to the size of the patient, by way of standardizing to the body surface area (BSA) (m^2). Cardiac index (CI) is given by the following equation:

$$CI = \frac{CO}{BSA}$$

The ejection fraction (EF) is the volumetric fraction of blood ejected in a single heartbeat, and is given by the following equation:

$$EF = \frac{SV}{EDV}$$

where the end-diastolic volume (EDV) is the volume of blood left in the ventricle at the end of diastole. End-systolic volume would be the volume of blood left in the ventricle at the end of systole. Despite a number of problems with reliance upon a single marker of cardiac function, ejection fraction is the most commonly used parameter for the assessment of systolic function across a number of different modalities.

The Fick principle states that if the oxygen concentration of arterial blood supplying a tissue, the oxygen concentration in venous blood leaving that tissue, and the rate of oxygen uptake by the tissue per unit time is known, then the cardiac output can be calculated by the following equation:

$$CO = \frac{VO_2}{C_a - C_v}$$

where VO_2 is the oxygen consumption (L/min), C_a is the oxygen concentration of the blood sample taken from the artery (L/L), and C_v is the oxygen concentration of the blood sample taken from the pulmonary artery (L/L). The blood samples are analyzed in a blood-gas analyzer to determine the oxygen concentration, and the oxygen consumption is measured by using spirometry. By assuming a value for oxygen consumption, cardiac output can be closely approximated to the actual value without the need for the spirometry equipment. The assumed oxygen consumption is typically calculated from the LaFarge equation:

$$VO_{2\sim males} = 138.1 - (11.49 \log_e age) + (0.378 HR)$$

and

$$VO_{2\sim females} = 138.1 - (17.04 \log_e age) + (0.378 HR)$$

where $VO_{2\ males}$ is the assumed oxygen consumption in males and $VO_{2\ females}$ is the assumed oxygen consumption in females ($mL/min/m^2$).

The pulmonary artery catheter, more commonly known as the Swan—Ganz catheter, allows the direct measurement of right atrial, right ventricular, and pulmonary artery pressures and recording of blood saturations in each location. It also allows the indirect measurement left atrial or wedge pressure by inflating the balloon when positioned in the pulmonary capillary. It is introduced through a venous sheath in the internal jugular or femoral vein. The catheter can be passed sequentially into the right atrium, right ventricle, and the pulmonary artery. Inflation of the balloon when the catheter is in a branch of the pulmonary artery allows the recording of pulmonary capillary wedge pressure (PCWP) which is an estimate of the left atrial pressure. The combination of these measurements allows the physician to measure a number of cardiovascular parameters including system vascular resistance index (SVRI), pulmonary vascular resistance index (PVRI), and oxygen consumption (VO_2). Assessment of saturations in each location also allows for the identification and quantification of shunts between the pulmonary and systemic circulation such as anomalous connection or septal defects.

The Swan—Ganz catheter is also used to perform the thermodilution method for determination of cardiac output. The catheter is advanced to the pulmonary artery. Inflation of the balloon can be used to float the catheter into an appropriate position. The tip of the catheter contains a temperature-sensitive thermistor which is used to measure the transient temperature change after injection of a small bolus (10 mL) of cold saline (0.9% NaCl). By measuring the blood temperature at a known distance from the tip of the catheter, cardiac output can be calculated by measuring the resistance change of the thermistor as a function of time as it responds to the pulmonary artery blood temperature change due to the injected bolus of saline. A greater temperature change will correspond to a lower cardiac output. Thermodilution-derived cardiac output measurement would normally be repeated 3 to 5 times and a mean measurement would then be taken as the true cardiac output.

Echocardiography

Ultrasound can be used in the clinical setting to produce useful information for diagnosis and treatment. Echocardiography is the common term for cardiac ultrasound. It provides detailed information on cardiac hemodynamics as well as structural images of the heart and vasculature. High-frequency sound waves (1—10 MHz) are produced and detected by a transducer with an array of piezoelectric crystals. These crystals deform under mechanical (pressure) and electrical load, termed the *piezoelectric effect*. A voltage signal is passed across the piezoelectric crystal to generate a mechanical pressure wave. Electrolytic coupling gel is used to transmit the ultrasound signal from the transducer and into the body. As the mechanical pressure wave passes through the body, the difference in acoustic impedance of the tissue interfaces cause a proportion of the ultrasound wave to be reflected back to the transducer. The transducer then receives the echo and the piezoelectric transducer converts the mechanical wave back into an electronic pulse to be processed by the ultrasound scanner. As the assumed speed of sound in soft tissue is $1540\ ms^{-1}$, the "time of flight" is then used to determine the depth of the tissue interface and is displayed as such on the monitor.

The interaction between ultrasound and the tissue it propagates through is fundamental to the diagnostic ability of the clinical measurement technique. This can happen by reflection, scattering, refraction, and absorption. For tissue interfaces larger than the ultrasound wavelength, the ultrasound will either undergo specular or diffuse reflection,[1] or Raleigh scattering when the tissue interface is smaller than the wavelength. Reflection is caused by the difference in acoustic impedance between two tissues at a boundary. The greater the acoustic impedance mismatch the greater the proportion of the transmitted pulse that is reflected back to the transducer. In specular reflection the strongest reflection occurs when the tissue interface is perpendicular to the transducer. A diffuse reflection results in weaker reflections being transmitted in multiple directions. If the ultrasound pulse was incident to a tissue boundary at an angle other than 90° and the two tissues were of a different speed of sound, the transmitted pulse would be refracted as it passes into the second tissue as governed by Snell's law and the resulting echo would be incorrectly displayed on the image:

$$\frac{\sin \theta_1}{\sin \theta_2} = \frac{v_1}{v_2}$$

where θ_1 is the angle of the incident pulse, θ_2 is the angle of the refracted pulse, v_1 is the speed of sound in the first tissue, and v_2 is the speed of sound in the second tissue.

Absorption is caused by the viscoelastic properties of tissue leading to the deposition of the mechanical energy in the pulse into thermal energy in the tissue. This is the primary mechanism for attenuation, described by the attenuation co-efficient and assumed to be approximately $0.5 \text{ dB cm}^{-1} \text{ MHz}^{-1}$ in soft tissue. Therefore, higher frequency sound waves are attenuated more, so there is a tradeoff between penetration depth and image resolution.

B-mode imaging uses the received timing and echo intensity to generate a 2D cross-sectional image of the heart. A group of piezoelectric crystal elements are excited with an electrical signal, this finite pulse is transmitted into the body, and each reflection provides information on the reflection strength for a specific time of flight. This information is used to create a scan line from the pulse-echo sequence, where the pixel brightness at each depth represents the strength of the reflector at that distance from the transducer, hence the name B-mode (brightness mode). The next group of elements are then sequentially activated to generate a 2D cross-section of the anatomy, or scan plane. The 2D image can then be used to visualize the cardiac anatomy, in addition to performing calliper measurements of the different parts of the heart.

Doppler ultrasound can be used to measure the frequency change in the Doppler pulse as it is reflected by a moving target, and the magnitude and direction of this frequency shift can be used to determine the velocity of the reflector as governed by the Doppler equation:

$$\Delta f = \frac{2vf \cos \theta}{c}$$

where Δf is the Doppler shift frequency, v is the velocity of the moving target, f is the frequency of the transmitted ultrasound pulse, θ is the angle between the ultrasound pulse and the target to be insonated, and c is the speed of sound of the transmitted ultrasound pulse.

There are two main types of Doppler, continuous wave (CW) and pulsed wave (PW), with PW Doppler being used in both spectral and colour Doppler. CW Doppler requires one element to continuously transmit the ultrasound pulse and one element to continuously receive the reflected ultrasound echo, and all reflector velocities along the line of sight are detected. PW spectral Doppler transmits an ultrasound pulse, similar to B-mode, and reflected ultrasound echoes are only measured if they fall within a set time period from transmission. The operator uses a range gate or sample volume indicator on the B-mode image to determine where the PW Doppler signal will be measured. The spectral Doppler trace is displayed as a graph of Doppler shift frequency (reflector velocity) versus time. As with any pulsed signal, Nyquist's theorem states that the sampling frequency must be at least twice the maximum frequency in the signal to be sampled, otherwise aliasing will occur. Since there is an upper limit to the pulse repetition frequency (PRF) there is a maximal blood velocity ($v_{\max}$) that can be detected, given by

$$v_{\max} = \frac{c^2}{8df \cos \theta}$$

where d is the depth of the target.

Similarly to spectral Doppler, colour Doppler transmits a pulse along a series of scan lines and reflected ultrasound echoes are only measured if they fall within a set time period from transmission defined by the position of the colour box. Each scan line is divided up into a number of sample volumes, the mean Doppler frequency is calculated for each of them

---

1. For smooth tissue boundaries the ultrasound pulse will undergo specular reflection. For rough tissue interfaces the ultrasound pulse will undergo diffuse reflection.

and then colour-coded on the image. The colour variation is then used to visualize the speed and direction of the blood flow. In general, red indicates flow toward the transducer and blue indicates flow away. However, the colours can be inversed and modern ultrasound scanners have many different colour options that can be selected by the operator. Colour Doppler also suffers from aliasing, where high frequency content will be incorrectly displayed as the wrong colour.

Although ultrasound is considered to be a safe imaging modality since it is nonionizing in nature, there are potential risks to the patient in both the thermal and mechanical form. The ultrasound pulse is attenuated as it passes through the tissue, the dissipation on the pressure wave leads to localized heating that may have the potential to cause permanent tissue damage. This potential for thermal harm is indicated to the operator by way of the thermal index (TI):

$$TI = \frac{W_i}{W_0}$$

where W_i is the incident ultrasound power and W_0 is the power required to raise the tissue temperature by 1 °C.

The mechanical pressure wave will also interact with small gas bubbles and fluids as it passes through the tissue in the form of streaming and cavitation (noninertial and inertial). Streaming is caused by the ultrasound pulse radiation force causing the forced flow of liquid within the body, and can be seen within the testes. Noninertial cavitation is caused by the oscillations in the pressure wave causing gas bubbles to expand and contract in synchronism, creating local shear stresses between the gas bubble and the surrounding tissue. Noninertial cavitation is caused by a prolonged exposure to an oscillating pressure waveform, hence would only be observed while using CW Doppler. Inertial cavitation is caused by a sufficiently large rarefactional pressure that causes the bubble to expand rapidly and violently collapse, leading to localized areas of high temperature and pressure, which may cause cell necrosis. This potential for mechanical harm is indicated to the operator by way of the mechanical index (MI):

$$MI = \frac{P_r}{\sqrt{f_{awf}}}$$

where P_r is the attenuated peak rarefactional pressure and f_{awf} is the acoustic working frequency. In practice these risks are extremely low in clinical practice using modern, well maintained ultrasound equipment. However, greater risks occurs during transesophageal echocardiography from the placement of the probe in the esophagus or stomach.

As with standard medical device management, an electrical safety test should be performed at acceptance and during any six-monthly or annual quality assurance (QA) or planned preventative maintenance testing. Firstly, a visual inspection should be performed to check the physical integrity of the device. This allows the operator to check for any signs of physical damage and to make sure all the controls and ergonomic adjustments function correctly. Ultrasound QA is then performed using phantoms or test objects of known acoustical property. Imaging and Doppler phantoms are used by a trained operator to ensure the accuracy and validity of an image or measurement taken using the device. For example, an imaging phantom can be used to check the accuracy of calliper measurements, imaging resolution, contrast sensitivity, and penetration depth. A Doppler phantom may be used to check the accuracy of velocity measurements, sample volume dimension and position, detectable velocity limits, and the accuracy of waveform estimations.

The clinical examination can be performed using 2D phased array and 3D matrix array transthoracic probes, and 2D and 3D transesophageal probes while the patient is under sedation to investigate cardiac hemodynamics and image the heart and vasculature. For a routine transthoracic scan the patient will be positioned to lay left lateral decubitus with their right arm by their side and their left arm by their head. This usually obtains an optimal image of the heart as gravity acts to force it toward the front of the chest cavity, and by positioning the left arm above the head the intercostal space between the ribs is increased to obtain a better view. Since the acoustic impedance of bone is much greater than that of soft tissue, ultrasound images cannot be acquired through bone, so by increasing the intercostal space the operator can scan the heart between the rib bones. Three silver chloride ECG electrodes are positioned on the patient's back so the patient's 3-lead ECG can be synchronized to the ultrasound scanner. An image or Doppler measurement is normally stored over 1—3 beats, however, if the heart rate is over 100 bpm, or the patient is in atrial fibrillation the information will be collected over more beats. Atrial fibrillation is a complex abnormal rhythm resulting from disordered electrical activity in the atria, resulting in an irregular heartbeat. By averaging the data collected over a series of heartbeats the parameters collected should better represent the patient's current physiology.

The operator will usually start the examination from the parasternal window and move on to the apical window (Fig. 16.3). Then the patient will be moved to the supine position to examine the heart and great vessels from the suprasternal and subcostal windows. By positioning the patient in this way, the heart can be scanned along standard planes and axes so that the information collected can be compared to normal data for diagnosis. A typical scan will involve

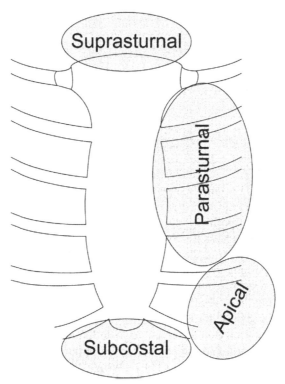

FIG. 16.3 Echocardiography scanning windows for transducer positioning.

assessment of all 4 chambers and valves, as well as the great vessels. Assessment of the left ventricle routinely involves measurement of the walls and chambers in systole and diastole. Increased wall thickness (left ventricular hypertrophy) can be caused by hypertension or inherited diseases such as hypertrophic cardiomyopathy. The chamber volumes can be measured by outlining the 2D area in orthogonal planes, and applying a calculation known as Simpsons rule. Measurement of the left ventricular volume in systole and diastole allows an estimation of ejection fraction. In heart failure, ejection fraction may be reduced. A value of 55−65% is considered normal, whilst below 30% is considered to be an indicator of severely impaired left ventricular systolic function. Detailed assessment of each segment of the left ventricular wall is usually performed in order to assess whether there are regional differences in function. This may be indicative of previous myocardial infarction or ongoing ischemia. Complex assessment using tissue Doppler can also be performed to assess the motion of individual segments of myocardium.

Valve assessment usually begins with structural assessment considering the movement of leaflets, thickness and abnormalities such as infection or thrombus seen on the valve. Colour Doppler can then be used to look for regurgitation into the preceding chamber. Doppler assessment can then be undertaken to assess both regurgitant jets and forward flow. Stenotic (narrowed) valves have an increased velocity across the valve with increasingly turbulent flow. This can be measured with Doppler and the degree of stenosis quantified.

Electrocardiography

We have already determined that the heart is excited by electrical signals which cause the heart muscle to contract during systole. This electrical signal is transmitted from the heart and into the thorax cavity, the voltage across the resistive tissue can be detected by electrodes positioned on the skin and recorded as an ECG. The ECG trace provides the observer with information on the electrical characteristics of the heart, the extent of damage to the heart, and the effects of drug or surgical intervention on cardiac function. As with the measurement of neurophysiological signals, ECG signals are measured using silver/silver chloride electrodes utilizing a driven right leg circuit. This provides a high common mode rejection ratio to remove the unwanted capacitive coupling induced electrical signals common across the body. The ECG is used to measure the voltages that arise from the differing contraction times of parts of the myocardium during the cardiac cycle. While at rest, myocardial cells have a negative potential across their membrane. An electrical signal is initiated at the SA node; it travels through the atria to the AV node, and via the bundle of His and Purkinje fibres into the ventricular

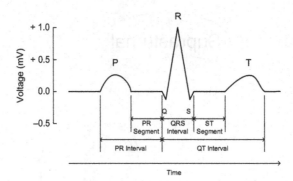

FIG. 16.4   The normal PQRST ECG waveform.

myocardium. The electrical signal floods positive ions into the cell creating a positive potential that depolarizes the myocardium and causes it to contract. The excess positive ions are then pumped back out of the cell and it repolarizes and relaxes. The depolarization and repolarization of the myocardium occur at different times throughout the heart and this variation in potential is detected by positioning leads across the chest and limbs in an ECG. On a conventional ECG a positive deflection indicates that the depolarized wave is travelling toward the electrode.

A typical ECG trace is shown in Fig. 16.4. The P wave corresponds to the depolarization of the atria. The PR interval is an assessment of the time taken for the impulse travel from the SA node across the AV node, into the ventricles. The QRS complex represents the ventricular depolarization (contraction), with the R wave the main ventricular depolarization. A widened QRS complex (>120 ms) indicates that the ventricle is not depolarizing at the same time, suggesting that the impulse is delayed in one of the fibres. This is known as a bundle branch block. The T wave is caused by the repolarization (relaxation) of the ventricles. The repolarization of the atria is covered up by the QRS complex. Ischemia such as that which occurs during myocardial infarction causes changes in the repolarization of the myocardium. This is seen as a number of different repolarization patterns on the ECG such as ST-elevation, ST depression and T wave inversion.

The apex of the T wave toward the ascending slope is a vulnerable period of the cardiac cycle and if a further electrical impulse arrives during this period ventricular fibrillation can occur. Ventricular fibrillation is the random contraction of the ventricular myocytes due to the random repetitive excitation of these cells. There is no coordinated ventricular contraction. Ventricular fibrillation is a cause of cardiac arrest and rapidly leads to global ischemia (particularly cerebral ischemia) as there is no cardiac output. Normal cardiac rhythm can be reestablished by defibrillating the heart. This involves passing a large electric current across the heart to put the entire myocardium in a refractory state where no impulse can occur, the SA node can then resume normal activity. Defibrillation may be unsuccessful and in this case death is likely to occur. Atrial fibrillation is characterized by the absence of organized contraction of the atria. The cause of atrial fibrillation remains open to debate. The AV node may receive signals at greater than 600 bpm. The refractory period of the AV node prevents most of these being passed to the ventricle but the resulting signals are irregular and often rapid.

A 12-lead ECG is used to monitor the heart's electrical activity from 12 different angles by selecting different pairs of electrodes, or combinations of electrodes, through a resistive network to give an equivalent pair, which is referred to as a lead. The 12 leads are summarized in Table 16.1. The first three leads are taken from electrodes placed on the left arm (LA), right arm (RA), and left leg (LL). These three electrodes form Einthoven's triangle (Fig. 16.5). Lead I is from RA to LA, Lead II is from RA to LL, and Lead III is from LA to LL. The electrical signal on each lead of Einthoven's triangle can be represented as a voltage source, thus we obtain Einthoven's equation:

$$I - II + III = 0$$

Leads I, II, and III are bipolar as they measure the voltage between two specific points. All other leads in a 12-lead ECG are unipolar as they measure the voltage at one electrode relative to a reference electrode, which is taken from the average of two or more other electrodes. The three unipolar limb leads, known as the *augmented limb leads*, are the voltage difference between one limb electrode and the average of the other two electrodes. Lead aVR is the voltage at RA referenced to the average of LA and LL; lead aVL is the voltage at LA referenced to the average of RA and LL; lead aVF is the voltage at LL referenced to the average of RA and LA. The first six leads I, II, III, aVR, aVL, and aVF are collectively known as the *limb leads*. The remaining six leads in the 12-lead ECG are known as the *chest leads*. The chest leads provide local information and are measured relative to the average of the limb electrodes. The accurate placement of the chest ECG leads is crucial to obtain reliable and repeatable ECG recordings. The incorrect placement of the chest electrodes can lead to artefacts within the measurement, ultimately causing serious misdiagnosis errors within the trace.

TABLE 16.1 The 12-lead ECG definitions.

Lead	Measurement
Lead I	Right arm to left arm (bipolar)
Lead II	Right arm to left leg (bipolar)
Lead III	Left arm to left leg (bipolar)
aVR	Right arm (unipolar ref. left arm and left leg)
aVL	Left arm (unipolar ref. right arm and left leg)
aVF	Left leg (unipolar ref. right arm and left arm)
Chest 1	Chest position 1 (unipolar ref. three limb electrodes)
Chest 2	Chest position 2 (unipolar ref. three limb electrodes)
Chest 3	Chest position 3 (unipolar ref. three limb electrodes)
Chest 4	Chest position 4 (unipolar ref. three limb electrodes)
Chest 5	Chest position 5 (unipolar ref. three limb electrodes)
Chest 6	Chest position 6 (unipolar ref. three limb electrodes)

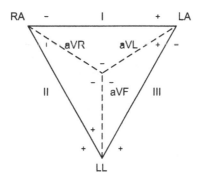

FIG. 16.5 Einthoven's triangle.

The frequency response required to accurately construct an ECG signal lies between 0.05 and 150 Hz. Thus it is not advisable to filter mains frequency as it would remove useful information. DC offsets are removed by using a 0.05 Hz high-pass filter and, likewise, high frequency noise from monitors and radio interference are removed by using a 150 Hz low-pass filter. The most common types of artefacts encountered during ECG measurement are mains noise, baseline wander, and jitter. Although mains noise is reduced by good instrumentation design (driven right leg circuit) it can be loaded on the system from poor connections within the circuit. This could be from electrical connections or high impedance contacts between the electrode and the patient. Baseline wander can be caused by respiration (observed on the chest electrodes as the chest cavity moves up and down during respiratory swing) cable motion, and faulty electrodes. Jitter is caused by unwanted muscle movement causing muscle noise on the ECG trace.

A resting 12-lead ECG is used extensively within a healthcare environment. It is a standard, noninvasive test that can be performed by a healthcare practitioner and then interpreted by a medically trained professional to provide information on the electrical characteristics of the heart. To continuously monitor the patient's ECG in a clinical ward environment, a 1-lead (lead II) can be taken and continuously displayed on a bedside monitor. This is used to monitor trends in the cardiac rhythm and to alarm the clinician to a too slow or fast heart rate. To avoid artefacts caused by mains, motion, and muscle noise, the frequency response would have to be reduced to 0.05−40 Hz. A simulated trace from the six chest leads is shown in Fig. 16.6.

Ambulatory monitoring, more commonly referred to as Holter monitoring, is the use of a portable device to record the patient's ECG for a prolonged period of time. This is normally performed over a 24-h period; however, it can be performed up for up to a 7-day period if clinically indicated. It is used to provide the clinician with long-term information on the

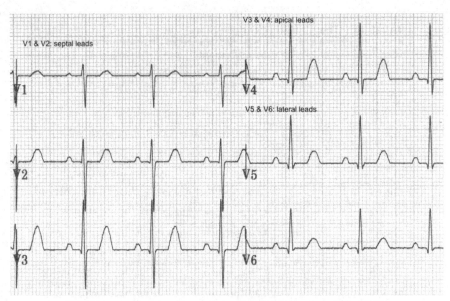

FIG. 16.6   A simulation of normal chest lead appearance in a 12-lead ECG.

patient's cardiac function to help identify the cause of the patient's symptoms, such as chest pain, angina, dizziness, and palpitations. Typically a 3-lead ECG monitor would be used. This will use four electrodes to obtain three leads; the neutral lead is positioned on the top of the sternum with the other three electrodes positioned on the chest to give modified bipolar views of chest electrodes V1, V3, and V5. The monitor is checked for good electrode contacts and that the trace is of high quality and artefact free. When the patient returns to the hospital the recorded trace can be transferred to a PC and analyzed digitally. A report can then be produced for the patient summarizing the findings of the test.

Exercise stress testing involves the measurement of a 12-lead ECG when the patient's heart is being stressed. It can be used in patients with known heart disease to determine the functional capacity and severity of the disease. Historically, it has been used to differentiate between ischemic heart disease and other causes of chest pain. A positive test result would indicate that cardiac ischemia is occurring on exercise and further investigations will be performed. The electrodes are positioned the same as with a resting 12-lead ECG, except the limb electrodes are positioned on the patient's torso to minimize artefacts generated from muscle motion. A standard clinical protocol will be followed where resting ECGs and blood pressure are recorded and then the patient is put on a treadmill. The treadmill will gradually increase in speed and incline and the patient's ECG and blood pressure will be recorded at set intervals according to the protocol being followed. Since the purpose of the test is to record the patient's ECG and blood pressure on a stressed heart, additional safety considerations must be observed. Exercise stress testing is contra-indicated for high-risk patients, due to the risk of severe myocardial ischemia or arrhythmia. Best practice would indicate that a defibrillator crash trolley should be kept in the room and that staff performing the tests are trained in cardiopulmonary resuscitation. A test would be stopped immediately if an exercise-induced arrhythmia occurred or if there were systems of altered cardiac function, such as a decline in blood pressure. There are also hazards to the patient from trips of falls while using the treadmill, and a test would be stopped if the patient's gait became unsteady or if they felt they had reached their maximum exertion.

In modern practice, exercise stress testing as a screening test for those with a low probability of angina, has largely been superseded by anatomical tests such as CT coronary angiography. The test remains useful in certain situations such as investigating ventricular ectopy and heart rate response to exercise.

Case study 16.1

A 43-year-old male presents to his local emergency department with a 6-h history of pain in the centre of his chest. The pain radiates to the left shoulder and into the jaw. It is associated with breathlessness and sweating. His heart rate is 80 beats per minute, with a blood pressure of 85/60 mmHg demonstrating that the patient is hypotensive and tachycardic. This suggests a diagnosis of shock. 12 lead ECG (Panel A) shows ST segment elevation in leads V1-5, I and aVL (the anterior and lateral leads, indicated with black arrow), with reciprocal ST depression seen in inferior lead III. The history and ECG findings are consistent with the diagnosis of an anterior ST elevation myocardial infarction, with cardiogenic shock. The patient underwent emergency coronary angiography, with an occluded left anterior descending artery and subsequent stenting to the left anterior descending coronary artery (fluoroscopy shown in Panel B, the occluded LAD is indicated with the asterisk and the stent is indicated with a white arrow).

(A)

(B)

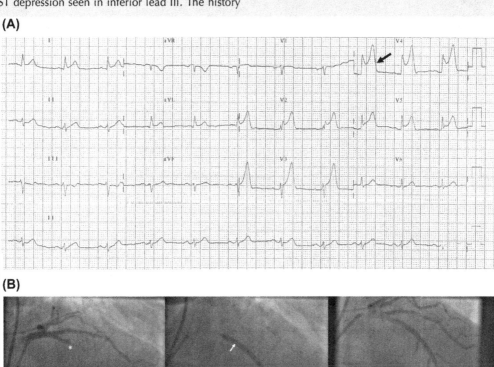

Case study 16.2

An 83-year-old female patient was reviewed by the community nurse. She has a past medical history of hypertension, and type 2 diabetes mellitus. Ambulatory blood pressure monitoring had demonstrated a mean systolic blood pressure of 143 mmHg, and a mean diastolic blood pressure of 56 mmHg (Panel A). During the review, the pulse was felt to be irregular. A 12 lead ECG demonstrated that the patient was in atrial fibrillation (Panel B). The QRS complex was not regular and no P waves could be seen. The tall QRS complexes suggest left ventricular hypertrophy, which is consistent with a diagnosis of hypertension. Since the elderly patient had hypertension and diabetes mellitus, she was commenced on oral anticoagulation to minimize the risk of stroke.

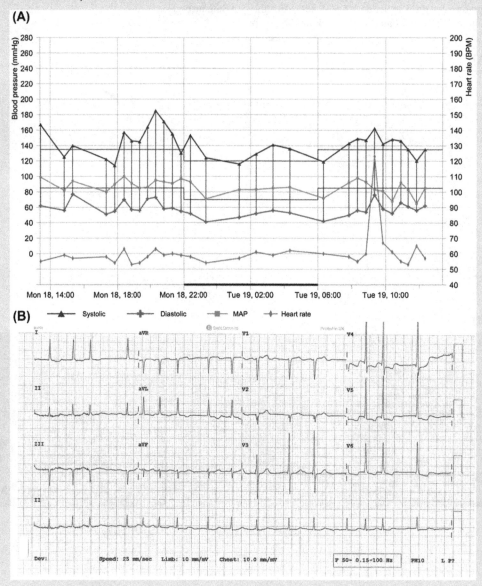

Abbreviations

AAMI Association for the Advancement of Medical Instrumentation
AV Atrioventricular
BP Blood Pressure
BPM Beats Per Minute
BSA Body Surface Area
CI Cardiac Index
CO Cardiac Output
CW Continuous Wave
DINAMAP Device for Indirect Noninvasive Automatic Mean Arterial Pressure
ECG Electrocardiography
EDV End-Diastolic Volume
EF Ejection Fraction
HR Heart Rate
LA Left Arm
LL Left Leg
MI Mechanical Index
NIBP Non-Invasive Blood Pressure
PCI Percutaneous Coronary Intervention
PCWP Pulmonary Capillary Wedge Pressure
PRF Pulse Repetition Frequency
PVRI Pulmonary Vascular Resistance Index
PW Pulsed Wave
QA Quality Assurance
RA Right Arm
SA Sinoatrial
SV Stroke Volume
SVRI System Vascular Resistance Index
TI Thermal Index
VO$_2$ Oxygen Consumption

References

British Standards Institution (BSI), 2019. Medical Electrical Equipment. Particular requirements for the basic safety and essential performance of automated non-invasive sphygmomanometers. BS EN IEC 80601-2-30:2019.

Darovic, G.O. (Ed.), 1995. Hemodynamic Monitoring: Invasive and Noninvasive Clinical Application, second ed. Saunders, London.

Nielsen, P.E., Larsen, B., Holstein, P., Poulsen, H.L., 1983. Accuracy of auscultatory blood pressure measurements in hypertensive and obese subjects. Hypertension 5, 122–127.

O'Brien, E., Waeber, B., Parati, G., Staessen, J., Myers, M.G., 2001. Blood pressure measuring devices: recommendations of the European Society of Hypertension. BMJ 322, 531–536.

U.S. Food and Drug Administration, Centre for Devices and Radiological Health, 1997. Non-Invasive Blood Pressure (NIBP) Monitor Guidance. www.fda.gov/cdrh/ode/noninvas.html.

Further Reading

Hoskins, P., Martin, K., Thrush, A., 2010. Diagnostic Ultrasound Physics and Equipment. Cambridge University Press.

Webster, J.G., 2008. Bioinstrumentation. John Wiley & Sons.

Chapter 17

Urodynamic measurement

Habiba Yasmin[a,b], Eskinder Solomon[c] and Richard G. Axell[a,b]

[a]University College London Hospitals NHS Foundation Trust, London, United Kingdom; [b]University College London, London, United Kingdom; [c]Guy's & St Thomas' NHS Foundation Trust, London, United Kingdom

Chapter outline

Introduction

The urinary system consists of two parts; the upper urinary tract formed of the kidneys and ureters; and the lower urinary tract (LUT) comprising of the urinary bladder and urethra. However, in men, the prostate (a glandular tissue that surrounds the proximal urethra) also contributes to LUT function. The upper and lower urinary tracts act as two dependent systems of conduits and reservoir that permit autonomic low-pressure storage of urine and intermittent higher-pressure voluntary micturition during two mutually exclusive phases of storage and voiding (micturition). The two phases are mediated by complex neural networks that when dysfunctional may generate bothersome lower urinary tract symptoms (LUTS). These symptoms may also arise from anatomical abnormalities in the LUT. This chapter describes urodynamic measurement techniques routinely used to assess the urinary system. Non-invasive urodynamic measurement techniques such as uroflowmetry, pad weight gains and the bladder diary are explored. Conventional urodynamic (cystometrogram – CMG) techniques used to investigate the LUT by measuring intra-vesical and intra-abdominal pressures when filling the bladder with saline, including the use of video-urodynamics (video-cystometrogram – VCMG) where pressure-flow studies are combined with radiographic imaging of the urinary tract, are described. Finally, a brief introduction into advanced techniques such as ambulatory urodynamics and urethral function tests are provided. Case study examples are included throughout the chapter to demonstrate how the various urodynamic techniques may be used to provide a urodynamic diagnosis and treatment for the patient's typical urinary symptoms.

Anatomy and physiology

A thorough understanding of the anatomy, physiology and neurology of the urinary system is crucial for accurate interpretation of urodynamic investigations to distinguish between normal and pathophysiological findings.

Clinical Engineering. https://doi.org/10.1016/B978-0-08-102694-6.00017-6

Upper urinary tract

The upper urinary tract is formed of the kidneys and ureters. Both kidneys continuously produce urine at an approximate rate of 0.5 mL/kg/h under normal function and adequate hydration, however, the maximal physiological filling rate is estimated by body weight (kg) divided by four (Rosier et al., 2017). The ureters function as low-pressure distensible conduits with intrinsic peristalsis properties to transport urine produced by the kidneys to the bladder. Each ureter terminates on either side of the bladder at the ureterovesical junction. The ureterovesical junction prevents retrograde transmission of urine back into the upper tract thus maintaining urine flow in one direction. This protects the upper tract from the higher pressures generated in the bladder during the micturition cycle and from urinary tract infections.

Lower urinary tract

The LUT comprises of the urinary bladder and urethra (Fig. 17.1). The bladder has two principal functions: to act as a low-pressure reservoir for storing urine and to intermittently expel urine at an acceptable pressure when socially convenient. The bladder is a distensible hollow muscular organ that sits behind the symphysis pubis in the shape of a flattened tetrahedron when empty. With increasing distension, the bladder rises in the shape of a dome well above the symphysis pubis. A full bladder can typically hold up to a capacity of 500 mL. The bladder wall comprises of three distinct layers: Serosa — an outer adventitial connective tissue layer; Detrusor muscle — a middle smooth muscle layer; and Urothelium — the innermost lining composed of transitional cell epithelium which provides an elastic barrier that is impervious to urine.

During the storage phase, the bladder exhibits a receptive relaxation property termed 'compliance' that enables it to increase in volume without a substantial rise in the bladder (intra-vesical) pressure. Normal compliance is up to 10 cm H_2O over 400 mL. Compliance is affected by the (i) passive elastic properties of the bladder wall, (ii) intrinsic ability of the smooth detrusor muscle to maintain constant tension with increasing distension and (iii) neural reflexes which control the detrusor muscle tension during bladder filling. During the voiding phase, the detrusor muscle changes from its state of constant tension (i.e. when the muscle is relaxed) to a brief contraction that raises the intra-vesical pressure to expel urine from the bladder.

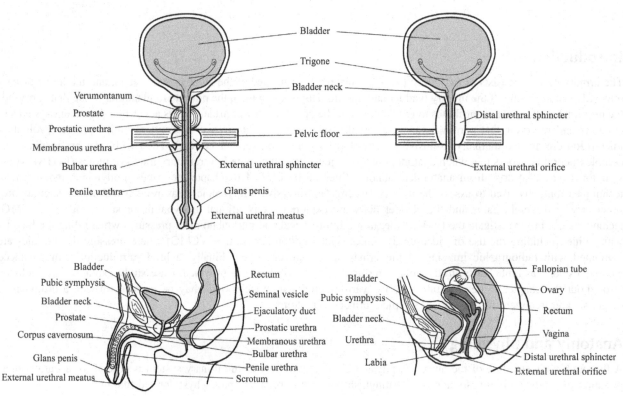

FIG. 17.1 Anatomy of the lower urinary tract (left) in males and (right) in females.

The urethra has two main functions: to maintain continence during the storage phase and to enable adequate emptying of the bladder by providing minimal resistance to urine flow during the voiding phase. During the storage phase, the urethra and sphincter mechanisms remain closed, thereby maintaining high outlet resistance and continence. During the voiding phase, the urethra and sphincter mechanisms open to reduce resistance and allow urine flow. Urine flow is facilitated by simultaneous external sphincter relaxation, a relaxation of the pelvic floor and funnelling of the bladder neck (the lowest part of the bladder), which precedes the detrusor contraction.

The male urethra is approximately 20 cm in length and composed of four sections; the prostatic, membranous, bulbar and penile urethra (Fig. 17.1). In men, urinary continence is maintained by two strong sphincter mechanisms, a proximal bladder neck mechanism and a distal membranous urethral mechanism at the apex of the prostate (beginning at the level of the verumontanum down to the distal aspect of the membranous urethra). The proximal bladder neck mechanism has a powerful inner layer of smooth muscle bundles that maintains continence and prevents retrograde ejaculation. The distal membranous urethral mechanism comprises mainly of extrinsic striated muscles capable of sustained voluntary contractions. Remarkably, the distal sphincter mechanism is powerful enough to maintain urinary continence in isolation of the proximal bladder neck mechanism, which can sometimes be rendered completely incompetent by surgical bladder neck incision or a prostatectomy. In men, the prostate acts as a further continence mechanism. The prostate is made up of smooth muscle (and glandular tissue) which contracts on release of noraadrenaline and provides an additional bladder outlet resistance. The proportion of smooth muscle can be increased in benign prostatic hyperplasia (an enlarged prostate) and is a common cause of bladder outlet obstruction among older men.

Conversely, women have a shorter urethra, at approximately 3.5 cm in length with weaker sphincter mechanisms than men (Fig. 17.1). A shorter urethra and more distensible urethra equates to a lower outlet resistance resulting in a typically higher urinary flow rate than men (approx. 30 mL/s in women). In women, the proximal bladder neck is poorly defined owing to a natural variation in sphincter mechanisms when compared to men. Therefore, urinary continence is mostly maintained by the urethral sphincter mechanism which extends throughout the proximal two-thirds of the urethra and similar to men has an extrinsic striated muscle component for voluntary contractions. In women, the pelvic floor muscles have a vital role in providing an additional continence mechanism. The pelvic floor acts as a supporting hammock for the urethra to compress against and remain shut during rises in intra-abdominal pressure (such as from coughs or sneezes). A weakness in the pelvic floor muscles can result in bladder descent and hypermobility. Consequently, the performance of the distal urethral mechanism is affected by pelvic floor muscle weakness, as well as intrinsic sphincter deficiencies or obstetric trauma, which predisposes women to a higher risk of stress urinary incontinence (SUI).

Neurology of the lower urinary tract

The LUT is controlled via a complex series of central and peripheral neuronal pathways, see Fig. 17.2 for a simplified representation. The peripheral innervations of the LUT are primarily from three groups of nerves: (i) hypogastric, (ii) pelvic, and (iii) pudendal, which allows for the storage and voiding phases to be mostly regulated by autonomic (involuntary) control and somatic (voluntary) control. These nerves contain efferent (motor) axons as well as afferent (sensory) pathways. The efferent pathways co-ordinate bladder and sphincter activity and relaxation to facilitate for the storage and voiding phases, whilst afferent pathways control the receptive relaxation (compliance) of the bladder, sense and communicate bladder fullness, and promote the guarding reflex (to maintain continence with increasing bladder fullness). The neural network supplying the LUT behaves as a circuit that accordingly switches between the storage and voiding phases when under normal neural control. However, abnormalities in the neural network and communication can result in neurogenic specific LUT dysfunctions. These can include storage phase abnormalities such as neurogenic detrusor overactivity (DO) and voiding dysfunctions such as detrusor underactivity (DU) or detrusor sphincter dyssynergia (DSD). The remainder of this section provides a simplified overview of the LUT nerve supply and neural control.

The storage phase is under predominant sympathetic control. Sympathetic nerves originate from the thoracic thoraco lumbar T10-L2 spinal level, via the hypogastric nerve. They relax the detrusor smooth muscle and contract the involuntary sphincteric smooth muscles at the bladder neck/prostate. The voiding phase is under predominant parasympathetic control. Parasympathetic nerves originate from the sacral level of the spinal cord, S2-S4 level (spinal micturition centre), via the pelvic nerve. They contract the detrusor muscle and relax the involuntary sphincteric smooth muscles. The pudendal nerve is under somatic control originating from the S2-S4 level and contracts the sphincteric striated muscle and pelvic floor. See Table 17.1 and Fig. 17.3 for a summary.

Sympathetic and parasympathetic pathways both also supply afferent (sensory) signalling along the hypogastric, pelvic and pudendal nerves for transmission of information on bladder fullness and the presence of any noxious (cold or chemical) stimuli. Consequently, involuntary storage reflexes and conscious sensation of bladder fullness are regulated by

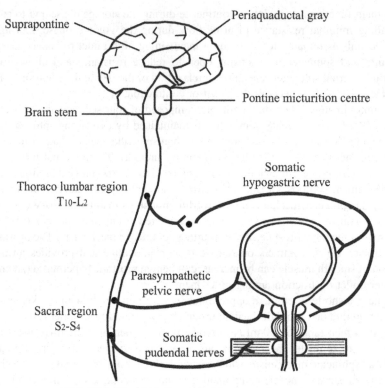

FIG. 17.2 Neurological control of the lower urinary tract.

TABLE 17.1 Nerve system.

Nerve	Type	Origin	Detrusor muscle	Sphincteric muscle	Predominant control of
Hypogastric	Sympathetic	T10-L2	Relaxes	Contracts smooth sphincteric muscle	Storage phase
Pelvic	Parasympathetic	S2-S4 (spinal micturition centre)	Contracts	Relaxes	Voiding phase
Pudendal	Somatic	S2-S4 (Onuf's nucleus)	N/A	Contracts striated sphincteric muscle (guarding reflex) during storage phase. Relaxes pelvic floor and external sphincter during voiding	Both

afferent control. A gradual distention of the bladder during the storage phase produces low-level involuntary afferent storage reflexes. Sympathetic and somatic activity is increased whilst parasympathetic activity is inhibited by these reflexes. Consequently, there are increases in the intrinsic and extrinsic sphincter tone termed "guarding reflex" and synchronous relaxation of the detrusor muscle (to inhibit contractions) with increasing bladder fullness. Once a threshold level of bladder fullness is reached (which varies between individuals and depends on circumstance), there is intense afferent firing from tension receptors in the bladder that activate reflex pathways from the parasympathetic afferents in the pelvic nerve via the spinal cord to the periaqueductal gray (PAG) area in the mid brain. Information on bladder filling is processed at the PAG and forwarded to the pontine micturition centre (PMC) in the brainstem and higher (suprapontine) brain centres. The PMC is the control centre in co-ordinating the micturition process and is governed by the suprapontine area. The suprapontine area has a role in delaying or initiating voiding based on inhibitory influences from the PMC and sensory perception of bladder fullness. If the bladder is sensed to be full but it is socially inappropriate to void, then the PMC sends descending signals to inhibit parasympathetic activity and increase sympathetic and somatic activity to relax the detrusor

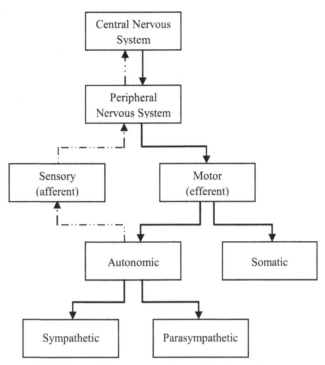

FIG. 17.3 Efferent signalling pathways of the lower urinary tract.

muscle and contract the urethral sphincter mechanisms and pelvic floor muscles. If the bladder is sensed to be full and it is appropriate to void, then the PMC switches the LUT to the voiding phase by sending descending signals to increase parasympathetic activity and inhibit sympathetic and somatic activity. This process is in effect the exact opposite to that occurring during involuntary storage reflexes. Consequently, there is an initial relaxation of the urethral sphincters, followed in a few seconds by contraction of the bladder, an increase in bladder pressure and flow of urine. The switch from involuntary storage to voluntary micturition can occur up to 5—7 times per day in healthy adults.

Non-invasive urodynamic measurement

Non-invasive urodynamics should always be the first line of investigation to gain insight into the storage and voiding function of a patient presenting with LUTS. There are four common non-invasive urodynamic investigations recommended by the International Continence Society (ICS): bladder diaries, pad testing, uroflowmetry and the measurement of post-void residuals (PVRs). These methods are simple, inexpensive and add objectivity when assessing the presence and severity of LUTS. They also serve as an effective screening method before referring patients for more comprehensive and invasive urodynamic investigations.

Bladder diaries

Bladder diaries are the simplest of all urodynamic investigations and frequently form part of the initial evaluation of LUTS, particularly storage symptoms such as urinary frequency and incontinence. Bladder diaries are recorded by the patient for at least 24 hours in line with ICS recommendations, although in clinical practice a period of 3 days is preferred. A good-quality bladder diary includes information on the time and volumes of each fluid intake and voided output (measured using a graduated jug), the type of beverage consumed (e.g. coffee, tea, etc), any occurrence of urinary leakage (graded in severity from damp, wet to soaking) and waking and sleeping hours are clearly indicated; see Fig. 17.4 for an example bladder diary. Bladder diaries offer a representative and objective assessment of the presenting LUTS since the information is recorded by the patient in their daily environment whilst undertaking their typical activities and lifestyle.

A number of findings can be deduced from the bladder diary, including daytime frequency, nocturia (waking up at night to void), increased fluid intake or output, frequency of incontinence episodes, maximum voided volume during a single micturition, among other things; see Table 17.2 for a list of the common urodynamics findings in association with

For three consecutive days please record as accurately as possible the amount of fluid you drink in the **'In'** column, and the amount of urine you pass in the **'Out'** column. Measure it in **millilitres (ml).** Please also record any leakage. Indicate whether you are **D-** damp, **W-** wet or **S-** soaking.

Please mark   **A** next to the box for the **time that you get up** and
                           B next to the box for the **time that you go to bed**

An example is shown in the shaded cells.

Day 1				Day 2				Day 3			
Time	In	Out	Leak	Time	In	Out	Leak	Time	In	Out	Leak
06:20 A	Tea 250			04:30		400					
07:00		230		07:00 A		300					
12:30			W	14:30			S				
22:00 B		400		21:00 B	300						

Time	In	Out	Leak	Time	In	Out	Leak	Time	In	Out	Leak

FIG. 17.4   Example patient bladder diary.

the parameters recorded in the bladder diary. However, interpretation of the bladder diary must be approached with caution for potential sources of error by verifying the information recorded with the patient. Common sources of errors include the patient estimating their output volumes rather than measuring, use of non-SI unit and retrospective completion of the bladder diary. It is also common for bladder diaries to remain incomplete. Moreover, factors such as changes in LUT function with increasing age must also be considered. For example, nocturia of up-to once or twice is common in the elderly, as is post-micturition dribble (small volume urinary leakage shortly after a void) in older men due to pooling of urine in the bulbar urethra (horizontal section of the urethra that loses its ability to elastically recoil following a void).

Pad testing

Pad testing is a simple, non-invasive and objective method for detecting and quantifying urinary incontinence, as often the presence and severity of urinary leakage can be difficult to distinguish from the history alone. The pad test aims to determine the volume of leakage during a timed test by measuring the pad weight gain (difference in pad weight from the start and end of the test). Urine loss is measured using an absorbent pad worn over a specified period of time and activities. The volume of urine loss in millilitres (mL) equates to the pad weight gain in grams (g). The activities are designed to provoke stress and urge incontinence, for example performing vigorous coughing and hand washing respectively. Only the 1 hour pad test is standardized by the ICS (Andersen et al., 1992), see Table 17.3, although a 24 hour pad test can be performed but this is difficult to standardize outside of the clinical facility. In routine clinical practice, patients are often simply asked to collect the pads they have worn over a 24 hour period for weighing in clinic to determine any significant pad weight gain. It is not possible to determine the cause of leakage from a pad test but it provides an objective assessment of the presence and severity of leakage. A pad weight gain that is greater than 1 g and 4 g following the 1 hour and 24 hour pad test, respectively, is considered as positive indicator for urinary incontinence. Severity is graded by the volume of urine lost during a specified time (Table 17.4) (Staskin and Cardozo, 2009). Another useful clinical utility of the pad test is as an outcome measure following an intervention to treat urinary incontinence.

TABLE 17.2 Common urodynamic findings associated with bladder diaries.

Parameter measured	Urodynamic finding
Increased number of voids during waking hours	Daytime frequency
Increased number of voids during sleeping hours	Nocturia
Increased total volume of urine voided during 24 hour period	Increased 24 hour production
More than 2.8L output in 24 hours	Polyuria
Increased total output at night	Nocturnal polyuria
Increased/reduced maximum voided volume in a single micturition	Increased/reduced bladder capacity
Total number of incontinence episodes in 24 hour	Frequency of incontinence episodes

TABLE 17.3 ICS standardized 1 hour pad test.

Time interval (mins)	Activity
0–15	Drink 500 mL sodium free liquid and rest
15–45	Walking, climbing stairs (up and down one flight or equivalent)
45–60	Sit to stand 10 times Vigorous coughing 10 times Running in one place for 1 min Picking up small objects from the floor 5 times Washing hands in running water for 1 min

TABLE 17.4 Severity of incontinence assessed from a 1 hour pad test.

Grade of incontinence	1 hour test pad weight gain (mL)	24 hour test pad weight gain (mL)
Mild	<10 mL	4–20
Moderate	11–50	21–74
Severe	>50	>75

Uroflowmetry

Uroflowmetry is a simple and non-invasive investigation in the assessment of patients with LUTS and is frequently used as first line screening assessment in most patients. Uroflowmetry findings can support the diagnosis of bladder outlet obstruction (BOO) or a poorly functioning detrusor and acts as a screening tool for BOO particularly when combined with the measurement of PVRs. Uroflowmetry is performed using a flow meter, a device that measures the volume of fluid voided per unit time. This measurement is referred to as the flow rate (Q) and is expressed in millilitres per second (mL/s). The simplest and most commonly used flow meter design is gravimetric. The principle is very similar to a load-cell weighing scale. The patient performs a void into a collecting container that is placed on top of a gravimetric flow meter (Fig. 17.5). The weight of the collecting fluid is measured by the flow meter and allows for the flow rate to be calculated as the change in weight per unit time. The key information extrapolated from uroflowmetry and utilized in routine clinical practice include the maximum flow rate (Qmax), voided volume (V, determined from the mass of fluid measured where 1 g equates to 1 mL), and flow pattern (which is simply a graphical representation of the flow rate per unit time), see Fig. 17.6 for an example of the flow rate recording. All of the uroflowmetry parameters are captured during a single void and provide insight into possible underlying voiding dysfunctions.

FIG. 17.5 Typical flowmeter used to perform uroflowmetry.

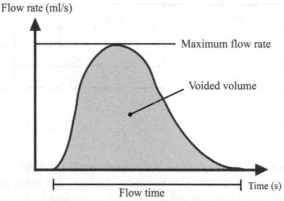

FIG. 17.6 Annotated uroflowmetry recording.

Women typically have a higher maximum flow rate than men, usually in the order of 5–10 mL/s more for a given bladder volume due to a shorter and more distensible urethra. This is because a longer and less distensible urethra in men results in an increase in the total resistance encountered by the flow of urine. Furthermore, flow rates decrease with age, whilst exaggerated maximum flow rates are typical in patients with marked DO and in women who have SUI, where the bladder outlet resistance is reduced. See Table 17.5 for a comparison in maximum flow rates between men and women.

The measured flow rate is dependent upon a number of factors including the strength of detrusor contraction, presence of BOO, function of sphincteric mechanism, patency of urethra and compensatory mechanisms such as abdominal

TABLE 17.5 Expected flow rates in men and women.

Sex	Maximum flow rate (Q_{max})
Male <40 years	>25 mL/s
Male >60 years and unobstructed	>15 mL/s
Women	>30 mL/s

straining. However, the flow rate is a composite of both the function of the detrusor and the bladder outlet or urethra. Therefore, it is impossible to distinguish the cause of voiding dysfunction using uroflowmetry alone. Only pressure-flow urodynamics can differentiate between such conditions. However, a number of characteristic uroflowmetry patterns have been described that may elude towards a particular cause of voiding dysfunction: A *normal* flow pattern is characterized by a smooth bell-shaped curve with a rapid rise to the maximum amplitude (Qmax), see Fig. 17.7A. The time to Qmax does not exceed one-third of the flow time. A normal flow pattern is associated with a normal detrusor contraction and an unobstructed bladder outlet. Any other patterns would suggest an abnormal void; a *fast bladder* is an exaggeration of the normal curve with higher peak amplitude and a faster flow time to reach the maximum amplitude (Fig. 17.7B). A *fast bladder* flow pattern is typically associated with a raised end-fill bladder pressure due to DO or may be due to a significant decrease in bladder outlet resistance in the presence of SUI; a *prolonged* flow is characterized by a flow with a prolonged time to reach Qmax and an extended flow time (Fig. 17.7C). Often the curve is asymmetric with prolonged decline in the amplitude towards the terminal end. This pattern is observed in both BOO and poor detrusor contractility; a *flat plateau* is described by a low maximum flow rate which plateaus for a prolonged time in a 'box like' fashion (Fig. 17.7D). This pattern is characteristic of a constrictive obstruction such as a urethral stricture and is typically referred to as an inelastic obstruction, seeing as the narrowing is fixed resulting in a constant flow rate for a prolonged period; an *intermittent (or irregular)* flow pattern is represented by irregular spiking along the curve which is frequently secondary to abdominal straining to overcome poor flow associated with BOO or a weak detrusor contraction (Fig. 17.7E). Sphincteric contractions can also transmit across the flow curve as sudden sharp rises in amplitude and may be contributing to the observed irregularities.

There are a number of factors and limitations to consider when interpreting uroflowmetry results. Low voided volumes of less than 100 mL lead to erroneous data due to poor repeatability of the flow rate therefore cannot be reliably interpreted. Flow meters must be calibrated to the density of fluid being voided, for example during a VCMG the flow meter would need to be calibrated to match the specific density of the contrast media instilled in the bladder. In addition, it is always important to verify with the patient if the void was typical of their normal voiding as often patients may be inhibited in the clinical space or may have adapted their typical drinking or voiding habits on the day of the assessment. A major limitation of uroflowmetry is that it is subject to artefacts especially when using the gravimetric type of flowmeter. A very common artefact occurs from accidently knocking the flow meter resulting in a sharp high amplitude spike, (Fig. 17.8). Careless interpretation from the electronically calculated values can lead to gross overestimation of the maximum flow rate. Other artefacts may also appear as irregularities in the flow pattern such as squeezing the prepuce of the penis during a void. Therefore, it is always important to verify the presence of irregularities with the patient to determine potential sources of artefacts.

Post-void residual

A simple flow rate can be used in combination with the measurement of a PVR to provide more detailed information on voiding dysfunction. The PVR is the volume of residual urine retained in the bladder following a voluntary void. A bladder is expected to be completely empty following a void in normal LUT function. Therefore, incomplete emptying is considered to be abnormal and an indication of an underlying voiding dysfunction. However, in practice, a PVR of less than 100 mL is commonly thought to be clinically insignificant. The clinical significance of an elevated PVR is also dependent on the patient's history and presenting symptoms. Commonly an elevated PVR may be associated with a poorly contractile bladder or the presence of BOO. However, the same voiding dysfunctions may present in the absence of an elevated PVR. Therefore, measurements of PVR should not be interpreted in isolation. However, patients that inadequately empty may be predisposed to recurrent urinary tract infections (UTI), may be at risk of

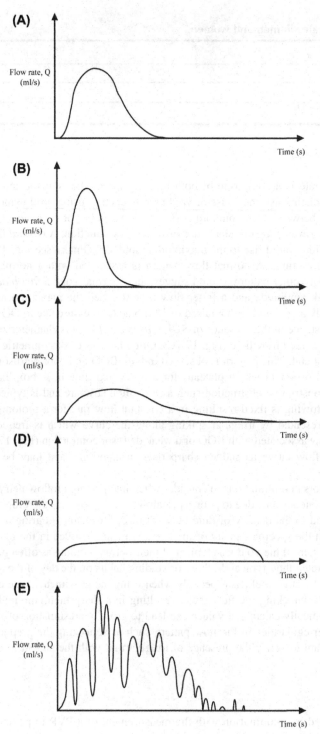

FIG. 17.7 Typical uroflowmetry patterns.

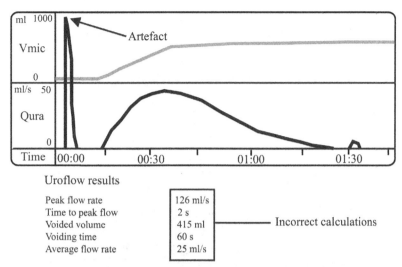

Uroflow results

Peak flow rate	126 ml/s	
Time to peak flow	2 s	
Voided volume	415 ml	Incorrect calculations
Voiding time	60 s	
Average flow rate	25 ml/s	

FIG. 17.8 Artefactual uroflowmetry trace recorded during an accidental knock.

retention, or could experience long term bladder or kidney damage. Therefore, the PVR may need to be regularly monitored or patients may be taught to perform intermittent self-catheterization to ensure the bladder is adequately emptied. The gold standard method of measuring the PVR is via urethral catheterization. However, this is an invasive method that puts the patient at risk of a UTI, discomfort and may inflict trauma to the LUT. Therefore, bladder or ultrasound scanners are routinely utilized in clinical practice to estimate the PVR. It is important to keep to a short interval between completion of a void and measurement of the PVR. This should ideally be within 5 min to estimate a representative PVR as a longer time period will result in an artefactually higher PVR measurement because the kidney's continuously produce urine.

Invasive urodynamic measurement

A pressure-flow CMG is the simultaneous measurement of bladder pressure and urine flow during both the storage and voiding phases of the bladder cycle. The aims of CMGs are to reproduce the patient's typical LUTS and determine any associations with the urodynamic findings. The technique involves the measurement of intra-vesical and intra-abdominal pressures; where the detrusor pressure can then be calculated in real time from the subtraction of the intra-abdominal pressure from the intra-vesical pressure. During a CMG the bladder is artificially filled with saline at a constant rate to simulate the storage phase and the described pressures are measured. During the storage phase there are typically five key parameters of interest: the capacity; compliance; sensations; presence of DO; and the cause of urinary incontinence. The patient is then asked to micturate with the bladder catheter in-situ to assess the pressure-flow relationship during the voiding phase. Therefore, a CMG allows for an accurate assessment of bladder and urethral function during both the storage and voiding phases. A normal bladder should relax during the storage phase and contract during voiding. Abnormal bladder function could be categorized by an overactive detrusor contraction (DO) during the storage phase and inadequate or unsustained detrusor contraction while attempting to void (underactive detrusor or acontractile detrusor). In normal urethral function the sphincter mechanism should contract to maintain continence during the storage phase and relax during the voiding phase to allow efficient micturition. Abnormal urethral function is characterised by an inadequate urethral closure pressure during the storage phase that attributes to SUI or a significantly increased urethral closure pressure during the voiding phase that obstructs voiding (resulting in BOO). A VCMG combines pressure-flow CMGs with radiological imaging when filling the bladder with contrast media. This allows for the visualization of the lower and upper urinary tracts during the storage and voiding phases. During the storage phase images are taken to assess the shape of the bladder (normal, diverticulae or trabeculated), assess the degree and type of SUI and to assess for vesico-ureteric reflux from the bladder to the kidneys. During the voiding phase images are taken to assess the urethral anatomy and to identify the cause of BOO.

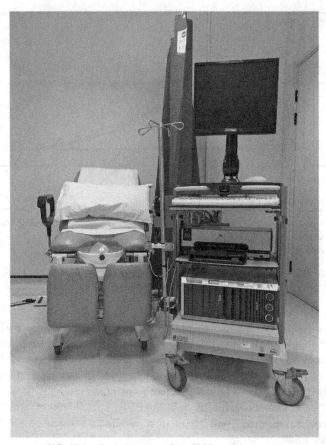

FIG. 17.9 Typical pressure-flow CMG machine set-up.

Equipment set-up

A typical pressure-flow CMG machine is shown in Fig. 17.9 and will include:

- a monitor to display the pressures and flow
- a peristaltic infusion pump for bladder filling
- external fluid filled pressure transducers to measure the intra-abdominal and intra-vesical pressures
- fluid filled catheters to measure the intra-abdominal and intra-vesical pressures. Typically, a dual lumen intra-vesical catheter is used to artificially fill the bladder and simultaneously measure the bladder pressure.
- a flowmeter and jug to measure the flow rate during the voiding phase. This can be used with a commode when seated or a funnel or cystaid when standing.

The urodynamicist must be able to correctly set-up the equipment, identify, and rectify any technical errors that may occur during the test. All equipment should have quality assurance and calibration schedule as per the manufacturer's guidelines.

External fluid filled pressure transducers deliver an accurate and easy to use measurement of pressure. The transducers are connected to an arm on the urodynamics machine to allow for a quick height adjustment of the transducers to the level of the superior edge of the symphysis pubis. The transducers are flushed with saline and zeroed to atmospheric pressure. The intra-vesical catheter is inserted into the bladder using an aseptic catheterization technique. The urethral opening is cleaned and then a sterile gel (antiseptic and local anaesthetic) is used to lubricate the urethra to insert the catheter. The catheter is then securely fixed to the patient taking care that the catheter and tape does not obstruct the urethral meatus. The intra-abdominal balloon catheter is then inserted in to the rectum using a lubricating gel. The balloon maintains a small volume of fluid around the catheter to prevent faecal blockage. The catheter lines are then connected to the transducers and directly transmit the intra-vesical and intra-abdominal pressures to the external transducers. The lines are flushed with saline, and the patient is asked to perform a cough to check for good subtraction, this should result in a rapid spike and return to baseline in both the intra-vesical and intra-abdominal pressure reading resulting in a small biphasic recording on the detrusor pressure trace. A rise or fall in the detrusor pressure would suggest that one of the intra-vesical and intra-abdominal pressure is damped. Care must be taken to ensure that there are no air bubbles in the fluid filled system. An air bubble will result in a reduced amplitude pressure wave being transmitted to the transducer and damping the signal. If there is poor cough subtraction the system can be flushed with saline to rectify. The urodynamicist must then check that the intra-vesical and intra-abdominal pressure readings are within the expected range (5–50 cm H_2O depending on patient position and body habitus) prior to starting the filling phase. Since the detrusor pressure is calculated from the subtraction of the intra-abdominal pressure from the intra-vesical pressure Pdet should be within ± 5 cm H_2O and ideally zero. If the pressures were outside this range it suggests there is a technical fault with the setup, the lines should be flushed, and all the connections checked to ensure there are no fluid leaks.

Performing a CMG

Clear communication between the urodynamicist and the patient is fundamental to a diagnostically successful CMG. This starts when the patient first enters the room and the urodynamicist takes a urodynamic history to fully understand the patient's main bladder symptoms and clearly explain the intimate and invasive test procedure to the patient. It is also a good opportunity to determine if the patient associates a specific activity with their urinary symptoms or incontinence, e.g. leaking on coughs or from a sudden urgency to void. This helps the urodynamicist formulate the main urodynamic question and tailor the test accordingly. The urodynamicist should then explain the aseptic catheterization technique to the patient and ensure they consent to proceed with the test.

The patient is asked to perform a uroflowmetry and empty their bladder to completion prior to starting the CMG. This allows the urodynamicist to obtain free-flow voiding information and perform a urinalysis test to ensure the patient is not showing any signs of a urine infection. Typically, if the urine test were positive for nitrites, the test would be postponed until a full urine culture can be performed and the urine infection is treated with an antibiotic. However, if the patient performs intermittent self-catheterization and is asymptomatic of a urine infection, the test can be performed under an injected antibiotic prophylaxis if nitrites were seen in the urine sample. A pressure-flow CMG is only performed after the urodynamicist has confirmed that the patient does not have any signs of a urine infection and the equipment is set-up correctly with good quality subtraction. Prior to the start of a standard CMG a bladder scan or intermittent catheterization would then be performed to make a subjective assessment of an initial PVR. During a VCMG an image is taken after filling the bladder with approximately 25 mL of contrast media to make an estimate of an initial PVR. The CMG is performed in two stages and allows the urodynamicist to assess the bladder and urethral function during the storage and voiding phases. The storage phase will begin once the infusion pump is turned on and ends once maximum cystometric capacity has been achieved and the urodynamicist has given the patient *permission to void*. The voiding phase commences once the patient is given *permission to void* and finishes once the patient has decided they have sufficiently emptied their bladder.

The urodynamicist starts recording and asks the patient to cough so that good quality subtraction is demonstrated at the start of the CMG and this is typically repeated at every 100 mL fill. The pump is then started at a predefined rate depending on the patient's history or neurological pathology. The ICS recommend that a *slow filling rate* of 10 mL/min is used for neurological patients, however, in practice many centres fill neurological patients between 20 and 40 mL/min due to the time pressures on the clinics. If the patient has early onset DO the filling rate is then reduced to try and attain a more accurate assessment of cystometric capacity. The majority of CMGs are performed with a *medium-filling rate* between 10 and 100 mL/min. The patient must be informed to inhibit voiding during the storage phase and inform the urodynamicist of any bladder sensation or onset of urgency or pain. If the patient experiences pain or is unable to suppress the bladder urgency, the storage phase is ended and the test moves on to the voiding phase when the patient is given permission to void. The urodynamicist must take care to mark any abnormal bladder sensations accurately on the urodynamics trace so they can be accurately associated with the bladder urodynamics and to mark when the voiding command was given for a clear distinction between the storage and voiding phases.

Filling cystometry

During a pressure-flow CMG, the patient should typically have a strong and persistent desire to void at a bladder capacity of approximately 500 mL. Bladder capacity is defined by the *maximum cystometric capacity* in patients with normal sensations, this is the volume at which the patient feels they can no longer delay micturition due to a strong and persistent desire to void. However, in patients who have abnormal sensations the *cystometric capacity* should be recorded along with the factors limiting the capacity and contributing to the abnormal sensations e.g. reduced capacity due to early sensations or DO; or filling phase stopped due to high volume infused (>500 mL) prior to the patient developing a strong and persistent desire to void (owing to either a reduced or absent bladder sensation).

As previously described, bladder compliance is the intrinsic ability of the bladder to change in volume without any substantial alteration in detrusor pressure. Therefore, a bladder can be compliant or poorly (reduced) compliant. After ensuring the pressures readings have adequate cancellation an initial baseline detrusor pressure can be recorded prior to filing the bladder. The bladder compliance can then be calculated by taking a second detrusor pressure reading after filling the bladder up to 400 mL. The detrusor pressure readings must be taken in the absence of an involuntary detrusor contraction (DO) or before leaking, as this would give a false reading of reduced compliance. Compliance can also be artefactually high due to the fast pump filling rate used during CMGs. Therefore, to confirm a poorly compliant bladder the pump should be stopped; if the detrusor pressure reduces then it is a non-physiological filling rate artefact; if the detrusor pressure remains the same it is a true measurement of a poorly compliant bladder; if the detrusor pressure were to continue to increase after stopping the pump this is likely DO and not a true loss of compliance.

Bladder sensations can be difficult to interpret as they are a subjective measure and the patient's awareness of their bladder is likely to be heightened during the CMG which may result in much earlier sensations than during their normal day-to-day life. The patient is asked to inform the urodynamicist about the sensations relating to their bladder fullness so they can be recorded on the trace. The ICS defines *first sensation* as the bladder fill volume when the patient first becomes aware of bladder filling; *first desire* as the bladder fill volume when the patient would pass urine at the next convenient moment, but voiding can be delayed if necessary; *strong desire* as the bladder fill volume when the patient has a strong and persistent desire to void without the fear of leaking; and *maximum cystometric capacity* as the bladder fill volume when the patient feels they can no longer delay micturition. Urgency is the sudden compelling desire to void that is difficult to delay. The patient should not feel any bladder pain during filling and if this occurs the bladder fill volume and exact site of the pain should be recorded on the trace. This allows the urodynamicist to make a subjective assessment of the patients typical bladder sensation during filling: *normal sensations* would indicate the patient has reached a strong and persistent desire to void at end-fill; *absent sensations* would indicate the patient has demonstrated no bladder sensations throughout filling; *reduced sensations* would indicate the patient has demonstrated some sensation of bladder filling but did not reach a strong and persistent desire to void at the end of the filling phase; and *early sensations* would indicate the patient has a persistent early desire to void which occurs at low bladder volumes.

The bladder should remain relaxed with little or no change in detrusor pressure during the storage phase and any involuntary detrusor contraction is abnormal. An involuntary detrusor contraction is referred to as DO and it is important for the urodynamicist to confirm and mark on the trace if the DO is associated with any urgency or leakage. The bladder volume at which DO first occurred should be recorded along with the peak detrusor pressure and if it was associated with an urge urinary incontinence (UUI). DO can be *spontaneous* or *provoked* (i.e. followed by coughing, hand washing and during postural changes); *phasic DO* is seen as repeated waves of involuntary detrusor contractions; *terminal DO* is a sustained involuntary detrusor contraction at cystometric capacity that the patient is unable to suppress and results in incontinence or voiding. If the patient has an underlying neurological condition then an involuntary detrusor contraction is known as *neurogenic* DO; when there is no underlying cause an involuntary detrusor contraction is known as *idiopathic* DO.

If a patient demonstrates terminal DO and is unable to suppress the detrusor contraction it is not possible to use this DO leak to accurately assess the voiding pressure-flow relationship and should be reported as the patient voided using DO pressure. High pressure terminal DO may incorrectly be suggestive of BOO and could lead to an incorrect diagnosis of obstructed voiding in addition to DO. Therefore, the patient should be refilled so that the voiding phase can be accurately assessed prior to the onset of terminal DO.

Case study 17.1

A 74-year-old male with multiple sclerosis presented with over-active bladder symptoms including frequency, urgency, nocturia and UUI (4 incontinence pads per day). The patient was initially treated with tablets designed to inhibit the symptoms of an overactive bladder but had reported no symptomatic benefit. Therefore, a CMG was performed and demonstrated that the patient had a reduced 165 mL capacity bladder limited by high-pressure terminal DO (peak pressure of 95 cm H_2O) and severe UUI that repeatedly emptied his bladder to completion despite

multiple attempts to refill. The patient was treated for UUI by injecting his bladder with Botulinum toxin (Botox) since conservative medical therapy had failed in the first instance. Botox is a chemical that causes muscle paralysis by inhibiting the release of the neurotransmitter acetylcholine from nerve fibres. When the effect of the Botox wears off the injection can be repeated, usually within 6–12 months.

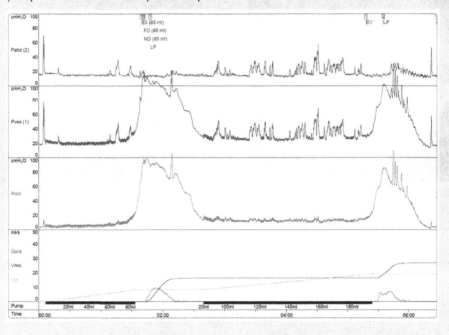

The normal urethra closure mechanism should remain competent in the presence of increased abdominal pressure (e.g. during a cough or Valsalva manoeuvre) during the storage phase to maintain continence. Urodynamic stress incontinence is the involuntary leakage of urine with increased abdominal pressure in the absence of an involuntary detrusor contraction. During the pressure-flow CMG the patient is asked to increase their intra-abdominal pressure by coughing or performing a Valsalva manoeuvre (an attempt to forcefully exhale against a closed airway — a closed mouth and nose) and leakage can be detected on the flowmeter. When performing a stress test during a VCMG, both the leakage of contrast along the urethra and the degree of urethral hypermobility can be visualized and assessed. During the storage phase it is also possible to use radiographic imaging to visualize the size and position of the bladder and to assess other bladder abnormalities including cystocele, diverticulae and vesicoureteric reflux (see Fig. 17.10).

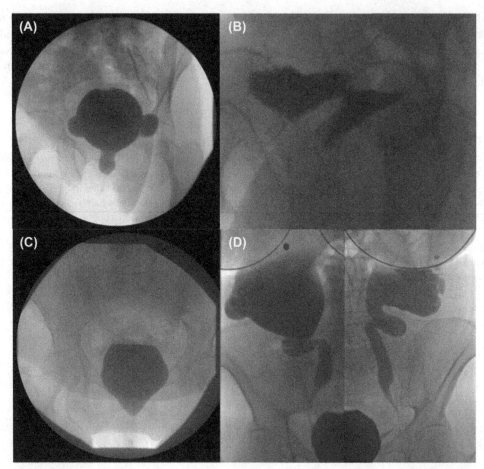

FIG. 17.10 Fluoroscopic imaging of the upper and lower urinary tract: (A) hutch diverticulum and urethral stricture on voiding; (B) vesicovaginal fistula; (C) cystocele; and (D) vesicoureteric reflux.

Case study 17.2

A 60 year old female presented with bladder symptoms including frequency, urgency and urinary incontinence. The VCMG demonstrated that the patient had a normal 525 mL capacity bladder with normal compliance, normal bladder sensations and no DO. The bladder base was positioned above the inferior border of the pubis symphysis on standing with significant hypermobility and leaks on coughs demonstrating SUI (2 mL leaked). The patient then had an unobstructed void to completion. The patient was treated for SUI surgically with an autologous fascial sling procedure. An autologous fascial sling procedure positions a sling underneath the urethra using a strip of the patients own tissue (fascia) taken from the wall of their abdomen to help reduce the degree of urethral hypermobility and subsequent SUI.

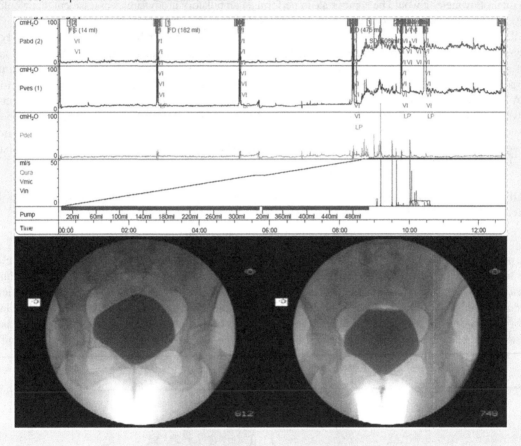

Voiding cystometry

A voiding study starts as soon as the urodynamicist has given the patient permission to void. During a conventional CMG the patient should be allowed to void in private to help minimize the effect of being asked to void in an unfamiliar or embarrassing environment. A limiting factor of a VCMG is that the void has to be performed within the fluoroscopy suite in front of the urodynamicist to acquire voiding images. Patients may feel inhibited and unable to void in front of the urodynamicist. Therefore, the voiding phase may be performed in private without any voiding images recorded. If the VCMG is performed in a conventional fluoroscopy suite, a female patient should be asked to attempt to void when standing using a cystaid (she-wee). However, this is not a natural voiding position for females and if the patient cannot void when standing the patient should be transferred to the commode to void in sitting. Any females who demonstrate an obstructed pressure-flow relationship when standing, but do not demonstrate any evidence of BOO on imaging, should be refilled and have the voiding study repeated with the patient sitting on the commode. Some females have a significant contribution from pelvic floor relaxation when voiding and standing inhibits this natural pelvic floor relaxation mechanism.

During voiding the detrusor muscle should voluntarily contract in a single smooth contraction to completely empty the bladder in an acceptable time span. High detrusor pressures can be encountered in patients with BOO as the bladder works harder to maintain a sufficient flow rate in the presence of increased outlet resistance. The detrusor muscle may also become underactive and is defined by the ICS as a contraction of reduced strength and/or duration, resulting in the prolonged bladder emptying and/or the failure to achieve complete bladder emptying within the normal time span. While this may result in a PVR, it would have to be associated with a patient being symptomatic of recurrent urine infections for the patient to require urological management. In other cases, the detrusor muscle can become acontractile where the patient does not demonstrate any contractility during the voiding study and is either unable to void or achieves voiding purely by abdominal straining. If the urodynamicist is concerned the patient is inhibited under the test conditions and has demonstrated a smooth void to completion on uroflowmetry it would be appropriate to perform an ambulatory urodynamics assessment that would allow the pressure-flow relationship to be recorded in private as discussed later in the chapter.

During the voiding phase the urethra should relax and remain open to allow the bladder to efficiently empty at normal detrusor pressures. The urethra may become obstructed from an anatomical obstruction such as a stricture or an enlarged prostate (in men). The urethra can also become obstructed due to a functional obstruction; this is where the urethra becomes overactive and fails to relax adequately to allow adequate voiding in pathologies such as a high tone non-relaxing sphincter. A conventional CMG allows the urodynamicist to accurately assess the degree of outlet obstruction and when combined with imaging during a VCMG the exact anatomical location of the outlet obstruction can be identified. BOO is used to describe an obstructed void from the pressure-flow relationship measured during the voiding phase. In males, an obstructed void can be calculated from the using the Bladder Outlet Obstruction Index (BOOI) nomogram (Abrams, 1999):

$$P_{det}Q_{max} - 2Q_{max} = BOOI$$

where BOOI < 20 is unobstructed; 20 < BOOI < 40 is equivocally obstructed; and BOOI > 40 is obstructed. In females an obstructed void can be calculated from the Solomon-Greenwell nomogram (Solomon et al., 2018):

$$P_{det}Q_{max} > 2.2Q_{max} + 5 = BOO$$

When a pressure-flow void is combined with imaging during a VCMG it allows the urodynamicist to visually identify the precise location of the outlet obstruction. It also allows for the identification for urethral anatomical abnormalities such as stricture, urethral diverticulum or fistulas. In males, a stop-test is performed by asking the patient to stop voiding suddenly mid-void. In the absence of bladder neck obstruction, contrast should milk back into the bladder from the posterior urethra soon after cessation of flow. When the bladder neck is obstructive, contrast cannot milk back, and is trapped between the bladder neck and the external sphincter. This has a characteristic appearance as shown in Fig. 17.11.

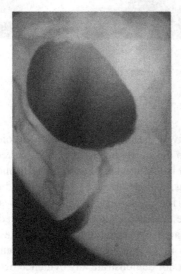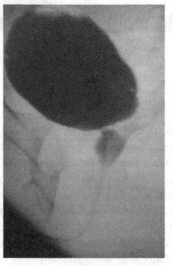

FIG. 17.11   Whiteside trapping stop test showing contrast trapped between the bladder neck and the external sphincter.

Case study 17.3

A 67 year-old male presented with refractory overactive bladder symptoms including frequency, urgency and nocturia. The patient denied any voiding dysfunction. The VCMG demonstrated that the patient had a normal 439 mL capacity bladder with normal compliance and bladder sensations on filling. No DO or SUI was demonstrated. However, upon attempting to void the patient was able to generate a sustained detrusor contraction between 60 and 70 cm H_2O but was unable to void until after the intra-vesical catheter was removed (arrow on image A). After removing the catheter the patient was able to void to completion with a flat-plateau flow pattern (Q_{max} 11 mL/s). After reviewing the voiding images, it was possible to determine the most likely cause of BOO was a meatal stricture (arrow on image B). This was treated surgically with a urethrotomy (incision of the urethral stricture) and then the patient was able to void with improved flow rates.

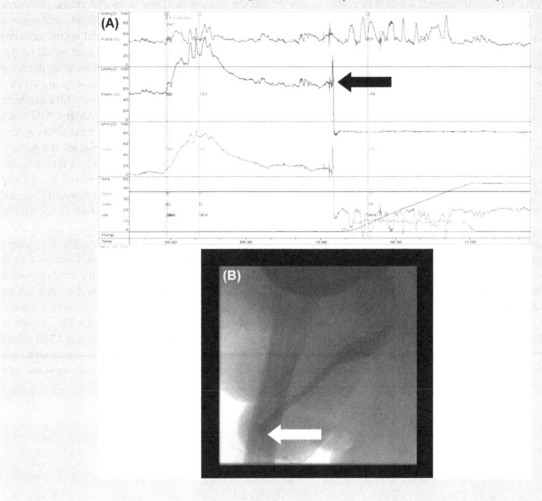

Ambulatory urodynamic measurement

An ambulatory (AMB) CMG is recognized as second stage investigation in patients with LUTS who have had an inconclusive conventional assessment (CMG or VCMG). The main advantage with AMB CMG is that it allows for orthograde (natural) filling of the bladder via the kidneys. After placing the catheters in the bladder and rectum the patient is able to get dressed, leave the clinic room and actively perform activities that the patient believes trigger their urinary symptoms, whilst the pressure readings are recorded by a portable data capture device that the patient carries with them. An AMB CMG has an increased diagnostic accuracy for detecting DO. However, there are some disadvantages. AMB CMG is an expensive time-consuming test that requires specialized equipment and a highly trained urodynamicist to perform and interpret the test. AMB CMG has also been associated with a high rate of abnormal detrusor contractions in asymptomatic controls. While SUI is typically better elucidated on VCMGs, there are cases where some complex patients may still require an AMB CMG to fully understand their urinary symptoms.

The patient is catheterized using the aseptic technique as previously described with a single channel fluid-filled catheter positioned in the bladder and a second balloon catheter placed in the rectum. The patient is asked to dress and a portable data capture device is worn similar to a side-bag. Disposable pressure transducers are connected to a belt positioned level with the bladder around the patient's waist. The transducers are zeroed, connected to the pressure lines, and then primed with saline. The patient is asked to cough to ensure that the intra-vesical and intra-abdominal pressures have good subtraction and accurately measure detrusor pressure. If the patient has presented with incontinence a conductance leak pad sensor can be placed in the patient's underwear (covering the urethral meatus) and is connected to the data capture device (when the leak pad detects fluid across the wires it creates an electrical conductance signal on the AMB CMG recording). This allows the urodynamicist to determine if the leak corresponds to an increase in detrusor pressure (DO) or to an increase in abdominal pressure (walking, coughing or sneezing). The data capture device connects to the CMG machine and flowmeter by bluetooth to record voiding and transfer the data to the CMG machine for review and analysis. The data capture device has a button that the patient can press to mark the AMB CMG trace with their typical urgency symptoms, if they feel they have leaked and a micturition button to connect the data capture device to the flow meter to record the uroflowmetry parameters in sync with the pressure readings. Before the patient leaves the clinic room the urodynamicist must confirm that the patient understands and can follow the test instructions. The patient's symptoms are directly compared to the test recording so it is essential that the patient accurately marks any urge or leaks, so that the symptoms can be directly compared to the data recordings. The patient is informed to drink approx. 1 L of fluid in the first hour and to drink diuretics (tea or coffee) if these are known to worsen their urinary symptoms.

The patient is asked to return to the clinic room ideally every hour so that the urodynamicist can ensure that the system is recording pressures accurately and to check the cough subtraction, if they feel one of the catheters has fallen out, or if they need to empty their bowels so that the rectal catheter can be replaced. During the hourly reviews, the urodynamicist must ensure that the pressure signals are recording correctly with adequate cough subtraction (if required the lines can be flushed with saline). An hourly review reduces the likelihood of an extended period where data is not accurately recorded and prevents the test from having to be excessively extended. The urodynamicist can also check that the patient is accurately recording their symptoms so that they can be correctly attributed to the urodynamic recordings. An AMB CMG test is typically performed over two to four hours, but the hourly review allows a test to be terminated early if a urodynamic diagnosis can be associated with the patient's typical symptoms; or if the patient is finding the test too tiresome and distressing.

Case study 17.4

A 30 year old female presented with refractory overactive bladder symptoms including frequency, urgency, nocturia and UUI. A VCMG was performed and demonstrated that the patient had a normal 439 mL capacity bladder with normal compliance and urgency in the absence of DO. The VCMG result suggested a diagnosis of sensory urgency and did not reproduce the patient's typical incontinence symptoms. Therefore, an AMB CMG was performed. Whilst the study confirmed that the patient's typical urgency symptoms were demonstrated prior to the onset of DO, DO was demonstrated (peak pressure of 28 cm H_2O) and was associated with UUI (21.5 mL leaked in total over multiple small leaks). Therefore, the AMB CMG resulted in a change in the patient's diagnosis from sensory urgency to DO and UUI that now matched the patient's typical incontinence symptoms. The DO and UUI was treated by injecting the patient's bladder with Botulinum toxin (Botox). Botox is a chemical that causes muscle paralysis by inhibiting the release of the neurotransmitter acetylcholine from nerve fibres. When the effect of the Botox wears off the injections can be repeated usually within 6–12 months.

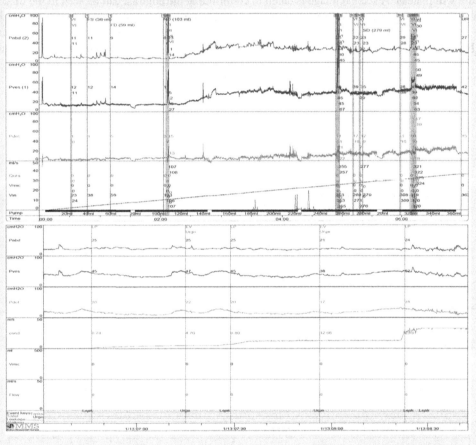

Urethral function measurement

The maintenance of continence requires the urethral pressure to exceed that of the intra-vesical pressure at all times except during micturition. Urethral function tests are used to determine the competence of the urethral sphincter in both men and women. A Retrograde Leak Point Pressure (RLPP) test is used to determine external sphincter closure pressure in men and a low RLPP suggests a sphincter weakness (often seen post-prostatectomy). A urethral pressure profilometry measures the intra-luminal pressure along the urethra to determine the urethral pressure profile (UPP) in men and women. An elevated UPP would suggest a high tone non-relaxing sphincter, however, this would be confirmed with a sphincter electromyography (EMG).

Retrograde leak point pressure test

A RLPP test measures the pressure of the urethral sphincter mechanism in men. The test is performed in the fluoroscopy suite where images are taken to confirm fluid has leaked from the urethra into the bladder. The patient is catheterized using an aseptic technique with a dual lumen catheter positioned in the bulbar urethra. The pressure transducer is zeroed, connected to the pressure line, and then primed with saline. The filling line is connected to the catheter, and then primed with contrast (typically Urografin or Omnipaque). An inflatable cuff is placed around the penile urethra to clamp the urethra and prevent urine flow out the meatus. Liquid is slowly (5 mL/min) infused into the bulbar urethra while simultaneously measuring the intra-urethral pressure. An image is taken to ensure the catheter is correctly positioned in the urethra and to confirm no contrast can be seen in the bladder. The infused liquid is trapped between the sphincter mechanism and the penile cuff. Therefore, as the bulbar urethra fills, the pressure inside the urethra increases. Eventually the pressure in the bulbar urethra will exceed the sphincter pressure, the liquid will "leak" into the bladder and the measured pressure will plateau. A second image is taken to confirm that the contrast can be seen in the bladder. The cuff is released to measure the resting urethral pressure and then the dual lumen catheter is removed from the urethra and held at the level of the superior edge of the symphysis pubis to measure the baseline bladder pressure. The RLPP is calculated by subtracting the baseline bladder pressure from the plateau pressure (see Fig. 17.12). Normal sphincter pressure in men is 75 ± 5 cm H_2O.

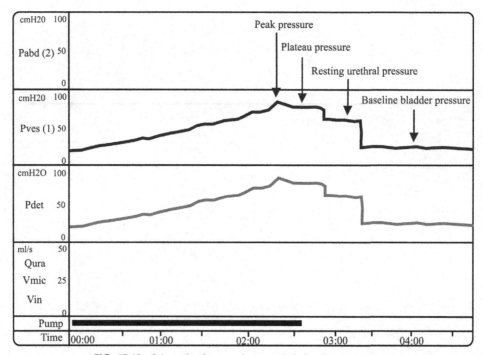

FIG. 17.12 Schematic of a normal retrograde leak point pressure test.

Case study 17.5

A 63 year old male presented with post prostatectomy incontinence following a radical prostatectomy for the treatment of prostate cancer. A RLPP test was performed and demonstrated the patient had sphincter weakness with a leak pressure of 29 cm H_2O, expected 70. This was treated surgically with an artificial urinary sphincter (AUS). An AUS is an implantable device to treat stress urinary incontinence in men. The AUS consists of a small cuff which is positioned around the urethra to supplement the function of the natural urinary sphincter and restricts urine flow out of the bladder.

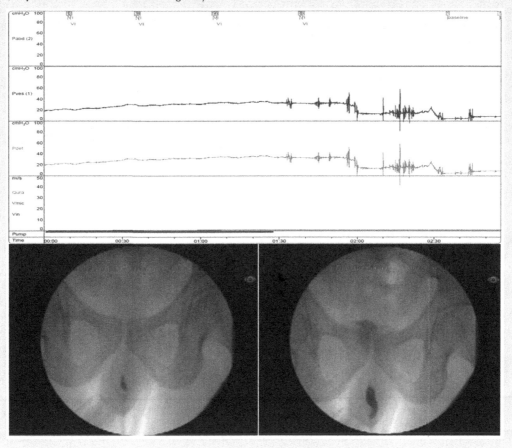

Urethral pressure profilometry

The intra-luminal pressure is measured along the length of the urethra to determine the UPP. The patient is catheterized using an aseptic technique and an 8 F dual lumen UPP catheter is positioned in the bladder. The pressure transducers are zeroed, connected to the intra-vesical and intra-urethral pressure lines, and primed with saline. The infusion pump is started (2-10 mL/m) and a cough test is performed to ensure that the pressure signals are recording correctly with adequate cough subtraction. The catheter is then withdrawn at constant speed (2-10 mm/s) to measure the UPP (Fig. 17.13). The resulting profile represents the fluid pressure required to open the urethra from the bladder neck to the meatus. The urethral closure pressure profile is calculated from the subtraction of the intra-vesical pressure from the urethral pressure (Fig. 17.14). The maximum urethral pressure is the peak pressure measured. The maximal urethral closure pressure (MUCP) is calculated by subtracting the intra-vesical pressure from the maximal urethral pressure. A normal MUCP can be calculated from subtracting the patient's age from a constant value of 92 (i.e. MUCP = 92 − patient's age) (Edwards and Malvern, 1974).

Case study 17.6

A 31 year-old female presented with bladder symptoms including frequency, urgency, nocturia, incomplete emptying and urethral pain. The VCMG demonstrated that the patient had a normal 492 mL capacity bladder with normal compliance and sensations on filling. No DO or SUI was demonstrated. However, the patient had an obstructed 417 mL void ($Q_{max} = 13$ mL/s; P_{det} at $Q_{max} = 48$ cm H_2O) with a prolonged flow pattern and a 75 mL post void residual. Radiographic narrowing was seen at the mid-urethra. A urethral pressure profile test was performed and demonstrated that the patient had a raised MUCP of 116 cm H_2O (expected 61) and was likely to be the cause of the patient's BOO. The patient's voiding dysfunction (raised MUCP) was treated with a sacral neuromodulator. This is a procedure where a small device is implanted in the buttock and attached to an electrode to stimulate the sacral nerves in an attempt to manage urinary dysfunction.

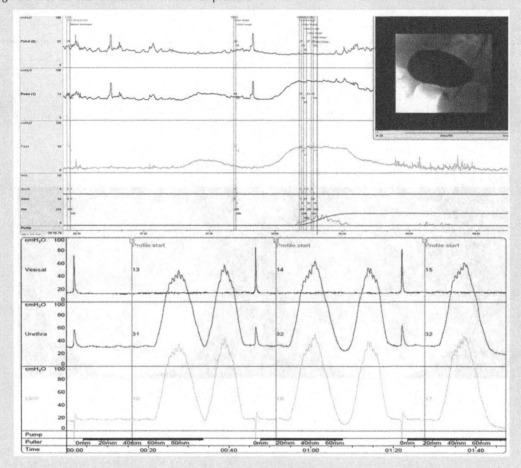

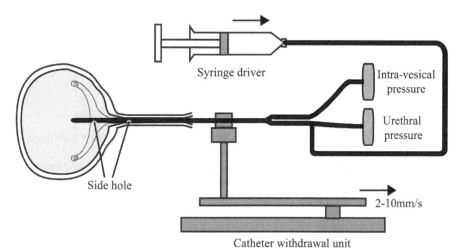

FIG. 17.13 Equipment set-up for a urethral pressure profilometry test.

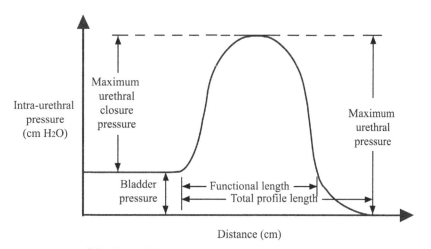

FIG. 17.14 Schematic of a normal urethral pressure profile.

Abbreviations

AMB Ambulatory
BOO Bladder Outlet Obstruction
BOOI Bladder Outlet Obstruction Index
CMG Cystometrogram
DO Detrusor Overactivity
ICS International Continence Society
LUT Lower Urinary Tract
LUTS Lower Urinary Tract Symptoms
MUCP Maximal Urethral Closure Pressure
PAG Periaquaductal Gray
PMC Pontine Micturition Centre
PVRs Post-Void Residuals
Q Urine Flow Rate
Q_{max} Maximum Urine Flow Rate
RLPP Retrograde Leak Point Pressure

SUI Stress Urinary Incontinence
UPP Urethral Pressure Profile
UTI Urinary Tract Infection
UUI Urge Urinary Incontinence
VCMG Video-Cystometrogram

References

Abrams, P., 1999. Bladder outlet obstruction index, bladder contractility index and bladder voiding efficiency: three simple indices to define bladder voiding function. BJU Int. 84, 14—15.

Andersen, J.T., Blaivas, J.G., Cardozo, L., Thuroff, J., 1992. Seventh report on the standardisation of terminology of lower urinary tract function: lower urinary tract rehabilitation techniques. Scand. J. Urol. Nephrol. 26, 99—106.

Edwards, L., Malvern, J., 1974. The urethral pressure profile: theoretical considerations and clinical application. Br. J. Urol. 46, 325—335.

Rosier, P., Schaefer, W., Lose, G., Goldman, H.B., Guralnick, M., Eustice, S., Dickinson, T., Hashim, H., 2017. International continence society good urodynamic practices and terms 2016: urodynamics, uroflowmetry, cystometry, and pressure-flow study. Neurourol. Urodyn. 36, 1243—1260.

Solomon, E., Yasmin, H., Duffy, M., Rashid, T., Akinluyi, E., Greenwell, T.J., 2018. Developing and validating a new nomogram for diagnosing bladder outlet obstruction in women. Neurourol. Urodyn. 37, 368—378.

Staskin, D.R., Cardozo, L., 2009. Baseline incontinence severity is predictive of the percentage of patients continent after receiving once-daily trospium chloride extended release. Int. J. Clin. Pract. 63, 973—976.

Further reading

Abrams, P., 2006. Urodynamics. Springer, London.

Chapple, C.R., Macdiarmid, S.A., Patel, A., 2009. Urodynamics Made Easy. Churchill Livingstone, New York.

Kaisary, A.V.A., Ballaro, A.A., Pigott, K.A., Blandy, J.P. Urology: Lecture Notes, 2016, Wiley-Blackwell, New Jersey.

Chapter 18

Neurological measurement

Christine Denby[a] and Thomas Stone[b]

[a]Royal Liverpool University Hospital NHS Foundation Trust, Liverpool, United Kingdom; [b]Cambridge University Hospitals NHS Foundation Trust, Cambridge, United Kingdom

Chapter outline

Introduction

Clinical neurophysiology is a medical speciality that examines the function of the nervous system through the recording of bioelectrical activity. This activity can be either spontaneous or stimulated. Evaluation can be at a cellular level, in which electrical signal generation and propagation in single cells and cellular networks are examined, or larger systems, such as the central and peripheral nervous system (CNS and PNS respectively). Clinical neurophysiology enables the study of the pathophysiology of the nervous system, and serves as a tool for the diagnosis of CNS and PNS diseases. Tests that are conducted are concerned with measuring the electrical functions of the brain, spinal cord, nerves, muscles and limbs. This chapter describes the clinical neurophysiological techniques used to examine the CNS and PNS. Typical Electromyography (EMG) measurement techniques are introduced, including nerve conduction studies and kinematic EMG. The chapter then goes on to explore how electroencephalography (EEG) measurements are used to monitor cerebral potentials, using ambulatory EEG recordings, invasive EEG and EEG combined with fMRI (Functional Magnetic Resonance Imaging).

Furthermore, it discusses how Sensory Evoked Potentials (SEP), Brainstem Auditory Evoked Potentials (BAEP) and Short Latency Somatosensory Evoked Potentials (SSEPs) allow an analysis of the structures in the midbrain and PNS. Finally the role of how SSEPs for intra-operative spinal monitoring is covered.

Anatomy and physiology of the nervous system

The Nervous System is a network of specialized cells for receiving, integrating and transmitting information. Systems have groups of nerve fibres running in a common direction or tract, and are surrounded by myelin sheaths, providing the characteristic appearance of white matter. The grey matter is comprized of neuronal cell bodies. In addition to neuronal cells, glial cells are also present in the nervous system and are more numerous ($5\times$) than the neuronal cells, occupying approximately 50% of the brain volume.

Clinical Engineering. https://doi.org/10.1016/B978-0-08-102694-6.00018-8

Neurons are specialized cells for transmitting signals, with each neuron consisting of a cell body, an axon, dendrites and synaptic terminals. The dendrites receive signals from other cells and the axons conduct signals from the cell body to distant targets, with the synaptic terminals transmitting signals to nearby cells.

The cerebral cortex is composed of two hemispheres, and both are involved in analyzing sensory data, performing memory functions, learning new information, making decisions and being involved in the thought process. The left hemisphere is primarily involved in sequential analysis, logic, language, mathematics, abstraction and reasoning; whereas the right hemisphere simultaneously processes multi-sensory input, and visual spatial skills. There are 4 lobes of the brain, each having specific functions. The frontal lobe comprises anterior and posterior regions. The anterior region, known as the pre-frontal cortex, is important for higher cognitive function and for determining personality and behaviour, with the posterior frontal lobe comprizing the pre-motor and motor areas. The temporal lobe is bilaterally located and situated beneath the temples. This region of the cortex is associated with auditory reception and association areas, expressed behaviour, language, learning, speech, memory, information retrieval and emotion. The parietal lobe is located behind the frontal lobes and above the temporal lobes and is concerned with processing nerve impulses (e.g. touch, pain, taste, pressure and temperature) and language function. The occipital lobe is the most posterior cortex, and is involved in object recognition and processing visual information. Any damage to the primary visual cortex produces vision loss opposite to the side of the damage.

The nervous system contains excitable cells, which can be stimulated to produce and respond to electrical signals (e.g. muscle cells, neurons, heart, secretory cells). The change in electrical potential associated with an impulse passing along nerve or muscle cell membranes is known as an action potential. Action potentials occur in all excitable cells. To facilitate the generation and propagation of electrical signals, the cell requires a membrane complex for the facilitation of ionic diffusion across biological membranes. Large polypeptides in the membrane complex contain hydrophobic (water hating) membrane-spanning domains, which are selectively permeable to sodium (Na^+), potassium (K^+), calcium (Ca^{2+}), and chloride (Cl^-); and can be opened by chemicals/neurotransmitters, voltage, or temperature. The Na^+ and K^+ ions move back and forth through the channels via Na^+/K^+ pumps on the membrane. The charge of the ion inhibits membrane permeability. All cells have a resting potential, which is the electrical charge across the plasma membrane, having a negative cell interior with respect to the exterior (charge separation across the membrane). The resting membrane potential is approximately -70 mV.

Action potentials are generated when a stimulus causes the cell membrane to depolarize past a threshold (usually -55 mV). The voltage gated Na^+ channels open allowing Na^+ on the outside of the membrane to rush into the cell and the neuron is depolarized (cell membrane becomes positively charged inside and negatively charged outside). Further depolarization follows (up to approximately $+30$ to $+50$ mV). After the membrane becomes flooded with Na^+, the gated ion channels on the inside of the membrane open to allow K^+ to move outside of the membrane. The Na^+ channels close (to stop inflowing positive charge). The K^+ channels open. As the K^+ moves outside the membrane, repolarization restores the electrical balance. Following this process, hyperpolarization occurs, with more K^+ ions being outside compared with Na^+ inside. This causes the membrane potential to drop slightly lower than the resting potential. After the impulse has travelled through the neuron the action potential is over, and the resting potential is resumed.

The refractory period enables K^+ to return inside and Na^+ to return to the outside of the cell. Whilst everything is returning to normal, the neuron cannot respond to any incoming stimuli. Once the polarized state has been achieved, the neuron stays polarized until another impulse arrives.

Electromyography

Electromyography (EMG) measures the activity of the nervous system as it manifests during the contraction of skeletal muscles. Movements, voluntary or reflex, originating in the brain or spinal cord will, in the absence of impairment, result in the depolarization of a peripheral nerve which in turn will activate skeletal muscles. The biochemical process by which a muscle contracts results in an electrical field that can be measured either intramuscularly or from the surface of the skin.

The electrical signal measured during electromyography originates from the depolarization of the sarcolemma, a gated plasma membrane that responds to the release of the neurotransmitter acetylcholine across the synaptic cleft, the gap between the muscle fibre membrane and the nerve that innervates it.

The muscle or fascia is formed of many muscle fibres or fascicles, which are formed of many myofibrils, a series of contractile elements connected end-to-end. Muscle fibres are innervated by efferent motor nerves. These are distinct from the sensory or afferent nerves that are also present, which originate within the grey matter ventral horn of the spinal cord and are contiguous with the alpha motor neuron – an all-or-nothing trigger that summates the huge number of inhibitive and excitatory inputs from the spinal and supraspinal centres. The alpha motor neuron, the nerve, and the muscle fibre it innervates are termed the motor unit. This is an important insight into the complexity of the electromyographic signal because any fascia, or collection of fascicles, may have many motor units and many fibre innervations. Therefore, many moving electrical fields generated by, almost certainly, phasically dissimilar and geographically distributed sources form any single electromyography signal. This can be expressed by the principle of superposition:

$$F(x_1 + x_2 + x_3 + \cdots + x_n) = F(x_1) + F(x_2) + F(x_3) + \cdots + F(x_n)$$

An EMG can be measured using essentially two different types of electrode: in-dwelling and surface. Whereas a fine wire or needle electrode will be influenced by only a small number of motor units, possibly only one, the surface electrode will capture the resultant electrical field from the multitude of motor units that make up any one muscle. Thus one technique is very selective, reflecting localized activity, and the other provides a generic view of the various muscle types within the heterogeneous muscle.

Electrode construction

Electrodes are used to transduce the electrical energy within the muscle to electrical energy within the recording system (the wires of the recording electrode). Electrodes used to measure a biopotential are typically constructed as nonpolarizable electrodes and commonly out of a silver/silver chloride (Ag/AgCl). Nonpolarizable electrodes allow the free passage of electrons across the electrode/electrolyte interface and do not rely on changes in charge distribution (capacitor-like action) which can be varied significantly by external factors such as electrode movement. Ag/AgCl forms a very stable half potential; the electrodes are constructed of a silver plate with an oxide layer that is in contact with an electrolyte impregnated sponge. With in-dwelling electrodes the intracellular fluid acts as the electrolyte.

A bipolar or differential amplifier amplifies the difference between its two inputs referenced to a common electrode. The differential amplifier has a low common mode gain (i.e. amplification of a signal appearing at both terminals at the same time) and a high differential gain. The ratio of common mode to differential gain forms the common mode rejection ratio; for a high quality biopotential amplifier for surface EMGs this should as high as possible:

$$CMRR = 20 \log_{10} \left(\frac{A_{diff}}{A_{com}} \right)$$

EMG and nerve conduction studies

Nerve conduction studies are used to query the integrity of the PNS, specifically by evoking an action potential within a nerve and recording its propagation to the muscle it innervates or to another part of the nerve.

Conduction studies can take the form of nerve, motor, or mixed studies. In the case of a motor study an innervating nerve is stimulated at two points proximal to the muscle. The difference ∂t between the time $t1$, for the stimulation to propagate from the most proximal point to the muscle, and the time $t2$, for the stimulation to propagate from the distal point to the muscle, is the conduction time. The conduction velocity, therefore, is the distance between the two stimulation points divided by the time difference.

Alternatively, it is possible to measure the conduction of the sensory nerve by stimulating a distal branch of a nerve and measuring the compound nerve action potential orthodromically from a proximal position. Equivalently, it is possible to make an antidromic measurement by stimulating proximally and measuring distally. As the nerve action potential is being measured directly and there is no delay introduced by the muscle depolarization, the conduction time can be calculated by dividing the time for the stimulus to propagate by the distance between stimulating and recording electrodes.

Nerve conduction velocities are highly repeatable measurements and can be related to standard data sets. However, there are several factors that can modify the conduction velocity, such as temperature.

Responses that are involved with the reflex arc can also be assessed using a combination of evoked response and biopotential measurement. Therefore, these techniques can extend the diagnostic potency from the PNS to the spinal cord. The pattern of the EMG within quiescent or voluntarily active skeletal muscle can reveal the presence of disease.

Kinematic EMG

The use of EMG in the analysis of isokinetics and kinetics requires a different set of analysis tools. The typical use is in biomechanics to understand muscle recruitment mechanisms, muscle fatigue, and activation patterns, however, this is still an interrogation of the nervous system. Equipment for kinematic analysis, although very similar in principle, is often required to measure from a larger number of neurological signals though may still focus on a single motor unit. The systems must be worn by the patient during the measurement time and during activity such as walking. Therefore there are different challenges in capturing viable signals during this clinical scenario. The equipment can be formed of wireless sensors allowing more free movement of the limbs and reducing the chances of movement artefacts being induced by the movement of wires or wires tugging the sensors themselves. When wires are present they are often designed to be very thin and flexible and very well screened to reduce noise being induced onto the signal. Commonly these systems have a small patient-worn unit which digitizes the signal information and structures it for communication to a main signal processing and acquisition unit. In addition, these systems must allow the synchronization of other measurement systems such as video or limb joint angle measurements.

Commonly the EMG is presented as a rectified and filtered linear envelope. This has the advantage of being easier to interpret by eye but it also permits calculating an ensemble average and amplitude normalization of multiple dynamic signals. Rectification for a set of n discrete samples creating a signal S_r is defined:

$$S_r = \sum_{i=0}^{n} |x_i|$$

Additionally, the root-mean-squared (RMS) value for a set of n discrete samples is defined by

$$S_{rms} = \sqrt{\frac{\sum_{i=0}^{n} x_i^2}{n}}$$

$$= \sqrt{(x)}^2$$

where in this nomenclature $< \cdot >$ denotes the mean.

Creation of the linear envelope can use many different filtering techniques but commonly a Butterworth or Bessel filter is used. These filters have maximally flat pass bands with rapid attenuation beyond the unwanted frequencies. Caution must be used if time lags are introduced and the signals are to be compared temporally.

Placement of EMG sensors is of critical importance, as surface sensors' orientation and position with respect to the muscle will greatly impact the signal measured. The propagation of muscle action potential is along the length of the muscle fibre. As the differential amplifier has greater differential gain for it to operate appropriately, the line of electrodes should be parallel to the line of propagation of the motor unit action potential (MUAP).

At the innervation zone, the region where the spinal nerves innervate the muscle, the electrical field can be less predictable and thus electrodes should be kept away from these areas. A general rule of thumb is to place electrodes over the belly of the muscle: a set of guidelines have been developed by the ISEK (International Society of Electrophysiology and Kinesiology) and SENIAM (Surface Electromyography for the Non-Invasive Assessment of Muscles) to guide good electrode placement. Finally, it is inadvisable to place electrodes near the edge of a muscle, for two reasons: (1) this increases the chances of cross talk from other muscles significantly affecting the signal quality, and (2) in a related way, the electrical field generated by the MUAP is less consistent in this area.

Possibly the most important difference between isokinetic and kinetic analysis of EMG is that the kinetic instance is likely to be a nonstationary signal. A stationary signal is one that has time invariant statistical properties. The EMG signal can be modelled on a stochastic process or, rather, a signal with values that can be defined probabilistically; they can be considered random (i.e., not deterministic). When the function that defines the probabilities remains constant for any time in the signal, the signal is stationary. However, if the probabilities vary over time, the signal is nonstationary. So, for example, a stochastic process is stationary when its mean (first moment) and variance (second moment about the mean) is a finite number that is not dependent on time:

$$\mu_x(t) = \mu_x(s+t)$$

The significance of this property becomes apparent in the analysis of frequency of a dynamic and isokinetic EMG signal.

Muscle fatigue manifests itself in a frequency shift in the EMG signal; the dominant frequency moves to a lower frequency bin. Frequency changes in EMG can reflect, among other things, a change in dominant action potential shape or change in muscle action potential conduction velocity. This is because muscle types have different frequencies and speeds of depolarization and different muscle types are recruited in different ways in the response to movement and load.

Pathology can adapt the frequency spectrum of an EMG signal due to the modification to the heterogeneity of muscle fibres and the predominance of often slower muscle fibre types.

Frequency analysis using familiar tools such as the Fourier series relies on some fundamental assumptions about the signal under analysis: continuous, infinite, and stationary. The reason for this is that the basic function of the Fourier method is a sinusoid and, thus, unless windowed in some way, it exists for all time (i.e. over the period of the whole signal under investigation). If a particular component of a signal exists at one frequency for all time then there is not a problem; however, what if a particular frequency component only exists for a finite time? Given this situation how are we to know when the "event" occurred if our basis function is infinite?

Observing the time series from an isokinetic exercise during testing on an isokinetic dynamometer we can measure the stochastic and wide-sense stationary[1] nature of the electromyogram. However, if we were to observe the EMG signal measured from the kinetic assessment of the quadriceps during walking, the requirements for a stationary signal are no longer met and we would be wise to use a different method for analyzing the frequency characteristics of the signal.

Signal analysis provides many opportunities to analyze the frequency characteristics of these types of signals; two commonly applied techniques to electromyography are short-time Fourier transforms (STFT) and wavelet analysis.

Evoked potentials

Electroencephalogram

Electroencephalography (EEG) is an electrophysiological technique for measuring cerebral potentials which are based upon the electrical activity and voltage fluctuations resulting from the active nerve cell populations and ionic current flow within the neurons of the brain occurring 1.5−4 mm from the surface of the cerebral cortex.

In nerve cells, ionic potentials are present due to differences in ion concentration, which are predominantly Na^+, Cl^- and K^+. The cell wall is a semipermeable membrane and is more permeable to K^+ and Cl^- than Na^+. A sodium-potassium pump keeps Na^+ outside the cell and K^+ inside, with the rate of sodium pumping being greater than potassium pumping (3 Na^+ to 2 K^+ ions) resulting in a difference in ionic potential. The resting membrane potential (electrochemical equilibrium) is between −70 mV to −75mV.

EEG recordings are measurements of the spontaneous activity (summation of the changes in current flow potential between dendrites and cell bodies) in the brain, typically over a 20−30 min recording period. EEG recordings are the main diagnostic tool for diagnosing and evaluating epilepsy, as well as retaining a role in evaluating brain activity in coma patients, assisting with the diagnosis of sleep disorders, and the diagnosis of encephalopathies, tumours and strokes. The routine clinical use of imaging techniques such as MRI and CT have reduced the need for EEG in some conditions as the spatial resolution can be limited; however temporal resolution is in the order of milliseconds.

Electrode positioning

The EEG recordings are performed using Ag/AgCl surface electrodes. The resultant voltage difference that can be measured on the scalp is of the order of 100 µV. However, cortical measurements can be measured at approximately 1−2 mV on the brain surface.

The placement of electrodes, which typically consists of 8−16 leads when performing conventional recordings, follows the International 10−20 system. This system utilizes anatomical landmarks on the skull to cover specific cortical areas. These areas are subdivided using intervals of 10%−20% of the distance between specific areas demarcated using a tape measure and marker pen for accurate electrode placement. The odd numbers in the electrode array denote the left side of the brain, whilst the even numbers represent the right side, with letters F, P, O and T representing the frontal, parietal, occipital and temporal lobes respectively, with Cz being the midline central electrode (Tatum, 2014). The recordings are obtained by placement of the electrodes on the scalp using a conductive gel or paste, following preparation of the scalp using light abrasion to remove dead skin cells to assist with decreasing impedance below 5 kOhms. Many systems use electrodes, each of which is attached to an individual wire, however, electrode caps and electrode nets can also be used. Each of the electrodes is connected to the input of the differential amplifier (i.e. one amplifier per electrode pair); a common reference electrode is also connected to the input of each differential amplifier. The voltage is amplified (typically 1000−100,000 times) between the active electrode and the reference electrode. The amplified signal is passed through a

---

1. Many signals are stationary over their first two moments, i.e., mean and standard deviation about the mean, but not necessarily for any higher moments. These signals are considered wide-sense stationary. A truly stationary signal must be stationary over all moments.

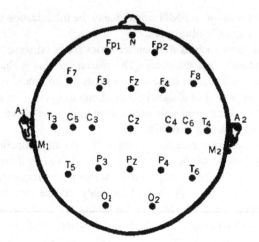

FIG. 18.1   Electrode positions based on the International 10–20 Standard. Cz: Central vortex electrode, F: Frontal, C: Central, T: Temporal, P: Parietal, O: Occipital, M: Mastoid, N: Nasion.

filter (anti-aliasing) and digitized using an analogue-to-digital converter. The rate of analogue-to-digital sampling occurs at 256–512 Hz in routine clinical scalp EEG, however, the sampling rates for research applications can reach 20 kHz.

The outpatient scalp-recorded EEG is the most commonly performed diagnostic study. Scalp EEG displays the difference in electrical potentials between two different sites on the cerebral cortex closest to the recording electrode. There are two different techniques in EEG measurements: unipolar and bipolar. Unipolar measurements are recorded with respect to a common reference. The main emphasis is on frequencies and amplitudes of the EEG signal. In bipolar measurements, recording is achieved from a series of electrodes in which the input of each amplifier is connected to the output of the next one. It is used mainly for visualizing phase reversals (loci of amplitude maxima) in the detection of epileptic foci (Fig. 18.1).

Artefacts

As with any physiological measurement recordings, patient, equipment and technical factors can affect recordings. Patients may introduce movement artefacts and contamination from other physiological signals, such as eye movement, electromyogenic and cardiovascular activity. The mains powerline can also provide interference, as well as movement of electrodes, electrode cables and skin impedance issues, particularly with ambulatory recordings.

Frequency bands

The frequencies measured during an EEG are measured in Hertz (cycles per second) and are categorized into fast, moderate and slow waves. The EEG is typically described in terms of rhythmic activity and transients. Rhythmic activity is divided into 5 frequency bands. Most of the cerebral signal observed in scalp EEG ranges between 1 and 20 Hz; with amplitudes recorded in the adult of approximately 10–100 µV. Transient waves are classified as abnormal waveforms having specific wave shapes and short time non-stationary properties. They are common in epilepsy (which has phenomena such as the single spike and the spike/wave complex). The 5 rhythmic bands are:

1. Delta waves: high-amplitude waves in the (low) frequency range of up to 4 Hz. They are located frontally in adults and posteriorly in children. They occur during slow wave deep sleep in adults (stage 3 of non-REM sleep) and are able to characterize the depth of sleep. Delta waves are common in infants under one year of age. The waves are thought to originate from the thalamus or the cortex (Fig. 18.2A).
2. Theta waves: have a frequency range of 4–8 Hz and are classified as being slow waves transiently seen during wakefulness. These waveforms occur most frequently during sleep, are more prominent when drowsy and are present in recordings from young children. They are also observed in cases of epilepsy and anxiety (Fig. 18.2B).
3. Alpha waves: have a frequency ranging between 8 and 13 Hz. They are located in the posterior regions of the head, both side and central sites. The rhythm is thought to be generated within the occipital lobes. They are normally associated with relaxation, closing of eyes, and inhibitory activity in different locations across the brain. Pathologically,

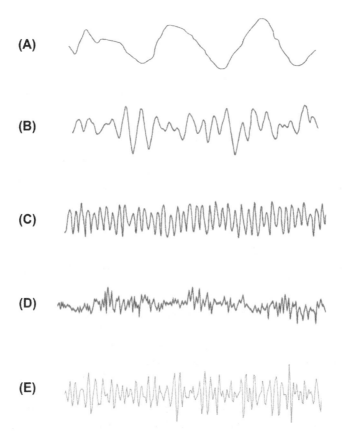

FIG. 18.2 Rhythmic EEG bands. (A) Delta waves, (B) Theta waves, (C) Alpha waves, (D) Beta waves, and (E) Gamma waves.

they are found in coma patients. On occasion, a prominent alpha-range frequency of 8−12 Hz is seen over the central head regions, and is described as being the mu rhythm (Fig. 18.2C).

4. Beta rhythms are low amplitude and have a fast frequency between 13 and 30 Hz, present bilaterally in the brain. They are typically detected in the frontal or central areas of healthy individuals. Beta brainwaves dominate the normal awake state of consciousness, when attention is directed towards cognitive tasks, and are therefore present when we are attentive, alert and engaged in problem solving and other activities. Beta waves are typically enhanced during drowsiness, which may be related to sensorimotor cortex function. Medication with a sedating effect, such as benzodiazepines and barbiturates produce beta waves with a prominent amplitude. Rolandic beta rhythms occur spontaneously when eyes are both open and closed, occurring predominantly in areas associated with sensorimotor activity. This rhythm typically has a frequency of approximately 20 Hz (Fig. 18.2D).

5. Gamma waves: are high frequency (26−100 Hz) low amplitude waves and are associated with the simultaneous processing of information from a variety of brain areas, linked to high attention states (Britton et al., 2016) (Fig. 18.2E).

Ambulatory EEG recordings

Ambulatory EEG recordings can be performed in cases where routine EEG recordings are not optimal, for example in patients with recurrent and unprovoked epileptic seizures that have been difficult to classify. Ambulatory recordings enable patients to be as minimally restricted as possible. Having the ability to capture the ictal EEG patterns is crucial in the classification and diagnosis of seizure disorder, along with establishing potential triggers, which is particularly useful in pre-surgical evaluation cases. The recordings can be performed either as an outpatient, or within a specialized monitoring unit. In the case of admission to a monitoring unit, additional physiological measurements can be recorded, such as EMG and cardiovascular recordings. Video-recording will normally be performed if a patient is an inpatient in an ambulatory facility. The disadvantages associated with ambulatory EEG recording include the introduction of additional movement and cable artefacts. This procedure can also be expensive when performed as an in-patient (Cascino et al., 2002).

Invasive EEG

Under certain clinical circumstances, invasive EEG recordings, known as foramen ovale (FO) recordings are necessary. These recordings have typically been involved in the pre-surgical evaluation of patients, particularly in the assessment of surgical suitability in patients with medial temporal lobe epilepsy. These electrodes are not routinely used in clinical practice, primarily due to the invasive nature of the recording and are therefore reserved for specific pre-surgical evaluation cases due to the superior detectability of the epileptogenic brain areas. Foramen ovale electrodes contain 4-6 contact wire electrodes which are inserted through the foramen ovale, and lie at the base of the temporal lobes. The electrodes are intracranially located and provide a more sensitive method for the lateralization of the epileptogenic areas in temporal lobe epilepsy patients. However, the routine use of MRI in epilepsy and pre-surgical evaluation programmes has reduced the requirement for FO electrodes in pre-surgical evaluation; therefore FO recordings retain a limited role in cases where the MRI and EEG lateralizations are discordant.

EEG and fMRI

Functional magnetic resonance imaging (fMRI) is a non-invasive imaging technique that enables the changes in neuronal activity to be localized, which can be detected during a task, such as motor or visual tasks. The experimental condition (activation or "ON" condition) is compared with a control condition ("OFF" condition). During active tasks the change in neuronal activity is accompanied by changes in oxy and deoxyhaemoglobin saturation levels. This response is known as the Blood Oxygen Level Dependent (BOLD) response (Kwong et al., 1992; Ogawa et al., 1992). fMRI typically evaluates cognitive, motor and sensory function. In some experiments, such as cognitive tasks, it is advantageous to simultaneously record the EEG response during these experimental tasks. However, the measurement of EEG signals in the MR environment is demanding as this environment introduces additional artefacts. Head motion can contaminate both fMRI and EEG recordings, although fixation of the head will improve the quality of the data. It is important to note that vibration produced by the rapidly switching gradient coils may potentially cause movement of electrode cables, introducing further artefacts into the EEG data. In addition to MRI pulse sequence artefacts and movement artefacts, electric currents in EEG wires can be produced along with potentially harmful radiofrequency heating. Despite these technical, equipment and patient artefacts and the MR environment, simultaneous EEG recordings and fMRI scans have been successfully obtained together; primarily due to advances in hardware and artefact processing (Ives et al., 1993). Additional technical difficulties include the presence of conductive materials, such as the EEG electrodes and associated cables, which can produce an electromotive force when moved within the static magnetic field (B0) (Huang-Hellinger et al., 1995). Currents induced in the electrodes and leads by the rapidly changing magnetic field gradients can introduce heating effects in addition to artefacts into the EEG recording process. It is therefore advantageous to utilize good equipment shielding and post-processing artefact removal (Krakow et al., 2000).

Diagnostic applications of the EEG generally focus on either event-related potentials or on the spectral content of the EEG recording. The later has been covered when describing the frequency bands. The former investigates potential fluctuations that are time locked to a stimulus event or a button press. Evoked potentials are acquired by averaging the EEG activity that is time-locked to the presentation of a stimulus such as a visual, auditory or somatosensory stimulus, commonly utilized in neuropsychology.

Sensory evoked potentials

Sensory Evoked Potentials (SEP) are recorded following stimulation of the sense organs, e.g. components of the visual or auditory system. The visual system can be stimulated using moving checkerboards or flashing lights. Auditory system evoked potentials can be acquired using either click or tone stimuli delivered through headphones. Somatosensory Evoked Potentials (SSEP) are evoked using electrical or tactile stimulation of sensory or mixed nerves, and are commonly employed during intraoperative physiological monitoring.

Brainstem auditory evoked potentials

Brainstem auditory evoked potentials (BAEPs) use hundreds, possibly a 1000 or more, auditory "click" stimuli to elicit a response in the eighth cranial nerve and auditory centres of the midbrain. The signal produced during BAEP characteristically has five peaks reflecting the different contributions of the eighth cranial nerve, cochlear nucleus, superior olivary complex, and colliculus and lemniscus. However, the true origins of the signals are still under conjecture. Wave 1 is considered to be the response predominately from the eighth cranial nerve and is measured from the earlobe. Waves 2 and 3 are most probably from activity originating in the cochlear nucleus and superior olivary complex, though Wave 2 is also thought to be produced by the proximal part of the eighth nerve. Waves 4 and 5 are considered to be a summation of the activity of multiple structures in the ascending lower auditory pathway. These waveforms are thought to include activity from the lower lemniscus and inferior colliculus. Waveforms 2−5 are best captured with electrodes placed on the vertex, Cz. BAEP allows an analysis of the structures in the midbrain and areas close to the auditory tract. Each waveform is related to an anatomical region. Disruption of different areas by, for example, a tumour may be reflected as a disruption to one of the typical waveforms. It is important to note, however, that an abnormal BAEP does not relate itself to any specific cause, rather this may be elucidated by the wider clinical picture.

Short latency somatosensory evoked potentials

SSEPs are sequentially generated by different neural structures in response to a stimulus. In the upper limb the medial, ulnar, or radial nerve is often used; in the lower limb the tibial or peroneal nerve is used. The stimulus can take the form of muscle stretch, tap, or electrical stimulation; with electrical stimulation being the preferred method. The stimulator provides a square wave stimulation pulse of frequency in the range $1 \text{ Hz} \leq f_{stim} \leq 100 \text{ Hz}$ with pulse widths of 100−200 µs and a maximum current of 50 mA, though a current of 15−20 mA is more common.

The latencies of the evoked response are measured at different points along the neural pathway.

Measuring locations are commonly the popliteal fossa, L1 and T12, and Erb's point (lateral route of the brachial plexus). Upper spinal and cortical regions are measured between C5 and Fz and Cz to C5. The areas of the premotor cortex (on the ipsilateral side of the stimulated limb) and the central scalp area over the primary motor cortex also provide a location for measuring the evoked response. Up to 1000 repeated stimulations are ensemble averaged to form a single observation, and several observations are routinely made to provide knowledge of measurement reliability.

Somatosensory evoked potentials spinal monitoring

Intra-operative spinal monitoring is performed using SSEPs to functionally assess the integrity of the nervous system during surgical procedures involving spinal manipulation, e.g. spinal surgery. The structures most at risk are the spinal cord and the nerve roots at the site of surgery. To record SSEPs the afferent pathway (the sensory pathway which sends signals to the cortex) is monitored. SSEPs are recorded by stimulating peripheral nerves (tibial, median and ulnar nerves) frequently using an electrical stimulus. The response can then be recorded from the patient's spinal canal or from the scalp.

The most common procedures requiring spinal monitoring are the correction of spinal deformities (such as scoliosis) where spinal fixation instrumentation is inserted to correct the curve of the spine, and retain a role in the treatment of spinal cord tumours. The recording involves the transcutaneous (electrical) stimulation of the peroneal (common fibula) nerve using two surface electrodes placed behind each knee at either side of the joint at the position of the nerve. The recording electrode (epidural) is placed within the spinal canal and lies along the surface of the dura entering the spinal cord. During monitoring, the legs are stimulated on an alternate basis, using a 20 mA current and 200 µs pulse between the two stimulating electrodes. The repetition rate is 25−30 Hz, with response traces being acquired every 3 min.

The amplitude and latency of the SSEP are of most interest during spinal recordings, which provide information relating to the integrity of the nerve pathway of interest and speed of the electrical response along the pathway. Any significant changes, such as an increase in latency or a decrease in amplitude can indicate neurological dysfunction.

It should be noted that the type and depth of anaesthetic can cause alterations in latencies and amplitudes, and can diminish a response in the most severe cases. Therefore the choice of anaesthetic is an important consideration when performing intra-operative monitoring.

Case study 18.1 (Top) Amplitude and latencies for the left and right leg, plotted against time. (Bottom) Initial and final SEP responses acquired during the monitoring session.

A twelve-year-old boy presented with severe scoliosis (100° curve), and underwent a two-stage procedure, which commenced with the anterior release. During the monitoring procedure, each event is documented and tabulated, for example fitting screws, placement of rods and any decline in amplitude is recorded. The amplitude and latency for each 3-min interval are recorded. The results are displayed in a graphical form to determine whether latency and amplitude varies over the course of the operation. New response traces are acquired every 3 min. The graph below demonstrates that the right and left latency readings were stable during the procedure. However, there was a decrease in right amplitude at approximately 17.20 h. The amplitude recovered soon after (within several minutes), which suggests that the event was temporary and equipment related, for example, the surgeon accidently knocking the recording electrode. No further events occurred during monitoring.

Continued

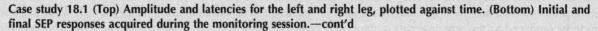

Case study 18.1 (Top) Amplitude and latencies for the left and right leg, plotted against time. (Bottom) Initial and final SEP responses acquired during the monitoring session.—cont'd

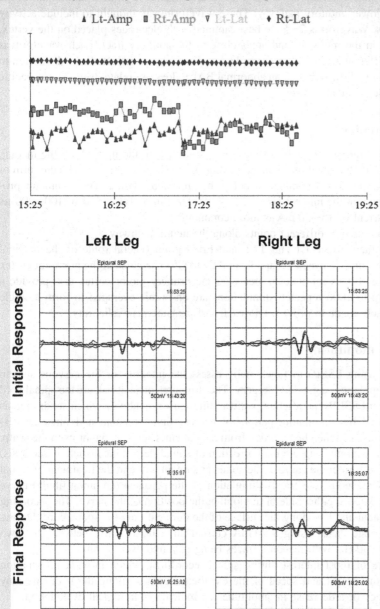

Abbreviations

BAEP	Brainstem Auditory Evoked Potentials
BOLD	Blood Oxygen Level Dependent
CNS	Central Nervous System
EEG	Electroencephalography
EMG	Electromyography
fMRI	Functional Magnetic Resonance Imaging
FO	Foramen Ovale

ISEK   International Society of Electrophysiology and Kinesiology
MRI   Magnetic Resonance Imaging
MUAP   Motor Unit Action Potential
PNS   Peripheral Nervous System
REM   Rapid Eye Movement
SENIAM   Surface Electromyography for the Non-Invasive Assessment of Muscles
SEP   Sensory Evoked Potentials
SSEP   Somatosensory Evoked Potentials

References

Britton, J.W., Frey, L.C., Hopp, J., et al., 2016. Electroencephalography (EEG). In: St Louis, E.K., Frey, L.C. (Eds.), An Introductory Test and Atlas of Normal and Abnormal Findings in Adults, Children and Infants. American Epilepsy Society, Chicago.

Cascino, G., 2002. Video-EEG monitoring in adults. Epilepsia 43 (Suppl. 3), 80–93.

Huang-Hellington, F.R., Breiter, H.C., McCormack, G., Cohen, M.S., Kwong, K.K., Sutton, J.P., Savoy, R.L., Weiskoff, R.M., Davis, T.L., Baker, J.R., Belliveau, J.W., Rosen, B.R., 1995. Simultaneous functional magnetic resonance imaging and electrophysiological recording. Hum. Brain Mapp. 3 (1), 13–23.

Ives, J.R., Warach, S., Schmitt, F., Edelman, R.R., Schomer, D.L., 1993. Monitoring the patient's EEG during echo planar MRI. Electroencephalogr. Clin. Neurophysiol. 87 (6), 417–420.

Krakow, K., Allen, P.J., Symms, M.R., Lemieux, Josephs, O., Fish, D.R., 2000. EEG recording during fMRI experiments: image quality. Hum. Brain Mapp. 10 (1), 10–15.

Kwong, K.K., Belliveau, J.W., Chesler, D.A., Goldberg, I.E., Weisskoff, R.M., 1992. Dynamic magnetic resonance imaging of human brain activity during primary sensory stimulation. Proc. Natl. Acad. Sci. U.S.A. 89, 5675–5679.

Ogawa, S., Tank, D.W., Menon, R., Ellermann, J.M., Kim, S.-G., 1992. Intrinsic signal changes accompanying sensory stimulation: functional brain mapping with magnetic resonance imaging. Proc. Natl. Acad. Sci. U.S.A. 89, 5951–5955.

Tatum IV, W.O., 2014. Handbook of EEG Interpretation.

Chapter 19

Visual electrophysiology measurement

Richard Hagan

Royal Liverpool University Hospitals NHS Foundation Trust, Liverpool, United Kingdom

Chapter outline

Introduction

Measuring electrical activity from the visual system is not something new, in fact the electrical response from a frog's eye was recorded by Holmgren in 1865 and later by Dewar (Dewar, 1877; Dewar and McKendrick, 1875) and McKendrick from human eyes around 1875. Electrophysiology has developed quite a bit since then and advances in technology such as electrodes and more importantly computers have made it possible to collect ensemble averages to time locked stimuli. This has meant that the collection of ever smaller potentials has become a reality, providing greater more specific clues to the eye doctor (ophthalmologist) for the treatment and management of their patients. Vision is a highly complex sense and the visual system operates almost seamlessly across several orders of magnitude in terms of brightness, can detect nearly an octave of the electromagnetic spectrum (this octave is more commonly known as light-higher frequency shorter wavelength is violet or blue with the lower frequency longer wavelength better known as red). Our visual system adapts to different backgrounds and hues, has fantastic spatial resolution and fairly good temporal resolution (flicker fusion of 60 Hz can be achieved at high luminance).

Often in conversation people discuss good vision as 20/20 which is often seen as the gold standard of vision. This is in fact a misnomer in the UK as the measurement is in imperial units (feet) whilst Europeans use metric (metre). Perfect vision in Europe might be described as 6/6, except this isn't perfect vision, just a realistically achievable level of vision. The denominator is what Snellen (the father of the letter chart) judged standard vision should be at 6 m; the numerator is what the subject being tested (patient) can see. Some say 6/6 is average vision, which may be true, though Snellen set out that letters subtending 5 min of arc separated by 1 min of arc be standard vision. Like anything with an average some people will be below the average and others above. So like many physiological measurements there is probably a range of Snellen acuities achieved by those thought to be visually normal.

Often fit and healthy young people often see beyond 6/6 such as 6/4. This means the subject sees at 6 m what Snellen defined as standard vision at 4 m (or a normal person sees at 4 m). Often people may become discouraged if they can't see to the very bottom of the letter chart, but there is often a line or more beyond 6/6, that ought to be beyond our expectation. Low vision is considered to be 6/18 or worse (up to 3/60) (Royal College of Ophthalmologists). Often with age, the optics begin to gain a yellow tinge, there is increased pigmentation at the back of the eye, there is some 'normal' neuronal decay and our vision may deteriorate a bit, and as we get older obtaining 6/6 vision may become challenging even without pathology being present. This is not to be confused with cataract, which is a clouding of the lens, which if left untreated can

Clinical Engineering. https://doi.org/10.1016/B978-0-08-102694-6.00019-X

cause a great deal of visual loss. Cataracts are now successfully taken out (and replaced with a new lens − pseudophakic) as day cases in most hospitals. Interestingly cataracts are the number one cause of blindness world-wide (51% of blindness), which suggests not every country offers surgery as a day case, which is currently a free life changing operation performed routinely by the NHS in the UK.

Another great threat to our vision as we get older is age related macular degeneration (AMD) and is third in the list of worldwide blinding disorders and the leading cause in industrialized countries. It is thought as many as 14% of white Americans over the age of 80 suffer from AMD (other ethnicities are around 2% at that age). This too needs to be identified as we get older and not seen as natural ageing.

As part of a driving test, most examiners will get the candidate to read a number plate at 20 m; clearly this is a different task to traditional eye tests, which have high contrast black letters on a white background. As well as managing this, the candidate ought to manage at least 6/12 in one eye (with glasses if needed).

For us to achieve a good Snellen score, our optics need to work well, the back of the eye (retina) also needs to function and in particular the central part of the retina called the macula needs to be healthy. There is however much, much more to human vision. Snellen acuity doesn't tell us how we will manage with close up work (reading vision); our visual fields (how well we see to the sides); our colour or contrast vision not to mention our vision in the dark; or how well our two eyes work together to develop a 3 dimensional scene (stereovision). So the next time someone tells you they have perfect 20/20 vision, you will know there are many, many other aspects of vision to consider rather than just one measure of distance vision conducted on near 100% contrast black on white letter chart.

Vision is complex and so requires numerous tests to fully describe. Vision is an extremely precious sense and its loss can impact our ability to work or care for ourselves (or others), it can also affect other activities such as reading, watching a movie, recognizing friends, identifying important non-verbal communication clues and pursuing hobbies. For this reason the study of vision merits the attention of scientists and/or engineers who may develop better or novel ways to test vision and add to the understanding of the underpinning mechanisms involved with vision from a clinical measurement perspective.

Visual electrophysiology is one of the less commonly used methods of assessing vision, largely due to cost of equipment, time to perform and expertize required to successfully interpret the complex waveforms produced. There are three main types of visual electrophysiology tests conducted in most laboratories: Visual Evoked Potential (VEP); Electroretinogram (ERG); and Electro-Oculargram (EOG). These will be discussed in turn, focusing on the more commonly used clinical tests, though there are many types of possible VEP and ERG.

Anatomy and physiology

For us to see, light must enter the eye via its aperture, the pupil, the size of which is governed by the iris (the coloured part around the pupil). Pupil size is a reflex and can be affected by a number of different things such as ambient light level, alertness or if we see something or someone we like to name but a few.

The light that enters the eye must then be refracted so it converges on the same point on the back of the eye, called the retina (see Fig. 19.1). Most of this convergence takes place at the cornea, which is a clear layer at the front of the eye that is very sensitive and delicate. The fine focus then occurs via the lens, which is controlled by the ciliary muscles. When we want to look at something close up the lens needs to work extra hard to bring divergent light together, this means the lens needs to have greater curvature or become 'fatter'. When light from far away objects enters the eye, the incoming light is closer to being parallel and so requires less refraction and the lens can remain less curved (thin). As we get older the lens becomes stiffer and more difficult for the ciliary muscles to alter its shape, this makes seeing things close up difficult, activities such as reading may become difficult. A pair of reading glasses might help the ciliary muscles focus the light together; reading glasses have concave lenses and refract light together. The refractive strength of glasses is measured in dioptres (D) and a single dioptre lens will focus parallel light to a point 1 m metre on the other side of the lens (2D-50 cm, 3D-33 cm). For short-sighted people (they see well close up) glasses convex in shape are needed, and these diverge light, -1D would bring together light virtually a metre on the same side of the lens that the light is coming from. Should a clinician suspect poor vision is due to the optics or inadequate optics they may get the patient to look through a pinhole, this obviates the optics and light will land directly on the retina via the principle axis (no bending of light, just the light passing through the pin hole and centre of the lens). Pinhole vision is the best possible vision a person can achieve (with correction/glasses) and so if this is still reduced the problem may lie elsewhere and need to be investigated. Whilst pinhole vision helps us see centrally it comes at the price of a very reduced visual field so could not be used as a treatment. Often when people reach their visual threshold they may bring their eyelids close together (squint) by doing this they are making light pass through the principle axis like a pinhole.

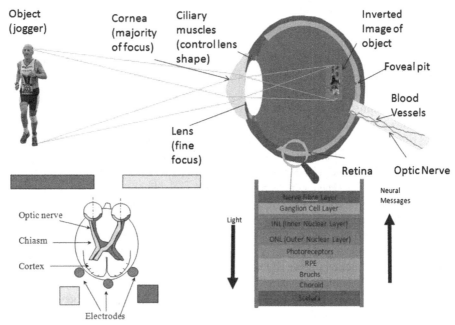

FIG. 19.1 Top showing how the optics of the eye allow for an inverted image to be formed at the back of the eye, a cross section of the retina, showing light must pass through several layers before stimulation the photoreceptors, which then pass the signal back up the retina. Bottom left how visual field information in processed, everything on the right visual field is processed by the left hemisphere, and everything from the left field is processed.

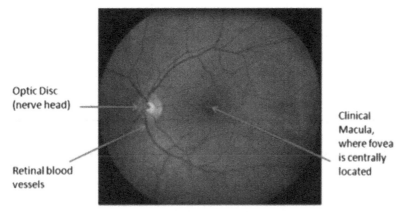

FIG. 19.2 Showing the retina, the central macular is where the fovea is located with greatest density of cones. The blood vessels coming out of the optic nerve head arc into the temporal retina and form the vascular arcades, outside the vascular arcades is the peripherally retina.

The back of the eye, the retina has several different areas (see Fig. 19.2) made up of several different cell types and cell densities. The first cell type to react to light is the photoreceptor. There are two main types of photoreceptors: cones, which mediate colour vision; and rods that are more sensitive to light and help us, see in the dark. The central part of the retina (macula) has the highest density of cones at the fovea (very centre of macula) and so the most detailed image is created here, our central vision is important for reading and face recognition etc. Another way to think about this is to imagine a camera phone, with the same size of sensor, but different number of pixels, the one with 8 MP, will have a sharper image than the one with just 1 MP or 100 kP, the higher density of light sensors you have (photoreceptors), the clearer the image. The peripheral part of our eye has a lower density of cones and does not provide the same level of detailed information, though is still very important for tasks such as navigation.

The cones are so named because they are conical in shape; this has a slight implication regarding its wave-guide properties, and means the cones are less forgiving in terms of seeing stray light. A cone at the centre of the eye will respond more readily to light coming through the middle of the pupil down its axis, whilst light coming in from the periphery of the pupil at an angle will appear dimmer to this central cone. This is the basis of the Stiles Crawford effect, which helps correct relative retinal illumination taking this effect into account. So whilst retinal illumination (trolands) is often considered to be room luminance x pupil area, as the pupil area gets larger the relative impact of the light on the cones is smaller due to this need for light to pass within a certain angle of its axis and so the Stiles-Crawford correction is needed.

Rods which are rod shaped, are better able to process various angles of light, and are much more sensitive to light energy. Due to their increased sensitivity they are the photoreceptor that can see best in dim illumination i.e. in the dark or night-time vision. Of note in normal light conditions the rods tend to be saturated or bleached by the ambient light and only cones function. In the dark our pupils naturally widen and so light will fall on the rods at a greater angle from the periphery of the pupil, their shape allows them to accept this light.

Three different types of cone detect colour vision. Each of these has a different wavelength spectral sensitivity (similar to the normal distribution in shape), and are often called blue, green and red cones. Some prefer to call them short (S), medium (M) or long (L) wavelength cones as peak sensitivity tend to be on average around 440 nm, 535 nm and 575 nm, which is blue, green and yellow/orange. The L-cone is more sensitive to red light than the others and indeed when this cone is more heavily stimulated than the M-cone we see red. It is thought on average there are around four and a half million cones and ninety million rods in the human eye. In the central fovea, the cones are most densely packed without any rods and this area is crucial for high-resolution vision. Light below 380 nm in length tends to be attenuated by the lens, cornea and vitreous and is termed ultra-violet.

The visual cascade in the retina involves primarily three neurones, the photoreceptor that passes its information to the bipolar cell layer, which in turn passes its information to ganglion cells whose axons form the optic nerve and leave the retina in bundles that form the optic nerve head (blindspot). The outer-plexiform layer between the photoreceptor and bipolar cell also has horizontal cells junctions which probably have a role in modulating responses across photoreceptors to the bipolar cells. The bipolar cells have both ON and OFF type cells. The ON-bipolar cells are excited by photo-receptors when light falls on the photoreceptors. OFF-bipolar are triggered when the cones stop being stimulated. Cones synapse to both ON and OFF bipolar cells whilst rods synapse to only ON-pathway bipolars. A cone from the central fovea might synapse directly to an ON-bipolar cell and OFF-bipolar cell, whilst in the peripheral there may be hundreds if not thousands of photoreceptors passing their information to a single bipolar cell. The same is true of central bipolar cells and ganglion cells. Centrally a single bipolar cell may synapse with a ganglion whereas in the periphery many bipolar cells will synapse to a single to ganglion cell. This means that the central area is subserved by many more ganglion cells than the periphery not just because of higher density of photoreceptors (cones) but because there is a higher ratio of ganglion cells to those individual photoreceptors. This is important as it enables crisp high-resolution vision in the centre of the vision.

It also means cortical electrical activity is dominated by central processes. Of note the ganglion cell bodies aren't directly in line with the photoreceptor in the fovea, this allows light to fall directly onto the foveal cones without the ganglion cell bodies getting in the way. This is because we have an inverted retina, with light coming into the eye, through the vitreous and into the retina, passing through the ganglion cell layer, then bipolar cell layer and finally stimulating the photoreceptors in the photoreceptor layer, most stray light is absorbed by the RPE (Retinal Pigment Epithelium), so glare is reduced (See Fig. 19.1). These cells then pass the information back up to the bipolar cell and then ganglion cell layer. There is a reduction in retinal thickness centrally, this is called the foveal dip and this reduction is caused by the ganglion cells that subserve the centre being pushed to the side. Also of note the blood supply for the central retina comes from the choroid a layer beneath the RPE, whilst elsewhere the inner retina is vascularized by the retinal blood vessels (see Fig. 19.2). This too is thought to ensure the high performance central vision isn't obstructed by blood vessels.

Visual evoked potential (VEP)

Visual Evoked Potential (VEP) refers to the evoked response recorded from the occipital cortex to a visual stimulus. This implies that a stimulus is required to generate the response. The different VEP names come from the different stimuli used. In this chapter we will focus on the Pattern Reversal VEP and the flash VEP. Most laboratories will use the same electrode montage for pattern reversal and Flash VEP. An active electrode should be placed over Oz (Jasper 10−20 system) (Jasper, 1958), a reference over Fz and a ground electrode over a visually inert location with similar background activity such as the forehead (Fpz), vertex (Cz) or either ear lobe (see Fig. 19.3). Oz tends to be located 3−4 cm above the Inion (a bony divot just above the base of the skull). The distance between Inion and Nasion tends to be about 30−40 cm (measured using a curved tape) hence an approximation of 3−4 cm above the Inion will usually suffice (of note most electrodes diameter are close to a centimetre in diameter and so precision above a centimetre would be difficult to justify). Also of note the Jasper system uses bony land markers to help guide electrode positions over brainy regions, in fact there maybe some variation in bony landmarks and brain location between subjects and this is a limitation of the technique.

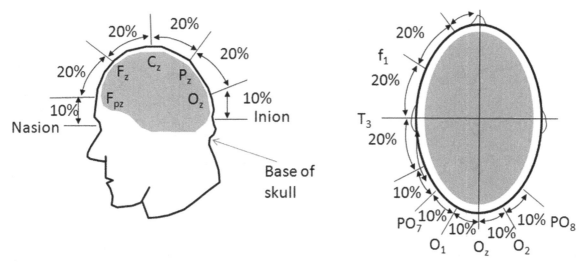

FIG. 19.3 Showing commonly used positions for electrodes, the first letter denotes brain region i.e. O for Occipital & F for Frontal etc, the subscript gives further information about the location, z is midline, 1 is shifted 10% of head circumference to the left, and 2 is 10% to the right-odd numbers refer to left side of the brain, even to right side of the brain.

Pattern reversal VEP

Pattern reversal VEP tend to be recorded to checkerboard patterns made up of black and white squares. ISCEV (International Society for Clinical Electrophysiology of Vision) suggest using a high contrast pattern (>80% Michelson) with white squares having luminance around 100 cd/m (Dewar and McKendrick, 1875). The screen should subtend at least 15°, ideally with a fixation spot or cross in the centre of the screen to help focus the subject. The black and white squares will alternate positions with one another without an increase or decrease in the overall screen luminance (to ensure the response is not to a luminance change but only a pattern change). ISCEV has identified CRT (Cathode Ray Tube) stimulators as having many desirable characteristics to achieve this whilst LCDs (Liquid Crystal Displays) tend to perform less well (Odom et al., 2016).

ISCEV recommends at least two check sizes be used, one large around 60′ and one around 15′. Of note there are 60 min of arc in a degree and 60 s of arc in a minute.

Pattern reversal VEP is very useful clinically as there is low variation in waveform between subjects with most people having a recognizable peak around 90−110 ms after being stimulated by a moderate size check (~50′). One factor that might affect the accuracy of this measure is how the stimulator delivers the stimulus, i.e. if a CRT runs at 60 Hz it takes close to 17 ms to draw the stimulus on the screen and return to the top of the screen, but a 100 Hz will do this in 10 ms, thereby possibly affecting peak time. Laboratories should identify how the stimulus is presented and the impact on recordings, so comparison with other labs can be facilitated.

An optimum recording will be made when the subject is alert, focused (optically & mentally) on the stimulus, has clear media, healthy macular, optic nerve function and cortical function. A typical PRVEP from a well seeing person is included (see Fig. 19.4). There are typically three cardinal points, a negativity at around 75 ms after stimulation termed N75, a positivity 100 ms after stimulation termed P100, a second negativity occurring around 135 ms, termed N135. Most centres look primarily at the size of the P100 (amplitude measure from bottom of N75 to top of P100) and P100 timing, now termed implicit time or time to peak measured from half way through stimulus delivery and the peak of the P100 (some have termed this latency though this is considered less correct now). When reporting a PRVEP particular attention is given to the amplitude of response, the time to peak (P100) and morphology (shape) of the waveform.

Often laboratories will calculate 95% reference ranges for amplitudes and latencies. This is usually an estimate of the values which will capture 95% of subjects of the same age as those tested clinically. Clinical decisions are often based on whether a result is within this range or outside it. A quick estimate of such a range is mean ± 2 S.D. (1.96 is more precise), though this would assume normality of distribution, which is unlikely to be the case for amplitude, which is almost certainly positivity skewed (practically taking logs of a low base might bring the data closer to a normal distribution, though with any model including non-parametric data, there are inaccuracies). The American society for neurophysiology has suggested for time to peak, the time needs to be delayed by 3.5−4 S.D. beyond average before considered abnormal. Of note when there is a large normative group (n > 40) non-parametric methods are recommended and for smaller samples

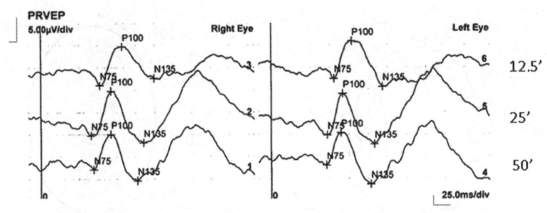

FIG. 19.4   Showing the PRVEP to a range of checks (50'-12.5').

(n < 40) Box-Cox transformation (Geffre et al., 2011) are recommended. In the Liverpool electrophysiology lab 90—110 ms is assumed to cover 95% of the normal population at the standard checksize, though responses are only considered suspicious of delay at around 115 ms and definitely delayed at 120 ms.

Fig. 19.4 shows how the VEP response alters in response to different checksizes in comparison to the standard large check size response (our representative normal). There is often an assumption that responses will reduce in size to smaller checks, this isn't always true as seen in Fig. 19.4. There is, however a tendency for responses to become later to smaller checks and this is often quite noticeable as the visual threshold is approached. When interpreting PRVEPs it is useful to have information from different checksizes as often subjects may have a small response to just one check size and this would give a misleading impression of the overall visual system. In true conductive problems, delayed responses will be seen at all checksizes and not just at small checks which can be caused by poor optics, amblyopia or subtle macular defects.

Amplitude of response can also provide some clues to visual function, though the spread of amplitudes within the normal population can make correctly identifying pathology challenging. Inter-ocular amplitude changes can be a strong indicator of unilateral loss of function, this could be for a number of reasons such as axonal loss, optic atrophy, glaucoma, compression due to glioma, hematoma, raised intracranial pressure (likely to be bilateral) etc. The ability to compare one eye to the other greatly increases the usefulness of the test and makes it easier to identify pathology.

A third characteristic to consider is the waveform shape, often termed morphology. In the example the responses are not particularly large but are very well defined, bifid peaks (a waveform with two peaks instead of one) (Rousseff et al., 2005) or a broad response (the timing of the N135 may be delayed or difficult to identify), may provide a subtle clue to pathology or indeed the risk of an evolving phenotype. It is of note that there is quite some variation of morphology in the normal group and drawing hard conclusions without other evidence should probably be refrained from.

Tan et al. (1984) describe how defocusing or eccentric fixation can defeat the test resulting in altered PRVEPs recordings. This emphasizes the need for vigilance of both the 'on-going' bio-electrical signal as well as monitoring of subject fixation either by a closed circuit camera or by an assistant coaching the subject to stay focused and fixed on the target. Tan's group also recommend using large check sizes (super-threshold) in these cases as defocusing has less of an impact on these large visual targets. Similarly, if a subject is not optimally corrected (with their glasses) when viewing the stimulus, then a sub-optimal response may well be collected. Opacities in the optics may blur the image causing a delay and/or reduction of the signal. It is therefore important to rule this out as a source of potential visual disruption prior to testing and reporting.

Flash VEP

The flash VEP (FVEP) is much more variable than the PRVEP, but does have the advantage that a response can still be detected even with minimal co-operation or in presence of compromised optics (Walsh et al., 2005). Due to the variability of response in the well-seeing population it is often difficult to determine if there is a bilateral abnormality, except in the most obvious cases of profound visual loss. It does however, have a role in identifying differences in function between the two eyes or in cases were there may be opacities of lens or media making it impossible for the Ophthalmologist (or retinal photographer) to image the back of the eye and assess the optic nerve head or retina.

The flash VEP ought to be conducted to full field stimulus (Ganzfeld), failing this the stimulus should at least cover the 20°. Most laboratories use a Ganzfeld bowl for testing, the German word Ganzfeld simple means full-field in English. Most

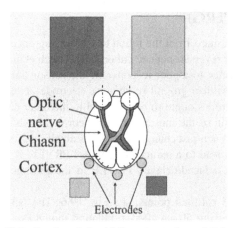

FIG. 19.5 Routing of visual information to the occipital cortex.

configurations use an integrating sphere with a light source (usually xenon flash or LEDs − Light-Emitting Diodes) shining from the top into the integrating sphere. If the geometry is right and surface is maximally reflective (most devices are usually coated white using a chemical process) the luminance achieved is equal regardless of direction of gaze. This is an important technical consideration to ensure the retina is fully and equally stimulated from all directions particularly when multi-channel VEP is undertaken. When testing, the patient is usually invited to place their chin on a chin rest that ought to sit within the integrating sphere (as opposed to the edge of a hemisphere). Brown's group described responses where the 'mini-Ganzfeld' had more of a hemisphere aperture with the same intensity and flash duration as the full-field Ganzfeld but smaller responses (Brown et al., 2009). This demonstrates the importance of the geometry of the integrating sphere being correct.

The single channel VEP recorded on Oz tends to evaluate the anterior optic nerve and global occipital cortex function. Any monocular visual abnormalities are unlikely to be cortical as it is the same cortex that is stimulated by each field. Fig. 19.5 shows the normal routing of vision. The right field of vision is seen on the nasal retina in the right eye, it travels along the anterior optic nerve, crosses at the chiasm, onto the left optic radiations, and finishes at the left occipital region. The right field of vision is seen on the temporal retina in the left eye, it travels along the anterior optic nerve, passes through the chiasm staying on the left, onto the left optic radiations and the signal finishes in the left occipital hemisphere (all light blue in Fig. 19.5). This has the advantage that the same cortical area is served by two different eyes seeing the same visual field, thus, allowing these neurons to have 2 different perspectives on the same visual scene that facilitates depth perception and 3-D vision.

Size and shadows of objects can give significant clues to how far away an object might be, particularly if we know the size of the object. Having information from 2 eyes about an object can give us further clues as the angle each eye views the object will be slightly different and will give an appreciation of how far away an object is.

From an electrophysiology point of view, the electrical response from each eye should be similar if both eyes are functioning well. The lateral channels (O1 & O2) ought to be similar from monocular testing if normal routing of the visual pathways is present. Possibly of note Oz will tend to be larger than O1 or O2, as an analogy it could be thought of as the vector summation of the electrical dipole of the left hemisphere with right hemisphere. Similarly VEP recordings with both eyes open tend to be larger than those recorded monocularly. If this isn't this case, one might suspect something isn't quite right, as in healthy vision information from each eye tends to reach the cortex at around the same time and summate. In pathology there may be cancellation of waves as they have slightly different phases.

In a scenario where the visual problem is anterior to the optical chiasm on the right side, we would expect the VEP from the Left Eye (LE) to be different to the Right Eye (RE) (usually larger and earlier). The patient would likely present with better vision in the LE than RE. In a scenario where the left hemisphere has been damaged, then the subject is likely to complain of not seeing the right visual field. The VEP recording would tend to be superior on the ROcc than LOcc to binocular, RE and LE viewing to a flash. Should a patient present with a bi-temporal field problem this might raise suspicions of a chiasmal lesion such as a tumour pressing on the chiasm. Were this the case, when testing the RE the right occipital response would be larger than left occipital response. When testing the LE there would be a larger left occipital response than right occipital. In ocular albinisim the opposite is true as there is an increase in the number of fibres that cross at the chiasm. When testing this condition in paediatrics with a flash stimulus, it would be expected that a larger response is seen on the LOcc when testing the RE and a larger response on the ROcc when testing the LE. This is often termed crossed asymmetry as the signal crosses over excessively at the Chiasm and the asymmetry crosses over depending on which eye is tested.

Pattern electroretinogram (PERG)

The PERG is the electrical response measured from the retina to a reversing checkboard similar to that used for PRVEP, though often with a faster reversal rate (4 reversals per second or 2 Hz) (Bach et al., 2013). It is a very useful adjunct to the PRVEP as often a poor PRVEP can be due to a poor response by the sensor (retina). Technically, recordings tend to be made with a sclereal/corneal electrode with a ground (common) electrode at forehead (or somewhere else electrically neutral like an ear lobe). Reference electrodes ought to be temporal to the outer canthus of the eye and ideally away from muscle mass to reduce electrical intrusion of the muscles. Optical correction should be worn for the distance the test is conducted. The PERG is very sensitive to contrast change, this means anything affecting the optics such as a subtle cataract can lead to a degraded PERG which can lead to a reduced or delayed PRVEP. A number of maculopathies (affecting the central vision) have reduced PERG. A reduced/delayed PRVEP in the presence of an intact PERG would be highly suggestive of a post retinal abnormality.

The PERG tends to be defined by 3 cardinal points, see Fig. 19.6. The N35 is a negativity occurring 35 ms after stimulation. The P50 is a positivity occurring 50 ms after stimulation thought to arise predominantly in the inner retina, though there is thought to be a substantial contribution to this wavelet from the ganglion cells. Finally the last wavelet, the N95 occurs around 95 ms after the stimulation, and is thought to arise from the ganglion cell layer. The ISCEV recommends recording with a corneal/sceleral electrode, but one that will not affect the optics (many of the contact lens electrodes do). The ISCEV also recommend repeat measurements be made as the PERG is often quite unreliable and technically difficult to perform, particularly if there is excessive blinking causing baseline shift or drift. It is important to identify baseline shift or drift which hasn't been rejected by the artefact rejection regime and either modify the report taking this into account or address the drift with post acquisition signal processing. One possible method may be to digitally filter the waveform with a high-pass filter. Often digital filters can be used that are superior in characteristic to analogue filters and can have rapid rise time and little or no phase distortion.

A reduced P50 can be due to macular dysfunction, optical blur or may be due to a reduced contribution to the P50 from the ganglion cell layer (thought to contribute on average around a third of the P50). The majority of the P50 is generated in the inner retina and often it is thought to reflect the health of this layer. A reduction in the N95 may suggest an abnormality at the ganglion cell layer. It is often clinically more useful to compare the size of the N95 to the P50 than N95 amplitude

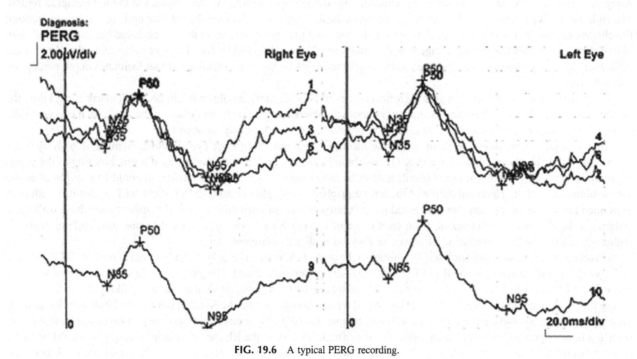

FIG. 19.6 A typical PERG recording.

alone. Cases with reduced N95 often have poor PRVEP also as it is the ganglion cell axons that form the optic nerve, which is important in transporting the visual signal from eye to brain.

Multifocal electroretinogram

In Ophthalmology, the term focal is often more closely associated with optics and focal length. In electrophysiology focal, tends to mean localized response. The Multifocal Electroretinogram (mfERG) elicits responses from many areas of the retina at approximately the same time. This is made possible by encoding the different areas' responses down a single channel with an m-sequence. The recorded signal is then decoded using the m-sequence, and a response relating to each stimulated area presented.

Eric Sutter patented the m-sequence's use with ERG around 1991. The technique as first described has an array of hexagons presented on a CRT monitor with a frame rate of around 75 Hz (base period $\sim$ 13 ms) (Sutter, 1985, 1991). Each hexagon is governed by the same m-sequence but cyclically shifted; this means each hexagon starts the m-sequence at a different position. The m-sequence is short for maximal length sequence, binary (0 or 1) and is pseudo-random. Pseudo-random just implies it is difficult to predict whether a hexagon will be ON or OFF in the next step of the sequence, particularly when viewing with the naked eye (a photodiode, spreadsheet and intimate knowledge of the m-sequence being used, may make this less random). The key feature of the m-sequence is its autocorrelation function is a Kronecker Delta at zero delay, and $-1/k$ everywhere else (were k is the number of steps in the sequence). M-sequences can be generated from shift registers and the length of the sequence is simply $2^n - 1$ were n is the length of the binary number seeding the shift register. The -1 is due to the fact that the shift register cannot operate at the all zero term so whilst a binary number length n has 2^n permutations, a -1 is required for the all zero term which cannot be achieved.

From this it is apparent that the longer the m-sequence the smaller the correlation with other hexagons. Even for a short sequence seeded with a 9-digit long binary number, will give a 511 long sequence, which would give minimal intrusion. Often systems are based on a 15 or 16-digit long number which results in very long m-sequences, with very little theoretical cross-correlation (contamination) from other areas. In the original publication, the m-sequence was run at quite a fast rate 13 ms which allowed a long sequence to be fully used and data collected in around 8 min of recording. At this rate there will be non-linearities, though the authors thought these are likely to be insignificant. In this context a linear response is one that does not change regardless of the time between flashes; a non-linear response is one that changes between flashes. When recorded with the laboratory lights on the mfERG tends to be a cone-mediate response, the cone pathway tends to recover from flashes more quickly than the rod system though even the cone system needs time to re-set. Temporally the central retina certainly doesn't operate beyond 50 Hz, the old CRTs achieved what seemed like a seamless picture, (except if viewed from the corner of one's eye when some might have been able to detect a flicker). The actual amount of time required to recover from a localized flash will probably depend on the area of the retina being tested, the intensity of the flash and the brightness of the background. Under normal recording conditions the macular will not be able to fully recover if two flashes are only 13 ms apart, Peter Gouras (Saeki and Gouras, 1996) looked at this in detail for the full field ERG. By having two flashes so close together creates a non-linearity with the response reduced due to the interference of the previous flash. This non-linearity can be mathematical modelled by higher order kernels. These are described by m-sequences and it is important that the calculated higher order kernels, such as the second order first slice, second order second slice and third order kernel do not overlap with the first order kernel m-sequence recording EPOCH.

The rate at which the stimulus is presented will affect the size and shape of response (Hood et al., 1997; Hagan et al., 2011). When the stimulus is slowed by the introduction of blank filler frames, responses tend to increase in amplitude, this effect tends to saturate with a base period (shortest time between flashes) around 100 ms with flash strength around 2 cd s/m^2. The morphology and implicit time is also likely to change and this altering of size and shape may well be different in pathology when compared to normal. Hood et al. (1997) concluded that slowing down the base period allowed the response to be closely mimic the response of the full-field ERG.

The method of stimulation presentation as well as rate is very important. It seems almost serendipitous that the characteristics of the CRT lend itself to being such a good method of stimulation for mfERG. In brief, the raster very quickly draws the image on the screen (hexagon), it has a very fast rise time, and very quick decay and so mimics a brief flash which is a very good stimulus for electrically recording the response from the retina. Compared to how an LCD or Plasma which would slowly go from dark to bright and stay bright until switched back to dark. An example might help to clarify this; if a hexagon is left on a 60 Hz CRT with luminance of 120 cd/m^2 then each flash will be 2 cd s/m^2. A Plasma might have a 400 cd/m^2 luminance but rather than being made up of 60 discrete flashes of 2 cd s/m^2 the first 1 or 2 ms (the time for a CRT to flash) would yield 0.4—0.8 cd s/m^2 and would not generate the same level of response (see Fig. 19.7). Also when testing, if the sequence had two 1 s together, the plasma instead of returning to black between flashes would

FIG. 19.7 Schematics representation of light characteristics of CRTs and Plasma screens, the 'brief flash' of the CRT helps facilitate recording.

stay white and there would be no response to this continued state for the second flash (this can be overcome in plasma's by programming dark steps in between m-sequence steps). A detailed examination of this is probably beyond the scope of this chapter though the reader is referred to Parks & Keating's excellent work in this area (Keating et al., 2001).

The mfERG can give topographical information of the function of the central macular. It is fairly robust to optical blur, though does require good fixation and concentration. Fixation ought to be monitored closely, though Hagan (Hagan et al., 2010) has demonstrated that the response from the central macular area in healthy controls are slower than off-centre areas and so this delay should be anticipated when recording and could be used to help validate or question (if not present) fixation. Technically the recording has a similar electrode montage to PERG, though pupils ought to be dilated and ideally optically corrected for the distance of recording. The ISCEV recommend using 61 or 103 hexagons, though some (Praidou et al., 2014) have noted the value of using a smaller number of hexagons in paediatrics where concentration may be limited and collecting good SNR quickly may be important. Chisholm et al. (2001) found using a Gadarian Eyetracker that the subjects gaze fell within 1.2° of target 51% of the time, suggesting that a high resolution stimuli of below 2.4° may be prone to fixation errors. However, this work was conducted in visually healthy individuals and fixation in those with central loss of vision may be worse.

The mfERG response consists of a mini array of 'ERGs' corresponding to the stimulus array. It consists of a negativity termed N1 and a positivity termed P1, under the right conditions these components can have similar morphology to the full field Photopic ERG and indeed the full field responses behave in a similar fashion to an increase in background luminance and stimulus intensity (Hood et al., 1997). Changes in amplitude, implicit time and morphology may give clues to dysfunction. Performing statistical analysis on 103 hexagons may be prohibitive without software and 95% reference ranges (limits of normal) may yield abnormalities in good sighted people. Often ring-averaged waveforms are created and these tend to be examined against reference ranges, as well as vigilantly looking for a pattern of depressed responses from the individual areas (of note the hexagon corresponding to the optic nerve head-blindspot ought to have a smaller response). Group averaged quadrants or hemifields can also be useful in determining a pattern of dysfunction.

Central mfERG responses are reduced in maculopathies such as Stargardt's or Sorsby. Peripheral areas are often reduced in disease that affects peripheral vision such as Retinitis Pigmentosa (RP) and the mfERG can monitor how much of the central vision is spared in this progressive disease. mfERG can detected changes in macular function due to toxicity from drugs such as Hydroxychloroquine. In cases where the optics may not be quite right the PERG (often described as a macular test) may be reduced, but the mfERG (being more robust to contrast change) may be normal suggesting macular function is in fact intact.

Electroretinogram

The Electroretinogram (ERG) was first recorded in a frog's eye in 1865 by Holmgren and has become a centre-piece in visual electrophysiology recording. Advances in electrode technology along with computer averaging of responses have allowed for high quality recordings to be made with no or only minor discomfort to most patients. Kriss et al. (Kriss, 1994) demonstrated that skin electrodes could give reliable responses in paediatrics, virtually removing any discomfort in recording. At present the ISCEV recommends 6 separate tests be used in a standard ERG session (McCulloch et al., 2015): Rod isolated ~ 0.01 cd s/m^2 after 20 min dark adaptation; mixed response 3.0 cd s/m^2 after 20 min dark adaptation; bright flash 10.0 cd s/m^2 after 20 min dark adaptation; oscillatory potentials to 3.0 cd s/m^2 after 20 min dark; photopic response 3.0 cd s/m^2 on a light background 30 cd/m^2; 30 Hz flicker 3.0 cd s/m^2 on a light background 30 cd/m^2. Testing should be

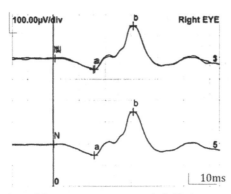

FIG. 19.8 Cone pathway 3.0 response, top traces are individual averages, bottom grand average.

conducted with similar electrode montage to PERG. Pupils ought to be maximally dilated, though Kriss has demonstrated clinically useful information can still be garnered in paediatrics without the use of mydratics (eye drop that increases dilatation of the pupil), without the risk of losing patient co-operation because of the stinging the eye drops cause. Testing should be conducted with fullfield stimulation via a Ganzfeld as for FVEP, though handheld stimulation providing at least 20° of stimulation can be used in paediatrics. Flash duration should be no more than 5 ms.

Cone pathway testing is conducted with a background light on (~ 30 cd/m^2) to saturate or bleach the rods so they cannot react to the flashes, thereby, isolating the cone pathway response. The first negativity is termed the a-wave and is largely generated at the photoreceptor layer (though there is some contribution from the post-photoreceptor ON/OFF pathways). Once the photoreceptors have been activated they synapse with the bipolar cells (ON/OFF depending on which ones they are connected to). The bipolar cells release potassium, which is then sequestered by the muller (glial) cells creating the electrical dipole measured as positive at the cornea and is termed the b-wave (see Fig. 19.8). The ISCEV have picked a flash intensity and duration that cause both the ON & OFF responses to overlap and summate. Whilst an increase in intensity results in a larger a-wave it won't necessarily result in an increase of the b-wave as the ON & OFF pathway responses become separated with a broader earlier ON response and later OFF response at higher intensities (Ueno et al., 2004) (the peak response is thought likely to be generated in most people around 4–6 cd s/m^2 with standard background illumination (Wali and Leguire, 1992)). Knowing what is expected in terms of amplitude and implicit time for these two waveforms helps to identify which are likely to be normal and those likely to be abnormal, often 95% reference ranges are calculated (sometimes referred to as the normal range).

The 30 Hz flicker isolates the cone pathway response via its background illumination and by the rate at which it stimulates the retina which is much too fast for the rods to recover from between flashes. It could be considered as a steady-state response as it over drives the retina and does not let it fully recover between flashes. The waveform tends to be characterized by measuring the amplitude between the first trough and first peak and the implicit time of the first peak. This peak is thought to be largely generated in the inner retina and tends to be smaller in amplitude than the transient 3.0 standard flash in light b-wave. Some systems perform a Fourier transform of the full wave.

Scotopic testing is conducted in the dark. The ISCEV recommends dark adapting the subject for 20 min prior to performing the test. It is thought that after 20 min the response will no longer grow (with further dark adaptation) to the ISCEV flashes. For dark adaptometry, a 40 min period of dark adaptation is required, though this is after a very strong bleaching light and so whilst in a Goldman-Weekes dark adaptometer it may be around 7 min for the cone-rod break to occur, without the bleaching light the rods start to adapt much faster. In paediatrics when co-operation is not guaranteed clinically useful responses can be recorded with shorter periods of dark adaptation.

The 0.01 is a very dim flash and only the rods are sensitive enough to detect this low level of photic energy. The response is a single late positivity at around 80 ms, which is generated via the bipolar/muller cell dipole. Although the test is often referred to as a rod isolating testing, it is in fact the next neuron (Bipolar Cell) in the visual cascade that is responsible for generating this positivity. Of note, the rods synapses in response to on-bipolar cells, so it is an on-pathway response. A technical issue to be vigilant of is the intrusion of a blink artefact masquerading as a healthy physiological response. Due to the simplistic nature of the response it is often difficult to tell these apart, though in our laboratory the b-wave's response tends to start at around 40 ms, whilst a blink may be much later. The stimulus ought to be present no more than once every 2 s (<0.5 Hz).

The 3.0 in the dark elicits a response from both rod and cone pathways and may be termed mixed response, maximal response or response to standard flash. The a-wave is generated predominantly by the photoreceptors (though there is likely a contribution from post-photoreceptoral ON and OFF pathways). Of note there is around twenty times the number of rods than cones, so the photoreceptor contribution to the a-wave is likely to be dominated by the rods. Cursoring of the a-wave may prove problematic for some, as often a high frequency component bi-sect the negativity, meaning the implicit time for this response in some is before this high frequency component (OP1) and for others after it. The b-wave is the positivity after the a-wave and tends to have its amplitude measured from the trough of the a-wave to the peak of the b-wave. The implicit time is measured from baseline, to peak of response. The ISCEV recommends the stimulus should be presented no more than once every 10 s to ensure full recovery between flashes, of note with corneal electrodes, averaging may not be necessary though a repeat is highly recommended.

The high frequency components of the dark adapted ERG, termed oscillatory potentials (OPs), are recommended to be collected with a high-pass filter set to at least at 75 Hz. There tends to be 3 main peaks often with a fourth smaller one present, though sometimes there can be 5 clear wavelets. OPs are highly variable and can be susceptible to subtle changes in adaptation or stimulus presentation. OPs are often sensitive to ischemic or toxic changes, however, they have been noted to be reduced in subjects with diabetes without retinopathy and can be altered by recent food intake in diabetics. It is recommended that the response to the first flash be ignored (as responses are highly non-linear) and flashes are presented at least 10 s apart.

The 10.0 flash or bright flash elicits a mixed rod cone response, which tends to be slightly larger than the 3.0. Of note the a-wave amplitude will tend to grow by more than the b-wave which will change the morphology of response. The a-wave peak now tends to be before the first OP reducing variability of the implicit time and some have suggested the slope of the a-wave can give clues to dysfunction.

Interpretation of the ERG

Absent ERGs would be highly suggestive of gross retinal dysfunction at the photoreceptor layer, in this scenario it would probably be wise to check electrode contact before drawing a firm conclusion (of note silicon oil can be used to treat detached retina and as it is an insulator can greatly reduce recording amplitude). Absent cone pathway responses with normal rod pathway responses would suggest severe cone dysfunction as seen in conditions such as achromatopsia, (though achromats with incomplete involvement may still have a residual response). Reduced or delayed cone pathway responses would suggest an abnormality of the cone pathway and as a group are termed cone dystrophies. Cone pathway responses are worse affected than rod pathway responses and tend to be termed as cone-rod dystrophies. A reduction in rod pathway responses with cone pathway responses less affected may suggest a rod-cone dystrophy such as RP (Retinitis Pigmentosa). A larger a-wave response than the b-wave to a 3.0 standard flash in the dark is termed a negative ERG and suggests post photoreceptor dysfunction and can be seen in Congenital Stationary Night Blindness (CSNB), X-linked retinoschisis, Duchenne muscular dystrophy, Melanoma Associated Retinopathy (MAR), Cancer Associated Retinopathy (CAR), unilaterally in Central Retinal Vein Occlusion (CRVO) or Central Retinal Artery Occlusion (CRAO), and siderosis. Negative ERGs can be caused by toxicity such as in quinine overdose or in autoimmune disorders such as birdshot chorioretinopathy. There are many possible causes and the differential diagnosis is usually made from fundus appearance and reviewing the patient's case history. After isolating the pathways and responses from different cellular layers it is possible to provide clues as to where in the retina the problem lies and which pathway is affected. This can help the referring ophthalmologist diagnose, manage, and possibly treat the individual patient effectively.

Electro-Oculargram (EOG)

The EOG (Marg, 1951) rose to prominence after Arden et al.'s (Arden and Fojas, 1962) work identifying that taking a ratio of the light peak to dark trough yielded the most clinically useful clues (though other information such as standing potential amplitude and peak light time rise may still be of some value). The front of the eye is electrically positive compared to the back to the eye. It is this potential that allows us to monitor the sweep (or saccade) of the eye as it passes from gazing from side to side. This is made possible by placing a skin surface electrode either side of the eye (beside the outer canthi, on the bony ridge if possible, and the side of the bridge of the nose beside the eye, usually with a forehead electrode acting as ground). In this scenario if the electrode on the side of the bridge of the nose is positive, then when the eye turns to towards this electrode the electrical recording goes positive and when looking towards the reference the trace goes negative. By giving the patient targets (usually red LEDs 30° apart) the saccade length can be controlled and with all other things being kept the same then stable electrical amplitude between each saccade should be obtained. Recordings should be achieved with as low a high-pass filter as possible (without causing serious saturation issues), this ensures when the subject is focused on one LED the recorded standing potential is as flat as possible (not drifting). While most systems calculate saccade amplitude automatically, the operator should be mindful of overshoots and should ensure saccades used for the calculation are as free from noise as possible.

Prior to testing care should be taken to ensure the patient has been in ambient lighting for approx. 30-minutes, being in the dark or exposed to bright lights will cause the standing potential at the back of the eye to oscillate between minimums and maximums for a period not dissimilar to a sine wave (amplitude y-axis) traveling through time (time-x-axis), with diminishing peak-to-peak the further from the light stimulus. Electrode placement is as above for right eye, and at the Liverpool laboratory for left eye the outer canthi electrode is the active to avoid cross talk between the two eyes with reference on the left-side of the bridge of the nose (Liverpool Laboratory would recommend this electrode convention though others are possible, probably the most important thing is to consistently place the electrodes on without cross-talk).

Testing should be conducted using a Ganzfeld bowl to control light phase luminance or similar with steady fixation targets 30° apart. It is important that the subject follows the fixation targets with their eyes only, keeping their head still and this may need to be explained prior to testing. Once electrodes have been located, it is recommended a couple of runs of saccades are made with the lights on (alternation between fixation targets should be around 1 per second). These first couple of runs afford the operator the opportunity to identify any problems with the electrode setup, or the subject's ability to perform the saccades. This gives the operator the opportunity to further coach the subject to keep their head still, not anticipate the next saccade and not to go past the target, slow and steady saccades should be encouraged. In cases of macular dysfunction the subject might not be able to see the fixation light with the background light on and this is better discovered prior to performing the dark phase. Some systems will allow for increasing the brightness of the target LEDs in these circumstances, which may aid the subject to perform the task. Using a close circuit camera to monitor fixation is highly recommended, to help the operator monitor the saccades and if eyes are open during the light phase.

Once the operator is happy with the subjects saccades, the room lights and Ganzfeld bowl (or similar) should be extinguished. Saccades should then be measured over the next 15 min in the dark, these could be at 2-min intervals to begin with, but after approx 6 min should be taken every minute. Each saccade run should contain at least 4 or 5 cycles of saccades, and if measuring the amplitude manually, it is important to ignore peak overshoots or saccades inconsistent with those in the same run. During this dark phase a minimum or trough should be identified and this amplitude and time of trough should be noted.

After 15 min the room lights and Ganzfeld bowl (or similar) lights should be switched on (achieving ~ 100 cd/m^2). The subject may be dazzled and it may be unpleasant for them to try to make saccades in this first minute. Asking them to sit back and get adjusted to the new light level may improve the patient experience without a detrimental impact to testing. The light peak tends to occur in most subjects after 6—10 min in the light so missing the first minute will not have a great impact on the overall result. Over the next 15 min saccades should be collected every minute, once a clear peak has been detected usually in the first 10 min, the test can be stopped. Some care is needed here as on some occasions the results plateau before increasing again and vigilance is required to ensure that a large result isn't due to an artefact such as an overshoot (by inspection of raw saccade).

The Arden ratio is calculated by dividing the light peak/dark trough, plotting the standing potentials against time may also help to identify outliers or noise so that robust peak and trough values are used. The ISCEV (Constable et al., 2017) recommends the Arden ratio now be termed the light peak to dark trough index. Arden's original work suggested a cut-off of around 1.85, whilst more recent work would suggest normal values may be as low as 1.6, which is around the lower limit suggested from the 46 normal data sets collected at the Liverpool laboratory. Normal cut-offs may be different between laboratories, due to light level used, whether pupils have been dilated or not (it is suggested that higher light phase luminance be used if undilated), amplifier settings or indeed method to establish saccadic standing potential or method for determining light peak to dark trough.

Calibration

Periodic photometric calibration is an essential part of the quality assurance (QA) of a visual electrophysiology laboratory. The calibration unit should be traceable to a national standard. At every stage there may be systemic error, so the fewer stages the better. It is essential the head of service can identify the route to that traceable standard so they can have confidence in their recordings. Only when the system has been calibrated can there be confidence in the performance since the previous calibration. Any detriment in function uncovered by calibration may have been present the whole time since the previous calibration, so regular calibration is warranted. Of note modern LED stimulators tend to be fairly robust so unless there is a significant failure the likelihood of subtle drift is small. The ISCEV recommends calibrating at least every 6 months and the effort required to calibrate should be balanced against a recall of the previous 6 months patients should a calibration fail.

A photometer is essentially a radiometer that has a filter tuned to the spectral sensitivity of the eye. A radiometer detects all electromagnetic waves, whilst light being that part of the electromagnetic spectrum describable by the eye, will only be detected by the photometer if its waves pass through the filter. The further away the wavelength is from peak transmission (555 nm), the more the filter attenuates it. For luminance of screen and Ganzfeld background light the photometer should be used in direct acquisition mode. For flashes the photometer needs to be able to integrate the light energy over time, it is recommended to build averages of flashes (~n = 10), repeat and control background lighting as far as practically possible. It is important to pay attention to any drift (caused by change in light or even electrical) and take account of this. Low level flashes can be challenging to calibrate.

Case study 19.1

A thirty year old female was referred for EDT testing after noticing a significant change in her LE vision. The patient's foggy vision cleared 3 weeks after its onset and apart from slight pain on extreme gaze everything was fine. She also mentioned that occasionally she had pins and needles in her extremities (possibly due to poor posture). She was seen 6 −8 weeks after initial visual loss. Testing started with Pattern Reversal Visual Evoked Potential (traces on left) to try and establish the quality of vision from each eye and more importantly the conduction time from each eye. Clear responses have been record of good amplitude but the LE responses are delayed by around 20 ms.

A PERG was performed (top right) to ensure each macular was developing similar signals, which they were. A full field ERG was conducted to ensure there was no unexpected pan retinal problem. This visual problem has been isolated to outside the retina and given the history is most likely an optic neuritis.

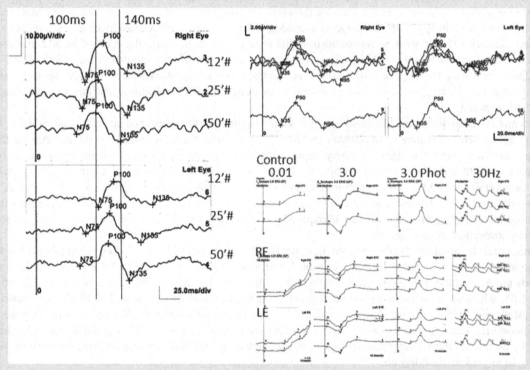

PRVEP to a range of checks (50′-12.5′). RE responses on top. Vertical line imposed at 100 ms to show delay of P100 peak. Vertical line imposed at 140 ms to show delay of N135 trough. PERG responses top right, group averages at bottom of panel, ERGs are bottom right.

Case study 19.2

A gentleman in his early 60s presented with reduced field of vision in his LE and had a RAPD (Relative Afferent Pupil Defect). An MRI scan was conducted with no obvious change. No gross fundus changes were noted. PRVEP are normal from each eye and similar (top left panel). A PERG was then conducted to check macular function. The PERG response is really very unusual from the LE with the P50 attenuated but the N95 intact (top right panel). This rather suggests disruption of the P50 as opposed to a maculopathy. An ERG was then performed with goldleaf electrodes and fully dilated pupils (bottom panel). The RE responses are all acceptable as normal. LE responses are much reduced and in particular the b-wave amplitude. The response to the standard flash in the dark (3.0) is termed a negative ERG, as the b-wave peak remains below the baseline (or the a-wave is larger than the b-wave). The LE a-wave is marginally smaller than the RE, though it is known that there is a contribution from post-photoreceptor processes to the a-wave amplitude. The most common cause of an acquired unilateral negative ERG is vascular: central retinal vein occlusion (CRVO) or central retinal artery occlusion (CRAO) often being the causes, though Siderosis (metal fragment in eye-usually resulting in fundoscopy changes) or Autoimmune cases have also been described.

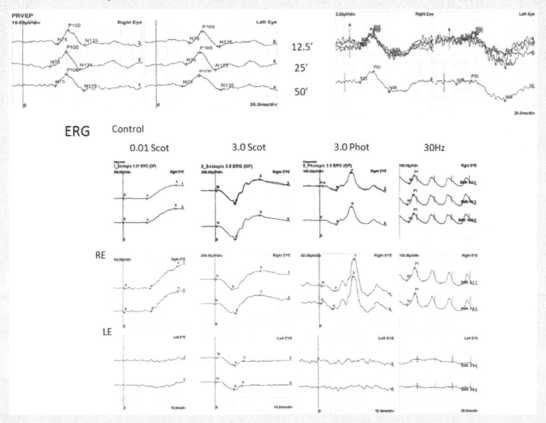

Top left panel normal PRVEP to range of checks, PERG top right- normal RE but disrupted P50 with normal N95 LE. Bottom panel is the ERG with starkly abnormal results LE, including a negative ERG to the 3.0 in the dark.

Case study 19.3

A lady in her forties presented to clinic with poor near vision. She had a beaten bronze fundus appearance similar to that of Stargardt Macular Dystrophy (SMD) or Fundus Flavimaculatus (FF). Vision is still fairly well maintained with RE 6/9 and LE 6/6.

Testing started with mfERG recorded with goldfoil electrodes and pupils dilated out to 8 mm diameter. Responses are clearly reduced from the central hexagon from each eye, though the group averaged response from the second ring although within normal limits is suspiciously small compared to the very healthy sized group averaged response from the third ring. This would suggest quite significant central dysfunction (though there is likely sparring at the very centre to facilitate her good visual acuity). The full field ERG shows fairly healthy responses and indicates the problem is isolated to the central maculae at this stage.

Given the fundus image is consistent with SMD or FF and the electrophysiology is consistent with both of these it is almost certainly one of these. Both SMD and FF have changes in the ABCA4 gene located on 1p22, SMD tends to present in the first two decades, whilst FF is later and thought to be an allelic subtype of SMD. Given the age of onset then, the most likely diagnosis is Fundus Flavimaculatus (FF).

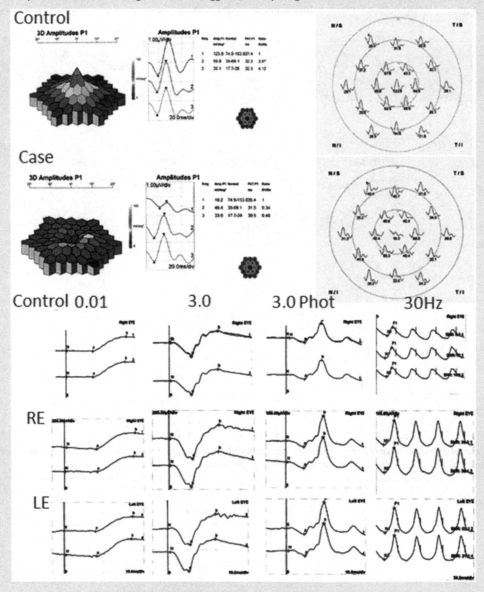

Top mfERG should an absent peak of response density centrally. Bottom ERG are within normal limits.

Case study 19.4

A lady in her twenties attended clinic due to difficulty seeing in the dark. Fundus appearance is consistent with retinitis pigmentosa (RP). Testing started with mfERG (top panel) recorded with gold leaf electrode and pupils fully dilated. Response from the central area is low-end normal for amplitude. Although the responses beyond this are clearly present they are slightly smaller than our reference range data. The ERG (bottom panel)

further reinforces the loss of function beyond this, with only vestigial cone responses and an undetectable isolate rod pathway response. RP often initially presents with complaints of poor nighttime vision (vision in the dark) and as in this case the rod pathway function is often worse affected than the cone pathway.

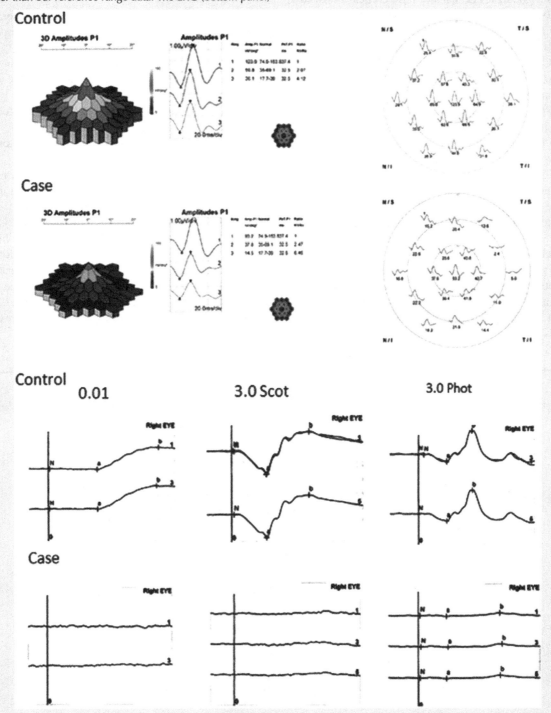

Top mfERG revealing central sparring, whilst (Bottom) ERG shows marked reduction of response outside this centrally area. Only a single eye's response is shown for brevity as the results were symmetrical between the two eyes.

Summary

This chapter has discussed the anatomy and physiology of vision. It has discussed some of the more commonly used electrophysiology tests. Table 19.1 is a summary of the salient technical setups of the various tests.

PRVEP has low variability and provides strong clues to overall visual function. As it is a cortical response, it is often thought to be a cortical test or an optic nerve test. In fact a pristine PRVEP requires good fixation, concentration, optics capable of resolving the stimulus, well functioning retina, optic nerve and cortex. If any of these is altered the PRVEP can be reduced. Of note the PRVEP only measures up to the primary visual cortex, if a lesion is beyond this then it is possible to record a good PRVEP but still have cortical visual loss.

FVEP is a much more robust and rudimentary test of vision. It has great use when opacities are present or cooperation is limited (paediatrics). Due to variation it may have limited input except when making inter-ocular or inter-hemispherical comparisons. Multi-channel VEP is useful in detecting lesions at the chasmal level or beyond.

PERG is a very useful adjunct to the PRVEP as it provides information about how the sensor (eye) is performing to the same sort of stimulus. Unless a PERG is performed it is difficult to be certain whether an abnormal PRVEP is due to optic nerve damage (or beyond) or whether it is due to macular dysfunction or poor optics.

mfERG provides topographic information about function of the macular. mfERG is thought to be more robust to changes in optics than PERG, and can detect localized areas of dysfunction.

ERG provides clues to the health of the rod and cone pathways; and whether pathology is at the photoreceptor layer, bipolar cell layer or beyond.

EOG is a measure of the RPE-photoreceptor complex and is useful in diagnosing Bests Macular Dystrophy where the ERG is normal and the EOG is badly affected. It will be reduced in disease with pan retinal dysfunction (often in these cases the a-wave is very reduced).

Using this battery of tests the visual electrophysiologist can give the Ophthalmologist clues as to whether there is visual dysfunction, the location of the dysfunction (retina/macular/photoreceptors/bipolar/optic nerve/chiasm/cortex) is likely to occur and with repeat testing or history can provide clues as to whether pathology is likely to recover, stay stationary or progress. Electrophysiology has an emerging use in monitoring retinal toxicity in drug treatments and evaluation of treatments for diabetic maculopathy and age related maculopathy. Reporting several different test results at once can be challenging and it is worth bearing in mind in these instances that one should try to make sense of the whole gestalt and each test should support or reinforce an overall story (however real-life electrophysiology often confounds the text book examples).

TABLE 19.1 Summary of technical details of testing.

	Field (min)	Adaption	Dilated	Michelson contrast (%)	Stim rate	Bandpass (min)	Recording EPOCH (min)	Luminance	Stim. Strength
PRVEP	15°	Ambient	No	80+	1.8–2.2 RPS	1–100	250 ms, 500 ms < 1 y.o.	40–60	
Pattern onset	15°	Ambient	No	80+	1.4–1.67 Hz	1–100	250 ms, 500 ms < 1 y.o.	40–60	
Flash VEP	20°	Ambient	No/Yes	n/a	0.9–1.1 Hz	1–100	250 ms, 500 ms < 1 y.o.	27–34	2.7–3.4
PERG	15°	Ambient	No	80+	3.2–4.8 RPS	1–100	150 ms	>30	
mfERG	40°–50°	Ambient	Yes	90+		10–100 to 3–300	100 ms		>100 cd/m²
EOG	Full field	Ambient 30 min	Yes	n/a	~1 Hz	≤0.1–30	10 s	Dark ~0	Light 90 –110 cd/m²
Dim flash 0.01 ERG	20°	Dark 20 min	Yes	n/a	≤0.5 Hz	0.3–300	50 ms pre-stim, 250+ms post	0	0.0063–0.016
Standard 3.0 ERG	20°	Dark 20 min	Yes	n/a	≤0.1 Hz	0.3–300	50 ms pre-stim, 250+ms post	0	2.7–3.4
OPs	20°	Dark 20 min	Yes	n/a	≤0.1 Hz	>75–300	50 ms pre-stim, 250+ms post	0	2.7–3.4
Bright 10 ERG	20°	Dark 20 min	Yes	n/a	≤0.05 Hz	0.3–300	50 ms pre-stim, 250+ms post	0	8.9–11.2
Ph. Standard 3.0 ERG	20°	Ambient 10+ min	Yes	n/a	≤2.0 Hz	0.3–300	50 ms pre-stim, 250+ms post	27–34	2.7–3.4
30 Hz Ficker	20°	Ambient 10+ min	Yes	n/a	28 –33 Hz	0.3–300	50 ms pre-stim, 250+ms post	27–34	2.7–3.4

Abbreviations

CRAO	Central Retinal Artery Occlusion
CRT	Cathode Ray Tube
CRVO	Central Retinal Vein Occlusion
CSNB	Congenital Stationary Night Blindness
ERG	Electroretinogram
EOG	Electro-Oculargram
FVEP	Flash Visual Evoked Potential
ISCEV	International Society for Clinical Electrophysiology of Vision
LCD	Liquid Crystal Display
LE	Left Eye
LED	Light-Emitting Diode
MAR	Melanoma Associated Retinopathy
mfERG	Multifocal Electroretinogram
PERG	Pattern Electroretinogram
PRVEP	Pattern reversal Visual Evoked Potential
QA	Quality Assurance
RE	Right Eye
VEP	Visual Evoked Potential

References

Arden, G.B., Fojas, M.R., 1962. Electrophysiological abnormalities in pigmentary degenerations of the retina. Arch. Ophthalmol. 68, 369−389.

Bach, M., Brigell, M.G., Hawlina, M., Holder, G.E., Johnson, M.A., McCulloch, D.L., Meigen, T., Viswanathan, S., 2013. ISCEV standard for clinical pattern electroretinogram (PERG): 2012 update. Doc. Ophthalmol. 126, 1−7.

Brown, M.C., Lowson, R.F., Hagan, R.P., Small, A., Fisher, A.C., 2009. Comparison of ERG responses from full size and mini Ganzfeld stimulators. Investig. Ophthalmol. Vis. Sci. 50. ARVO E-Abstract 4520.

Chisholm, J.A., Keating, D., Parks, S., Evans, A.L., 2001. The impact of fixation on the multifocal electroretinogram. Doc. Ophthalmol. 102, 131−139.

Constable, P.A., Bach, M., Frishman, L.J., Jeffrey, B.G., Robson, A.G., 2017. ISCEV Standard for clinical electro-oculography (2017 update). Doc. Ophthalmol. 134, 1−9.

Dewar, J., 1877. The physiologic action of light. Nature 15, 433−435.

Dewar, J., McKendrick, J.G., 1875. On the physiological action of light. Trans. R. Soc. Edin. 27, 141−167.

Geffre, A., Concorde, D., Braun, J.P., Trumel, C., 2011. Reference value advisor: a new freeware set of macroinstructions to calculate reference intervals with Microsoft Excel. Vet. Clin. Pathol. 40, 107−112.

Hagan, R.P., Small, A., Fisher, A.C., Brown, M.C., 2010. Can central hexagon peak latency provide a clue to fixation with the mfERG. Doc. Ophthalmol. 120 (2), 159−164.

Hagan, R.P., Fisher, A.C., Brown, 2011. Investigation of the temporal properties of the retina using the m-sequence. Doc. Ophthalmol. 123, 179−185.

Hood, D.C., Seiple, W., Holopigian, K., et al., 1997. A comparison of the components of the multifocal and full-field ERGs. Vis. Neurosci. 14, 533−544.

Jasper, H.H., 1958. The ten twenty system of the International Federation. Electroencephalogr. Clin. Neurophysiol. 10, 371−375.

Keating, D., Parks, S., Malloch, C., Evans, A., 2001. A comparsion of CRT and digital stimulus delivery methods in the multifocal ERG. Doc. Ophthalmol. 102, 95−114.

Kriss, A., 1994. Skin ERGs: their effectiveness in paediatric visual assessment, confounding factors, and comparison with ERGs recorded using various types of corneal electrode. Int. J. Psychophysiol. 16, 137−146.

Marg, E., 1951. Development of electro-oculography. Arch. Ophthalmol. 45, 169−185.

McCulloch, D.L., Marmor, M.F., Brigell, M.G., Hamilton, R., Holder, G.E., Tzekov, R., Bach, M., 2015. ISCEV Standard for full-field clinical electroretinography (2015 update). Doc. Ophthalmol. 130, 1−12.

Odom, J.V., Bach, M., Brigell, M., Holder, G.E., McCulloch, D.L., Mizota, A., Tormene, A.P., 2016. Doc. Ophthalmol. 133, 1−9.

Praidou, A., Hagan, R., Nayak, H., Chandna, A., 2014. Multifocal electroretinogram contributes to differentiation of various clinical pictures within a family with Bardet-Biedle syndrome. Eye 28 (9), 1136−1142.

Rousseff, R.T., Tzvetanov, P., Rousseva, M.A., 2005. The bifid visual evoked potential-normal variant or a sign of demyelination? Clin. Neurol. Neurosurg. 107, 113−116.

Royal College of Ophthalmologists, 2008. Low Vision the Essential Guide for Ophthalmologists. The Guide Dogs For the Blind Association. ISBN:978-0-9559268-0-8.

Saeki, M., Gouras, P., 1996. Cone ERGs to flash trains: the antagonism of a later flash. Vis. Res. 36, 3229−3235.

Sutter, E.E., 1985. Multi-Input VER and ERG Analysis for Objective Perimetry. Proceedings of the Seventh Annual Conference of Engineering and Medical Society, pp. 414−419.

Sutter, E.E., 1991. The fast m-Transform: a fast computation of cross-correlations with binary m-sequences. SIAM J. Comput. 20, 686−694.

Tan, C.T., Murray, N.M.F., Sawyers, D., Leonard, T.J.K., 1984. Delibrae alteration of the visual evoked potential. J. Neurol. Neurosurg. Psychiatry 47, 518–523.

Ueno, S., Kondo, M., Niwa, Y., et al., 2004. Luminance dependance of neural components that underlies the primate photopic electroretinogram. Invest. Ophtalmol. Vis. Sci. 45, 1033.

Wali, N., Leguire, L.E., 1992. The photopic hill: a new phenomenon of the light adapted electroretinogram. Doc. Ophthalmol. 80, 335–345.

Walsh, P., Kane, N., Butler, S., 2005. The clinical role of evoked potentials. J. Neurol. Neurosurg. Psychiatry 76, 16–22.

Further reading

Fishman, G.A., Birch, D.G., Holder, G.E., Brigell, M.G., 2001. In: Electrophysiologic Testing in Disorders of the Retina, Optic Nerve, and Visual Pathway, second ed. American Academy of Ophthalmology. ISBN:1-56055-198-4.

Haliday, A.M. (Ed.), 1992. Evoked Potentials in Clinical Testing, second ed. Churchill Livingstone. ISBN:0-443-04050-8.

Section IV

Rehabilitation engineering & assistive technology

Chapter 20

Introduction

David Long

AJM Healthcare, UK & Oxford University Hospitals NHS Foundation Trust, Oxford, UK

Chapter outline

Introduction to rehabilitation engineering

It is hoped that the reader of this chapter will be provided with some foresight into the world of rehabilitation engineering and assistive technology, particularly in relation to dealing with face-to-face patient contact, an area in which engineers are often less experienced. Much of what is presented may be applied broadly to the various subject areas. Whilst disability may not on the face of it be the most attractive area in which to work, it is, to quote Tom Shakespeare (2018), "… both extremely interesting and rather complicated."

Acknowledgements

I should personally like to acknowledge the following people who I have had the privilege to work alongside and who, in different ways, have influenced my thinking: Dave Calder, Paul Dryer, Dr Barend ter Haar, Margaret Hannan, Rick Houghton, Henry Lumley, Dr Linda Marks, David Mitchell, Wendy Murphy, Roy Nelham, Bex Oakes, Steve Peck,

Pauline Pope, Dr David Porter, Pat Postill, Paul Richardson, Nathan Robson, Nigel Shapcott, Phil Swann, Linda Walker and Jon Ward.

Titles for engineers

The term rehabilitation engineering is not universally defined. In this book it is used to encapsulate a broad spread of clinical areas. Engineers working in these fields are referred to either as *rehabilitation engineers*, *clinical engineers*, *bioengineers, clinical technologists* or, less commonly these days, *technical officers*. Technicians may support the work of an engineer (or therapist) and it is generally the case that clinical engineers and bioengineers will carry out clinical assessment independently, but in some countries this role is termed *rehabilitation engineer*, and what is referred to in some areas as *rehabilitation engineer* is referred to in others as *rehabilitation technician*. In the UK, clinical and bioengineers are usually state registered under the protected title of *clinical scientist*. Furthermore, *orthotists* and *orthopaedic engineers* may be involved in the clinical casting process for the production of custom contoured wheelchair seating.

One must be aware of this inconsistency in terms when communicating with different services/organizations who may have little understanding of engineering applied to the clinical setting.

Principles of communication and patient assessment

Asking questions

A fundamental part of the engineer's role is to ask questions in order to find out precisely what has been requested. However, it is often tempting to want to jump ahead with getting a result or finding a "solution". In his book "The Hitchhiker's Guide to the Galaxy", Adams describes how a computer is asked a question, and eventually produces a result:

> The answer to the great question ... of life, the universe and everything ... is ... forty-two" said Deep Thought, with infinite majesty and calm. "I checked it very thoroughly," said the computer, "and that quite definitely is the answer. I think the problem, to be quite honest with you, is that you've never actually known what the question is ... so once you do know what the question is, you'll know what the answer means.

Adams (1979)

This is particularly true in clinical practice where it is vital that a reliable method of communication with the patient is established, but with the problem that it is often deeply flawed. We make sometimes sweeping assumptions about what we have heard and are thoroughly convinced that what we have said has been crystal clear, but as George Bernard Shaw has pointed out:

> The single biggest problem with communication is the illusion that it has taken place.

How many times have you later realized that the outcome from a previous conversation was interpreted entirely differently by the other person involved? Translating this into the clinic environment: a question has been proffered and an answer received. Did that elicit the "correct" information? It often becomes clear in the course of an assessment that the question has been interpreted differently from how it was intended, and/or there is more to a situation than the person is reporting. This is not usually because there is anything to hide, rather that the question was asked in a way that was not accessible to the recipient. If you are to get to the root of a problem then you need to be patient, persistent and perceptive. You need to develop the ability to perceive when the response you receive does not contain all the information you require. You must then ask the question in a different way, or come back to it later in the appointment. Consider the construction of a robust survey questionnaire: some questions will be asked more than once, but will be worded differently. To sum up, take the time to understand, then be sure to be understood.

Taking the time to make a thorough assessment

Clinic schedules are often packed too full, forcing the assessor to cut short clinical assessments. Unfortunately, this tends to lead to subsequent problems as insufficient data was gathered at the start, in other words "save now, pay later". This produces poor outcomes for the patient, possibly producing more problems than they had before, and certainly wasting time (and by inference, money) for both them and the healthcare professional/service. Far better to allow more time up front and to proceed with something that is more likely to succeed.

In developing a solution to the problems presented, there are usually conflicting factors, such as the need for a high level of postural support in a wheelchair combined with the requirement for manual self-propulsion. Time will be needed to determine priorities and come to an agreement as to how to proceed. Added consideration should be given to the person having difficulties with communication, and/or who needs to use a communication aid, where additional time will, in most cases, almost certainly be required.

Involving the person

Regardless of their age and ability, the patient must remain central in the assessment process, their requirements, needs, wishes and desires being the focus. It may not be possible to provide everything that is requested, but this must still be acknowledged if the person is not to feel that their wishes are being ignored. The same applies to the family and carers who play a crucial part in the person's life. In the case of equipment provision, their support is often vital to a successful outcome. One must be careful, however, that family and carers do not control the outcome where the person is able to advocate for themselves, i.e. their ability to self-advocate must be safeguarded. The family and carers (almost always) have the best interests of the person at heart, but it is worth making a point of speaking to the person, using their name, and even saying "I'd like to know what Jabeen thinks", leaving enough time for her to collect herself and provide a response. An additional challenge is where the patient has a mild intellectual disability, and you believe that the carer is right, while the person continues to make their point to the contrary. There are no rules about how to respond in these situations, but the assessor must slowly and sensitively work their way through to a conclusion, taking care to acknowledge what the person is saying. It may be necessary to involve a further person close to and respected by the patient or, in some cases, to utilize formal advocacy or safeguarding channels.

Further points include maintaining eye contact and avoiding physical contact without first (a) gaining consent, and (b) establishing a rapport. Be aware that some disabled people are particularly prone to fatigue and may struggle with a long appointment or one that is timed later in the day. Equally, the person's morning routine can be particularly complex and an afternoon appointment may be better.

Is there a carer sitting quietly in the background? Ask them if there is anything they want to contribute. Get alongside people when you have the chance; develop opportunities for people to talk to you. With care, humour can be used to establish a rapport, but over-familiarity should be avoided. Don't feel the need to fill what might seem an uncomfortable lull in conversation − that might be just the opportunity someone will take to speak.

Using a clinical methodology

Whatever branch of this field we happen to work in, a methodology is required if we are to achieve consistency in approach and outcome. Returning to the Hitchhiker's "trilogy", Arthur Dent (the main character), in attempting to find in modern times the location of the cave in which he had lived temporarily on pre-historic earth, wrote a computer programme to carry out the calculations, and:

> … decided not to mind the fact that with the extraordinary jumble of rules of thumb, wild approximations and arcane guesswork he was using he would be lucky to hit the right galaxy, he just went ahead and got the result. He would call it the right result. Who would know? As it happened, through the myriad and unfathomable chances of fate, he got it exactly right, though he of course would never know that.

Adams (1984)

Let us not fall into the trap of hoping for lucky guesses because for every one of these which turn out to be right there will be many, many more which are wrong. Even if your guess, or corner cutting, turns out right you will have no idea how you got there, and obtaining the same result a second time will be troublesome.

Clearly, a clinical methodology is required. This will vary according to the specific area of interest but should be scrutinized for sensitivity to the question in hand. The most basic form of methodology will follow this pattern:

1) Clarify what has been requested by the referrer and the patient/carer
2) Compile a detailed list of requirements and current issues
3) Take the relevant functional, social, environmental, medical, physical and psychological details
4) Define the problems, i.e. those issues which can be overcome
5) Define the constraints, i.e. those issues which cannot readily be overcome or that are fixed
6) Evaluate all the data collected
7) Produce a list of aims and objectives in conjunction with the patient/carer, acknowledging and resolving any conflicting priorities
8) Develop conceptual solutions
9) Finalize the outcome, detailing the specification of any equipment to be prescribed
10) Form a plan of action

There are many sub-stages within this process, of course, but this at least provides an overview. Clinical assessment may be thought of as akin to the assembly of a complicated jigsaw puzzle where all the pieces must be fitted together in a specific way and which are not all visible at the beginning of the process. As pieces are assembled, the picture becomes clearer and it is more obvious where other pieces might fit.

Prescription

In the case of equipment provision it is difficult to prescribe without first having sight and touch of the equipment. As a result, it will be necessary to invite companies to demonstrate their products, or to attend a suitable exhibition. Be analytically critical, ask difficult questions and, as the saying goes, if it looks/sounds too good to be true, it probably is. It is also worth remembering that whilst the clinician is the expert in the needs of their particular patient, the company representative is (usually) more knowledgeable about the product and will bring useful experience from having worked alongside a wide range of people.

There will be restrictions on funding which will vary according to the source. It will be necessary, on occasion, to form an argument for something out of the ordinary. This should be made significantly easier by having completed the assessment in the manner defined above. However, it is prudent to under-promise and over-deliver.

Finally, it can be helpful to ask oneself the following questions:

- Is the piece of equipment needed?
- Is it wanted?
- Do the patient and carers know how to use it?
- Can the patient and/or the carers manage it?
- Does it fit in with their lifestyle?
- What is the trade-off? (adapted from Pope, 2006)

Fitting the equipment to the person

It sounds obvious, but equipment should be made to fit the person: it would be reasonable to expect this to be the case. However, in services that are under pressure, either financially or from a lack of time/staff/training/understanding, the tendency is for the person to be made to fit the equipment, the assessor possibly managing to convince themselves of the opposite. There is a balance to be struck: if the person uses the equipment seldom, a precise fit will probably be less critical. If use is likely to be regular and prolonged, tailoring to the individual is imperative. We use the same decision making processes in everyday life.

Equipment for children

Consideration must be given to the needs of children who require equipment designed to promote their development. This may be to develop the physical skills required to control other equipment, or to be provided with equipment that will grow with them. It is important that children are engaged with the assessment process wherever possible. They have an opinion and it is important that this is heard. The other aspect of provision to children is, of course, that they have a habit of growing.

The overall aim of provision

It is all too easy to become so embroiled in the provision of equipment or a service that sight is lost of the original purpose of the intervention. As such, it is important that reference be made to the aims and objectives at regular intervals during the process. The art is in balancing these often conflicting requirements. Honest and open discussion with the patient is critical in order to achieve a satisfactory outcome.

The potential for learning

Sadly, it is often the case that equipment is denied because the person cannot demonstrate that they can control it adequately. However, one is not born with the ability to drink without spillage, or to read poetry without first learning nursery rhymes. In other words, clinical assessment and provision must allow for the potential of a person to learn a new skill. If you are a car driver, recall the moment you first attempted to wrestle with and co-ordinate the clutch, gear lever, brake pedal, accelerator and steering wheel. Oh and the handbrake, mirror, lights, … Did you manage smooth gear changes straight away, and remember to put your indicator on at every turn? No. You built up this skill over time and it started to become second nature as your brain laid down new neural pathways so you could avoid having to re-learn every move.

This applies to people with disabilities in just the same way. Where someone has an intellectual disability, the process may take a little longer. People can be fearful of using equipment, perhaps because they are worried they will damage something, or because they lack self-belief. It is your job to facilitate (not to pressure) them in learning a new skill.

Consent to assessment and treatment

One must be cognisant and respectful of the wishes of an individual. "Well, of course", you may say. But this presents challenges where the person has difficulties with communicating, has an intellectual disability or has impaired cognition. If a person does not wish to be assessed or to be treated, and cannot be persuaded otherwise, that is their decision and must be respected, in the UK within the bounds of the Mental Capacity Act (2005). One should tread very carefully in casually taking action in the person's "best interests" — you are taking a judgement on their behalf.

Increasingly in the UK, professionals such as occupational therapists, physicians and social workers are being given formal, Master's level training to enable them to act as "best interests assessors" to carry out deprivation of liberty assessments for people who are not able to be sectioned under the Mental Health Act. Best interests assessments are descended from the above mentioned UK Mental Capacity Act and set in place deprivation of liberty safeguards (DOLS) which protect people having been formally diagnosed as lacking capacity from being unlawfully restrained/constrained. At present, this applies only to adults living in a residential setting or who have been admitted to hospital.

A common example is where an elderly person with dementia lives in a care home, requiring total assistance with all aspects of care, and who must be constantly supervised as they have a history of walking out into the main road without checking for traffic. The care home locks the doors to prevent this from happening. The best interests assessor will investigate whether the care home is depriving the person of their liberty and breaching their human rights by effecting complete and total control of their life and, if so, whether or not it is being done in their best interests. If the assessment concludes that it is in the person's best interests they will grant a DOLS authorization.

"Challenging" behaviour

Some people, notably those with profound intellectual disabilities, an acquired or traumatic brain injury, or dementia, may exhibit what is sometimes termed "challenging behaviour". This is behaviour that is not culturally acceptable and/or puts the person or others at risk, and includes aggression, self-harm, destructiveness and disruptiveness (NHS Choices, 2012). People displaying these symptoms are less able to participate in daily life, which is likely to include conforming to a clinical assessment process. Such behaviours are likely to be heightened by anxiety brought about by the presence of strangers and unfamiliar surroundings. Pain can also be a contributory factor, as can boredom (NHS Choices, 2012). One must be mindful to work with the family, and professional and care staff in order to minimize the effects of such behaviour and the distress of the person.

Outcome measures

Having completed your clinical assessment and made your intervention, how do you know that it met its requirements and will continue to meet them? This leads us to enter what some might call the "murky" world of outcome measurement, of which there are myriad tools. It can be difficult to identify one that is appropriate to the question being asked, particularly in determining whether it is sufficiently sensitive to detect changes in the specific area of interest (Laver Fawcett, 2007). As an example, if you desired to measure changes in sitting ability as a result of an active rehabilitation programme, a tool providing only the options of the person being able to "sit without support" or "requiring additional support to sit" would not detect small, incremental changes in ability as rehabilitation progressed.

Having identified a suitable tool, it is then necessary to ask whether it has been tested for validity, i.e. does it measure what it is said to measure. Taking the survey questionnaire as an example it is simple enough to produce a set of questions, but to form these questions so that they have validity is a very complicated subject and far easier to get wrong than right. Have you ever struggled to answer a question on a survey either because the wording could be interpreted in different ways, or because you were not able to select from the options presented? Have you ever felt a question to be leading? Herein lies the challenge, and the science.

It is not possible to cover within this book the range of outcome measures that might be suitable in the field of rehabilitation engineering and assistive technology, but Cowan and Najafi (2019) describe a range of options that are suitable for consideration for use within assistive technology services.

Documentation

This is a critical factor for all clinical, technical and scientific work. It is important that healthcare decisions are clearly described for future reference, be that a colleague taking over the care of an individual, or yourself in being able to recall precisely what was decided. When we have multiple patients on our caseloads it is all too easy to forget or confuse critical details at a future date, even if they appear with absolute clarity in your mind at the time of assessment.

Registered professionals are, of course, required by statute to keep adequate records. This is not only to promote good practice and quality outcomes, but also to protect themselves and their employer against any potential future legal case made against them. It should also be remembered that, in the UK at least, patients have the right to request access to their own notes.

Patient groups and their characteristics

There are thousands of medical diagnoses used to explain a person's clinical presentation. As a result, it is often necessary to carry out research into a particular condition, looking for certain characteristics that will inform the assessment and provision process. These may be grouped as follows:

- Prognosis
  - Is the condition terminal, rapidly deteriorating, slowly deteriorating, fairly stable, or temporary, i.e. is the person expected to recover? Is there a specific life expectancy?
- Rehabilitation
  - Is it possible that the person will recover some or all of the function they have lost? Does your provision need to reflect this, both in terms of the potential for adjustment and the time taken to supply?
- Physical impairment
  - How is the person likely to be affected? Are there specific difficulties, e.g. limited joint mobility/pain, poor balance, spasticity.
- Intellectual disability
  - Are there aspects of the condition that limit learning or understanding, or the ability to make judgements or form opinions that are based on logical reasoning?
- Specific risk factors
  - Are there aspects to the condition that are critical to understand, e.g. potential for bone fracture for those with osteoporosis.

The following conditions are among those more commonly seen by clinical and biomedical engineers:

- Acquired brain injury (ABI)
- Amputation (see section on prosthetics for further details)
- Arthritis (osteoarthritis (OA) or rheumatoid arthritis (RA))
- Cerebral palsy (CP)
- Cerebrovascular accident (CVA) or stroke
- Dementia (including Alzheimer's disease)
- Multiple sclerosis (MS)
- Muscular dystrophy (MD)
- Parkinson's disease (PD)
- Spinal cord injury (SCI)
- Spinal muscular atrophy (SMA)
- Traumatic brain injury (TBI)

There is a wealth of information available on the internet but the usual precautions apply: look for a known organization and/or check information across two or three sites, particularly in the case of rare conditions.

Rehabilitation

Rehabilitation implies recovery, or part thereof. There are many centres specializing in rehabilitation and which are typically, but not exclusively, for people having had a stroke, acquired/traumatic brain injury or spinal cord injury. There is window of opportunity in which it is possible for improvements to the person's condition to be made through a formalized

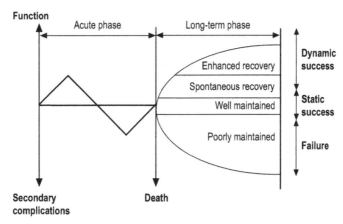

FIG. 20.1   Ranges of outcomes (Pope, 1988).

and intense treatment process. This usually involves a multi-disciplinary team including physicians, physiotherapists, occupational therapists, speech and language therapists and nurses. Engineers can play an important role, particularly where provision of equipment is required.

Change in the body can happen very quickly, particularly in respect of plastic adaptation of the musculoskeletal system. Muscle starts to waste and to shorten surprisingly quickly, leading to contracture and joint range limitation. These changes can be extremely difficult, and sometimes almost impossible, to overcome. Posture management, of which physiotherapy is a core component, plays a crucial role in maintaining joint ranges and body symmetry.

On the other hand, the plasticity of the nervous system, known as neuroplasticity i.e. the ability of the brain to lay down new or revised neurological pathways, is remarkable. A substantial amount of recovery can take place with an intense treatment programme as skills are re-learnt and practised, embedding movement patterns within the brain.

The diagram above (Fig. 20.1) illustrates a range of outcomes from rehabilitation, time being shown along the X-axis. After the acute phase, a number of long term outcomes are possible. Following the end of the programme of rehabilitation, further significant increases in function and ability are less likely, the focus often being on preventing deterioration.

There are many resources available on the subject of rehabilitation. The reader is directed to any good bookshop for a formal text book, or to relevant journals for the most up to date research findings.

Case study — pay now, save later

A referral was received for an adult male (Mark) regarding postural support in his wheelchair. It was necessary to conduct the assessment in Mark's home, which was a 1 h drive from the clinic. The outcome was to prescribe a moulded seat.

A second appointment was made at a later date to take a cast of Mark's body shape. This was completed satisfactorily.

At the third visit the completed system was handed over. Or rather it wasn't. Once Mark had been hoisted into position he reported that he was much more comfortable than in his old wheelchair. Those around him commented on how well he was sitting. Everyone was delighted, but then his primary carer enquired as to how Mark would use his urinal bottle.

Skilfully, the shape of the seat had been produced to control the tendency for Mark's knees to clench together, but in so doing there was no space for the bottle.

The result was that:

a) The seat had to be taken back to the workshop for a significant alteration, including the padded covers

b) A fourth appointment was necessary

c) Mark had to wait an additional month to receive his seat

All this incurred delays to provision, significant additional expenditure and loss of reputation for the service. Had a little more time been taken in the assessment to explore in greater detail the functional requirements of the system, all the problems could have been avoided.

References

Adams, D., 1979. The Hitchhiker's Guide to the Galaxy. William Heinemann, pp. 128–129.

Adams, D., 1984. So Long, and Thanks for All the Fish. William Heinemann, p. 521.

Cowan, D., Najafi, L., 2019. Chapter 4: Assessment & outcomes. In: Handbook of Electronic Assistive Technology. Elsevier.

Laver Fawcett, A., 2007. Principles of Assessment and Outcome Measurement for Occupational Therapists and Physiotherapists. John Wiley and Sons Ltd.

NHS Choices, 2012. Dealing with Challenging Behaviour. Available from: http://www.nhs.uk/CarersDirect/guide/practicalsupport/Pages/Challenging-behaviour.aspx.

Pope, P.M., 1988. A model for evaluation of input in relation to outcome in severely brain damaged patients. Physiotherapy 74 (12), 647–650.

Pope, P.M., 2006. A Physical Management Programme for People with Severe Disability. Lecture Notes: Posture Management for Adults and Children with Complex Disabilities, Oxford.

Shakespeare, T., 2018. Disability: The Basics. Routledge.

Medical engineering design

Mike Hillman

University of Bath, Bath, UK

Introduction to medical engineering design

Clinical engineering is about finding a solution to the specified need of a client. Usually this will be through the use of an existing product or application of an existing process or procedure. There will be times, however, when an existing product is not appropriate: it may need modifying or a new piece of technology may need designing and producing. The discipline of "design" applied to medical engineering is wide, but in the context of clinical engineering it is about solving the stated need of a client/patient by designing a new (or modified) piece of technology.

There are many models and methodologies described in the literature for the design process (Pugh, 1990; Pahl and Beitz, 1988; Ulrich and Eppinger, 2011; Design Council; BS7000-2), as well as more general project management (Prince2).

Some are more appropriate for a product design environment while others are more suitable for the design of a "one-off" item. In general terms they all contain the following aspects.

- Understand the problem
- Identify and evaluate concepts
- Embody & develop the design
- Build or manufacture the device
- Verify/validate/hand over.

For medical engineering design the identifying features are that the work (A) starts with an identified need, (B) is by definition "user centred", and (C) ends with a device delivered to the client. This is different from product design which starts with an idea and ends with a product. A description of such a design process is given by Orpwood (1990).

In order to conform as closely as possible with one of the well documented design methodologies, the method described here is based upon that described by Pahl and Beitz (1988). Using their headings, the phases, with their main deliverables, are:

- Clarification of the task → Specification
- Concept design → Concept
- Embodiment design → Preliminary layout/definitive layout
- Detail design → Documentation
- Final deliverable = Solution

N.B. As this book does not attempt to repeat what is already well covered in the engineering literature, particularly in the area of engineering design, it is the aspects of the model which are distinct for clinical engineering which are highlighted, and does not attempt to cover the aspects of engineering which should be covered in a good engineering degree syllabus (e.g. tolerancing, technical drawing, stress analysis, electronic circuit design).

Clarification of the task

The input to this phase is the specified task, alternatively described as the project brief in the Prince2 project management method, or problem definition (e.g. Orpwood, 1990). It will initially be described in terms of the user (in rehabilitation technology, the patient or end-user is not the only person using the technology: it may include a carer, formal or voluntary, therapist, as well as the end user) and the functional need to be met.

At the outset this will be in qualitative terms. The engineer must develop this to a more detailed and, where possible, quantitative specification. Some aspects will be known in quantitative terms from the start (e.g. weight of the user), while others will be determined in this and later phases of the project. Some parts of the specification will be defined as demands (what the product must meet) and wishes (what the product should meet). A detailed specification is vital to allow evaluation of the design at all stages (evaluating concepts, design review, verification and validation).

Other aspects involved in clarification of the task include an understanding of the environment the device must fit into: both the physical environment and the regulatory framework. There will be financial constraints for the project, either in terms of an overall budget, or a cost/benefit judgment, or the cost of other solutions. There must obviously be a clear understanding of the clinical (physiological etc) aspects of the problem to be addressed.

Concept design → concept

An engineering device has a primary function which can be divided into a number of sub functions. The first stage of concept design is to identify the essential problems, establish the overall functions and the sub functions and then to find a number of solution principles to fulfill the sub-functions. For a typical assistive or rehabilitation device the user interface will be a critical part of the design. It can be useful to separate the user interface aspects from the supporting engineering features (Orpwood, 1990). Technical aspects will often (but not always) be well known technology; it is the user interface aspects which are likely to be the most challenging. As an example, a patient with impaired sitting ability and balance requires a perching seat/stool for their professional work which results in it needing to be transportable. The design considerations are:

- Folding/dismantling mechanism
- Must not slip or become unstable
- Structural — strength, stiffness
- Position/angle of main seat
- Other body supports
  - Back
  - Thoracic
  - Feet
  - Knees
- Material/shape/padding of seat
- Aesthetics (needs to look professional)

It is the skill of an engineer to identify a wide range of solution principles. At this stage it is less important whether they are in detail feasible. Quantity is more important than quality. A brainstorming or mind mapping technique (whether carried out individually or with a team) is valuable in generating a large number of potential solutions. There are many sources of inspiration, both technical and aesthetic. For example other assistive technology products, literature review, mainstream and consumer products, nature.

The feasibility of these solutions is often investigated through the use of prototypes. A prototype may not necessarily be physical; it could be a sketch or CAD drawing to illustrate a point to the client, or a computer model for stress analysis. To be effective, prototypes need to answer a question and need to be as simple as possible to get the required answer. It is important to try to get as much iteration done at this stage before funds are committed to the final device.

It should be noted at this point that for every test with an end user, an adequate risk assessment should be in place, although that assessment must bear in mind the constraints within which the evaluation is taking place.

It is important that evaluations consider the reaction of the user (be this the patient, carer or healthcare professional). At one extreme it is important not to unrealistically raise expectations, but at the same time the appearance of the prototype should not produce negative reactions. In this respect, simple materials such as cardboard are a very useful tool as they are clearly not the finished device but can communicate the function and scale of the final device. In all such interactions a good working relationship with the user is essential.

Having identified a range of solution principles these are then evaluated (with reference to the specification) and the most promising combined to produce a small number of concept variations. At the start of this phase the functional requirements were separated. Now the task is to put them back together. Using the same features to solve more than one functional demand produces the most economical and efficient solution. These concepts are then evaluated against the specification. Those which do not meet the "demands" of the specification must be either discarded or modified. This will leave a number of concepts which are evaluated against the criteria described in the specification "wishes". Although an engineer's judgment will often lead to a preferred concept, it is valuable to use a quantitative selection method in which the concepts are scored against the product specification. The simplest is to score a concept as +1/0/−1 against a datum concept for each specification point. More sophisticated methods use a wider scoring range and introduce weighting for the importance of each specification point. In order to avoid or reduce bias, the weighting and scoring should be carried out, or at least reviewed, by someone other than the project engineer.

Embodiment design → preliminary layout/definitive layout

In the embodiment phase, a concept which is still loosely defined is refined first to a preliminary layout and finally to a definitive layout. This is an iterative stage as the functions are fitted into an overall solution.

Certain features will define the size of the solution. For most rehabilitation devices the overall size will be based around the human scale and the interface support features. Also to be considered are size determining features such as power and strength requirements and any known standard components. It is now possible to start laying out the overall spatial arrangements.

Pahl and Beitz (1988) make no reference to the need to consider the aesthetics of a design. However, the words of William Morris are pertinent "Have nothing in your house that you do not know to be useful, or believe to be beautiful" (William Morris). This is particularly important for equipment which relates so closely to the user. Pullin (2009) has discussed these issues in detail in his book "Design meets disability". The question to ask is whether the design gives a sense of value — does the user feel valued by using this piece of equipment? Appropriate aesthetics can be incorporated into a device without an unacceptable cost penalty; they are not a final detail but must be iteratively included throughout the embodiment phase, and sometimes even earlier in the concept generation phase.

Starting with the main functions which define the embodiment, the design is developed, including the auxiliary functions. Materials are chosen and the form of the individual components defined. Preliminary analysis of stresses and performance is carried out. As a preliminary design is developed it must be checked against the product specification. Design review may be carried out informally or more formally, e.g. BS EN 61160:2005.

Design freeze is an important discipline (Pietzsch et al., 2009). This has already happened once in choosing which concept to take forward to embodiment design. It must also be implemented after the preliminary layout has been selected.

When the preliminary layout has been fixed the details are optimized and weak points are improved or eliminated. Checks for errors must be made on both detail points and the overall design. This gives the definitive layout which must again be checked against the product specification.

Detail design → documentation

In this stage the parts are defined in detail and documents prepared for manufacture. The most important document is obviously the manufacturing drawing. This will include accurate material specification, tolerances and guidance for manufacture and assembly. Parts lists will be prepared for manufactured and bought in parts. As documentation is developed, the (European) requirements of the technical file for regulatory purposes will be met — see regulatory section for further details. This will include the identification of relevant standards to allow appropriate testing to take place. Documentation will not only include manufacturing instructions, but also risk assessment and user instructions.

Final deliverable = solution

The final device must undergo verification and validation. Verification asks the questions — does it meet the quantitative specification. Validation concerns whether the device works for the user, in his or her environment. This is why it is so important to have defined in detail the requirements of the user(s). Making assumptions about intended use/function is very likely to lead to the development of a device which is, at best, ineffective or worse, useless.

In an ideal world the device would work perfectly first time. The reality of rehabilitation devices is that there may be some need for modification/fine tuning. At earlier stages, intelligent use of prototypes should minimize the risk of this happening. To de-risk the solution, the design should include the facility for adjustment and fine tuning without the need for major changes. A device will often be tested with the client in the "bare metal" before being disassembled, finished, and reassembled.

References

BS EN 61160:2005 Design Review.
BS7000-2 Design Management Systems — Part 2: Guide to Managing the Design of Manufactured Products.
Design Council, no date. The design process. Available from: http://www.designcouncil.org.uk/designprocess.

Morris, W., no date. British Craftsman, Early Socialist, Designer and Poet, Whose Designs Generated the Arts and Crafts Movement in England (1834–1896).

Orpwood, R.D., 1990. Design methodology for aids for the disabled. Med. Eng. Technol. 14 (1), 2–10.

Pahl, G., Beitz, W., 1988. Engineering design – a systematic approach. In: Wallace, K. (Ed.), The Design Council. Springer-Verlag.

Pietzsch, J.B., Shluzas, L.A., Paté-Cornell, M.E., Yock, P.G., Lineham, J.H., 2009. Stage gate process for the development of medical devices. J. Med. Dev. Vol. 3/0201004-1, ASME.

Prince2, no date. Available from: http://www.prince2.com.

Pugh, S., 1990. Total Design – Integrated Methods for Successful Product Engineering. Prentice Hall.

Pullin, G.M., 2009. Design Meets Disability. MIT Press.

Ulrich, K., Eppinger, S., 2011. Product Design and Development. McGraw Hill.

Regulations and risk management

David Long[a] and Mike Hillman[b]

[a]AJM Healthcare, UK & Oxford University Hospitals NHS Foundation Trust, Oxford, UK; [b]University of Bath, Bath, UK

The EU medical devices regulations 2017/745 (MDR)

Introduction

Where rehabilitation equipment is placed on the open market there are nearly always regulatory requirements which must be met. In Europe, the relevant legislation is Regulation (EU) 2017/745 of the European Parliament and of the council of 5 April 2017 on medical devices. It is referred to as the MDR 2017 and replaces the Medical Devices Directive which originated in 1993 and which was last updated in 2007. MDR 2017 must be fully implemented by May 2020.

N.B. At the time of writing (summer, 2019) there is some uncertainty about the continued application of the MDR within the UK, assuming Britain leaves the EU. It seems unlikely that use of the regulations will be abolished but this is not known for certain. Regardless, the regulations will continue to provide a robust framework of reference for anyone seeking to design a medical device.

Further information on this subject may be found in Chapter 8.

Definitions

Most equipment that is used in the field of rehabilitation engineering is classed as a medical device. The MDR offers the following definition in Article 2:

The term 'medical device' means any instrument, apparatus, appliance, software, implant, reagent, material or other article intended by the manufacturer to be used, alone or in combination, for human beings for one or more of the following specific medical purposes:

- *Diagnosis, prevention, monitoring, prediction, prognosis, treatment or alleviation of disease*
- *Diagnosis, monitoring, treatment, alleviation of, or compensation for, an injury or disability*
- *Investigation, replacement or modification of the anatomy or of a physiological or pathological process or state*
- *Providing information by means of in vitro examination of specimens derived from the human body, including organ, blood and tissue donations,*

and which does not achieve its principal intended action by pharmacological, immunological or metabolic means, in or on the human body, but which may be assisted in its function by such means.

The MDR also states in Article 2

The term 'accessory for a medical device' means an article which, whilst not being itself a medical device, is intended by its manufacturer to be used together with one or several particular medical device(s) to specifically enable the medical device(s) to be used in accordance with its/their intended purpose(s) or to specifically and directly assist the medical functionality of the medical device(s) in terms of its/their intended purpose(s).

And in relation to custom-made devices we have the following

The term 'custom-made device' means any device specifically made in accordance with a written prescription of any person authorized by national law by virtue of that person's professional qualifications which gives, under that person's responsibility, specific design characteristics, and is intended for the sole use of a particular patient exclusively to meet their individual conditions and needs.

However, mass-produced devices which need to be adapted to meet the specific requirements of any professional user and devices which are mass-produced by means of industrial manufacturing processes in accordance with the written prescriptions of any authorized person shall not be considered to be custom-made devices.

The following should be noted regarding software

It is necessary to clarify that software in its own right, when specifically intended by the manufacturer to be used for one or more of the medical purposes set out in the definition of a medical device, qualifies as a medical device, while software for general purposes, even when used in a healthcare setting, or software intended for life-style and well-being purposes is not a medical device. The qualification of software, either as a device or an accessory, is independent of the software's location or the type of interconnection between the software and a device.

This is particularly relevant for assistive technology where software is used increasingly in a clinical context for improving functional ability.

Purpose

The MDR allows manufacturers to trade throughout Europe without having to comply with multiple national legislation. It is based on standards of quality and safety accepted across the member countries. Other countries have similar legislation, for example the USA Food and Drug Administration (FDA) requirements. It is critical that a device complies with the requirements of the country in which the device is to be sold and used.

Categorization of devices

Medical devices are categorized according to the level of risk, often in terms of whether a device is invasive or applies energy to a patient. Most rehabilitation equipment will come within the lowest level of risk, but its manufacture and provision must still be properly regulated. Some equipment, for example in functional electrical stimulation, will be classified as slightly higher risk, in this case because the use of surface electrodes transmits energy to the body. There are rules which govern risk categorization and these are detailed within the regulation.

CE marking

It is necessary to place a CE mark on a device before it is put into service. This demonstrates that the manufacturer has considered the requirements of the MDR and believes their product to comply. In the case of custom-made devices the CE mark should not be used.

Regardless of whether the device is custom-made, the manufacturer must still ensure that the device meets the general safety and performance requirements of the MDR, which were previously known as the "essential requirements" of the MDD. It should be noted that the term "manufacturer" applies not only to commercial organisations but to any person or organization manufacturing medical devices.

General safety and performance requirements (GSPR)

These define how the device should be designed and manufactured. There are a set of general requirements and then a more detailed lists of design and construction requirements. Full information is available in the full regulations. These requirements are aligned with both good engineering practice and common sense, giving no surprises to a competent engineer. A helpful summary was provided in the 2007 amendment to the original document, but which is still applicable:

The devices must be designed and manufactured in such a way that, when used under the conditions and for the purposes intended, they will not compromise the clinical condition or the safety of patients, or the safety and health of users or, where applicable, other persons, provided that any risks which may be associated with their intended use constitute acceptable risks when weighed against the benefits to the patient and are compatible with a high level of protection of health and safety. This shall include:

- *reducing, as far as possible, the risk of use error due to the ergonomic features of the device and the environment in which the device is intended to be used (design for patient safety), and*
- *consideration of the technical knowledge, experience, education and training and where applicable the medical and physical conditions of intended users (design for lay, professional, disabled or other users)." (MDD 2007)*

Regulatory process

While it is not appropriate to go into any level of detail here, the most important parts of the regulatory process are:

- The MDR 2017 requires a quality management system (QMS) to be in place where products are being manufactured; this was previously optional for class 1 devices. The QMS may be an accepted national or international standard, such as BS EN ISO 9001 "Quality Management Systems", or BS EN ISO 13485 "Medical devices — Quality management systems — Requirements for regulatory purposes", or an in-house standard. In the case of devices in higher risk categories, quality must be audited by a designated body.
- Risk assessment. Is the level of risk posed by the intervention acceptable within the context of the benefit to the patient? This must be justified, and the way in which residual risks will be minimized and controlled must be documented.
- Conformance with standards/requirements. These may be specified as national or international standards, or with a list of the relevant GSPR. Conformance with 'harmonized standards' may infer compliance with the GSPR in specific respects but at the time of writing this has not been confirmed by the European Commission.
- A technical file. This will describe fully the design and manufacture of the product, and include the risk assessment and standards conformance data. It will also include information provided to the client, such as user instructions and labelling.

Health institution exemption (HIE)

There has been much concern over paragraph 4 of chapter II in the regulations which states that *"Devices that are manufactured and used within health institutions shall be considered as having been put into service"* because this would require one-off products such as rehabilitation engineering devices to be CE marked. Paragraph 5 and article 10 (referred to as the HIE by MHRA) tempers this and provides requirements that, if met, mean that CE marking is not required. The main points are as follows:

- The devices are not transferred to another legal entity
- Manufacture and use of the devices occur under appropriate quality management systems
- The health institution justifies in its documentation that the target patient or patient group's specific needs cannot be met, or cannot be met at the appropriate level of performance by an equivalent device available on the market
- The health institution reviews experience gained from clinical use of the devices and takes all necessary corrective actions
- HIE shall not apply to devices that are manufactured on an industrial scale

  Further details may be found in Chapter 8 of this book.

Risk management

Introduction

On any day, any one person carries out a number of risk assessments, e.g. crossing a road, driving a car, pouring boiling water. We are used to taking risks: we would go nowhere and do nothing if we were to attempt to avoid them. What we are less used to doing is documenting the process — we have little requirement for this when the main person affected is ourselves. In respect of rehabilitation engineering and assistive technology it is necessary to manage risks and document the process so that safe and efficient solutions to problems are provided, and that this can be demonstrated at any point in the future.

Definitions and process

Risk can be considered in three parts: (1) the potential for harm to occur, i.e. a hazard, (2) the nature and severity of that harm, and (3) the likelihood of it occurring. Management can mean many things but perhaps in this context it is best described as being in control, having an awareness of the end goal, ordering and applying logic, monitoring and problem solving. BS EN ISO 14971 (Application of risk management to medical devices) describes risk management as "... a framework within which experience, insight and judgment are applied systematically to manage risks ..." (ISO, 2012).

Once the risk has been defined, consideration should be given as to whether it can be avoided, either altogether or in part — a different method or product may achieve the same aim. Next, one must determine whether the risk is acceptable. This requires a knowledge of the potential harm and likelihood of this harm occurring (see section below). Unacceptable or high risks must be reduced by putting in place specific control measures. A risk/benefit analysis will be needed to justify the acceptance of risk. This is a complex area to manage and, ultimately, comes down to objective clinical judgement and practical control measures. Some interventions, diagnostics and pieces of equipment carry an inherent risk with use, making removal of risk impractical.

Worked example: the parent of a child with quadriplegic cerebral palsy has requested that a powered wheelchair be provided since manual self-propulsion has become difficult. Such a device has the potential to cause significant harm to the child, other people and the environment, were the child to lack or lose control of the chair. It is anticipated that this could happen often, at least initially. However, there is the potential for clinical benefit if the child is able to learn to drive, i.e. greater independence and participation. Following initial assessment, the service agrees to supply the chair and, to reduce the risks, stipulates that it can be used only indoors initially and always with adult supervision. A training programme is organized. The service puts in place a review for six weeks' time to establish if the child has learnt the requisite driving skills for use without adult supervision and driving outdoors.

Rating likelihood and severity

Many risk assessment policies use a matrix to determine whether a risk is acceptable. An example is shown in Fig. 20.2 where the shading provides an outcome. For example, if the perceived harm is likely to occur regularly (probable) and is serious (major), the risk is deemed unacceptable and must be avoided or reduced to an acceptable level. If the harm is negligible (insignificant) and unlikely to occur regularly (remote), no additional action need be taken. Many risks fall into the middle bracket and it is here that clinical benefit must be shown to outweigh the inherent risks. Note that:

1) The shaded areas should be adjusted to suit the application
2) Any matrix combination is possible, e.g. three by three, four by six, to ensure that the risk assessment is specific to context
3) This table displays three risk outcomes: it is appropriate to have more, depending on the application

The above mentioned standard (BS EN ISO 14971) provides further examples and explanation in the appendices.

It will quickly be realized that categorizing harm and its likelihood can be extremely difficult to achieve quantitatively, accurately and objectively. Figs. 20.3 and 20.4 provide further guidance on choosing appropriate levels. There is still a problem, of course, because determining likelihood numerically requires a precise knowledge of past events. If this information is not available (often/usually the case in rehabilitation engineering and assistive technology) then one can only produce an estimate based on experience and knowledge of similar incidents, or lack of incidents. An estimate is worth making, however, because it demonstrates that the risk has been considered, were this ever to be called into question.

Fault detection

In some applications it will be appropriate to consider the likelihood of a fault being detected before it causes harm. In advance of a component of a device failing, the problem may be detected, e.g. a rattle that gets progressively louder. Other

FIG. 20.2 A five by five risk assessment matrix, derived from BS EN ISO 14971 Medical devices — Application of risk management to medical devices (ISO, 2012).

		Severity				
		Insignificant	Minor	Moderate	Major	Catastrophic
Likelihood	Frequent					
	Probable					
	Occasional					
	Remote					
	Improbable					

	Insignificant / broadly acceptable
	Reduce if possible / ALARP (As Low As Reasonably Practicable)
	Unacceptable

Likelihood rating	Score	Guideline definitions
Frequent	5	Expected to occur in most circumstances / almost certain 1:1 – 1:10 Once per day/week/use
Probable	4	Likely to occur / will probably occur, but not persistently 1:10 – 1:100 Once per week/month/100 uses
Occasional	3	May occur occasionally 1:100 – 1:1000 Once per month/year/1,000 uses
Remote	2	Unlikely to occur / not expected but possible 1:1000 – 1:10,000 Once per year/decade/10,000 uses
Improbable	1	May occur only in very exceptional circumstances / rare 1:10,000 – 1:100,000 or more Once per decade/100,000 uses

FIG. 20.3 Guideline likelihood ratings for risk management.

Severity rating	Score	Guideline definitions
Catastrophic	5	Death
Major	4	Major permanent harm / disability Extensive injury
Moderate	3	Semi-permanent harm (up to 1 year) Significant injury Medical treatment required
Minor	2	Non-permanent harm (up to 1 month) First Aid treatment required
Insignificant	1	Inconvenience or temporary discomfort

FIG. 20.4 Guideline severity ratings for risk management.

times, the chances of detection will be almost none, e.g. sudden failure of an electrical switch. In the case of safety critical components/operations it is safest to assume that the risk will not be detected.

Methodologies for identifying and analyzing failures/faults

Failure Mode and Effects Analysis (FMEA) is a qualitative tool used to identify and evaluate the effects of a specific fault or failure mode at a component or sub-assembly level. Human error is considered, which makes it particularly suited to this field. In contrast to a FMEA, a fault tree analysis (FTA) takes an undesirable event and works backwards to identify potential failure modes. This has the advantage of allowing the process to be evaluated, as opposed to looking at the failure in isolation. The hazards identified in a FMEA can be used within a FTA.

There is extensive literature available on these and other methodologies within many engineering text books to which the interested reader is directed.

Areas for consideration in a clinical context

The following table (Fig. 20.5) lists some of the more common areas for consideration in rehabilitation engineering and assistive technology; it is by no means exhaustive and is not in any particular order. The full set of hazards applicable will be derived from the clinical assessment and the context of use.

FIG. 20.5 Example areas for consideration in risk management.

Clinical
Communication difficulties
Muscle weakness
Limited range of movement
Involuntary movements
Cognition
Poor skin condition
Development/deterioration of pressure ulceration
Management of future changes in condition (requirement for review)
Use of wheelchairs as vehicle seats
Use
User error
Reasonably foreseeable misuse
Complexity of use/operation related to the ability of the person/carer
Manual handling
Context, e.g. delicate equipment in a busy school environment
Technical
Interfaces and compatibility of equipment from multiple manufacturers
Durability
Wheelchair stability
Service / review interval

Further resources

There is a wealth of literature available on the general principles of risk management. In addition, the following two documents provide specific information:

- Risk Management and its Application to Medical Device Management (IPEM, 2008)
- Guidance on the Stability of Wheelchairs (Medicines and Healthcare Products Regulatory Agency, 2004)

Local employer risk assessment tools may provide useful information and guidance, but are unlikely to be suited to all applications.

References

IPEM, 2008. Risk Management and its Application to Medical Device Management. Report 95 Institute of Physics and Engineering in Medicine. ISBN:9781903613337.

ISO, 2012. BS EN ISO 14971 Medical Devices — Application of Risk Management to Medical Devices. International Organization for Standardization.

Medical Devices Regulation (EU) 2017/745 of the European Parliament and of the Council of 5 April 2017 on Medical Devices, Amending Directive 2001/83/EC, Regulation (EC) No 178/2002 and Regulation (EC) No 1223/2009 and Repealing Council Directives 90/385/EEC and 93/42/EEC.

Medicines and Healthcare products Regulatory Agency, 2004. Stability of Wheelchairs DB2004(02) Medicines and Healthcare Products Regulatory Agency.

Chapter 21

Functional electrical stimulation

Duncan Wood and Ian Swain

Salisbury NHS Foundation Trust, Salisbury, United Kingdom

Chapter outline

Introduction

Functional electrical stimulation (FES) is a means of producing useful movement in paralyzed muscle. Electrical stimulation is not a new technique: it dates back to the Ancient Greeks who used rubbed amber and torpedo fish to produce a number of physiological responses, primarily to cause muscle contractions. Its development followed that of advances in physics by Volta and Faraday during the 18th and 19th centuries which led to more reliable and controllable sources of electricity and advances in our understanding of neurophysiology as a result of the work of Galvani and Duchenne during that same period. Following these advances, various groups showed that denervated muscle only responded to stimulation by connecting and disconnecting a direct current source and not to alternating or Faradaic current. However, in the case of an innervated muscle (i.e., where there was an intact motor neuron), a contraction did occur with Faradaic current. This opened up the possibility of using electrical stimulation to restore some level of muscle contraction, with the goal to aid function, and remains the focus for this chapter.

Since those early days, electrical stimulation has been used in many medical conditions to restore function and movement. These include assisting cardiac function through the use of pacemakers, controlling bladder, bowel, and sexual function in spinal cord injured persons, and improving hearing ability through implanted devices in the cochlear. Some applications are now widely used in the clinical environment, including the applications listed above, whereas others, such as restoring visual feedback, are still in the research stage with limited clinical trials. One other major application is in the use of electrical stimulation to restore limb movement and hence improve function and activities of daily living. Though this application is certainly applicable clinically, in some cases without the direct need for clinical engineering support, it is still an emerging field in rehabilitation. This chapter describes one of the more successful applications, drop foot correction, concentrating more on the thought processes undertaken during the initial design as well as giving a basic overview of how electrical stimulation works.

Defining FES

As stated, FES is a means of producing useful movement in paralyzed muscle. This differs from perhaps the wider definition for electrical stimulation (sometimes called neuromuscular electrical stimulation) and that in itself presents some of the main clinical engineering challenges. For example, if it is possible to produce a muscle contraction in an innervated muscle by the simple technique of applying a Faradaic current, what methods can be used to control both that contraction

Clinical Engineering. https://doi.org/10.1016/B978-0-08-102694-6.00021-8

and the resulting limb movement? Both aspects therefore need to be considered: the physiological principles underlying FES and the design concepts relating to the desired application to make it functional and clinically relevant.

Physiological principles of FES

In FES, small electrical impulses are applied to the nerves that supply the affected muscles using either self-adhesive electrodes placed on the skin or implanted electrodes on the nerve or muscle close to the motor point. The electrical current generates an electric field between the pair of electrodes (Fig. 21.1), and, with the right conditions, may induce a nerve impulse that is propagated along the nerve to the muscle, causing the muscle to contract in a manner very similar to natural contraction. Though there are obvious differences between these two delivery techniques, for this section they can be considered in the same way.

As a result, each nerve in the vicinity of this electric field may be excited. What is meant by the phrase "the right conditions" is that a nerve is required to be in an excitable state and that the level of stimulation intensity needs to be sufficient to cause excitation. It needs to be remembered that just as in normal nerve excitation, the all-or-none principle is maintained. The characteristics of the electrical pulses are therefore important: the amplitude, the pulsewidth, and frequency of electrical pulses. This perhaps over-simplifies the nature of these pulses, but is fundamental to how a train of pulses can generate a required movement useful for function.

The amplitude and pulsewidth can be regarded as being synonymous with the stimulation intensity. Below a certain level of intensity there is no muscle response because the level is insufficient to cause any nerve excitation. The point where nerves begin to become excited is called the threshold of stimulation. As the intensity increases, the response curve follows the classic S-shape, with a steep linear slope over much of the middle part of the curve, leading to a plateau, where the resulting muscle response does not increase even with an increase in intensity (Fig. 21.2). This increase in muscle response over the S-shaped curve is caused by more motor units being recruited, partly due to the electric field penetrating deeper (i.e., more nerves are in its vicinity) and partly because the intensity is now above the excitability threshold of more nerves. The plateau is at the point where no additional nerves can be excited.

The effect from the frequency of the stimulation pulses is slightly different. Increasing the frequency (i.e., reducing the inter-pulse interval) also causes an increase in force produced from the muscle, but not from exciting more motor units. The cause here is from summating contractions from the same nerve (or nerves) being excited, since increasing the frequency does not allow the muscle to return to its state of rest between pulses (Fig. 21.3). At a certain frequency, these contractions summate to the point where they become fused; this is termed *tetany*. For most functional activities, a fused, or smooth, contraction is required, demanding a higher frequency, however a higher frequency shortens the rest time between pulses and therefore has the disadvantage of increased muscle fatigue (Fig. 21.4). A compromise between a sustained smooth contraction and muscle fatigue must therefore be considered when selecting the stimulation frequency.

Designing a practical FES system

We have now examined the characteristics of the train of electrical impulses and how setting the stimulation intensity (amplitude or pulsewidth) and frequency can affect the muscle response. The next stage is how this technique can be integrated into an FES system for a specific application, and this is perhaps best achieved by posing a series of questions:

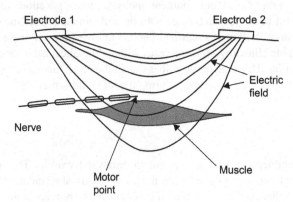

FIG. 21.1 Electric field between a pair of stimulation electrodes on the skin surface. The closeness of the electric field lines nearer the electrodes indicates the higher current density in that region.

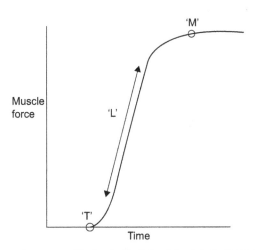

FIG. 21.2 Effect of stimulation intensity on muscle response. The threshold of stimulation is indicated by "T," the region where the stimulation response plateaus is indicated at levels above "M," and the steep linear slope is indicated by the region "L". *Adapted from Baker, L.L., McNeal, D.R., Benton, L.A., Bowman, B.R., Waters, R.L., 1993. Neuromuscular Electrical Stimulation — A Practical Guide. Rancho Los Amigos Research and Education Institute.*

- What outcome is desired for the patient?
- Which muscles and nerves will produce the desired response?
- How will the required muscle response be generated?
- How will the stimulated movement be controlled for the specific application?

It would be wrong, though, to assume that FES systems are necessarily simple in their design. As inferred earlier, FES has been used for different outcomes in mobility, such as grasping, standing, and walking and with many patient groups. In these cases, individual patients often present with individual movement patterns and deficits that need addressing, even though there are some generic characteristics. Their different needs and expectations, along with the recent advances in technology, have therefore led to different solutions being applied to FES systems. These have included:

- Using FES with multiple muscle groups, such as in the study by Kim et al. (2012), which demonstrated improvements in spatiotemporal parameters of gait when stimulating gluteus medius in the stance phase, alongside stimulating tibialis anterior in the swing phase. In the work that has come out of Cleveland in the United States, one example demonstrates an 8-channel implanted system to assist persons with spinal cord injuries to exercise, stand, and maneuver (Rohde et al., 2012).
- Using skin surface electrode arrays to accurately detect optimal electrode positions (e.g., Heller et al., 2013), demonstrates the principle of an automated setup which could lead to FES becoming more viable for patients who, at present, have difficulty in setting up current commercial stimulators.

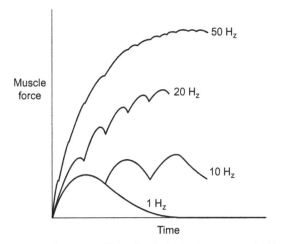

FIG. 21.3 Effect from stimulation frequency on muscle response, illustrating the higher force generated with a higher frequency and the level of graded control (or smoothness in response) at the different frequencies. *Adapted from Baker, L.L., McNeal, D.R., Benton, L.A., Bowman, B.R., Waters, R.L., 1993. Neuromuscular Electrical Stimulation — A Practical Guide. Rancho Los Amigos Research and Education Institute.*

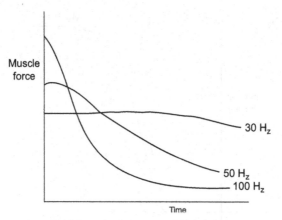

FIG. 21.4 Effect from stimulation frequency on muscle fatigue, showing that with a sustained contraction at an increased frequency the response reduces more quickly. *Adapted from Baker, L.L., McNeal, D.R., Benton, L.A., Bowman, B.R., Waters, R.L., 1993. Neuromuscular Electrical Stimulation — A Practical Guide. Rancho Los Amigos Research and Education Institute.*

- Applying stimulation through implanted systems, two examples being the BION device from the Alfred Mann Institute in the United States which is injected in or near muscles (Popovic et al., 2007) and the STIMuSTEP device from Finetech Medical in the United Kingdom which uses electrodes inserted into the epineurium of a nerve (Kottink et al., 2007), as well as the previously mentioned work from Cleveland.
- Detecting physiological signals to control FES devices, such as cutaneous nerve signals to induce grasp force (Inmann and Haugland, 2012) and intramuscular (or surface) muscle activity (EMG) to detect the intention to step (Dutta et al., 2009).
- Applying new sensor detection methods to more accurately detect specific events in a movement pattern; for example, gyro and accelerometer measurements for gait events (Park et al., 2012).
- Employing different control methodologies to determine stimulation envelopes, such as the work of Kordjazi and Kobravi (2012) which used measured activity from a "healthy" muscle to train an artificial neural network to predict the activation pattern for a disabled muscle, in this case for drop foot correction.

This introduces the reader to the complexity of FES systems, but for simplicity and clarity of thought in discussing the steps involved in the concept design of an FES system, only one case study will be considered here, as mentioned above. That case is of using FES to correct for dropped foot following neurological damage, such as from a stroke, and is probably the most widely used application for FES in the United Kingdom. Its beauty is that it is relatively simple in nature, but has the potential of prompting further discussion when answering the previously posed questions.

The desired outcome for the patient

Dropped foot is the inability to lift the foot as the leg swings forward when walking. It is caused by weakness in the muscles that lift the foot, the dorsiflexors such as tibialis anterior, and/or excessive activity (typically spasticity) in the antagonist muscles, such as the gastrocnemius. It is very common in stroke patients and can result in increased trips and falls, and reduced mobility, leading to loss of confidence, reduced social participation, and loss of independence. The problem can be addressed by using a passive ankle splint or ankle foot orthosis (AFO) and though these can be very effective, some people believe that a more active means, such as from using FES, can have additional advantages, such as promoting a more normal movement pattern following a stroke. Patients also often walk with excessive inversion that leads to poor foot placement into the stance phase of gait and can often mean the patient being unstable as they bear weight through their affected side (the ankle sometimes "turns over"), as well as weight transference being limited since the foot becomes flat on the floor too early into stance, with the tibia having not advanced forward. Other more proximal problems and compensatory strategies also play a part in the gait of a person who has had a stroke, but these will be ignored at the current time for simplicity.

An FES system therefore needs to provide floor clearance during the swing phase and improved stability into stance. The first could be achieved by eliciting dorsiflexion, whereas the second could be addressed through ensuring a positive heel strike with eversion at initial contact and through the loading response phase to aid weight transference. This can be shown pictorially with reference to a gait cycle, as shown in Fig. 21.5. It is perhaps worth noting here, however, that for

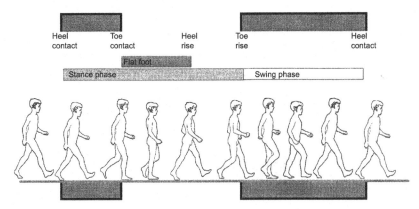

Heel contact Toe contact Heel rise Toe rise Heel contact

Flat foot

Stance phase Swing phase

FIG. 21.5 Representation of the gait cycle and stimulation phases for drop foot correction. A typical gait cycle from an unimpaired person is illustrated, with the stimulation phases represented by blocks from toe rise through to toe contact for floor clearance and tibial progression, respectively.

some people a well-tuned AFO could provide more effective control during the stance phase, but would limit dorsiflexion during swing. (Further information on the gait cycle may be found in Chapter 25, "Clinical Gait Analysis.")

Correct muscles and nerves to produce the desired response

In this application, dorsiflexion with eversion is required (again, the more proximal muscles have been ignored in this case study). This is produced by activating the tibialis anterior muscle, but since this also produces inversion its response needs to be somewhat compensated for by activating the peronei muscles for eversion. Pairs of electrodes could be placed over both muscle groups, but by understanding the physiology and also how unimpaired walking is achieved, another solution can be achieved by considering not the muscle groups and motor units, but the nerve supplying those two muscle groups, that is, the common peroneal nerve. By using just two electrodes, one over the motor point of tibialis anterior and the second over the fibula head, where the common peroneal nerve typically branches into its deep and superficial branches (with motor units at tibialis anterior and peronei muscles, respectively), careful electrode positioning can produce the desired response (Fig. 21.6). The added advantage of stimulating at the nerve is that it can also sometimes result in a flexion withdrawal reflex by stimulating the 1a afferent fibres causing hip flexion with abduction and external rotation, knee flexion, and dorsiflexion and eversion, and hence improved responses at the more proximal joints.

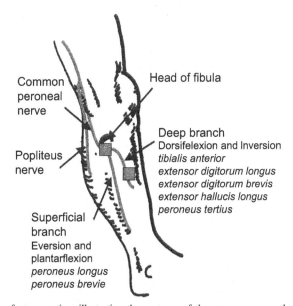

Common peroneal nerve

Head of fibula

Popliteus nerve

Deep branch
Dorsiflexion and Inversion
tibialis anterior
extensor digitorum longus
extensor digitorum brevis
extensor hallucis longus
peroneus tertius

Superficial branch
Eversion and plantarflexion
peroneus longus
peroneus brevie

FIG. 21.6 Electrode positions for drop foot correction, illustrating the anatomy of the common peroneal nerve with both the deep and superficial branches shown. One electrode is placed over the fibula head, and the other is placed more anteriorly and distally over the bulk of tibialis anterior. *From Odstock Medical Ltd. Clinician's Instruction Manual 2012.*

FIG. 21.7 Basic design of an FES system illustrating the envelope and pulse generator. Two main components are shown: a pulse and an envelope generator. Though it is possible for both components to be placed under some level of control (with or without feedback), in this case only the timing and control aspects of the envelope generator are shown.

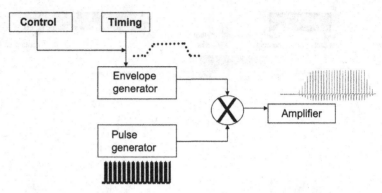

Generating the required muscle response

It has already been explained how a series of electrical stimulation pulses can produce a muscle response. However, before discussing how these can be controlled for this application, it may be worthwhile considering how to "set" the three basic parameters, that is, amplitude, pulsewidth, and frequency. Stimulation intensity (amplitude-pulsewidth) is generally set to be at the middle portion of the steep slope in the muscle response—intensity curve (Fig. 21.3). This allows the patient (or clinician) the dynamic range to either turn up or turn down the intensity as the day progresses to accommodate different scenarios; such as increasing the intensity when the patient begins to fatigue and the foot starts to drop again, or when walking over uneven ground and more foot lift is required. In this application the stance phase is generally when the stimulation is "off," hence there is no requirement for the contraction to be sustained over a long time and hence fatigue occurring. The frequency can therefore be set slightly higher than for other FES applications, with the added advantage of increased speed of muscle response and possibly high enough to more likely elicit the withdrawal reflex. For stimulation of more postural muscles, where stimulation is continuous, it may be necessary to reduce the frequency.

How to control the stimulated movement for the specific application

The FES system consists of a simple pulse generator which is amplified to deliver the stimulation pulses to the body to cause a contraction. However, for this application the stimulation is required to be "on" at certain times of the gait cycle and "off" at others. This perhaps provides the most challenging, and at the same time interesting, aspects of designing a practical FES system: How will the muscle responses be controlled for the required application? A simple way of looking at this is to think of the FES system being the pulse generator plus amplifier, alongside an envelope generator, as shown in Fig. 21.7.

Looking now just at the envelope, Fig. 21.8, the transition points need to be determined. For the simple envelope described, these transition points are at "turn on" and "turn off" (i.e., at the start and end of the ramp periods). Earlier it was illustrated that the stimulation needs to be on during the swing phase, with some extension into early stance (see Fig. 21.5). For this relatively simple case study, gait events at the foot (i.e., heel/toe strike/rise) could be considered to be used for these two trigger points, that is, turn on and turn off. One solution may be to use toe rise (to turn the stimulation on at the start of swing) and toe strike (to turn the stimulation off toward mid-stance). This would work, but it does require the stimulation to turn on instantly at toe rise to ensure sufficient lift at early swing. Bringing this trigger point further forward in the gait cycle would now take it to the previous gait event (i.e., heel rise), ensuring that the foot is sufficiently prepared

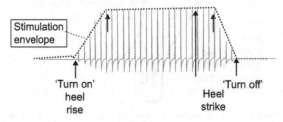

FIG. 21.8 Representation of the FES envelope. The simple transition points are indicated by the arrows, alongside the solution selected for their practical implementation in a dropped foot system.

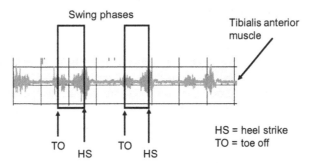

FIG. 21.9 Surface EMG recording from tibialis anterior muscle in unimpaired walking. Two bursts of muscle activity are observed: the first during the first part of the swing phase for floor clearance, and the second toward the end of swing, but extending into early stance for eccentric activity to control the lowering of the foot to the ground for weight transference.

prior to the start of swing. It also allows for there to be an up ramp period which is essential to minimize any responses from stretching the antagonist muscle too quickly and eliciting a spastic response and plantarflexion. Such a system now has its "on" trigger at heel rise and its "off" trigger at toe strike. This would require switches under both the heel and the toe (or first metatarsal head), so a simpler solution could be to use just one switch under the heel, with the "off" trigger now at heel strike and just simply extending the stimulation into stance for a fixed time, hence turning off by mid-stance. This is the approach taken by the team at the National Clinical FES Centre, Salisbury, United Kingdom with its Odstock Dropped Foot Stimulator system (www.odstockmedical.com).

This envelope is relatively straightforward, but, even for this simple application, there are some strong grounds to make it more complex. First, it could be argued that the "off" trigger should reflect the actual time when the tibia has progressed forward into stance. Using a second switch at the toe goes some way to achieving this, however a sensor on the tibia could make that more accurate by determining its actual position relative to the vertical, or by investigating the acceleration and deceleration components of its movement. Second, in the scenario described, a simple up-hold-down envelope is used when, in fact, the tibialis anterior muscle in unimpaired physiological gait is seen to have two bursts of activity, as shown in Fig. 21.9. The first burst is replicated with the dropped foot system for floor clearance and the second burst relates to eccentric activity of that muscle as the tibia advances forward, as replicated in the extension phase of the stimulation envelope. The issue here is that the second burst is typically stronger than the first and so perhaps the envelope should be more like that shown in Fig. 21.10. The challenge, then, is how to control the two levels of the envelope and also when to make the transition from the first to the second burst. Again, this would need to be quite accurately timed to ensure that the gait is not to be impeded and therefore would require additional movement or positional sensors. Examples of this work can be found in the papers by Chen et al. (2010) and O'Halloran et al. (2004). This may make the system more complicated, however, possibly less reliable, and certainly more expensive and hence less likely to be used routinely in a healthcare system such as the NHS.

Conclusions

FES has been around for many years, but has tended to stay in the research laboratories of academic and clinical institutions. There have been some successes in using FES more clinically, but these have been slow, partly reflecting the

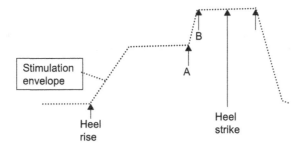

FIG. 21.10 A proposed new FES envelope to reflect the real activity in tibialis anterior. This has an envelope similar to Figure 18.8, but with an increased stimulation intensity at the time relating to the second burst of unimpaired EMG activity. The challenge, then, is to accurately determine the appropriate point for A and B (*note*: there is no floor contact since these points are during swing).

limited resources applied to this emerging field. However, as a technique, it does have considerable potential to restore limb movement and as such needs to be taken further.

In this chapter, the basic principles of FES have been considered alongside the specification and design of an FES system for a specific application, that is, dropped foot. It is imperative for there to be cooperation between engineering, scientific, medical, and therapy staff in the clinical environment to specify, design, test, and evaluate such products for patients. Clinical engineers need to be at the forefront of that to ensure that the design requirements and specification are correct, and not just contributing to the engineering design and construction of the product. The testing and evaluation is equally important for all staff to be involved with so that the ergonomics and usability of the product, for both clinicians and patients, can be appropriate and that the functional outcomes from patients using the products can be assessed objectively.

For further information related to the medical applications of electrical stimulation visit the websites of the International FES Society (http://ifess.org/) and the International Neuromodulation Society (www.neuromodulation.com).

For a more detailed description of how nerves are excited, the reader is referred to standard text books on (neuro) physiology.

References

Chen, M., Wang, Q.B., Lou, X.X., Xu, K., Zheng, X.X., 2010. A foot drop correcting FES envelope design method using tibialis anterior EMG during healthy gait with a new walking speed control strategy. Conf. Proc. IEEE Eng. Med. Biol. Soc. 4906−4909.

Dutta, A., Kobetic, R., Triolo, R., 2009. Development of an implanted intramuscular EMG-triggered FES system for ambulation after incomplete spinal cord injury. Conf. Proc. IEEE Eng. Med. Biol. Soc. 6793−6797.

Heller, B.W., Clarke, A.J., Good, T.R., Healey, T.J., Nair, S., Pratt, E.J., Reeves, M.L., van der Meulen, J.M., Barker, A.T., 2013. Automated setup of FES for drop foot using a novel 64 channel prototype stimulator and electrode array: results from a gait lab based study. Med. Eng. Phys. 35 (1), 74−81.

Inmann, A., Haugland, M., 2012. Regulation of FES-induced grasp force based on cutaneous nerve signals: experiments and modelling. Med. Eng. Phys. 34 (1).

Kim, J.H., Chung, Y., Kim, Y., Hwang, S., 2012. FES applied to gluteus medius and tibialis anterior corresponding gait cycle for stroke. Gait Posture 36 (1), 65−67.

Kordjazi, N., Kobravi, H.R., 2012. Control of tibialis anterior FES envelope for unilateral drop foot gait correction using NARX neural network. Conf. Proc. IEEE. Eng. Med. Bio. Soc. 1880−1883.

Kottink, A.I., Hermans, H.J., Nene, A.V., Tenniglo, M.J., van der Aa, H.E., Buschman, H.P., Ijzerman, M.J., 2007. A randomised controlled trial of an implantable 2-channel peroneal nerve stimulator on walking speed and activity in post-stroke hemiplegia. Arch. Phys. Med. Rehabil. 88 (8), 971−978.

O'Halloran, T., Haugland, M., Lyons, G.M., Sinkjaer, T., 2004. An investigation of the effect of modifying stimulation profile shape on the loading response phase of gait, during FES-corrected drop foot: stimulation profile and loading response. Neuromodulation 7 (2), 113−125.

Park, S., Ryu, K., Kim, J., Son, J., Kim, Y., 2012. Verification of accuracy and validity of gait phase detection system using motion sensors for applying walking assistive FES. Comput. Methods Biomech. Biomed. Eng. 15 (11), 1129−1135.

Popovic, D., Baker, L.L., Loeb, G.E., 2007. Recruitment and comfort of BION implanted electrical stimulation: implications for FES applications. IEEE Trans. Neural Syst. Rehabil. Eng. 15 (4), 577−586.

Rohde, L.M., Bonder, B.R., Triolo, R.J., 2012. Exploratory study of perceived quality of life with implanted standing neuroprostheses. J. Rehabil. Res. Dev. 49 (2), 265−278.

Further Reading

Baker, L.L., McNeal, D.R., Benton, L.A., Bowman, B.R., Waters, R.L., 1993. Neuromuscular Electrical Stimulation − A Practical Guide. Rancho Los Amigos Research and Education Institute.

Rushton, D.N., 2003. Functional electrical stimulation and rehabilitation − an hypothesis. Med. Eng. Phys. 25 (1), 75−78.

Swain, I.D., Taylor, P.N., Franklyn, J., 2004. The clinical use of functional electrical stimulation in neurological rehabilitation. In: Franklyn, J. (Ed.), Horizons in Medicine 16 − Updates on Major Clinical Advances. Pub. Royal College of Physicians, London, pp. 315−322.

Functional Electrical Stimulation for drop foot of central neurological origin: Buyer's Guide (CEP10010), Market Review (CEP10011) and Economic Report (CEP10012). An independent evaluation by the NHS − visit the Cedar website (www.cedar.wales.nhs.uk/home) for access.

For a more detailed description of how nerves are excited, the reader is referred to standard text books on (neuro) physiology.

Chapter 22

Posture management

David Long

AJM Healthcare, UK & Oxford University Hospitals NHS Foundation Trust, Oxford, UK

Chapter outline

Introduction

The content of this chapter has been drawn principally from the subject matter of the posture management courses provided in Oxford, UK, by physiotherapists Wendy Murphy, Pat Postill and the author (clinical scientist), which were developed originally by physiotherapist Pauline Pope and educational advisor Janet Wells. The underpinning theories and principles are documented in the book *Severe and Complex Neurological Disability* (Pope, 2007), published by Elsevier. The work of Dr Linda Marks, a consultant in rehabilitation medicine, physiotherapist Dr Linda Walker, and clinical scientist Phil Swann has also been influential.

The chapter is aimed primarily at nonambulant individuals having significant limitations to movement, although the principles may be applied more broadly. Please note that it should be considered an outline of posture management, this being a highly complex subject area.

Clinical Engineering. https://doi.org/10.1016/B978-0-08-102694-6.00022-X

Posture

One often hears of good postures and bad postures, but posture can be a difficult concept to define. What might be a good posture for typing an email would be a bad one for relaxing, or a good posture adopted within a military parade a bad one for talking casually with friends. Pope (2007) suggests that posture is "… the attitude or configuration of the body." Expanding on this, she suggests that it is the ability to organize and stabilize the body segments relative to one another, and then to be able to offload one segment without losing overall stability. Able-bodied people take for granted the ability to lean forward or to one side to reach for an object out of their immediate grasp, but for the physically disabled person this can be enormously challenging, if not impossible. This brings us to functional activity which is a critical aspect of posture management because, ultimately, we arrange ourselves according to the task in hand. Consider how your posture changes as you carry out different activities. One makes these changes to optimize functional performance and to conserve energy. We organize, balance, and stabilize our body segments relative to the supporting surface and are able to respond to changing requirements and external forces.

Able-bodied people are able to move in and out of position at will and in response to stimuli, such as tiredness or discomfort/pain. Importantly, what might be considered a good posture for a particular activity might also be a damaging one if it is sustained over an extended period of time. Those less able to move are at high risk of damage to the body system (i.e., plastic change), which can take place in two ways:

- Orthopaedic: The development of soft tissue contracture (muscles, tendons, and ligaments) and change in bony shape, leading to secondary complications such as impaired internal organ function and pressure ulceration.
- Neurological: The laying down of altered neural pathways through repetitive asymmetrical, atypical, unusual, or anomalous movements, having a negative effect (Scrutton, 1991).

The ability to organize one's posture is learnt: it is not something with which we are born. We gradually adapt our primitive reflexes to functional movement, learning how to hold our head up, roll over, sit up, crawl, stand, walk, and run. The steps in this process have been researched extensively by Chailey Clinical Services which published the Chailey Scales of Postural Ability for sitting, standing, and lying (Pountney et al., 2004).

Effects of gravity

The effects of gravity are profoundly important for posture. They can be used positively to secure body segments in a particular position and can have significant negative effects in causing the body to buckle and bend. Gravity is (more or less) a constant force, that is to say one cannot escape it. There is, however, a common, misplaced conception that gravity has no impact on posture in lying. It has just as much effect, of course, the difference being that the body is orientated to it in a different plane from sitting or standing.

A helpful visualization of posture was described by Whitman (1924): "a constant struggle against the force of gravity." This was further developed by Hare (1987) who presented the idea of the "human sandwich" (Fig. 22.1), where as people we are the filling being held in place and compressed between the force of gravity and the surface of the Earth (or the supporting surface). When able-bodied people become tired of standing, they sit to conserve energy; when they become tired of sitting, they lie down. In this position, minimum energy is required, thus resting the musculoskeletal system. This is a profoundly important concept in relation to people with a physical disability.

The role of the supporting surface

The supporting surface has a vital part to play in posture control. Take, for example, sitting erect on a stool. One must be able to balance on a small area of support and sustain relatively high pressures because the load is being distributed over a small area. One tires of such a position relatively quickly and so additional support is recruited, perhaps by moving the stool near a wall against which one's back can be leant. The legs may also be crossed to secure the position of the foot in contact with the ground/support surface to help secure the position of the pelvis. These changes in position not only offload some of the weight from the ischial tuberosities but also widen the base of support, making the posture more stable and energy efficient. As further tiredness creeps in, one may wish to sit in an armchair which offers a more tilted position, allowing gravity to help secure a position. Some people choose to sit with their legs flexed and placed to one side, the heels positioned close to or even underneath the pelvis, perhaps leaning on the arm of a couch. It is becoming clear, then, that functional postures are not necessarily symmetrical.

Gravity

Ground reaction

FIG. 22.1 Human sandwich.

While we require stability to function, it should be remembered that in offloading body segments we create partial instability. It is critical that in providing a piece of equipment for posture management we do not provide so much stability that function is impaired; there has to be a balance between the two. One must ascertain the level of support required set against the functional requirements.

24-Hour postural management

In providing a piece of equipment for posture management it is necessary to consider the full 24 hour period of each day (Gericke, 2006; Pope, 2007; Pountney et al., 2004). There is often great focus on providing seating for use in the daytime, whether this be an armchair, classroom chair, or wheelchair, but an area often neglected is positioning requirements at night. It is not difficult to conceive that the amount of time spent in bed can consume anywhere between a quarter and two-thirds of the 24 hour period. Even the smaller of the two figures is a significant proportion of time and this is important because postures adopted at night can have a profound effect on postures adopted during the day (Goldsmith et al., 1998). Tissue adaptation caused by poor positioning in bed affects positioning in sitting; discomfort in lying may transfer to sitting; lack of sleep caused by discomfort may reduce sitting tolerance in the day; pressure management issues in bed may create difficulties in sitting.

Getting the right balance of support, comfort, and ease of use is a difficult result to achieve, but this should not stop the clinician involved in one area of posture management from addressing the other areas, which may require making onward referral to other professionals or services.

Biomechanics as applied to postural management

This section does not cover basic mechanical concepts, nor does it provide any degree of depth in what is a very complex subject. The concepts of biomechanics most critical to the implementation of 24 hour postural management are discussed. There are many texts available for both mechanics and biomechanics for those who wish to pursue the subject further.

Shearing forces

Where two masses pass each other in opposite directions, shear forces are generated at the interface. These comprise a mixture of tensile and compressive forces which also develop heat. An example of this is in the development of tissue ulceration, typified by the hospitalized patient being propped up in a semi-sitting position with the legs out straight and the head of the bed raised (Fig. 22.2), but is applicable to many seated postures. The ischial tuberosities and sacrum travel

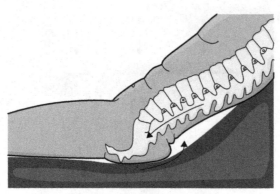

FIG. 22.2 Patient sliding in bed.

forward because the center of mass of the person falls behind (outside) their base of support and because a slope has been created down which the trunk can slide. However, motion of the soft tissues between the pelvis and supporting surface is impeded by friction at the surface of the skin.

Development of pressure ulceration is discussed in greater detail in Chapter 20 "Pressure Ulceration."

Stability and instability

These concepts are central to posture management. We require stability to conserve energy and to improve certain functions, but we also require instability to facilitate other functions. Static stability has three basic attributes:

1. The center of mass must fall within the base of support
2. The wider the base of support, the greater the stability
3. The lower the center of mass, the greater the stability

It translates, then, that a tilted seating system (or, indeed, any armchair) will create greater stability than an upright (wheel)chair. These principles are carried through the whole of this chapter, both in terms of securing a position and in facilitating functional movement.

Stress and strain; elasticity and plasticity

We know that an elastic response to loading means that a material will return to its original shape and length when the load is removed. We also know that too much loading will give a plastic response when the elastic limit of the material is passed, causing permanent deformation. These properties are depicted by a stress/strain curve, as shown in Fig. 22.3.

What we are generally more concerned with in posture management is sustained loading/positioning over time, often measured in hours and days in a rehabilitation setting post-stroke, spinal cord injury, or head injury, and in months and years for anyone with a long-term condition with reduced or impaired movement. In materials science the term *creep* refers to the situation where an increase in strain can be detected while the applied load remains constant over time, as shown in Fig. 22.4. This leads ultimately to failure in static materials, but in biological materials we can observe plastic adaptation to structure, both in bone and soft tissue, which presents clinically as fixed postural asymmetry or enhanced shape, such as scoliosis and kyphosis, and as joint contracture (i.e., a limitation in movement). Notice in the graph that there is an immediate jump in strain as the load is applied, which corresponds to the elastic response of the material, but that after this the rate of increase is reduced.

Moments

Moments help us to describe the actions and results of forces applied about a pivot point or fulcrum; they are the product of force and distance (Fig. 22.5).

In the human body we have long levers in the arms and legs. The spine is multijointed and many moments act simultaneously. As a result, supporting the body and/or facilitating movement requires an understanding and application of the theory of moments. If the leg of a seated person tends to fall out to the side of the chair, a corrective force can be applied to control the position of that leg. The force is most effective when placed distally (i.e., at the knee), and so may be

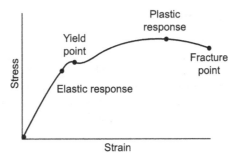

FIG. 22.3 Sample stress/strain curve.

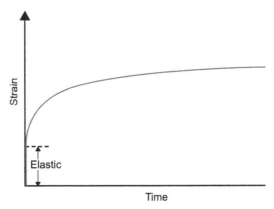

FIG. 22.4 Sample strain/time curve for a constant applied load.

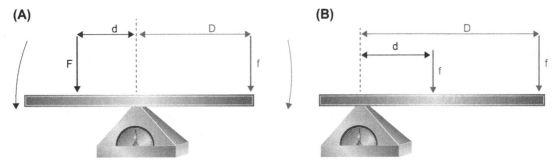

FIG. 22.5 Moments: (A) the smaller force is able to balance the larger force because it is placed further away from the fulcrum; (B) the same force produces less mechanical leverage if applied closer to the fulcrum.

reduced in magnitude compared to application at mid-thigh. One may go a step further and support the thigh along its length so that the load is distributed over a larger area, reducing the applied force at any given point. Moments link with postural stability in that it is more effortful to stand up from a low settee than it is from a dining chair: the centre of mass must be moved further forward and be raised through a greater height, all linked with the length of the levers rotating around the ankles, knees, hips and vertebrae in the spine. It follows, then, that a tilted seat position is more stable than one which is upright.

Day-to-day clinical applications

These biomechanical principles are readily applied to many other clinical scenarios. To some, this is intuitive, perhaps most of all to the engineer, but the ability to explain what is happening and communicate this in a meaningful way to the patient is very important. Why is a support needed in a particular place? Why is a particular orientation of sitting/standing/lying required? The person and/or their relatives or carers must be convinced of the value of the advice they are being given, a clear description of the reasoning behind decisions greatly aiding this process.

Introduction to the physical assessment

General principles of patient assessment for rehabilitation engineering and assistive technology were covered in Chapter 17. To develop a programme of physical management over a 24 hour period, one must take great care to establish all relevant physical abilities and limitations. This is not a quick process and with some patients will be physically demanding of the assessor, as well as of the patient. It is important for the patient to feel comfortable with being physically handled/touched. What may be routine for the professional may feel extremely intrusive to the person concerned. In some instances it will be appropriate to request the presence of a chaperone.

Body configuration

Introduction

The process starts with an assessment of the presenting body configuration, usually in sitting. It is important that this is a typical presentation: there is always a temptation for the person or their carers to correct what they deem to be a "poor" posture. It is necessary to see the person as they typically sit to establish any postural tendencies and patterns of movement; for example, leaning to the side, sliding forward in the seat, or head dropped forward/to the side. It is advisable to take photographs, one from the front and one from each side, keeping the camera on the level of the person to avoid perspective distortion.

The international standard ISO 16840-1:2006 "Wheelchair seating − Part 1: Vocabulary, reference axis convention and measures for body segments, posture and postural support surfaces" provides a method for defining body configuration in sitting. This standard is designed to "… specify standardized geometric terms and definitions for describing and quantifying a person's anthropometric measures and seated posture, as well as the spatial orientation and dimensions of a person's seating support surfaces" (ISO, 2006). The method is extremely comprehensive, providing a full data set of measures. While it clearly has a very useful place in a research setting, the level of detail included makes it more difficult to apply in clinical practice, although Waugh and Crane (2013) have developed an accompanying document that provides clinical guidance on its application. There are elements that may clearly be applied successfully, although the terminology is inconsistent with that used widely in healthcare settings, certainly in the UK, and notably by physiotherapists (or physical therapists), acknowledging that this terminology itself is not always applied consistently.

More significantly, it is not possible to apply the standard readily to the practice of 24 hour posture management because it does not provide a means to describe lying or standing postures. In addition, the detail of spinal shapes, notably those of a complex nature, are also difficult to describe using the prescribed terminology. The standard does, on the other hand, illustrate clearly the complexities of describing body orientation and shape and has, undoubtedly, moved forward the science underpinning our understanding of body configuration.

In this chapter we use the more conventional terms and reference this standard where applicable to illustrate its potential use.

Pelvic orientation

The first measurement is of pelvic symmetry or asymmetry and is described in three planes of motion: obliquity, rotation, and tilt. It is important that these are understood clearly as they form the basis of postural support, which then allows the more complex picture of body segment organization to be established (Pope, 2007; Frischhut et al., 2000).

To define the position of the pelvis, it is first necessary to find two alike bony landmarks, typically the anterior superior iliac spines (ASISs). These are easily visible in an anatomy text and on people having little excess tissue, but may be difficult to find on some patients. Where the pelvis is so oblique that one ASIS is tucked up inside the lower portion of the rib cage, one cannot usually reach the ASIS and so some other landmark must be used. In these cases it is possible to palpate for the posterior superior iliac spines, iliac crests, or the ischial tuberosities. It is also possible to palpate for the greater trochanters of the hips but this may lead to a false reading where the hip is asymmetric or dislocated, so should be avoided.

- Pelvic obliquity, measured relative to the horizontal, is identified where one ASIS is higher than the other (Fig. 22.6A). It is referred to in ISO16840-1 as the *frontal pelvic angle*. Ideally, an angular measurement would be recorded, but it can be difficult to align a goniometer with the ASISs and reliable visual estimation of small angles can be difficult to achieve (Parker, 2012, 2014). An alternative is to make a visual estimation of the linear difference in height of one

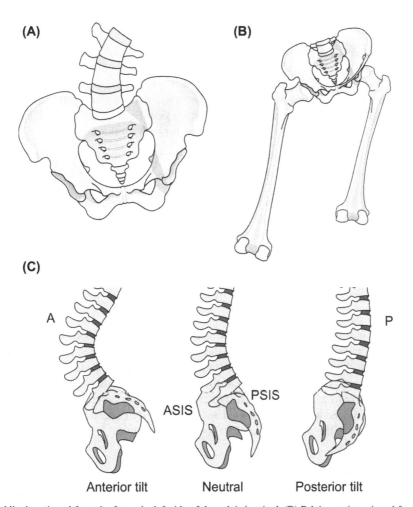

FIG. 22.6 (A) Pelvic obliquity: viewed from the front, the left side of the pelvis is raised. (B) Pelvic rotation: viewed from above the pelvis is rotated forward on the right side, toward the left. (C) Pelvic tilt: anterior, neutral, and posterior orientations.

ASIS compared to the other. However, the significance of this will vary according to the overall distance between the ASISs, most notably between small children and adults. In spite of this limitation, a linear measurement allows comparison between postures and between clinic appointments, having greater reliability where it is taken by the same assessor (Parker, 2014). Note that the ischial tuberosities are closer together than the ASISs, so the differences in their height will be less.

- Pelvic rotation, referred to in ISO16840-1 as the *transverse pelvic angle*, describes the situation where one ASIS is forward of the other (Fig. 22.6B), i.e., one is more forward of an imaginary or real symmetrical flat seat back. Again, an angular measurement would be ideal but a visual linear estimation is easier to attain, acknowledging that it has the same limitations as described above.

- Pelvic tilt: Where a line drawn between the ASIS and PSIS (posterior superior iliac spine) is horizontal, as viewed in the sagittal plane, the pelvis is said to be in neutral tilt (Fig. 22.6C). Pelvic tilt is referred to in ISO16840-1 as the *sagittal pelvic angle*. If this line tips down at the front (relative to the horizontal) the pelvis is in anterior tilt (Fig. 22.6C) and will usually be accompanied by an enhanced (hyper) lumbar lordosis (see the following subsection "Spinal Alignment"). If the line tips down at the back, the pelvis is in posterior tilt (Fig. 22.6C) and will usually be accompanied by a flattened lumbar spine. Remember that in normal anatomy one would expect to find a gentle inward curve (lordosis) in the lumbar region of the spine. An angle would be helpful to record but without instrumentation this is difficult to estimate. Physiotherapists use the terminology of "+" to indicate a slight increase from normal/neutral, "++" and "+++" to indicate increasing amounts. Alternatively, the descriptors of *minimal*, *moderate* and *maximal* may be used.

Alignment of the hips

Having noted the alignment of the pelvis, the symmetry or otherwise of the hips may then be determined, but it is important to remember that you are now noting position relative to the *pelvis* and not to any other plane or body segment. In this way, the *actual* position of the body segment is described, that is, it is a relative measurement, not an absolute, and it is a measurement relative to the more proximal segment. A measurement to a neutral plane may mask the severity of, say, hip adduction where there is also pelvic rotation forwards on the opposite side. Equally, a hip which appears adducted relative to a neutral plane may not be adducted where the pelvis is rotated forward on the same side.

- Abduction/adduction is measured relative to pelvic rotation in sitting, i.e., the amount of true abduction is increased where the pelvis is forward on the same side as the measured hip, and is decreased where the pelvis is forward on the opposite side.
- Internal/external rotation is measured relative to pelvic obliquity in sitting, i.e., the true amount of external rotation is less than the apparent measurement where the pelvis is oblique up on the opposite side, and is more where the pelvis is raised on the same side.

Again, the "+" and "++" terminology can be a useful means of denoting the severity of asymmetry and in making comparisons between hips. An angular measurement could also be used, according to ISO16840-1.

Position of feet

Next, the position and orientation of the feet is described. Are they resting on the supports or falling off the back, front, or sides? Do they become trapped between the footplates? Are they restrained by strapping and, if so, why, and is this all the time? Are the feet angled down at the front (plantarflexed), at the back (dorsiflexed), supinated (turned in, as if to clap the soles together), pronated (turned out), varus (toes closer together than heels), or valgus (toes further apart than heels)? Are shoes worn? Oftentimes, it is clearer to take a photograph than attempt a written description. If the person intends to stand, description of any asymmetry will need to be more detailed and more clearly understood because the feet will be bearing weight; in a classroom chair, though, the issues are likely to be far less critical.

Orientation of the shoulder girdle

Having completed the assessment of the pelvis and lower limbs, we start to think about the trunk, but before this it is necessary to analyze the orientation of the shoulder girdle. Obliquity and rotation is described in the same way and with the same reference planes as the pelvis, but one must be mindful that the shoulder girdle is not a fixed structure like the pelvis. The shoulders can independently protract (move anteriorly from neutral), retract (move posteriorly from neutral), elevate, and drop, often with minimal impact on the shape of the spine.

Spinal alignment

Analyzing this can be challenging as the spine is multijointed and highly flexible, allowing very complex shapes to emerge. The term *scoliosis* is used to describe a sideways curve, as viewed in the frontal plane, and is referred to as either convex or concave. It is not important which of these terms is used, only that one is used consistently. Fig. 22.7A) shows a simple scoliotic curve, running from sacrum to occiput, which could be described as either convex left or concave right.

ISO16840-1 would refer to the frontal sternal angle to describe such a curve, although this becomes more challenging in Fig. 22.7B which shows a more complex shape having two component curves: convex right in the thoracolumbar region and convex left in the upper thoracic region.

Scolioses give rise to and are caused by rotation in the spine and this in turn causes asymmetry in the ribs, usually referred to as a rib "prominence" or "fullness." The term rib "hump" is considered derogatory and has fallen largely into disuse, certainly within the UK. The term "deformity" is still fairly common parlance but has a negative connotation. A typical prominence is shown in Fig. 22.8, in this example on the right side. Also note that the pelvis is significantly oblique up on the left, which has resulted in the person sitting on and taking weight not only through the right ischial tuberosity but also the right greater trochanter.

Posterior prominences are very important as they can throw postural alignment if not adequately accommodated: they will cause rotation of the shoulders, trunk and pelvis if set against a flat surface. Anterior prominences are less critical for support surfaces unless the person lies prone at night, but they do indicate significant complications with the spine and, most likely, internal organ function. They usually appear on the opposite side to the posterior prominence.

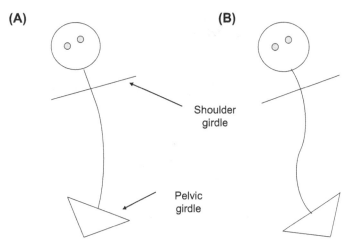

FIG. 22.7 (A) Simple scoliotic curve. (B) Complex scoliotic curve.

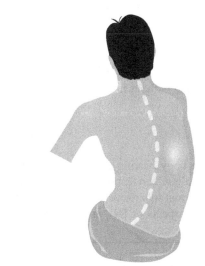

FIG. 22.8 Prominent ribs posteriorly on the right.

In the sagittal plane, an outward curvature of the spine is referred to as a kyphosis and an inward curve a lordosis, as previously mentioned. Fig. 22.9 demonstrates a significant upper thoracic kyphosis which has resulted in the person only being able to look into their lap, with obvious functional and social implications. Also note that the lumbar spine has flattened, that the pelvis is in posterior tilt, and that the hip is more extended than flexed.

It is difficult to define precise measurements that can be taken to describe spinal asymmetry. Instead, descriptive language is required, such as *subtle*, *enhanced*, *pronounced*, *marked*, or *significant*. A photograph will assist in the description.

When making an assessment it is necessary to remember that the spine has a natural lumbar lordosis and thoracic kyphosis which can vary significantly between people. The apex of the kyphosis is more posterior than the most posterior point of the sacrum. This means that unless support surfaces are shaped to stabilize the sacrum, posterior tilt will result, with associated kyphosis, problems with head control, and a tendency to slide forward in the seat.

While the neck forms part of the spine, one tends to refer to either neck extension, meaning lordosis, or flexion, meaning kyphosis. One also describes movement in the neck in terms of lateral flexion and by axial rotation to the left/right.

Position and movement of the arms

The significance of the arms is easily neglected but they play a vital role. Where they are functional, it is important to understand their movement. Where they are dysfunctional they tend to pull forward and down on the shoulder girdle due to

FIG. 22.9   Implications of an enhanced thoracic kyphosis.

their weight, which is often significant. When describing position, consideration should be given as to whether the shoulders are abducted or adducted, internally or externally rotated, extended or elevated. Following this, it should be established if the elbows and wrists are flexed or extended as this clearly has implications for function. It is necessary to make a detailed assessment of arm function where functional movement is required. People with higher level spinal cord injuries in particular use a variety of "trick" movements to facilitate function and independence that will sometimes limit the amount of postural support that can be provided, e.g. they will hook one elbow behind a wheelchair push handle in order to lean forward (to take a drink, for example) without falling, which they would otherwise do due to having limited muscular control of their trunk.

Weight bearing

It is helpful to define in detail the areas of the body bearing weight, which can be surprisingly few. This will provide additional information to the description of posture developed from the assessment outlined. Bony prominences are particularly vulnerable to damage, notably the ischial tuberosities, greater trochanters, coccyx, sacrum, lateral/medial knee condyles, lateral/medial malleolus, heels, lateral aspects of feet, apex/rib prominence of scoliosis/kyphosis, scapulae, elbows, and the back of the head.

Patterns of movement and neurological phenomena

Throughout the assessment, observe any movement the person is making, be this volitional or involuntary. The latter, is typically caused by neurological phenomena, including hypertonia, hypotonia, spasticity, spasm, clonus, ataxia, athetosis, chorea, and rigidity, and any reflexes such as the asymmetric tonic neck reflex (ATNR) or startle. Each can have a profound effect on posture and make day-to-day management extremely difficult. It is sometimes necessary to refer the person to their physician for a medical review prior to or in conjunction with the development of a posture management programme.

There are some familiar patterns of postural asymmetry, as described by Porter et al. (2007) and as often clinically observed; for example, windsweeping of the hips to one side with an associated scoliosis convex to the contralateral side. An adducted hip tends to be internally rotated and an abducted hip to be externally rotated. In supine lying, flexed hips and knees will usually cause the legs to fall to one side whereupon the pelvis will be pulled forward on the contralateral side. These are not rules, and many variations will be observed in clinical practice.

Lying position

Having completed the assessment of body configuration in sitting, it is then necessary to repeat the process in lying. It is tempting to think if one is assessing for seating that lying is irrelevant. I should like to propose that it is difficult, if not impossible, for a satisfactory assessment of seating to be carried out without having also assessed posture in lying. In sitting, gravity is having a profound impact on posture, most noticeably on the spine, but in lying this effect is reduced. With the person positioned in supine, it is possible to explore just how much correction of spinal asymmetry is possible. Having supported the legs and stabilized the pelvis, the trunk can be manipulated to establish how much of the curve is fixed and how much is flexible, that is, whether there is contracture and what internal forces are at work. Having done this, the process is to carry out the same measures of pelvic asymmetry, hip position, shoulder girdle asymmetry, and spinal alignment as with sitting. Only then is it possible to accurately determine the amount of correction that may be achieved in sitting.

Note that when assessing hip position, the pelvic plane against which one is measuring is opposite to that in sitting, that is to say hip abduction and adduction become relative to pelvic obliquity and hip rotation relative to pelvic rotation. This is caused by the legs being in an extended position rather than flexed, that is, their position relative to the pelvis has been transposed through 90°. Where the legs do not straighten fully one must take care in describing hip orientation.

Summary

The body is a complex, organic structure that can give rise to an almost infinite number of physical presentations. The job of the assessor is to pick out the critical elements, most notably to determine what is fixed and what is flexible, and not to dwell on detail that has little impact on the end result. Knowing where to focus can only truly be learnt with practise.

Critical measures: joint range of motion and pelvic/trunkal asymmetry
Introduction

The next step, with the patient lying supine, is to measure joint ranges of motion, most notably the hips, knees, and ankles, and to identify critical limitations in the alignment of the pelvis and trunk. Together, these are referred to as *critical measures*. They are dealt with in the following subsection, "Critical Measures to Consider for Sitting, Lying, and Standing." These measures are critical because without consideration being given to each one, the postural management strategy may be jeopardized. Prior to their introduction we briefly discuss the reasons why we take measurements and general points on carrying out a physical assessment.

Reasons for taking measurements

Why do we measure ranges of joint motion? We are interested in the presence of limitations and the effect of these on posture and positioning. Joints undergo plastic change that impairs their ability to move. Pain can also limit range and has many potential sources, often being difficult to control and resolve.

In which joints are we interested? This depends on the clinical question we are trying to answer. In terms of postural management, we are most interested in the ranges of motion of the hips, knees, and ankles. The feet, arms, and hands are also important and we are also interested, of course, in any limitations of movement in the (multijointed) spine.

How precise do our measurements need to be? Again, this depends on the clinical question. A paediatric physiotherapist working in a school will carry out a physical assessment of a child with the aim of determining the present range available in a given joint. This data will then be compared to past measurements to determine if there has been a change and, if so, whether treatment should be adapted to suit. As a result, the physiotherapist is interested in the extremes of motion available to the child. In posture management, we are often seeking to find out if the joint ranges allow the person to be positioned in either sitting, lying, or standing. We are interested more in the *critical measures* and less in the extremes of motion (Pope, 2007).

General points on carrying out a physical assessment

It is possible to carry out an assessment of lying position on a bed mattress, but it is far preferable to use a physiotherapy plinth as there is less movement compared to a mattress and, as a result, less margin for error. A floor mat can also be used as an alternative to a plinth but this is best suited to children as hoisting to the floor can present difficulties, as can manual handling at that level.

If you are unused to measuring joint ranges, work alongside an experienced colleague such as a clinical scientist/ engineer, physiotherapist, occupational therapist, or consultant in rehabilitation medicine. In terms of taking a measurement, it is possible to use visual estimation or goniometry. The latter is limited in cases where anatomical landmarks are altered or not in their normal positions, as is often the case with people having complex postural presentations. If your spatial awareness is less developed, however, goniometry might be a helpful way of improving the accuracy of your estimations.

An assistant is always required to stabilize the more proximal body segment, particularly the pelvis. Trying to carry out a physical assessment alone is extremely difficult and prone to error. If a fellow professional is unavailable, carers can be recruited for such tasks but only with very clear instruction as to what they are to look for. There is less certainty that the assessment will be valid in such circumstances.

When moving the limbs, be sure to provide support such that the joint is not loaded abnormally. Support the resting position with pillows or towels where required. Move around the person to ensure you can support them without injuring yourself, particularly your back. Adults have heavy limbs and when mixed with spasticity can make a physical assessment an extremely demanding process. Use postural supports and manual handling aids, such as slide sheets, to aid your assessment.

Where neurological phenomena persist (e.g., spasticity), try a different approach with holding the limb or joint and return to it later in the assessment if need be. It can be surprising to see full range in a joint that was previously thought to have significant restriction.

Immobile and/or older people are more prone to bone fracture due to osteoporosis. The soft tissues around a joint that has reduced movement will have adapted to the new position. As a result, it is important to move joints slowly and within comfortable range. If the person is able to tell you that they are in pain, ask them to do so (people will often mask pain). If not, keep a check on their face or ask a carer known to the person to advise. Some people call out in the anticipation of pain, which is misleading to the assessor but demonstrates their anxiety, to which the assessor should by alert.

It is important to display confidence (without being over-confident or patronizing) when manipulating joints. Plan your next move and don't dwell too long on any one range. It is possible to be too gentle. The person is more likely to relax if they have faith in your ability. Be tactful in what you express verbally to people having profound postural asymmetry — simply state what you observe in plain language and without emotion.

Critical measures to consider for sitting, lying, and standing

This section describes which joints, joint positions, and other critical measures to focus on for posture management in respect of sitting, lying, and standing. It is a guide and will require interpretation for each individual being assessed. Some joint ranges become critical, or more critical, where there are proximal limitations.

Sitting

- Hip flexion (Fig. 22.10A)
- Measured relative to pelvic tilt (a posterior tilt will mask a reduced range of hip flexion and an anterior tilt will make the range appear less than is available).

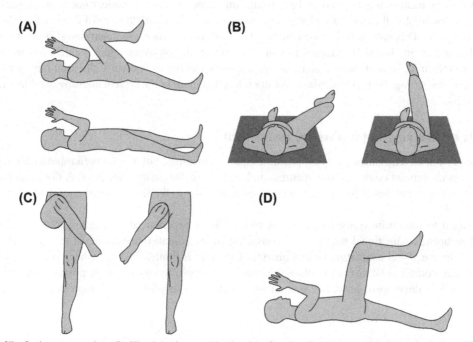

FIG. 22.10 (A) Hip flexion to extension. (B) Hip abduction to adduction (hip flexed). (C) Hip external to internal rotation (hip flexed). (D) Knee extension with the hip flexed.

- If the hip will not flex to 90°, a normal sitting position cannot be attained; positioning the person in a normal wheelchair or seating system will result in posterior pelvic tilt and sliding forward if the limitation is bilateral, or in the pelvis lifting and rotating forward on one side if the limitation is unilateral (sliding forward may also occur).
- Hip abduction (with the hip flexed as close to 90° as possible; Fig. 22.10B)
- Measured relative to pelvic rotation, e.g., what appears to be an abducted right hip may in fact be neutral or even adducted where the pelvis is rotated forward on the left.
- Ideally for sitting, the hips should be able to be positioned in 10° of abduction bilaterally to widen the base of support, thus increasing stability.
- If the hip is fixed in an abducted position but the seat demands a less abducted position, the pelvis will tend to rotate forward on the same side as the abducted hip due to tightness in the abductor muscles.
- Hip adduction (hip flexed as close to 90° as possible; Fig. 22.10B)
- Measured relative to pelvic rotation, e.g., what appears to be an adducted left hip may in fact be neutral or even abducted where the pelvis is rotated forward on the left.
- If the hip is fixed in an adducted position but the seat demands neutral, the pelvis will tend to rotate forward on the opposite side to the adducted hip due to tightness in the adductor muscles.
- Hip rotation (hip flexed as close to 90° as possible; Fig. 22.10C)
- Measured relative to pelvic obliquity, e.g., what appears to be an externally rotated left hip may in fact be neutral or internally rotated where there is a pelvic obliquity raised on the right.
- If the hip is fixed in external rotation but the lower leg is forced into neutral by the foot support, significant forces will be applied to the knee joint which is likely to lead to pain, and the pelvis may rise on the side of the affected hip.
- If the hip is fixed in internal rotation but the lower leg is forced into neutral, the knee will again be placed under great stress, and the pelvis may rise on the opposite side to the affected hip.
- Knee extension (with the hip flexed as close to 90° as possible; Fig. 22.10D)
- Measured relative to the line of the femur.
- The hamstring muscles pass over two joints, the hip and the knee. As such, the position of one joint will affect the available range in the other. In sitting, a flexed hip position is required and this consumes some of the available hamstring length. It is in this position that knee extension must be measured. If there is insufficient range then the conventional position of the feet, i.e., just in front of the knee, will either result in the feet sliding back or, if the feet are fixed in position, in the pelvis being dragged forward in the seat with resultant posterior pelvic tilt, thoracic kyphosis, and difficulties with head control, not to mention the generation of shear forces under the buttocks/thighs which may give rise to skin damage.
- A hip unable to flex to 90° will demand a greater amount of extension at the knee if feet are not to be tucked back under the front edge of the seat.
- This measurement is usually taken between the tibia and an imaginary line projected distally from (and in line with) the femur, being somewhere in the region of 30°−40° in a healthy subject. It is *not* normal to gain full knee extension with the hip flexed to 90° due to the hamstrings length being consumed by virtue of the fact that they pass over two joints. The measurement is sometimes taken as the angle between the posterior aspects of the femur and tibia, called the "popliteal angle," i.e., somewhere in the region of 140°−150° in a healthy subject.
- Ankle dorsiflexion/plantarflexion
- Measured relative to the tibia.
- For the foot to sit flat on the supporting surface, the ankle must be able to attain a neutral, or plantigrade, position.
- The foot is a complex structure, being able to adopt a variety of profoundly asymmetrical shapes. Where this is the case, a simple measurement of dorsi/plantarflexion is not possible, a fuller description of shape being required (and probably a photograph).
- Pelvic asymmetry
- This is determined by analyzing the presenting postures in sitting and lying.
- If the pelvis is unable to attain neutral in obliquity, rotation, or tilt, the sitting base is compromised and must be accommodated to provide postural stability and to avoid high peak pressures in soft tissues.
- A certain amount of asymmetry may be accommodated in modular seating, but for the more pronounced presentations, a custom contoured support surface is required.
- Spinal asymmetry
- Again, the previous analysis of presenting postures will be called on at this point.
- If there is fixed kyphosis and/or scoliosis, it is not possible to sit in the conventional manner. The fixed component of spinal asymmetry must be accommodated and stabilized.

- The potential for complexity of shape in the spine is greater than in the pelvis due to the significantly greater number of joints. As a result, it is more difficult for modular seating to offer appropriate support for an asymmetrical spine. The decision to use a custom contoured support surface will, therefore, come sooner.
- Neck flexion/extension
- To facilitate respiration, a safe swallow, and a functional and social line of vision, it is necessary to accommodate any limitation in neck flexion or extension. More commonly, it is a loss of range into extension that presents, i.e., chin on or close to chest. Loss of range into flexion usually occurs where there is a marked anterior tilt to the pelvis and the person has adopted a leant-forward position.

Lying

- Hip extension: Can the hip be extended fully to allow supine lying? (Fig. 22.10A)
- Measured in side lying and relative to pelvic tilt.
- Where there is a limitation and it is intended that the person will be positioned in side lying, the leg must be supported, otherwise it will tend to fall to one side or the other, pulling the pelvis into rotation and axially rotating the spine, predisposing to scoliosis; a limitation in hip extension (where the knee is able to reach full extension) will tend to pull the pelvis into anterior tilt which can be uncomfortable: again, the legs must be supported under the knees.
- The ankle must also be supported, usually with a resting night splint, to prevent it remaining in a plantarflexed position for extended periods, which is likely to lead to a shortened Achilles tendon.
- Knee extension with the hip extended: Can the knee be extended fully to allow supine lying?
- Measured in side lying and relative to the line of the femur.
- Again, the leg must be supported, otherwise it will tend to fall to one side or the other; limitations in hip and knee extension will tend to cause increased loading under the heel if the leg is not supported, with the potential for pressure ulcer development.
- Hip abduction/adduction
- Measured relative to pelvic *obliquity*, i.e., opposite to sitting, as the femur is now transposed through 90° to that of full extension.
- Where the hip is fixed in a degree of abduction or adduction, any attempt to straighten the leg will cause the pelvis to become oblique and the spine to develop scoliosis.
- Pelvic asymmetry
- If the pelvis is unable to attain neutral in obliquity, rotation, or tilt, the base of support is compromised and must be accommodated to provide stability.
- Fixed kyphosis
- An increased kyphosis that is fixed reduces the surface area over which weight is borne, tending to lead to pressure marking; it also creates instability, the trunk effectively being able to roll to either side, potentially giving rise to asymmetry in other body segments.
- Fixed scoliosis
- There is usually a fullness to the ribs accompanying a lateral curve; a scoliosis tends to have a posterior rib prominence associated with it on the same side as the convexity, and an anterior prominence on the opposite side; any posterior fullness can have the same effect as an enhanced kyphosis (see previous).
- Neck flexion/extension
- Any limitation in this respect must be accommodated within the supports used for bed positioning.

Standing

- Pelvic asymmetry
- Fixed obliquity, rotation, or tilt will destabilize posture and may be a contraindication to standing, depending on severity.
- Ability to achieve a plantigrade foot
- The feet bear all the person's weight in free standing and often a significant proportion in a standing frame. As a result, little fixed asymmetry is tolerated before rendering standing for any period unsuitable (note that some people with asymmetric feet may bear weight through them temporarily to facilitate a standing transfer).
- Hip abduction/adduction

- If the hip is fixed in adduction, the base of support is smaller and the feet are at different heights. Without support this will lead to a pelvic obliquity and scoliosis; if one hip is more abducted than the other, the same results will occur.
- Hip/knee extension: Is the hip/knee fixed in a degree of flexion?
- Standing requires full extension of the hip and knee if it is not to be substantially effortful; where supports are used to block the knees, care must be taken to avoid high shearing forces within the knee joint.
- Severe fixed spinal curvatures cannot be accommodated in a standing frame and are a contraindication in their own right; they are likely also to present a challenging head position.

Modeling a stable and functional seated posture

Having identified the critical measures for your patient it is now time to sit them over the side of the physiotherapy plinth. It is possible to use a bed for this purpose but the mattress will not provide the stability required to assess pelvic orientation accurately. A further complication occurs where the person has tight hamstrings and the feet need to tuck back under the surface, something which is not possible with most beds and particularly so where side rails are fitted.

All the critical results of your physical assessment are combined at this point to determine a realistic position for sitting. Supports and bolsters are added to accommodate joint range limitations and to assist in aligning and stabilizing the body segments relative to each other and the supporting surface. Limitations in hip flexion are accommodated by building up under the pelvis to let the femurs drop; minimisation of any pelvic obliquity is achieved by iteratively adjusting the heights of supports under the ischial tuberosities. Limitations in hip abduction/adduction and rotation are accommodated, as are tight hamstrings (limited knee extension with the hip flexed). The trunk is supported manually and the best possible alignment determined through the application of forces to the skeletal structure.

The assessor will kneel behind the person to take their weight and hold the trunk. A second person is required to remain in front of the person to ensure they remain in position on the plinth. The arms should be raised to reduce the drag on the shoulder girdle and spine to open out the chest to enhance respiration (Chan and Heck, 1999). Small stick-on spots may be applied to each spinal vertebra to highlight spinal shape and to facilitate evaluation. Photographs will assist in subsequent clinical reasoning. Fig. 22.11 shows how a flexible scoliotic curve can be corrected with application of forces to the apex of the curve on the convex side and to points on the trunk above and below this on the concave side, the weight of the arms being supported.

This part of the process must be adapted to the individual, making each assessment slightly different from the next. It is important to keep the person safe as they are in a potentially precarious position on the side of the plinth. If practicable, a tilted position should be modeled and is particularly relevant where a kyphosis is flexible or where the head tends to drop forward but the neck has range for this to be reduced.

Throughout this process one must keep in mind the differences between the presenting postures in sitting and lying. That attained in lying will usually provide a best possible reference point. During this stage of the assessment process, that is, sitting over the side of the plinth, one determines a realistic optimal position. What is achieved is an understanding of

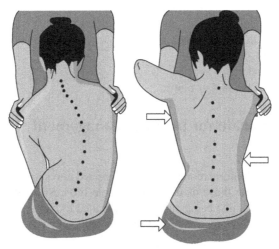

FIG. 22.11 Correction of a flexible scoliosis.

the type and amount of support required. This information will feed directly into the process of making recommendations for the seating system as a full understanding of the postural requirements will have been determined.

Case Study − sitting over the edge of the plinth

You have just completed your assessment of presenting postures, compared the two, determined the best corrected spinal position and assessed joint ranges. The critical measures for sitting are:
- Pelvic obliquity up on the right by 2 cm at the ASIS
- Neutral pelvic rotation and tilt
- Partially correctable scoliosis convex left
- Right hip flexes only to 80 degrees
- Right hip moves in a range of abduction from 20 to 30 degrees, i.e. does not reach neutral and cannot be adducted
- Left hip moves in a range of adduction from 5 to 20 degrees, i.e. does not reach neutral and cannot be abducted
- Knees will not extend beyond 90 degrees, i.e. hamstrings are tight

How will you arrange the person seated on the plinth to determine a realistic position for seating?
1) First, accommodate the limitations in movement
   a. Place a folded towel under the distal aspect of the left femur to support it in 90 degrees of flexion (to increase stability)
   b. Allow the right hip to rest directly on the plinth in 80 degrees of flexion: the thigh is conical meaning that the knee will be lower than the hip when resting on a flat surface, i.e. around 10 degrees less than 90 degrees
   c. Initially, do not make any accommodation for the pelvic obliquity: to be confirmed with the second assessor in step 2)
   d. Allow the right hip to abduct to 20 degrees and the left to adduct to 5 degrees, i.e. to avoid inducing rotation of the pelvis
   e. Allow the feet to tuck under the front edge of the plinth to avoid pulling the pelvis into posterior tilt
2) Now explore what can be corrected
   a. Your colleague is kneeling behind the person, preventing them from falling if necessary
   b. You will be in front of the person with your hands on their ASISs
   c. Your colleague will rock the person's trunk to the right until the pelvis is brought level
   d. Whilst you hold firmly to the pelvis your colleague will rock the person's trunk slowly to the left whilst you determine if the pelvis can be retained in a level position, or if it rises back to 2 cm up on the right; the latter would indicate that the obliquity is fixed and so must be accommodated; the former that the aim should be to retain it in a level position
   e. Next, you will switch positions with your colleague and whilst they hold firmly to the pelvis, you will explore how much scope there is to correct the scoliosis; you will do this by placing one hand on the apex of the curve on the left, and one on the right side of the thorax just under the arm, thereby creating a three point force system; it will become apparent how much correction is possible; if possible, lift the person's arms to take their weight off the trunk

You now know a realistic position which might be attained in a seat. The final position may be different to what you achieved on the plinth because your hands are more responsive than a passive set of supports in a seating system.

Summary of the physical assessment process

1. Describe the presenting posture in sitting
2. Describe the presenting posture in lying
3. Consider the differences between the two
4. Define the best corrected position in supine lying
5. Assessment of joint ranges
6. Identification of all critical measures
7. Sitting the person over the edge of the bed or plinth

Recommendations and rationale for posture management

Setting objectives

This is the point where all the assembled information must be synthesized into a meaningful and realistic set of objectives, balancing conflicting priorities (including those of initial and whole-life cost). These objectives will allow the development of a posture management programme being sufficiently detailed to allow precise recommendations to be made. They will list postural abilities and limitations, functional requirements, environmental restrictions, and psychological considerations.

Sitting

Seating is prescribed for wheelchairs, armchairs, classroom chairs, office chairs, toilet seats (commodes), shower chairs, and car seats. The same principles apply regardless of what type of seating is required; it is the application that differs.

The first question is what shape of material is needed, for example, plain slab, contoured, or custom contoured? What properties must it have, for example, for pressure relief, postural support/correction, dynamic properties, and potential for adjustment? What are the functional requirements, for example, transfers, toileting, folding? What size is required?

These initial questions allow conceptual ideas to be developed and from this it is possible to appraise individual pieces of equipment to determine suitability. Very often it is necessary to combine products from different manufacturers. In this case the method of assembly must be considered. It may be necessary or appropriate to liaise with the manufacturers about compatibility. Consider that a different set of products may need selecting. There may be nothing available commercially to meet clinical need and it is here that bespoke manufacturing is indicated. This will require a substantial amount of design work, risk assessment, and technical documentation, although if a service is set up to carry out this type of work routinely, the additional workload will be diminished.

The structure of the support surface can have a significant effect on activities of daily living, particularly the ability of a person to reach beyond their base (Aissaoui et al., 2001). Some surfaces are inherently more stable than others. A very high level of stability can hinder function. The structure can also have an effect on the pressure distributing qualities of the cushion (Apatsidis et al., 2002).

It is beyond the scope of this book to list specific types of seating (and lying or standing equipment), with the exception of custom-contoured seating, a subset that is detailed in Chapter 22 "Wheelchair Prescription." Any form of seating equipment must be appraised for suitability and will usually require trialing with the person. The results of the assessment process should be used as a guide to determine suitability, with particular reference to the list of objectives. Most statutory services in the UK have a preferred list of equipment or manufacturers, this making sense from the perspective of holding stock and maintaining a fleet out in the field, but this periodically requires revision where better equipment becomes available. Equipment designs and specifications evolve, mostly for the better but sometimes to cut costs. Where this happens, it may be necessary to review other products on the market.

The choice of base support (e.g., wheelchair, armchair, etc.) is critical to the success of the seating system. Some base supports lend themselves better to the fitting of seating than others. The articulations of the base in terms of tilt and recline will be critical, as will its ability to support appropriate peripheral supports such as those for the legs, arms, and head. With wheelchairs, there is often a requirement for a seating system to be transferred between two bases, typically between a powered chair and a manual chair. Depending on the type of seating that is being used and its method of interface, this can present significant technical challenges, and it is sometimes necessary to use a different combination of wheelchair bases to obtain a satisfactory result.

Lying

As has been identified previously, posture in lying is a crucial part of the 24 hour programme of management. A supported posture can facilitate sleep for the individual and their spouse, parents, or carers. It can reduce moving and handling requirements, discourage detrimental bony and soft tissue adaptation, facilitate respiration and the management of saliva, cause a reduction in neurological phenomena, and assist in the management of tissue integrity.

The principles are the same as for prescribing seating, with the following additional considerations which are brought about by there being a reduced amount of supervision at night:

- Increased risk of asphyxia where there is an ability of the person to move into a compromised position and where there is also the inability to move out of such a position.
- Increased risk of aspiration/choking/asphyxia if the person is known to vomit.

There are a variety of commercially available sleep systems, each having particular attributes that can be appraised against the requirements of the individual. Additionally, simple positioning aids such as bean bags, which come in a wide variety of shapes and sizes, can be used for less formal systems. It is often preferable to start with very basic, commonly available items to explore the possibilities for support. These are as follows:

- Pillow folded lengthways and wrapped in a bath towel to create a simple support for the legs where the hips and knees do not extend fully; a central "funnel" can be created to separate the knees.
- Pillows placed *under* an additional bed sheet orientated at 90° to normal, the trailing ends of which are tucked back under the pillow and slightly under the person, thereby stabilizing the position of the support.

- Folded towels placed under a pillow to create a nest for the head where it tends to turn to the side.
- Any combination or variation on the above to support other body segments as necessary.

These simple supports are sometimes appropriate for long-term use. Most sleep systems support supine lying but it is possible with some to support side lying or, more commonly, semi-side lying. This is required typically where there is a posterior rib prominence caused by scoliosis, the person being unable to attain a stable supine position. Severe kyphosis may also be an indicator for side lying, again due to instability.

Very great care should be taken in making any recommendation for bed positioning due to the reduced levels of supervision, as mentioned above. Sleep systems, in being supportive, can also cause problems with temperature regulation, although some manufacturers claim to have materials that will assist in maintaining a normal body temperature. Where a person uses a urinal bottle independently at night, the level of support able to be provided will be significantly reduced. It would be unacceptable to demand that bottle use be ceased as this would cause a loss of dignity and the requirement for alternative means of bladder management.

It is worth noting that support at night is usually contraindicated where the person moves around significantly. It is possible that the introduction of supports may help to stabilize their position, but where this does not happen there is often little that can be introduced without compromising safety.

It should also be noted that a further contraindication can be where the introduction of a sleep system places a higher burden of care on carers or family members such that their sleep is disturbed regularly through the night. In all likelihood the equipment will not be used and the regime not followed.

Standing

This can be broken down into two broad areas, as follows, noting that other forms of therapeutic standing equipment exist:

1. Standing/stand-up wheelchairs: There are a small number of wheelchairs that translate from a seated posture to one of standing. They are mechanically/electromechanically complex and allow increased independence and participation for many people. Typically, significant forces are taken through the knees which are blocked to stabilize the joint so that standing is achieved, although some systems move the person into lying before standing which avoids this scenario. It is difficult to fit custom-contoured seating to such chairs as the articulation of the seat does not match the biomechanical joint centers of the person, and also because body shape changes between sitting and standing.
2. Standing frames: These are typically used in conjunction with physiotherapists in schools and rehabilitation units, and sometimes in private homes, clinical engineers rarely becoming involved. The same principles of assessment apply. Standers are either prone, upright, or supine and come in a wide variety of models, shapes, and sizes. They are static devices and so functional tasks should be given to the person while they have their period of therapy.

The joint range limitations for standing must, of course, be considered, with particular attention paid to the symmetry and loading of the foot, knee, and hip. Marked spinal asymmetry will be an additional contraindication. It can be difficult to maneuver a person into a standing frame, sometimes making the procedure unsafe from the perspective of manual handling.

Complementary interventions

Alongside postural support for sitting, lying, and standing, there are a number of other interventions that will require consideration. Onward referral to other services is often required, for example, for physiotherapy, orthotics, speech and language therapy, surgical opinion, medical review, or nursing review.

It may be appropriate to initiate a physiotherapy stretching regime and to arrange periods of time where "counter" postures are adopted, that is, those which oppose postures adopted for the majority of the day. This may involve lying over a wedge in the prone position, or using side lying to oppose the normal position of a flexible scoliosis. Orthotics are often used as part of a physical management programme. Further details are available in the relevant chapter of this section. The involvement of speech and language therapists can be sought where there are particular difficulties with swallowing.

A surgical opinion can be useful in relation to management of an orthopedic condition, particularly the hips and spine. Where there is pain that cannot be controlled by position, or where there is spinal instability that cannot, or is only partially, controllable through postural support, the view of an orthopedic surgeon may be sought. They may not recommend surgery straightaway, there being an (anecdotal) tendency nowadays toward conservative management, at least in the United

Kingdom, but they will be able to take a surgical overview and refer on to other parts of the medical profession as appropriate.

A medical review can be helpful to ensure that the drug regime continues to be appropriate. It can be difficult to predict the effect of a drug on an individual. Some people respond well to a certain medicine where others do not. When more than one drug is being taken, the effect becomes even more difficult to predict.

Where there is spasticity and where muscles have shortened, typically in the hips, knees, and ankles in relation to postural management, consideration may be given to the use of botulinum toxin injections. This temporarily blocks nerve transmission at the neuromuscular junction of specific muscles, that is, it has a targeted rather than a global effect, this being the case with oral administration of, typically, baclofen. It has a short-term effect, usually around three months, during which time an active physiotherapy programme of stretching is required to make the most of the available time that joint motion is not resisted by spasticity. It should be noted that botulinum toxin will have no effect on contracted muscle. Many people have repeated doses at three-month intervals.

An increasingly common method of managing severe spasticity in the lower limbs is the use of intrathecal baclofen (ITB). Oral administration requires a higher dose to have an effect on severe spasticity but one of the most significant side effects of baclofen is drowsiness. An intrathecal dose, being targeted, can be significantly smaller. It is administered into the spinal tract by a catheter connected to a pump which is surgically inserted into the abdomen. There is a reservoir for the drug which must be refilled periodically. ITB can be extremely effective, making postural management significantly easier and, as a result, allowing the person to function far more effectively.

Pressure sores are usually managed by nurses who will have a variety of techniques at their disposal. In the case of sores that do not respond to conservative treatment, it is sometimes necessary to carry out plastic surgery to repair the skin. This is not straightforward and the area affected will not return to normal state. The area from where the skin graft was taken must also then be allowed to heal. Where there are pronounced postural asymmetries that are part of the cause of the pressure sore, typically bony prominences such as the ischial tuberosities, clinical engineers have an important role to play in the use of pressure mapping equipment to determine peak loads and pressure distribution, and in the provision of bespoke equipment shaped to the individual. Further information is available in Chapter 20 "Pressure Ulceration."

Overview

It is important to consider the effects of a postural management programme that is too intense, that places too great a burden on the carers or family, and that lacks scientific evidence to support its use (Gough, 2009). One should take care in using words like "prevent" in the context of managing a scoliosis. This is likely to lead to false hope by the person and their family. It would be more realistic to use words like "discourage" or "to slow down the development of," and so on. If the end result is that deterioration *is* prevented, no one will be unhappy. In some circumstances, an improvement in condition can be brought about. This requires a very active physiotherapeutic regime and can be extremely advantageous to the individual. However, as mentioned, placing too great a burden on carers and family members can be counterproductive and it should be remembered that we cannot always say with confidence that our recommendations will have the desired effect.

It is a valiant aim to attempt to reduce discomfort, but the truth is that this can be very difficult for a person with altered neurology and posture (Crane et al., 2004). Comfort relates very strongly to functional attainment and is impacted by many physiological, environmental, and psychosocial factors. In the same way that a pair of shoes do not immediately induce discomfort, so it is with postural support that the person must be allowed time to become familiar with the new support surfaces and the forces they apply to the body.

In certain circumstances it is necessary to initiate a multidisciplinary review (case conference) where there are a number of interlinked strands needing to be resolved. Trying to address one area in isolation may be unproductive or could even make the situation worse.

Secondary complications

Many medical conditions are static, such as cerebral palsy or head injury, but the medical and functional condition of people having such diagnoses often deteriorates. This is caused by what are termed secondary complications, that is, those difficulties experienced that are secondary to the main diagnosis. Of course, people with progressive conditions, such as multiple sclerosis or muscular dystrophy, are also affected by secondary complications.

As an example, postural instability tends to lead to unequal loading of tissues which, in turn, can lead to pressure ulceration, treatment for which includes extended periods of bed rest. Where an open pressure sore exists there is a risk of infection to the surrounding soft tissue and, eventually, to the underlying bone itself. Prolonged immobility can, in extreme cases, lead to profound shortening of muscle and critically reduced ranges of joint movement, which renders some people unable to adopt a sitting position.

Altered spinal postures have an impact on internal organ function. Organs become compressed, stretched, or even displaced. This leads to impaired respiratory and gastrointestinal function. According to Stewart (1991), "Seating imposes significant effect on the cardiovascular, respiratory, abdominal, renal and neurological systems." Swallowing can become profoundly impaired, leading to food and drink being aspirated into the lungs. Where the person's ability to cough is impaired, this food and drink may cause a chest infection, potentially requiring hospitalization.

Immobility causes bones to become osteoporotic. At the simplest level it is the dynamic loading/unloading cycles of normal movement that keep bone structures healthy. Osteoporotic bones are more prone to fracture, which may further impact the person's quality of life. The clinician manipulating joints should be mindful of the condition.

Summary

Postural management is a highly complex but rewarding clinical area in which to work. It presents multiple, simultaneous challenges to the clinician and engineer, requiring considerable thought and the development of sound clinical reasoning. It has a significant impact not only on the person's health, but on their functional ability and participation in society. It is a building block for electronic assistive technology since without postural management, operation of such equipment can be extremely difficult, if not impossible.

References

Aissaoui, R., Boucher, C., Bourbonnais, D., Lacoste, M., Dansereau, J., 2001. Effect of seat cushion on dynamic stability in sitting during a reaching task in wheelchair users with paraplegia. Arch. Phys. Med. Rehabil. 82, 274–281.

Apatsidis, D.P., Solomonidis, S.E., Michael, S.M., 2002. Pressure distribution at the seating interface of custom molded wheelchair seats: effect of various materials. Arch. Phys. Med. Rehabil. 83, 1151–1156.

Chan, A., Heck, C., 1999. The effects of tilting the seating position of a wheelchair on respiration, posture, fatigue, voice volume and exertion outcomes in individuals with advanced multiple sclerosis. J. Rehabil. Outcomes Meas. 3 (4), 1–14.

Crane, B., Holm, M.B., Hobson, D., Cooper, R.A., Reed, M., Stadelmeier, S., 2004. Development of a consumer-driven wheelchair seating discomfort assessment tool (WcS-DAT). Int. J. Rehabil. Res. 27 (1), 85–90.

Frischhut, B., Krismer, M., Stoeckl, B., Landauer, F., Auckenthaler, T., 2000. Pelvic tilt in neuromuscular disorders. J. Pediatr. Orthop. B. 9, 221–228.

Gericke, T., 2006. Postural management for children with cerebral palsy: consensus statement. Dev. Med. Child Neurol. 48.

Goldsmith, E., Goldsmith, J., Lacey, P., Ouvry, C., 1998. Physical management people with profound and multiple learning disabilities: a collaborative approach to meeting complex needs. In: Lacey, P., Ouvry, C. (Eds.), People with Profound and Multiple Learning Disabilities: A Collaborative Approach to Meeting Complex Needs. David Fulton Publishers, pp. 15–28.

Gough, M., 2009. Continuous postural management and the prevention of deformity in children with cerebral palsy: an appraisal. Dev. Med. Child Neurol. 51, 105–110.

Hare, N., 1987. The Human Sandwich Factor Congress Presentation. Chartered Society of Physiotherapy, Oxford.

International Organization for Standardization (ISO), 2006. ISO 16840-1:2006 Wheelchair Seating – Part 1: Vocabulary, Reference axis Convention and Measures for Body Segments, Posture and Postural Support Surfaces. International Organization for Standardization, p. vi.

Parker, K., 2012. Reliability of Visual Estimation of Angles Relating to Joint Range of Motion in Rehabilitation (unpublished).

Parker, K., 2014. Validating the MPD 24/7 form: testing the reliability of measuring joint ranges for adults with complex postures (unpublished).

Pope, P.M., 2007. Severe and Complex Neurological Disability. Elsevier.

Porter, D., Michael, S.M., Kirkwood, C., 2007. Patterns of postural deformity in non-ambulant people with cerebral palsy: what is the relationship between the direction of scoliosis, direction of pelvic obliquity, direction of windswept hip deformity and side of hip dislocation? Clin. Rehabil. 21, 1087–1096.

Pountney, T.E., Mulcahy, C.M., Clarke, S.M., Green, E.M., 2004. The Chailey Approach to Postural Management: An Explanation of the Theoretical Aspects of Posture Management and Their Practical Application through Treatment and Equipment. Chailey Heritage Clinical Services.

Scrutton, D., 1991. The causes of developmental deformity and their implication for seating. Dev. Med. Child Neurol. 15, 199–202.

Stewart, C., 1991. Physiological considerations in seating. Prosthet. Orthot. Int. 15, 193–198.

Waugh, K., Crane, B., 2013. A Clinical Application Guide to Standardized Wheelchair Seating Measures of the Body and Seating Support Surfaces Assistive Technology Partners. University of Colorado.

Whitman, A., 1924. Postural deformities in children. N. Y. State J. Med. 24, 871–874.

Chapter 23

Pressure ulceration

Dan Bader

Faculty of Health Sciences, University of Southampton, Southampton, United Kingdom

Chapter outline

Skin and soft tissues

The skin represents the largest organ of the body with a surface area of 1.8 m^2 for a standard person. It is divided into three separate layers, the epidermis, the dermis and the sub-dermis. The former outermost layer is approximately 75−150 μm thick, although it is considerably thicker in the palms and plantar aspects of the feet. The epidermis is divided into five strata, the deepest of which, the stratum basale, is the site of cell division to form the main epidermal cells, the keratinocytes. As these cells migrate outwards they increase in size, change to a flattened morphology, and their organelles start to change and degrade. The most superficial layer, the stratum corneum, consists of 15−20 layers of dead anucleated cells that are hexagonal thin flat squames. At this stage the cells represent terminally differentiated keratinocytes, termed corneocytes.

The epidermal-dermal junction provides a physical barrier for cells and large molecules, and forms a strong molecular attachment enhanced by parts of the epidermis penetrating the outermost dermis resulting in large cones and rete ridges, or papillae.

The human dermis constitutes the major thickness of human skin, contributing between 10% and 20% of the total body weight. It contains many structural features including blood and lymph vessels, nerve endings, skin appendages, such as hair follicles, sebaceous glands and sweat glands. The predominant cell type in the dermis, the fibroblast, is responsible for synthesizing a moderately dense extracellular matrix of solid constituents, typically:

- Collagen fibres − approximately 75% of the fat free dry weight and 18%−30% of the dermal volume. The relatively inextensible collagen fibres bundles form an irregular network that runs almost parallel to the epidermal surface. The collagen orientation is distinctive for each body area, a feature known as Langer's lines, which is routinely used during surgical procedures to enhance wound healing.
- Elastin fibres − approximately 4% of the fat free dry weight and 1% of the dermal volume. The extensible elastin fibres, interwoven among the collagen bundles, is important in restoring the fibrous array to its original dimensions and organization when an external load is removed.
- A supporting matrix of amorphous ground substance, composed of long chain glycosaminoglycans (GAGs), which attract and bind a high proportion of water, forming a biological hydrogel.

Clinical Engineering. https://doi.org/10.1016/B978-0-08-102694-6.00023-1

The dermis is divided into two arbitrary layers. The outermost thin papillary dermis contains relatively small and loosely distributed collagen and elastin fibres associated with considerable ground substance. The reticular dermis, representing the majority of the dermal thickness, contains dense larger collagen and elastin fibres interspersed with small amounts of ground substance.

The subcutaneous fat, or hypodermis, is a fibro-fatty layer which is loosely connected to the dermis. Its thickness varies with anatomical site, age, gender, race, endocrine and nutritional status of the individual. It acts as an insulating layer and protective cushion, constituting about 10% of the body weight. Subjacent to this layer can be a muscle layer, which overlies either bony prominences or internal tissues and organs.

The complex skin structure interfaces with the external environment where it is exposed to a range of insults, which may be mechanical, physical, biological and chemical in nature. Of its many functional roles, the highly organized skin structures are designed to permit gas/fluid transport across its surface and, critically, maintain the internal body homeostasis.

In a normal state, skin exhibits viscoelastic behaviour similar to other biological tissues, such as muscles, articular cartilage, blood and lymphatic vessels. Accordingly the skin demonstrates creep, stress relaxation and load-rate dependent properties. The most common form of loading reported in both *in vivo* and *in vitro* studies, involves either uniaxial or biaxial tension. The resulting force-extension curves from the uniaxial tests are non-linear in form and vary in magnitude depending on whether the direction is either parallel or perpendicular to the preferred orientation of the underlying collagen fibres − the characteristic anisotropic behaviour of skin. By contrast there are relatively few studies in which the compressive behaviour of skin and underlying tissues has been investigated. One exception, revealed an *in vivo* viscoelastic response, which varied considerably with both subject age and tissue site (Bader and Bowker, 1983). Indeed structural changes in the soft tissues associated with age and disease will inevitably affect their tolerance to compressive loading and endanger internal body organs.

Pressure ulcers

The condition known as pressure ulcers, bed sores, pressure injury or decubitus has represented a problem since time immemorial − indeed there is evidence of its presence in the Egyptian section of the British Museum (Rowling, 1961). It has been recognized in the nineteenth century by Florence Nightingale that there is a relationship between effective nursing care and the incidence of pressure ulcers. It has been defined as a localized injury to skin and/or underlying tissue, usually over a bony prominence, as a result of pressure, or pressure in combination with shear (NPUAP/EPUAP/PPPIAP Guidelines, 2014).

Pressure ulcers (PUs) are generally categorized in terms of the extent of the associated tissue damage. Thus PUs confined to the epidermal tissues are referred to as Grade (or Stage) I ulcers, and are often indistinguishable from incontinence associated dermatitis (IAD) or moisture lesions. Grade II ulcers affect deeper dermal tissue. Both of these PU grades should, with time and effective management, lead to successful healing. By contrast, damage affecting subcutaneous tissues is classified as grade III and IV PUs, which may account for between 11% and 31% of the total (Vanderwee et al., 2007), and may require some form of surgical intervention to close the wound. Another form of extensive damage initiating in vulnerable muscle tissues close to bone and progressing outwards undetected towards the skin is termed Deep Tissue Injury (DTI). The prognosis of a DTI is highly variable and might even prove fatal. Indeed the high profile actor, Christopher Reeves, developed a deep pressure ulcer following a spinal cord injury, which later resulted in his untimely death due to septicaemia.

PUs can occur in any situation where people are subjected to sustained mechanical loads, and are particularly common in those who are bedridden supported on mattresses or confined to sitting in chairs for much of their waking day. This situation will only be exacerbated at loaded tissue sites when exposed to a hostile microclimate involving elevated temperatures and humidity, such as at the plantar aspects of the foot, the residual amputee stump-socket interface of amputees or at tissues where high forces are transmitted to enable orthotic control. It has been reported that over 30% of PUs acquired in hospitals were a direct result of interventional medical devices (Black et al., 2010). These so-called Medical Device-Related Pressure Ulcers (MDRPUs) contribute to the financial and personal burden imposed on many patients with vulnerable skin. Indeed many clinicians have noted that long term useage of a range of orthotic and prosthetic devices may cause incidences of skin irritation, pain, maceration and PUs, although these events are rarely reported in the UK. This is surprising given that existing devices are often rejected leading to inadequate intervention and wasted resources. Common sites of soft tissue damage invariably involve locations adjacent to bony prominences, as indicated in Fig. 23.1, such as the sacrum, ischial tuberosity, heels and the back of the head. However, with respect to MDRPUs, any site exposed to pronged mechanical loading through an orthosis is vulnerable e.g. bridge of nose during application of respiratory masks.

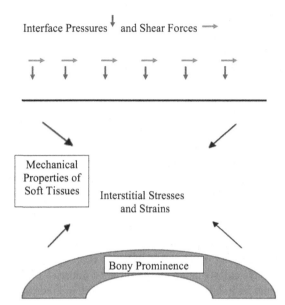

Interface Pressures ↓ and Shear Forces →

Mechanical
Properties of
Soft Tissues

Interstitial Stresses
and Strains

Bony Prominence

FIG. 23.1   External load transmission into soft tissue areas adjacent to bony prominences.

Subjects who are insensate and/or immobile are particularly at high risk of developing soft tissue breakdown. Additionally, the skin tissues of some individuals are compromised by intrinsic factors and, as a consequence, exhibit mechanical properties which are not able to tolerate even normal mechanical loading conditions. PUs have been traditionally associated with the elderly population, particularly those who are malnourished and dehydrated with additional medical complications (Hahnel et al., 2017). However PUs affect a wider age range including neonates nursed in incubators, young patients in intensive-care paediatric units and, commonly, the spinal cord injured population, for which PUs may occur throughout their lifetimes. With respect to Body Mass Index (BMI), it is generally accepted that subjects with extreme values of BMI (<19.0 kg m^{-2} and >30.0 kg m^{-2}) may be predisposed to PUs (Kottner et al., 2011). However, this criteria does not exclude the development of PUs in individuals within the normal BMI range who exhibit intrinsic characteristics which are known to predispose to tissue damage, such as immobility, lack of sensation and metabolic disorders.

Care quality and financial implications

Pressure ulcers represent a massive burden to individual sufferers and their carers worldwide, and health services and the community at large across each nation. Traditionally the perceived importance of PUs, particularly by medical doctors, has been under estimated and PUs have been considered to be a direct result of poor nursing care. In the last two decades, however, a number of factors have raised awareness worldwide, associated with the ever-ageing population in many countries. As an example, in 1997, results from a financial audit within the health system in the Netherlands indicated that the treatment of hospital-acquired PUs represented the fourth costliest of all medical conditions, representing 1.4% of the total budget care (Schuurman et al., 2009). This led to considerable activity in the Netherlands, where prevalence measurements were recorded in a range of healthcare settings, including nursing homes and rehabilitation centres. Most recent data have indicated a significant reduction most probably due to the heightened awareness and education of carers — as an example, in general hospitals the prevalence decreased from 23% to 10.5% between 1997 and 2011. By contrast there was no change from the 13% prevalence in academic hospitals, with 75% of these ulcers being classified as hospital-acquired pressure ulcers. This issue is particularly relevant when considering the laws passed in the US, which state that if a patient was not considered to be at risk on entering a hospital but subsequently acquired a PU during their stay, no financial support would be given to the hospital from insurance companies for any of the treatment costs of the patient.

Prevalence rates of PUs among hospitalized patients across Europe remain consistently high at about 10%. There is also strong evidence that a proportion of individuals with PUs reside in the community, with recent prevalence rates ranging between 0.40 and 0.77 per 1000 population. It is interesting to note that there is a disparity in the management of seated high risk patients when compared to their management in bed (Vanderwee et al., 2007; Phillips and Buttery, 2009). Indeed, it was reported that over 50% of at-risk patients did not receive specialist chair equipment and were not repositioned at regular time intervals (Gerbhardt and Bliss, 1994; Vanderwee et al., 2007). Indeed one epidemiological study revealed that the highest percentage of patients with PUs were chair-fast, but totally dependent upon others to mobilize them (25%), with a smaller proportion (19%) occurring in bed-fast individuals (Jordan et al., 1977). The seated group also exhibited the highest percentage of the most severe PUs (4.0% with Grade 4 PUs). The totality of this data provides compelling evidence for the need for effective preventative strategies in sitting and lying postures to reduce the unacceptable high incidence of PUs.

Apart from the inevitable human suffering and the high risk of complications, treatment costs are significant in cash-strapped health services in many countries. Indeed average costs of treating PUs in the UK range from £1214 (grade I) to £14,108 (grade IV) (Dealey et al., 2012). Costs increase with ulcer severity because the time to heal is longer and the incidence of complications is higher in more severe cases. Despite the increased attention within health services, the incidence rates of PU and diabetic foot ulcers (DFUs) remain unacceptably high with corresponding costs of treating all chronic wounds estimated at £5 billion per annum in the UK (Guest et al., 2015). These costs will inevitably increase in association with the financial burden of PU treatment and the aging population.

Epidemiological research using subjective clinical assessment of risk factors highlights general characteristics of patients at risk, but these factors are generally indirect measures of the causative factors. Current 'macro' measures of immobility (moves a lot, moves a little etc.) do not provide sufficiently sensitive data to identify those at risk of developing a PU, and of those, approximately 90% will not develop a PU (Nixon et al., 2006). Health-related quality of life literature highlights that PUs impact greatly on physical, social and psychological domains of the patient resulting from one or more of the following: distressing symptoms including pain, exudates and odour; increased care burden; prolonged rehabilitation; requirement for bedrest; hospitalization; prolonged work-related sickness (Gorecki et al., 2009).

Current knowledge on the pathogenesis of pressure ulcers

The aetiopathogenesis of PUs has long been considered to involve the obstruction of blood vessels within loaded soft tissues leading to pressure-induced ischemia. This mechanism will result in a limited delivery of vital nutrients, such as oxygen, to the cell niche. The resulting cell death would restrict any remodelling processes and lead to the accumulation of soft tissue breakdown. Other mechanisms had been proposed but their examination had largely been limited to hypothetical concepts (Reddy et al., 1981; Krouskop et al., 1983) or to the use of invasive techniques, such as radioisotope tracers (Miller and Seale, 1985). In the last decade these mechanisms have been revisited using bioengineering techniques and it is now recognized that, in addition to pressure-induced ischaemia, pressure ulcers can result from other mechanisms (Bouten et al., 2003), namely:

- Impaired interstitial and lymphatic flow − this will result in an accumulation of toxic intercellular waste products, which are both damaging to the cells and can influence the local cellular environment e.g. reduced levels of local pH. The development of non-invasive techniques has enabled this mechanism to be recently investigated in humans (Gray et al., 2016).
- Ischaemia-reperfusion injury associated with load removal − this results in the reperfusion of blood and transport of other nutrients, which may result in an over production and release of oxygen-derived free radicals, which are known to be damaging to many tissues and organs (Pierce et al., 2000; Unal et al., 2001).
- Cell and tissue deformation − tissue deformation triggers a variety of effects, which may be involved in early cell damage, such as local membrane stresses leading to buckling and rupture of the membrane. This loss of membrane integrity will lead to altered transport of biomolecules and ions, volume changes and modifications of cytoskeletal organization, all of which can affect cell viability and limit the remodelling capacity of the tissues.

To examine these mechanisms a multi-scale approach has been adopted involving a range of cell-based studies (Gawlitta et al., 2007), tissue and animal models and human studies. Alternatively, *in vivo* animal models have been used to visualize real time damage with Magnetic Resonance (MR) Imaging. The acuity of these MR images enabled the development of Finite Element (FE) models to predict the internal mechanical state (Ceelen et al., 2008). Soft tissue damage due to large deformations as reflected in MRI parameters, such as T2 weighted index, has been shown to occur earlier than pressure-induced ischaemia, with damage evident after 10 min (Stekelenburg et al., 2007; Loerakker et al., 2010). The reperfusion phase can evoke additional tissue damage (Loerakker et al., 2011). A similar approach, examining both seated able-bodied and spinal cord injured (SCI) subjects (Linder-Ganz et al., 2008), has established threshold values for internal strain above which damage can occur. At the present time, research involving MRI represents the "gold standard" for imaging the soft tissue composite overlying bony prominences. However, it is a complex and expensive modality and, as such, could not be considered for routine use of assessing risk of developing PUs in a clinical setting.

Extrinsic factors

Effective prevention of PUs is possible if early signs of tissue breakdown can be detected and rigorous intervention strategies are introduced. From a bioengineering perspective there are a number of goals related to PU prevention, which could be achieved in the research and clinical setting, as summarized below:

- Development of an integrated system to monitor conditions at the loaded body-support interface
- Prediction of the interface/interstitial conditions which may lead to tissue breakdown
- Integration of novel materials to provide effective support systems and medical devices
- Establishment of objective screening techniques, which are reliable and robust, for use with individuals, particularly at risk of developing PUs

The following sections will focus on the first two goals. With respect to the interface conditions, there are a number of measurable factors at the loaded patient support interface including pressure, shear, temperature, humidity and time. Pressure and shear have long been known to be relevant in load-induced ischaemia (Fig. 23.1). There is also a growing realization of the importance of the microclimate at the loaded patient support interface. For example, a 1 °C rise of temperature increases the metabolic demands of the skin tissues by approximately 13%. Thus tissue demands an increased delivery of vital nutrients, typically oxygen, although the critical blood supply will inevitably be compromised by the localized mechanical environment within the soft tissues. In addition, an increase in skin temperature is likely to lead to an increase in moisture released in the form of sweat at the loaded interface. This will increase skin susceptibility to damage and increase frictional forces at the interface.

In a much-quoted retrospective study, Reswick and Rogers (1976) confirmed that both magnitude of pressure and time of exposure are critical in determining the risk of developing a PU. A sustained pressure of low magnitude can result in a PU, as well as a high pressure existing for shorter time periods, as reflected in a hyperbolic risk curve. However, more recent work (Stekelenburg et al., 2007; Ceelen et al., 2010; Linder-Ganz et al., 2007), have indicated that the curve of internal mechanical state as a function of the loading period must be adapted to a sigmoidal form, because of the damage mechanisms associated with high deformation at short loading periods.

Mechanical loading at the patient-support interface

Knowledge of the nature of the stresses occurring at the interface is essential in the assessment of the potential damage to soft tissues. Thus body tissues can support high levels of hydrostatic pressure, with equal components in all directions, with no resulting tissue distortion. This may be illustrated in the case of deep sea divers, who are regularly exposed to hydrostatic pressures in excess of 750 mmHg (100 kPa) for prolonged periods with no deleterious effects to the soft tissues. However, if the pressures are applied non-uniformly then localized tissue distortion and associated damage can result. This can arise if the pressures are applied locally or if pressures are applied in association with external shear forces (Hobson, 1992). In the former case, maximum pressure gradients will often be focused at the periphery of the locally compressed area. This establishes the need for the measurement of interface pressures.

Interface pressure mapping

External pressures are always present when either the body forces are transmitted through support surfaces or, alternatively, when an orthosis applies correctional forces through soft tissues. Accordingly for many years, bioengineers have focused their attention on developing accurate and reliable pressure measuring systems. These have incorporated sensors based on a number of physical principles involving pneumatics, electro-pneumatics, force-sensitive resistance materials and capacitance methods. A number of these systems have become commercially available to map interface pressure distribution over a relatively short time period i.e. 10s of minutes, using a range from single cells to arrays incorporating in excess of 1000 discrete measurements.

Pressure measurement systems are generally used in either a research or clinical setting. In the former, the systems can be used in the laboratory to evaluate the relative performance of different pressure relief/redistribution systems under controlled conditions. In order to compare products, two alternative approaches have been adopted. Protocols have been designed to simulate the loading patterns at the patient support interface, often involving a domed indenter incorporated with anthropomorphic mannequins with an internal skeleton covered by simulated soft tissues (Bain et al., 1999). Meaningful data can also be obtained from measurements on human subjects, provided that the experimental protocols are standardized, hence minimizing the inherent variability. Alternatively interface pressure monitoring systems can be used, typically in a seating clinic involving therapists and clinical engineers in a multidisciplinary team (MDT), as an adjunct to subjective risk assessment e.g. Braden or Waterlow scales, as well as providing an aid to clinical prescription of an appropriate support surface. Such measurements can also be used as a biofeedback tool to the individual providing evidence of postural factors associated with pelvic obliquity, tilt and rotation and the efficacy of pressure relief regimes. A critical analysis of these systems is provided in Table 23.1. Irrespective of how the tests are performed, regular calibration must be undertaken for all pressure measuring systems.

It is generally accepted that interface pressure measurements are subject to great variability resulting from differences between anatomical sites, individuals and even when the sensor is kept on a single anatomical site on a given individual due to small changes in posture (Table 23.2). There are also differences due to clothing/covering materials at the interface, the type of measurement system used and the interpretation of the data. This is particularly relevant when using systems which provide a vast data set to be processed into a pressure index, which can be used in research and/or clinical settings (Bogie et al., 2008). Common parameters include peak pressure, peak pressure gradient, average pressures, contact areas and symmetry index i.e. comparing values on two sides of the body. However, it is inevitable that no one parameter can provide a ubiquitous index of pressure distribution, which is applicable to all subjects at risk of developing PUs.

As pressure is force per unit area it is obvious that the shape of a subject will influence the resulting interface pressure distribution. Both shape and form of a subject in a load-bearing site will depend on the bony skeleton, the quantity, tone and shape of the musculature and the amount of subcutaneous fat, as well as the resilience of the intervening skin tissues. Accordingly, there is a complex interaction and there are many cases for which subjects with very similar body types can exhibit quite different interface pressures. This was exemplified by a series of studies examining the performance of mattresses with able-bodied volunteers commissioned by the UK Department of Health and several healthcare companies, as described by Swain and Bader (2002). As an example, two subjects with a similar height and BMI (1.57 m and 23.5 kg/m^2) recorded mean interface pressures under the sacrum when semi recumbent in bed of $61.9 + 9.2$ mmHg ($8.3 + 1.2$ kPa) and $86.4 + 12.2$ mmHg ($11.5 + 1.6$ kPa). This effect is even more marked with the heels due to their small radius of curvature, and thus any slight difference in contact area will have a major effect on interface pressures, and thus sensor placement is critical. Therefore the range of interface pressures on various anatomical sites vary widely with the underlying anatomy and thus it is not possible to predict the interface pressures from individual body type.

Although seminal studies involving animal models have indicated that the presence of shear forces effectively reduces the skin tolerance to applied pressure e.g. Dinsdale (1974), there is a dearth of studies measuring shear forces at the human body-support surface interface. This is mainly due to the technical challenges inherent in developing compliant, thin and flexible sensors that can distinguish between signals associated with normal forces with those forces acting parallel to the skin surface. Recently, research has exploited the use of 3D printing with elastomeric materials to create sensors which are capable of simultaneous measurements of pressure and shear forces (Laszczak et al., 2015, 2016). Based on a capacitance design, these novel tri-axial pressure and shear (TRIPS) interfacial sensors have been developed for measurements at the stump-socket interface of lower limb amputees, where shear forces can be high. The sensor unit has also been successfully integrated into prototype silicone liners and pads. The data acquisition (DAQ) unit, design to be worn outside of the socket by the amputee, is small and enables multiple sensor units to be used simultaneously. Wireless data transmission via

TABLE 23.1 Critical evaluation of interface pressure measurements.

Potential of interface pressure monitoring

- Well-established clinical measure to compare support surfaces for individual subjects
- Ideal to provide feedback for individuals to indicate support postures and areas of high pressures
- Useful lab-based tool for comparative evaluation of new materials and support surfaces

Limitations of interface pressure monitoring

- Analysis of large data sets (Bogie et al., 2008)
- Relevance to interstitial pressures?
- Relevance to site of initial tissue breakdown?
- There is no reliable indicator of safe pressure, or band of pressures, in association with time, which would be appropriate for all patients at risk

Conclusions

- Pressure measurements alone are not sufficient to alert the clinician to potential areas of tissue breakdown
- It is important to examine the effects of interface pressure on tissue viability/status

TABLE 23.2 Sources of variability associated with interface pressure monitoring.

Source of variability	Examples
Measurement system	Spatial and temporal resolution of sensor Methods of recording, displaying and interpreting data
Positioning	Change in footrest height Changes due to leaning forwards/side lying Tilt manoeuvres, including change of head of bed angle Subject posture
Anatomical location	Local body curvature Proximity to bony prominences
Inter-subject	Subject morphology Body mass index

Bluetooth™ allows the data to be transmitted to a smart phone or tablet. The TRIPS sensor system presents high resolutions of approximately 0.9 kPa for pressure and 0.2 kPa for shear and high linearity. However, the use of the TRIPS sensors with the lower shear forces and pressures in lying and sitting postures has yet to be established.

It is evident from the above factors that the monitoring of interface pressures alone will not prove sufficient to alert the clinician to potential areas of tissue breakdown. This has motivated a number of investigators to utilize additional measurement techniques, which can provide early objective indicators of compromise to the health of soft tissues in the loaded state. These include physical sensors, typically involving transcutaneous gas tensions and Laser Doppler fluxmetry and biosensing systems, involving the analysis of blood and urine markers, sweat metabolites and inflammatory biomarkers (Worsley et al., 2016a, 2018). In some cases these have been combined to evaluate the effects of different loading regimens on able-bodied (Knight et al., 2001) and SCI patients (Bogie and Bader, 2005), as well as to evaluate the effectiveness of specialized support surfaces (Goossens and Rithalia, 2007) and medical devices. For a more comprehensive summary of some of these multi-sensor approaches the reader is directed to a review article (Bader and Oomens, 2005).

Internal mechanical state of loaded soft tissues

The externally applied pressures will inevitably deform the soft tissue composite over the bony prominences establishing an internal mechanical state. However, the relationship between interface or external pressures, which can be measured, and the resulting mechanical state i.e. the internal interstitial stresses/strains, is necessarily complex in nature (Fig. 23.1). It is important to note that shear can be present externally at the skin surface, due to subject sliding and transfer across a support surface, as well as internally within the soft tissue structures due to pressures applied normal to the skin surface.

Experimentally there are a few studies, using invasive methods, which have examined the load transfer across the interface. As an example, Sangeorzan and colleagues (1989) reported that the values of interface versus interstitial pressures were not equivalent and were highly dependent on the nature and the mechanical properties of the intervening soft tissues. Thus the thickness, tone and mechanical integrity of subcutaneous tissues, and the proximity of bony prominences will influence this relationship (Fig. 23.1). An investigation of subjects during surgical procedure examined the response of tissues adjacent to the lateral aspect of the proximal thigh. Results indicated that skin interface pressures were dissipated within the depth of the tissues resulting in reduced internal stresses (Bader and White, 1998). Indeed linear models of the data suggested interstitial stresses range between 29% and 40% of the applied interface pressures. This highlights the protective nature of tissues to attenuate the effects of sustained pressure.

An alternative approach to analyze load transmission across the patient interface, involves developing mathematical solutions to the problem. A number of studies reveal considerable variation in the ratio values relating interface pressures and predicted interstitial pressures, as detailed in Table 23.3. A description of this mathematical approach is beyond the scope of this chapter, but it is worth noting that the more recent models incorporating non-linear and hyper-elastic behaviour are more realistic in terms of the mechanical response of the soft tissues. Additionally, appropriate values of mechanical parameters for all layers (skin, fat and muscle) within the human soft tissue composite are essential if the models are to predict critical internal threshold levels (Then et al., 2009). Early MRI studies revealed marked differences in structural stiffness values in healthy tissues adjacent to ischial tuberosities when compared to atrophied buttock tissues of an age-matched paraplegic with flaccid paralysis (Reger et al., 1990). The latter tissues were more distorted under load,

TABLE 23.3 The relationship between interface pressures and interstitial pressures as determined by a selection of experimental and computational approaches.

Study	Model system	Values	Interface pressures: interstitial pressure ratio
Bader and White (1998)	Loaded greater trochanter of surgical patients		0.28—0.57
Lee et al. (1984)	Pressure sensors implanted in a pig model		3—5
Ragan et al. (2002)	Axisymmetric 3D (FE) model of buttock	37 kPa/ 10 kPa	3.7
Oomens et al. (2003)	3D FE model — variable properties of muscle, fat and skin	120 kPa/ 50 kPa	2.4
Gefen et al. (2005)	3D FE model	4 MPa/ 15 kPa	266
Sun et al. (2005)	FE model based on non-sitting MRI	76 kPa/ 21 kPa	3.5

suggesting an increased risk of tissue trauma. More recently the use of elastography, combined with either MR or ultrasound imaging, has been proposed as a reliable means of estimating soft tissue properties under compressive loading in the research environment (Deprez et al., 2011). Although such techniques have been introduced to evaluate structural inclusions in breast and liver tissues, they are still to be used to detect the onset of pressure ulcers in a clinical setting.

Support surfaces and pressure relief regimens

Support surfaces at the patient interface should provide a safe, stable and comfortable means of transmitting loads to the body. Their design should provide a fairly uniform pressure distribution over a significant contact area, such as that envisaged with low air-loss systems. In addition, the choice of materials should account for other physical, functional and aesthetic factors, including durability, permeability to water vapour and heat dissipation. Additionally, materials should be biocompatible with host tissues, not evoking any skin irritations or allergic reactions. Compliant viscoelastic materials form the basis of many support surfaces. As an example for seating materials, a combination of foam, gel and air supports are regularly used at a thickness, which will minimize the risk of "bottoming out" without compromising other postural effects associated with arm and footrest supports.

If pressures are relieved periodically, they can be tolerated for longer periods. This forms the basis of pressure relief and redistribution regimens, which are performed by regular turning, lift-off from the support surface, and alternating pressure air mattresses (APAMs) and cushions. Nonetheless the relative merits of these high technological interventions, as assessed in a Cochrane systematic review (McInnes et al., 2015), still remain unclear. In recent studies the performance of APAMs have been evaluated using a range of bioengineering parameters. As an example, the performance of a prototype APAM, incorporating an in-built pressure sensor to adjust the internal pressures under the sacrum to subject morphology and BMI, was examined (Chai and Bader, 2013). Internal mattress pressures and transcutaneous gas tensions ($TcPO_2$ and $TcPCO_2$) at the sacrum and a control site were monitored. The skin response to alternating support pressures in a cohort of healthy volunteers were divided conveniently into three distinct categories (Fig. 23.2), namely:

- Category 1: Minimal changes in both T_cPO_2 and T_cPCO_2 values
- Category 2: Decrease in T_cPO_2 with minimal change in T_cPCO_2
- Category 3: Decrease in T_cPO_2 associated with an increase in T_cPCO_2

In the majority of test conditions the internal support produced sacral T_cPO_2 values, which demonstrated adequate viability, either remaining similar to those at the control site (Category 1) or fluctuating in concert with the cycles of alternating support pressures (Category 2). In both cases, the associated T_cPCO_2 levels remained within the normal range of 35—45 mmHg (4.7—6.0 kPa). However, in a few cases when the head of bed (HOB) was raised (>45°), there was compromise to the sacral viability, as reflected in depressed T_cPO_2 levels associated with an elevation of T_cPCO_2 levels above the normal range (Category 3). In all cases, interface pressures at the sacrum rarely exceeded 8 kPa (60 mmHg).

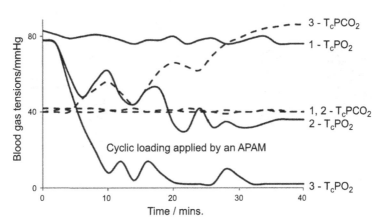

FIG. 23.2 Three categories of skin response at the sacrum in terms of transcutaneous gas tensions when individuals are supported supine on an alternating pressure mattress. *Based on Chai CY, Bader DL. 2013. The physiological response of skin tissues to alternating pressure in able-bodied subjects. J. Mech Behav Biomed Mater. 28, 427–435.*

This categorization was also adopted in a study examining the differences between lateral rotation provided by an active mattress system and the manual repositioning regularly performed by clinicians (Woodhouse et al., 2015). In a further study involving a fluid immersion simulation mattress the majority of participants (82%) exhibited minimal changes in gas tensions at the sacrum during all test conditions. However, three participants exhibited a Category 3 response for all three immersion settings, specifically in the high sitting position (Worsley et al., 2016b). Clearly, more robust trials are indicated for which individual characteristics are taken into account. Future developments could include establishing a range of optimal design features for support surfaces — the concept of a "personalized support surface" to match the physiological response of the individual.

Medical devices

Recent studies have examined the effects of different orthotic devices at the skin interface, using a range of biomechanical and biomarker responses. As an example, two different types of non-invasive ventilation masks, commonly used for respiratory support, were fitted on a group of able-bodied volunteers at three different strap tensions (Worsley et al., 2016a). Masks were worn for 10 min at each tension followed by a 10-min refractory period. Both physical sensors and biomarkers were employed in conjunction with subjective comfort scores. Results indicated significantly higher interface pressures at the bridge of the nose (Fig. 23.3A) compared to the cheeks for both masks ($p < 0.05$), with nasal interface pressures significantly increasing with elevated strap ($p < 0.05$). In addition, the inflammatory cytokine, IL-1α, increased following mask application at the highest tension, with median increases from baselines ranging from 21% to 33% (Fig. 23.3). Temperature and humidity values under the mask were elevated from ambient conditions and discomfort was reported over the bridge of the nose. A similar approach was adopted to examine the effects of prolonged loading using C-Collars, routinely used for immobilization of a serious trauma to the head or neck in the non-acute setting to manage cervical injury (Worsley et al., 2018). Three separate collar tensions (TL, TO, TH) were utilized, each for 15 min with a 10 min refractory period. The interface pressures at each tissue site (Fig. 23.3B) increased monotonically with collar tension ($p < 0.01$). Biomarker analysis revealed that IL-1α was elevated during collar application, with a 4-fold increase during the tight fit condition (TH) compared to the unloaded state. Regardless of collar tension or type, there was an increase in temperature of $1.5 \pm 0.8 \, ^{\circ}C$ and relative humidity of $6.1 \pm 3.6\%$ compared to baseline values. The greater strap tensions through the collars restricted the ranges of motion, with an associated increase in discomfort.

These two studies highlight the importance of both correct fitting of medical devices and regularly examining the interface when a device is applied for prolonged periods on patients with vulnerable skin.

Microclimate control

There is increasing evidence that thermodynamic conditions around skin tissues strongly influences susceptibility to PUs. This has culminated in the use of the term "microclimate" to describe the local temperature and moisture conditions at the loaded skin-support interface (Clark et al., 2010). This is particularly relevant for individuals with excess sweating or who experience urological dysfunction leading to urinary and, possibly, faecal incontinence. There has been recent interest

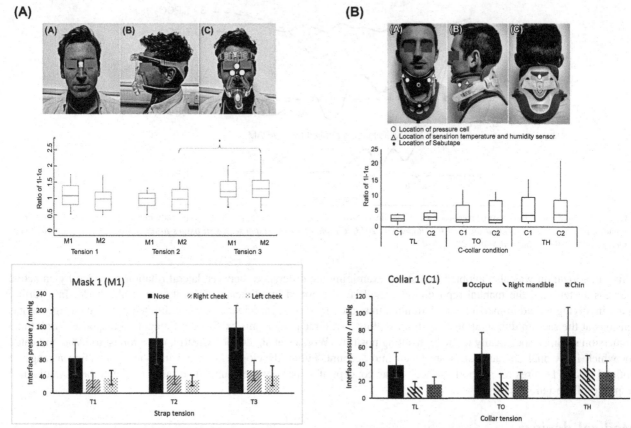

FIG. 23.3 The response of skin to loading applied with (A) respiratory face mask and (B) C-collar designs in terms of IL-1 expression and interface pressures. *Based on Worsley, P.R., Prudden, G., Gower, G., Bader, D.L., 2016a. Investigating the effects of strap tension during non-invasive ventilation mask application: a combined biomechanical and biomarker approach. Med. Devices (Auckl) 9, 409–417 and Worsley, P.R., Stanger, N.D., Horrell, A.K., Bader, D.L., 2018. Investigating the effects of cervical collar design and fit on the biomechanical and biomarker reaction at the skin. Med. Devices (Auckl) 11, 87–94.*

among support surface manufacturers to address this issue by designing mattresses and cushions which regulate the microclimate. A number of manufacturers have introduced novel fabric technologies and active air flow at the patient-support surface interface, designed to facilitate the transport of moisture and heat away from the loaded site. Recently, technological advances in woven manufacturing techniques have given rise to new 3D spacer fabrics, designed to have superior cyclic compression–recovery properties (Mao and Russell, 2007), which can be incorporated as overlays within support mattresses. Traditional spacer fabrics are composed of co-planar knitted structures that are joined together by yarns of known rigidity to provide a well-defined and pressure-tolerant inter-space between the different knitted layers. In addition, the 3D knitted spacer fabrics generally exhibit high air permeability and low thermal resistance. However, their performance has still to be comprehensively evaluated.

Summary

- Soft tissues represent an important interface with the outside world.
- When the integrity of soft tissue is compromised, prolonged external loading can lead to the development of pressure ulcers which, in extreme conditions, can be life-threatening.
- Pressure ulcers affect a wide range of individuals in both hospital and community settings, leading to personal suffering and considerable financial burden to health services.
- There are a number of mechanisms associated with the aetiology of pressure ulcers, each of which influences the viability at both cellular and tissue levels.
- The transmission of load across the body support interface establishes internal mechanical conditions which are, in part, determined by the mechanical properties of the soft tissues.

- Interface pressure measurements alone are not sufficient to define a damage threshold for pressure ulcer prevention.
- A range of bioengineering strategies should be adopted to provide early detection of soft tissue damage and minimize the incidence of pressure ulcers.
- Medical device related PUs must be reported to inform manufacturers when medical devices need improved design features to minimize soft tissue damage. Also, clinicians must take care when attaching any medical device to the skin surface.
- There is a need for the optimal design of support surfaces coupled with effective pressure relief/redistribution strategies and microclimate control to match the individual risk of pressure ulcers developing.

References

Bader, D.L., Bowker, P., 1983. Mechanical characteristics of skin and underlying tissues *in vivo*. Biomaterials 4, 305–308.

Bader, D.L., Oomens, C.W.J., 2005. Recent advances in pressure ulcer research. In: Romanelli, M., et al. (Eds.), Science and Practice of Pressure Ulcer Management. Springer-Verlag, Berlin, pp. 11–26.

Bader, D.L., White, S.H., 1998. The viability of soft tissues in elderly subjects undergoing hip surgery. Age Ageing 27, 217–221.

Bain, D.S., Scales, J.T., Nicholson, G.P., 1999. A new method of assessing the mechanical properties of patient support systems (PPS) using a phantom. A preliminary report. Med. Eng. Phys. 21 (5), 293–301.

Black, J.M., Cuddigan, J.E., Walko, M.A., et al., 2010. Medical device related pressure ulcers in hospitalized patients. Int. Wound J. 7, 358–365.

Bogie, K.M., Bader, D.L., 2005. Susceptibility of spinal-cord injured individuals to pressure ulcers. In: Bader, D.L., Bouten, C.V.C., Oomens, C.W.J., Colin, D. (Eds.), Pressure Ulcer Research: Current and Future Perspectives. Springer-Verlag, Berlin, pp. 73–88.

Bogie, K.M., Wang, X., Fei, B., Sun, J., 2008. New technique for real-time interface pressure analysis: getting more out of large image data sets. J. Rehabil. Res. Dev. 45 (4), 523–536.

Bouten, C.V.C., Oomens, C.W.J., Baaijens, F.P.T., Bader, D.L., 2003. The aetiology of pressure sores: skin deep or muscle bound? Arch. Phys. Med. Rehabil. 84, 616–619.

Ceelen, K.K., Stekelenburg, A., Loerakker, S., Strijkers, G.J., Bader, D.L., Nicolay, K., Baaijens, F.P.T., Oomens, C.W.J., 2008. Compression-induced damage and internal tissue strains are related. J. Biomech. 41 (16), 3399–3404.

Ceelen, K.K., Gawlitta, D., Bader, D.L., Oomens, C.W.J., 2010. Numerical analysis of ischaemia- and compression-induced injury in tissue-engineered skeletal muscle constructs. Ann. Biomed. Eng. 38 (3), 570–582.

Chai, C.Y., Bader, D.L., 2013. The physiological response of skin tissues to alternating support pressures in able-bodied subjects. J. Mech. Behav. Biomed. Mater. 28, 427–435.

Clark, M., et al., 2010. Microclimate in Context. International Guidelines. Pressure Ulcer Prevention: Pressure, Shear, Friction and Microclimate in Context. A Consensus Document. Wounds International, London, pp. 19–25.

Dealey, C., Posnett, J., Walker, A., 2012. The cost of pressure ulcers in the United Kingdom. J. Wound Care 21 (6), 261–262.

Deprez, J.F., Brusseau, E., Fromageau, J., Cloutier, G., Basset, O., 2011. On the potential of ultrasound elastography for pressure ulcer early detection. Med. Phys. 38 (4), 1943–1950.

Dinsdale, S.M., 1974. Decubitus ulcers: role of pressure and friction in causation. Arch. Phys. Med. Rehabil. 55, 147–152.

Gawlitta, D., Li, W., Oomens, C.W.J., Bader, D.L., Baaijens, F.P.T., Bouten, C.V.C., 2007. Temporal differences in the influence of ischemic factors and deformation on the metabolism of engineered skeletal muscle. J. Appl. Physiol. 103 (2), 464–473.

Gebhardt, K., Bliss, M.R., 1994. Preventing pressure sores in orthopaedic patients – is prolonged chair nursing detrimental? J. Tissue Viability 4, 51–54.

Gefen, A., Gefen, N., Linder-Ganz, E., Margulies, S., 2005. In vivo muscle stiffening under bone compression promotes deep pressure sores. J. Biomech. Eng. 127 (3), 512–524.

Goossens, R.H., Rithalia, S.V., 2007. Physiological response of the heel tissue on pressure relief between three alternating pressure air mattresses. J. Tissue Viability 17 (1), 10–14.

Gorecki, C., Brown, J.M., Nelson, E.A., Briggs, M., Schoonhoven, L., Dealey, C., Defloor, T., Nixon, J., 2009. Impact of pressure ulcers on quality of life in older patients: a systematic review. J. Am. Geriatr. Soc. 57 (7), 1175–1183.

Gray, R.J., Worsley, P.R., Voegeli, D., Bader, D.L., 2016. Monitoring contractile dermal lymphatic activity following uniaxial mechanical loading. Med. Eng. Phys. 38 (9), 895–903.

Guest, J.F., et al., 2015. Health economic burden that wounds impose on the National Health Service in the UK. BMJ Open 5 (12), e009283.

Hahnel, E., Lichterfeld, A., Blume-Peytavi, U., Kottner, J., 2017. The epidemiology of skin conditions in the aged: a systematic review. J. Tissue Viability 26 (1), 20–28.

Hobson, D.A., 1992. Comparative effects of posture on pressure and shear at the body seat interface. J. Rehabil. Res. Dev. 29, 21–31.

Jordon, M.M., Clark, M.O., 1977. Report on Incidence of Pressure Sores in the Patient Community of the Greater Glasgow Health Board Area on 21 January 1976. University of Strathclyde, Glasgow.

Knight, S.L., Taylor, R.P., Polliack, A.A., Bader, D.L., 2001. Establishing predictive indicators for the status of soft tissues. J. Appl. Physiol. 90, 2231–2237.

Kottner, J., Gefen, A., Lahmann, N., 2011. Weight and pressure ulcer occurrence: a secondary data analysis. Int. J. Nurs. Stud. 48 (11), 1339–1348.

Krouskop, T.A., 1983. A synthesis of the factors that contribute to pressure sore formation. Med. Hypothesis 11, 255–267.

Laszczak, P., Jiang, L., Bader, D.L., Moser, D., Zahedi, S., 2015. Development and validation of a 3D-printed interfacial stress sensor for prosthetic applications. Med. Eng. Phys. 37, 132−137.

Laszczak, P., McGrath, M., Tang, J., Gao, J., Jiang, L., Bader, D.L., Moser, D., Zahedi, S., 2016. A pressure and shear sensor system for stress measurement at lower limb residuum/socket interface. Med. Eng. Phys. 38, 695−700.

Le, K.M., Madsen, B.L., Barth, P.W., Ksander, G.A., Angell, J.B., Vistnes, L.M., 1984. An in-depth look at pressure sores using monolithic silicon pressure sensors. Plast. Reconstr. Surg. 74, 745−756.

Linder-Ganz, E., Shabshinb, N., Itzchakb, Y., Gefen, A., 2007. Assessment of mechanical conditions in sub-dermal tissues during sitting: a combined experimental-MRI and finite element approach. J. Biomech. 40, 1443−1454.

Linder-Ganz, E., Shabshinb, N., Itzchakb, Y., Yizhar, Z., Siev-Ner, I., Gefen, A., 2008. Strains and stresses in sub-dermal tissues of the buttocks are greater in paraplegics than in healthy during sitting. J. Biomech. 41 (3), 567−580.

Loerakker, S., Stekelenburg, A., Strijkers, G.J., Rijpkema, J.J., Baaijens, F.P.T., Bader, D.L., Nicolay, K., Oomens, C.W.J., 2010. Temporal effects of mechanical loading on deformation induced damage in skeletal muscle. Ann. Biomed. Eng. 38 (8), 2577−2587.

Loerakker, S., Manders, E., Strijkers, G.J., Nicolay, K., Baaijens, F.P.T., Bader, D.L., Oomens, C.W., 2011. The effects of deformation, ischemia, and reperfusion on the development of muscle damage during prolonged loading. J. Appl. Physiol. 111 (4), 1168−1177.

Mao, N., Russell, S.J., 2007. The thermal insulation properties of spacer fabrics with a mechanically integrated wool fibre surface. Text. Res. J. 77 (12), 914−922.

McInnes, E., Jammali-Blasi, A., Bell-Syer, S., Dumville, J., Cullum, N., 2015. Preventing pressure ulcers − are pressure redistribution surface effective? Int. J. Nurs. Stud. 49 (3), 345−359.

Miller, G.E., Seale, J.L., 1985. The mechanics of terminal lymph flow. J. Biomech. Eng. 107 (4), 376−380.

Nixon, J., Cranny, G., Iglesias, C., Nelson, E.A., Hawkins, K., Phillips, A., Torgerson, D., Mason, S., Cullum, N., 2006. Randomised, controlled trial of alternating pressure mattresses compared with alternating pressure overlays for the prevention of pressure ulcers: PRESSURE (pressure relieving support surfaces) trial. BMJ 332, 1413−1415.

NPUAP/EPUAP/PPPIA, 2014. Prevention and Treatment of Pressure Ulcers: Clinical Practice Guideline Cambridge Media, pp. 1−292.

Oomens, C.W.J., Bressers, O.F.J.T., Bosboom, E.M.H., Bouten, C.V.C., Bader, D.L., 2003. Can loaded interface characteristics influence strain distributions in muscle adjacent to bony prominences? Comput. Methods Biomech. Biomed. Eng. 6, 171−180.

Peirce, S.M., Skalak, T.C., Rodheheaver, G.T., 2000. Ischaemic-reperfusion injury in chronic pressure ulcer formation: a skin model in the rat. Wound Repair Regen. 8, 68−76.

Phillips, L., Buttery, J., 2009. Exploring pressure ulcer prevalence and preventative care. Nurs. Times 105, 34−36.

Ragan, R., Kernozek, T.W., Bidar, M., Matheson, J.W., 2002. Seat-interface pressures on various thicknesses of foam wheelchair cushions: a finite modeling approach. Arch. Phys. Med. Rehabil. 83, 872−875.

Reddy, N.P., Palmieri, V., Cochran, G.V., 1981. Subcutaneous interstitial fluid pressure during external loading. Am. J. Physiol. 240 (5), R327−R329.

Reger, S.I., McGovern, T.F., Chung, K.C., 1990. Biomechanics of tissue distortion and stiffness by magnetic resonance imaging. In: Bader, D.L. (Ed.), Pressure Sores-Clinical Practice and Scientific Approach. Macmillan Press, pp. 177−190.

Reswick, J.B., Rogers, J.E., 1976. Experience at Rancho Los Amigos Hospital with devices and techniques to prevent pressure sores. In: Kenedi, R.M., Cowden, J.M., Scales, J.T. (Eds.), Bedsore Biomechanics. Macmillan, London, pp. 301−310.

Rowling, J.T., 1961. Pathological changes in mummies. Proc. R. Soc. Med. 54, 409−415.

Sangeorzan, B.J., Harrington, R.M., Wyss, C.R., Czerniecki, J.M., Matsen, F.A., 1989. Circulation and mechanical response of skin to loading. J. Orthop. Res. 7, 425−431.

Schuurman, J.P., Schoonhoven, L., Defloor, T., van Engelshoven, I., van Ramshorst, B., Buskens, E., 2009. Economic evaluation of pressure ulcer care: a cost minimization analysis of preventive strategies. Nurs. Econ. 27, 390−400.

Stekelenburg, A., Strijkers, G.J., Parusel, H., Bader, D.L., Nicolay, K., Oomens, C.W., 2007. Role of ischemia and deformation in the onset of compression-induced deep tissue injury: MRI-based studies in a rat model. J. Appl. Physiol. 102 (5), 2002−2011.

Sun, Q., Lin, F., Al-Saeede, S., Ruberte, L., Nam, E., Hendrix, R., Makhsous, M., 2005. Finite element modeling of human buttock-thigh tissue in a seated posture. In: Summer Bioengineering Conference, June 22−26, Vail, Colorado.

Swain, I.D., Bader, D.L., 2002. The measurement of interface pressure and its role in soft tissue breakdown. J. Tissue Viability 12, 132−146.

Then, C., Menger, J., Vogl, T.J., Hübner, F., Silber, G., 2009. Mechanical gluteal soft tissue material parameter validation under complex tissue loading. Technol. Health Care 17, 393−401.

Unal, S., Ozmen, S., DemIr, Y., Yavuzer, R., LatIfoğlu, O., Atabay, K., Oguz, M., 2001. The effect of gradually increased blood flow in ischaemia-reperfusion injury. Ann. Plast. Surg. 47, 412−416.

Vanderwee, K., Clark, M., Dealey, C., Gunningberg, L., Defloor, T., 2007. Pressure ulcer prevalence in Europe: a pilot study. J. Eval. Clin. Pract. 13, 227−235.

Woodhouse, M., Worsley, P.R., Voegeli, D., Schoonhoven, L., Bader, D.L., 2015. The physiological response of soft tissue to periodic repositioning as a strategy for pressure ulcer prevention. Clin. Biomech. 30, 166−174.

Worsley, P.R., Prudden, G., Gower, G., Bader, D.L., 2016a. Investigating the effects of strap tension during non-invasive ventilation mask application: a combined biomechanical and biomarker approach. Med. Devices (Auckl) 9, 409−417.

Worsley, P.R., Parsons, B., Bader, D.L., 2016b. An evaluation of fluid immersion therapy for the prevention of pressure ulcers. Clin. Biomech. 40, 27−32.

Worsley, P.R., Stanger, N.D., Horrell, A.K., Bader, D.L., 2018. Investigating the effects of cervical collar design and fit on the biomechanical and biomarker reaction at the skin. Med. Devices (Auckl) 11, 87−94.

Chapter 24

Introduction to mobility and wheelchair assessment

David Long

AJM Healthcare, UK & Oxford University Hospitals NHS Foundation Trust, Oxford, UK

Chapter outline

Introduction to mobility

Historical context

Within the field of rehabilitation engineering, mobility devices are normally thought of in terms of wheelchairs, accepting that there are other forms of assisted mobility such as tricycles and mobility scooters, etc. Wheelchairs often come under the remit of an occupational therapist or physio/physical therapist, but clinical engineers have an important role in understanding the effective use of such devices, their prescription, modification and design, particularly where commercially available equipment does not meet a specific need meaning that something bespoke must be created.

It is difficult to say precisely when the wheelchair was invented, but it seems clear that they have existed since at least the 19th century. Early examples were literally ordinary chairs to which wheels were attached. Designs progressed through the early part of the 20th century and use became more prominent in the rehabilitation of veterans returning injured from the two world wars and subsequent conflicts. Use of more advanced materials was adopted through the second half of the 20th century and the knowledge of the concept of posture as related to the wheelchair began to take off.

A number of factors have led to the more widespread use of wheelchairs in society:

- The emergence of specialist spinal injury units leading to a more advanced understanding of wheelchair propulsion, postural biomechanics and pressure ulcer prevention, coupled with advances in materials technology, and the application of this to functioning from a wheelchair
- The integration into society of disabled people previously living in large, specialist hospitals and "asylums"
- An ageing population
- Advances in medical science which have resulted in people surviving very traumatic accidents and babies surviving very premature birth, often resulting in profound and complex levels of disability

This last point may give rise to difficult moral questions about the sanctity of life, quality of life, prolonged suffering of individuals and their families, the potential for having to grieve for the loss of a loved one whilst they are still medically alive, the individual's wishes stated pre-trauma, whether these may have changed post-trauma, and their capacity to consent to treatment or the withdrawal of treatment (life support machine).

Pooled resources

Most wheelchairs are provided for and used by an individual. However, it is common in some settings, e.g. residential homes, to find a "pool" of wheelchairs that are available for use by a number of people. This makes sense where not everyone needs a wheelchair all the time and where a standard chair can be used by many people. Hospitals have portering chairs, used purely within the hospital context to move people from one department to another. They are usually more sturdy than standard wheelchairs, but the resultant weight penalty is less of an issue because the chair is not intended to leave the premises.

State provision

In many countries wheelchairs are provided by the state for those who have need. They are also often purchased privately, sometimes because a particular model is not provided by the state. Charitable organizations also provide wheelchairs alongside other necessary equipment.

In England, wheelchair users are able to top up state funding of their equipment to allow themselves more choice. This was known as the "voucher scheme", which became available in 1996, and is now called a "personal wheelchair budget", or PWB (National Health Service, 2016). The two are identical in structure but the intention with PWBs is that everyone has one, regardless of whether they choose to top up funding:

- No voucher/notional PWB: the person accepts the equipment provided by the state
- Partnership/notional with top-up: the person either (a) chooses a higher specification chair from within the wheelchair service range or (b) adds an additional feature; since maintenance continues to be provided by the state there is no financial risk to the person; the state can only (realistically) provide an effective maintenance service for chairs within its range, hence why this limitation is in place; some services may choose not to provide maintenance for some additional features, dependent upon cost
- Independent/third party: to allow the person to choose any wheelchair they wish using funds from any source they can find; the value of the voucher/PWB is calculated as the cost of chair to the NHS plus an amount towards maintenance; a higher specification chair could be sought to meet or offset other health, social, educational or vocational needs

Table 24.1 describes how the schemes are aligned, who owns the equipment, the duration of the voucher/PWB and maintenance responsibilities.

Mobility devices

At the simplest level we have a walking stick — a device used for centuries. This has developed into a number of variations and then to the elbow crutch for those who have less weight bearing ability through their legs. These simple devices provide support, security and stability. In the case of regular users, an ergonomic design of handle can improve comfort to the hand by spreading the load over a larger surface area.

Those with more advanced mobility needs but still being able to bear weight through their legs may be supported by a frame (often referred to as a Zimmer). At the simplest this will have four rubber ferrules at the base of each corner shaft, but variations will have wheels or castors replacing some or all of the ferrules (these devices are often referred to as rollators). Other variations include seats and luggage carrying capability. In recent years there have been a number of more aesthetically pleasing designs come onto the market, ones which look less out of place in the home environment.

Moving onto wheelchairs, these devices in essence offer a means of mobility for people who are less able or unable to walk. However, they also have a critical role in facilitating the completion of functional tasks, e.g. eating/drinking, using a computer, visiting the lavatory. Added into this mix is the need for the person to be comfortable, which in turn leads to the requirement for the wheelchair to provide postural support, particularly for those having higher levels of physical impairment. Very quickly, our simple means of mobility has become a complex, multi-faceted device which, in many cases, will need to be prescribed/designed very specifically for the individual.

There are a vast array of wheelchairs, seating and accessories available on the market today. Some of these will be described to aid explanation but an exhaustive list would be impossible to compile and out of date by the time of publication. It is more important that the reader knows how to determine what is needed from a wheelchair, which will enable them to be able to appraise the options available. Without gathering this knowledge, the approach to provision would be rather "hit and miss", with questionable outcomes for the patient and poor efficiency for service provision. More detail is given in the next chapter on what considerations should be made specifically for wheelchair provision.

TABLE 24.1 Alignment of voucher/personal wheelchair budget schemes.

Voucher	PWB	Equipment ownership	Maintenance responsibility	Duration
None	Notional	State	State	n/a
Partnership	Notional with top up	State	State	Usually five years for adults & three for children, unless clinical needs change
Independent	Third party	Individual	Individual	Usually five years for adults & three for children, unless clinical needs change

Environmental issues and adaptation

Mobility is not just assisted by devices but also by careful attention to the environment. There is a general trend towards improving accessibility for wheelchair users and those who find walking difficult. New buildings are required to have a level access entrance, and buses and trains are slowly becoming more accessible. Air travel, however, can still present substantial difficulties for those who are wheelchair dependent.

Environmental features such as grab rails, hand rails, escalators and lifts will improve mobility for those with varying degrees of disability. Dropped kerbs are widely used to gain access to/from the pavement/sidewalk, although these vary in height and their effectiveness can be reduced by a very steeply cambered roadway or drain grate that is difficult to cross. Access ramps of restricted slope allow wheelchair users entry to buildings.

Side slopes can be particularly difficult to navigate using a wheelchair because there is a tendency for the chair to roll down the slope, i.e. to turn away from its intended trajectory. This problem is not isolated to manual wheelchairs because rear wheel drive powered chairs rely on adhesion/traction of the drive wheel at the top of the slope to provide a braking effect, this being reduced by slippery surfaces. The effect is significantly reduced in mid wheel drive powered wheelchairs but ultimately it is determined by weight distribution over the drive wheels compared to the castor wheels.

Surface treatments can help or hinder mobility: some surfaces, e.g. cobbles, grass, make it more difficult for wheelchair users, while at the same time textured surfaces help those with visual impairment. Another issue for those with visual impairment is to avoid overhanging architectural features such as "open" stairs. The design of the environment is often the preserve of architects but engineers can understand the advantages and problems of such features, and can offer advice.

Children and mobility

There are specific mobility needs related to children. Normally developing children progress from lying to sitting to crawling and then to walking within the space of about a year. Children with disabilities are often encouraged to develop as much as possible by their own abilities rather than through use of a device such as a wheelchair. There is an opinion, however, that use of a mobility device from a young age can improve the chances of a child developing their abilities through play and social interaction because they are able to move within and explore their environment more independently (Nilsson et al., 2011; Durkin, 2009). On this basis there is a strong argument that even very young children with delayed mobility development should be given a powered mobility device which they can control independently. Ideally this should not look like a wheelchair: styling as a toy (or similar) may provide added appeal. There are a small number of products on the market that fill this niche.

Not forgetting the adults …

Equipment and services for children with disabilities righty receive a lot of attention from government and the general public. However, it is often (seemingly) forgotten that these children grow into adults whose needs, rather than reducing, often increase at the person ages. Even those with so-called non-progressive conditions, e.g. cerebral palsy, often go on to develop profound complications secondary to the primary diagnosis. Someone with impaired motor function is likely to struggle with postural control which can lead to the repeated utilization of sustained asymmetric positioning, which itself can cause muscle shortening and deterioration in joint ranges/condition. It is vital that sufficient resource and attention is given to equipment and services for adults so that the effects of these secondary complications is minimized.

The broader picture of wheeled mobility

Physiotherapy departments often use walkers which support a person in a standing position but allow use of the legs for mobility. A wide range of products are available with myriad levels of support. Used in therapy less commonly than in years past are tricycles which require the child to be able to pedal to some extent, or perhaps just to enjoy the experience with the assistance of another. In the context of paralympic sport, however, people having difficulties with balance, but who are able to pedal, can compete in road cycling events.

Mobility scooters are becoming increasingly common in the UK. These are different to wheelchairs in that they have a pivotting seat to allow access from the side, and a tiller to steer the front wheel(s) rather than a joystick. One would not ordinarily expect to be hoisted into a scooter, and the inability to transfer independently would suggest a level of postural inability not able to be accommodated within a scooter. They are designed primarily for use outdoors but some of the more compact versions are also suitable indoors where large distances have to be covered, for example in a residential home. There is far less scope for modification than with wheelchairs and so clinical engineers do not tend to have so much involvement.

Wheelchair assessment process

Introduction

As will be clear from the section above, selecting the right wheelchair is not only complex but is also critical in allowing the person to achieve their functional aims. In order to determine the most appropriate model it is necessary to carry out a clinical assessment to discover what the person wishes to achieve coupled with an analysis of their impairments and any constraining factors such as the size of their house.

Factors to be considered in each wheelchair assessment

The following list should be used as a guide for enquiry when assessing for a wheelchair. It will be the case that priorities alter according to the nature of the referral and the precise circumstances of the person. It should be noted that an assessment form in its own right will not necessarily lead the assessor to an appropriate conclusion. It is a prompt sheet which requires the assessor to analyze and synthesize the information collected in order to draw a meaningful and effective conclusion.

List of problems and aims, as identified by the person

Prior to carrying out a full assessment, it is first necessary to elicit from the person and family/carers what it is that they would like — the difference between the reason for referral stated by the referring healthcare professional and the stated aims of the person themselves can be surprising.

Some aims may be outside the scope of the service but should be acknowledged because they might be met by funding from another source, or (in England) by use of a personal wheelchair budget.

Use of an outcome measurement tool will assist with determining the aims and objectives of the person, and with determining the suitability and effectiveness of provision. Care should be taken in choosing a tool for use with assistive technology, as described by Cowan and Najafi (2019), who suggest that measurement of outcomes is becoming increasingly important because the focus of service commissioners is not only on waiting list times but also on the quality of care delivered.

Tuersley et al. (2018) have developed the wheelchair outcomes assessment tool for children (WATCh) which is a validated, patient-centred instrument for young wheelchair users. They have also developed but not yet validated a version for adults (WATCh-Ad). The tools support the person to choose their top five aims, to grade these using their current equipment, and then again after three to six months of use. Further information is available at the following URL: https://cheme.bangor.ac.uk/watch.php

Medical	
• Primary and secondary **diagnoses**	• Relevant **medication**, e.g. for pain, spasm, epilepsy, bowel function
• **Prognosis**, i.e. likely progression of disease and timescale	• Ability to **swallow**, i.e. implications for head positioning and orientation of posture in space
• Stage in **rehabilitation** programme, if applicable, i.e. does equipment need to be adjustable	• **Communication**, i.e. can the person reliably give a yes/no response to questions, is speech impaired, is a communication aid in use
• **Age** of person, particularly concerning child development	
• Current **state of health**, including respiratory status	• **Cognition**: This is a complex area that is beyond the scope of this book; it is important that lack of cognition is not
• **Pain** and whether it is likely that this can be reduced by altering the wheelchair, e.g. is it relieved when lying down	

- **skin condition** and susceptibility to pressure ulcers, including sensation; past history of pressure ulceration
- **Neurological phenomena**, e.g. spasm, spasticity, movement disorders, persistent reflexes; observation will elicit useful information
- Past or planned **surgical procedures**, e.g. hip, spine, abdomen
- **Hip joint status**, particularly for those who have never walked
- **Continence** and how this is managed; for example a urinal bottle used to empty the bladder will preclude certain fixed seat shapes

- assumed due to impaired communication, and that a judgement is made concerning aspects of safety, i.e. can the person demonstrate that they are able to use their wheelchair without coming to harm or harming others
- **Vision**: Implications for safety, communication and use of equipment, e.g. buttons on a powered wheelchair joystick module
- **Hearing**: Implications for safety and communication
- **Height**, e.g. impact on a standing transfer or access into a vehicle
- **Weight**, in relation to the capacity of the chair to carry the person and any items of additional equipment, usually seating or medical equipment

Social/functional/environmental

- Current or intended **pattern of use** of wheelchair, i.e. is it to be used all day, or for brief periods only; if the latter, a simpler solution may be appropriate and more effective
- **Type of mobility**, i.e. manual or powered; occupant or attendant propelled
- **Occupation/education/leisure pursuits/household duties**, mostly in relation to the environment, either access to buildings or to work spaces/surfaces
- Ability to carry out **self care tasks** and the potential impact of prescribed equipment on these
- Difficulties **eating/drinking**, i.e. is there a required postural orientation

- Method of **vehicular transport**: is the wheelchair to be folded and stowed in the luggage compartment, or does the person travel seated in their chair
- **Social situation**: Does the person live at home with family, on their own, or in a care setting; who are the primary carers
- **Other equipment in use**, such as other wheelchairs, any form of armchair, office chair or classroom chair, orthotic splints, prostheses
- Restrictions in the home or work **environment**, i.e. narrow doorways, tight turns, through floor lifts
- Method of **transfer** – see below

Transfers

- **Standing pivot** – the person is able to stand in front of the wheelchair and lower themselves, sometimes with help, into the seat. A pivoting frame (turntable) can be used for assistance.
- **Slide** from side – the person is unable to carry out a standing transfer but has sufficient strength in their arms to lift their weight across from one surface to another, the armrests having been removed or swung back. A slide board is often used to provide assistance.
- **Lift** – the person is unable to bear weight either through their feet or hands/arms, and is light enough not to pose a moving and handling risk to the assistant. This type of transfer tends to be limited to small children, though parents often continue to lift their child into their teens and adulthood, and spouses frequently carry the person in order to avoid the limitations to lifestyle imposed by the requirement to use a hoist.
- **Hoisted** – where the person cannot be lifted, a hoist and sling are used. Hoists are either mobile or mounted on a ceiling track system. A wide variety of slings are available.

Physical measurements

It is necessary to take linear measurements to determine the appropriate size of wheelchair. Ideally, this should be carried out on a firm surface, such as a physiotherapy plinth, as softer surfaces tend to mask anatomical landmarks. The following measurements should be considered but will not all be necessary on every occasion.

- **Hip width**: Across the widest point; consider relationship to shoulder width
- **Seat depth**: Back of the knee, or popliteal crease, to the back of the buttock; care should be taken not to measure with the pelvis in posterior tilt (see posture management section) where this is mobile, as the seat depth will be too long, causing postural complications
- **Lower leg length**: From the popliteal crease to the bottom of the heel
- **Back support height**: Taken from the underside of the buttock to a point on the trunk where support is no longer required, which is a matter for clinical judgement based on the shape of the spine, the use of tilt-in-space and the requirement for shoulder movement, particularly related to manual propulsion of the wheelchair

- **Sacral support height**: It is a common failing of wheelchair seating that posterior support to the sacrum is not considered; without such support, the pelvis tends to fall into posterior tilt; the height at which support stops must be determined
- **Head height**: The height needed to be achieved by a headrest
- **Elbow height**: To determine the required height of arm support
- **Thoracic width**: In relation to the shape of the back cushion and positioning of lateral trunk supports
- **Shoulder width**: Related to seat width and which is required to avoid impingement of shoulders on the back posts of the wheelchair

Postural assessment

Usually required for a full-time wheelchair user and adapted according to complexity. Full details are available in the posture management chapter but note here that for those having even moderate postural impairment, failure to address postural positioning at night may impact heavily on equipment used in the day:
  - Asymmetrical postures repeatedly sustained through the night may cause tissue adaptation affecting sitting postures
  - Discomfort in lying may give rise to discomfort in sitting
  - Fatigue caused by lack of sleep may result in reduced sitting ability in the day
  - Pressure management issues not addressed at night may have an impact on the effectiveness of wheelchair seating
The service may not have the remit to address issues of positioning at night but onward referral should be made to fellow healthcare professionals where necessary.

Objective setting

Having completed the information gathering sections above, it is necessary to define the objectives for provision, i.e. what it is that is needing to be achieved. This provides a basis for the prescription, clarifies the reasons for intervention, is a way of identifying conflicting demands and can help in the measurement of outcomes.

There is no definitive method but it is important to pull out the critical elements of the assessment. It can be helpful to describe an overall aim, such as in this example:

It is the intention of this prescription to prevent X sliding down in their wheelchair, for them to be able to sit out for up to four hours without back pain, and for the carer to be able to take X out to the local shops.

Further detail can then be added, potentially in the form of a list, such as this:

- Support and stabilize pelvis in neutral alignment
- Accommodate limited left hip flexion
- Stabilize trunk in central alignment
- Support head in neutral position
- Protect skin over ischial tuberosities and sacrum
- Facilitate ease of attendant propulsion
- Facilitate the hoisted transfer
- Facilitate use of the urinal bottle

This list can be used to discuss priorities with the person and their carers. In this example, we may wish to prescribe a tilt-in-space wheelchair to stabilize posture and allow sitting for a longer period, but this will not be light weight in terms of pushing to the local shops. However, such a solution might be acceptable if comfort is significantly improved and has been prioritized ahead of mobility. It can also be helpful to use the SMART goal setting methodology which is widely used in the clinical setting. Here is an example:

- **S**pecific (allow the carer to independently push X to the local shops twice per week)
- **M**easurable (was the aim achieved?)
- **A**ttainable (the carer does not have any significant physical impairments)
- **R**ealistic (suitable equipment is available)
- **T**ime defined (the journey should not take more than 15 min each way)

There are many other goal setting/planning methodologies but their suitability to the task in hand should be analysed prior to use.

Conceptual ideas

Having gathered the assessment data and defined aims and objectives, an outline of a prescription may be developed. It is often tempting to jump directly to a particular piece of equipment through familiarity, but this may preclude the identification of potentially better solutions. Questions to ask include:

- What sort of wheelchair is appropriate: manual or powered?
- What type of seating should be used: basic foam slab, contoured, custom contoured?
- What properties must the material have: pressure relief, postural support/correction, adjustability?

- What orientations should the wheelchair move through, e.g. need for tilt-in-space?
- What are the functional requirements?
- In what setting will the equipment be used?

This will generate a performance specification which provides a basis from which to judge potential pieces of equipment as different options are explored.

Prescription

Finally, one is able to make specific recommendations. These should be detailed and include the full remit of what is needed. A clear, clinical rationale supports each recommendation and is developed through clinical reasoning. Assembly techniques must be considered because it is likely that equipment contained in the prescription will come from more than one manufacturer.

Further information on prescription is contained in the first chapter of this section as the principles apply across a wide range of clinical services.

References

Cowan, D., Najafi, L., 2019. Chapter 4: Assessment & outcomes Elsevier. In: Handbook of Electronic Assistive Technology. Elsevier.

Durkin, J., 2009. Discovering powered mobility skills with children: 'responsive partners' in learning. Int. J. Ther. Rehabil. 16, 331–342.

National Health Service, 2016. Personal Wheelchair Budgets. https://www.england.nhs.uk/personal-health-budgets/personal-wheelchair-budgets/.

Nilsson, L., Eklund, M., Nyberg, P., Thulesius, H., 2011. Driving to learn in a powered wheelchair: the process of learning joystick use in people with profound cognitive difficulties. Am. J. Occup. Ther. 65 (6), 652–660.

Tuersley, L., Bray, N., Edwards, R.T., 2018. Development of the Wheelchair outcomes Assessment Tool for Children (WATCh): a patient-centred outcome measure for young wheelchair users Bangor University. PLoS One 13 (12), e0209380. https://doi.org/10.1371/journal.pone.0209380.

Chapter 25

Wheelchair prescription

David Long

AJM Healthcare, UK & Oxford University Hospitals NHS Foundation Trust, Oxford, UK

Chapter outline

Getting into the detail

Having considered in the previous chapter the outline of the assessment process, we shall now examine some of the more detailed designs/sections/components of a wheelchair.

The frame/chassis/base

Wheelchairs frames can generally be split into two major types: folding and fixed. The former usually has a cross brace arrangement which allows the wheelchair to be flattened to aid stowage in a car or cupboard. It also allows the chair to flex, one side frame relative to the other, tending to keep all four wheels in contact with the ground over rougher surfaces. The additional tubing components add weight to the chair and the moving parts can work loose and wear over time (Fig. 25.1).

Fixed frame chairs do not fold flat but usually have a backrest that folds down onto the seat. In manual wheelchair form they are generally used for more active people because they are lighter and stiffer, meaning that less energy is required for propulsion. With the wheels removed (there is a quick release mechanism) and the backrest folded, some car drivers can

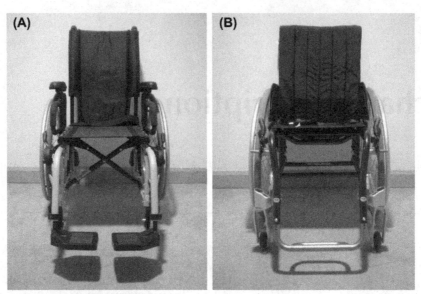

FIG. 25.1 (A) Folding frame wheelchair (note the cross brace). (B) Fixed frame wheelchair.

pull the wheelchair frame between themselves and the steering wheel, placing it on either the passenger or rear seat. The rear wheels of the chair are stowed separately inside the car.

As they are fixed, these chairs do not conform so well to less even surfaces but this can be less of an issue since they tend to be set up with more weight over the rear axle to allow the user to perform "wheelies", a critical aspect of negotiating kerbs and rough terrain.

Most powered wheelchairs have a fixed frame, only a small number being designed to be folded and lifted into a car boot. More commonly, the user will travel seated in their wheelchair as this avoids both them having to transfer and the manual handling issues associated with lifting a heavy chair into a car boot, even if it does break down into a number of smaller components. Wheelchair hoists installed in the car are available where the person is able to transfer to a normal car seat.

Wheels (manual chairs)

Usually measured in imperial units, the rear wheels of an occupant propelled wheelchair are between 20″ and 26″ (in 2″ increments). The smaller size is used with children and the largest by adults wanting higher "gearing". Tyres can be fitted with pneumatic tubes or solid inserts. The latter will clearly avoid punctures but some people prefer the ride of a pneumatic tyre which can provide improved comfort. Solid inserts also add weight.

Attendant propelled manual wheelchairs usually have 12″ or 16″ rear wheels and are usually fitted with solid tyres. Simpler rear wheels like this may help reduce maintenance costs compared to larger, spoked wheels fitted with pneumatic tyres. They are easier to stow in a car boot but many attendants prefer to have the larger diameter wheel as it makes the wheelchair easier to push: it overcomes obstacles with significantly more ease than the smaller wheel.

Push rims (manual chairs)

These are the secondary rim, distanced from the wheel rim itself, used to grip and turn the wheel by the person. Different materials and surface coverings are available to suit individual need and preference. The distance of the rim from the wheel can be critical, particularly for those with reduced hand function. Also available are "capstan" rims, having a series of projections against which someone with reduced or inability to grip can push.

Castor wheels

These are the smaller wheels positioned at the front and/or the back of a chair, depending on wheel layout. They should ideally be used as stabilizers and not bearers of significant weight. Why? Because the more weight that is applied, the more difficulty the castor has in rotating about its stem, having a profound impact on the manoeuvrability of the wheelchair. The axle having the largest wheels would, in an ideal world, bear all of the weight, but in reality we know that because this would be unstable there is a need for some form of stabilization. This is discussed in more detail in the stability section, below.

Brakes

There are three groups of braking mechanism on a wheelchair:

1) Those which act directly on the tyre and which are either on or off (manual and powered chairs)
2) A drum or disc braked hub (manual chairs only) which can be used to slow the wheelchair when descending a hill, and/ or a mechanism to allow them to be used as parking brakes
3) Those which are intrinsic to a powered chair gearbox

Brakes acting directly on the tyre might be considered a crude engineering solution because they use a simple metal bar with/without a plastic shoe pushed into and distorting the face of the tyre, which is locked in place by an over-centre mechanism. Hub brakes, operated using a handle and cable, are operated only by an attendant and whilst they may add a little convenience in not having to stoop either side of the chair, they also add weight and cost to production/ongoing maintenance.

Foot and lower leg support

Providing support for the feet is a challenge to the wheelchair designer and prescriber alike. Supports must offer sufficient adjustment to cater for varying leg length whilst at the same time being of sufficient strength to bear the weight of the feet and lower legs. Added to this is the common requirement for them to swing to the side to allow access for a standing transfer. Footplates are in a vulnerable position at the front of the chair and often become entangled with door frames, drop kerbs and all manner of other obstructions, leading to distortion of the supports and loss of position.

Some manual wheelchair designs are inclusive of a fixed foot support in the front section of the frame and do not, as a result, swing away. They are less susceptible to damage but do not offer so much scope for adjustment.

Powered chairs frequently have available a central foot board, i.e. one that is suspended from a mounting fitted centrally under the front of the seat pan. The advantage is that there are no lateral hangers meaning that the turning circle of the chair is reduced and there is less chance of the foot support becoming snagged in a door frame. Central footplates tend to be more robust, being well suited to people who push strongly through their feet. The drawbacks are that many are produced in one piece meaning that footplate height cannot be adjusted individually, although this is not always the case. Secondly, they demand that the feet sit close together, which means there must be sufficient range of movement in the hips.

Elevating leg rests (ELRs) are used to support the knees in an extended position but there are two potential problems:

1) They do not always travel so far back (when lowered) as a normal foot plate, which extends the length of the wheelchair, which can give rise to problems with access
2) Where the hamstrings are tight (see chapter on postural management), elevated leg rests will tend to pull the pelvis into a posterior tilt, causing the buttocks and legs to slide forward in the seat which in turn creates problems with skin damage; alternatively, raised leg rests may cause the (flexed) knees to rise and then, because they lack support in this position, fall to one side, causing a rotation in the pelvis and trunk

ELRs can be manually adjusted or powered, which may allow independent adjustment by the occupant. Where there is sufficient joint range, they can be a useful adjunct to the wheelchair user having problems with swelling in their ankles or with pain. Furthermore, having an alternative position can extend the period able to be tolerated sitting in the wheelchair, which may in turn improve independence and participation.

Third party components are often fitted, such as brackets to position support outside the scope provided in the original design, and means of locating the feet more securely, i.e. moulded plates and straps.

Arm support

These are most commonly used to support the weight of the arms through the elbows/forearms, with hands tending to fall in the lap. Arm supports are also used as a surface against which to push when rising to stand from a chair. Some are reduced in depth to allow access under desks. Others are adjustable in height to suit individual need. Most are removable, either completely or swing back out of the way to allow the person to transfer sideways out of their chair onto another surface.

Arm support is usually accompanied by some form of clothes guard on the inner side to protect clothing from entanglement and dirtying on the rear wheel. Clothes guards also help to contain the seat cushion and can provide lateral location to the pelvis to aid postural stability. Wheelchairs for more active users often dispense with armrests as they can hinder access to the wheels.

Trays can be used to support the weight of the arms, reducing the drag on the shoulder girdle, and/or to provide a surface on which to carry out functional tasks. They can be wooden or of some form of plastic. They are frequently ill fitting and are prone to failure, mostly because of the number of times they are fitted and removed. They can also be a barrier to social inclusion, e.g. in not allowing the person to join others at the meal table, or in not allowing a small child to climb/be placed onto the person's lap.

Weight of the chair (manual chairs)

Whilst it is true in theory that a lighter wheelchair might be easier to push, both for the occupant and attendant, it is entirely possible to make a heavier wheelchair feel lighter if the position of the centre of gravity is placed over the axle having the larger wheels. Many chairs have adjustable axle positions but they are frequently left in the default position as the chair left the factory, i.e. the most stable position, the wheels being set back as far as they will go.

The weight of the chair is a particularly critical factor for people who need to routinely perform awkward lifts of the wheelchair e.g. wheelchair users who are independently transferring into the driver's seat of a car.

The weight of the individual will also, to some extent, dictate the weight of the wheelchair. Heavier people require stronger chair frames, and this adds weight. Again, though, the potential for adjustment of the axle positions is critical.

Methods of propulsion (manual chairs)

By far the most common method of propulsion in manual wheelchairs is with the hands on the wheel push rims. An alternative method of propulsion is with one hand and one foot, as in the case of someone having had a stroke leading to hemiparesis. Less commonly, both feet can be used without assistance from the hands. The wheelchair will then typically be propelled backwards since to gain sufficient grip on the floor and to pull forwards is extremely demanding of the leg muscles and will tend to pull the person down in the seat.

A further derivative is the one-arm drive manual wheelchair. Here, one wheel has a push rim as normal, and the other wheel has none. Instead, a linkage connects one wheel to the other, with a second, smaller rim being presented to the user on the same side as the normal rim. It is then possible to propel with one arm/hand, but a high level of dexterity is required to manipulate the rims either together or individually. It also requires a reasonably high level of cognitive functioning to be able to dissociate movement of the adjacent rims and to associate each rim to a particular wheel. The linkage between the wheels either concertinas or is telescopic, where the chair has a folding frame.

Many attempts have been made over the years to develop lever propulsion, i.e. similar to rowing but with the "oars" vertical and with both being pushed forward at the same time, rather than pulled. The levers may act either directly on the tyre or may activate the hub via a geared linkage.

Self propulsion biomechanics

The biomechanical action of manual propulsion is a complex subject which cannot be covered in detail within the context of this book. The principle considerations are to bring the rims as close to the hips as possible and for the rear axle to be as far underneath the person as possible whilst maintaining an acceptable amount of instability (see section below). A very stable wheelchair, of course, is not efficient to push and will prevent the pulling of a wheelie to allow access up/down steps/kerbs and over rough ground. The main considerations in terms of adjustment to the wheelchair are as follows:

- Size of rear wheel (diameter & tread width)
- Type of wheel construction
- Type and tread pattern of tyre
- Type and position of push rim
- Position of rear wheel centre, in terms of fore/aft and up/down, relative to the shoulder
- Camber angle of rear wheels — negative camber, i.e. tops of wheels leaning inwards, improves the straight line stability of the wheelchair as a leaning wheel will, when rolling, tend to turn in the direction of the lean
- Size of castor wheel (diameter & tread width)
- Type and tread pattern of tyre

- Castor trail angle — a small angle of trail will assist straight line stability because to turn, the front of the chair must be elevated slightly

It is critical for a wheelchair to be adjusted to suit the person and their intended use (Engström, 2002). There are many adjustments possible and each can have a profound effect, both positive and negative, on the functionality of the wheelchair.

Seat cushions and back supports

The former term usually refers to seating placed under the buttocks and thighs; the latter to support for the trunk. There are hundreds, if not thousands, of seat cushions available on the market. As such, it is necessary to define a specification for what is desired. This will include consideration of:

- Shape
- Comfort
- Stability
- Tissue integrity
- Ease of interfacing with a specific wheelchair
- Function, e.g. type of transfer
- Weight
- Durability
- Cost
- Local service preferences

Of course the individual may also have preferences and past experience of different cushions which must also be considered. Additional shaping/support is often available in the form of inserts for the cushion.

Modular seats

Mostly confined to paediatric equipment, modular seats include both seat and back in a package that can be fitted to a range of different bases and can be adjusted for growth. They usually include a variety of seat cushion shapes, options for lateral pelvic and trunk support, and a variety of head, knee and foot supports.

"Special seating"

This is a commonly used term without a common definition. It generally includes custom contoured seating (see section below) but may also include the more complex forms of modular seating, together with "comfort" chairs (see below). As such, it is a term that is perhaps best avoided, or at least used with further explanation.

"Comfort" chairs

This, again, is a commonly used term, but not consistently. It generally refers to a complete, modular wheelchair system, i.e. chassis and seating, having a high level of postural support coupled with adjustable tilt-in-space and recline, with the option to fit a variety of postural supports. It sits in the gap between a standard wheelchair and custom contoured seating, i.e. where someone can be positioned symmetrically but where a posteriorly tilted position is required to maintain such a position.

Mostly prescribed for adults, there are a smaller number of children's versions available.

Customisable modular seating

In recent years there have been introduced to the market a number of seating systems which are modular in the sense that they can be configured into different sizes and levels of support, but which accommodate more asymmetry than "standard" modular seating. Typically this will include:

- A seat base which can be adjusted to accommodate pelvic obliquity, pelvic rotation, leg length discrepancy, uni or bilateral hip flexion limitation, limited hip ab/adduction

- A back support being able to accommodate mild/moderate kyphoscoliosis, lumbar hyperlordosis, and/or posterior rib prominences

These systems allow the clinician to supply a specifically shaped seating system to meet the needs of someone with moderate postural need who would, otherwise, have needed to have been supplied with a custom contoured seating system. This has the advantage of reducing the number of appointments and, to some extent, purchase cost, and also gives greater scope for adjustment into the future.

Inevitably there comes a point where the level of postural need is too high, either because body shapes are more extreme, or because the required level of stability for the supports cannot be facilitated in such a system.

Tilt-in-space versus recline

The former term refers to a system of support which moves the body in one unit and in one orientation in the sagittal plane, where the hips, knees, ankles, spine and head maintain their relative positions. Recline, by contrast, refers to motion of the back support alone, hinged at the base, which opens the hip angle, leaving the legs in the same position.

Reclining wheelchairs were developed to provide an alternative position for people having/choosing to sit for extended periods. The problem, of course, is that there is a natural tendency to slide in a seat where the backrest is reclined and the seat is level (try this out yourself) caused by the person's centre of mass falling behind their pelvis, i.e. outside their base of support. Able bodied people are able to correct such a position but people using wheelchairs are less able. The result is unsustainable shearing forces in the soft tissues under the ischial tuberosities caused by friction between the skin, clothing and surface of the seat. This is ultimately likely to lead to the development of tissue damage and pressure ulceration.

Tilt-in-space, on the other hand, reduces these problems because although the person's centre of mass still falls outside their base of support, their ischial tuberosities are resting on an inclined surface and do not experience the same degree of damaging, shearing forces (care is taken not to suggest that shearing forces are absent).

Having suggested that recline alone can lead to harmful forces in soft tissues, if used in conjunction with tilt-in-space it can, in contrast, provide improved postural alignment and reduced energy expenditure since gravity is used powerfully to secure a position. This is found in a variety of wheelchairs and also in riser-recliner armchairs which often tilt by a small amount as they recline. Note that a tilted and reclined position is likely to be less functional and socially interactive, so may be of limited use for some people.

The other use for recline is in reducing pressure on the lower abdomen. Immobile people often have difficulties with digestion and bowel movement. Opening the hip angle may help with this, much as sitting back in one's chair after a big dinner is more comfortable. In some cases, recline is required to allow a urinal bottle to be placed effectively between the legs, particularly in the case of an anteriorly tilted pelvis where opening the hip angle draws the urethra up and back from its otherwise very low position where access can be difficult.

Further information is available in the paper by Michael et al. (2007) which is a systematic review of nineteen previous studies looking into the effectiveness of tilt-in-space. It was found that little evidence existed for function derived from a tilted position, but that tilting posteriorly beyond an angle of 20° reduced tissue interface pressures for those with spinal cord injury.

Tilt-in-space and stability

When the tilt mechanism of a chair is adjusted, the weight distribution is altered (Fields, 1992) where there is a fixed point of rotation between seat frame and chassis. Where two pivots or centres of rotation are used, the centre of mass moves far less, keeping the stability characteristics more constant. This mechanism may also be referred to as a "floating pivot/tilt" and allows for a shorter wheelbase dimension (distance between front and rear axles) compared to a fixed point tilt (Fig. 25.2).

Tilt-in-space base

A common term to define a chassis onto which seating can be fitted or interfaced, coupled with the ability to tilt to a variable angle. Many of these bases also have the ability to vary the angle of recline (seat to back angle), either with a gas strut/sprung pins, which may or may not be preferable, and some require use of a tool. They generally offer a lower seat to ground height to allow space for a seating system without making the knee height too great. Many have space between the seat rails to allow a seating system to be "sunk" further into the chassis.

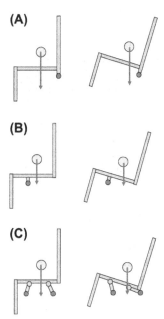

FIG. 25.2 Larger circles indicate centre of mass of person; arrows indicate where this falls relative to pivot point(s) on wheelchair chassis, shown as small circles, (A) — fixed pivot (rear): centre of mass moves backwards (and up) as seat is tilted, reducing rearward stability, (B) — fixed pivot (front): centre of mass moves backwards as seat is tilted, reducing rearward stability, (C) — floating pivot: centre of mass broadly maintains its position relative to the chassis; note that there are variations on the linkage mechanism which have the same effect.

Buggies

There are a wide variety of buggies available for small children having additional postural need. As well as extra supports, many also include a tilt-in-space mechanism. Many have a reclining mechanism, which can present fewer issues for a small child than an adult, and mirrors mainstream buggies in that there is an expectation that the child will need to sleep during the day. Increasingly, aesthetics are being addressed with many systems looking very similar to those available on the high street.

The transition from a buggy to a wheelchair can be a difficult issue for parents. It can be perceived as confirmation of disability since transition from a buggy is normally to a walking child. Where the parent is not ready to take the step into the world of wheelchairs and a buggy still offers appropriate support, function and mobility, provision of a buggy should continue: it is suggested that it is unwise to make hard and fast rules about an age where a buggy is no longer appropriate. As always, the decision should relate to the individual and their circumstances.

Straps and harnesses

There are a large number of straps and harness available for use with wheelchairs. Beyond a basic safety belt fitted across the pelvis, one should take great care in prescribing such equipment as it can act, or be seen to act, as a form of restraint. If the person is able to move and this does not cause any particular issues, why contain the movement? Clearly there are reasons of safety, e.g. preventing feet falling into the wheels of the chair, but this should be explored in detail prior to prescription. It is often the case that straps are fitted because straps have always been fitted, and that straps are only used because they are fitted.

The following questions may be helpful: What is the aim of the strap/harness? Will it, realistically, achieve its aim? Is the person happy with its use? What are the chances of it being used as intended? What are the chances of it not being used as intended? Will it be used at all? If satisfactory answers can be provided, a harness may be indicated.

It is worth reviewing the paragraph in the first chapter in this section on consent to assessment and treatment. Where the fitting of a strap/harness could be construed as a form of restraint a risk assessment should be used to cover the situation and must include a risk/benefit analysis, for example in the case of a forearm strap to prevent the arm falling off the side of the armrest leading to a risk of entanglement with the spokes of the wheel.

Adaptations, modifications and "specials"

There is a substantial range of components and devices available commercially which negate the need for manufacture of commonly used items. It is optimal to use such equipment where possible, rather than to manufacture such equipment, as costs are reduced and the relevant regulations will (should) have been covered.

However, one of the most crucial roles for the clinical engineer in the field of rehabilitation engineering is in adapting and modifying equipment, and in some cases producing a bespoke design to meet particular clinical needs.

Adaptations maintain the original purpose and function of the piece of equipment whereas the term modification implies that the piece of equipment has been taken outside its original purpose. Specials are bespoke, one-off items of equipment designed and manufactured to meet the needs of an individual. They may comprise readily available components but will use them in a unique manner. Within Europe it is necessary to comply with the requirements of the Medical Devices Regulations.

Powered seat raise/lower

On some powered chairs it is possible to fit a raiser unit which alters the height of the entire seat unit. Some systems focus on raising the seat up to allow improved social integration and/or access to cupboards/book shelves normally out of reach in sitting. Others focus on lowering the seat to the ground, typically children's chairs designed for use in a play/school environment where being able to communicate to peers at an appropriate level is important. A small number of wheelchairs are designed around the need to adjust height and so may offer both the ability to raise and to lower.

Standing wheelchairs

Some wheelchairs are designed specifically to allow the person to stand, offering the ability to move from sitting to standing, according to function and social circumstance. This can work very well for some but the complexity of the necessary mechanisms adds weight, which is critical in a manual wheelchair in terms of self propulsion. The chairs tend to be more bulky which can create problems with access.

All systems maintain the lower leg and knee in position with a footplate and anterior support just below the knee. Some systems then raise the person from this position, extending the knee and hip in the process. Others first elevate the legrest and recline the backrest so that the person is supine, then rotate the person into a standing position, as if they were on a tilt table in a physio gym.

Adding even minimal postural support can be very difficult, or even contra-indicated, as the body changes shape between sitting and standing, and the mechanism of levers do not articulate in exactly the same way as the hips, knees and ankles, resulting in postural supports being aligned correctly in one orientation but not in the other.

Such chairs can be anything up to ten times more expensive than a chair without a standing mechanism which, for most people, removes the possibility of even considering the acquisition of such a chair.

Sports chairs and adaptations for sport

There are many manual wheelchairs made for the sole purpose of a particular sport (e.g. track racing, basketball, rugby, etc). Being highly tuned to a specific activity will preclude routine everyday use and so it is unreasonable to expect one wheelchair to meet all requirements. Powered wheelchairs can be fitted with additional components (bumper guards) to allow participation in some ball games. It can also be necessary to alter seating components to allow participation in sport, particularly Boccia (Ibrahim, 2012).

Transportation

Wherever possible, wheelchair users should be transferred to a standard vehicle seat for the purposes of transportation, with the wheelchair being stowed as luggage. There are instances where this is either unsafe due to lack of postural support or not possible because the person cannot transfer without a hoist. It is then a requirement that the wheelchair be suitable for use in transportation.

In 2010 a group of experts developed by consensus a best practice guideline in this respect. This was updated in 2018 and published the following year (Appleyard, 2019). It is recommended that reference be made to this work for further information.

Over the last 10−15 years there has been a marked increase in the number and quality of vehicles adapted to transport an individual seated in their wheelchair. These are known as wheelchair accessible vehicles, or "WAVs", tend to carry one person and are often based on a small van, being modified by specialist firms. They can be relatively inexpensive to purchase. Access can be via a ramp, which may also come with a winch, or via a powered lift either at the rear or side of the vehicle. Difficulties can arise where the person is tall, more in passing through the door aperture than in relation to the height available inside. Width and length can also cause problems in some cases. A further option is an adapted car although these tend to be considerably more expensive than their van-derived cousins.

Maintenance, repairs and insurance

Well used wheelchairs require regular attention to their mechanical and electrical systems. Costs may not be insignificant in the case of the more complex or technologically advanced systems. In some countries this is paid for by the state but where purchase of equipment is undertaken privately, the likely costs of ongoing maintenance and repairs should not be overlooked.

As well as considering insurance protection for oneself in the event of an accident, it may also be appropriate to consider third party insurance cover. A powered wheelchair is capable of substantial, if unintentional, damage to both property and people.

Custom contoured seating

Background

This is a form of seating moulded uniquely for an individual, interfaced to a wheelchair, shower chair base or some form of static seat, and which is not re-useable by another person. It is indicated where modular or "off the shelf" systems cannot give the required level of support or shaping, and is typically used for those having:

- Established asymmetry in the pelvis and/or spine
- Critical limitation in hip/knee joint range
- Low postural ability

It may also be suitable for those having movement disorders and/or high levels of discomfort.

Materials

There are a variety of materials available, as described in Table 25.1 and in Fig. 25.4. All capture body shape using either a process of direct fitting to the patient (used only for "instant" systems and by some matrix fitters) or, far more commonly, vacuum consolidation (bead bags with a valve through which air is either introduced to soften the bag or extracted to produce a firm shape). In the case of the latter technique, the shape is captured either:

1) As a digitized image using some form of scanner, an example of which is seen in Fig. 25.3, or
2) A plaster cast, but this is a messy process in comparison and so is avoided where possible

It is not possible simply to scan body shape directly as tissues are unloaded and corrective forces have not been applied.

This image may be used, with a CNC machine, to mill either a carved foam seat or a high density foam "positive" over which a thermoplastic or interlocking material sheet can be draped. Such a "positive" may also be formed in plaster, although for a one piece seat/back being vacuum formed it must be solid, meaning that the weight of the unit can be significant.

Lynx is able to be expanded and contracted (within limits) without the need to add or remove cells. With Matrix this is achieved by arranging cells/joiners accordingly. Second Generation Matrix has the capability to fit expanding cells (through rotation of the unit). It is also available with flexible components which can be used to introduce trunk support anteriorly without impeding transfers. A skilled fitter will be able to manipulate any of the interlocking materials rapidly to fit body shape.

There is a perception (a natural reaction) that foam seats are more comfortable than either interlocking or thermoplastic moulds. However, one should remember that with custom contoured seating, the applied load is distributed over a large area, thus reducing point loads and improving comfort.

TABLE 25.1 Materials used in custom contoured seating.

	Carved/moulded foam	Interlocking (matrix, 2nd and 3rd genera-tion matrix, lynx)	Thermoplastics (ABS, HDPP, HDPE[a])	Instant systems (foam-in-place system (FIPS); bead seats)
Material	Combustion modified foams & plasterzotes of varying densities, stiff-nesses and performance characteristics	Flat sheets of interlock-ing components having a distance between cell centres of between 35 mm and 55 mm	Sheet material, usually 10 mm thickness for ABS or 6 mm for HDPP/ HDPE	FIPS: Constituent chemicals of visco-elastic foam Bead: Polystyrene beads/ bonding agent
Construction method	Foam carved out to body shape from body casts using either (a) a panto-graph arrangement comprising a tracer on the bead bag and router bit on the foam, or (b) digitized image and CNC router; waterproof membrane; usually sup-ported by a thermo-plastic or aluminium shell; removable covers in a flame retardant fabric	Either (a) direct fit with sheet hung from frame on which patient sits, or (b) draping of sheet over plaster cast taken from body casts; supportive aluminium tubing struc-ture; removable covers in a flame retardant fabric	Heated sheet material is draped over a high den-sity foam or re-enforced plaster cast of body shape with a vacuum forming machine, then trimmed and covered in a flame retardant fabric	Both are rapid setting. FIPS: Chemicals mixed in clinic and poured into poly-ethylene bag behind patient to form around body shape (a few minutes of working time). Bead: Bead bag is shaped around person; bonding agent poured and moulded whilst setting (around an hour). Both are covered in a flame retardant fabric
Speed of construction (1 being fastest)	3	4	2	1
Interfacing to chassis	Variety, attached to ther-moplastic shell	Variety, attached to tubular aluminium structure	Variety	Variety
Heat dissipation	Poor; improved by boring ventilation holes, by electrical fan assis-tance, or by using an open cell foam	Good	Poor; improved by boring series of ventila-tion holes through material	Poor
Ease of casting	Very good	Very good	Very good	Difficult as time for moulding limited to a few minutes
Potential for adjustment	Poor, due to shape being irregular and three dimensional	Extensive, but being limited ultimately by la-bour costs and skill of fitter	Least adjustable of all; some materials have very narrow period of transition between solid and liquid, making them particularly difficult to work, ABS having a wider transition period than polypropylene, for example	Very poor
Weight	Comparable with inter-locking systems once shell and interface added to foam	Comparable with a moulded foam system	ABS moulds are compa-rable with foam due to the required material thickness; others are significantly lighter due to thinner material and reduced interfacing	Dependent upon interface method

Continued

TABLE 25.1 Materials used in custom contoured seating.—cont'd

	Carved/moulded foam	Interlocking (matrix, 2nd and 3rd generation matrix, lynx)	Thermoplastics (ABS, HDPP, HDPE[a])	Instant systems (foam-in-place system (FIPS); bead seats)
Absorption of odour	Yes, over time, despite waterproofing/use of covers	Minimal (except in covers which can, of course, be laundered/replaced)	Yes, over time, despite waterproofing/use of covers	Yes, over time, despite water-proofing/use of covers
Structural integrity	Foam degrades over time, particularly where applied loads are high, leading to reduced performance; thermoplastic shells can fracture (rare); waterproofing can fail leading to rapid degradation of foam	Edges of sheet can loosen if lacking support from framework; tubing can fracture (rare) unless poorly constructed	ABS can crack, although this is less likely with thicker walls; all are dependent upon material not becoming too thin when being draped over the "positive" of body shape during vacuum forming	Foam degrades over time, particularly where applied loads are high
Areas of use	Wheelchairs, static seating	Wheelchairs, static seating	Wheelchairs, toilet seats/shower chairs	Wheelchairs, static seating
Initial costs (1 being lowest)	3	4	2	1
Long term costs	Interlocking systems offer the most scope for adjustment and so can offer a very cost effective long term solution; however, this is dependent upon the shape being correct and the seat being constructed effectively to allow future change			

[a]*Thermoplastic materials: ABS (acrylonitrile butadiene styrene), HDPP (high density polypropylene), HDPE (high density polyethylene).*

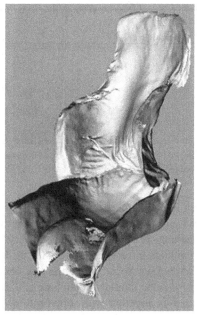

FIG. 25.3 Scanned digital image.

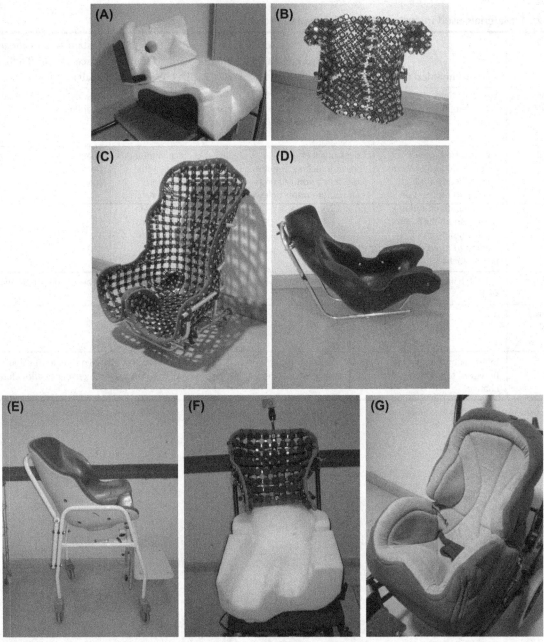

FIG. 25.4 Examples of materials, (A) Moulded foam, (B) Matrix (backrest as part of a hybrid), (C) Lynx, (D) Thermoplastic wheelchair seat, (E) Thermoplastic shower chair/commode, (F) Hybrid (moulded foam seat and Lynx backrest), (G) Custom contoured seat with covers.

Thermoplastic moulds can be lighter than interlocking and foam systems but this is dependent upon material, material thickness and method of interfacing. Lighter weight is an advantage in the slightly less common scenario of someone being able to self-propel but having the need of a custom contoured seat. There is very little scope for adjustment post-production and heat retention can be a problem. Some moulds have ventilation holes drilled at intervals.

Increasingly, hybrid seats are being prescribed, i.e. those where the seat base is made from one material and the back from another. Perhaps the most common hybrid is the moulded foam base and interlocking back. This provides protection, to a degree, against mis-positioning of the pelvis, together with a perception of comfort, coupled with the potential for adjustment in the back where fine tuning is often required due to the multi-jointed and often unstable spine/trunk/head unit. It would, in theory, be possible to create any combination of materials to meet a particular need.

Instant systems are quick to use but offer very little opportunity for adjustment of shape before the material cures. The person must be able to remain still and, in the case of foam-in-place, tolerate the heat given off by the chemical reaction of the foam constituents. Instant systems are generally suited to less complex shapes and whilst initial costs are low, these can increase where a significant amount of finishing is required post-cast.

Material choice should be guided by the particular needs and circumstances of the patient and their carers, coupled with what is available locally in terms of materials and skilled engineers. A further consideration is whether to use a one or two piece system. A one piece unit offers greater structural integrity, which may be critical for very strong individuals, whereas two piece systems offer greater scope for adjustment.

Taking a shape

The single most important determinant of a successful outcome is the configuration of the moulded material, hence one must be equipped with a full set of assessment data, including relevant background information, functional considerations and physical limitations. These limitations are used to determine an optimized postural position, further information on which may be found in the posture management section.

The skill lies in negotiating the best compromise between function and posture, within the limits set by patient and carer. This takes time to determine and may require an element of iteration, i.e. slowly adjusting the material until an optimal shape is achieved. An example is shown in Fig. 25.5, guidelines for positioning: *pelvis and legs*.

- Position casting chair upright to allow gravity to effect a shape in the casting bag
- Check and re-check pelvic position against assessment recommendations
- Ensure that the pelvis is supported posteriorly at the sacrum
- Position legs according to any joint range limitations
- Extend medial and/or lateral thigh support for control at point furthest away from hip (fulcrum)
- Ensure that the front edge of the seat is shaped to allow for tight hamstrings (check for pressure on tendons and chamfer back to form a "shark nose" where the limitation is severe)

Guidelines for positioning: *trunk*.

- Position the casting chair in posterior tilt to allow gravity to effect a shape in the back casting bag
- De-rotate the trunk relative to the pelvis, according to assessment recommendations
- Correct trunk lateral bending as far as possible without compromising pelvic position
- Completely accommodate fixed component of kyphosis — ensure there is enough depth of casting bag and soften the bag to let the shape sink in
- Ensure the shoulders are not protracted and that the shape is not encouraging an enhanced kyphosis where one is not present — pull back through the chest and shoulders
- Check the person can be removed — it is too easy to cast a seat that provides ideal support but from which it is not possible to extract the torso

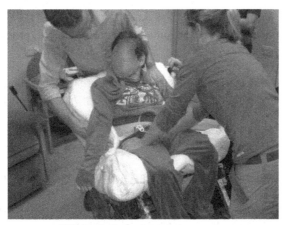

FIG. 25.5 Example of casting process.

Guidelines for positioning: *head.*

- Check alignment for breathing/swallowing/vision
- Allow for any lateral offset caused by scoliosis and pelvic obliquity
- Accommodate fixed side flexion/rotation
- Use tilt-in-space to facilitate position
- Remember that if the person has been positioned with an asymmetric head position for a long time, they may find it disturbing to be positioned in a more symmetrical position because their brain may have undergone neuroplastic adaptation to the asymmetric position

Guidelines for positioning: *feet.*

- Support where the feet want to rest relative to the knee and hip (consider tight hamstrings)
- Consider how this might conflict with the wheelchair frame/wheels
- Treat the feet as individuals
- Trial a removal of support where excessive whole body extension is an issue

Guidelines for positioning: *arms.*

- Support the weight of the arms which may otherwise pull the trunk into an enhanced kyphosis, and the head/neck into forward flexion
- Consider support from a tray or bead bag
- Remember that a natural position for the arms is with the shoulders internally rotated, i.e. hands in lap

The casting process is physically demanding of the person and the assessors, and requires a great deal of time and patience to achieve satisfactory outcomes. It is necessary to be calm, resourceful and, at times, politely authoritative, to achieve the desired aims.

Case study examples

1) A child with a deteriorating condition, having a highly complex shape, tending to get hot and have frequent issues with management of continence: may be advised to proceed with an interlocking system.
2) A child with cerebral palsy, having a moderately complex body shape, being prone to developing pressure ulcers under the ischial tuberosities and having parents who place a high priority on comfort: may be advised to use a moulded foam seat and back.
3) An adult with cerebral palsy, having a moderately complex shape, self propelling a manual chair (indoors), frequently needing to remove the seat from the chassis to allow transit in a car, and having no significant postural changes or weight gain/loss in the last few years: may wish to pursue the option of one of the lighter thermoplastic moulds, mostly because of the need for self propulsion. In this circumstance it would also be appropriate to explore whether powered mobility would be viable.
4) An adult with cerebral palsy, displaying powerful, full body extension when communicating, tending to get hot and to bruise easily, presents more of a challenge as a one piece system would provide increased structural integrity but less in the way of protection against bruising. There are a number of possible options:
   - Thermoplastic mould with holes bored for ventilation and extra padding to protect skin
   - One piece interlocking system with extra padding
   - Two piece interlocking system mounted to a seat frame having a dynamic backrest, i.e. one that has a sprung loaded and damped joint between seat and back, with the aim of accommodating powerful movements
   - Another combination according to precise circumstances of the person and what services and skills are available locally

Contraindications

There are times where custom contoured seating may appear the appropriate choice but where there are additional confounding factors which negate its use. Where someone is in a rehabilitation setting they may change shape, increase joint range, or gain increased postural ability whilst they are waiting for seating to be manufactured, rendering it unsuitable at the point of issue. Rapidly growing children are a particular challenge and there is a point at which one must accept a

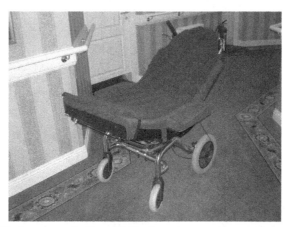

FIG. 25.6   Platform seat to facilitate mobility for someone unable to attain a seated posture.

certain amount of "wastage". People having rapidly deteriorating conditions, such as motor neurone disease or multi-systems atrophy, may deteriorate faster than the manufacturing processes for seating.

Where there are very significant issues with pain, the process of casting and fitting may be intolerable. Extreme lower limb contractures may render the person unseatable in the traditional sense. In these instances it may be appropriate to provide a small, padded and upholstered platform on a wheelchair base to facilitate mobility (Fig. 25.6).

Wheelchair stability

Overview

This is a key concept for wheelchair provision. There is a danger, in our increasingly risk-averse society, that we pay too much attention to making things safe and not enough to making them functional. If the primary purpose of a wheelchair is to enable someone to travel from A to B, then surely ease of propulsion is a significant consideration. A failure to do so may lead to dysfunctional mobility, reduced quality of life and reduced participation in society.

A very stable wheelchair is unlikely to fall over, but it is also likely to be difficult to push, either for the occupant, attendant, or both, in the following respects[a]:

- Propulsion
  - o Where the centre of mass is far forward of the rear drive wheels, the front castor wheels bear a higher proportion of the weight than if the centre of mass were farther back (see Fig. 25.7). This causes two problems:
    - Being small, castor wheels offer greater resistance to motion and so a greater pushing force is required
    - Castor wheels are less free to spin in their stems when they are loaded with increased weight causing the wheelchair to resist turning
  - o An added complication for the occupant in pushing a very stable wheelchair is that they must reach back for the wheels, reducing biomechanical efficiency and increasing the risk of shoulder injury
- Reduced straight line stability, caused by
  - o An increased tendency for the wheelchair to roll down a slope that is being traversed due to the moment created by the centre of mass being ahead of the rear axle line, coupled with the natural tendency of the castor wheels to swivel (Fig. 25.8); with powered wheelchairs, loss of traction to the drive wheel at the top of a slope will have the same effect, resulting in the wheelchair turning and slipping down the pavement towards the road
  - o Imperfections in the ground surface being more likely to throw the chair off line because the overall mass, being centred forward of the rear axle, having more effect due to a larger moment than if the centre of mass were placed closer to the rear axle
- Turning, due to the increased leverage required, caused by the centre of mass being at a distance from the fulcrum (rear axle)

---

[a] The above discussion relates mostly to the traditional large rear wheel, small front castor arrangement. The same considerations will be relevant to alternative configurations, but will need transposing.

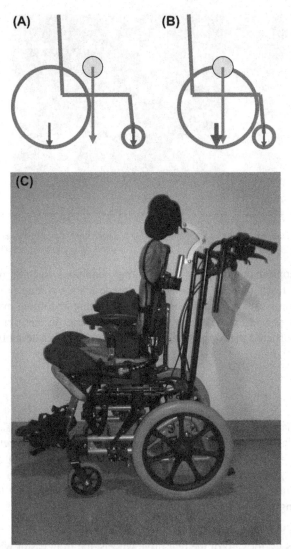

FIG. 25.7 An altered centre of mass within the frame increases the weight taken by the castor wheels (thin rimmed circle indicates combined centre of mass of wheelchair and occupant), (A) – Centre of mass forward in frame relative to rear wheel centre, (B) – Centre of mass further back in frame relative to rear wheel centre, (C) – Clinical example of seating unit bringing centre of mass forward.

- Negotiating tight turns due to a long wheelbase (distance between front and rear axle centres)
- Negotiating kerbs/obstructions, caused by the action of tipping requiring more leverage

It is necessary, then, to optimize the balance between stability and instability, a process which should be carried out jointly with the patient and their family/carers. Where there is a specific problem of stability with a particular wheelchair, it is worth considering if an alternative model might be more suitable.

Further, helpful information is available in the MHRA publication, Guidance on the Stability of Wheelchairs (2004), which can be downloaded freely within the UK.

Risk assessment

A risk assessment should be used to document considerations of stability. As mentioned above, it is all too easy to be over cautious, and whilst it is important to optimize levels of safety, it is also important to facilitate mobility, i.e. to balance risk with direct benefit or potential for benefit. To help justify decisions taken, risk assessment can be used in a positive and facilitatory manner. This is covered in more detail in the first chapter of this section.

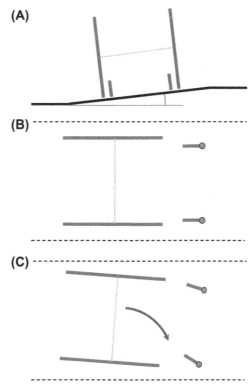

FIG. 25.8 Wheelchair tends to roll down a slope being traversed, (A) − Front view showing large rear wheels with axle and front castors, (B) − Plan view static on slope; small circles indicate castor stems, (C) − Plan view rolling across slope, rotation of castor stems turning the chair down the slope.

"Active" wheelchair users

People with very good upper body control and strength, typically paraplegics, are able to propel a manual wheelchair extremely effectively, but this is only possible because the wheelchair has been set up to have significantly reduced stability. This instability is controlled with balance of the trunk, arms and head to adjust the centre of mass during controlled manoeuvres. The occupant has also learnt the skills through practising techniques and experimenting, sometimes making mis-judgements and falling out of their chair. This is a necessary part of the process. We do not suddenly become good at something. It is necessary, then, to allow wheelchair users the chance to develop their skills and to support them as their equipment needs adjusting, or even replacing.

Effect of specific body configurations and movement patterns/disorders

It will be necessary in certain circumstances to have different approaches to stability, for example:

- Double amputees may need to have the rear wheels set back to offset the loss of mass at the front of the chair; this is likely to compromise shoulder and arm biomechanics and so alternative options may need to be explored, perhaps the use of anti-tip levers (see below) or provision of a powered wheelchair
- People with very extended hip positions may be more suited to mid-drive configurations
- Those with uncontrolled movements, such as Huntington's chorea, may need to prioritize stability over manoeuvrability

Anti-tipping levers/wheels

These are devices which are attached to the wheelchair frame, almost always at the rear, to "catch" the wheelchair, should it start to tip. They are very useful aids but are not without their problems:

- When pushing, the attendant's feet can catch the levers, particularly on narrow chairs

- Access up and down kerbs can be blocked: whilst most anti-tippers can be raised, there is then a risk that they are left in the "off" position
- They can be adjusted to be completely ineffectual, leading to false confidence
- Many can be removed altogether, even without the need for tools
- Their performance is reduced where the wheelchair is on a slope facing up the incline as the line of the centre of mass is drawn backwards: if the wheelchair starts to tip, the anti-tipping levers will be easier to overcome

Used appropriately, and in controlled circumstances, they can be an extremely effective means to facilitate improved manoeuvrability whilst maintaining safety.

Stability assessment

It is necessary to carry out a formal assessment of stability when the wheelchair has been substantially modified or where it is no longer being used within the scope defined by the manufacturer. This will apply where a seating system has been fitted since the position of the centre of mass will have changed from the original design, so stability tests carried out by the manufacturer will be nullified. This will also apply to a wheelchair prescribed for a lower limb amputee.

There are a few approaches to formal stability testing and those in clinical use generally measure static stability in four directions (facing up/down a slope, facing across a slope, left/right side higher):

- Fixed angle ramp (often 12°/16° in the UK)
  - Limited to a pass/fail result
  - Can still be useful as an indication
  - Helpful for training the user/carer
- Variable angle ramps
  - Powered and manual versions
  - Allow the determination of a precise angle of instability
  - Helpful for training the user/carer
- Force plate systems
  - Take readings of force under each wheel at two angles, typically at 0° and ∼5° to the horizontal, which together with measurement of certain dimensions of the wheelchair, allow calculation of angles of tip in all four directions
  - Reduces manual handling for operative
  - Reduces user anxiety in relation to being placed on a steep ramp
  - No opportunity for training the user/carer

It is arguable that all these methods have flaws. First and foremost, none measure dynamic stability and at the time of writing there are no known, validated methods for assessing dynamic stability, although research continues in this extremely complex subject area: assessment in motion gives rise to a startling array of variables. Secondly, there are any number of intrinsic and extrinsic variables that will affect stability: inflation pressure of tyres, angle of tilt or recline (where these are adjustable), fluctuation in weight of the occupant, additional equipment carried on the wheelchair (typically bags hung on the back of the chair).

In any assessment, then, one must consider the errors that are likely and make provision for these in any recommendations for use. A method of testing stability that is particularly flawed is to tip the wheelchair on its front and rear wheels by hand. This is more likely to produce a false positive result, i.e. that the wheelchair is sufficiently stable, because the wheels are on a flat surface rather than a slope, causing the centre of mass to be more likely to fall within the wheelbase. No measurement is taken and so no hard data can be recorded. On the other hand, in the absence of any form of measuring equipment, this method does give a very rough indication and can be used with care if its limitations are taken into consideration.

To summarize: any decision on wheelchair stability is a clinical judgement on risk versus benefit and should be recorded appropriately. All methods of stability measurement have flaws and these must be recognized. Training should be provided to occupants and attendants as appropriate.

References

Appleyard, R., 2019. International Best Practice Guidelines: BPG1 Transportation of People Seated in Wheelchairs, 1st Revision Posture and Mobility Group as derived from Tiernan, J., Appleyard, R., Arva, J., Bingham, R., Manary, M., Simms, C., Wretstrand, A., 2010. International Best Practice Guidelines: Transportation of People Seated in Wheelchairs 4th International Conference on Posture and Wheeled Mobility.

Engström, B., 2002. Ergonomic Seating: A True Challenge when Using Wheelchairs. Posturalis Books.

Fields, C.D., June 1992. Living with Tilt-In-Space. Team Rehab Report, pp. 25–26.

Ibrahim, D., Summer 2012. Seating requirements to maximise performance in Boccia. Posture Mobil. 29, 7–12.

Medicines and Healthcare products Regulatory Agency, 2004. Guidance on the Stability of Wheelchairs. Medicines and Healthcare Products Regulatory Agency, DB2004(02).

Michael, S.M., Porter, D., Pountney, T.E., 2007. Tilted seat position for non-ambulant individuals with neurological and neuromuscular impairment: a systematic review. Clin. Rehabil. 21, 1063–1074.

Chapter 26

Powered wheelchairs

Ladan Najafi[a] and David Long[b]

[a]Kent and Medway Communication and Assistive Technology Service (KM CAT) − Adults, Kent, United Kingdom; [b]AJM Healthcare & Oxford University Hospitals NHS Foundation Trust, Oxford, United Kingdom

Chapter outline

Introduction

Where an individual is unable to self-propel a manual wheelchair due to limitations in muscle strength, muscle control, or fatigue, the use of a powered wheelchair may need to be considered. Although usually more costly than manual wheelchairs, they are expected to increase an individual's independence and to improve quality of life.

There are three basic categories:

1) *Indoor:* designed to be compact and to turn in tight spaces, usually being unsuitable for any form of outdoor driving due to reduced stability, less powerful motors and batteries having less capacity
2) *Indoor/outdoor:* dual use, but more biased towards the indoor environment and limited to smoother surfaces outdoors
3) *Outdoor/indoor:* dual use, but more biased towards use outdoors, being more capable over rougher surfaces, having greater range and having greater top speed; their potential for use indoors will be governed by the amount of space available and the surfaces over which the chair will be driven − heavier chairs with courser tyre tread will tend to ruck/"chew" up carpets/rugs

In the UK, the state provides Electrically Powered Indoor (wheel)Chairs (EPIC) and Electrically Powered Indoor/Outdoor (wheel)Chairs (EPIOC). There is occasional reference to Electrically Powered indoor/Outdoor Chairs (EPOC) but these are not usually provided by the UK state.

Research indicates that provision of powered mobility in children and adults has resulted in significant improvements in several social components such as expressive behaviour, cooperation, interacting with family, in the quantity of motor activities, and in the quality of interactive and symbolic play (Rosen et al., 2009; Nilsson et al., 2011).

Appropriate postural management is a prerequisite in successful assessment and provision of a powered chair (see relevant chapter). It is then important to establish an access site that is consistent and reliable and that will enable the user to safely control the powered wheelchair. In general, a holistic assessment by a specialist multidisciplinary team will support the prescription of an appropriate seating system as well as the decision on the type of wheelchair (De Souza and Frank, 2018). This process will be similar to assessment of accessing all other assistive technologies (see relevant chapter). An additional factor when assessing for powered mobility is to determine that the user is able to initiate or cease a movement as required because safety may be compromised if they are unable to stop the chair in a timely manner. This may be caused by impaired cognitive function, poor muscle control, including involuntary movements, or a medical complication, such as poorly controlled epilepsy.

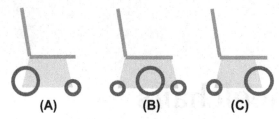

FIG. 26.1   Powered wheelchair wheel layouts, (A) — rear wheel drive, (B) — mid wheel drive, (C) — front wheel drive.

Wheel layout

The type of powered wheelchair may have direct impact on manoeuvrability, which is an important factor to consider during prescription for those users where space is an issue. Manoeuvrability will depend on the position of the drive wheels as illustrated in Fig. 26.1:

- In Rear Wheel Drive (RWD) the drive wheels are behind the centre of mass and the castor wheels are in front
- In Mid Wheel Drive (MWD), the drive wheels are directly below, or very close to, the centre of mass, the front and rear castor wheels being designed to be in contact with the ground at all times; note that at least one of the axles must be sprung so that the chair can negotiate uneven ground without 'beaching'
- In Front Wheel Drive (FWD) the drive wheels are in front of the centre of gravity and the rear castor wheels behind

Koontz et al. (2010) constructed an environment in which 90°, 180° and 360° turns were carried out both with and without barriers. The purpose was to determine the minimum space required to perform specified manoeuvrability tasks. They concluded that MWD powered wheelchairs required the least space for the 360° turn and that FWD and MWD performed better than RWD in all other tasks.

In many services, though, rear wheel drive continues to dominate, partly due to cost, partly to custom of practice, and partly because it is more intuitive to learn, particularly for people having been used to driving a car. It is important to note that there are differences in manoeuvrability between commercially available electric wheelchairs belonging to the same category (Pellegrini et al., 2010) and therefore a trial period following an assessment is advised.

The choice of wheel layout may also be driven by the person's posture: tight hamstrings may preclude some FWD and MWD chairs as the battery box tends to be placed forward in the chassis, preventing the feet from being placed behind the normal support position. The provision of a RWD chair to obese and bariatric patients, having a centre of mass in a more forward position, may give rise to (a) loss of traction at the drive wheels, (b) high rate of wear at the castor tyre/bearing/fork/stem, (c) forward instability. A FWD chair would usually be the more preferable option in this scenario. The same issues can arise with a bespoke seating system or the carriage of additional medical equipment, e.g. a ventilator, both of which can alter the position of the centre of mass.

It is also necessary to consider changes in centre of mass that occur under dynamic conditions. The effects of an adult moving within the seat when driving off a low kerb, for instance, will be greater than with a small child. A tall adult has a longer trunk and so the moments caused by movement of the shoulder girdle, arms and head are amplified compared to someone who is shorter. The centre of mass of an amputee will be further back and will reduce rearward stability. This may be particularly important when the chair is accelerated suddenly from rest when pointing up a slope. Many other examples exist and it is the job of the clinical engineer to ensure that they are considered.

Powered adjustment to position

Over the last 50 years, powered wheelchairs have become extremely diversified, allowing users with physical disabilities the option of different postural positions (Edlich et al., 2004) through various powered articulations:

- *Tilt:* orientation of the whole seating unit at an angle posterior to the vertical, allowing gravity to assist in maintaining a sitting position, or, less commonly, anterior to the vertical, enabling a forward lean position to be adopted, or to facilitate a standing transfer
- *Recline:* rearward movement of the backrest only, pivoting at the base, to allow an alternative position but which will usually induce sliding in the seat and the potential to develop pressure ulceration; recline is usually combined with tilt
- *Elevation of the legs/feet:* to assist with management of oedema and for comfort, **not** for placing the hamstrings on passive stretch; often referred to as elevating leg rests, or ELRs

- *Elevation of the whole seating unit:* to allow access to objects on higher shelves or to bring the user's head in line with those standing nearby (social inclusion)
- *Lowering of the whole seating unit:* to allow access to objects dropped on the floor or, for younger children, to allow them to be at the same height as their peers sitting on the floor or, for some adults, to allow working at an office desk
- *Passive standing:* there is a wealth of literature on the benefits of standing for people with physical disabilities, but it should be noted that standing wheelchairs are not without their problems: firstly, loss of postural support during the process of moving from sitting to standing caused by the fact that body shape changes, precluding/compromising postural support; secondly, the increased engineering complexity which can result in higher production and maintenance costs

Aspects of clinical assessment specific to powered wheelchairs

To ensure that as many of the user's needs as possible are met, all factors must be considered (see chapter on wheelchair assessment) which, specific to this context, will include:

- *Environment:* steps, ramps, door thresholds, width of corridors, tightness of turns, heights of work surfaces, access to the toilet
- *Transport:* most powered wheelchairs cannot be readily folded or dismantled to fit into a small car boot
- *Control options:* the method by which the user will control the chair must be determined, together with any limitations in control
- *Vision:* the user must have sufficient visual ability that they can see hazards such as other people, furniture, steps; in some conditions, such as stroke, people can suffer with "neglect" on the affected side which means they cannot see hazards in certain fields of vision; it is possible to drive a powered wheelchair with visual impairment if compensatory strategies are in place, e.g. turning the head to check for objects out of the field of vision, or learning and committing to memory a route from A to B
- *Epilepsy:* the onset of an epileptic seizure can cause loss of control of a powered wheelchair; this might result in coming to a sudden stop when crossing a road, or pushing and holding (involuntarily) the joystick in the full forward speed position; the condition is sometimes nocturnal or may be suitably controlled with medication; if the person drives the chair within a controlled environment and is suitably supervised, it might be deemed that the risks are minimal despite the presence of epilepsy.
- *Cognition/insight/anticipation:* the user must be able to anticipate danger and understand the implications of their actions, e.g. that running into someone could cause that person significant injury

It must be remembered that independent mobility is a significant feature of human existence and so it is important that as healthcare professionals we first open[HYPHEN]mindedly explore all means to facilitate it before concluding that it is inappropriate or not possible (Long, et al., 2019).

Control interfaces for powered wheelchairs

There are two types of control interface available: proportional and switched examples of which are shown in Fig. 26.2. Proportional control enables the user to drive the chair in whichever direction the joystick is displaced, and the greater the

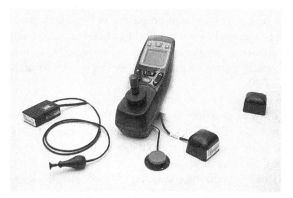

FIG. 26.2 A selection of control options.

displacement the faster the chair drives. This is not possible when switched controllers are used where it can be extremely slow to change direction and where the chair moves only at a pre-selected speed, regardless of displacement. However, switched control will be the only viable option in some scenarios/presentations.

Correct configuration of a system enables use of a powered chair to its full potential whilst maintaining safety and control. If parameters such as speed, acceleration and deceleration are not programmed appropriately, the user may feel insecure. As an example, the chair may turn too quickly, giving rise to a feeling of insecurity, and which may make the person reluctant to drive the chair. Each powered wheelchair must be set up/programmed to meet the individual's needs and preferences, according to the environment in which they drive the chair i.e. indoor, outdoor, or both. Most powered chairs can be programmed using a computer or a hand held device that plugs into the system directly.

When driving with a joystick and travelling in a straight line it is possible to make fine adjustments to direction to take account of veer caused by uneven surfaces. This highlights one of the main disadvantages of switched controllers which cannot compensate for unwanted veer or turn as they do not have the required level of control. Take the example of an individual having been set up to drive their chair with a clock face scanner and a single switch. If the chair veers to the right, they must release the switch to stop driving forward, wait for the scanner to offer the left direction (it scrolls through the directional options), select the left direction to correct the veer, wait for the chair to move sufficiently to the left, release the switch to stop driving left, wait until the forward option is offered on the scanner, select forward, and finally carry on driving forward, until a further change of direction is required when the whole procedure must be repeated.

Veer is caused by gravity affecting the castors that are swivelling in the direction of the slope on which the chair is being driven (Langner et al., 2008) and is most evident in RWD and FWD configurations. Even the direction of the pile of carpeted floor will cause a powered wheelchair to veer. Veer can be corrected to a very limited extent through programming. Some manufacturers have addressed this problem through the use of additional electronic components, for example using a gyroscopic system which detects and corrects position.

Specialized controls

The most common method for control of a powered wheelchair, the proportional joystick, is typically positioned for use with the hand on the side of the chair or in midline. Joysticks may also be positioned for access by chin, tongue or foot (please refer to the "access" chapter). Where an individual is not able to use a standard setup an alternative option, commonly known as specialized controls, will need to be considered. This is necessary where, for example, the user is unable to exert sufficient force to operate a standard joystick, has limited range of active movement, or has only one reliable access site, but requires access to more than one assistive device. Specialized controls may provide more efficient access to powered mobility and other assistive devices (please refer to the "integrated access" chapter).

It is critical that a thorough assessment is conducted in order to identify precisely what is required from the controls. Of particular importance is to understand any physical limitations. It is also necessary to modify the approach according to the age and cognitive abilities of the user. The input of carers and family members will be invaluable.

The following list includes commonly used examples of specialized controls:

- *Switch arrays:* this setup uses several switches with each one allocated to a specific direction; these can be positioned separately as required for ease of the individual's access; switches may be mechanical or electronic (refer to "access" chapter); the powered chair control system can be set up in either momentary or latched mode
  - o In momentary mode, the chair is only driven whilst the user is in contact with the switch: for those users who cannot maintain the contact but are able to press and release the switch quickly, latched mode can be used
  - o The latched option requires a detailed assessment because it is important that the user, or attendant, can stop the chair immediately, as and when required; when the latched option is considered, the chair is usually programmed so that the switch has to be pressed at regular intervals, e.g. every 10 s, to reactivate the latch; it is necessary to provide an emergency stop switch for reasons of safety — this would be activated either by the user and/or an attendant
- *Scanner using a single switch:* a sequence of directions, often in the form of a clock face, is offered to the user at a set interval of time; the user is required to press the switch when the desired direction is offered; the interval between offered directions can be adjusted to the individual; single switch scanning is time consuming, cognitively demanding and requires timing skills, but for some users with limited motor skills and one reliable access site, single switch can be faster and less effortful than using two switch scanning
- *Scanner using two switches:* one switch is used for scanning through directions and the other to select the desired direction and drive the chair, thus it can be faster or more controlled than timed scanning

- *Sip and puff:* the technology is used for those with good oral motor skills where no other means of access can be established e.g. for people with very high level spinal cord injuries; the set up can be customized for each user, for example hard puff − forward, soft puff − right, soft sip − left and hard sip − reverse; this can also be set up with both latched and momentary modes but because this is a form of switched system, the same limitations exist; one must also have sufficient controlled head movement to be able to negotiate the end of the tube
- *Mini/light joysticks:* these are designed for those individuals with restricted movement and poor strength where fine motor control is intact, e.g. people with muscular dystrophy; this can be set up/positioned to be used by hand, chin or tongue; the smallest type requires force exertion of less than 10 g with the joystick itself being approximately the same cross-sectional size as a match stick and about 10 mm in length, thus requiring minimal movement to reach full displacement; as a result, it is necessary to have very fine motor skills
- *Tablet control:* this is a flat, touch proportional control which can be operated by only touching and remaining in contact with the surface of the tablet
- *Heavy duty joystick:* for those who, due to their physical impairment, may damage standard joysticks due to the exertion of very large amounts of force and extreme gross motor movement caused by a lack of fine motor skills
- *Foot control:* suitable for those who are unable to use their hand or head but have reasonable, reliable and consistent movement to activate a foot control system that may be switch, joystick or a combination
- *Finger pot steering control:* this is a proportional control which does not require any physical contact to drive a wheelchair; the position of the user's finger is detected, as if it were a joystick shaft; if the user's finger is in the centre of the control, this is recognized as the joystick being in neutral and the wheelchair will be stationary; it will then drive in the direction that the finger moves
- *Assisted driving options:* in normal development, children experience mobility at an early age, i.e. crawling at around seven to ten months of age; assisted driving options are intended for those children and young adults with complex physical and/or cognitive disabilities who may not be able to drive a powered wheelchair independently but who otherwise are not able to experience mobility; this may be in the form of using a track system through infrared technology such as the Smart Wheelchair (Nisbet et al., 1988) or Sensing Collision Avoidance Device (SCAD) through ultrasonic technology (Langner, 1996); SCAD creates a safe environment for the user by detecting obstacles and helping avoid collisions which could otherwise increase anxiety about driving; sometimes, use of such technology is a first step for introduction of driving and as the child develops the appropriate skills, it may be appropriate to change to a standard or specialized controls option

Controls should be tailored to the individual, a range of possibilities being considered for each situation. There may also be the requirement to take into account other equipment which may include integrated systems (see relevant chapter), as shown in Fig. 26.3.

Powered assistance to manual wheelchairs

Pushrim activated power assisted wheelchair (PAPAW)

The PAPAW augments the power applied to the push rims by the occupant through the use of motors and batteries. They can either be retro-fitted to an existing wheelchair, or purchased as part of a complete system. When the push rims are

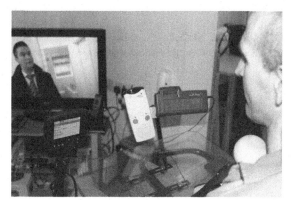

FIG. 26.3 Access with a chin joystick and integrated access including an environmental control.

moved, the effect is amplified, resulting in less effort being required to achieve motion. Some systems also amplify the braking effect from resistance applied by the occupant to the rims. A microprocessor is used to determine the amount of acceleration or braking effect based on the input received from its sensors. It can also be tuned to provide differential input to each wheel, or an increased coasting effect between pushes (Cooper et al., 2004).

Powered wheelchairs can be difficult and clumsy to control in an indoor environment. The PAPAW allows the control of a manual chair indoors but provides assistance to propulsion outdoors, meaning that in some instances two wheelchairs are not required. Since the PAWPAW augments rather than replaces manual propulsion, the motors and batteries need not be so large as those contained in a fully powered wheelchair. This has the effect of reducing weight which allows the use of lighter weight wheelchair frames and easier manoeuvring of the wheelchair into a car, either by the occupant or an attendant. Degeneration of the shoulder joint is a common problem amongst people having propelled manual wheelchairs for many years (Cooper et al., 2004). The PAPAW may help to delay the onset of such injuries or may help those who already have an injury.

Add-on power packs

Manual wheelchairs can be heavy to push for the attendant, particularly where the occupant is an adult. A powered wheelchair is one solution to this problem but it is (a) expensive, (b) difficult to drive as an attendant due to not being seated in the moving vehicle, and (c) difficult to drive in an indoor environment compared to a manual chair, as mentioned above. Instead, it is possible to fit a device known as an "add-on power pack" to a manual chair which comprises a battery, motor/gearbox and drive wheel which is fitted as one unit between the rear wheels of the chair using a special bracket. A simple lever fitted to one of the push handles controls speed. Some systems offer a reverse function.

The system is particularly effective at enabling transit over greater distances but must be detached or disengaged to allow turning in very small spaces such as in the home or small shops.

References

Cooper, R.A., Cooper, R., Schmeler, M., Boninger, M., March 2004. Push for power. Rehab. Manage. 17 (3), 32–36.
De Souza, L.H., Frank, A.O., 2018. Clinical features of electric powered indoor/outdoor wheelchair users with spinal cord injuries: a cross-sectional study. Assist. Technol. 23, 1–8.
Edlich, R.F., Nelson, K.P., Foley, M.L., Buschbacher, R.M., Long, W.B., Ma, E.K., 2004. Technological advances in powered wheelchairs. J. Long Term Eff. Med. Implant. 14 (2), 107–130.
Koontz, A.M., Brindle, E.D., Kankipati, P., Feathers, D., Cooper, R.A., May 2010. Design features that affect the manoeuvrability of wheelchairs and scooters. Arch. Phys. Med. Rehabil. 91 (5), 759–764.
Langner, M., 1996. The development of special mobility systems at Chailey Heritage. In: 1st Symposium on Powered Vehicles for Disabled Persons. ISBN:0 9527524 0 9.
Langner, M., Sanders, D., 2008. Controlling wheelchair direction on slopes. J. Assist. Technol. 2 (2), 32–41.
Long, D., McConnell, J., Harbach, G., 2019. Powered mobility. In: Cowan, D., Najafi, L. (Eds.), Handbook of Electronic Assistive Technology. Elsevier Academic Press.
Nilsson, L., Eklund, M., Nyberg, P., Thulesius, H., November–December 2011. Driving to learn in a powered wheelchair: the process of learning joystick use in people with profound cognitive disabilities. Am. J. Occup. Ther. 65 (6), 652–660.
Nisbet, P.D., Loudon, I.R., Odor, J.P., 1988. The CALL centre smart wheelchair. In: Proc. 1st International Workshop on Robotic Applications to Medical and Health Care, Ottawa.
Pellegrini, N., Bouche, S., Barbot, F., Figère, M., Guillon, B., Lofaso, F., June 2010. Comparative evaluation of electric wheelchair manoeuvrability. J. Rehabil. Med. 42 (6), 605–607.
Rosen, L., Arva, J., Furumasu, J., Harris, M., Lange, M.L., McCarthy, E., Kermoian, R., Pinkerton, H., Plummer, T., Roos, J., Sabet, A., Vander Schaaf, P., Wonsettler, T., Winter 2009. RESNA position on the application of power wheelchairs for paediatric users. Assist. Technol. 21 (4), 218–225.

Chapter 27

Electronic assistive technology

Chapter outline

Clinical Engineering. https://doi.org/10.1016/B978-0-08-102694-6.00027-9

Introduction and assessment

Donna Cowan[a], Jodie Rogers[b] and Ladan Najafi[b]

aChailey Clinical Services, East Sussex, UK; bKent and Medway Communication and Assistive Technology Service (KM CAT) – Adults, Kent, UK

Introduction

Equipment such as alternative computer access, environmental control systems, communication aids and powered mobility are some of the main examples of Electronic Assistive Technology (EAT). All of these devices provide different functions; some of them can be integrated into a single device e.g. a communication aid will often have facility to control an environmental control system, and computers can be used as communication aids. The range of commercially available solutions suitable for consideration both as equipment and as access methods is constantly evolving, many mainstream devices having applications directly intended to meet the needs of someone with a disability, or having accessibility options built into the standard software e.g. Windows "Ease of Access" or iOS "Accessibility" options. In assessing for the optimal access method, a team should always look for the most efficient and reliable method available for the client for that given activity. It follows, then, that different solutions may be required for different activities.

EAT and posture management

A prerequisite to achieving successful access and control of technology is appropriate postural management. The individual needs to be in a position that is supported, comfortable and promotes function (Chantry and Crombie, 2019, p. 53). A functional seating position is one that enhances function and postural control whilst simultaneously decreasing effort, spasticity or involuntary movements (Pope, 2007; Pountney et al., 2004; Trefler and Taylor, 1991; Steen et al., 1991). When sitting in a supported position, an individual can attend to a task without the distraction of trying to control their posture. If the client is comfortable, they will be more likely to maintain their position for an appropriate period of time, ensuring that the access method can be placed in the same position repeatedly which means they should be able to reach and activate it consistently and reliably.

As a result, it is often recommended that, where possible, an individual's postural management is addressed prior to assessment for access to EAT (please refer to postural management section).

Assessment

Once posture management needs have been addressed, motor, sensory-perceptual, cognitive, linguistic and psycho-social skills need to be assessed along with a discussion around what the client wishes to achieve using the equipment (Cowan and Najafi, 2019; Cook and Polgar, 2014). This information can be gathered in a number of ways including observation, assessment and reports from family and other professionals/teams associated with the client. Examples of assessment charts/templates are available from a variety of sources, such as websites, or directly from AT services or companies.

Observation of the client will reveal their range of movements and over which part of the body the client has the greatest control. This will form the starting point for determining how the interface will be activated. Consideration of movement patterns such as asymmetric tonic neck reflex (ATNR), extensor patterns, tremor etc, need also to be known such that accidental activation is avoided, or if this cannot be avoided that the client's safety is not compromised e.g., if considering powered mobility.

Any visual or hearing impairment needs to be known as this can affect the shape, size and position of an interface, and the number of options which a client can access at any one time. Cognitive issues must be considered so that the client remains safe and that the activity is presented at an appropriate level. Whilst EAT can help fill the gap between a client's physical skills and their cognitive skills, providing them with a device of which they do not have an adequate understanding will not enhance their independence. In some instances, clients find it difficult to learn new skills, remember instructions, or have an awareness of danger.

When looking for activities for an assessment, consideration of the client's interests and identifying a subject which motivates them is necessary in order to promote best efforts. This is particularly important when assessing children and in particular those who cannot communicate verbally.

The assessment is a complex process that requires a cycle of initial assessment, implementation and evaluation. Furthermore, as technology develops, more suitable devices may become available or, as an individual's abilities change, the device may no longer meet their needs. A process of regular review should ideally take place to ensure that the user's needs continue to be met in the long term.

The end goal of any assessment is to provide a solution that has value, therefore assessment is not the end point for determining a solution. In order to promote confidence in the use of the device, trialling of options should be offered wherever possible along with appropriate instruction on how to use the device. This should include advice on how to troubleshoot minor issues and also what to do in the event of a breakdown that cannot be solved locally. In this way, the use of the device can be assimilated into everyday lifestyle with confidence and ease.

Where clients have complex or multiple disabilities, it is highly recommended that a multidisciplinary team approach is adopted when assessing for both equipment and access as this offers a mix of skills which allows holistic consideration of a client's needs. It may be necessary to consider whether the task should be simplified or broken down into small steps in order to facilitate best use of equipment, indicating that therapeutic input is required alongside technical input.

Selection of an appropriate EAT device and access method

Having carried out an assessment, the information gathered can then be matched against a range of devices. Other aspects such as where the device is to be used, what support is available and the user's own preference must also be taken into account.

Successful use of assistive technology is dependent upon identifying an appropriate means of accessing and controlling that device. Technology is continually developing and a growing multitude of access devices are available, making the selection of an appropriate device for an individual an inherently complex process. AT models, such as HAAT (Cook and Polgar, 2014), SETT (Zabala, 2005), and Matching Person to Technology (Scherer et al., 2007; Scherer, 2008), propose a predictive feature matching based approach. This systematically matches the individual's needs, skills and abilities with the characteristics of AT devices. It requires an in-depth knowledge of both the individual and the AT, and a multi-disciplinary approach, involving the AT clinician, the user and their families, to ensure all aspects are considered (Herman and Hussey, 1998; Hoppestad, 2006, 2007; Cowan and Najafi, 2019).

It should always be kept in mind that clients with complex disability are likely to have in place EAT from other services or private purchase. Any piece of equipment provided should fit into the collection already provided and should not adversely affect usage of another device. If a user with a single reliable voluntary movement has been issued with a switch to operate an environmental control, consideration should be given to providing an integrated access system if providing them with a second piece of equipment (see relevant section later in this chapter).

References

Chantry, J., Crombie, S., 2019. Functional posture. In: Cowan, D., Najafi, L. (Eds.), Handbook of Electronic Assistive Technology. Elsevier, pp. 53–80.

Cook, A., Polgar, J., 2014. Assistive Technologies Principles and Practice, fourth ed. Mosby, Inc.

Cowan, D., Najafi, L., 2019. Handbook of Electronic Assistive Technology. Elsevier, pp. 81–103.

Herman, J.H., Hussey, S.M., 1998. Module III assistive technology provision module part I: assessment. In: Herman, J.H., Hussey, S.M. (Eds.), Fundamentals in Assistive Technology, third ed. RESNA, Arlinton, VA, pp. III 1–III 38.

Hoppestad, B., 2006. Essential elements for assessment of persons with severe neurological impairments for computer access utilizing assistive technology devices: a Delphi study. Disabil. Rehabil. Assist. Technol. 1 (1–2), 3–16.

Hoppestad, B., 2007. Inadequacies in computer access using assistive technology devices in profoundly disabled individuals: an overview of the current literature. Disabil. Rehabil. Assist. Technol. 2 (4), 189–199.

Pope, P.M., 2007. Severe and Complex Neurological Disability. Elsevier.

Pountney, T.E., Mulcahy, C.M., Clarke, S.M., Green, E.M., 2004. The Chailey Approach to Postural Management: An Explanation of the Theoretical Aspects of Posture Management and Their Practical Application Through Treatment and Equipment. Chailey Heritage Clinical Services.

Scherer, M., Jutai, J., Fuhrer, M., Demers, L., DeRuyter, F., 2007. A framework for modelling the selection of assistive technology devices (ATDs). Disabil. Rehabil. Assist. Technol. 2 (1), 1–8.

Scherer, M., 2008. Institute for Matching Person and Technology, Inc. Available at: http://www.matchingpersonandtechnology.com/.

Steen, R., Lanshammer, Fristedt, 1991. (1997) AAC assessment strategies: seating and positioning. In: Glennon, S., Decoste, D. (Eds.), The Handbook of Augmentative and Alternative Communication. Singulair Publishing Group, p. 193.

Trefler, E., Taylor, S., 1991. Prescription and Positioning: evaluating the physically disabled individual for wheelchair seating. Prosthet. Orthot. Int. 15, 217–224.

Zabala, J., 2005. Using the SETT Framework to Level the Learning Field for Students with Disabilities. Available at: http://www.joyzabala.com/uploads/Zabala_SETT_Leveling_the_Learning_Field.pdf.

Further reading

Greenwood, R.J., 2003. Handbook of Neurological Rehabilitation Psychology. Press E, Sussex.

Nisbet, P., 1998. Special Access Technology. Call Centre, Scotland.

Environmental control systems

Donna Cowan

Chailey Clinical Services, East Sussex, UK

Introduction

Environmental control systems enable a person with disabilities to have control over a range of appliances installed around the house. In general these systems consist of a central controller operated by the individual using their most reliable method of access e.g. direct touch, switches, voice activation or eye gaze. The central controller generally outputs either infra-red or radio frequency codes to a range of peripheral devices.

Using these systems a person with the most complex physical disabilities, with perhaps only one reliable movement (i.e. able to operate a single switch), can have independent access to a wide range of activities. As well as providing a degree of independence for the user, these systems can also provide support for the family or carers as they are no longer solely responsible for ensuring the comfort of their family member. In some instances it can give additional confidence to enable a carer to leave the house for short periods of time without having to worry because if anything were to happen, the person at home can seek help independently and immediately.

In general these systems can offer access to four areas of function. These are:
leisure, communication, comfort and security.

- Leisure:
  - Devices such as a television or music appliances, computer access or page turners can be operated using these systems
- Communication:
  - Components under this area can include intercom systems and hands free telephones, with some systems being able to output a number of phrases for those with communication difficulties
- Comfort:
  - Altering the temperature and light levels of a room are possible e.g. remote control of heating and overhead lighting, motorized windows, control of position of a chair or bed, as well as curtain and blind control, and mains operation for devices such as lamps, fans or heaters
- Security:
  - Support from others can be sought using pagers or call alarms; allowing entry to the home can be screened using door openers/release mechanisms with intercom via television or telephone for interrogating whoever is at the door

The central controller can take a variety of shapes and sizes and the interface and format of information presented to the user can be altered to meet the individual's sensory and cognitive needs (Fig. 27.1).

A typical example of a menu would be where the user is presented with a display of options, perhaps relating to a single room. Within that room they might have control of intercom, alarm, lighting, a mains socket, curtains, television and telephone. If the user can only operate a single switch this would be mounted appropriately such that access was maintained. When activated, the system would scroll through the menu until the option of choice is reached, e.g. television operations. The user will then press the switch to select that option. If the user has a visual impairment the options can be read out loud as the system scrolls through the menu. If the user cannot recognize text, symbols can be used. The speed of scrolling can be adjusted to meet the reaction times required from the user in order to make a selection. Having made a selection such as television operations, a second set of options may open up. This set will include the operations required to control the television e.g. channel up, channel down, volume up, volume down, etc. Again, the user is taken through this list and they select the option required when offered.

Systems can also be programmed to deal with certain known "scenarios"; for example, when the phone rings the system can be set to automatically mute the television or the music appliance (if it is on) and then switch automatically to the phone option in the menu and output a given message if the user cannot speak. Similarly, if someone knocks at the door it can be programmed to switch on the intercom, switch on the television to the channel where the door CCTV camera can be viewed, so that the person inside the home can be assured of who is calling before allowing entry.

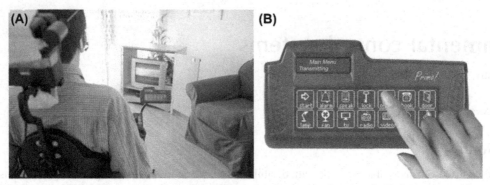

FIG. 27.1 Primo and Vivo infra red controllers offering different interface options for users. *By kind permission of Possum Ltd.*

Environmental control systems are provided through NHS services in the UK but some additional items such as internal door openers for users of powered mobility must be purchased privately. Eligibility criteria also apply.

These systems need to be regularly maintained as they often have safety critical systems incorporated, e.g. calling for help or operating entry and exit to the house.

Assessment

The assessment process for such a system should be undertaken as a multidisciplinary process. Like all areas of assistive technology, the user and carer need to be at the centre of the assessment. There needs to a clear understanding of what motivates the user and what they wish to have control over in their environment. This then needs to be aligned with their physical and sensory needs to enable the team to identify the correct hardware and software. The user's cognitive skills need also to be taken into account as there may be a mismatch between what the user/carer expects of the system versus what they can actually achieve: with some acquired conditions or injuries, cognitive deficit can occur. Language skills also play an important part in determining the most suitable piece of equipment.

The assessment of the method of operation of the controller and where it is best placed/mounted requires careful consideration. Often for adults this is one of the few opportunities to have a switch assessment for alternative access of their equipment. Clients with highly compromised physical abilities frequently require postural or specialist seating to enable them to be in a position whereby they can access a reliable voluntary movement. When out of their seat, their access option may need to change, i.e. they may be unable to control the device in the same way when in lying compared to sitting.

There needs to be consideration of all the equipment in use and how this can be best used to meet the needs of the individual without affecting any other area of function. An example would be if the user has a single switch operating a voice output communication aid (VOCA). By providing them with another device requiring single switch access, the user will need support switching between the VOCA and the environmental control system. However, by considering a device which allows integrated access they can retain their independent use of both devices and, as a result, the goal of improving independence is achieved. Sometimes this requires different agencies or health services to work together. In some instances, devices that the user already owns have infra-red output capability (e.g. VOCAs). In these cases, consideration should be given to using the VOCA as the central controller instead of supplying a separate device. This helps to rationalize the equipment in use, creating the most economic and acceptable form of system (see sections below on access to EAT (electronic assistive technology) and integrated systems).

NHS services in the UK provide systems for meeting complex needs but also where needs are relatively simple. Younger children, for example, do not require control of such a broad range of household functions, although it is supportive of their development to be able to control certain aspects of the home environment, just as typically developing children do as they grow. This might include operating a food mixer in the kitchen by pressing a switch while another person holds and moves the mixer. Alternatively, they might control devices such as sensory toys or some functions of the television. Simple devices are available to facilitate this and provide a useful introduction to environmental control. Adults may have problems seeing the small buttons on a standard remote control or find them too complex. Again, there are a range of simple remote controls, with or without large buttons, to meet this level of need (Fig. 27.2).

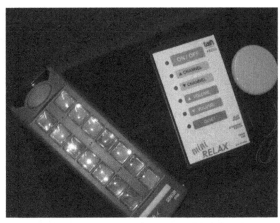

FIG. 27.2 Simple scanning (right) and large buttoned programmable infra red operated remote control (left).

Mainstream devices accessed using speech (e.g. Alexa, Google home-hub) are increasingly being used by the wider population to operate certain environmental control functions within the home, e.g. lighting, mains sockets and TV operation. These types of device might start to be used as part of larger installations (Woodcock and Newman, 2019).

Case study

Hannah is 56 and was referred to the service by her local speech and language therapist. She has multiple sclerosis (MS) and lives with her husband in a one story apartment.

Hannah is a full-time wheelchair user and is beginning to find holding and operating TV remote controls more complex because of her changing vision and decreased fine motor skills. She has recently been issued with a voice output communication aid via a regional communication aid service. She operates this using a switch.

Hannah spends time in the home on her own when her husband goes out to work; carers attend during the day to support her.

The environmental controls service team attended and discussed with Hannah, her husband and a member of care staff her needs. The device she has been issued with by the communication aid service can also be used as a controller for environmental control. The two services liaised with each other prior to the assessment to ensure that the specification of the device was suitable to meet Hannah's simultaneous communication and environmental needs.

Discussion included where in the home Hannah spent her time and what equipment would be helpful. Assessment was undertaken to ensure Hannah could access her switch reliably when out of her seating, e.g. resting in a comfy chair or her bed. Consideration of mounting the switch was required to ensure it remained in place in these different settings.

- Heating control was important for Hannah as she often felt cold.
- Operation of the TV and her radio was also important
- Hannah wanted to be able to see who was at the door and allow entry independently because on occasion her carers have not been able to access the key safe outside the home
- She wanted to operate lamps and overhead lighting
- Control of the position of her bed was a key issue as she became uncomfortable when in bed and had to wait for help to alter her position
- Operation of the blinds was requested as the sun often prevents her from being able to see the TV during the day and at present her husband closes these before leaving which means she sits in a room without sunlight until carers arrive; while automated blind operation was not available through the state service, discussion was had over where to purchase these such that this function could be subsequently programmed into the system, understanding that maintenance of these was to be organized separately from the remainder of the installation

Grid sets were developed to offer the above functions in her bedroom and lounge and added to the existing communication aid software. An emergency alarm was also added and set up as a separate device to the communication aid to ensure that Hannah always had access to a call for assistance regardless of whether her communication aid was functioning and in place.

References

Woodcock, A., Newman, G., 2019. Environmental controls. In: Cowan, D., Najafi, L. (Eds.), Handbook of Electronic Assistive Technology. Academic Press, pp. 149–180.

Further reading

Greenwood, R.J., 2003. Handbook of Neurological Rehabilitation. Psychology Press, East Sussex.
Cook, A.M., 2008. Assistive Technology: Principles and Practice. Mosby Elsevier.
Hooper, B., Verdonck, M., Amsters, D., Myburg, M., Allen, E., 2018. Smart device environmental control systems: experiences of people with cervical spinal cord injury. Disabil. Rehabil. 13 (8), 724–730.

Augmentative and alternative communication (AAC)

Ladan Najafi, Fiona Panthi and Georgina Overell

Kent and Medway Communication and Assistive Technology Service (KM CAT) — Adults, Kent, UK

Introduction to AAC

Communication is a vital part of everyday life. Living with a communication impairment can reduce social participation and the overall quality of life. The United Nations Convention on the Rights of Persons with Disabilities (United Nations, 2006) highlights the right of disabled people to freedom of expression and opinion through communication of their choice, including AAC. Communication impairments in children can affect speech and language development, cognitive, literacy development and access to education. As a result, timely AAC intervention is critical (Drager et al., 2010; Fried-Oken et al., 2011; McNaughton and Bryen, 2007). In adults with acquired communication disorders following a stroke or traumatic brain injury, reduced or loss of participation in work and leisure activities can lead to social isolation.

In the World Report on Disability (2011), Professor Stephen Hawking stated that "we have a moral duty to remove the barriers to participation". AAC intervention endeavours to help break down some of these barriers to reduce the detrimental effects of the communication difficulty in a person's life. Enabling people to develop social networks gives the potential for greater independence. In some cases this enables people to follow their aspirations. Comedian Lee Ridley, who has cerebral palsy and is also known as "Lost Voice Guy", uses his communication aid on stage. Winner of the 2018 TV series 'Britain's Got Talent', he performs to sell-out audiences. In an interview before the final he said "When I am performing, it's as if I have finally found my voice — and it's a great feeling to make people laugh". (BBC News, 4 June 2018).

AAC refers to a wide range of techniques which supplement or replace speech and handwriting. There are many strategies, techniques and tools that can enable people with complex communication needs (CCN) to communicate more effectively. These strategies may be unaided, whereby the individual uses their own body movement to communicate, such as gestures, facial expression, eye pointing and signing. Aided communication systems require tools and equipment, such as pen and paper, picture or symbol based communication books and voice output communication aids (VOCA). Aided communication systems are generally categorized into low, light/medium and high tech AAC.

Low tech AAC systems

These are non-electronic and generally inexpensive. They are often paper based and designed specifically to provide symbol/picture/photo communication books/charts (Fig. 27.4) for individuals with no or impaired literacy skills. Alphabet charts, E-Tran frames and other text based systems can be provided for literate individuals (Fig. 27.3).

Access methods for low tech AAC:

Methods are categorized into direct and indirect:

- Direct access: The communicator is able to point directly to the desired letter or symbol using a body part such as finger, hand, elbow, foot, knee or head. Sometimes a pointing aid, such as a head pointer or a mouth stick, can be used for ease of access.
- Indirect access: Those with CCN may also have other physical disabilities that could prevent them from using a direct method of access. In these circumstances, partner assisted scanning can be used. The conversation partner points to/ reads out the letters, words or symbols on the communication page. The communicator indicates the desired item by an eye blink, gesture or any other previously agreed method, until the message is conveyed.

The responsibility for achieving effective communication is shared, with the communication partner taking a significant part in working out the final message. As a result, the conversation partner needs to be aware of the potential for misunderstandings or misinterpretations.

A low-tech system can be a very powerful method of communication and may, in some circumstances, be the only suitable method. Even when an individual uses an electronic communication aid it is good practice to use low tech AAC as an adjunct since the electronic technology can fail. On some occasions, use of low tech AAC might be more practical.

FIG. 27.3 An E-Tran frame (low tech): The communicator eye points to a block, then a colour, to indicate the desired letter; the communication partner confirms the letters and words as the message is created.

FIG. 27.4 Symbol based communication book (low tech): The communicator navigates their way around the book and points at the desired words/phrases. Where the communicator is unable to point directly, the communication partner reads out the words and phrases. The communicator then selects the required word/phrase by nodding, eye blinking or other method of confirmation that has been established between the two.

Light/medium tech AAC systems

Battery operated VOCAs, such as recorded message devices, are defined as medium or light tech. These communication aids range from providing a single to a number of spoken messages. At a glance, these devices are limited in the number of voice output messages they can offer, but for some users they are the most suitable aids and offer an effective method to communicate. Light tech AAC can be accessed via direct or indirect methods (Figs. 27.5 and 27.6).

High tech AAC

High tech VOCAs can be comprised of vocabulary packages installed on standard computers or dedicated communication aid systems sometimes referred to as speech generating devices. High tech AAC has the advantage of being able to provide a wealth of vocabulary, literally thousands of words, which could not be provided by low or light tech AAC.

Dynamic communication display is an important feature of high tech AAC systems. The communicator is able to make a selection of a particular topic or category, e.g. sport, which automatically displays another page of the relevant items within that category, such as football or tennis, together with other related vocabulary. Dynamic pages reduce the time spent on finding words, phrases and composing messages. It enables links to a multitude of relevant vocabulary items and pages.

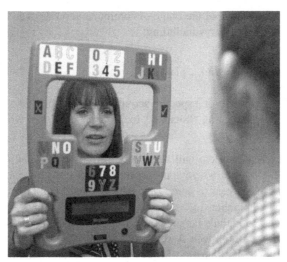

FIG. 27.5 MegaBee™. This medium tech, battery operated device works similarly to the E-Tran frame, except that the communication partner presses keys which correspond to the colour of the blocks and colours of the letters, the message then being displayed on the screen in view of the communicator. Quicker communication can be achieved by using abbreviations to display messages.

FIG. 27.6 GoTalk20+. This battery operated VOCA has the capacity to record 100 messages using communication overlays over five levels. The communicator selects the cells to play the message.

A consistent layout facilitates learning and motor planning skills. These are aided further by colour coding frequently used words such as pronouns and verbs (core vocabulary) and placing function keys, including 'Home' and 'Speak', in the same position on each page (Cowan and Najafi, 2019; Drager et al., 2010; Light and Drager, 2007).

Another feature is word prediction which can enable quicker retrieval of words and phrases and help individuals with impaired spelling skills. Pre-stored, personalized phrases can also speed up communication.

There are a number of important considerations in the implementation of high tech AAC which must be addressed by the multidisciplinary assessment team during the assessment process. These factors include language and voice options, ease of use of the device, reliability, the availability of technical support in addition to the time required to generate a message, personal preferences, family perceptions and support (Baxter et al., 2012, Light and McNaughton, 2014; Lund and Light, 2007; Rackensperger, 2012). Access methods and integration of technologies are areas that need to be addressed by the practitioner when assessing a person for an appropriate VOCA.

Vocabulary packages: High tech AAC devices contain symbol or text based systems. Deciding on the most appropriate vocabulary package for an individual is based on language and literacy skills, cognitive abilities and sensory impairments.

The specialist AAC team will have knowledge of the range of communication devices with pre-loaded language software. Vocabulary can be arranged in a number of ways including:

- Grammatically - using core vocabulary
- Semantically - in categories e.g. clothes, drinks, places
- Alphabetically - requiring a level of literacy
- Schematically - where vocabulary required for a specific activity or context e.g. going out for a meal, is placed together, sometimes with a visual scene display using 'hotspots' to produce messages when selected/activated (Cowan and Najafi, 2019; Light and McNaughton, 2013).

It is important to note that every AAC system will need to be set up or modified to meet the individual's needs and considerations given to language development where appropriate. Regular updating and development of the vocabulary is essential to ensure the communicator has access to language enabling them to talk about recent events and new activities. However, AAC does not have to be comprehensive: some individuals with progressive neurological conditions, such as motor neurone disease, may only wish to include language regarding their palliative care at the latter stage of the disease.

Generally speaking, all low, light and high tech AAC systems will require planning and interventions for today *and* tomorrow, an integral component of The Participation Model (Beukelman and Mirenda, 2013), a systematic process for conducting AAC assessments and intervention.

Physical features: These considerations include portability of the device, ruggedness, speech, volume, aesthetics, battery life and mounting. There may be other considerations that need to be taken into account that are usually led by the communicator, such as lighting conditions and the effects on the screen in the environment that the individual is intending to use the device.

Access method: prior to assessment of VOCAs, a person's postural management needs must be addressed. Accessing VOCAs requires the development of physical skills, whether direct or indirect. It takes practise to develop these skills which are generally taught separately to those required to access the VOCA. In children and adults with complex disabilities, physical skills are usually taught through ~~fun~~ activities such as playing games. This is to ensure that lack of motor silks are not misinterpreted as lack of communication skills, and vice versa. As part of the process, positioning the device to enable ease of access and optimum function must also be assessed (see chapters on access and postural management for more details).

Integration features: VOCAs can be integrated with computers, environmental control systems and mobile phones, i.e. for texting. Increasingly, most dedicated VOCAs are on computers running Windows and are used as computers as well as communication aids, and have built in environmental control modules.

There are a number of high tech AAC systems on the market. They may be keyboard based for those who are literate and have the ability to type, handheld, or less portable where usually they can be positioned on a desk or mounted onto a wheelchair.

The last few years have seen mainstream technology being used increasingly in place of dedicated communication aids (Fig. 27.7). However, dedicated equipment is still preferred and more appropriate for those who:

- Are not familiar with Windows/iOS based devices and prefer a simple VOCA with a standard keyboard, such as a Lightwriter
- Are familiar with a device and already able to communicate with a specific vocabulary package
- Require an alternative method of access: not all methods of access can be used with all applications on mainstream devices
- Require simple setups: some dedicated communication aids have built in interfaces for access such as a switch module which allows the direct connection of switches to the VOCA; mainstream devices such as tablet PCs may require additional components/software to enable switch access

FIG. 27.7 iPad with Grid for iPad software (Smartbox Software).

Conclusions

Through the assessment process the skills of the individual are matched to the features of the AAC system, regardless of whether it is low/light or high tech AAC, and more than one device might be considered in the early stages of intervention. Not all people with CCN have the same skills and difficulties. Cognition, sensory and motor skills, language, literacy and the ability to learn can differ considerably person to person. In addition, psycho-social considerations, such as the communicator's attitude to technology, can play an important role in the decision making process. Some communicators may prefer to use light or low tech AAC. It is also worth noting that high tech AAC may place considerable learning demands on the individual and their family in supporting them.

A trial period should be part of an assessment process whereby the communicator can receive training and plenty of opportunities to practice with their AAC device, along with regular support provided by their family/carers and AAC practitioners. On-going evaluation and reviews will establish whether the communication device is appropriate and whether it continues to meet the individual's needs.

References

Baxter, S., Enderby, P., Evans, P., Judge, S., 2012. Barriers and facilitators to the use of high-technology augmentative and alternative communication devices: a systematic review and qualitative synthesis. InternationaAmyournal of Language & Communication Disorders 47 (2), 115–129.

BBC News, Entertainment and Arts, Britain's Got Talent: Is Lost Voice Guy's Win a Watershed Moment for Disability? https://www.bbc.co.uk/news/entertainment-arts-44354287.

Beukelman, D.R., Mirenda, P., 2013. Augmentative and Alternative Communication, Supporting Children and Adults with Complex Communication Needs, fourth ed. Paul H. Brookes Publishing Co. Inc.

Cowan, D., Najafi, L., 2019. Handbook of Electronic Assistive Technology. Elsevier Academic Press.

Drager, K., Light, J., McNaughton, D., 2010. Effects of AAC interventions on communication and language for young children with complex communication needs. J. Pediatr. Rehabil. Med. 3 (4), 303–310.

Fried-Oken, M., Beukelman, D.R., Hux, K., 2011. Current and future AAC research considerations for adults with acquired cognitive and communication impairments. Assist. Technol. 24 (1), 56–66.

Light, J., Drager, K., 2007. AAC technologies for young children with communication needs: state of the science and future research directions. Augmentative Altern. Commun. 23 (3), 204–216.

Light, J., McNaughton, D., 2013. Putting people first: Re-Thinking the role of technology in augmentative and alternative communication intervention. Augmentative Altern. Commun. 29 (4), 299–309.

Light, J., McNaughton, D., 2014. Communicative competence for individuals who require augmentative and alternative communication: a new definition for a new era of communication? Augmentative Altern. Commun. 30 (1), 1–18.

Lund, S.K., Light, J., 2007. Long-term outcomes for individuals who use augmentative and alternative communication: Part III–contributing factors. Augmentative Altern. Commun. 23 (4), 323–335.

McNaughton, D., Bryen, D.N., 2007. AAC technologies to enhance participation and access to meaningful societal roles for adolescents and adults with developmental disabilities who require AAC. Augmentative Altern. Commun. (AAC) 23 (3), 217–229.

Rackensperger, T., 2012. Family Influences and academic success: the Perceptions of individuals using AAC. Augmentative Altern. Commun. 28 (2), 106—116.

United Nations, 2006, Convention on the Rights of Persons with Disabilities, https://www.un.org/development/desa/disabilities/convention-on-the-rights-of-persons-with-disabilities.html

World Report on Disability, 2011. Produced Jointly by WHO and the World Bank. whqlibdoc.who.int/publications/2011/9789240685215_eng.pdf.

Further reading

Ace Centre (e-books and low tech resources) https://acecentre.org.uk/.

Binger, C., Kent-Walsh, J., 2010. What Every Speech and Language Pathologist/audiologist Should Know about Augmentative and Alternative Communication. Allyn and Bacon, Boston.

Communication Matters http://www.communicationmatters.org.uk/.

Access to electronic assistive technology (EAT)

Jodie Rogers and Ladan Najafi

Kent and Medway Communication and Assistive Technology Service (KM CAT) — Adults, Kent, UK

Introduction

The term 'access' refers to the means by which an individual interfaces with the assistive technology, for example, an individual using a computer is typically using a standard keyboard, mouse and display. However, a person who has suffered an illness or accident which has resulted in a disability may not have full use of their upper limbs, and is therefore unable to use a computer in this way. Alternative access technology allows those individuals with disabilities who cannot use standard controls to achieve independent control of their chosen device. The access method needs to be considered in the provision of all EAT devices, and whether it is for computer access, high-tech augmentative and alternative communication (AAC), environmental controls or powered wheelchair driving, the underlying principles are the same.

This section gives a basic overview of alternative access, the process involved in selecting an appropriate EAT access method, and an overview of some of the more commonly used access devices.

The principles of alternative access

The aim in the provision of alternative access is to enable the individual to independently control their chosen device. This control needs to be both reliable and effective for the individual to be able to use the device functionally. Within the literature there are no agreed measures of efficacy for EAT access. Quist and Lloyd (1997) state that the underlying principles in the successful use of alternative access should include best fit to the user's abilities, minimum effort, minimum learning and maximum output. For example, a user of AAC will wish to be able to communicate their message quickly in a conversation, without experiencing undue fatigue from the effort of doing so.

When considering alternative access methods, the AT clinician also needs to ensure that the method being considered does not have any contraindications for the user, such as inducement of pain, harmful patterns of movement, or increased muscle tone, all of which can have long-term implications.

The components of alternative access

Access can be divided into several component parts, as described below:

- *Control interface, or input device:* the hardware that an individual uses to operate a device.
- *Selection set:* the set of items from which the user is making a choice, these can be letters, pictures or symbols, and can be presented in visual, auditory or tactile formats.
- *Selection method:* is the method by which the individual makes a selection using the control interface. The selection method can be divided into two categories: direct and indirect.
   Direct selection: The user is able to directly select their choice using direct access. This could include using their hand to touch a screen, using a mouse or eye-pointing.
   Indirect selection: The user has to take intermediary steps to make their selection. The most common method is scanning, whereby items from the selection set are each presented in turn and the user waits to select their chosen item. Input devices that enable direct selection should be considered first as there are no intermediary steps involved, enabling quicker and less cognitively demanding access.
- *Output:* This is how the information is fed back to the individual. This could be in the form of text, pictures or sounds and speech.

An overview of access methods

There is a wide range of access devices and systems available and these are continually developing. Here follows an overview of some of the devices currently used.

Pointer control

- Ergonomically designed mice: These are an adaptation of the 'standard' mouse design. They may be mini, ergonomically shaped, or upright but will operate in the same way to that of a 'standard mouse.
- Trackballs: The user rolls the ball in the desired direction to correspondingly move the on-screen cursor. These are available in many different shapes and sizes and can be operated with just a thumb, single finger or whole hand.
- Joysticks: The user pushes the joystick in the desired direction to correspondingly move the cursor. These are available in a range of shapes, sizes and require varying degrees of force. There are joysticks available to be controlled by movements of the hand, chin, tongue or foot.
- Touchpads: A pad with a tactile sensor, where movement of the finger on the pad controls the cursor.
- Mouse emulators: Usually consist of software that allows the user to mimic the functions of a mouse, such as directing the cursor and mouse clicks, when using an alternative access method. An example of this is Windows® 'Mousekeys' which allows the user to control the cursor using a number pad.
- Dibbers, mouth sticks, head pointers and alternative styluses: These are physical pointers that the user holds or wears and allows them to press the keys or touchscreen of their device.
- Head trackers: The user's head movement controls the movement of the on-screen cursor (Fig. 27.8). These systems are typically infra-red (IR) based, where the user wears a dot that reflects the IR emitters; video tracking and gyroscopic versions are also available. To perform mouse 'clicks' the user can use either a switch or dwell selection where the cursor is held still (for a specified length of time) over the chosen icon in order to select it.
- Eye gaze technology: The most common commercial eye tracking systems are comprised of a camera unit that tracks the reflection of emitted IR light from the user's retinas without the need for the user to wear any additional component i.e. lens or glasses (Fig. 27.9).

  The degree of compensation for involuntary movements and repositioning varies in different systems, a factor which is very important to take into account when assessing an individual with complex disabilities. For example users with cerebral palsy may require a system that can accommodate their involuntary movements, but this is not usually a consideration when assessing those with spinal cord injuries. Touchscreens: The user is able to move the cursor or activate an icon on the screen by touching it directly. There are two types of touchscreens; resistive and capacitive. Resistive touchscreens work on the basis of pressure applied to the screen. They can be used with a finger, fingernail or stylus. Capacitive touchscreens work by using the conductive properties of an object, typically the skin on finger or other parts of the hand. Most commercially available devices now use capacitive screens. However, resistive screens are still available to purchase and can be useful for those individuals who tend to hit the screen with their nail or run their finger along the screen before making a selection.

Keyboards

There is a wide range of keyboard options available such as large keys keyboards, mini keyboards, one handed keyboards and key guards to aid key selection. The keys can be presented according to an individual's needs and preferences. Options include ABC or frequency based layouts, instead of QWERTY, or can be in contrasting colours for those with visual impairment (Fig. 27.10).

Switches

These come in a large range of shapes and sizes (Fig. 27.11) and are typically activated by limb or head movement. Switches can only perform one action and so the user may need to use a range of switches or use scanning to perform a task.

- Mechanical switches: these need to be physically moved, depressed, touched or released to initiate a command. They vary in activation force, shape, size, travel (the physical displacement required to activate the switch) and some provide auditory feedback.
- Proximity switches: these do not require physical contact from the user. Proximity switches are activated when the user is close but not necessarily touching the switch. The activation can be by facial muscle movement, eye blink or finger or head movement.
- EMG (electromyography) switches: these are activated by the electrical impulse of muscle activations.
- Sip and Puff stitches: these use air pressure by sipping (inhaling) or puffing (exhaling) on a straw or tube. The varying amount of pressure can be set for each individual through a calibration process initially.

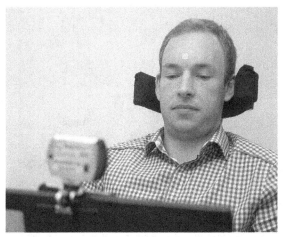

FIG. 27.8 Headmouse Nano. This is a head operated mouse that consists of an infra-red camera that is placed above the monitor. The user wears a reflective dot on their forehead or glasses. The camera follows the user's head movement which controls the position of the on-screen cursor. This can be used with an on-screen keyboard or mouse control software to enable the user to fully operate their computer hands free.

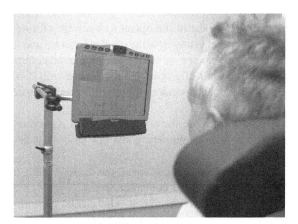

FIG. 27.9 Eye gaze system.

FIG. 27.10 A range of alternative keyboards and mice.

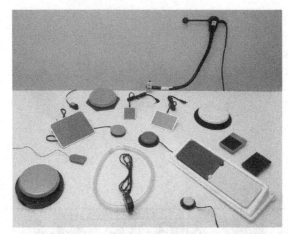

FIG. 27.11 Example switches which vary in shape, size, activation force, activation travel i.e. the distance by which they must be displaced for activation, and auditory feedback.

Software and control enhancers

- Speech recognition software: This is software that allows the user to control their device using their speech and is most commonly used for computer control where the user can dictate into a document or perform computer tasks using a range of voice commands.
- Accessibility options: These are options that exist in the operating software of a device that can be adjusted to suit an individual user's needs. Options can include adjusting how the display is set up and how the mouse or keyboard operate.
- Voice control systems: The use of voice activation systems for environmental control has now become widely available as a mainstream technology. Whilst not specifically designed for people with disabilities, they can offer benefits for clients with physical disabilities who have intact speech or those with speech impairment that use their communication aids to access it e.g., Amazon Alexa.
- Word prediction software: This is used to increase the text output when typing and is already widely used in mobile phone technology. It is available for use with computers; some AT devices such as communication aids have word prediction software built in.
- Screen readers: These will interpret and read out the content of the display, using a synthesized voice. Screen readers can be used by those with visual impairments to aid computer access.
- Screen magnifiers: Software that magnifies the screen content. This can be presented as whole screen magnification or the magnification of sections of the screen. These sections are displayed in a second box and change in correspondence to the on-screen cursor, i.e. as you move the cursor over a section of the screen, that section is magnified.
- On-screen keyboards: A graphical representation of a keyboard, or other type of selection set, is displayed on the screen. The keys or cells can be activated by switch or pointer control (see above options) and will then appear as text in the user's chosen application.
- Interface positioning: The position of an individual in relation to their technology interface can have a significant impact upon the ease of use of that device. For example, if an individual is unable to place their legs under their desk and therefore has to lean forward to use their mouse and keyboard, they are likely to find their computer difficult to use. Correct positioning of the device, whether it is a keyboard, mouse or switch, is essential in enabling the user to achieve optimum function with minimum effort.

Other considerations

Once an appropriate control interface has been identified, it may be necessary to consider mounting the device such that it is kept in the position which enables optimum function. Mounting options can include angled rests, desk-mounts, floor-stands to place a device next to a bed or chair, wheelchair trays and mounting poles that fit the device to the user's wheelchair (where applicable).

Future of access

The range of access technology options for individual with disabilities is rapidly growing. Examples of new technologies that are emerging:

Brain computer Interface (BCI): this technology is explained in more detail in the BCI section. Presently, most human BCI systems used for alternative access use the non-invasive electroencephalographic (EEG) based technologies; however the development of functional BCI to serve as alternative access is still an area that requires further research.

Eye gaze technology for driving: the technology is widely used for computer and AAC access. Use in powered mobility is a topic that is consistently brought up by the users of such technology and discussed amongst professionals. There are, at present, safety issues which require further research and development in order to evaluate its suitability for controlling powered wheelchairs.

Gesture recognition: These can range from interfaces that recognize a few symbolic gestures to recognition of sign language. Similarly, interfaces may recognize static hand/head poses, or dynamic hand/head motion, or a combination of both. In all cases, each gesture has an unambiguous semantic meaning associated with it that can be used in the interface. Currently, there is some use of gesture recognition already integrated into mainstream devices such as AssistiveTouch on iPhone. Fager et al. (2011) suggests that predictive gesturing promises to substantially reduce the cognitive and physical workload for people with severe disabilities when writing. Further research is required to investigate accuracy and efficiency of these new technologies for those client groups with limited physical abilities.

Tongue Drive System (TDS): this is a wireless assistive technology which can enable those with severe physical disabilities, such as spinal cord injuries, to access computers, environmental control systems and drive powered wheelchairs using their tongue movements. The system allows the user to send commands by pointing their tongue in different directions. This is still an area of research and currently those systems available are prototypes and for research purposes alone.

References

Quist, R.W., Lloyd, L.L., 1997. Principles and uses of technology. In: Lloyd, L.L., Fuller, D.R., Arvidson, H.H. (Eds.), Augmentative and Alternative Communication: A Handbook of Principles and Practices. Allyn and Bacon Inc, Boston, pp. 107–126.

Further reading

Abilitynet, 2012. My Computer My Way. Available at: http://www.abilitynet.org.uk/myway/.

Church, G., Glennen, S., 1992. The Handbook of Assistive Technology. Singulair Publishing Group, Inc.

Communication by Gaze Interaction (COGAIN) Website. http://www.cogain.org/wiki/COGAIN_Reports.

Cook, A., Polgar, J., 2008. Cook and Hussey's Assistive Technologies Principles and Practice. Mosby, Inc.

Cowan, D., Najafi, L., 2019. The Handbook of Electronic Assistive Technology. Elsevier.

Donegan, M., Oosthuizen, L., Bates, R., Daunys, G., Hansen, J.P., Joos, M., Majaranta, P., Signorile, I., 2005. D3.1 User Requirements Report with Observations of Difficulties Users Are Experiencing. Communication by Gaze Interaction (COGAIN). IST-2003-511598: Deliverable 3.1. Available in PDF format. http://www.cogain.org/results/reports/COGAIN-D3.1.pdf.

Duchowski, A.T., 2003. Eye Tracking Methodology: Theory & Practice. Springer-Verlag, London, UK.

Fager, S., Beukelman, D.R., Fried-Oken, M., Jakobs, T., Baker, J., 2011. Access interface strategies. J. Assist. Technol. 24 (1), 25e33

Emptech: http://www.emptech.info/.

Majaranta, P., Aoki, H., Donegan, M., Witzner Hansen, D., Hansen, J.P., Hyrskykari, A., Räihä, K., 2012. Gaze Interaction and Applications of Eye Tracking: Advances in Assistive Technologies, first ed. IGI Global.

Integrated systems

Ladan Najafi

East Kent Adult Communication and Assistive Technology (ACAT) Service, Kent, UK

Introduction

Integrated systems use the same control interface to operate more than one device. As an example, an individual may use their joystick to drive their powered wheelchair and, using the same joystick, access other assistive devices such as a communication aid, environmental control and computer.

The concept of integration of assistive devices is relatively new and the literature goes back only to the early 1990s. With the advances made in electronics and software in recent years, the integration of EAT devices has become more widely available to those individuals with disabilities.

Reasons for integration

The advantages of integrated control are that persons with limited motor control can access several devices with one access site and without assistance, and the user does not need to learn a different operating mechanism for each device (Ding et al., 2003).

The finding of one study indicates that integrated access may be useful when:

- The user has one single reliable control site
- The optimal control interface for each assistive device is the same
- Speed, accuracy, ease of use, or endurance increases with the use of a single interface
- The user or the family prefers integrated controls for aesthetic, performance, greater independence and control, or other subjective reasons (Judge, 2019; Guerette and Summi, 1994).

When making a decision to either use integrated access or separate control interfaces, commonly known as distributed controls, a number of factors need to be taken into account.

Factors to consider when recommending integrated access

Although integrated control is beneficial for the reasons stated above, there is always a danger that if one aspect fails, all aspects fail. Breakdown in an integrated system can cause significant disruption for an individual who may be reliant on EAT for mobility, communication and/or environmental controls. When recommending such systems, a backup system should be also considered, for example if the single method of access is a joystick, a stand-alone joystick that can be used with the VOCA in isolation from the integrated access may need to be considered so that the user is not left without a voice for a period of time.

It is important to ensure that accessing one technology is not compromising the performance and efficacy of the other. The skills required to perform one task are not necessarily the same as the other e.g., driving a powered wheelchair requires a different set of skills to those required to access a computer, therefore access to both must be assessed to ensure the setup is appropriate for the user.

Any progression in a condition should be considered at the assessment. Some models of integration require daily setups which need third party support e.g., a carer or a family member to plug in a switch. This is indicative of the importance of the network of support when considering integration (Judge, 2019, p. 299).

Guerette and Summi (1994) also conclude that integrated access may not be appropriate when:

- Performance on one or more assistive device is severely compromised by integrating control
- The individual wishes to operate an assistive device from a position other than a powered wheelchair
- Physical, cognitive, or visual/perceptual limitations preclude integration
- It is the individual's personal preference to use distributed controls
- External factors such as cost or technical limitations prohibit the use of integrated controls

Most factors stated above are still valid today but with advances in technology some external factors are no longer a deciding factor, for example more and more mainstream technology now can be integrated with minimum technical support, and the prices of specialized controllers are more or less the same as standard controllers.

Another important factor to consider is the ownership of assistive devices and the consequent network of support and inter-service co-operation that the user requires to maintain the system. Responsibility for maintenance and troubleshooting problems with equipment can be complex when a single device is used to control a number of pieces of equipment provided through different agencies (Nisbet, 1996). Assistive devices may be owned by various organizations such as wheelchair services, environmental control services, AAC services and/or privately funded equipment. In such circumstances, the organization recommending and setting up the integrated system must, in agreement with all parties, deliver a maintenance plan to the user.

Case study

Background information

Amy is a 27 year old woman with cerebral palsy and spastic quadriplegia. She has no speech but is highly motivated to communicate. She lives independently with the assistance of 24 h carers and has a supportive family nearby. Amy has limited literacy (single letters and some short words) and has used high tech AAC with a symbol based software package in the past, but has not used this since leaving school.

Since she had not used high tech AAC for a number of years it was necessary to assess what communication package and access methods would now best meet her needs.

Communication

Amy's current communication strategies include: eye contact, facial expression, vocalizations and using her low tech communication book, with picture based symbols organized into categories. This is accessed with the assistance of a communication partner using partner assisted scanning (PAS). She knows how to navigate to every picture in her communication book, but this relies on someone being trained to use PAS and is quickest with someone who knows the book well.

Assessment and trial of high tech AAC

Amy wished to be able to create novel messages independently, so she was assessed by a specialized AAC service to establish the most suitable high tech system.

The assessment for a suitable access method was carried out in parallel with, but distinct from, the assessment for a suitable vocabulary package; both aspects of high-tech AAC are interdependent and influence the decision-making of the other.

Access

Amy had accessed her previous device with a switch. The specialist AAC team knew she was a competent switch user but supported her goal to trial an eye gaze system to see if this was a practical/quicker direct access method for her to communicate on her high tech device. This decision was based on the assessment session when she showed potential to access the technology. After the trialling both eye gaze and switch access, both Amy and the specialist team agreed that switch access best met her needs. This was because use of eye gaze was effortful and not as reliable/consistent as the switch. In addition it was recognized that Amy benefited from having auditory feedback because she was not literate, had not used her communication aid for years, and therefore had forgotten some of the symbols and the layout of the system.

It was recognized that Amy would need to practise to familiarize herself with the location of categories and their contents. Her new vocabulary package uses a 'More' button to access additional categories and words. This means there is a richer choice of vocabulary but a disadvantage is the time it takes to scan to the 'More' button to select it with the switch; it is located on the bottom line of each grid. During the trial period Amy started with single cell switch scanning to familiarize herself with the vocabulary package and layout. This was then changed to block row cell switch scanning to help her speed up her selections, including the 'More' button, (see section on access methods for more explanation).

Vocabulary

Amy's previous picture based symbol package was explored first (each cell contained a picture symbol with the word typed below). Amy demonstrated that she was no longer familiar with it and she expressed that she was open to trying new options when presented with a choice.

The rationale for changing her picture based symbol package was that there was no advantage to having her old one as she could not remember it. Newer packages offered more vocabulary and a wider range of features, for example to speed up communication and/or to control the environment, computer activities, etc. It was also acknowledged that a period of learning/familiarization would be required.

Picture based symbol packages were compared in order to select the most suitable for Amy to trial. Due to her limited literacy it was established that Amy benefitted from symbol support for all words. It was important that the package selected should not be too complicated or overwhelming. It was also felt that there should be scope for her to expand her vocabulary further in the future.

Given these parameters, a dedicated AAC device and software were chosen (48 cells per grid page, each containing a picture based symbol with word below). This had a considerably larger vocabulary than her previous AAC package. It also allowed for the possibility at a later date of progressing to a) 63 cells per grid page and b) a dynamic display, both of which would enable her to say even more.

Use of AAC post trial

Amy was issued with a dedicated AAC device and software so she now has a choice of using her high tech device or her low tech book to augment her communication. A key person has been trained on editing her software vocabulary so that new

Continued

Case study—cont'd

cells can be added e.g. names of family and friends. They have also been shown how to re-order some of the vocabulary e.g. in the 'Food' category so that Amy's favourites appear first and can be scanned and selected quickly.

She now has access to emails and Facebook (as well as other functions) added onto her AAC device by the local environmental controls service (ECS). This enables Amy to communicate with friends and family whenever she wants using her device. ECS have also programmed her TV, music player and lights into her device so that she can also control her environment independently.

Amy drives a powered wheelchair and due to her limited physical abilities she was considered a good candidate for integrated communication, mobility and environmental control. The aim of this is to achieve more independence as currently the switch must be set up by someone else and in the exact place of her switch for driving. At the time, Amy's powered wheelchair was not compatible with the integrated options but the wheelchair service and family were informed that when she is due for a replacement to consider integrating her powered wheelchair and communication aid. This will require joint working between the wheelchair and communication aid services.

References

Ding, D., Cooper, R.A., Kaminski, B.A., Kanaly, J.R., Allegretti, A., Chaves, E., Hubbard, S., 2003. Integrated control and related technology of assistive devices. Assist Technol. Winter 15 (2), 89—97.

Guerette, P., Summi, E., 1994. Integrating control of multiple assistive devices: a retrospective review. Assist. Technol. 6 (1), 67—76.

Judge, S., 2019. Assistive technology integration and accessibility. In: Cowan, D., Najafi, L. (Eds.), Handbook of Electronic Assistive Technology. Elsevier, pp. 289—310.

Nisbet, P., 1996. Integrating assistive technologies: current practices and future possibilities. Med. Eng. Phys. 18 (3), 193—202.

Further reading

Abilitynet, 2012. My Computer My Way. Available at: http://www.abilitynet.org.uk/myway/.

Church, G., Glennen, S., 1992. The Handbook of Assistive Technology. Singulair Publishing Group, Inc.

Communication by Gaze Interaction (COGAIN) Website. http://www.cogain.org/wiki/COGAIN_Reports.

Cook, A., Polgar, J., 2008. Cook and Hussey's Assistive Technologies Principles and Practice. Mosby, Inc.

Emptech: http://www.emptech.info/.

Majaranta, P., Aoki, H., Donegan, M., Witzner Hansen, D., Hansen, J.P., Hyrskykari, A., Räihä, K., 2012. Gaze Interaction and Applications of Eye Tracking: Advances in Assistive Technologies, first ed. IGI Global.

Using and adapting mainstream technology for assistive technology

Will Wade

ACE Centre North, Manchester, UK

The need for mainstream

Mainstream technology, that is technology not specifically designed for people with disabilities, is ubiquitous. All individuals use mainstream technology every day, whether they are disabled or not. Many items from microwaves, televisions and fridges to cars and mobile phones, come as standard un-specialized. A service supporting individuals with disabilities, or the user themselves, has two options when looking at equipment: to purchase mainstream or to adapt, and the answer to the question may not become clear without some thought.

Specialist assistive technology products are often developed to meet as many needs as possible by having a large array of configurability. Although this can increase a product's breadth within a population, costs tend to be increased and a relatively high level of knowledge is required for configuration and maintenance.

A small number of services have workshop facilities, staff expertise and the time available to develop bespoke equipment, which is obviously desirable in some circumstances. A custom made device for an individual that has been designed to meet a specific set of needs will hopefully last a long period of time with minimal configuration being required. This can, however, lead to problems with repair and maintenance where the client moves area or where the service is no longer available, the client being left helpless with a broken device and a reduced level of independence. The lifetime of any assistive technology, often used repetitively every day in compromising situations, for example at the front of a wheelchair, is unknown. Where budgets are tight, this may have an impact on what is supplied.

With this in mind, services are increasingly tending to look first at what is available on the consumer market to see if a mainstream product will meet the needs of the client. This applies equally to services having bespoke development opportunities. As an example, small children operating a computer may require a small mouse. It makes more sense to look at hardware that is available on the mainstream market than elsewhere. If what is available is unsuitable, the next question is whether adaptation of a mainstream device is possible. This is not without its difficulties, notably that adaptions may invalidate warranties or compromise device safety. Hardware adaptions may include the use of technology such as modeling silicone, e.g. http://sugru.com/Sugru (2012) and Polycaprolactone based products such as ShapeLock (2012), to help the handling of objects (see Fig. 27.12).

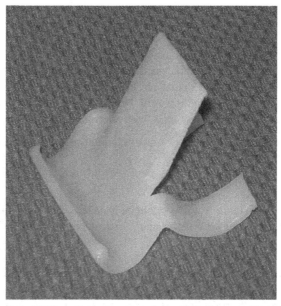

FIG. 27.12   Example of Shapelock (2012) used to create a prop for an iPod. *Courtesy of Luke Duncan/Flickr: lucianvenutian.*

Other items held by the user can be used to help facilitate access to mainstream technology, e.g. "dibbers" or "touch enabling devices" are terms used to describe technology that when strapped onto or held in the hand of a user, can increase functional usage to, say, a touchscreen device or keyboard. This can include everything from small T-bar shaped pipes from local DIY stores held in the hand, to toy fingernail extensions to provide better "point" for a client's finger.

Adapting "high-tech" technology

Unlike mechanical equipment, is not always so obvious how to adapt and modify technology based on computer systems for a client's needs. Due in part to legislation and government incentives, all popular operating systems now have a number of common accessibility features built in as standard (Field and Jette, 2007). A range of features include:

- Keyboard access:
  - Key repeat/filter keys
  - Key delay until repeat
  - Acceptance delay
  - Sticky keys (Fig. 27.13)
- Mouse access:
  - Mouse keys
  - Mouse speed/delay
  - Mouse cursor size
  - Click & scrolling speed
- Vision assistance:
  - In-built screen reader
  - Magnifier functionality
  - Contrast variability

Many of these options provide a huge array of configurability to allow a large number of people with physical and cognitive difficulties to access a computer. However, access to the computer alone is sometimes insufficient: a client may wish to access a particular programme which is not entirely accessible, needing modification to work successfully. One advantage of a modern computer is that developing unique software or scripts within the operating system is usually not as difficult as might be thought. Many tasks can be achieved with relatively little experience in software development. To highlight this we will use two case studies.

George is a 6 year old boy with cerebral palsy who has difficulty accessing a computer. His occupational therapist went through a number of activities, for example drawing on the computer and typing. After trying a number of keyboards, both specialist and mainstream, it was decided that typing on a conventional keyboard with a specialist key guard was suitable. Keyboard accessibility settings were assessed and configured using Keyboard Wizard (2012). George could operate the mouse well for drawing, accurately using the left click button. However, he kept hitting the right click button accidently. His therapist wanted a solution that would mean George could learn to use the mouse but be introduced to the right click functionality at a later date, i.e. he should not have to spend time correcting errors. A number of options were considered, including free software. With limited access to the internet, his therapist wrote a script in http://autohotkey.com/AutoHotkey (2012), a free program that allows remapping of any key to another, and simple scripting of the operating system at a low level. This script was turned into a self-running executable that the therapist created on her computer and then placed on the user's "Startup" folder so it would run when the computer was started up. It was also configured so that a helper could pause the script.

The "script" in this example is remarkably straightforward. Note this is written in a plain text file. Lines beginning with a semicolon are comment lines, i.e. lines that are not read by the computer programme but there to provide explanation.

```
; Map right button to left button. All presses of any mouse button act as a left button click
RButton::LButton
; Press cntrl+s keys together to suspend the programme. Operated by a helper or applied to a switch
^s::Suspend
```

Note: AutoHotkey scripts generally require AutoHotkey to be installed. However, it is possible to do this on a machine without the software installed by converting to a self-running executable using the "Convert .ahk to .exe" programme installed by AutoHotkey.

Here is another example:

Susan is a 19 year old student with an acquired brain injury (ABI) who has been working with her therapist on switching skills. As part of this, it was identified that Susan wishes to control music independently. Knowing that operating a music player fully can be difficult, her therapist develops an intervention programme where, for the first few days, Susan

(A)

(B)

Set up Filter Keys

☐ Turn on Filter Keys

Ignore or slow down brief or repeated keystrokes and adjust keyboard repeat rates.

Keyboard shortcut

☑ Turn on Filter Keys when right SHIFT is pressed for 8 seconds

When using keyboard shortcuts to turn Ease of Access settings on:

☑ Display a warning message when turning a setting on

☑ Make a sound when turning a setting on or off

FIG. 27.13 Examples of keyboard accessibility settings in (A) Mac OS X (10.8.2 "Mountain Lion") and (B) Windows 7.

presses the switch to here 45 s of music. To hear the next 45 s of music, Susan has to hit the switch again. This will help Susan build up her experience of using a switch for repeated action and also help make sure the team have located the switch in the best place. Next, her therapist wishes Susan to start investigating a second switch for other functions in her music player.

There are many ways for Susan to operate a music player with a single switch. Most media programs simply operate on the space key/bar to play music and pressing again to pause the music. Thus linking a switch up to "space" should be enough. However, Susan's therapist wants to achieve timed switching. This is difficult without developing something specific or using specialist hardware. Although slightly more complex, the essence of the script for this is as follows:

```
; Define a variable for length of delay
DelayTimeMS := 45000 ; 45 seconds in milliseconds
; Our shortcut will be shift control t. We could use anything in truth.
^+t::
; DetectHiddenWindows means look for windows not at the front.
; This means Susan could work on something else and iTunes is not at the front
DetectHiddenWindows,On
; This line, although hard to remember (copy & paste!)
; means send a space command to iTunes. Space to iTunes means Pause/Play toggle
ControlSend, ahk_parent, {space}, iTunes ahk_class iTunes
; Our script is now quietly not going to do anything for the period of time (45sec)
```

```
Sleep, DelayTimeMS
; Ok now wake up after 45 s and press space to iTunes
ControlSend, ahk_parent, {space}, iTunes ahk_class iTunes
; Hopefully iTunes has now paused
return
```

This script is not without fault, for example, iTunes needs to be running, a playlist highlighted and not playing to start with. Improvements can be found here: http://wllw.de/K14nkE.

Other, more advanced alternatives for scripting a computer are available. Regedit, for example, allows you to edit the registry of windows (Windows Registry, 2012). Useful if a user needs to regularly change their accessibility settings, a registry file can change back and forth settings by simply importing registry files each time. Scripting languages such as Visual Basic are also popular on Windows based operating systems for doing even more complex tasks with applications. Alternatively, languages such as Python (Python, 2012) allow more cross-compatibility between different operating systems.

The future of "high-tech" technology — new interface methods and new challenges

At the time of writing, traditional desktop PC's are still a mainstay of schools & workplaces. However, outside of these settings there is a considerable change in the way consumers control and access online content. Currently, 29% of US adults own a modern tablet/e-Reader (Kleiner et al., 2012). Unlike the traditional computing platform of the past, where the focus of interaction was turning an indirect method of control (a keyboard or mouse) into a graphical user interface element (mouse pointers, cursors and screen elements to access these), interaction with these newer devices is based on natural user interface methods to control the system, i.e. speech, touch and gesture. Some are suggesting that the pace of sales in this new arena will lead to traditional desktop based PCs being outsold by tablet devices by 2013 (Grabham, 2012; http://www.asymco.com/2012/03/02/when-will-the-tablet-market-be-larger-than-the-pc-market/Deidu, 2012a). This is depicted in Fig. 27.14.

Along with the redefined user interfaces, there is also a redefining of a number of services and systems that were traditionally whole markets in themselves (Kleiner et al., 2012). Car navigation systems, software distribution, media delivery, telephony, photography and banking are just a few sectors which have had to change direction to cope with this new interest. In some areas, assistive technology has redefined itself to make use of these new technological opportunities.

Developing tablet computing that is responsive, bright, loud and having sufficient battery life, even compared with high-end laptops, is not without its downsides. To achieve these features, manufacturers have used hardware that is power-efficient and software to match. This means that programmes are often compartmentalized or modular, not easily interfacing with each other, creating problems for assistive technology software which needs to provide a single point of control for a user. Projects such as http://komodoopenlab.com/tecla/Tecla (2012) aim to work on devices having either Google's Android or Apple's iOS system in order to provide a single point of access for assistive technology developers and modifiers (Fig. 27.15). Also of significance is that methods of access users and services had become accustomed to, such as keyboard debounce, switch boxes and common interface methods such as USB, have been abandoned in some areas.

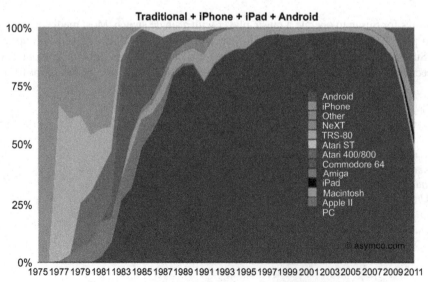

FIG. 27.14 The rise and fall of personal computing (Deidu, 2012b).

FIG. 27.15 Tecla (2012); a system built on an open-source hardware and software architecture aiming to facilitate access to mobile devices, such as smartphones and tablets.

The marginal number of sales for companies in the assistive technology sector, combined with an ever present demand for lower costs, leads to difficulties innovating rapidly (Harwin, 1998). Tecla (2012) was created as a social enterprise with support from academia and with the aim of creating an open-source hardware and software solution. This means that a company can sell a product and provide support to end users in a traditional sense, but if required, services can make alterations to the software and hardware since the structure is freely available. Companies in the assistive technology sector have traditionally had a highly conservative approach to development (Harwin, 1998) making sure any intellectual property is carefully guarded. This new model allows for faster development and reaction to user needs. As the pace of change in technology ever increases, this model allows professionals who have the skills to provide innovative and well-supported solutions.

References

AutoHotkey, 2012. AutoHotkey. Available at: http://www.autohotkey.com.

Deidu, H., 2012a. When Will Tablets Outsell Traditional PCs? (Asymco). Available at: http://www.asymco.com/2012/03/02/when-will-the-tablet-market-be-larger-than-the-pc-market/.

Deidu, H., 2012b. The Rise and Fall of Personal Computing (Asymco). Available at: http://www.asymco.com/2012/01/17/the-rise-and-fall-of-personal-computing/.

Field, M.J., Jette, A.M., 2007. Institute of Medicine (US) committee on disability in America. In: Field, M.J., Jette, A.M. (Eds.), The Future of Disability in America. National Academies Press (US), Washington (DC), 7, Assistive and Mainstream Technologies for People with Disabilities. Available from: http://www.ncbi.nlm.nih.gov/books/NBK11418/.

Grabham, D., 2012. Microsoft: Tablets Will Outsell Desktops Next Year: Windows 8 Is "both an Old and New Bet" (techradar.computing). Available at: http://www.techradar.com/news/software/operating-systems/microsoft-tablets-will-outsell-desktops-next-year-1087076.

Harwin, W.S., 1998. Niche product design, a new model for assistive technology. In: Porrero, I., Ballabio, E. (Eds.), Improving the Quality of Life for the European Citizen: Technology for Inclusive Design and Equality. IOS Press, p. 449452.

Kleiner, P., Caufield, Byers, 2012. 2012 KPCB Internet Trends Year-End Update (. Available at: Slideshare.Net http://www.slideshare.net/kleinerperkins/2012-kpcb-internet-trends-yearend-update.

Python, 2012. Python.org. Available at: http://python.org.

Shapelock, 2012. Shapelock. Available at: http://shapelock.com.

Sugru, 2012. Sugru. Available at: http://sugru.com/about/.

Tecla, 2012. Tecla KomodoOpenLab. Available at: http://komodoopenlab.com/tecla/.

Wizard, K., 2012. KPR-Keyboard Wizard. Available at: http://www.kpronline.com/kbwiz.php.

Further reading

Windows Registry and Regedit, Windows Registry — Wikipedia Available at: http://en.wikipedia.org/wiki/Windows_Registry#.REG_files.

Brain computer interfaces

Robert Lievesley

Oxford University Hospitals NHS Foundation Trust, Oxford, UK

Introduction

A brain computer interface (BCI) is a device which enables messages and commands to be conveyed directly from the brain to the external world via a computer. Ordinarily, intentions at the brain are converted into physical actions via the nervous and musculoskeletal systems. However, disease or old age may cause these systems to become impaired, leaving a person unable to interact with the environment as they would wish. BCIs offer the possibility of bypassing the body's motor systems and returning functionality to those who may otherwise be severely disabled by their impairments.

The technology is still in its infancy, and while there is much research in academic departments there are few commercial products available targeted for individual use. The more established methods of access are more suitable for the vast majority of people in need of assistive technologies but conditions such as motor neurone disease (MND) or a brain stem stroke may lead to a person developing locked-in syndrome. In these cases, a fully functioning healthy brain may be trapped within a body that is unable to move, and BCIs offer the only possibility of interaction with the external environment.

This section of the chapter gives a basic overview of how BCIs work, and what has been achieved to date. Those interested are referred to the further reading suggestions at the end.

Detecting intentions at the brain

A BCI must firstly be able to detect intentions at the brain, and secondly convert these intentions into actions on the external environment. The first task is extremely difficult. The brain is a complex organ made up of over 100 billion neurones, and the mechanisms by which it works are far from being fully understood. While techniques such as positron emission tomography (PET) and functional magnetic resonance imaging (fMRI), are able to provide some useful information about brain activity, they currently have the disadvantage of being large and expensive. For this reason, most BCI research has instead centred on using surface electroencephalography (EEG) to detect intentions at the brain.

Surface EEG

Messages are transmitted within the brain by electrical activity in the neurones. Each time a neurone is activated, its electrical potential alters by approximately 100 mV. In order to successfully detect and understand intentions at the brain, a BCI needs to acquire this signal, process it, and then recognize patterns within it.

The signal is acquired by placing electrodes on the scalp. The electrodes must be extremely sensitive, as by the time the signal reaches the scalp it is attenuated to only a few microvolts (Fig. 27.16).

The signal must then be processed to remove artefacts caused by the electrical activity associated with muscle (electromyography/EMG) or eye (electrooculography/EOG) movements, which would interfere with the EEG signal.

Once processed, the signal must be interpreted. However, at such a distance from the brain it is impossible to distinguish the activity of an individual neurone. Each electrode will be picking up activity from billions of neurones and only an overall idea of activity within a certain area of the brain can be ascertained. This means that pattern recognition is needed, and three different methods have proved to be successful with BCIs:

1) Sensorimotor rhythms
2) The P300 signal
3) Steady State Visual Evoked Potentials (SSVEP)

Sensorimotor rhythms

Sensorimotor rhythms are particular frequencies of EEG signal detected near the motor and sensory areas of the brain. It has been shown that when a movement is planned (but before it is carried out), there is a decrease in sensorimotor activity.

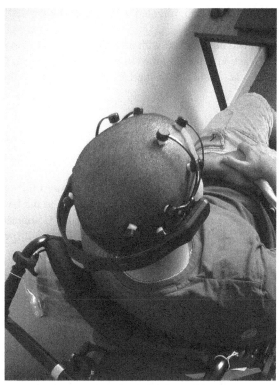

FIG. 27.16 Emotiv EPOC neuroheadset in use.

Conversely, after a movement has been carried out there is an increase in sensorimotor activity. BCI systems can take advantage of this knowledge by detecting the change in EEG activity when movements are planned.

P300

The P300 is a peak in the EEG signal detected approximately 300 ms after a stimulus is presented. The effect is strengthened by using the "oddball" paradigm: a strong signal is evoked from a low probability stimulus interspersed among many high probability stimuli. BCI systems can take advantage of this effect by showing users a number of options and detecting the peak in EEG signal when the desired option is viewed. Unlike sensorimotor rhythms, where a user must learn how to imagine movements that create detectable changes to the EEG signal, the P300 is evoked automatically.

Steady state visual evoked potentials (SSVEP)

In this technique, a range of stimuli are shown to the user, each pulsating at a different frequency. When the user focuses on the desired stimulus, the EEG signals in the occipital cortex lock into its phase. A BCI that measures this frequency can therefore identify the selected stimulus. This technique is often considered not to be a true BCI, since it detects a response to a stimulus rather than an intention formed in the brain.

Device control

Once intention has been detected at the brain, the next task of a BCI is to convert this to interaction with the real world. Examples of devices that can be successfully controlled by BCIs are wheelchairs, communication aids and computers.

Powered wheelchairs can be controlled using sensorimotor rhythm pattern recognition. The BCI is set up to distinguish when a user thinks about moving their left arm, and when they think about moving their right. These actions are then programmed into the left and right controls of a powered wheelchair, allowing a user to steer just by using their thoughts.

Communication aids can be controlled by BCIs that use the P300 signal to spell out words. A grid of letters is displayed on a computer screen. The user concentrates on the letter they want, while the computer randomly highlights different rows and columns in turn. Each time the desired letter is highlighted, a P300 signal is evoked automatically, allowing the correct letter to be selected.

Simple navigation of computer apps can be achieved with an SSVEP BCI, e.g. a basic music app may display choices such as play, pause, skip track etc. Each action is programmed to pulsate at a particular frequency; the BCI identifies which choice the user has made by comparing the frequency of the EEG signal to that of the desired stimulus.

The future

BCIs are currently only able to offer limited benefits, even to people with severe impairments, due to the relatively slow speed of interpreting the EEG signal. However, if the technology continues to develop, then there are great possibilities for what can be achieved in the future.

One area of research is the surgical implantation of electrodes directly onto the brain cortex to detect the activity of individual neurones. It has been shown that such systems can detect intention to the level of the individual words a person would like to speak, or the specific hand movements they would like to make. Combined with sophisticated engineering, it is possible to imagine future BCIs giving precise control over robotic arms or full speech, simply by thought.

Further reading

Akbari, H., Khalighinejad, B., Herrero, J., Mehta, A., Mesgarani, N., 2019. Towards reconstructing intelligible speech from the human auditory cortex. Sci. Rep. 9 (874). https://doi.org/10.1038/s41598-018-37359-z.

Bansal, D., Mahajan, R., 2019. EEG-based Brain-Computer Interfaces, first ed. Academic Press.

Diez, P., 2018. Smart Wheelchairs and Brain-Computer Interfaces. Academic Press.

Hassanien, A., Azar, A., 2015. Brain Computer Interfaces: Current Trends and Applications. Springer.

Hochberg, L., Bacher, D., Jarosiewicz, B., Masse, N., Simeral, J., Vogel, J., Haddadin, S., Liu, J., Cash, S., van der Smagt, P., Donoghue, J., 2012. Reach and grasp by people with tetraplegia using a neurally controlled robotic arm. Nature 485, 372−375. https://doi.org/10.1038/nature11076.

Nam, C., Nijholt, A., Lotte, F., 2018. Brain−Computer Interfaces Handbook: Technological and Theoretical Advances. CRC Press.

Web resources

Links to BCI sites having information about current projects:
http://bnci-horizon-2020.eu/.
http://www.bci2000.org/BCI2000/Home.html.

YouTube videos of BCI applications:
Robotic arm: https://www.youtube.com/watch?v=cg5RO8Qv6mc.
Wheelchair: https://www.youtube.com/watch?v=1VPY1d2t_FE&playnext=1&list=PL9AF5A92ADF45B2D9.
Communication aid: https://www.youtube.com/watch?v=eLT0G7d5y2M.
Music app: https://www.youtube.com/watch?v=uekFQ6X5Gg0.

Disability and smart house technology

Tim Adlam

University College London, London, UK & Designability, Bath, UK

Introduction

People with disabilities, physical and cognitive, use technology to offset their impairments and enhance their ability to function. Common examples of assistive technology include wheelchairs, walking sticks and reminders. These devices are useful to the disabled person and enable them to do things they would not otherwise be able to do. However, these are simple devices that perform their specific role without coordination with other systems. They are technology that is additional to the technological context in which the person lives.

An alternative approach to assistive technology is to adapt the *environment* in which the disabled person lives, building the ability to offset disability into building infrastructure. When such infrastructural technologies are integrated with control and coordination systems in a domestic setting, then a "smart house" is created. The Institution of Mechanical Engineers (2018) go further by suggesting that "creating a home which encourages its occupants to stay mobile and active as they age has the potential to keep them both mentally and physically fit for longer."

A smart house is a domestic dwelling fitted with sensors, controllers and assistive devices that can offset functional losses caused by physical or cognitive impairment, and enhance quality of life.

This section is about smart houses for people with disabilities. A smart home requires several key technologies to function:

- Sensors to detect the activity or status of the occupant
- Control system to assess the sensor data and decide on appropriate interventions
- Actuators to effect the desired interventions
- A network to link the sensors, control system and actuators
- Communications technology to enable information from the smart home to be sent to external stakeholders

Sensors

Sensors are used to detect and measure the activities of the occupant of a smart home so that the controller can provide appropriate support when it is needed. Common examples include passive infrared motion sensors as used in security systems, light level sensors, floor pressure pads and bed occupancy sensors. These sensors can be used to determine what activity the occupant is engaged in, or whether a problem has occurred that needs to be addressed. The information from the sensors can be used in the short term to direct an immediate response to a situation, or in the longer term to adjust the system's response to better suit the individual, or to detect and track trends that may indicate a slowly developing problem that can be flagged and responded to by an external stakeholder such as a doctor or social worker.

Controllers

The control system in a smart home is what differentiates it from an environmental control system or a telecare system (see other sections). The smart home controller should be able to integrate information from a variety of sources, including the installed sensors, and make decisions about interventions based upon that information. This computing platform may be centralized or distributed around the building. Simple controllers use rules based systems to make decisions such as:

IF "The bath water is 150 mm deep" THEN "the occupant should be prompted to turn off the taps"
IF "the bath water is 300 mm deep" THEN "the bath taps should be turned off"
OR
IF "there has been no activity for 6 h" THEN "the occupant's daughter should be informed"

More complex systems will integrate multiple sensor inputs and make probabilistic judgements about the safety of the occupant or a task that he is trying to complete. The COACH system controller, for example, provides context sensitive voice and video prompts to assist people with dementia with completing a hand washing task, based on inputs from a video camera.

An area requiring further research is the programming and configuration of smart house controllers by non-technical stakeholders. At the moment, configuring a smart house is the job of a technician at best, but an expert in information technology may also be required. There is a great need to develop means of configuring smart house controllers that can be understood and carried out by people without technical training such as the occupants themselves, social workers and sheltered housing managers.

Actuators

So what can a smart home do? This depends upon who the home is designed to support and the nature of their needs. To support a person with a spinal injury who uses a wheelchair for most of the day, a smart home will enable that occupant to reach things that might ordinarily be out of reach, perform tasks that are difficult from a wheelchair such as opening and closing doors and windows, and controlling lighting. Where there is no cognitive disability, the difference between a smart home and an environmental control system may be smaller. Where the occupant has a cognitive disability, such as dementia or a brain injury, then the type of support provided is likely to be more complex. The system will need to offset the cognitive disability and its symptoms which may include memory loss or difficulty with orientation in time and space. Examples of interventions in this context include voice prompts to tell an occupant to turn off a cooker where smoke has been detected and reminders to go back to bed at night time if the occupant is confused about the time of day. Other examples include lighting the way to the toilet at night to assist with route finding.

Networks

Many different network systems have been used to link sensors, controllers and actuators together. Some have been based upon existing automation systems within buildings and others on more generalized networking systems. Buildings' automation systems applied to smart homes include KNX, EnOcean, and LonWorks. These networking systems are robust and designed to be reliable for many years in the infrastructure of a building. They are typically available in wired and wireless versions. Ethernet, WiFi, ZigBee and Z-Wave are also being used increasingly for smart home installations. ZigBee is of particular interest as it is based on the IEEE 802.15.4 standard and is designed for the low-power networking of many small devices such as would be found in a smart home. Z-Wave differs from the other wireless systems in that it is proprietary and not an open standard.

Ethics and autonomy

The design and implementation of smart homes raises some ethical questions regarding the autonomy and privacy of the occupant. It is important that systems with such potential to be intrusive and controlling are not imposed upon people. They should be sensitively designed and configured, taking into account the needs, desires and autonomy of the individual. When designing a smart home system, what do the people who will be living with it think about the design? It is important to take the time to find out what they think at the beginning of the process, rather than assumptions being made.

Further reading

Abowd, G.A., Bobick, I., Essa, E., Mynatt, Rogers, W., 2002. The aware home: developing technologies for successful aging. In: Workshop Held in Conjunction with American Association of Artificial Intelligence (AAAI) Conference 2002, Alberta, Canada, July 2002. Workshop Publication Accepted of Collection: Proceedings of AAAI Workshop and Automation as a Care Giver.

Boger, J., Hoey, J., Poupart, P., Boutilier, C., Fernie, G., Mihailidis, A., 2006. A planning system based on Markov decision processes to guide people with dementia through activities of daily living. Inf. Technol. Biomed. IEEE Trans. 10 (2), 323—333.

Dewsbury, G.A., Taylor, B.J., Edge, H.M., 2002. Designing dependable assistive technology systems for vulnerable people. Health Inf. J. 8, 104—110. https://doi.org/10.1177/146045820200800208.

Diane, F., Mahoney, R.B., Purtilo, F.M., Webbe, M.A., Ashok, J., Bharucha, T.D., Adlam, T., Holly, B., Jimison, B.T., Becker, S.A., Working Group on Technology of the Alzheimer's Association, 2007. In-home monitoring of persons with dementia: ethical guidelines for technology research and development. Alzheimer's Dementia 3 (3), 217—226. https://doi.org/10.1016/j.jalz.2007.04.388. ISSN:1552-5260.

Institution of Mechanical Engineers, 2018. Healthy Homes: Accommodating an Ageing Population. Institution of Mechanical Engineers.

Martin, S., Kelly, G., Kernohan, W.G., McCreight, B., Nugent, C., 2008. Smart home technologies for health and social care support. Cochrane Database Syst. Rev. (4), CD006412.

Mihailidis, A., Bardram, J., Wan, D., 2006. Pervasive Computing in Healthcare. CRC Press. ISBN-13:978-0849336218.

Mihailidis, A., Cockburn, A., Longley, C., Boger, J., 2008. The acceptability of home monitoring technology among community-dwelling older adults and baby boomers. Assist. Technol. 20 (1), 1−12.

Orpwood, R., no date. Smart Homes, International Encyclopaedia of Rehabilitation. Available at: http://cirrie.buffalo.edu/encyclopedia/en/article/155/.

Orpwood, R., Gibbs, C., Adlam, T., Faulkner, R., Meegahawatte, D., 2005. The design of smart homes for people with dementia − user-interface aspects. Univers. Access Inf. Soc. vol 4 (2), 156−164. Springer-Verlag. ISSN:1615-5289.

Park, K.H., Bien, Z., Lee, J.J., Kook Kim, B., Lim, J.T., Kim, J.O., Lee, H., Stefanov, D.H., Kim, D.J., Jung, J.W., Do, J.H., Seo, K.H., Hui Kim, C., Song, W.G., Lee, W.J., 2007. Robotic smart house to assist people with movement disabilities. Aut. Robots 22 (2), 183−198. https://doi.org/10.1007/s10514-006-9012-9.

Technology enabled care services

David Long

AJM Healthcare, UK & Oxford University Hospitals NHS Foundation Trust, Oxford, UK

Definition

According to NHS England (2019) "Technology enabled care services (TECS) refer to the use of telehealth, telecare, telemedicine, telecoaching and self-care in providing care for patients with long term conditions that is convenient, accessible and cost-effective, [recognizing] the potential of these solutions to transform the way people engage in and control their own healthcare, empowering them to manage their care in a way that is right for them." With an ageing population it seems sensible to exploit technology wherever possible in order to make optimal use of the healthcare funding that is available.

Telehealth and telecare

The idea behind telehealth and telecare is to use the technological advances of recent years to provide improved and more efficient delivery of healthcare to people in their own homes, reducing the need for attendance at a clinic or costly residential care. This is particularly relevant to older people and those with long term conditions (Davis, 2012). One of the main drivers for this is that people are living longer and with increasingly complex health needs, putting increased strain on already stretched budgets.

The concept behind telehealth is remote patient monitoring. Point-of-care technologies are used to take various physiological measurements, for example blood pressure or heart rate. If a measurement falls outside what is expected, action can be taken and hopefully this would occur prior to the situation becoming critical, thereby reducing the rate of hospital admission (King's Fund, 2012).

Telecare is again remote patient monitoring, but focussing on the personal safety of the individual. It uses elements of a "smart" home (see separate section), such as a sensor to detect if the patient has fallen, to transmit important information to the relevant person. It can also include a personal alarm which the patient can trigger if they get into difficulty (King's Fund, 2012).

Videoconferencing

The use of videoconferencing is starting to emerge as a means of providing healthcare. In some instances it is possible to carry out an assessment and/or to make changes to someone's care using this facility, which would not be possible with a telephone/teleconference method of contact. It allows multiple people to meet and to share a problem and, with the help of a visual display, to find a way to solve that problem. Dedicated videoconferencing suites are available in some organizations but low cost and widely available technologies are now available to most people in their own homes. Arthur (2017) suggests that video consultations generate efficiencies, are convenient for patients and do not impair the quality of consultation.

There are limitations, of course. Camera placement is crucial and may not reveal the full picture, e.g. views from different angles, environmental context. Getting the technology operational for everyone involved in the appointment can take time and is dependent upon sufficient broadband speed and technological ability. Some organizations do not permit the use of the widely available technologies for fear of a breach of data security.

Despite these limitations, it seems likely that we will see an increase in the use of this technology as it becomes available more commonly.

Remote access

Many information technology support services already solve problems by taking control of a computer remotely, even within the same organization. This reduces significantly the need for travel to individual computers. This same technique can be applied to electronic assistive technology, allowing a clinician, engineer or technician to work on a patient's computer from their office, negating the need to spend time travelling, thereby reducing costs. At the time of writing, use of this technique is not widespread but it is anticipated that this will increase in the coming years.

References

Arthur, H., 2017. Steal with Pride: The Benefits of Digital Technology NHS Providers. Available at: https://nhsproviders.org/news-blogs/blogs/steal-with-pride-the-benefits-of-digital-technology.

Davis, D., 2012. 3 million lives Programme: Turning the Spotlight on Telehealth and Telecare. Department of Health (UK). Allied Health Professions Bulletin No. 91 gateway 18271.

NHS England, 2019. Technology Enabled Care Services NHS England. Available at: https://www.england.nhs.uk/tecs/.

Further reading

Schwartz, J., 2012. What Impact Does Telehealth Have on Long Term Conditions Management? King's Fund. Available at: http://www.kingsfund.org.uk/topics/telecare-and-telehealth/what-impact-does-telehealth-have-long-term-conditions-management.

Chapter 28

Gait and clinical gait analysis

Adam P. Shortland

Guy's and St. Thomas' NHS Foundation Trust, London, United Kingdom; School of Biomedical Engineering and Imaging Science, King's College London, London, United kingdom

Chapter outline

Introduction

In many clinical conditions and disorders, walking ability is highly correlated with health-related quality of life. In cerebral palsy for example, independent mobility seems to be linked to the probability of forming long term romantic relationships, of gaining and maintaining employment, and of happiness (Murphy et al., 2000). Even amongst typically developing older adults, there is a positive relationship between level of walking ability and the ability to carry out the activities of daily living, and to participate in life events (Fagerström and Borglin, 2010). No wonder then that interventions to enable, improve or maintain walking are commonly formulated, attempted and evaluated. Clinical gait analysis (CGA) is the assessment of movement in children and adults to monitor ambulatory function. A common output from these analyses are treatment recommendations to improve walking patterns, and, by doing so, improve overall physical function, participation and quality of life in affected individuals.

To place CGA in context it is necessary to understand something of the evolution of walking and of its emergence in the infant.

The evolution of bipedalism in humans

Bipedal ambulation is the preferred and usual method of walking in very few mammalian species, including the giant pangolin and the human being. Palaeontologists have identified skeletal adaptations necessary to walk functionally in the ancestors of modern humans who existed as far back as 5 million years. These include adaption of the *foramen magnum* so that the skull sits above the spinal column and adaptations to the femur to allow our feet to point in the direction of progression. Why early humans evolved to walk bipedally is not completely clear although it does not seem to be related to the use of hand tools which came much later. More likely, early humans developed bipedal ambulation secondary to the rearing of defenceless infants, requiring one of the parents for protection and requiring the other to gather greater amounts of food. The theory goes that it was necessary to walk bipedally in order to free the upper limbs to perform food collection.

Clinical Engineering. https://doi.org/10.1016/B978-0-08-102694-6.00028-0

Certainly, it is plausible that infant insecurity was the driving cause of bipedalism. The central nervous system in the human infant undergoes extraordinary development during the first year of life with the brain increasing in mass by 100%. It is thought that this level of growth would be impossible to sustain metabolically within the mother's womb, so, unlike other (quadrupedal) species, which are effectively "ready to go" when born, the human infant still requires a lot of development. Interestingly, one of the reasons the human infant might take so long to progress is the need to walk bipedally, which requires extraordinary sensori-motor and muscular development.

The development of walking in infants

The motor development of infants occurs in a characteristic rostro-caudal (head to tail) manner. At around 2 months of age, the typically-developing baby may be able to turn its head towards a parent. At 4 months, the infant raises its chest and can hold her head steady. By 6 months, she can sit supported, and by nine months, crawl and pull to stand. It is typically at around 1 year that the infant can stand and take her first independent steps. However, adult patterns of walking do not emerge until 4 or 5 years age. But why does this process take so long and why does it take place in this sequential head-to-tail manner?

Firstly, the mechanical challenge to stand on two limbs with stability is enormous. To stand effectively, we must learn to actively control our body position when our centre of mass is at a height which is much greater than the length of our base of support. Being susceptible to a small *toppling moment* requires us to respond to minor perturbations to avoid falling over. We do this by controlling the levers of all our lower limb joints but especially of our feet. Large distal muscles insert either side of the ankle to facilitate changes in the position of the centre of pressure to maintain our balance.

Secondly, our sensori-motor control must be sufficient to detect changes in the centre of pressure with respect to our body centre of mass, and react to those changes, to maintain stability in standing, and to co-ordinate the movement of our limb segments to progress.

The development of distal muscle mass and the ability to control it has not developed at the time of birth. Rather, neural pathways are remodeled and refined during the first few years of life but particularly during the first two. The first independent movements of the foetus occur at around 8–10 post-conception weeks (Prechtl et al., 1993), upon innervation of the muscle precursors and from the spontaneous action of motor neurons in the spinal cord. Up until 17 weeks of gestation it appears that the development of cortical circuitry and peripheral reflex circuitry are largely independent (Fig. 28.1A). After 17 weeks, the cortico-spinal tract (CST) (and other tracts) enter the spinal cord but will not completely innervate the neurons of the ventral horn along the full length of the spinal cord until 35 weeks. The dense connections made by the muscle afferents now have to compete with the invading axons of the CST (Fig. 28.1B). In the normally-developing human, the descending connections displace the afferent connections such that the connections to the spinal neurons are dominated by descending input at maturity. Clowry suggests that the arrival of corticospinal neurons begins a critical period in the development of the cord circuitry, in particular the development of inhibitory interneurons (inhibition is required to turn off excited α-motor neurons) (Clowry, 2007). Concurrent activity in segmental and descending pathways appears to reinforce and strengthen connectivity while other non-useful connections are lost.

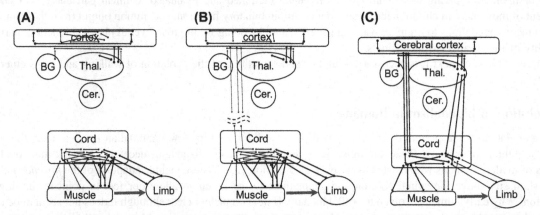

FIG. 28.1 The development of the central nervous system in early life. (A) 8–17 weeks gestation: neural circuits separately in cerebral grey matter and between α motor neurons and target muscles. Afferent axons on the spinal cord may terminate diffusely. Spinal cord circuitry is not fully formed. There is weak efferent output to the musculature. There is no connection between the cortex and the α-motor neurone; (B) 17–31 weeks gestation: the CST enters the spinal cord; 31–35 weeks gestation: axons of the CST invade the ventral horn and synapse with the α motor neurons; (C) 35 weeks -2 years post natal: CST competes for space with the afferent fibres; monosynaptic reflex pathway diminished; the development of inhibitory interneurones; the development of spinal cord circuits and the facilitation of motor output results in stronger and sustained efferent flow to muscles, and greater reciprocal inhibition of antagonists.

During the first 2 years of age (Fig. 28.1C), refinement and elimination of connections within the spinal cord occurs which depends on the movements of the growing and developing individual, and thus motor control develops. As well as an increase in the number of connections made by axons of the descending tracts, changes in the facilitation of neuron activation by the CST occurs tending to boost activation of the target muscles. The implication of stronger facilitation is that as the corticospinal system develops, the motor cortex can activate spinal motor circuits—and produce movement—with lower levels of activity. CST neurons initially appear responsible for development and refinement of intraspinal connections, and later for transmitting motor commands. The presence of low threshold excitation by descending input is probably responsible for the development of a sustained activation of the musculature necessary for muscle growth and the production of antigravity postures and walking (Eken et al., 2008).

The sequential rostro-caudal acquisition of motor milestones in the infant is probably related to the rostro-caudal progression of the CST with caudal nervous connections and distal musculature developing later than rostral ones. This notion is supported by the electromyographic recordings in infants made by Ivanenko and his colleagues (Ivanenko et al., 2013). They demonstrated that spinal cord output to activate the musculature develops rostro-caudally in typically developing children between the ages of 1 and 2 years. This is accompanied by maturation of intersegmental movement patterns probably as a consequence of the refinement of specialized neuronal circuits (central pattern generators) in the spinal cord (Forssberg, 1985). In contrast, in children with cerebral palsy who have a damaged CST, primitive infant patterns of muscle activation are maintained and intersegmental coordination of the lower limb do not mature (Cappellini et al., 2016).

The following points can be made in summary:

1. Cortical and spino-muscular neural circuitry develop independently until 17 weeks gestation.
2. Development of spinal circuits necessary for non-spontaneous movement do not begin to develop until mid-way through gestation after the arrival of the CST.
3. Inhibitory neurons in the spinal cord develop late in foetal development and during early post-natal development, along with the refinement of spinal cord circuitry, the facilitation of α-motor neurone output and the elimination of afferent connections.
4. Muscle development occurs secondary to sustained innervation of the musculature.
5. Innervation and activation of the lower limb musculature follows a proximal to distal pattern until a mature pattern emerges.
6. In children with cerebral palsy (in whom the cortico-spinal tract is damaged) adult patterns of muscle activation and intersegment co-ordination do not emerge and motor control is limited.

It is in the context of an understanding of normal neurological and muscular development that clinical gait analyses should be performed.

Describing gait

There are multiple ways of describing gait, from the distance we cover with each stride, to the movements of our limbs and the forces acting them, and the activation of the muscles contributing to movement. In a typical clinical gait analysis, more than one aspect of walking will be measured to help clinicians understand the patient's gait problem.

One of the most convenient ways of assessing gait is to observe and/or record the patient walking. There are scores and charts available to help the clinician classify the gait pattern, for example the Edinburgh Visual Gait Score (del Pilar Duque Orozco et al., 2016). These measures are very useful for evaluating outcome but their limited reliability and validity may make them inappropriate for treatment decision.

Spatio-temporal parameters

Gait can be considered as the advancement of one limb in front of the other in a regular pattern. In a walking gait, at least one foot remains in contact with the floor (in contrast with running, hopping or skipping where there is a period of flight). The repeated advancement of alternate limbs gives rise to phases where both limbs are in contact with the floor and periods where only one limb is in contact. These phases of gait are circumscribed by events. Let's look in a little more detail at the events and phases that make up a *gait cycle*.

A gait cycle is defined as the interval between successive foot contacts on the same limb. *Foot contact* defines the start of a period of double support called *loading*. In this period, weight is transferred from the trailing limb to the leading limb (Fig. 28.2). This phase of gait comes to an end when the subject raises the contralateral (opposite) limb from the floor, an

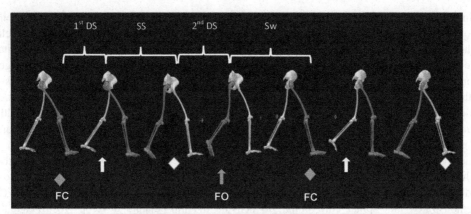

FIG. 28.2 The phases and events of the gait cycle. The green limb is the ipsilateral limb and the grey limb is the contralateral or opposite limb. FC, OFO, OFC, and FO refer to the gait cycle events — Foot Contact, Opposite Foot Off, Opposite Foot Contact and Foot Off. First DS, SS, second DS and Sw refer to the phases of the gait cycle — first period of Double Support (or loading), single support, second period of double support or preswing, and swing.

event called *opposite foot off*. In typical mature walking, this period of loading lasts about 10% of the gait cycle. Opposite foot off defines the beginning of a period of single support. During this phase the ipsilateral limb is solely responsible for maintaining a straight leg position and preventing the body from collapsing. In this period, the contralateral limb is in swing. In symmetrical walking, the period of single support and swing make up about 40% of the gait cycle. The period of single support is terminated when the contralateral limb makes contact with the ground, or *opposite foot contact*. The second period of double support (sometimes called preswing) starts with opposite foot contact. In this period load is transferred to the contralateral (now leading) limb and the ipsilateral limb is released to promote forward progression of the limb. The stance phase of gait is ended when the ipsilateral limb leaves the floor (*foot off*).

An individual's gait can be usefully described using spatial and temporal parameters derived from the concept of a gait cycle. Table 28.1 documents the most common parameters and gives typical values in the mature adult.

The measurement and interpretation of spatio-temporal parameters

Spatio-temporal parameters can be measured using simple equipment such as a stop watch, chalk dust and a marked-out area. Chalk dust on the floor permits the measurement of spatial parameters, and a stop watch allows the mean stride time and cadence across a number of cycles to be measured (the temporal parameters). Often, specialized services will employ optoelectronic cameras and forceplates, or pressure mats to do the same.

TABLE 28.1 Spatio-temporal parameters and their typical adult values.

Parameter	Description	Typical adult values
Stride length	The distance between successive foot contacts on the same limb.	1.3–1.6 m
Stride time	The time taken between successive foo contacts on the same limb.	~1 s
Cadence	The frequency of walking and the reciprocal of stride time. This is generally expressed in steps per minute.	110–120 steps/min
Speed	The mean speed of the centre of mas of the subject over the course of the gait cycle.	1.2–1.6 m/s
Step length	The distance in the direction of progression between initial contact on the contralateral limb and the ipsilateral limb.	0.65–0.8 m
Step width	The distance between two feet in when both on the floor perpendicular to the direction of walking	~0.3 m
Single support percentage	The percentage time of the gait cycle spent supported by a single limb.	~40%

Primitive interpretations of a patient's gait may be conducted solely using spatio-temporal parameters. For example, walking speed is often used as an outcome measure before and after intervention to monitor patient recovery and to evaluate the effectiveness of the treatment. Changes in specific parameters may be in some way diagnostic. A reduced period of single support may indicate instability or weakness of the lower limb and reduced stride length may be caused by an element of muscle tightness. However, the use of spatio-temporal parameters alone to diagnose patient conditions is fraught with ambiguity. For example, a shortened period of swing may be related to limited power generated by the plantarflexors on the ipsilateral limb to accelerate the swing limb forward. Equally, it may be a compensation for a weak contralateral limb (the period of swing on one limb is necessarily equal to the period of single support on the other limb).

Comparing the spatio-temporal parameters between individuals is not straightforward because the lengths of their limbs vary. Because the movement of the lower limb behaves like a pendulum in swing and the movement of the trunk can be thought of as an inverted pendulum, the principal spatio-temporal parameters are often scaled to dimensionless parameters based on dynamics of a pendulum to account for inter-subject variation in leg length (Hof and Zijlstra, 1997).

Describing joint movement

Spatio-temporal parameters may provide some insights into the walking difficulties of a patient but to obtain a more detailed analysis of the issue it useful to describe the motions of the limb segments, and particularly of the lower limb joints. Most commonly, 3D gait laboratories use most optical motion capture equipment which record the 3D position of retroreflective markers which are attached to the skin using double-sided sticky tape. These marker positions along with anthropometric measurements of the body are used to construct reference frames for the body segments (Fig. 28.3).

In general, in gait analysis, one makes two simplifying assumptions about the properties of the limb segments and of the joint rotations.

The first assumption is that limb segments are rigid bodies i.e. that the distance between any two points on the body remain constant during movement. Obviously, in the human body, the bones can be considered as rigid bodies but the skin, muscles and fat surrounding them cannot. We use this simplifying assumption because it is very difficult to model soft tissue movement though many attempts have been made (Leardini et al., 2005).

The second assumption is that joints move around a single axis or centre of rotation throughout their range of motion. This approach is valid for some of the joints that we are interested in movement analysis (e.g. the hip, the wrist, the talocrural joint) but is not strictly satisfied by others (e.g. the knee joint and the subtalar joint). Although, attempts have been made to model the variation in position of joint axes and centres of rotation with movement, the utility of these approaches

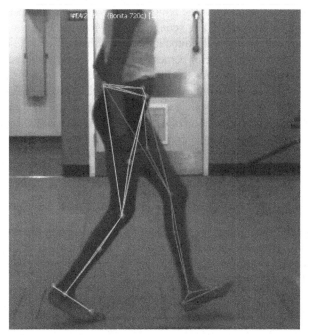

FIG. 28.3 A subject walking with retroreflective markers attached to their skin over particular bony landmark. In this visualization, the positions of the markers are projected on a sagittal plane video recording.

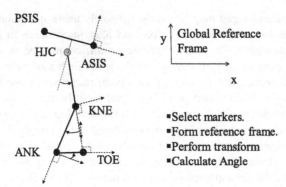

FIG. 28.4 The formation of reference frames and the calculation of angles in a 2D multisegmented model of the human body.

is confounded by the relatively small displacements of joint axes in the presence of skin movement and short neighbouring body segments. Think of the small movements within your foot as you walk! However, many movement analysis units have used complex marker sets and calibration procedures in attempts to model the movements within the foot (Leardini et al., 2019) and the shoulder (Duprey et al., 2017).

Having made these assumptions, the first task in producing a model of movement is to define the body segments to be considered. In the case of clinical gait analysis, we often model the lower limbs as having 7 rigid body segments: the pelvis, two thighs, two tibial segments or shanks and the feet. One must model the relative orientations of the body segments and calculate the angles between them.

Perhaps the best way of appreciating how to build a biomechanical model is to do it in 2D in the x-y plane. Let's imagine a pelvic segment, a thigh, a shank and a foot all connected by pin joints (Fig. 28.4).

Our first task is to describe the orientation of the parent segment, the pelvis, relative to the space we are walking in. We make an *orthogonal axis system or reference frame* for the space based on some vectors that we can define. In the case of a typical room it is most convenient to employ horizontal and vertical axes with a common origin. Let's call this the *global reference frame*. Next, we can define the reference frame for the pelvis. It is useful to form the axis system using a vector (defining line) with some anatomical meaning. In this case, we choose bony prominences on the pelvis (the anterior and posterior superior iliac spines, ASIS and PSIS). Then we can form a reference frame from the unit vector in the direction of line joining the posterior and anterior spines and a unit vector perpendicular to this line, and make the origin of this reference frame the anterior spine. To make an anatomically meaningful reference frame for the thigh is a little bit more problematic because the proximal end of the femur (the femoral head) is hidden internally within the body. However, the centre of the femoral head, or hip joint centre (HJC) in a congruent hip joint, can be estimated with respect to the reference frame of the pelvis. We can define a unit vector in the direction between the HJC and the knee marker (KNE) and make its origin at the KNE. We can also construct a unit vector perpendicular this vector to form a reference for the thigh segment. In a similar way, we can define reference frames for the tibial (shank) segment and for the foot segment.

Having established the reference frames for our body segments, we can calculate the angular rotations that would make neighbouring reference frames align. The rotations are expressed formally using rotation matrices. Eq. (28.1) shows the equivalent rotation matrix for an anti-clockwise rotation of α, around the z-axis (our 2D body is moving in the x-y plane, so the body segments are rotating around the z-axis).

$$P_P = \begin{bmatrix} P_{XP} \\ P_{YP} \end{bmatrix} = \begin{bmatrix} \cos\alpha & -\sin\alpha \\ \sin\alpha & \cos\alpha \end{bmatrix} \cdot \begin{bmatrix} P_{XD} \\ P_{YD} \end{bmatrix} = [R] \cdot [P_D] \qquad (28.1)$$

where $\begin{bmatrix} P_{XP} \\ P_{YP} \end{bmatrix}$ and $\begin{bmatrix} P_{XD} \\ P_{YD} \end{bmatrix}$ are points in the proximal and distal reference frames respectively.

This matrix based on the angle of rotation has an equivalent formulation using the *direction cosines* (the projection of one axis on another axis) (Eq. 28.2). Here, each matrix element is formed from the projection of one of the parent axes onto one of the distal axes. You can solve a multisegmented 2D model for movement using these rotation matrices and calculate the angle of rotation throughout the recorded movement.

$$P_P = \begin{bmatrix} P_{XP} \\ P_{YP} \end{bmatrix} = \begin{bmatrix} \cos_{XPXD} & \cos_{XPYD} \\ \cos_{YPXD} & \cos_{YPYD} \end{bmatrix} \cdot \begin{bmatrix} P_{XD} \\ P_{YD} \end{bmatrix} = [R] \cdot [P_D] \qquad (28.2)$$

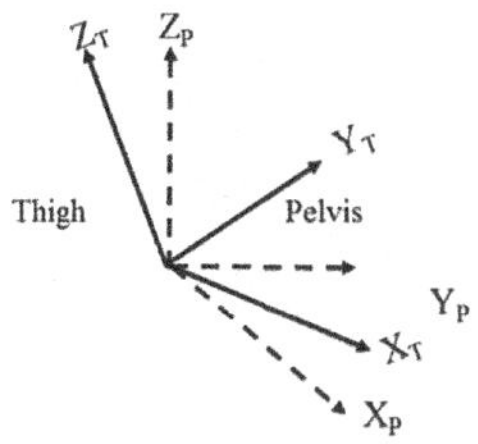

$$\begin{pmatrix} \cos X_t X_p & \cos X_t Y_p & \cos X_t Z_p \\ \cos Y_t X_p & \cos Y_t Y_p & \cos Y_t Z_p \\ \cos Z_t X_p & \cos Z_t Y_p & \cos Z_t Z_p \end{pmatrix}$$

$$\begin{bmatrix} 1 & 0 & 0 \\ 0 & \cos\gamma & \sin\gamma \\ 0 & -\sin\gamma & \cos\gamma \end{bmatrix} \begin{bmatrix} \cos\beta & 0 & -\sin\beta \\ 0 & 1 & 0 \\ \sin\beta & 0 & \cos\beta \end{bmatrix} \begin{bmatrix} \cos\alpha & -\sin\alpha & 0 \\ \sin\alpha & \cos\alpha & 0 \\ 0 & 0 & 1 \end{bmatrix}$$

FIG. 28.5 Calculation of the 3D Cardan hip angles. The 3D rotation matrix can be constructed from the direction cosines of the between a reference frame representing the thigh ($X_TY_TZ_T$) and a reference frame representing the pelvis ($X_PY_PZ_P$). Cardan angles can be calculated by decomposing the rotation matrix into 3 component matrices representing independent rotations around the X, Y and Z axes.

In 3D, the principles are precisely the same. An anatomically meaningful reference frame is created for each body segment, rotation (direction cosine) matrices are solved from the relative orientation of neighbouring reference frames, and angles of rotation are calculated (Fig. 28.5). The direction cosine matrix is unique to a particular relative orientation of the two reference frames, and this matrix can be formed from the multiplication of 3 component matrices that represent rotations that represent (2D) rotations each axis. However, the magnitude of the 3 angular rotations around the x, y and z axes derived from the decomposition of this matrix depends on the order taken. For example, the *Cardan* angles (α, β, γ) produced for a sequence of component rotations around the z-axis first and then the y and x axes are not the same as those produced by a sequence starting with a rotation around the x-axis followed by rotations around the y and z axes. Where there is a potential ambiguity, it is important to establish convention, and in this case, the convention is to perform the rotation in the flexion-extension axis first followed by the ab/adduction axis and then the transverse (or rotational) axis. One could argue that the formulation of Cardan angles in this way from the decomposition of the direction cosine matrix can be deceiving since the angles produced are not the classical projection angles of anatomy but a convenient mathematical abstraction that produces something similar but not the same. This may cause some confusion for the clinician when reviewing gait data and videos of the patient walking. At the pelvis, a change in the sequence of rotations has been proposed so that the Cardan angles produced more closely match the projection angles that the clinician may be familiar with (Baker, 2001).

The result of the construction of reference frames and the computation of Cardan angles is a set of graphs representing the movement of the individual over the gait cycle. A patient's data may be compared to those of an age-matched control group to identify gait abnormalities (Fig. 28.6).

Joint forces and moments

Forces act on the body due to gravitational acceleration and to *inertial* accelerations of the body and its segments. Let's consider a very large man standing on the earth. The force acting on him is given by the Newton's equation $F = \frac{GMm}{r^2}$ where G is the universal gravitational, M is the mass of the earth, m is the mass of the man, and r is the distance between the centre of mass of the man and the centre (of mass) of the earth. We also know that the acceleration due to any force is given by Newton's second law $a = \frac{F}{m}$. In this special case $a = g = \frac{GM}{r^2}$ or approximately 9.81 ms^{-2}. The man doesn't accelerate towards the centre of the earth because there is a *reaction force* acting on the man which is equal and opposite to the force of gravity (Newton's third law). This keeps the man in *equilibrium*, and there are no net forces acting on him.

The reaction force which opposes the force owing to gravity is measured by our bathroom scales when we stand on them. When we move on the scales (try bouncing up and down on your tiptoes), the digital readout or the position of the analogue pointer changes because the scale is now measuring a combination of the force owing to gravity (your body weight) and the force owing to our inertial acceleration. Force plates that are used to measure ground reaction forces in walking in a gait laboratory are more sophisticated versions of weighing scales. They measure the 3D reaction force originating from the floor including components in the vertical, medio-lateral and fore-aft directions. They also measure the origin of the reaction force, known as the *centre of pressure*. The combination of the component orthogonal forces and the centre of pressure give the Ground Reaction Force Vector or GRFV.

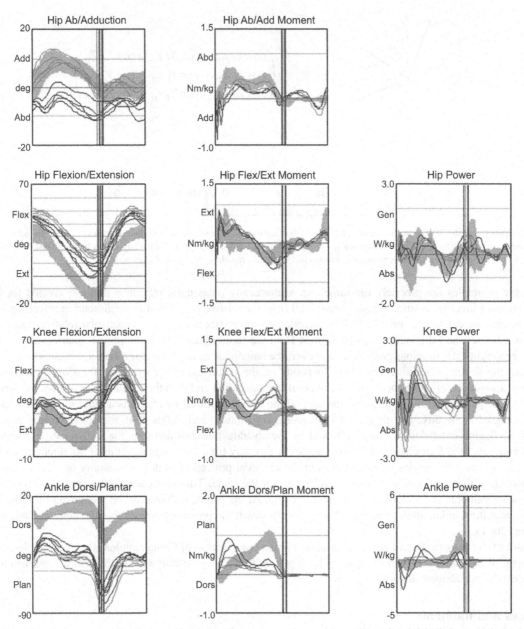

FIG. 28.6 Examples of kinematic and kinetic data (red and green lines represent the movement of the left and right limbs respectively) from a patient compared to some control data from and aged matched group (grey band, mean ± 1 SD).

If we assume that the inertial accelerations in walking are small compared to the gravitational acceleration, then estimates of the angular forces (or *moments*) around the joints can be made by projecting the GRFV on to a spatial representation of the joints of the lower limb. In Fig. 28.7, the vector passes in front of the ankle producing an external *dorsiflexing* moment, behind the knee producing a external knee flexing moment, and in front of the hip producing an external hip flexing moment. To maintain equilibrium, the muscles at these joints must produce equal and opposite net *internal* moments — in this case, a plantarflexor moment at the ankle, a knee extensor moment and a hip extensor moment. The magnitude and direction of these moments is given by the cross product of the perpendicular distance between the GRFV and the joint centre and the GRFV.

In general, joint moments during walking can be estimated accurately by the projection method. However, during portions of the gait cycle where the rotational accelerations and/or mass moments of inertia are large (such as at the hip in late stance/early swing), one must use an alternative technique called *inverse dynamics* to estimate joint moments. In this method, the equations of motion are solved for the foot segment in order to estimate the reaction forces and moments at the

FIG. 28.7 Using the GRFV to estimate the joint moments. In this case the vector passes infront of the ankle behind the knee and in front of the hip. In order to maintain equilibrium these external moments must be counterbalanced by internal moments generated by the ankle plantarflexors, the knee extensors and the hip extensors.

ankle. The forces and moments produced by rotational and linear accelerations of the tibia and the forces and moments at the ankle are used to solve for the forces and moments and the knee. In a similar way, the forces and moments at the hip are estimated from the forces and moments produced from the rotational and linear accelerations of the thigh segment and the knee joint forces and moments.

Joint power is the scalar product of joint moment and angular joint velocity. One can think of it as the rate of transfer of energy between neighbouring segments. When the internal joint moment and the angular joint velocity act in the same direction then positive power is produced and when they act in the opposite directions there is negative power. So, for example, when the positive power is generated at the ankle in preswing (see Fig. 28.6), then energy is transferred from the foot to the shank.

Describing muscle activity

Muscles are the only tissues in the body which actively generate forces. Skeletal muscles execute commands from the central nervous system (CNS) to generate joint motion, moments and powers. Abnormal patterns or magnitudes of muscle activation secondary to a damaged CNS (such as in cerebral palsy, stroke or spinal cord injury) are often responsible for abnormal movements.

Surface electromyography is the recording of electrical activity of muscles from sensors placed on the skin. The signal is amplified by a differential instrumented amplifier. In gait analysis units, surface electromyograms (sEMGs) are often recorded synchronously with the motion and force plate data (see Fig. 28.8).

An sEMG is a complex signal being formed from action potentials travelling down fibres in the muscle at different depths. The contribution of a single action potential to the sEMG depends on the distance between the muscle fibre and the skin surface, the electrical properties of the tissues between the action potential the electrodes, the orientation of the muscle fibres with respect to the placement of the electrodes, and the distance between the electrodes. Consequently, directly inferring a level of muscle activation is fraught with error. Nonetheless, EMG can be useful in determining the origin of the patient's problem and directing treatment (Fig. 28.8).

Other instrumentation used to assess gait

Kinematics, kinetics and electromyography are amongst the most commonly used instrumented assessments in gait analysis but other assessments can be employed to elucidate particular aspects of the patient's pathology.

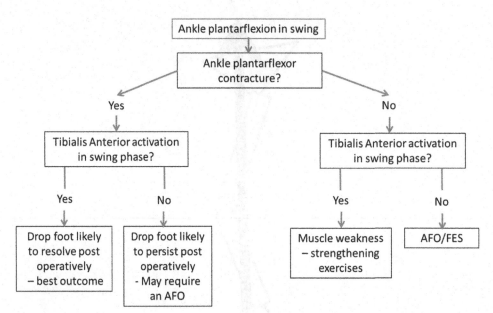

FIG. 28.8 Electromyography can be used to assist in decision making. In this example, the patient has foot drop in swing. The decision tree uses electromyography to help decide the course of treatment for the patient.

Individuals with foot pathologies or with conditions which make them susceptible to foot ulceration (such as diabetes) can be assessed using pressure mats or insole pressure systems. In these systems a high-resolution array of *sensels* (typically, 4 per square cm) are used to measure the pressure under the foot. Pressure mats can identify areas of high pressure underneath the foot during walking or standing. The information gathered can be used to evaluate the outcomes from foot surgery or to design insoles or footwear to reduce loading at specific sites on the sole of the foot (Fig. 28.9).

Energy is required to maintain our resting state (keep us breathing, maintain our heart rate and allow turnover of proteins etc). Energy demands greatly increase when we walk or run. The ubiquitous energy molecule in the body is adenosine triphosphate (ATP). This is manufactured by aerobic and anaerobic means. In most everyday activities, we use our aerobic metabolism (requiring oxygen) to produce the energy required to manufacture ATP. Although, the best way of measuring energy consumption is to measure the heat produced by a body (*direct calorimetry*), the difference in concentration of inhaled and exhaled oxygen or CO_2 (*indirect* calorimetry) can be considered a good surrogate measurement of energy expenditure, if we can assume that there is little anaerobic metabolism (for review see (Levine, 2005)).

Typically, in gait laboratories, oxygen consumption is measured by expiratory collection open circuit systems (which are portable), prior to and during a prescribed walking task. In these systems, the oxygen or CO_2 content is measured and a formula used to relate gas concentration to energy expenditure. In a walking test in a laboratory, the oxygen consumption is measured at rest and then at steady state period within the task. Data may be normalized to account for variation in body size and for the distance travelled (energy cost).

Children with cerebral palsy and adults with stroke have much higher energy costs than their typically developing peers. Energy expenditure is a useful outcome measure from interventions aimed at making gait more efficient.

Non-technical assessments used in clinical gait analysis services

The primary purposes of a clinical gait analysis are (a) to provide treatment recommendations; (b) to establish a baseline analysis or (c) to monitor the stability or progression of a movement problem. To provide a complete analysis it is necessary to combine the technical assessments described previously in this chapter with clinical assessments such as a physical examination, a clinical interview, and a functional assessment or questionnaire.

A physical examination is typically a series of measurements of passive and active joint range, bony torsion, neurological function and muscle strength. It can be considered as an assessment of the neurological and musculoskeletal impairments of the patient that are complementary to the measurements made in the instrumented assessment of gait. In our unit a physical examination is carried out by two personnel. The assessor manipulates the lower limb and asks the patient to perform certain tasks while the other makes measurements with a goniometer and records the data on to a form.

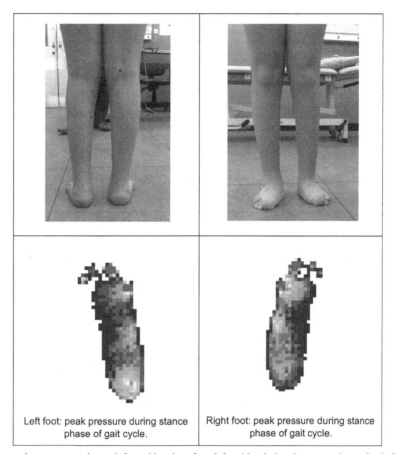

FIG. 28.9 Illustration of the peak pressures underneath feet with valgus foot deformities during the stance phase of gait. Brighter areas represent high loads.

During a passive range of movement assessment, the patient's joints are slowly rotated until the assessor encounters resistance to further motion. At this point, the member of staff who is measuring aligns the goniometer with its centre over the centre of the joint with the arms of the goniometer placed along the axes of the neighbouring limb segments, and measures the angle made by the two segments. During assessment of torsion of the long bones, the assessor palpates bony prominences of the patient and the measurer aligns the goniometer between distal and proximal landmarks along the principal axis of the bone and records the angle between them. Fig. 28.10 gives examples of measurements of passive range of motion and bony torsion made at the One Small Step Gait Laboratory.

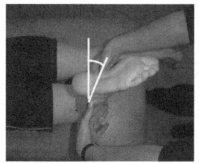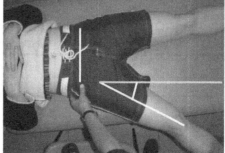

FIG. 28.10 Two examples of physical examination measurements made at the One Small Step Gait Laboratory. In the left hand photo, the knee axis has been aligned parallel to the end of the bed. The shank is made vertical and the projection angle between the bimalleolar axis and the knee joint axis is estimated. In the right hand photo, the hip is abducted until resistance is felt, and then the angle between the long axis to the thigh and an axis perpendicular to the line joining the anterior superior iliac spines is made.

TABLE 28.2 The modified Ashworth score is a clinical measurement of muscle tone.

Grade	Description
0	No increase in muscle tone.
1	Slight increase in muscle tone, manifested by a catch and release or by minimal resistance at the end range of motion when the affected part is moved in flexion or extension.
1+	Slight increase in muscle tone, manifested by a catch, followed by minimal resistance throughout the remainder (less than half) of the range of motion.
2	More marked increase in muscle tone through most of the range of motion, but the affected part is easily moved.
3	Considerable increase in muscle tone, passive movement is difficult.
4	Affected part is rigid in flexion or extension.

Neurological assessment of the patient may involve tests of hyperreflexia, tone and selective motor control. Tests of tone involve moving a limb segment at a particular speed and grading the resistance of the limb to the movement. A common schema used for the assessment of resistance to motion is the Modified Ashworth Scale (Table 28.2) (Meseguer-Henarejos et al., 2018).

Selective motor control is the ability of the patient to isolate joint movements. Fowler and colleagues (Fowler et al., 2009) developed a score for selective motor control called SCALE (the Selective Controlled Assessment of the Lower Extremity) which assesses active movement at each joint in the lower limb is scored at 0 if the patient is unable to perform the movement, 1 if the movement is impaired in some way (lack of range or movement at another joint) or 2 if there is good selectivity. As SCALE is an indirect measurement of the integrity of the corticospinal tract, the test is attractive for the assessment of patients with upper motor neuron lesions. The test appears to be a good predictor of gross motor function (Noble et al., 2019) and of normality of the gait pattern (Chruscikowski et al., 2017).

Muscle strength is commonly assessed qualitatively by the MRC manual muscle test (MMT). In one version of the test, the assessor asks the patient to move a joint to a position of flexion or extension and hold the limb in position. The assessor then tries to 'break' the held position of the joint by applying pressure. For example, the patient may be asked to hold their hip in flexion while lying in supine and the assessor applies pressure to the thigh in an attempt to move the hip towards a less flexed position. The test can be repeated at different joint angles to assess strength through range, and scored on a scale from 0 to 5 (see Table 28.3).

Physical assessments tend to be subjective and unreliable. There may also be some ambiguity in the meaning of the measurements. For example, children have much more extensible tendons than adults, and a passive range of motion test may differentially stretch the tendon and mask an underlying shortness of the muscle belly. In the case of the MMT, voluntary muscle strength is the combination of muscle properties (size, organization etc) and the capacity to activate the tissue. Individuals with UMN lesions may find it difficult to fully activate muscles in a voluntary test, and may be able to activate more fully when walking. In our laboratory, we stopped performing MMT in children with spastic cerebral palsy because we couldn't reconcile the results of the MMT with the joint moments we observed during walking.

TABLE 28.3 The MRC manual muscle test. The patient's voluntary strength is graded according to a categorical scale from no observable movement (0) to normal strength (0).

Grade	Description
5	Full active range of motion & normal muscle resistance
4	Full active range of motion & reduced muscle resistance
3	Full active range of motion & no muscle resistance
2	Reduced active range of motion & no muscle resistance
1	No active range of motion & palpable muscle contraction only
0	No active range of motion & no palpable muscle contraction

Taking a clinical history is an important element of a clinical gait analysis for the following reasons:

a) It establishes the relationship between the clinician and the patient.
b) Identifies how the condition has progressed
c) Identifies if any treatment has responded to treatment.
d) Explores the impact of the condition on the patient (and their carers).
e) Identifies the social and environmental impacts on the patient's condition.
f) Explores the patient's expectations.
g) Often leads to a change in treatment, or even diagnosis.

An interview should try to include elements of questioning across the domains of impairments (pain, weakness etc), functional performance (activities of daily living performed in the patient's environment) and participation in social activities. It should explore the personal and environmental factors that might influence the patient's mobility (these may be more influential than their physical impairments or their gait pattern).

To extract the most information from the patient, the interviewer should adopt a friendly, calm and supportive manner. They should find a private space to conduct the clinical history and introduce themselves and wear their hospital ID. They should give the patient a rough idea of how long the interview will last and document the identity of the people accompanying the patient. The interviewer should try to ask *open* rather than *closed* questions. Open questions such as "Can you tell me something more about your problem?" or "How do you feel about your wheelchair provision?" can be more revealing than asking questions that require a Yes or No answer (e.g. "Are you happy with your wheelchair provision?).

There are special concerns when interviewing a child or an adult with a learning disability, the interviewer should make sure that those accompanying the patient have the authority to take consent for the assessment and answer questions on behalf of the patient. Sometimes it is useful for a professional carer (physiotherapist, teaching assistant) to be present, especially if the patient is "looked after" or at an institution where they board. Often the professional carer may know as much about the child as the parental carer. The interviewer should take the views of the child, the parent/guardian and the professional carer and document them as individual contributions may be conflicting. They should use language appropriate to the patient's understanding — they may need to slow your speech and use more body language. It is often useful to encourage storytelling ("Tell me about what you did yesterday") in those who have more difficulty answering direct questions. Interview styles that allow patients to give a wider range of responses, and often a lot of detail, makes it more difficult for the interviewer to remember and record the prescient facts. To facilitate an accurate description of the interview, it is advisable to summarize the content verbally to the patient and their carers at the end of the interview, and use an interview proforma to make sure that all the area of the clinical history have been covered.

Questionnaires are useful instruments in the (self-) assessment of the patient. In questionnaires, questions are asked within specific domains (walking ability, dressing, personal hygiene etc) and the patient or their representative scores the response. In one sense, questionnaires may be considered superior to a clinical interview because they are more structured and impersonal. On the other hand, interviews help to explore the areas of concern that the patients have. In the One Small Step Gait Laboratory, we provide the patient and their family with the Gillette Functional Assessment Questionnaire before they enter the laboratory (Gorton et al., 2011). We use responses on this questionnaire to help us to develop the content of the clinical interview.

Interpreting and reporting clinical gait analysis data

The quality of any clinico-technical report is as important as the quality of the data themselves. The challenge in clinical gait analysis is to produce a report that is logical, transparent, short and unsophisticated in the face of enormous amounts of clinical and complex technical data, some of which may appear to be conflicting. For the last twenty years, we have adopted a simple reporting model that enables us to formulate opinions of the functional and impairment status of the patient while accommodating differential evidence and explaining our thinking to the reader. We call this method of reporting the "opinion-evidence model". Any recommendations for intervention mentioned in the report are then linked to a series of findings based upon this model.

In our laboratory, an opinion-evidence segment has the following template.
Opinion: A statement indicating the presence and severity of an impairment or functional deficit.
Evidence: observations from the gait analysis that support the opinion.

Notes:

a) observations that are differential to the opinion.
b) further explanation of an opinion and or evidence.
c) possible further consequences of an impairment or functional deficit.

A simple example of this model would be the evaluation of a bony torsion.

Increased internal femoral torsion bilaterally (evidence: increased internal hip rotation in walking bilaterally {kinematics}; increased angle on the greater trochanteric prominence test bilaterally {clinical examination}; much greater internal than external passive hip rotation bilaterally {clinical examination}).

Note: the level of internal hip rotation in stance is greater than 30° and varies only a little over the gait cycle.

Here, our opinion is that the patient has increased femoral torsion and we support that view with the evidence collected from the analysis with increased internal hip rotation during walking and two measures from the clinical examination: the Greater Trochanteric Prominence Test is an estimate of the projection angle made of the axis of the femoral condyles on the axis defined by the femoral neck and measurements of the passive range of motion at the hips. The note we make further supports our opinion by explaining that the internal rotation of the hip remains at an increased level throughout the gait cycle (a hip rotational kinematic profile with a significant dynamic component that would cast doubt on our opinion).

Sometimes, the evidence for an opinion isn't very strong, and the uncertainty should be expressed within the *Notes* portion of the opinion-evidence segment.

Weakness of the plantarflexors bilaterally (evidence: reduced periods of single support bilaterally {spatio-temporal parameters}; reduced plantarflexor moment in terminal stance and ankle power in preswing bilaterally {kinetics}; increased knee extensor moment in late stance bilaterally {kinetics}).

Note: Z develops a lot of power in early stance at his ankle, knee and hip. This may be secondary to a mass extensor response utilizing the storage and release of energy in muscle extensors of the lower limbs, particularly the gastroc-soleus complex. This is likely to lead to two phenomena. Firstly, a ballistic and unstable gait, and secondly a shortened position of some of the muscle groups at the end of stance, reducing their ability to produce power in this phase.

In the notes section here, we are explaining that the reduced ankle moment and powers that we observe in late stance may be related to an altered way of walking due to a neurological problem rather than an intrinsic muscular one. Under such circumstances, the utility of an exercise programme to restore plantarflexor strength may have little impact on the gait of the patient.

In our reports, we construct a series of opinion-evidence segments to form a "Summary of Findings" section (see the anonymized example below). If you study the content, you can see that opinions are often related, share evidence and may have multiple components.

Summary of findings

Z coped well with the demands of gait analysis. We collected 3D movement, force plate, and electromyographic (EMG) data of his barefoot independent walking. Below, we detail our findings.

Mildly limited independent ambulator (evidence: reduced independent walking distance limited by fatigue; mild difficulties with stairs; score of 10/10 on the Gillette Functional Assessment Questionnaire {clinical history}).

Note: Z walked at a normal self-selected speed in the laboratory.

Mild lower limb length discrepancy, shorter on the right (evidence: mild anatomical lower limb length discrepancy shorter on the right by 1 cm {clinical examination}; mild pelvic obliquity lower on the right side {kinematics}).

Fixed shortness of the right hamstrings (evidence: increased popliteal angle on the right {clinical examination}; increased knee flexion at initial contact on the right {kinematics})

Note: Z hyperextends his right knee in single support.

Mild fixed shortness of the right ankle plantarflexors (evidence: plantarflexion contraction on the right {clinical examination}; plantarflexed in single support on the right {kinematics}).

Weakness of the right ankle plantarflexors (evidence: unable to perform any single leg heel raises on the right {clinical examination}).

Note: Z generated normal levels of power at the right ankle in walking.

Weakness of the ankle dorsiflexors on the right (evidence: plantarflexed foot position in swing on the right which is greater than in the stance phase {kinematics}; poor selective control of dorsiflexion on the right {clinical examination}; continuous activation of the right tibialis anterior in stance and swing {EMG}).

Note: Z's stance phase tibialis anterior activity in stance may contribute to his inverted foot position in this phase.

Mild fixed shortness of the posterior tibialis on the right (evidence: varus hindfoot foot position just correctable on the couch {clinical examination}; varus hindfoot position in standing on the right {video}).

The opinion-evidence model is not only a formal and clear method of expressing our views on the patient's status but also a way of improving our practice. It allows us to reconsider which observations should be used as evidence to support an opinion, by incorporating new clinical research findings and refining our own rationale. For example, to help us to distinguish the neurological and muscular contributions to weakness, we recently introduced ultrasound imaging in to our routine clinical practice to measure muscle size and assess muscle composition. Our opinion above of Weakness of the ankle plantarflexors may now be supported by an evidence statement such as *"reduced muscle volume and reduced myofibrillar content in the medial gastrocnemius {ultrasound imaging}"*.

Quality control and assurance in gait laboratories

Clinical measurement services need quality control (QC) and assurance (QA) measures to verify and validate their output. It is important because an error of 10° in a kinematic profile may result in the wrong treatment being suggested at the clinical review. QC refers to the specific repeated tests performed in the laboratory to check the operational performance of a piece of equipment or method. QA refers to the processes in place to prevent errors occurring which may affect performance.

QC measures in a gait laboratory might include the static and dynamic checks of force plate performance, a spatial calibration of the motion capture equipment or the reliability of a measurement in a clinical examination. Often, the limits of acceptability of the test are set rather arbitrarily but it is advisable to define tolerances according to the impact of error on clinically meaningful outcomes. We simulated the effect of errors in the centre of pressure and the direction of the GRFV on kinetic variables. Our objective was to determine what magnitude of errors would produce a significant change (1 standard deviation of the values in our control sample) in the mean value of the hip moments from a group of patients. We found that "safe" tolerances were 20 mm in centre of pressure and 2° in the direction of the vector. We use these values as pass/fail criteria for a dynamic pole test (ref Lewis).

QA can be assessed by carrying out audits against a set of agreed standards. In the UK and Ireland, the Clinical Movement Analysis Society (CMAS) developed a set of standards covering all aspects of gait and movement laboratory functions including environment, data collection and processing and reporting (www.cmasuki.org). Participating centres are audited against these standards every one or two years (depending on the extent of each audit) by a team of expert professionals, and if successful, are accredited by the society.

CMAS auditing and accreditation have been successful at maintaining minimum acceptable standards in the clinical gait analysis laboratories of the UK. The future is likely to see the accreditation of NHS clinical measurement services being governed by an external body such as the United Kingdom Accreditation Service (UKAS) under a programme similar to IQIPS (Improving Quality in Physiological Services) (www.ukas.com/services/accreditation-services/physiological-services-accreditation-iqips/).

The future of clinical gait analysis

Clinical gait analysis measures a phenomenon on the outside (the pattern of walking) and clinicians use the information to make interventions to the inside (a muscle lengthening, an injection of a pharmaceutical etc). Treatment decision making is based on a set of assumptions about the relationship between an abnormal pattern of walking and the pathophysiological factors that caused it. The process is akin to investigating the poor performance of a car by measuring its velocity and acceleration. One can tell that something's wrong with the car but under many circumstances you can't tell exactly what the problem is!

One approach to resolving these ambiguities in gait analysis is to make and interpret measurements in the context of our understanding of pathophysiological mechanisms. In an earlier part of this chapter, we briefly discussed how neuronal circuits in the spinal cord develop during childhood. These circuits are likely to regulate muscle activity in repeated movements such as walking, with reciprocal activation of agonist and antagonist muscles and co-activation of synergists. Often, they are referred to as central pattern generators or CPGs. The patterns of muscle activations generated by the CPGs become more complex as the child matures with more sophisticated combinations of muscle activations allowing a smoother and more controlled gait. These fundamental combinations of muscle activation are referred to as *synergies*. Using the powerful mathematical technique of non-negative matrix factorization, the magnitude of these synergies can be computed from analysis of surface electromyograms. In mature walking, just 5 synergies can describe the vast majority of variance in normal EMG patterns. However, there are fewer significant synergies in a toddler's gait, the gait of a child with spastic cerebral palsy, or that of a person recovering from a stroke. It appears that the complexity of motor synergies is a powerful predictor of success from intervention in cerebral palsy, of greater importance in fact than the selection of the intervention itself (Schwartz et al., 2016). In the future, we are likely to witness the greater incorporation of instrumented measurements of motor control to better understand our neuropathological patients, and to devise better interventions.

Clinicians will often use "pattern recognition" to identify characteristics in the gait analysis and associated data to "match" the patient under review with previous patients under their care. In this way, they select with some level of confidence the interventions best-suited to their current patient. It is possible to formalize the clinician's approach by adopting black box statistical methods such as machine learning. Higher order statistical methods like these require large databases of patient data where historic patients have been evaluated comprehensively and consistently, and their outcomes from intervention measured. Schwartz and colleagues from Gillette Children's Hospital in the United States have used the *Random Forest Algorithm* to successfully predict outcomes in candidates for femoral derotation surgery and for intramuscular psoas lengthenings (Schwartz et al., 2014, 2013). Few individual centres have the volume of data to match that of Gillette Children's and therefore it may be difficult to execute methods like the random forest. To take advantage of machine learning, it may be necessary to merge databases from different centres to gain adequate statistical power. That would require some harmonization across gait analysis units of their technical methods and outcome measures.

Because machine learning methods are capable of optimizing current practice there is also the danger that they may also crystallize it. Novel technical or clinical methods may not provide any immediate advantage to the clinician in decision-making, in the absence of large datasets to support them. In this case, we may need to be mindful that potential advances in technology and findings from prospective clinical research may need a longer period to bed in and make a difference to patient outcomes.

One way of improving our understanding of the impairments influencing an abnormal gait pattern is to reverse engineer the problem. Movement is a product of the activation of combinations of muscles and the properties of the individual musculo-tendinous units (their size, fibre length, tendon length etc) as well as the paths of these units between origin and insertion defined largely by the shape of the bones. If we are able to characterize the properties of these musculotendinous units and model the underlying anatomy, we can find the activation of these muscles (according to certain optimization criteria) that would simulate a movement that matched a recorded one (Seth and Pandy, 2007). In this way, it is possible to estimate the contributions of individual muscles to the acceleration of the body segments and, therefore, in principle, work out which muscles are interfering with function of a person with a physical disability. Although, musculoskeletal simulations are useful in teaching us about the complex mechanics of movement, researchers are still some way from directly using simulations to inform clinical practice due to the difficulty in obtaining the properties of muscle of individual patients and, more importantly, validating algorithms that estimate accurately the contributions of individual muscles to a net joint moment during a movement.

Summary

Clinical gait analysis is a complex set of clinical measurements that are used to characterize the movement of patients with physical disabilities so that clinicians can recommend treatments to improve their mobility. The ideal clinical gait analyst is a person who has a combination of technical and people skills, as well as biomechanical, anatomical and clinical knowledge.

Clinical gait analysis is an exciting area for the clinical engineer to work in because it combines clinical and biomechanical knowledge with patient contact, data analysis and report writing.

References

Baker, R., 2001. Pelvic angles: a mathematically rigorous definition which is consistent with a conventional clinical understanding of the terms. Gait Posture 13 (1), 1—6. Retrieved from: http://www.ncbi.nlm.nih.gov/pubmed/11166548.

Cappellini, G., Ivanenko, Y.P., Martino, G., MacLellan, M.J., Sacco, A., Morelli, D., Lacquaniti, F., 2016. Immature spinal locomotor output in children with cerebral palsy. Front. Physiol. 7, 478. https://doi.org/10.3389/fphys.2016.00478.

Chruscikowski, E., Fry, N.R.D., Noble, J.J., Gough, M., Shortland, A.P., 2017. Selective motor control correlates with gait abnormality in children with cerebral palsy. Gait Posture 52. https://doi.org/10.1016/j.gaitpost.2016.11.031.

Clowry, G.J., 2007. The dependence of spinal cord development on corticospinal input and its significance in understanding and treating spastic cerebral palsy. Neurosci. Biobehav. Rev. 31 (8), 1114—1124. https://doi.org/10.1016/j.neubiorev.2007.04.007.

del Pilar Duque Orozco, M., Abousamra, O., Church, C., Lennon, N., Henley, J., Rogers, K.J., et al., 2016. Reliability and validity of Edinburgh visual gait score as an evaluation tool for children with cerebral palsy. Gait Posture 49, 14—18. https://doi.org/10.1016/j.gaitpost.2016.06.017.

Duprey, S., Naaim, A., Moissenet, F., Begon, M., Chèze, L., 2017. Kinematic models of the upper limb joints for multibody kinematics optimisation: an overview. J. Biomech. 62, 87−94. https://doi.org/10.1016/j.jbiomech.2016.12.005.

Eken, T., Elder, G.C.B., Lømo, T., 2008. Development of tonic firing behavior in rat soleus muscle. J. Neurophysiol. 99 (4), 1899−1905. https://doi.org/10.1152/jn.00834.2007.

Fagerström, C., Borglin, G., 2010. Mobility, functional ability and health-related quality of life among people of 60 years or older. Aging Clin. Exp. Res. 22 (5−6), 387−394. https://doi.org/10.1007/BF03324941.

Forssberg, H., 1985. Ontogeny of human locomotor control. I. Infant stepping, supported locomotion and transition to independent locomotion. Exp. Brain Res. 57 (3), 480−493. https://doi.org/10.1007/bf00237835.

Fowler, E.G., Staudt, L. a, Greenberg, M.B., Oppenheim, W.L., 2009. Selective control assessment of the lower extremity (SCALE): development, validation, and interrater reliability of a clinical tool for patients with cerebral palsy. Dev. Med. Child Neurol. 51 (8), 607−614. https://doi.org/10.1111/j.1469-8749.2008.03186.x.

Gorton III, G.E., Stout, J.L., Bagley, A.M., Bevans, K., Novacheck, T.F., Tucker, C.A., 2011. Gillette functional assessment questionnaire 22-item skill set: factor and rasch analyses. Dev. Med. Child Neurol. 53 (3), 250−255. https://doi.org/10.1111/j.1469-8749.2010.03832.x.

Hof, A.L., Zijlstra, W., 1997. Comment on "Normalization of temporal-distance parameters in pediatric gait. J. Biomech. 30 (3), 299, 301−302. Retrieved from: http://www.ncbi.nlm.nih.gov/pubmed/9119833.

Ivanenko, Y.P., Dominici, N., Cappellini, G., Di Paolo, A., Giannini, C., Poppele, R.E., Lacquaniti, F., 2013. Changes in the spinal segmental motor output for stepping during development from infant to adult. J. Neurosci. 33 (7), 3025−3036. https://doi.org/10.1523/JNEUROSCI.2722-12.2013.

Leardini, A., Caravaggi, P., Theologis, T., Stebbins, J., 2019. Multi-segment foot models and their use in clinical populations. Gait Posture 69, 50−59. https://doi.org/10.1016/j.gaitpost.2019.01.022.

Leardini, A., Chiari, L., Della Croce, U., Cappozzo, A., 2005. Human movement analysis using stereophotogrammetry. Part 3. Soft tissue artifact assessment and compensation. Gait Posture 21 (2), 212−225. https://doi.org/10.1016/j.gaitpost.2004.05.002.

Levine, J.A., 2005. Measurement of energy expenditure. Public Health Nutr. 8 (7A), 1123−1132. Retrieved from: http://www.ncbi.nlm.nih.gov/pubmed/16277824.

Meseguer-Henarejos, A.-B., Sánchez-Meca, J., López-Pina, J.-A., Carles-Hernández, R., 2018. Inter- and intra-rater reliability of the modified Ashworth Scale: a systematic review and meta-analysis. Eur. J. Phys. Rehabil. Med. 54 (4), 576−590. https://doi.org/10.23736/S1973-9087.17.04796-7.

Murphy, K.P., Molnar, G.E., Lankasky, K., 2000. Employment and social issues in adults with cerebral palsy. Arch. Phys. Med. Rehabil. 81 (6), 807−811. https://doi.org/10.1016/S0003-9993(00)90115-1.

Noble, J.J., Gough, M., Shortland, A.P., 2019. Selective motor control and gross motor function in bilateral spastic cerebral palsy. Dev. Med. Child Neurol. 61 (1), 57−61. https://doi.org/10.1111/dmcn.14024.

Prechtl, H.F., Ferrari, F., Cioni, G., 1993. Predictive value of general movements in asphyxiated fullterm infants. Early Hum. Dev. 35 (2), 91−120. Retrieved from: http://www.ncbi.nlm.nih.gov/pubmed/8143572.

Schwartz, M.H., Rozumalski, A., Novacheck, T.F., 2014. Femoral derotational osteotomy: surgical indications and outcomes in children with cerebral palsy. Gait Posture 39 (2), 778−783. https://doi.org/10.1016/j.gaitpost.2013.10.016.

Schwartz, M.H., Rozumalski, A., Steele, K.M., 2016. Dynamic motor control is associated with treatment outcomes for children with cerebral palsy. Dev. Med. Child Neurol. 58 (11), 1139−1145. https://doi.org/10.1111/dmcn.13126.

Schwartz, M.H., Rozumalski, A., Truong, W., Novacheck, T.F., 2013. Predicting the outcome of intramuscular psoas lengthening in children with cerebral palsy using preoperative gait data and the random forest algorithm. Gait Posture 37 (4), 473−479. https://doi.org/10.1016/j.gaitpost.2012.08.016.

Seth, A., Pandy, M.G., 2007. A neuromusculoskeletal tracking method for estimating individual muscle forces in human movement. J. Biomech. 40 (2), 356−366. https://doi.org/10.1016/j.jbiomech.2005.12.017.

Chapter 29

Mechanical and electromechanical devices

Chapter outline

Clinical Engineering. https://doi.org/10.1016/B978-0-08-102694-6.00029-2

Aids for daily living

Donna Cowan
Chailey Clinical Services, East Sussex, UK

Introduction

Aids for daily living are a range of products which support activities generally known as activities of daily living. These are in the main self-care activities such as:

- Bathing and toileting
- Dressing and grooming
- Eating and drinking

The ability of people to undertake these activities is routinely taken as a measurement of the functional status of a person.

As with all assistive technology, the key to success is matching the equipment accurately to the client's needs. As a result, it is important to identify the core issues associated with an activity and what the client is likely to accept as assistance, then to match the two accurately.

The range of aids offers support to users with a wide range of conditions, congenital and acquired, incorporating sensory impairment and physical restriction. It is perhaps most usually associated with older people compensating for changes in physical ability with age, enabling some to remain independent and safer in undertaking these activities.

Occupational therapists will often work with clients to develop strategies which support a different approach to the activity and incorporate the use of an aid. This may be as simple as sitting whilst dressing to prevent falling due to imbalance caused by raising the arms above the head, through to using a dressing frame to assist donning of tops and jackets.

Increasingly, this range of equipment is becoming mainstream and is finding its way onto the shelves of supermarkets and department stores as well as being found in specialist outlets.

Dressing

A wide range of products are available to aid this activity such as dressing sticks and hooks, sock aids and shoe horns. Clothing itself can also be adapted, such as replacing buttons and ties with velcro, or shoelaces with elastic laces. People require these aids due to reduced dexterity, motor movement or physical mobility.

Bathing

Aids for this activity range from a bath mat to improve safety (an aid many use now in their home) through to personally moulded shower chairs with adaptations to allow for postural impairment and movement patterns. Standard shower seats/chairs provide stability for users and seats can be fitted into a bath to enable safe entry and exit.

Products comprising a long handle attached to a sponge or brush allow users with restricted limb mobility to undertake activities of washing and grooming independently.

In some instances, holders are required, e.g. for users with limb deficiency a holder and mount is required to allow a toothbrush to be placed. The user then moves their head relative to the brush, rather than having to bring the brush to their mouth.

Toileting

Cleansing aids and wipers are available to promote independent personal care. A range of toilet seats and raisers can be found to ease the difficulty of sitting and then rising from a toilet seat. Steps are also used to promote stability in sitting for young children. The seat surfaces can also be made in a variety of materials to provide a more conforming surface for users and thus increase comfort and surface area contact to promote stability. Personally moulded toilet seats/commodes are available for those having particularly pronounced postural impairment. These can also double as shower chairs.

Toilets which offer washing and warm air drying can also be purchased to provide additional support in undertaking this personal activity.

Eating and drinking

The International Classification of Functioning, Disability and Health (WHO, 2001) defines the task of eating as the ability to carry out the coordinated tasks and actions of eating food that has been served, bringing it to the mouth and consuming it in culturally acceptable ways, cutting or breaking food into pieces, opening bottles and cans, using eating implements, having meals, feasting or dining. The aids which are available to support this include angled cutlery with a range of handles and grips. A single tool that incorporates the use of two of these items e.g. a fork with a serrated edge can enable someone with only one functional limb to cut and eat their food independently. Plates shaped to ease manipulation of food are also available. Non-slip mats underneath crockery prevents movement of the plate. Drinking vessels are available which have double grips for those with reduced movement in their hands. Lids on mugs avoid spillage. Mechanical and electromechanical eating aids have also been developed (Fig. 29.1).

Writing and drawing

Grips for pens and pencils enable standard writing implements to continue to be used. Holders for pens and pencils via helmets and mouth sticks can also be found. Consideration of the individual is essential in all assistive technologies. In addition, where aids are held in the mouth, consideration of the risk associated with controlling a pen or pencil is required as injury is possible if the user has sudden movements or works in a busy environment (such as a classroom).

Grips to support access to the computer to press the keys of a keyboard can also be found. Standard software packages (e.g. Windows) have settings to accommodate some access needs (e.g. screen magnifier, text narrator, or the ability to offset the effect of tremor). In addition, aids such as key guards and different sized keyboards can be used to provide simple solutions to these problems (further information on this subject is available in the "access to EAT" section of the EAT (electronic assistive technology) chapter).

Personalized devices

Some items, however, are not commercially available. In some cases there is a need to provide personalized solutions for a range of activities. This is usually carried out in specialist centres having multidisciplinary teams able not only to assess the client, but also able to provide solutions. The starting point may be a commercial item which may be adapted to meet a particular need. In other cases there is a need to design and manufacture something bespoke. Specialist centres have engineers who are able to synthesize the functional and physical requirements requested by a therapist with the lifestyle

FIG. 29.1 "Neater Eater" by kind permission of Neater Solutions Ltd.

FIG. 29.2 Two piece foam lying support.

requirements of the client who may be a child, young adult or older person. The engineer's role is to design a solution to bring these sometimes opposing sets of requirements together (Figs. 29.2 and 29.3).

In order for the design to be successful it is critical that the client and their family/carers are at the heart of the design process. They must take an active role in identifying when a solution will work or not. Aesthetics is also important, as to how it will fit into the user's and their carers' daily life/lifestyle.

Choice of materials will be governed by biocompatibility issues, temperature regulation of the user, the environment to which it will be exposed, cleaning and/or decontamination requirements, maintenance and lifespan, coupled with aesthetics.

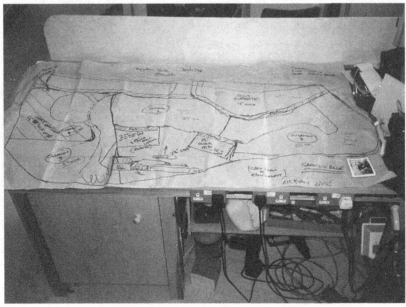

FIG. 29.3 Personalized lying support design.

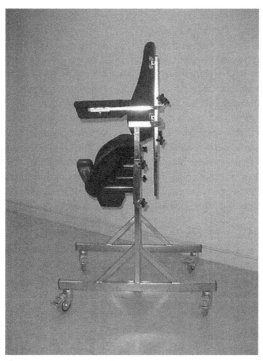

FIG. 29.4 Custom made toilet seat for client with arthrogryposis achieving only 5° hip flexion.

The engineer is a key element of the team in these circumstances and must not only take into account a number of design and technical considerations, but also risk assessment in terms of how it might be used or misused and what fault conditions may occur. Further information is available in the chapters on medical engineering design and regulation & risk management (Figs. 29.4 and 29.5).

A potential pitfall

It is important not to "inflict" assistive technology on people through over-enthusiasm. One must be sensitive to the personal situation and circumstances of the person and only seek to solve the problems that the person believes exist. One can introduce new ideas but this must be done with care and sensitivity to avoid overloading the person with technology which might result in wasted resource through lack of use.

FIG. 29.5 Standard static exercise bike with adaptations to provide additional postural support.

Case study

Jon was referred to the specialist service by a local therapy team and has a diagnosis of Lesch Nyhan disease, which presents as a four limb motor disorder with self-injurious behaviours. He has been known to the service since he was 3 years old (he is now 11) and has been provided with support to provide safe care in his home environment and at school.

The self-injurious behaviour has led to several harmful incidents. Jon bites his fingers and lip, particularly if anxious or stressed. He will arch his back and hyper-extend his neck, putting himself into dangerous postures affecting his airway when being showered and when undergoing personal care. Jon becomes very distressed when these occur but is unable to stop himself.

At clinic appointment to discuss ADL are Jon, his family, his local team and a multidisciplinary team from the specialist service. Risk assessments are undertaken before equipment is provided and help to ensure all are aware of the risks associated with the use of each piece of equipment. Materials used are carefully considered to ensure equipment can be cleaned and retains mechanical integrity.

Alongside the equipment is the use of strategies to ensure that Jon knows what is happening; training for staff who work with him and understand the purpose and limitations of the devices provided.

A range of equipment has been designed, tested and supplied to Jon and his family over the years including:
- Changing mats designed to support safe nappy changing when very young and to enable a single person to manage personal care
- "Sleeping waistcoats" attached to the bed which prevent Jon from moving around excessively and hurting himself on bedsides, walls, becoming entangled in bedding, etc.
- Shower trolley inserts designed to prevent excessive movement and to enable personal care to be carried out
- Mittens designed to be used in different environments to manage finger biting
- Additional padding for standard equipment such as wheelchairs, buggies and seating systems, where commercially available options were not found to be sufficient to prevent harm
- Bespoke mounting of switches and technology to facilitate intentional use whilst simultaneously protecting Jon and the technology from harm; trays with padding at the elbows and elbow stops to keep the arms in place and support access to the technology
- Additional padding and postural elements added to commercially available "comfort" seating to provide a safe place to sit and enjoy relaxing opportunities with the family

References

World Health Organisation, 2001. International Classification of Functioning, Disability and Health. http://www.who.int/classifications/icf/en/.

Further resources

As described above, there is a vast array of assistive technology available commercially. A simple internet search will yield plentiful results. In the UK, the Disabled Living Foundation (http://www.dlf.org.uk/) is a charity offering independent advice on these types of products and can be an extremely useful resource.

Wielandt, T., String, J., 2000. Compliance with prescribed adaptive equipment: a literature review. Brit. J. Occup. Ther. 63 (2), 65–75.

Lacey, G., MacNamara, S., 2000. User involvement in the design and evaluation of a smart mobility aid. J. Rehabil. Res. Dev. 37 (6), 709–723.

Resnik, L., Allen, S., Isenstadt, D., Wasserman, M., Lezzoni, L., 2009. Perspectives on the use of mobility aids for a diverse population of seniors: implications for intervention. Disabil. Health J. 2 (2), 77–85.

Wintergold, A., 2019. A multidisciplinary approach to the provision of custom equipment for children and adults with Lesch Nyhan Disease. In: Posture & Mobility Group Conference.

Prosthetics

Martin Smith[a] and Vicky Gardiner[b]
[a]Oxford University Hospitals NHS Foundation Trust, UK; [b]Opcare, Abingdon, UK

Introduction

Rehabilitation healthcare concerning externally applied prosthetic devices and known as "prosthetics" does not usually require engineering support at a clinical level, the clinical engineer being more likely to be involved in research and development. In certain circumstances, however, a clinical engineer may assist in setting up a prosthesis in an instrumented gait laboratory, but this is limited to those clinics having such facilities.

Demography

The national amputee statistical database was set-up in 1997. Figures show that annually, approximately 5000 new referrals are made to the 44 prosthetic centres in the UK. Of these, 95% are for lower limb amputations, 50% of which are trans-tibial (below knee) level. There are twice as many males referred as females. The most prevalent cause of amputation is dysvascularity accounting for 75% of referrals. The second most common cause is trauma which accounts for 9% of referrals.

Pre-amputation and surgery

The amputation level and choice of surgical technique will generally be dictated by the presentation of the affected limb; however, consideration should be given to the length of residual limb remaining below a joint. It is important that sufficient length remains to ensure good muscle power to control a prosthesis and adequate area to distribute socket forces. On the other hand, leaving a residual limb too long may compromise the space required to accommodate prosthetic componentry such as an artificial knee joint.

Amputation through a joint (disarticulation) is likely to heal more quickly than cutting through bone, and this kind of surgery offers greater surface area for force distribution; often it is possible to weight bear through the distal end. However, there are disadvantages to this. Disarticulation can limit space for componentry and compromise aesthetics with sockets appearing bulky around the distal end. One exception to this is disarticulation in paediatric users since the bones do not develop in the same way, becoming generally shorter and less well defined distally (Fig. 29.6).

The human lower limb consists of 3 main joints; hip, knee and ankle, and supporting bony structures of the thigh (femur) and shank (tibia and fibula). These provide the stability and articulation required for bipedal motion. In addition, feet form an intricate structure consisting of 26 bones each which perform three key functions; shock absorption, compliance over uneven ground and propulsion that are achieved effectively at varying speeds. Further reading is suggested on anatomy of the musculoskeletal system and anatomical reference terminology.

Post-amputation management

When a person loses a limb it is the job of a professional prosthetist to provide a suitable artificial replacement. With the aid of a prosthesis, the clinician aims to restore function according to the will and needs of the user, enabling the person to safely continue life as normally as possible compared to that prior to surgery.

Prostheses

External prosthetic appliances can be purely cosmetic, but in most cases a more functional solution is required; the complexity of the restoration is essentially dependent on the level and extent of amputation. Energy demand increases with complexity, a problem that is particularly apparent for mobilizing with a prosthesis.

The majority of prosthetic limbs prescribed are modular systems. A socket forms the interface with the patient. Depending on amputation level, prosthetic hip joints, knees or feet are connected via tubular pylons. Commercially manufactured components are CE marked, but the prosthesis as a whole is considered a custom made device due to the requirement for a bespoke socket. As a result, compliance with the medical devices directive, according to the guidance for custom made devices, is mandatory.

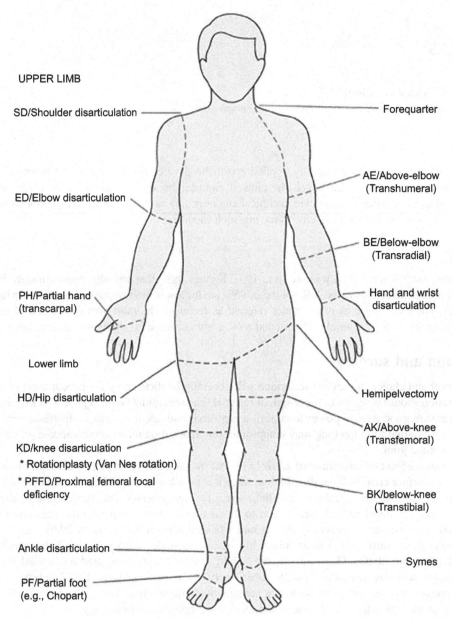

UPPER LIMB

SD/Shoulder disarticulation ——————————————— Forequarter

ED/Elbow disarticulation ———————

————— AE/Above-elbow
(Transhumeral)

————— BE/Below-elbow
(Transradial)

PH/Partial hand
(transcarpal) ————————

————— Hand and wrist
disarticulation

Lower limb

HD/Hip disarticulation ——————————

————— Hemipelvectomy

————— AK/Above-knee
(Transfemoral)

KD/knee disarticulation ——————
* Rotationplasty (Van Nes rotation)
* PFFD/Proximal femoral focal
deficiency

————— BK/below-knee
(Transtibial)

Ankle disarticulation ——————————

————————— Symes

PF/Partial foot
(e.g., Chopart)

FIG. 29.6 The main upper and lower limb amputation levels; these may be considered unilateral (affecting a single side), or bi-lateral (affecting both sides). *Copyright 2012, the War Amps National Amputee Centre.*

Sockets

The vast majority of users rely upon a socket as a means of interface between the residual limb and distal components of the artificial limb. An alternative method is by osseointegration. This technique involves a component being surgically implanted in the residual bony structures. Time is required for stabilization before an additional procedure to fit an abutment that permanently penetrates the soft tissues. In the case of amputees for whom socket interface is not suitable, the technique offers the possibility to use a prosthesis. However, infection and loosening of the implant means the technique is not widely applicable, with most cases requiring revision surgeries. Research continues to attempt to overcome such limitations in an area of promising advancement. Further reading is suggested on biomaterials and osseointegration.

Socket design is entirely bespoke and could be discussed extensively. It is the most specialized skill of the prosthetist requiring detailed knowledge of anatomy and a sound understanding of biomechanics as well as a certain "feel factor".

There are several well established styles of design for lower limb sockets: Patellar-Tendon Bearing, Total Contact, Quad, Ischial Containment and the Marlow Anatomical Socket. Further reading is suggested if knowledge of socket design is required. In general, the following factors are important when designing a socket and should also be considered if recruiting amputees for research purposes.

The socket must bear load where tolerable and relieve sensitive areas as much as possible. Forces applied in weight bearing, during the gait cycle and whilst mobilizing with a prosthesis must be carried by the residual limb and transmitted to proximal joints. Residual tissues are not well suited to this and so surgical quality, the chosen technique and the residual stump condition have a major bearing on how well load may be tolerated.

Besides the lack of control an amputee will experience from a poor fitting socket, movement that occurs in relation to the stump is likely to incur pain. Satisfactory fit of a socket is determined by assessment. Key signs are resistance to rotation about the stump, minimal "pistoning" and an absence of any red areas on the skin which do not disperse readily.

It is not uncommon for amputees to experience blisters, pressure ulcers, fragile or sensitive scar tissue, bone spurs and phantom limb pain at some stage. If an amputee is experiencing socket issues or discomfort they will often develop compensatory strategies during gait. The actual tactic employed varies between individuals, but a reduction in walking speed is commonly observed.

It is normal for the residual limb to swell and contract to some degree in response to activity, temperature and hydration. To maintain an optimal fit, amputees wear stump socks in varying thickness and number to accommodate this natural fluctuation. However, the period immediately following surgery is a time when the stump is particularly swollen due to oedema. Following surgery, amputees are encouraged back to their feet as soon as possible to optimize their rehabilitation, minimize secondary complications such as flexion contractures, and reduce oedema in the residual limb. The time for the residual limb to stabilize varies between individuals and during this period they are likely to require several changes of socket. For this reason they endure a long repetitive cycle of re-adjustment to new sockets that inevitably load their stump differently. It is difficult to say with any confidence when an amputee will reach steady state but there is satisfactory agreement that 18−24 months post amputation is reasonable.

Amputees can manage residual limb volume fluctuations with stump socks. Incorrect use of these can lead to socket problems and create a functional leg length discrepancy if too few or too many socks are worn with the prosthesis. Incorrect length may also be a consequence of the design and/or manufacturing of a prosthesis. Insufficient evidence exists to firmly quantify the amount of leg length inequality required to affect amputee gait, but it is recognized that when present, compensatory strategies emerge that may otherwise be avoided.

Construction

The process of designing and manufacturing a prosthetic socket begins by capturing the shape of the residual limb. Traditionally, this is done by plaster casting which allows the prosthetist to manipulate the soft tissues and feel the location and degree of pressure applied. This is then back filled with plaster to form a positive cast which can be rectified to achieve the loading/relief required. Alternatively, CAD/CAM may be employed whereby a 3-D representation of the residual limb is electronically scanned into a PC and processed via software to rectify the shape. A positive model is created by means of 3-axis computer numerical control (CNC).

Modern prosthetic sockets are largely constructed from solid thermo-softening plastic or laminated glass-reinforced (GRP)/carbon fibre-reinforced plastic (CFRP). The former is heated to a particular temperature and draped over a cast of the residual limb under vacuum; the latter is manufactured by means of a wet lay-up lamination process. This method of lamination requires the cast or model to be isolated from the structural materials that are impregnated with liquid resin under vacuum. A plastic dummy is commonly used in both methods to form a precise shape at the distal end of the socket corresponding with the interface component being used (Figs. 29.7 and 29.8).

Lower limb prostheses

Interface components may also incorporate the suspension method to keep the limb on the person. Silicone or polyurethane based liners are commonly used to improve tissue stability and comfort. These may incorporate a locking pin at the distal end that is released by a push button. Alternative means of suspension may be by vacuum, locking lanyard, straps or elasticated cuffs. Each method has a bearing on the design of the socket, particularly in the case of self-suspending sockets.

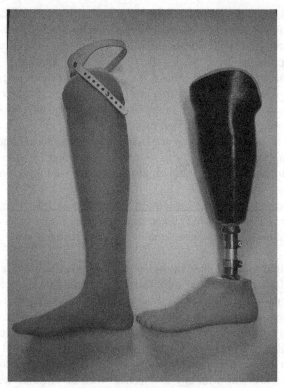

FIG. 29.7 Example of a trans-tibial prosthesis with cosmesis.

FIG. 29.8 Example of a trans-femoral prosthesis.

Prescription of lower limb prosthetic componentry is largely based on the weight and activity level of the user. There is no industry standard for activity levels so manufacturers have developed their own, but they are simple to use and provide a useful reference for the clinician as to what components are suitable for a particular user in terms of their functional demands.

Almost all lower limb prostheses require an artificial foot. Traditionally, prosthetic feet were designed to restore basic ambulation. Evolution from the rigid pylon (historically referred to as the "peg leg") to better reflect natural appearance and function, resulted in the solid-ankle-cushioned-heel (SACH) foot. These remain in wide use today in a variety of forms. However, more active individuals benefit from a foot better suited to their activity levels, particularly if they wish to partake in sport. The development of feet capable of storing and releasing energy to assist forward propulsion came in response to this requirement. Since the introduction of the "flexfoot" in 1987, which saw a radical departure from earlier versions, there have been a plethora of design variants on the theme. These passive devices are predominantly made from laminated carbon fibre and/or glass reinforced plastics. Essentially they form a system of elastic leaf springs that deform under the weight of the body, storing potential energy that is released when the load is removed. However, as is the case with most mechanical springs, they are not 100% efficient and suffer some degree of hysteresis. Loss of energy to the system is undesirable because it means there is less available to assist the residual limb through the swing phase of gait. Many prosthetic feet are designed to replace the function of the ankle, which through the action of the plantar-flexors has the ability to generate more energy than it absorbs. The lack of active energy generation by most current prosthetic feet is one of the major barriers to normal gait replication.

To overcome these problems a dynamic solution capable of active power generation is thought to be necessary. Some powered devices have been developed, but these are very expensive, heavy and bulky.

Prosthetic knees and hips vary considerably in complexity depending on the needs of the user. The most basic form consists of a simple locking mechanism that stabilises or releases a single axis joint. More functional knee units employ mechanical linkages to improve dynamic stability. These swing freely and may incorporate spring assisted extension. The requirement for more natural gait replication led to development of swing and stance control mechanisms. There are many different types of hydraulic and pneumatic damping systems incorporated in prosthetic knees that control the rate of swing and adapt to a certain extent to different walking speeds. Progression from simple mechanical systems resulted in "intelligent prostheses" incorporating a microprocessor. These control the damping system in response to feedback from strain gauges, accelerometers and transducers in real-time as well as "learning" the style of a particular user. One such approach applies magnetorheological technology to alter the viscosity of the damping fluid, varying its resistance to angular motion.

Alignment

One of the most critical elements to the success of a prosthesis is how it is aligned. This refers to the orientation and position of the prosthetic joints relative to the socket and proximal anatomy. It has the potential to fundamentally alter a person's gait and ability to use a prosthesis and, as a result, correct alignment must be achieved and maintained in order for function to be optimized.

In general, lower limb prostheses are set up with the socket flexed to $5°-10°$ in the sagittal plane. A straight vertical line should link the hip, knee and ankle joint centres, and in the coronal plane the mid posterior aspect of the socket should fall on a straight vertical line to the centre of the heel. Beyond this, alignment must accommodate any excessive varus, valgus or flexion by shifting the foot laterally, medially or anteriorly accordingly. Misalignment results in instability, discomfort and poor gait associated with the generation of unwanted moments that act about the joints.

Amputee gait

Amputee gait can appear remarkably normal to an inexperienced observer, which is a testament to the skill of the prosthetist and design of components.

Visual gait analysis is routinely used as a means of assessment in prosthetic clinics. For example, when a new foot is fitted, the prosthetist aligns the prosthesis to what they consider optimal. This is a subjective means of assessment but is suitably quick and effective. Various scales have been developed to assist in quantifying the technique for ease of recording and future comparison.

Visual gait analysis is limited when attempting to identify the causes of subtle deviations, for which the use of instrumented gait analysis may be considered appropriate. This powerful means of collecting objective data, measured from several parameters at once, is not free from limitations of its own. See chapter on clinical gait analysis.

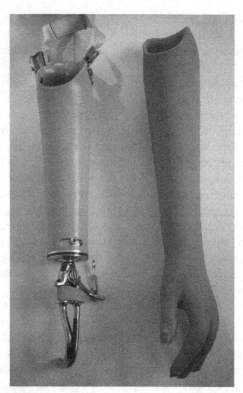

FIG. 29.9 Example of a trans-radial hook and cosmesis.

Upper limb prostheses

Many upper limb amputees choose not to use prostheses due to their shortcomings. Even the most complex myo-electric limbs are crude in relation to the complexity of the anatomy they are designed to replace. Upper limb prostheses usually fall into three categories; cosmetic, body powered and myo-electric. Cosmetic prostheses are designed to match the users sound side as closely as possible and provide very little functional use. Body powered prostheses are operated by a harness and pulley system employed to flex joints and open and close a terminal device such as a split hook (Fig. 29.9). Myo-electric prostheses detect the users' residual limb muscle movements which can be employed to control a prosthetic hand.

Advances in materials and innovative design have provided the clinician with components that offer superior function compared with traditional equipment. However, mechanical devices fail to accurately replicate the complex natural structures they replace, primarily because they are mostly passive. This means that amputees compensate by adopting strategies that are energy efficient and functional, but may not necessarily be considered a good outcome from a medical perspective. Further reading is suggested on the world health organization medical and social models of disability.

Prosthetics case study

Alan is a 28 year old ex serviceman who was injured by an improvised explosive device three years ago. He sustained traumatic injuries resulting in right trans-femoral and trans-radial amputations. His right arm was amputated mid forearm. There is minimal scarring and normal range of movement at the elbow and shoulder joints. He has a very short, right residual lower limb. The skin sustained burns during the explosion and there are some areas of tissue grafting. Sensation across the residual limb is impaired in places.

Alan benefited from an intensive program of rehabilitation and through military support was provided with high specification prostheses. He has achieved a good level of function using a self suspending myoelectric upper limb prosthesis. Mobilization with his lower limb prosthesis has been more difficult. His lower limb prosthesis consists of an ischial containment socket with locking liner suspension, microprocessor knee and energy storing foot. Alan is able to mobilize well but he experiences frequent skin breakdown in the groin area. The main reasons for this are skin fragility and short residuum which has resulted in a reduced surface area for socket force distribution and propulsion of a prosthesis. Skin breakdown limits the amount of time and the type of activities for which Alan can use his prosthesis. He also has periods where he is unable to use his prosthesis and will instead mobilize using an energy efficient wheelchair. Different prosthetic options have been tried to

Prosthetics case study—cont'd

resolve this problem, including alternative socket designs, interface materials and suspension methods. Lighter weight prosthetic componentry has also been trialled but the issue persists.

Another option in Alan's case would be osseointegration to surgically implant a titanium abutment into the distal end of the residual limb. The technique provides a secure means of attachment for a prosthesis, eliminating the need for a socket. The procedure involves a lengthy rehabilitation period and is not regularly carried out due to post surgical complications, such as infection.

Questions for the reader

Why is osseointegration not carried out more widely?

What are the advantages and disadvantages of using a myoelectric prostheses?

Are microprocessor knees suitable for amputees of all activity levels?

Further reading

Levine, D., Richards, J., Whittle, M.W., 2011. Whittle's Gait Analysis, fifth ed. Butterworth Heinemann.

Lusardi, M., Nielsen, C., 2012. Orthotics and Prosthetics in Rehabilitation, third ed. Elsevier.

Özkaya, N., Nordin, M., Goldsheyder, D., Leger, D.L., 2012. Fundamentals of Biomechanics — Equilibrium, Motion and Deformation, third ed. Springer.

Ratner, B.D., Hoffman, A.S., Schoen, F.J., Lemons, J.E., 2008. Biomaterials Science, third ed. Elsevier.

Smith, D.G., Michael, J.W., Bowker, J.H., 2004. Atlas of Amputations and Limb Deficiencies — Surgical, Prosthetic and Rehabilitation Principles. American Academy of Orthopaedic Surgeons.

Tortora, G.J., Derrickson, B.H., 2011. Principles of Anatomy and Physiology, thirteenth ed. Wiley.

Orthotics

Paul Horwood

Oxford University Hospitals NHS Foundation Trust, Oxford, UK

Introduction

Orthoses are externally applied devices which compensate for impairments or modify the musculoskeletal or neuromuscular systems (ISO, 1989a). Orthotists are healthcare professionals specifically trained to assess, fit and advise how an orthosis can be designed and constructed. Orthoses are prescribed to achieve clinical objectives such as to prevent/discourage deformity or to improve function. Orthoses can be stock (off the shelf) items taken from a range of sizes, modular (limited amount of changes to a stock product) or custom-made. This latter process can include measurements, casts or digital scans of the body. Custom-made orthoses can be moulded from plastics, such as copolymers, and will incorporate judiciously placed straps and padding in order to achieve their objectives with satisfactory comfort.

The use of new materials such as carbon fibre composites, polyolefin elastomers, a large range of Ethyl Vinyl Acetate (EVA) foams, mixed materials such as EVA/Low Density Polyethylene (LDPE) and other tri-laminate cushioning materials has helped to replace the traditional use of leather covered metal sub-structures.

The assessments required to design an orthosis will include passive and active range of motion of the anatomical joints, muscle control and strength, joint congruency and integrity, the level of sensation and presence of any associated impairments. The range of conditions treated with orthoses is extensive with anything from foot functional deficits to complex neurological conditions such as cerebral palsy.

Biomechanical principles

The means by which orthoses work is biomechanical using the application of force and lever systems. Typically the forces that orthoses apply are 'reaction' forces generated in response to gravity, where muscles are weak, and/or to counter forces of muscle imbalance. Key biomechanical principles underpinning orthotic management are that using longer lever arms means less force is required, and that applying forces over larger surface areas means less pressure is applied to the body. To maintain stability the centre of mass must be within the base of support. Knowledge of gait analysis is necessary to understand how orthoses can improve the efficiency of walking.

Functions, objectives, goals & design

The functions of an orthosis can be considered as follows:

- Correct/reduce/accommodate deformity
- Protect against further progression of deformity
- Pain relief — limit motion/weight bearing
- Relocate axial load centrally
- Improve function/activity limitations

All orthoses will have a clinical goal and these can include:

- To relieve pain
- Protect tissues/promote healing
- Correct/accommodate deformity
- Improve function
- Compensate for limb/segment length deficiency
- Compensate for abnormal muscle function

When designing an orthosis the orthotist will consider within the criteria the following:

- Functional objectives
- Biomechanical objectives

- Treatment objectives
- Strength
- Weight
- Reliability
- Patient interface
- Cosmetics

Terminology

A standard system of anatomical terminology that is familiarly abbreviated is used. This describes an orthosis by the joints that are encompassed in the device (ISO, 1989b). As an example, an orthosis enclosing the ankle and foot but finishing below the knee is an ankle-foot-orthosis, AFO. Extending proximally to the thigh would then encompass the knee joint, so the term knee-ankle-foot-orthosis, KAFO, is appropriate. Similarly, a spinal orthosis encompassing the thoraco-lumbar and sacral spine is referred to as a TLSO. Sometimes the aim or function of the orthosis is included in the name, such as hip abduction orthosis.

Confusion can occur when orthoses are named nominally after people, places or referred to by trade names.

Foot orthoses

Insoles, foot orthoses (often known as functional foot orthoses, FFO), supportive footwear and shoe modifications can all be used to increase stability during standing and walking. Mild plano-valgus or varus deformities can be controlled by foot orthoses that are designed to encourage better skeletal alignment. Foot orthoses occasionally extend just above the ankle to gain greater control, these designs being termed supra-malleolar orthoses (SMOs). Rigid thermoplastic or composite materials are used to provide maximum control with an element of strength and durability. Softer, more accommodating insoles can be moulded to redistribute the plantar pressure under the foot utilizing cushioning materials such as EVA or polyurethane foams.

Ankle foot orthoses

To control weakened dorsiflexion muscles (as described in the chapter on functional electrical stimulation), over active plantarflexion muscles, an equinus or calcaneus deformity, or moderate to severe valgus or varus deformities, an orthosis needs to encompass the ankle and foot and extend proximally to below the knee.

Ankle foot orthoses (AFOs) provide longer leverage and control in the sagittal plane. They may be trimmed to create a flexible, posterior leaf spring AFO, incorporate hinges to allow dorsiflexion, or made rigid to provide maximum control. AFOs are widely prescribed for flaccid foot drop, hemiplegia subsequent to cerebral vascular accident (CVA, or stroke), cerebral palsy and other neuromuscular conditions to improve gait efficiency. They can be used to immobilize painful joints in musculoskeletal conditions such as osteoarthritis.

AFOs are also used to control foot position and prevent deformity in non-ambulant people. They are sometimes used at night for stretching calf muscles and preventing tightening of calf muscles, although if this is found to disturb sleep, softer, resting night splints can be used which maintain a reasonable position through the night with the muscles on less stretch (Fig. 29.10).

Knee orthoses

A knee orthosis (KO) encompasses the knee joint only and can be provided for a broad spectrum of conditions. In their simplest form they can range from soft elasticated materials, including neoprene variants, and are supplied for such issues as mild arthritic joints or patella tracking problems. The range then extends to a combination of soft with rigid materials such as metal hinges added to a main fabric base to offer increased support and stability. More rigid alloy or composite material framed orthoses are used in functional knee bracing. These are commonly provided in the management of anterior or posterior cruciate ligaments (ACL/PCL) injuries or deficits.

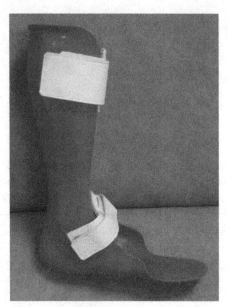

FIG. 29.10 Example ankle foot orthosis (AFO).

KAFO case study

64 year old male with poliomyelitis diagnosis from age 2. Polio has affected both lower limbs with flaccid paralysis to right leg resulting in a lifetime use of a KAFO to allow ambulation. This KAFO has locked knee joints in the stance phase. Mobility is aided with the use of bilateral crutches that has allowed a career in engineering.

Left leg has significant weakness but this gentleman has managed over the years with only mild support or simple orthoses. The left knee has increasing ligament laxity with resultant hyperextension and resultant pain becoming a greater issue starting to limit mobility. In 2019 he has been supplied with a long length knee orthosis to control the hyperextension but allow free knee flexion. This is made from polypropylene shells with metal hinged free knee joints and fixing straps.

Images show left knee unsupported (Fig. 29.11), orthosis at trial stage (Fig. 29.12) and when completed (Figs. 29.13 and 29.14).

Knee ankle foot orthoses

A knee ankle foot orthosis (KAFO) extends from the thigh and includes the ankle and foot; a hinge is usually included at the knee to enable flexion during sitting but these are often designed to be locked in extension for standing and walking. These devices typically consist of thermoplastic or composite shells at the thigh and foot/ankle sections with metal joints to hinge at the knee.

More recent innovations have developed stance control knee joints that will unlock on the swing phase of gait and automatically lock on the stance phase to maintain the knee securely in extension (more information on the gait cycle may be found in the chapters on functional electrical stimulation and clinical gait analysis).

Patients with neuromuscular conditions such as poliomyelitis, muscular dystrophy or spinal muscular atrophy may find that KAFO's enable them to stand and walk, although gait patterns have to be modified to compensate for a knee locked in extension.

Hip knee ankle foot orthoses

Hip knee ankle foot orthoses (HKAFOs) can enable standing and upright locomotion in people who are normally unable to maintain standing unaided. HKAFOs extend from the trunk and control the whole lower limbs and pelvis. People with spina bifida or paraplegia can learn to use custom-fitted modular orthoses such as the Swivel Walker or ParaWalker.

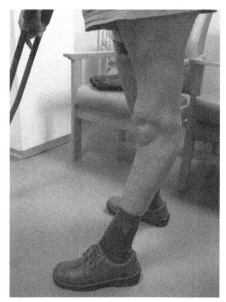

FIG. 29.11   KAFO case study: left knee unsupported.

Thoraco-lumbar sacral orthoses

Spinal orthoses (TLSOs) are used to support the trunk by controlling scoliosis or supporting weakened musculature. These orthoses are typically moulded from a range of rigid to semi-flexible thermoplastics, laminated foam materials or, less commonly, fabrics. Spinal orthoses may be provided to improve trunk control, improve sitting posture or to try to prevent the progression of scoliosis. TLSOs are often prescribed for people with neuromuscular conditions where the aim is to reduce the rate of scoliosis progression and delay the need for surgical stabilization, assist sitting posture or when surgery is not possible (Fig. 29.15).

Upper limb orthoses

Orthoses can be used to position the arm, wrist and hand to improve manual ability. Wrist hand orthoses (WHOs) usually hold the wrist in extension, and may extend to control thumb posture in order to promote a functional position. 'Paddle'

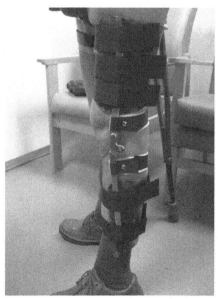

FIG. 29.12   KAFO case study: orthosis at trial stage.

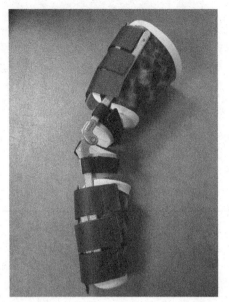

FIG. 29.13 KAFO case study: completed orthosis.

type designs of orthoses may be used to resist flexion deformities in the wrist and fingers. It should be noted that occupational therapists also mould and provide WHOs, often as part of a rehabilitation programme, although those made by an orthotics department are often more durable in the longer term due to the more advanced manufacturing techniques available.

Orthoses for the elbow joint or for the entire upper limb can have the objective of providing support or stabilization. An example is a brachial plexus injury where the orthosis will encompass the limb from the shoulder to wrist as an attempt to gain function in a flaccid arm.

Head orthoses

A protective helmet may be indicated to reduce the risk of injury when a person is prone to falling, for instance during seizures, or after craniectomy surgery. There are some applications where helmets are provided as 'cranial moulding'

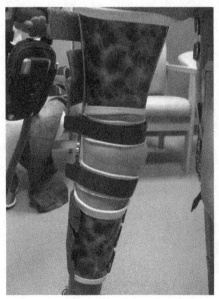

FIG. 29.14 KAFO case study: completed orthosis in use.

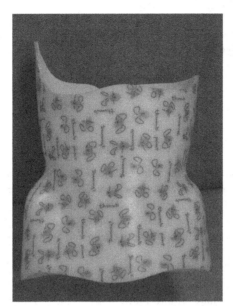

FIG. 29.15 Example thoraco-lumbar sacral orthosis (TLSO).

devices in the treatment of infants with plagiocephaly. Helmets vary in design dependent on the objectives to be met. Some are constructed from low density foams and fabric covers offering mild protection, whilst other designs have high density thermoplastic shells offering far greater prevention of further injury.

Summary

Orthoses can be very useful to improve functioning or reduce pain in adults and children with musculoskeletal or neuromuscular conditions and may reduce the rate of progressive in some deformities. Appropriate fitting and design of orthoses is required to prevent problems with pressure or rubbing and to ensure that attainment of clinical goals is maximized. There can be stigma associated with using equipment that identifies people as different to their peers, so the benefits of orthoses for individuals should be carefully assessed and re-evaluated over time.

References

International Organization for Standardisation, 1989a. ISO 8549-1 Prosthetics and Orthotics — Vocabulary, Part 1: General Terms for External Limb Prostheses and External Orthoses. ISO, Geneva.

International Organization for Standardisation, 1989b. ISO 8549-1 Prosthetics and Orthotics — Vocabulary, Part 3: Terms Relating to External Orthoses. ISO, Geneva.

Recommended reading

Mosby, C.V., 1985. Atlas of Orthotics, Biomechanical Principles and Applications. American Academy of Orthopaedic Surgeons, St. Louis.

Rose, G.K., 1986. Orthotics — Principles & Practice. William Heinemann, London.

Morris, C., Dias, L. (Eds.), 2007. Paediatric Orthotics Clinics in Developmental Medicine No. 175. MacKeith Press.

Edelstein, J., Moroz, A., 2010. Lower-Limb Prosthetics and Orthotics: Clinical Concepts. Slack Incorporated.

Lusardi, M., Jorge, M., Nielsen, C., 2012. Orthotics and Prosthetics in Rehabilitation. Elsevier Health Sciences, W.B. Saunders & Co.

Orthopaedic biomechanics

Tim Holsgrove
University of Exeter, Exeter, UK

Engineering requirements of orthopedic implants

The aim of orthopedic[1] implants is generally to restore normal functional biomechanics to the affected area. This may be in the form of a fracture fixation device or a joint replacement device. The device should work in such a way that once implanted, pain is reduced or eliminated entirely, the body should be able to move through normal ranges of motion, and should be able to cope with the normal loads present in everyday life. An exception to this is fusion procedures,[2] which aim to remove physiological motion at the operated level to reduce pain and allow the normal load transfer characteristics to be restored.

The body is constantly adapting to the conditions to which it is subjected. If an implanted device shields the skeleton from normal loads, bone may be resorbed and this may lead to injury, pain, or loosening of the implant. Such complications may result in clinical failure and may require further surgery. It is therefore imperative to thoroughly assess the mechanical properties of implants and how they integrate with the natural structures of the musculoskeletal system prior to clinical use.

The design of orthopedic implants requires a certain level of compromise with regard to the geometry and materials that may be used. The implant must fit within the existing framework of the musculoskeletal system, with minimal effect on any other systems present. The materials used must be biocompatible and able to cope with the corrosive environment of the body. This difficult task must be completed bearing in mind that the implant should work, and continue to work, without any adjustment or alteration for many years, under high loading conditions and millions of cycles.

Use of synthetic biomaterials[3] in orthopedics

It is crucial that any foreign material implanted into the body has been thoroughly assessed for biocompatibility (Goel et al., 2006; Ratner et al., 1996). Over time, this has led to a limited number of materials that have been shown to be stable and safe in the body over prolonged periods. Commonly used metals include alloys of titanium, stainless steel, and cobalt-chromium. The compromise in choosing an appropriate alloy is in achieving a suitable level of stiffness, strength, corrosion resistance, and biocompatibility.

Polyethylene is a polymer frequently used as an articulation surface in arthroplasty[4] devices. It can be coupled with either a metal or ceramic component. Increased resistance to polyethylene wear can be achieved using ultra-high molecular weight polyethylene (UHMWPE) and by cross-linking the material (Kurtz et al., 1999; Morrey, 2003; Ries, 2011). Polyaryletheretherketone (PEEK) is a thermoplastic resin that can be injection molded and is commonly used in spinal applications such a posterior stabilization devices and fusion cages. The elastic properties of silicone have been exploited in the one-piece design of the NeuFlex (DePuy Orthopaedics, Inc.) finger joint replacement. Polymethylmethacrylate (PMMA) is a material used as a bone cement to provide fixation for arthroplasty devices. The bone cement is mixed intraoperatively by combining powdered PMMA with a liquid monomer, usually in a vacuum, before injecting it into the required area of the body.

Ceramics are also used as articulation surfaces in arthroplasty devices due to the low wear that can be achieved. Alumina and zirconium are two such materials. Ceramics may be paired in articulation (ceramic on ceramic) or combined with another material, such as a ceramic femoral head articulating on a UHMWPE acetabular component. Hydroxyapatite is a ceramic used for coating cementless implants to provide secondary fixation via bone ongrowth.

---

1. Orthopedics is the branch of medicine concerned with the musculoskeletal system.
2. The fusion of a joint in the body through surgical procedure is known as arthrodesis.
3. Biomaterial is a material found in the body or synthetically implanted into the body.
4. Arthroplasty is the restoration of a joint in the body through surgical procedure.

It is important to consider the amount of wear in an arthroplasty device, not only in terms of the eventual wearing out of the device, but also because the wear particles produced can be a significant contributor to osteolysis and implant loosening (Bozic and Ries, 2005; Morrey, 2003; Wang et al., 2004).

Mechanical load requirements

It must be demonstrated that all devices, whether for fracture fixation, joint arthroplasty, or fusion procedures, be able to cope with the loading environment for which the implant is intended. Preclinical tests are used for this appraisal and generally include both static and dynamic tests. Static tests may be completed to assess the strength, stiffness, and yield point of a device. Dynamic tests may assess wear and fatigue characteristics over the predicted life cycles of the device. There are standard recommendations for such testing published by ASTM International and the International Organization for Standardization (ISO).

In addition to wear, fatigue, and yield tests, it may also be necessary to complete further tests to assess the efficacy of a device, or the effect that an implant may have on the surrounding tissue when used in-vivo.

Approaches to device fixation

Orthopedic implants may be screwed, cemented, or press-fitted into place. In addition to these primary methods of fixation, secondary fixation may be achieved through bone ingrowth or ongrowth.

Screws are often used to fix fracture plates and pins to bone. Pedicle screws and rods are used for posterior fusion of the spine. Other orthopedic devices such as dental implants, acetabular cups, and spinal fusion cages may use screws for primary stability.

Bone cement can be used to provide the fixation of an implant. The cement is normally injected into the required space when doughy in consistency, then pressurized to minimize void formation. The implant is subsequently inserted and held in place until the cement has cured. Cement is less stiff than trabecular and cortical bone (Zivic et al., 2012; Zysset et al., 1999), and may therefore act as a good medium for load transfer between the stiff implant and the host bone.

Cementless fixation can also be achieved by using specific reaming instruments that provide a close fit between the implant and bone. Secondary fixation through bone ingrowth or ongrowth is generally used in cementless devices.

Bone ingrowth can occur when the surface of an implant is porous, for example with titanium beads or mesh. Over time, the bone grows into the pores of the surface and provides stability to the bone and implant interface. Bone ongrowth is achieved through a similar means as ingrowth. An implant may be sprayed with a material such as hydroxyapatite (HA), which promotes bone growth and osseointegration[5] (Solomon, 1992). An HA sprayed surface is generally combined with a textured surface as this is more effective than an HA coating alone (Rodriguez, 2006). It is crucial for both ingrowth and ongrowth that primary stability is achieved. If the displacement of the implant relative to the host bone that occurs during loading (referred to as micromotion) is greater than approximately 150 μm, soft tissue rather than bone will grow into, or onto, the implant surface (Gortchacow et al., 2012; Jasty et al., 1997; Kienapfel et al., 1999) and this can prevent long-term stability through osseointegration.

Common orthopedic implants

Fracture plates are commonly used to align bones and allow bone to grow across the fracture (Fig. 29.16). Titanium alloys are frequently used for this type of implant due to their low stiffness compared to other metals used for implants. Small amounts of micromotion induced at the fracture surfaces as loading occurs provide the necessary stimulation for bone repair. Should this micromotion be too large, soft tissue will grow across the fracture first, and the fracture will take longer to fully heal or result in a fibrous union as opposed to bony union (Nordin and Frankel, 2001).

Dental implants are commonly used to reassemble a tooth, or provide a base onto which a prosthesis may be fixed. They are commonly titanium alloy and comprise a screw that is driven into the bone onto which an abutment is fixed. The threads of the screw may be coated to provide secondary fixation via bone ongrowth or ingrowth.

---

5. Osseointegration is the development of a functional interface between an implant and the host bone.

FIG. 29.16 Example fracture plate.

FIG. 29.17 Example hip prosthesis.

Hip arthroplasty (Fig. 29.17) is a common procedure that has good clinical success rates (Kärrholm et al., 2017; National Joint Registry, 2018) and a long history of progressive development in both design and materials. Generally, the affected joint is treated by removing the femoral head and neck, reaming into the femoral canal, and inserting a femoral component. This may be cemented into place, or a cementless device may be used. The femoral component may be one piece, or modular in design. Modular designs allow an increased number of sizing options and reduced stock inventory, but also lead to more taper fits, which may lead to an increased potential for failure. The femoral stem is metal, and the femoral head may be metal or ceramic. The acetabular component often comprises a metal outer shell that may be either cemented or cementless, though in cementless procedures additional screws may be used for primary stability. Once the shell is in place, the liner is inserted, which is most commonly UHMWPE, or ceramic.

Knee arthroplasty (Fig. 29.18) is also a well-established and generally successful joint replacement procedure (National Joint Registry, 2018; Swedish Knee Arthroplasty Register, 2018). A knee arthroplasty device comprises a tibial and femoral component and features metal on UHMWPE articulation. Both components may have a stem for fixation and stability. The tibial plateau is generally comprised of a metal tray with a UHMWPE insert, and although one-piece tibial components produced from UHMWPE are available, they are only currently used in a small proportion of procedures (1.3% of primary knee arthroplasties in England Wales, and Northern Ireland in 2018 (National Joint Registry, 2018)). The femoral component is comprised entirely of metal, with highly polished condyles for articulation on the UHMWPE insert in the tibial tray. In revision knee arthroplasty, and in situations where the soft tissue is compromised, a prosthesis with a hinged knee design may be used in order to provide the required stability to the joint.

Degenerative disc disease in the spine is common and can be severely debilitating (Adams et al., 2006; Cassinelli and Kang, 2000). An affected level may be fused to restore disc height, correct load transfer, and reduce pain. However, this is carried out at the cost of motion at the operative level. Fusion cages may be inserted into the disc space after a discectomy has been completed. This may comprise one or two cages of a metal or PEEK that are combined with allograft bone. Over time, bone grows into the cages and entirely fuses the vertebral level.

Fusion may also be achieved through posterior procedures (Fig. 29.19) using screws that are driven into long pedicles and into the vertebral bodies of the levels to be fused. The screws are then linked via a rod. This assembly may be inserted

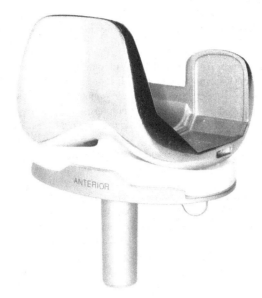

FIG. 29.18 Example knee prosthesis.

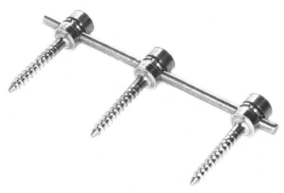

FIG. 29.19 Example fusion device.

along the pedicles on one side only, or two parallel assemblies may be inserted, which may also be linked together to increase the rigidity of the structure.

Fusion procedures may also combine both anterior and posterior fusion devices to provide more stability than the implantation of one system alone.

Case study – the exeter hip: small design changes can make a big difference

The way that orthopaedic implants interact with the host materials and structures of the body are often complex and multifaceted, and a small change in the design of an implant may have far-ranging implications on the success, or failure of the design. This was found to be the case with the development of the Exeter double-tapered hip stem.

The Exeter hip stem was developed in 1969, and the double-tapered collarless design was designed to provide a taper-locking fit with the cement into which it was implanted. The original stem was produced from EN58J stainless steel, with a polished finish and initial clinical results were good. However, the design was updated in 1976 using a stronger 316L stainless steel in order to reduce the incidence of stem fractures (Ling, 2018). At the time of this change, the surface finish was not considered critical to the performance, so a rougher finish was used, as this was more cost effective. However, after several years it became apparent that although the 316L stainless steel had greatly reduced the incidence of implant fractures, the problem of bone lysis and aseptic loosening was more common (Ling, 2018), which led to an increased revision rate of rough stems (Howie et al., 1998). Therefore, in 1986 the Exeter stem was updated to continue using the 316 stainless steel, but the polished surface of the original design was reintroduced (Ling, 2018).

Whilst the polished tapered stem allowed for a taper-lock mechanism, with the subsidence of the stem under loading increasing the stability of the implant, the rough surface finish of the same stem led to greater shear and tensile loading between the stem/cement interface. A retrieval study comparing rough and polished stems identified abrasive wear at the stem/

Continued

Case study – the exeter hip: small design changes can make a big difference—cont'd

cement interface of rough stems (Howell et al., 2004), which could lead to an increase in the release of wear particles and a reduction in stem stability. An in-vitro study of cement surface finish also found that following 1 million load cycles, the stem/cement interface pressure was not changed in a polished tapered stem, whereas it significantly increased with a rough tapered stem, and led to increased rotational micromotion (Bartlett et al., 2009), which could contribute to the increased aseptic loosening observed clinically.

The Exeter stem has maintained the polished surface finish since the reintroduction in 1986. More than 2 million Exeter stems have now been used worldwide, and it is regarded as one of the most successful femoral components for total hip arthroplasty, with an estimated survivorship of 97%–98% at 10 years based on the latest National Joint Registry Data (National Joint Registry, 2018).

The above case study highlights the importance of investigating and assessing even small design alterations, as a modification aiming to improve performance in one area, may detrimentally impact performance in another. However, it also emphasises the value of the thorough clinical follow-up of orthopaedic devices. The early performance of the Exeter stem was monitored closely at the Princess Elizabeth Orthopaedic Centre. Now, many countries have national joint registries, and this means that it is possible to assess the effect of changes in surgical practice using larger patient cohorts than ever before; the National Joint Registry of England, Wales, and Northern Ireland now has data relating to approximately 1 million hip arthroplasty procedures. However, identifying trends using registry data can take several years, so it is still critical to complete thorough pre-clinical testing prior to the introduction of new designs, or alterations in the design of existing devices.

References

Adams, M., Bogduk, N., Burton, K., Dolan, P., 2006. The Biomechanics of Back Pain, second ed. Elsevier Ltd, Philadelphia, PA, USA.

Bartlett, G.E., Beard, D.J., Murray, D.W., Gill, H.S., 2009. In vitro comparison of the effects of rough and polished stem surface finish on pressure generation in cemented hip arthroplasty. Acta Orthop. 80, 144–149.

Bozic, K.J., Ries, M.D., 2005. Wear and osteolysis in total hip arthroplasty. Semin. Arthroplast. 16, 142–152.

Cassinelli, E.H., Kang, J.D., 2000. Current understanding of lumbar disc degeneration. Oper. Tech. Orthop. 10, 254–262.

Goel, V.K., Panjabi, M.M., Patwardhan, A.G., Dooris, A.P., Serhan, H., 2006. Test protocols for evaluation of spinal implants. Journal of Bone and Joint Surgery. American Volume 88 (Suppl. 2), 103–109.

Gortchacow, M., Wettstein, M., Pioletti, D.P., Müller-Gerbl, M., Terrier, A., 2012. Simultaneous and multisite measure of micromotion, subsidence and gap to evaluate femoral stem stability. J. Biomech. 45 (7), 1232–1238.

Howell Jr., J.R., Blunt, L.A., Doyle, C., Hooper, R.M., Lee, A.J., Ling, R.S., 2004. In vivo surface wear mechanisms of femoral components of cemented total hip arthroplasties: the influence of wear mechanism on clinical outcome. J. Arthroplast. 19, 88–101.

Howie, D.W., Middleton, R.G., Costi, K., 1998. Loosening of matt and polished cemented femoral stems. J. Bone Joint Surg. Br. 80, 573–576.

Jasty, M., Bragdon, C., Burke, D., O'Connor, D., Lowenstein, J., Harris, W.H., 1997. In vivo skeletal responses to porous-surfaced implants subjected to small induced motions. J. Bone Joint Surg. Am. 79, 707–714.

Kärrholm, J., Mohaddes, M., Odin, D., Vinblad, J., Rogmark, C., Rolfson, O., 2017. Swedish Hip Arthroplasty Register – Annual Report 2017. Swedish Hip Arthroplasty Register. Göteborg, Sweden.

Kienapfel, H., Sprey, C., Wilke, A., Griss, P., 1999. Implant fixation by bone ingrowth. J. Arthroplast. 14, 355–368.

Kurtz, S.M., Muratoglu, O.K., Evans, M., Edidin, A.A., 1999. Advances in the processing, sterilization, and crosslinking of ultra-high molecular weight polyethylene for total joint arthroplasty. Biomaterials 20, 1659–1688.

Ling, R., 2018. The Exeter stem over 30 years – taking the rough with the smooth. Orthop. Proc. 84-B.

Morrey, B.F., 2003. Joint Replacement Arthroplasty, third ed. Churchill-Livingstone, Philadelphia, PA, USA.

National Joint Registry, 2018. 15th Annual Report 2018 – National Joint Registry for England, Wales, Northern Ireland and the Isle of Man – Surgical Data to 31 December 2017. National Joint Registry. Hemel Hempstead, Herfordshire, UK.

Nordin, M., Frankel, V.H., 2001. Basic Biomechanics of the Musculoskeletal System, third ed. Lippincott Williams & Wilkins, Philadelphia, PA, USA.

Ratner, B.D., Hoffman, A.S., Schoen, F.J., Lemons, J.E., 1996. Biomaterials Science: An Introduction to Materials in Medicine, second ed. Academic Press, San Diego, CA, USA.

Ries, M.D., 2011. Highly crosslinked ultrahigh molecular weight polyethylene in total hip arthroplasty: No further concerns-opposes. Semin. Arthroplast. 22, 82–84.

Rodriguez, J.A., 2006. Acetabular fixation options: notes from the other side. J. Arthroplast. 21, 93–96.

Solomon, L., 1992. Hip replacement: prosthetic fixation. Curr. Orthop. 6, 153–156.

Swedish Knee Arthroplasty Register, 2018. Annual Report 2018. Lund University, Department of Clinical Sciences, Skånes University Hospital, Lund, Sweden.

Wang, M.L., Sharkey, P.F., Tuan, R.S., 2004. Particle bioreactivity and wear-mediated osteolysis. J. Arthroplast. 19, 1028–1038.

Zivic, F., Babic, M., Grujovic, N., Mitrovic, S., Favaro, G., Caunii, M., 2012. Effect of vacuum-treatment on deformation properties of PMMA bone cement. J. Mech. Behav. Biomed. Mater. 5, 129–138.

Zysset, P.K., Edward Guo, X., Edward Hoffler, C., Moore, K.E., Goldstein, S.A., 1999. Elastic modulus and hardness of cortical and trabecular bone lamellae measured by nanoindentation in the human femur. J. Biomech. 32, 1005–1012.

Mobile arm supports

Tori Mayhew[a] and David Long[b]

[a]Oxford University Hospitals NHS Foundation Trust, Oxford, UK; [b]AJM Healthcare, UK & Oxford University Hospitals NHS Foundation Trust, Oxford, UK

Introduction

Believed to originally have been developed in the 1950s in California, USA, mobile arm supports (MAS) are devices fitted to a wheelchair, table, desk or stand which allow people with weak arm muscles to carry out, with less effort, functional tasks such as eating, using a computer or communication aid and, increasingly, accessing a tablet computer/ e-reader. They can also be used to aid page turning, for drawing/painting and grooming (e.g. brushing teeth, shaving, applying make-up).

Construction

The device can be either a passive mechanical device or one which is powered. It will comprise:

- Trough for the forearm fitted to a pivot or swivel which allows vertical movement of the hand and rotates in the horizontal plane
- Hinged and balanced linkage comprising a proximal and distal arm
- Where mounted to a wheelchair, an adjustable bracket which can be varied in angle and rotation about the vertical plane; this is critical in allowing the device to be adjusted to swing with gravity in specific directions, according to clinical and functional requirements

It may be necessary to manufacture a custom mount to hold the angle adjustable bracket, depending on the structure of the device to which the MAS is to be fitted.

Where hand function/strength is impaired, the distal part of the trough can have attachments fitted to a custom sized and shaped T-bar, such as:

- Pointer for turning pages and accessing keyboards
- Stylus for keypads/touch screens
- Self-levelling spoon (food falls off a fixed angle spoon)
- Palm support, where the wrist is weak but the fingers have functional movement (Figs. 29.20—29.22)
- Examples are shown in figures 21.20 to 21.22.

Applicable client groups

Mobile arm supports are typically used for people having:

- Motor Neurone Disease (MND), also known as Amyotrophic Lateral Sclerosis (ALS), where movement of the shoulder girdle is initially retained whilst the arms and hands are weakened
- Spinal Muscular Atrophy (SMA) having, in this context, similar clinical features to those with MND, but being stable in their condition for longer
- Muscular Dystrophy (MD), where there is proximal weakness, the hands tending to retain their function for longer, but additional hand support being required as the disease progresses
- Spinal Cord Injury (SCI), the type of support varying according to the level of the lesion
- Multiple Sclerosis (MS), the type of support varying according to the nature of the impairment and progression of the disease
- Cerebrovascular Accident (CVA or stroke), but mostly in the context of rehabilitation, i.e. improvements in function may develop over time

There is application for many other health conditions but those listed are the most common groups.

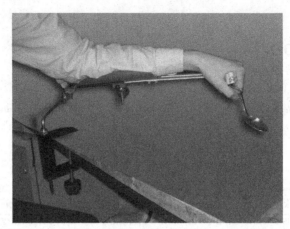

FIG. 29.20   Occupied MAS with T-bar and self-levelling spoon fitted to a table top.

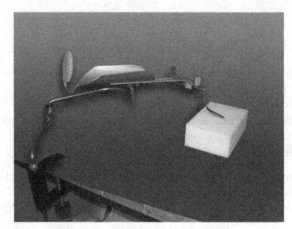

FIG. 29.21   Detail of the trough and T-bar.

Assessment and trial

It is necessary to carry out a detailed clinical assessment prior to the trial or issue of equipment. Initially, this will be to determine what is required and what is desired. There may be a need to arrange additional equipment for the MAS to work successfully, which might typically involve the supply of an over-chair table with a split top to allow mounting of the MAS on a level surface, the sloped surface being used to angle a magazine towards the client, for example. This will usually involve liaison with a community occupational therapist and typically relates to people with MND whose neck muscles will often be weak. Referral to a speech and language therapist may also be required, particularly in respect of facilitating a safe swallow. Critically, there is a requirement for care support to facilitate use of the MAS, either from family members or from carers. Without this support, a MAS is very unlikely to succeed in its objectives.

Having gathered the relevant background information, a physical assessment of the arm and shoulder must then be carried out (this assumes that, where necessary, there is satisfactory postural management in place in terms of wheelchair or static seating). The aim is to check for pain free range of movement in the arm and shoulder such that a MAS can be used, taking time to analyse muscle weakness and imbalance. The assessor takes the arm through a standard set of joint ranges:

- Shoulder abduction
- Shoulder internal to external rotation

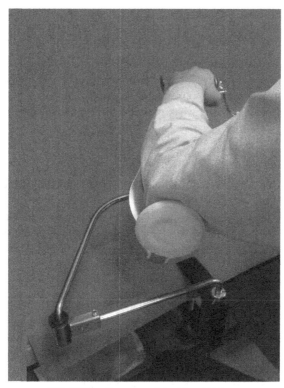

FIG. 29.22 Operation of the hinged linkage.

- Shoulder elevation
- Elbow flexion to extension
- Supination of the forearm
- Wrist flexion and extension

The assessor also checks wrist strength and hand grip which will guide the prescription of distal components.

Handedness is an important factor as the impairment may have occurred on the person's dominant side. Additionally, use of a MAS will be tiring because it involves learning a new skill. This will become more natural as new neural pathways are laid down for the new pattern of movement.

Setting up

Having made this assessment, a MAS is set up in the relevant context and environment. This usually dictates that the appointment takes place in the client's home as it is almost impossible to mimic this in a clinic setting.

Adjustments are generally made in the following order:

1. Length of trough
2. Orientation of elbow dial/pad
3. Length and shape of T-bar
4. Distal componentry
5. Balance point of trough and T-bar
6. Orientation of the angle adjustable bracket (the person is asked to carry out simple tasks, such as to scratch their nose, the assessor observing what adjustments are necessary to make this easier/more efficient)

Stops can be added to limit movement from beyond where, due to weakness, recovery is not possible. Offset swivels suspend the trough, as opposed to it pivoting over a joint, in order to lower the centre of gravity relative to the pivot and to reduce the effort of control.

Additional equipment may be needed to support the head in the form of a collar, of which a wide variety are available. Shoulder cuffs may also be required to stabilize the joint, and supports for a flail arm may be necessary.

Contraindications

There are any number of reasons why a MAS might be contraindicated, but listed below are those most common:

- Unhelpful movements produced by spasticity and tremor can be dampened by use of a MAS due to the reduced effort involved with its use, but they can also be exaggerated which reduces the smoothness of movement
- Insufficient range of (pain free) motion in the joint ranges described above
- Whilst the MAS is designed for people having weak muscles, there must be some available muscle power in order to initiate and sustain movement

Other issues

- The task of writing can be difficult because the whole arm moves, making difficult the precise hand movements required for letter formation
- Drinking is challenging because the weight of the cup/glass and fluid tend to unbalance the support; even if the drink can be raised it may be difficult to tip, so a straw would be needed, in which case it would usually be easier to have the cup positioned on the table with a long straw and non-return valve

On-going care

Once set up correctly for the person, it is unusual for regular adjustment to be necessary. Required more commonly, however, are changes to componentry as a result of disease progression and/or change in task/function. As any change is likely to unbalance the MAS, a similar assessment and setting up process must be followed.

Case study – MAS Provision

LM eating a snack using her wheelchair mounted MAS with custom adaptation (swivelling spoon).

LM has MND and the resulting muscle weakness makes it difficult for her to use her arms functionally. Activities such as eating, texting, emailing, or even playing with pets, are very fatiguing.

LM was visited at her home for an assessment where the following were discussed: daily routine, home environment, level of independence, equipment already in use, care provision. The passive, pain free range of movement in the arms and shoulders was then analyzed, together with an assessment of movement control.

LM uses a powered wheelchair which was considered the best mounting option for the MAS at the time of the intervention. An assessment kit was set up for LM to try out with various activities.

The prescribed equipment and accessories were made up and taken out to LM two weeks later. At this appointment fine adjustments were made to trough balance and rotational bias. The assembly and maintenance of the unit was demonstrated in detail and a user guide was issued.

Robotics

Mike Hillman

University of Bath, Bath, UK

Definitions

A robot is traditionally described (by The Robot Institute of America in 1979) as "A re-programmable, multifunctional manipulator designed to move material, parts, tools or specialized devices through variable programmed motions for the performance of a variety of tasks". This definition is still relevant for a traditional industrial application. However, the application of robotics in a non-industrial application, such as healthcare or rehabilitation, requires a more advanced definition. "The integration of enabling technologies and attributes embracing manipulators, mobility, sensors, computing (IKBS, AI) and hierarchical control to result ultimately in a robot capable of autonomously complementing man's endeavours in unstructured and hostile environments." (described by the UK Department of Trade and Industry's "Advanced Robotics Initiative" in 1987) (Hillman, 2004). From these definitions we see that a robot is not limited to either the humanoid representation of science fiction (as well as much research across the world, not least in Japan), or the traditional industrial definition. Within rehabilitation, robotics have been applied in the following areas.

Assistive robotics

Assistive robotics aims to help those with often severe levels of disability to live as independently as possible in a relatively unmodified environment. Examples of applications are:

- Fixed site — the disabled user is able to use the robot (often a variation on a small industrial robot arm) in a workstation environment set up to optimize specific tasks. These may be of an "office" type or more personal areas such as eating or personal hygiene (Van der Loos, 1995; Hammel et al., 1989). Although many research groups have developed such systems which have been used effectively, and a small number of commercial products have been available, the limitations are obvious. Though no commercial products are currently available, one of the most cost effective systems was the Handy 1 (Topping, 2001).
- Mobile — for some, the ideal has been to provide a robotic carer. The most notable implementation of this was the Movar system developed at Stanford University (Van der Loos et al., 1986). More recently, this concept has been extended to the care of the elderly but with the emphasis on communications rather than manipulation.
- Wheelchair mounted — for wheelchair users having compromised upper limb mobility and dexterity, the ideal might be a "third arm" mounted to the wheelchair. The Manus (Kwee et al., 1989; iArm, Exact Dynamics, no date) is the most successful product in this area and still continues in production. Though popular in its home country of the Netherlands, costs can be prohibitive. The two main obstacles to a wider use of wheelchair robotics (besides price) are of an efficient human machine interface and the problems of integrating the system to a wheelchair without compromising overall width, stability and battery life of the wheelchair. Two examples of wheelchair mounted robot arms are shown in Figs. 29.23 and 29.24 below.

Therapy

At the time of writing, the greatest interest in robotics in rehabilitation both in terms of research and commercial products is in providing therapy to the hand, upper limb and lower limb. Much of this has concentrated on the rehabilitation of stroke survivors. Effective stroke rehabilitation therapy makes use of the ability of the human brain to rewire itself (neuroplasticity) following damage to a part of the brain. It has been found that intensive repetition of movement promotes motor recovery following a stroke (Dipietro et al., 2012). Therapy can be given in the following ways (Lum et al., 2002):

- Passive: movement is externally imposed by the robot while the patient remains relaxed.
- Active: patient initiates the movement, but the robot assists along a predefined path.
- Active resisted: patient must move against a resistance generated by the robot.

FIG. 29.23 Robot arm in use to provide increased reach.

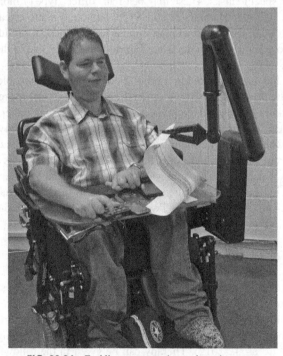

FIG. 29.24 Enabling access to the work environment.

As the potential of robot mediated therapy is explored, the research questions that are being addressed are: is it an effective therapy? Is it more effective than current exercise therapies by physiotherapists? Is it cost effective?

Apart from physical rehabilitation it should be noted that robotics are also being used for cognitive therapy of children with autism (Robins et al., 2004).

Exoskeletons

At a completely different level of technical complexity are exoskeletons which are now starting to appear on the market. These are robotic devices requiring actuators, sensors and power packs. Much of the initial research was pushed by potential for military application to assist soldiers in carrying heavy loads over rough ground. However, the application to people with disabilities was recognized early, the challenges being to decrease the weight needing to be carried and finding a way to provide integration with the patient (Zoss et al., 2006; Suzuki et al., 2007).

Other application areas

Robotics have also been applied in the areas of smart wheelchairs with long range and short range navigational functions, and smart prosthetics, notably of the knee and the hand. Other areas of potential application are in education & communication.

References

Dipietro, L., Krebs, H.I., Volpe, B.T., Stein, J., Bever, C., Mernoff, S.T., Fasoli, S.E., Hogan, N., 2012. Learning, not adaptation, characterizes stroke motor recovery: evidence from kinematic changes induced by robot-assisted therapy in trained and untrained task in the same workspace. IEEE Trans. Neural Syst. Rehabil. Eng. 20 (1), 48—57.

Exact Dynamics. http://www.exactdynamics.nl.

Hammel, J., Hall, K., Lees, D., Leifer, L., Van der Loos, M., Perkash, I., Crigler, R., 1989. Clinical evaluation of a desktop robotic assistant. J. Rehabil. Res. Dev. 26 (3), 1—16.

Hillman, M., 2004. Rehabilitation robotics from past to present — a historical perspective. In: Zenn, B.Z., Stefanov, D. (Eds.), Advances in Rehabilitation Robotics. Springer, pp. 25—44.

Kwee, H., Duimel, J., Smits, J., Tuinhof de Moed, A., van Woerden, J., 1989. The MANUS wheelchair-borne manipulator: system review and first results. In: Proc. IARP Workshop on Domestic and Medical & Healthcare Robotics, Newcastle.

Lum, P., Reinkensmeyer, D., Mahoney, R., Rymer, W.Z., Burgar, C., 2002. Robotic devices for movement therapy after stroke: current status and challenges to clinical acceptance. Top. Stroke Rehabil. 8 (4), 40—53.

Robins, B., Dautenhahn, K., Boekhorst, R., Billard, A., 2004. Effects of repeated exposure to a humanoid robot on children with autism. In: Keates, S., Clarkson, J., Langdon, P., Robinson, P. (Eds.), Designing a More Inclusive World. Springer Verlag, London, pp. 225—236.

Suzuki, K., Mito, G., Kawamotot, H., Hasegawa, Y., Sankai, Y., 2007. Intention-based walking support for paraplegia patients with robot suit HAL. Adv. Robot. 21 (12), 1441—1469.

Topping, M., 2001. Handy 1, A robotic aid to independence for severely disabled people. In: Mokhtari, M. (Ed.), Integration of Assistive Technology in the Information Age. IOS, Netherlands, pp. 142—147.

Van der Loos, M., 1995. VA/Stanford Rehabilitation Robotics Research and Development Program: lessons learned in the application of robotics technology to the field of rehabilitation. IEEE Trans. Rehabil. Eng. 3 (1), 46—66.

Van der Loos, M., Michalowski, S., Leifer, L., 1986. Design of an omnidirectional mobile robot as a manipulation aid for the severely disabled. In: Foulds, R. (Ed.), Interactive Robotic Aids. World Rehabilitation Fund Monograph #37. New York.

Zoss, A.B., Kazerooni, H., Chu, A., 2006. Biomechanical design of the Berkeley lower extremity exoskeleton. IEEE/ASME Trans. Mechatron. 11 (2), 128—138.

Further reading

Hillman, M., 2004. Rehabilitation robots from past to present — a historical perspective. In: Bien, Z., Stefanov, D. (Eds.), Advances in Rehabilitation Robotics. Lecture Notes in Control and Information Sciences, vol. 306. Springer, New York. ISBN:3-540-219866.

Sirlantzis, K., Larsen, L.B., Kanumuru, L.K., Oprea, P., 2019. Robotics. In: Cowan, D., Najafi, L. (Eds.), Handbook of Electronic Assistive Technology. Academic Press.

Index

Printed in the United States
By Bookmasters